ANSI STRUCTURED COBOL

Advanced

THE IRWIN SERIES
IN INFORMATION AND DECISION SCIENCES

Consulting Editors

Robert B. Fetter
Yale University
Claude McMillan
University of Colorado

ANSI STRUCTURED COBOL

Advanced

Steve Teglovic, Jr.
University of Northern Colorado
Kenneth D. Douglas
Southwest Missouri State University

1986
IRWIN
Homewood, Illinois 60430

ISBN 0-256-03287-4

Library of Congress Catalog Card No. 86-80110

Printed in the United States of America

2 3 4 5 6 7 8 9 0 ML 3 2 1 0 9 8 7 6

For years, the full power of the COBOL language has lain dormant in the manuals of computer vendors. It has only been recently that industry representatives and professional organizations such as Data Processing Management Association (DPMA) and Association of Computer Machinery (ACM) have encouraged those teaching COBOL to expose potential programmers and analysts to the advanced concepts and techniques of the language. To help develop this knowledge of the COBOL language, the authors present the needed skills using a modular approach. They start with a review of some of the basic concepts from beginning and intermediate levels of the language and progress into more difficult concepts. This approach allows the potential programmer to more quickly gain confidence in how to use these advanced concepts and to develop good programming techniques.

Chapter 1 is a discussion of structured design. The needs for structured design and structured design concepts are presented. Important programming standards for COBOL are also discussed. Chapter 2 starts with a review of table manipulation. Since this is such an important topic the creating, accessing, and searching of two and three level tables has been given comprehensive coverage. In a similar fashion, Chapter 3 starts with simple ideas of internal COBOL sorts and progresses into detailed uses of various types and techniques of sorting. The use of variable length records is introduced as well as the merging of files.

The correcting of program errors is always a time-consuming task. Chapter 4 discusses several techniques to reduce the time involved. The Debugging Module of the language is fully discussed and programs to monitor the execution of files, fields, and procedures are explained. The validation of input files is fully discussed and applied in Chapter 5.

File maintenance is one of the strongest features of the COBOL language. The text presents complete coverage of sequential, indexed-sequential, and relative files in Chapters 6, 7, and 8. Creation, updating, and reporting for these files are carefully presented for each type of file. Variable length records, error detection, and the use of primary and alternate keys are illustrated by using many program examples. Randomizing algorithms are explained for use in relative files.

The use of subprograms is becoming very important in many data processing installations. Chapter 9 covers the concepts of calling and called programs, including the nesting of subprograms. The often misunderstood use and need for the Report Writer feature of COBOL is explained at length in Chapter 10. The chapter progresses from the basic syntax of this feature to complex programs illustrating the concepts and techniques necessary to take advantage of most of its features.

The difficult topic of character manipulation is discussed in Chapter 11. The STRING, UNSTRING, and INSPECT statements and their various options are explained in detail. Examples are provided to help the programmer understand how to use these instructions. Chapter 12 introduces interactive concepts. Screen development and menu-driven systems are examined.

Important features of the text are the sections on programming style and on common errors encountered when using the topics in a particular chapter. Each chapter starts with a listing of the terms and statements that should be understood while studying that chapter. Also Chapters 2 through 11 use complete program examples with solutions to cover the new material. These program examples have a statement of the problem, an explanation of the data input and output, a complete program listing, and a discussion of the program logic. Where appropriate, documentation is covered with structure and printer spacing charts. In addition, the authors have implemented their own self-documenting technique for numbering and naming procedures in the structure charts and the procedures used in the programs. It is referred to as the Z Technique.

Several chapters in the text have been written to be relatively independent of each other. This enables users to cover topics in a different sequence than the one presented in the text. For example, the chapters covering debugging, subprograms, Report Writer, and character manipulation can be introduced in the course wherever the instructor desires without causing problems with the material in the remaining chapters. The topics covered in the text are more than adequate for an advanced course in COBOL. When using an advanced text in COBOL many users find it beneficial to also have available a beginning text. One such text is *ANSI STRUCTURED COBOL: An Introduction,* in which the authors utilize the same general format and style used in this text.

The appendixes in the text cover COBOL language formats and reserved words, provide complete data sets of all chapter programs and problem assignments, provide answers to selected exercises from each chapter, and explain the uses of line and full-screen editors for creating programs and data sets. In addition, there is coverage of general concepts of Virtual Storage Access Method and its utilities. Also there is a useful reference summary of all I/O statements and file status values that can be used with the text material on file maintenance.

An instructor's manual is available with the text. It contains solutions to all of the text exercises and a bank of objective questions and executed programs with output results for all chapter problems. There are copies of many of the figures from the text that can be used as transparencies. The manual saves many hours of programming and preparation time.

The authors wish to thank their many colleagues for their comments, suggestions, and moral support. Special thanks are due to William Cornette, William Duff, and Robert Lynch. The useful suggestions and constructive insights of the following reviewers are sincerely appreciated:

Norman D. Brammer
Colorado State University

R. Wayne Headrick
Texas A&M University

Satya P. Saraswat
San Diego State University

Bennett L. Kramer
Massasoit Community College

We are deeply indebted to our spouses Mary and Cecil and our children; Linda, Mike, Mary-K, Brent, Brenda, and Brandon, for their continued support and sacrifices during the many months of writing this text.

Acknowledgment

The acknowledgment required by the American National Standards Institute for the use of copyrighted material follows:

COBOL is an industry language and is not the property of any company or group of companies, or of any organization or group of organizations.

No warranty, expressed or implied, is made by any contributor or by the CODA-SYL Programming Language Committee as to the accuracy and functioning of the programming system and language. Moreover, no responsibility is assumed by any contributor, or by the committee, in connection herewith.

The authors and copyright holders of the copyrighted material used herein FLOW–MATIC (trademark of Sperry Rand Corporation), Programming for the UNIVAC I and II, Data Automation Systems copyrighted 1958, 1959, by Sperry Rand Corporation; IBM Commercial Translator Form No. F28–8013, copyrighted 1959 by IBM; FACT, DSI 27A5260–2760, copyrighted 1960 by Minneapolis-Honeywell

have specifically authorized the use of this material in whole or in part, in the COBOL specifications. Such authorization extends to the reproduction and use of COBOL specifications in programming manuals or similar publications.

Steve Teglovic, Jr.
Kenneth D. Douglas

CONTENTS

Chapter 3   *Sorting and Merging Files*   *78*

Chapter 4   *Debugging*   *117*

Chapter 5   *Validation of Input Data*   *146*

Chapter 6   *Sequential File Processing*   *178*

Chapter 7   *Indexed Files*   *220*

Chapter 8   *Relative Files*   *270*

Chapter 9   *Subprograms*   *305*

Chapter 10   *Report Writer*   *333*

Structured Design and Programming Standards

The structured design of programs provides a proven framework for improved program design resulting in less time to develop programs and less difficulty in modifying programs, particularly when the programmer doing the modification is someone other than the person who originally developed the program. Structured program development is but one of many programming standards that an organization uses to ensure that every programmer in the organization is programming in essentially the same manner. That way when a programmer is called on to modify someone else's program, there are no surprises and little difficulty in deciphering another's logic.

Throughout the text many terms and statements are introduced. At the beginning of each chapter a list of these terms and statements is provided to assist the users in organizing their thoughts related to each concept. Additionally, each term and statement introduced is boldfaced. Terms and statements discussed in this chapter appear below.

TERMS AND STATEMENTS

Case structure	GO TO/	Priming READ
Cohesion	DEPENDING ON	Program nucleus
Common modules	statement	Programming
Coupling	Iteration structure	standards
Dead code	PERFORM	Selection structure
Fall-through logic	statement	Sequence structure
Forward GO TO	PERFORM/THRU	Span of Control
statement	statement	Structure chart

Need for Structured Design

Before structured programming techniques were widely implemented a linear approach to programming existed. That is, the program was written so that execution would begin at the top of the program with necessary OPEN and initializing statements, the major processing routine would come next, and ending routines would be placed at the bottom of the source program. A high-level flowchart of a typical program illustrating this linear approach for a report program is shown in Figure 1–1.

Program 1–1 provides an example of an unstructured control break program. Notice the major loop caused by the GO TO statement at line 1540 and the exit from the loop caused by the AT END clause of the READ statement at line 1290. It is typical in unstructured programs to have performed modules, but generally only for those procedures that are needed from more than one place in the program, such as for the printing of the headings and the printing of the region totals. Notice the location of the CLOSE and STOP statements at the end of the program.

Several problems exist with unstructured programs, particularly when modifications are necessary. First, it is difficult to determine what the program is supposed to accomplish without reading the entire program and following the entire logic of

Figure 1–1   *Unstructured Flowchart*

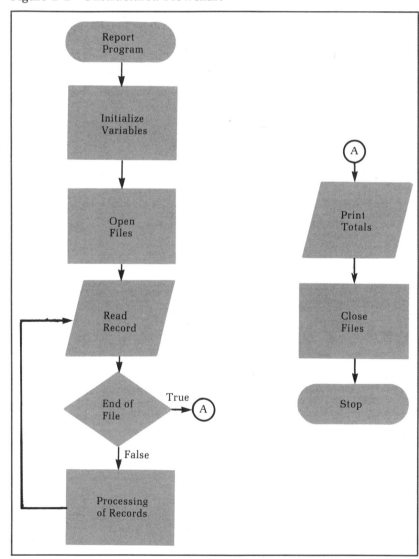

Program 1–1

```
000010 IDENTIFICATION DIVISION.
000020 PROGRAM-ID.    CTRLPAY.
000030**********************************************************
000040*   PROGRAM EXAMPLE 1-1 UNSTRUCTURED CONTROL BREAK PROGRAM      *
000050**********************************************************


001200 PROCEDURE DIVISION.
001210 TOTALS-BY-REGION.
001220     OPEN INPUT PAYROLL-INPUT-FILE
001230            OUTPUT CONTROL-BREAK-REPORT.
001240     MOVE ZEROES TO WS-PAGE-NUMBER
001250                     WS-ACCUMULATORS.
001260     MOVE 'YES'  TO WS-FIRST-RECORD-INDICATOR.
001270     PERFORM PRINT-HEADINGS.
001280 READ-RECORDS.
001290     READ PAYROLL-INPUT-FILE
001300         AT END GO TO PRINT-REGION-TOTALS.
001310     IF FIRST-RECORD
001320         MOVE 'NO'            TO WS-FIRST-RECORD-INDICATOR
001330         MOVE PI-REGION-NUMBER TO PR-PREVIOUS-REGION-NUMBER.
001340     IF PI-REGION-NUMBER NOT = PR-PREVIOUS-REGION-NUMBER
001350         PERFORM PRINT-REGION-TOTALS.
001360     IF WS-LINES-USED > WS-LINES-PER-PAGE
001370         PERFORM PRINT-HEADINGS.
001380     MOVE PI-EMPLOYEE-NAME        TO DL-EMPLOYEE-NAME.
001390     MOVE PI-DEPARTMENT-NUMBER    TO DL-DEPARTMENT-NUMBER.
001400     MOVE PI-PLANT-NUMBER         TO DL-PLANT-NUMBER.
001410     MOVE PI-REGION-NUMBER        TO DL-REGION-NUMBER.
001420     MOVE PI-YTD-GROSS-PAY        TO DL-YTD-GROSS-PAY.
001430     MOVE PI-YTD-FEDERAL-TAXES    TO DL-YTD-FEDERAL-TAXES.
001440     MOVE PI-YTD-FICA-TAXES       TO DL-YTD-FICA-TAXES.
001450     MOVE PI-YTD-STATE-TAXES      TO DL-YTD-STATE-TAXES.
001460     MOVE DL-DETAIL-LINE TO CB-CONTROL-BREAK-RECORD.
001470     WRITE CB-CONTROL-BREAK-RECORD
001480         AFTER 1.
001490     ADD 1 TO WS-LINES-USED.
001500     ADD PI-YTD-GROSS-PAY     TO RT-TOT-YTD-GROSS-PAY.
001510     ADD PI-YTD-FEDERAL-TAXES TO RT-TOT-YTD-FEDERAL-TAXES.
001520     ADD PI-YTD-FICA-TAXES    TO RT-TOT-YTD-FICA-TAXES.
001530     ADD PI-YTD-STATE-TAXES   TO RT-TOT-YTD-STATE-TAXES.
001540     GO TO READ-RECORDS.
001550 PRINT-HEADINGS.
001560     ADD 1               TO WS-PAGE-NUMBER.
001570     MOVE WS-PAGE-NUMBER    TO HD-PAGE-NUMBER-OUT.
001580     MOVE HD-HEADING-LINE-1 TO CB-CONTROL-BREAK-RECORD.
001590     WRITE CB-CONTROL-BREAK-RECORD
001600         AFTER PAGE.
001610     MOVE HD-HEADING-LINE-2 TO CB-CONTROL-BREAK-RECORD.
001620     WRITE CB-CONTROL-BREAK-RECORD
001630         AFTER 2.
001640     MOVE HD-HEADING-LINE-3 TO CB-CONTROL-BREAK-RECORD.
001650     WRITE CB-CONTROL-BREAK-RECORD
001660         AFTER 1.
001670     MOVE SPACES TO CB-CONTROL-BREAK-RECORD.
001680     WRITE CB-CONTROL-BREAK-RECORD
001690         AFTER 1.
001700     MOVE 5 TO WS-LINES-USED.
001710 PRINT-REGION-TOTALS.
001720     MOVE SPACES              TO TL-TOTAL-LINE.
001730     MOVE RT-TOT-YTD-GROSS-PAY    TO TL-YTD-GROSS-PAY.
001740     MOVE RT-TOT-YTD-FEDERAL-TAXES TO TL-YTD-FEDERAL-TAXES.
001750     MOVE RT-TOT-YTD-FICA-TAXES   TO TL-YTD-FICA-TAXES.
001760     MOVE RT-TOT-YTD-STATE-TAXES  TO TL-YTD-STATE-TAXES.
001770     MOVE 'REGION TOTALS'       TO TL-STUB-HEADING-NAME.
```

Program 1–1 *(concluded)*

```
001780        MOVE PR-PREVIOUS-REGION-NUMBER TO TL-REGION-NUMBER.
001790        MOVE TL-TOTAL-LINE          TO CB-CONTROL-BREAK-RECORD.
001800        WRITE CB-CONTROL-BREAK-RECORD
001810            AFTER 2.
001820        MOVE SPACES                 TO CB-CONTROL-BREAK-RECORD.
001830        WRITE CB-CONTROL-BREAK-RECORD
001840            AFTER 1.
001850        ADD 3 TO WS-LINES-USED.
001860        ADD RT-TOT-YTD-GROSS-PAY     TO GT-TOT-YTD-GROSS-PAY.
001870        ADD RT-TOT-YTD-FEDERAL-TAXES TO GT-TOT-YTD-FEDERAL-TAXES.
001880        ADD RT-TOT-YTD-FICA-TAXES    TO GT-TOT-YTD-FICA-TAXES.
001890        ADD RT-TOT-YTD-STATE-TAXES   TO GT-TOT-YTD-STATE-TAXES.
001900        MOVE ZEROES TO RT-REGION-TOTAL-ACCUMULATORS.
001910        MOVE PI-REGION-NUMBER        TO PR-PREVIOUS-REGION-NUMBER.
001920 PRINT-GRAND-TOTALS.
001930        MOVE SPACES                  TO TL-TOTAL-LINE.
001940        MOVE GT-TOT-YTD-GROSS-PAY     TO TL-YTD-GROSS-PAY.
001950        MOVE GT-TOT-YTD-FEDERAL-TAXES TO TL-YTD-FEDERAL-TAXES.
001960        MOVE GT-TOT-YTD-FICA-TAXES    TO TL-YTD-FICA-TAXES.
001970        MOVE GT-TOT-YTD-STATE-TAXES   TO TL-YTD-STATE-TAXES.
001980        MOVE 'GRAND TOTALS'          TO TL-STUB-HEADING-NAME.
001990        MOVE TL-TOTAL-LINE           TO CB-CONTROL-BREAK-RECORD.
002000        WRITE CB-CONTROL-BREAK-RECORD
002010            AFTER 1.
002020        CLOSE PAYROLL-INPUT-FILE
002030              CONTROL-BREAK-REPORT.
002040        STOP RUN.
```

the program. There is no controlling module that would let the programmer know at a glance the major functions of the program.

Second, the mixing of GO TO and PERFORM statements makes it difficult to follow the logic. For example, the IF statement at line 1340 will cause PRINT–RE GION–TOTALS to be performed when a control break occurs and the AT END at line 1300 causes an unconditional branch to PRINT–REGION–TOTALS. Since a GO TO has been used, the flow of logic falls through to PRINT–GRAND–TOTALS and the eventual end of the program. Consider what it would be like modifying a very large program and having to keep track of whether a module was performed or referenced by a GO TO statement utilizing **fall-through logic.**

Third, because of the mixing of GO TO and PERFORM statements, placement of the referenced paragraphs is critical. What would happen to program execution if the PRINT–REGION–TOTALS paragraph were to be placed ahead of PRINT– HEADINGS. In a structured program it would make no difference. In this unstructured program the headings would be printed after the last region totals were printed and before the grand totals were printed. The placement of all modules is critical when using fall-through logic; when using structured design only the placement of the first control module is important.

Structured Design Concepts

Program Nucleus

Structured design of programs calls for a main **program nucleus**, which has as its purpose the invoking of statements or sets of statements called modules. The emphasis at this stage of development is on major functions that the program will perform. For most COBOL programs this involves three major functions: (1) beginning routines,

Figure 1–2 *Main Program Nucleus*

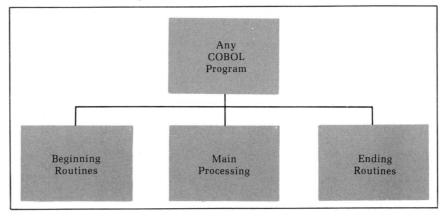

(2) main processing routines, and (3) ending routines, and can be depicted by the high-level structure chart shown in Figure 1–2.

To develop any COBOL program the modules in the main program nucleus represented by the boxes are simply expanded until there is sufficient detail to solve the problem at hand. To illustrate the concept of module expansion, consider the control break program that was shown in unstructured form as Program 1–1.

The functions that would be part of the beginning routines would include the opening of the files, initializing necessary variables, and the printing of headings. Ending routines include the printing of the last region totals, the printing of the grand totals, and the closing of the files. All other routines are main processing routines. (Note that the printing of the region totals would also be a main processing routine.) Since the beginning and ending routines are usually the easiest to expand and develop, consider the expanded **structure chart** illustrated in Figure 1–3.

One function has been added at the main program nucleus level, that of reading the first record from the input file. This is termed a **priming READ** and allows the first iteration through the main processing routines to operate on the first record. There will be another READ statement within the main processing routine to prime the pump for subsequent iterations through the module. The AT END clause of the READ statement is used to terminate additional iterations when the end of the file (EOF) has been reached.

Next the main processing routine would be expanded to an additional level of detail as shown by the abbreviated structure chart in Figure 1–4.

At this point in the development, the amount of expansion has been the same for each of the major functions, but is there sufficient detail for a programmer to complete the detailed program planning and subsequent coding? If so, the programmer may proceed to a detailed planning and design tool such as pseudocode, flowchart, or other method. If there is not sufficient detail, the programmer should consider additional factors to sufficiently expand the structure chart. It is always up to the programmer to decide when the structure chart is sufficiently expanded.

In the case of this program some additional factors that have not been considered are page break control and the resetting of regional total accumulators to zero after a region control break has been detected. A complete structure chart is depicted in Figure 1–5. Note that the authors do not use a strict interpretation of the beginning and ending routines and do not include the opening or closing of files as a main module. Note also the boxes that are shaded in the upper right-hand corner to depict modules that are invoked from more than one place in the program, called **common modules.** Also note the labeling of each block. This labeling will be explained later in the chapter when the complete COBOL source listing developed from this structure chart is presented.

Figure 1–3 *Expanded Structure Chart*

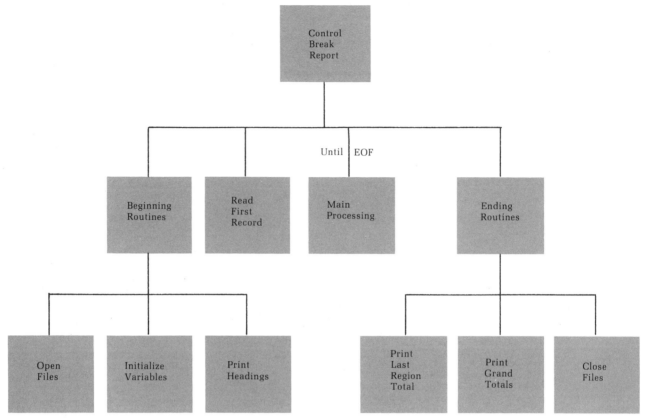

Control Structures

Control structures are used to expand modules eventually into suitable COBOL code. There are three basic control structures that can be used to code any COBOL program. These control structures are called the **sequence structure,** the **selection structure,** and the **iteration structure.**

Sequence Structure   The sequence structure simply indicates that statements or sets of statements are executed in sequence. To illustrate, consider the flowchart in Figure 1–6, which is a flowchart of the main program nucleus from the previous structure chart.

Figure 1–4 *Main Processing Routine Expanded*

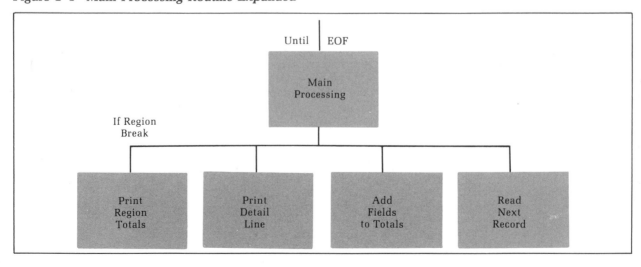

Each block, which may be comprised of one or more statements, is executed in sequence, one after the other. The only apparent break in this sequence is that the main processing routine will have to be executed several times, causing the need for the iteration structure. However, the main processing can still be considered to be but one of several procedures executed in sequence.

Selection Structure   The selection structure enables a decision to be made between two alternative paths. Each path may be represented by one or more statements and/or control structures. The flowcharts in Figure 1–7 illustrate the concept of the selection structure along with some examples of COBOL code.

In all four examples, processing continues in sequence immediately after the appropriate paths have been executed Note that all of the process blocks could be a performed procedure or could be a statement or set of statements coded as a part of the IF statement. In no case should any GO TO statement be included as a part of the executed procedure. A GO TO statement would break the sequence. All control structures should have only one entry point and one exit point. The GO TO statement violates this concept.

Iteration Structure   The iteration structure allows the execution of a statement or set of statements through the use of one of the options of the **PERFORM statement.** Figure 1–8 provides a review of all of the available options of the PERFORM statement.

Option A is a simple PERFORM statement, which allows the execution of the named procedure for one iteration. When repeated iterations of a procedure are required, the PERFORM/UNTIL, the PERFORM/TIMES, or the PERFORM/VARY ING option is used. Both the PERFORM/TIMES and the PERFORM/VARYING options find their major application in the manipulation of tables, while the PERFORM/ UNTIL is primarily used to control the execution of the main processing routine. A major concern to remember when using the PERFORM/UNTIL option is that a statement in the performed procedure must eventually cause the tested condition to be true. Also remember that in no case should a GO TO statement be contained as a part of the performed procedure; otherwise the sequence structure would be broken.

Any option of the PERFORM statement can actually reference a procedure in one of four different ways. First, a PERFORM statement can reference a single paragraph as shown in Figure 1–9.

In this example, statements in the PRINT–HEADINGS paragraph are executed in sequence until another paragraph name or the end of the program is detected. Control then returns to the next statement in sequence after PERFORM PRINT–HEADINGS.

Figure 1–10 illustrates the ability to execute multiple paragraphs with a single PERFORM statement by using the optional THRU clause. The paragraphs named in the PERFORM/THRU define the beginning and ending paragraph to be executed in sequence. As many paragraphs as desired may be physically placed between the two named paragraphs.

In this example, when the PERFORM statement is executed, control is transferred to the first named paragraph, WRITE–DETAIL–LINE. All statements in that paragraph are executed in sequence, but control falls through to execute the statements in ADD–FIELDS–TO–TOTALS and on to the statements in the READ–RECORD paragraph. Only when all statements in the second named paragraph are executed does control return to the statement after the PERFORM/THRU. Several concerns should arise in a programmer's mind. What happens to the ability to follow the logic of a program when a performed paragraph is expected to return to a PERFORM statement, but it does not? Chaos! What would happen if the paragraph named ADD–FIELDS–TO–TOTALS was physically moved outside of the range of the PER FORM/THRU? That paragraph would become unreachable and become what is

Figure 1-5   Complete Structure Chart for Program 1-2

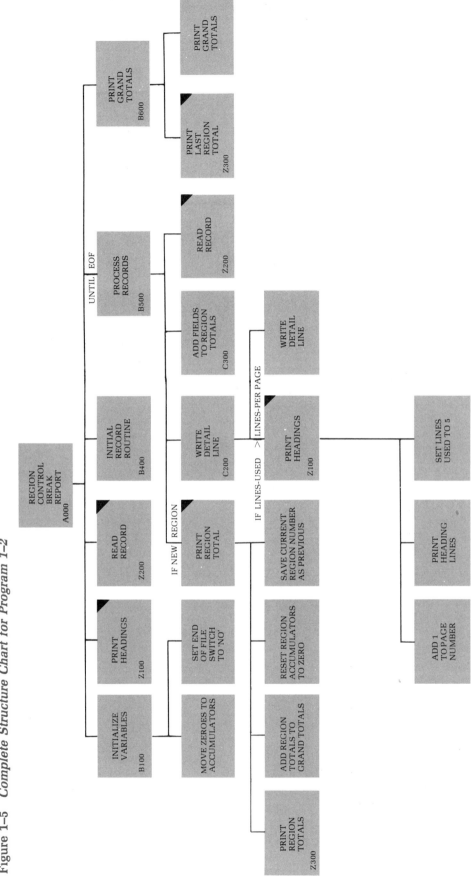

called dead code. What happens if a programmer who is modifying the program happens to place an added paragraph inside the range of the PERFORM/THRU by mistake. This added paragraph would then be executed twice. It should be obvious that the PERFORM/THRU is fraught with problems even though it appears to be a powerful option. It is preferable to use the code shown in Figure 1–11 instead of the PERFORM/THRU so as not to violate the single-entry, single-exit concept. It requires the keying of a few extra statements, but it eliminates many severe problems.

Figures 1–12 and 1–13 depict the last two methods of referencing procedures with the PERFORM statement by using sections.

The end of a section is detected by the compiler by the presence of another section name, the end of the source program listing, or a paragraph that contains the single entry EXIT. Since a section can contain multiple paragraphs, its application is much like the use of the **PERFORM/THRU statement** with paragraph names. When used with or without the PERFORM/THRU statement, sections cause the same difficulties previously described with the PERFORM/THRU statement. These same arguments suggest that the programmer not use sections except were required by COBOL syntax, such as with the use of either an INPUT or OUTPUT PROCEDURE when using the SORT or MERGE statements.

Figure 1–6 *Sequence Structure Illustrated*

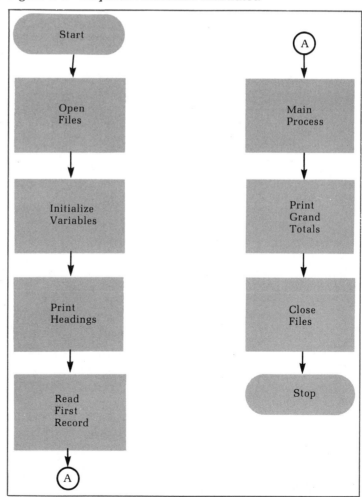

Case Structure
There is one additional control structure that can be implemented. This control structure is called the **case structure**, which uses either a linear nested IF statement or the GO TO/DEPENDING ON statement. An example of the case structure using the linear nested IF statement is shown in Figure 1–14.

The **GO TO/DEPENDING ON statement**, with either a performed section or a set of performed paragraphs with a PERFORM/THRU, enables an alternative way to implement the case structure.

In both Figure 1–15 and Figure 1–16 the GO TO/DEPENDING ON statement evaluates the value of TRANSACTION–CODE; transfers control to ADDITION–ROUTINE if TRANSACTION–CODE is a 1, transfers control to DELETE–ROUTINE if TRANSACTION–CODE is a 2, and so on. IF TRANSACTION–CODE does not contain a numeric value from 1 through 5, control falls through to the next statement in sequence after the GO TO/DEPENDING ON statement, which is an error routine.

In any case transfer of control occurs, which requires additional GO TO statements at the end of each routine. If these GO TO statements were not present more than one paragraph would be executed. In all cases the GO TO statements transfer control to an exit paragraph, which indicates a common exit to the UPDATE–ROUTINE. This type of GO TO statement is called a **forward GO TO statement** and is typically the only allowed use of the GO TO in organizations that utilize structured design. The next version of COBOL should certainly have a statement that can be used to replace the GO TO/DEPENDING ON statement so that a true case structure will be available in COBOL.

Figure 1–7 *Selection Structure*

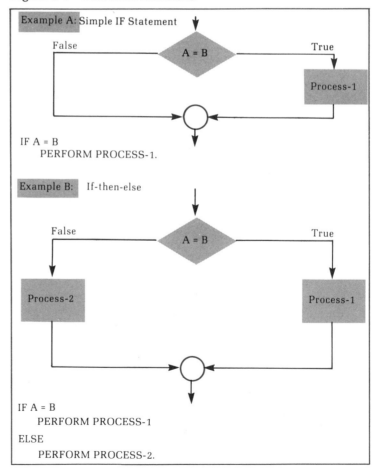

Figure 1–7 *(concluded)*

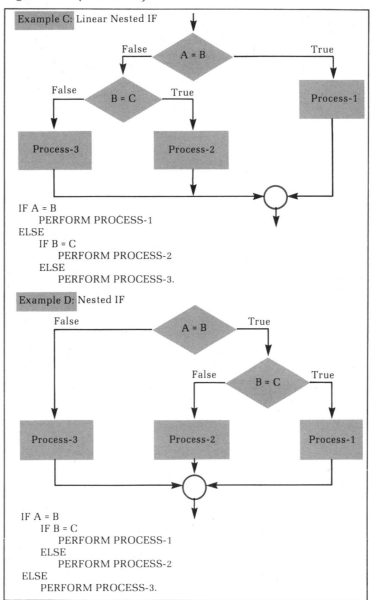

Example C: Linear Nested IF

```
IF A = B
    PERFORM PROCESS-1
ELSE
    IF B = C
        PERFORM PROCESS-2
    ELSE
        PERFORM PROCESS-3.
```

Example D: Nested IF

```
IF A = B
    IF B = C
        PERFORM PROCESS-1
    ELSE
        PERFORM PROCESS-2
ELSE
    PERFORM PROCESS-3.
```

Module Expansion

Once control structure concepts are understood it is a fairly simple process to expand modules by inserting the appropriate control structure in place of a named module. Each of these control structures will then be executed in sequence. Remember, every procedure still utilizes the basic sequence structure. To illustrate, Figure 1–17 shows the expansion of the previous flowchart of the main program nucleus for the control break report program.

First, notice that the main processing module has been replaced by an iteration structure in order to allow repeated iterations of this module. This module is then expanded to allow the execution of four procedures in sequence. They are the testing for the existence of a control break, the writing of the detail line, the adding of the fields to region totals, and the reading of the next record. The testing for

Figure 1–8   *Options of the PERFORM Statement*

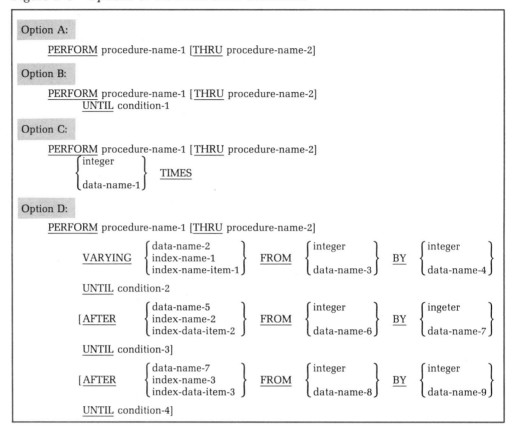

Figure 1–9   *A Performed Paragraph*

```
    PERFORM PRINT-HEADINGS.
        .
        .
        .
PRINT-HEADINGS.
    ADD 1                 TO WS-PAGE-NUMBER.
    MOVE WS-PAGE-NUMBER       TO HD-PAGE-NUMBER-OUT.
    MOVE HD-HEADING-LINE-1 TO CB-CONTROL-BREAK-RECORD.
    WRITE CB-CONTROL-BREAK-RECORD
        AFTER PAGE.
```

Figure 1–10   *Use of the THRU Option of the PERFORM Statement*

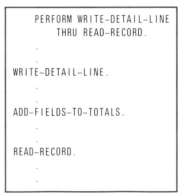

```
    PERFORM WRITE-DETAIL-LINE
        THRU READ-RECORD.
        .
        .
WRITE-DETAIL-LINE.
        .
        .
ADD-FIELDS-TO-TOTALS.
        .
        .
READ-RECORD.
        .
        .
```

Figure 1–11 *Alternative to the PERFORM/THRU*

```
      PERFORM WRITE-DETAIL-LINE.
      PERFORM ADD-FIELDS-TO-TOTALS.
      PERFORM READ-RECORD.
          .
  WRITE-DETAIL-LINE.
          .
          .
  ADD-FIELDS-TO-TOTALS.
          .
          .
  READ-RECORD.
          .
          .
```

the control break has also utilized a selection structure in order to select the region total routine when appropriate. Additional module expansion would also be possible for each of modules at this level as well as for remaining modules in the main program nucleus. However, the process of module expansion is the same no matter what level of module being considered. All that is necessary is to determine which type of control structure is required and which sequence of procedures is correct. Continued module expansion will eventually result in the listing of procedures that can be directly translated into individual COBOL statements.

Cohesion and Coupling

There are two additional concepts that provide guidelines regarding the relationships that exist within and among the logic modules of a program. **Cohesion** is the relationship of statements within a given module, and **coupling** refers to the relationships among modules in a program. The objectives related to these two concepts are to strive for high cohesion and low coupling. That is, a module should be structured so that all statements in the module relate to one function, and each module should be relatively independent of other modules at the same level.

Figure 1–12 *The Use of Sections in the PROCEDURE Division*

```
      PERFORM DATA-VALIDATION.
          .
          .
  DATA-VALIDATION SECTION.
  VALIDATE-YTD-SALES.
          .
          .
  VALIDATE-NAME.
          .
          .
  VALIDATE-ADDRESS.
          .
          .
  DATA-VALIDATION-EXIT.
      EXIT.
  OTHER-SECTION-NAME SECTION.
          .
          .
```

Figure 1–13   *The Use of Sections with the PERFORM/THRU*

```
      PERFORM DATA-VALIDATION
          THRU READ-RECORD.
              .

  DATA-VALIDATION SECTION.
  VALIDATE-YTD-SALES
              .

    VALIDATE-NAME.
              .        .

    VALIDATE-ADDRESS.
              .

  DATA-VALIDATION-EXIT.
      EXIT.
  CALCULATIONS SECTION.
  ADD-YTD-SALES.
              .

    ADD-CURRENT-SALES.
              .

  CALCULATIONS-EXIT.
      EXIT.
  READ-RECORD SECTION.
              .

  READ-RECORD-EXIT.
      EXIT.
```

Figure 1–14   *Case Structure and a Linear Nested IF Statement*

```
    PERFORM UPDATE-ROUTINE.
              .
UPDATE-ROUTINE.
    IF TRANSACTION-CODE = 1
        PERFORM ADDITION-ROUTINE
    ELSE
        IF TRANSACTION-CODE = 2
            PERFORM DELETE-ROUTINE
        ELSE
            IF TRANSACTION-CODE = 3
                PERFORM CHG-YTD-SALES
            ELSE
                IF TRANSACTION-CODE = 4
                    PERFORM CHG-YTD-RETURNS
                ELSE
                    IF TRANSACTION-CODE = 5
                        PERFORM CHG-COMMISSION-RATE
                    ELSE
                        PERFORM TRANS-CODE-ERROR.
```

Several types of cohesion have been identified and have been placed on a continuum from low to high, as shown in Figure 1–18.

Coincidental cohesion means that parts of a module just happen to be placed together with no apparent reason. The programmer will have difficulty trying to

Figure 1–15 *Case Structure and the GO TO/DEPENDING ON Using Sections*

```
        PERFORM UPDATE-ROUTINE.
                .
UPDATE-ROUTINE SECTION.
        GO TO ADDITION-ROUTINE
                DELETE-ROUTINE
                CHG-YTD-SALES
                CHG-YTD-RETURNS
                CHG-COMMISSION-RATE
                DEPENDING ON TRANSACTION-CODE.
TRANS-CODE-ERROR.
                .
                .
        GO TO UPDATE-ROUTINE-EXIT.
ADDITION-ROUTINE.
                .
                .
        GO TO UPDATE-ROUTINE EXIT.
DELETE-ROUTINE.
                .
                .
        GO TO UPDATE-ROUTINE-EXIT.
CHG-YTD-SALES.
                .
                .
        GO TO UPDATE-ROUTINE-EXIT.
CHG-YTD-RETURNS.
                .
                .
        GO TO UPDATE-ROUTINE-EXIT.
CHG-COMMISSION-RATE.
                .
                .
        GO TO UPDATE-ROUTINE-EXIT.
UPDATE-ROUTINE-EXIT.
        EXIT.
```

name this kind of module. A module that is said to have logical cohesion contains activities that are alike, such as all activities in an edit routine. Temporal cohesion relates to activities that take place at the same time. Beginning of job routines are a good example of temporal cohesion. A module that has procedural cohesion contains procedures that are necessary to accomplish a job, but these procedures are not functional. That is, they do not all relate to one function. Communicational cohesion identifies all processing that takes place on one logical record. This type of module is frequently the main loop through a program. Sequential cohesion contains tasks, in which the output from one becomes the input to another task. Functional cohesion, the highest on the cohesion continuum, should be strived for as much as possible since it provides a module that is the easiest to modify. The programmer should also find that a module that is functionally cohesive is easy to name.

Several types of coupling have also been codified and can be placed on a continuum similar to that for cohesion. This continuum is shown in Figure 1–19.

Low coupling is to be strived for because it minimizes the difficulty in modifying a program. When high coupling exists multiple modules at the same level are affected by a single change, thereby making the modification process more costly, time-consuming, and prone to error.

Content coupling occurs when statements in one module modify the data content

Figure 1–16 *Case Structure and the GO TO/DEPENDING ON Using PERFORM/THRU*

```
       PERFORM UPDATE-ROUTINE
           THRU UPDATE-ROUTINE-EXIT.
       .
UPDATE-ROUTINE.
       GO TO ADDITION-ROUTINE
            DELETE-ROUTINE
            CHG-YTD-SALES
            CHG-YTD-RETURNS
            CHG-COMMISSION-RATE
          DEPENDING ON TRANSACTION-CODE.
TRANS-CODE-ERROR.
       .

       .
       GO TO UPDATE-ROUTINE-EXIT.
ADDITION-ROUTINE.
       .

       .
       GO TO UPDATE-ROUTINE-EXIT.
DELETE-ROUTINE.
       .

       .
       GO TO UPDATE-ROUTINE-EXIT.
CHG-YTD-SALES.
       .

       .
       GO TO UPDATE-ROUTINE EXIT.
CHG-YTD-RETURNS.
       .

       .
       GO TO UPDATE-ROUTINE-EXIT.
CHG-COMMISSION-RATE.
       .

       .
       GO TO UPDATE-ROUTINE-EXIT.
UPDATE-ROUTINE-EXIT.
      · EXIT.
```

of another module. Common coupling means that data is shared among multiple modules and causes problems because the programmer must be aware of changes in data-items wherever they may occur. Control coupling and stamp coupling are related to the sharing of data structures. Data coupling, the most desirable form of coupling, can best be implemented using subprograms, where individual fields are passed from one adjacent module to another, and the separate programs cannot share larger portions of the data structures. Remember that coupling is a concept of the horizontal relationships among adjacent modules. Passing of control fields and data structures from a module downward to a subordinate module generally means that the subordinate module is logically cohesive. Coupling problems occur because of horizontal interdependencies, not vertical interdependencies.

A single question can be asked to determine whether a program has low coupling. Can a given module be changed without affecting another module that is not in the same vertical span of control at the same level on the structure chart? If so, low coupling exists, which reduces the amount of code that must be changed during program modification.

Additional considerations related to the structure of a program are the number of modules that should be performed by another process, called **span of control**, and the amount of detail that each module contains.

In an organizational setting, the span of control should be somewhere in the

Figure 1–17   *First Level Module Expansion Illustrated*

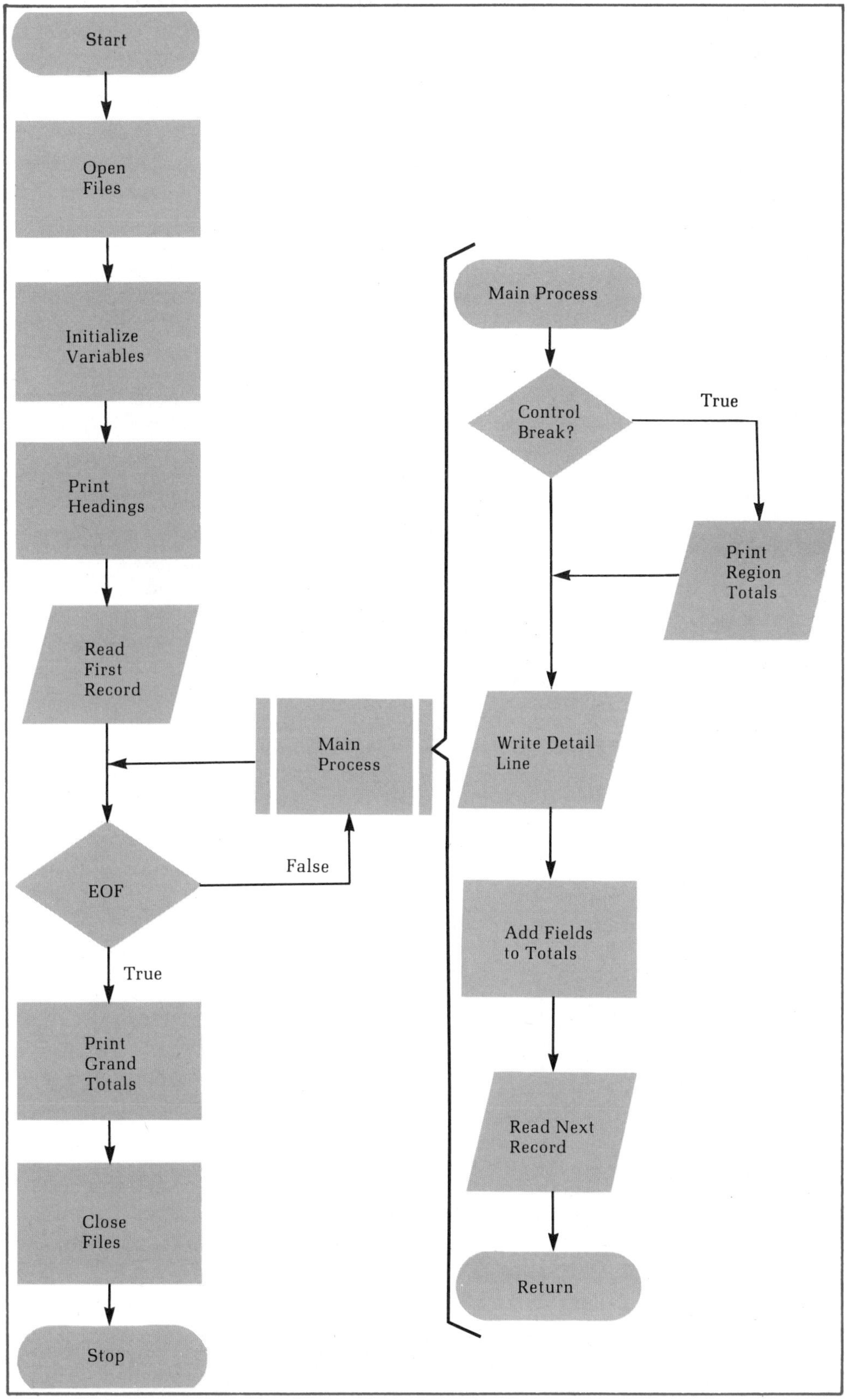

Figure 1–18 *Cohesion Continuum*

Low Chesion						High Cohesion
Coincidental	Logical	Temporal	Procedural	Communicational	Sequential	Functional

Figure 1–19 *Coupling Continuum*

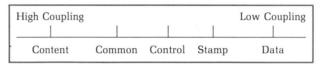

High Coupling				Low Coupling
Content	Common	Control	Stamp	Data

range of two to six modules. In a related vein, each module should contain the right amount of detail, which should not exceed the size of one printed page, so that it is easy to understand when read by a programmer during modification.

Programming Standards

Since programmers in any organization spend a large share of their time in program modification (in some organizations as much as 80 percent), the development of **programming standards** within the organization is imperative. This is particularly important because the modifications may occur to a program over several years by many different programmers. If everyone used their own methods of program structure or conventions for data-item naming, chaos would surely result.

Program 1–2, a structured version of the control break program, is provided as a means of discussing coding standards. In some cases, these standards are generally agreed upon; in others there is room for decisions to be made by the organization. In any case, this codification should serve a useful purpose in the development of programming standards.

Program 1–2

```
000010 IDENTIFICATION DIVISION.
000020 PROGRAM-ID.    CTRLPAY.
000030*
000040*··············································································
000050*            PROGRAM EXAMPLE 1-2
000060*··············································································
000070*    PROGRAM PURPOSE:   TO PRODUCE A PAYROLL REPORT BY REGION
000080*                       WITHIN THE COMPANY.
000090*    DATE WRITTEN    :  OCTOBER 13, 1988.
000100*    AUTHOR          :  JOHN J. DOE.
000110*    REVISIONS       :  NOVEMBER 20, 1988.
000120*    PERIODICITY     :  WEEKLY AFTER EACH PAYROLL.
000130*    DISTRIBUTION    :  ACCOUNTING
000140*                    :  REGION MANAGERS
000150*    DOCUMENTATION   :  STRUCTURE CHART, PSEUDOCODE LOCATED IN
000160*                    :  DOCUMENTATION LIBRARY - COMPUTER SERVICES.
000170*··············································································
000180*
000190 ENVIRONMENT DIVISION.
000200 CONFIGURATION SECTION.
000210    SOURCE-COMPUTER.  AMDAHL.
000220    OBJECT-COMPUTER.  AMDAHL.
000230*
```

Program 1–2 *(continued)*

```
000240 INPUT-OUTPUT SECTION.
000250 FILE-CONTROL.
000260     SELECT PAYROLL-INPUT-FILE
000270         ASSIGN TO UT-S-PAY.
000280     SELECT CONTROL-BREAK-REPORT
000290         ASSIGN TO UT-S-PRINTER.
000300*
000310 DATA DIVISION.
000320 FILE SECTION.
000330*
000340*················································
000350*    OUTPUT IS ON FOUR-PART STANDARD 132-COLUMN PAPER.
000360*    ANY AVAILABLE HIGH-SPEED PRINTER.
000370*················································
000380*
000390 FD  CONTROL-BREAK-REPORT
000400     RECORD CONTAINS 132 CHARACTERS
000410     LABEL RECORDS ARE OMITTED.
000420*
000430 01  CB-CONTROL-BREAK-RECORD          PIC X(132).
000440*
000450*················································
000460*    INPUT TO THIS PROGRAM IS FROM TAPE BACKUP CREATED AS A RESULT
000470*    OF PRODUCING THE WEEKLY PAYROLL.
000480*················································
000490*
000500 FD  PAYROLL-INPUT-FILE
000510     RECORD CONTAINS 61 CHARACTERS
000520     LABEL RECORDS ARE STANDARD.
000530*
000540 01  PI-PAYROLL-INPUT-RECORD.
000550     05  PI-EMPLOYEE-NAME            PIC X(20).
000560     05  PI-DEPARTMENT-NUMBER        PIC X(2).
000570     05  PI-PLANT-NUMBER             PIC X(2).
000580     05  PI-REGION-NUMBER            PIC X(1).
000590     05  FILLER                      PIC X(1).
000600     05  PI-YTD-GROSS-PAY            PIC 9(6)V99.
000610     05  FILLER                      PIC X(1).
000620     05  PI-YTD-FEDERAL-TAXES        PIC 9(6)V99.
000630     05  FILLER                      PIC X(1).
000640     05  PI-YTD-FICA-TAXES           PIC 9(6)V99.
000650     05  FILLER                      PIC X(1).
000660     05  PI-YTD-STATE-TAXES          PIC 9(6)V99.
000670/
000680 WORKING-STORAGE SECTION.
000690*
000700*················································
000710*    CONTROLS FOR PAGE SIZE AND PAGE NUMBERING.
000720*················································
000730*
000740 01  WS-REPORT-CONTROLS.
000750     05  WS-PAGE-NUMBER              PIC 9(4).
000760     05  WS-LINES-PER-PAGE           PIC 9(4) VALUE 40.
000770     05  WS-LINES-USED               PIC 9(4).
000780*
000790*················································
000800*    INITIALIZED AND TESTED IN THE PROCEDURE DIVISION TO DETECT
000810*    THE END OF THE TAPE FILE.
000820*················································
000830*
000840 01  WS-RECORD-INDICATORS.
000850     05  WS-EOF-INDICATOR            PIC X(3).
000860         88 WS-END-OF-EMPLOYEE-FILE  VALUE 'END'.
```

Program 1–2 *(continued)*

```
000870*
000880*·················································································
000890*    USED TO DETECT A NEW REGION - INITIALIZED AFTER A PRIMING
000900*    READ AND TESTED ON EVERY SUBSEQUENT RECORD.
000910*·················································································
000920*
000930 01  PR-PREVIOUS-RECORD-INDICATORS.
000940     05  PR-PREVIOUS-REGION-NUMBER    PIC X(1).
000950*
000960*·················································································
000970*    USED TO ACCUMULATED REGION AND GRAND TOTALS FOR REPORT.
000980*·················································································
000990*
001000 01  WS-ACCUMULATORS.
001010*
001020     05  GT-GRAND-TOTAL-ACCUMULATORS.
001030         10  GT-TOT-YTD-GROSS-PAY      PIC 9(7)V99.
001040         10  GT-TOT-YTD-FEDERAL-TAXES  PIC 9(7)V99.
001050         10  GT-TOT-YTD-FICA-TAXES     PIC 9(7)V99.
001060         10  GT-TOT-YTD-STATE-TAXES    PIC 9(7)V99.
001070*
001080     05  RT-REGION-TOTAL-ACCUMULATORS.
001090         10  RT-TOT-YTD-GROSS-PAY      PIC 9(7)V99.
001100         10  RT-TOT-YTD-FEDERAL-TAXES  PIC 9(7)V99.
001110         10  RT-TOT-YTD-FICA-TAXES     PIC 9(7)V99.
001120         10  RT-TOT-YTD-STATE-TAXES    PIC 9(7)V99.
001130*
001140*·················································································
001150*    THREE HEADING LINES FOR THE REPORT PRINTED ON EACH PAGE.
001160*·················································································
001170*
001180 01  HD-HEADING-LINE-1.
001190     05  FILLER                        PIC X(26) VALUE SPACES.
001200     05  FILLER                        PIC X(28)
001210                          VALUE 'PAYROLL CONTROL BREAK REPORT'.
001220     05  FILLER                        PIC X(19) VALUE SPACES.
001230     05  FILLER                        PIC X(5)  VALUE 'PAGE '.
001240     05  HD-PAGE-NUMBER-OUT            PIC Z9.
001250*
001260 01  HD-HEADING-LINE-2.
001270     05  FILLER                        PIC X(8)  VALUE 'EMPLOYEE'.
001280     05  FILLER                        PIC X(22) VALUE SPACES.
001290     05  FILLER                        PIC X(5)  VALUE 'GROSS'.
001300     05  FILLER                        PIC X(8)  VALUE SPACES.
001310     05  FILLER                        PIC X(7)  VALUE 'FEDERAL'.
001320     05  FILLER                        PIC X(19) VALUE SPACES.
001330     05  FILLER                        PIC X(5)  VALUE 'STATE'.
001340*
001350 01  HD-HEADING-LINE-3.
001360     05  FILLER                        PIC X(4)  VALUE 'NAME'.
001370     05  FILLER                        PIC X(17) VALUE SPACES.
001380     05  FILLER                        PIC X(12)
001390                          VALUE 'RN PN DN PAY'.
001400     05  FILLER                        PIC X(10) VALUE SPACES.
001410     05  FILLER                        PIC X(10)
001420                          VALUE 'INCOME TAX'.
001430     05  FILLER                        PIC X(3)  VALUE SPACES.
001440     05  FILLER                        PIC X(8)  VALUE 'FICA TAX'.
001450     05  FILLER                        PIC X(5)  VALUE SPACES.
001460     05  FILLER                        PIC X(10)
001470                          VALUE 'INCOME TAX'.
001480*
001490*·················································································
```

Program 1–2 *(continued)*

```
001500*    FORMATTED DETAIL LINE FOR THE REPORT.
001510*········································································
001520*
001530 01  DL-DETAIL-LINE.
001540     05  DL-EMPLOYEE-NAME              PIC X(20).
001550     05  FILLER                        PIC X(1) VALUE SPACES.
001560     05  DL-REGION-NUMBER              PIC Z9.
001570     05  FILLER                        PIC X(1) VALUE SPACES.
001580     05  DL-PLANT-NUMBER               PIC Z9.
001590     05  FILLER                        PIC X(1) VALUE SPACES.
001600     05  DL-DEPARTMENT-NUMBER          PIC Z9.
001610     05  FILLER                        PIC X(1) VALUE SPACES.
001620     05  DL-YTD-GROSS-PAY              PIC $ZZZ,ZZ9.99.
001630     05  FILLER                        PIC X(2) VALUE SPACES.
001640     05  DL-YTD-FEDERAL-TAXES          PIC $ZZZ,ZZ9.99.
001650     05  FILLER                        PIC X(2) VALUE SPACES.
001660     05  DL-YTD-FICA-TAXES             PIC $ZZZ,ZZ9.99.
001670     05  FILLER                        PIC X(2) VALUE SPACES.
001680     05  DL-YTD-STATE-TAXES            PIC $ZZZ,ZZ9.99.
001690*
001700*········································································
001710*    FORMATTED TOTAL LINE USED FOR BOTH REGION AND COMPANY TOTALS.
001720*········································································
001730*
001740 01  TL-TOTAL-LINE.
001750     05  TL-STUB-HEADING-NAME          PIC X(21).
001760     05  TL-REGION-NUMBER              PIC Z9.
001770     05  FILLER                        PIC X(1) VALUE SPACES.
001780     05  TL-PLANT-NUMBER               PIC Z9.
001790     05  FILLER                        PIC X(1) VALUE SPACES.
001800     05  TL-DEPARTMENT-NUMBER          PIC Z9.
001810     05  FILLER                        PIC X(1) VALUE SPACES.
001820     05  TL-YTD-GROSS-PAY              PIC $ZZZ,ZZ9.99.
001830     05  FILLER                        PIC X(2) VALUE SPACES.
001840     05  TL-YTD-FEDERAL-TAXES          PIC $ZZZ,ZZ9.99.
001850     05  FILLER                        PIC X(2) VALUE SPACES.
001860     05  TL-YTD-FICA-TAXES             PIC $ZZZ,ZZ9.99.
001870     05  FILLER                        PIC X(2) VALUE SPACES.
001880     05  TL-YTD-STATE-TAXES            PIC $ZZZ,ZZ9.99.
001890/
001900 PROCEDURE DIVISION.
001910*
001920 A000-TOTALS-BY-REGION.
001930*
001940*········································································
001950*    MAIN CONTROL MODULE - CONTROLS EXECUTION OF SIX MAJOR MODULES
001960*········································································
001970*
001980     OPEN INPUT PAYROLL-INPUT-FILE
001990          OUTPUT CONTROL-BREAK-REPORT.
002000     PERFORM B100-INITIALIZE-VARIABLES.
002010     PERFORM Z100-PRINT-HEADINGS.
002020     PERFORM Z200-READ-PAYROLL-RECORD.
002030     PERFORM B400-INITIAL-RECORD-ROUTINE.
002040     PERFORM B500-PROCESS-RECORDS
002050          UNTIL WS-END-OF-EMPLOYEE-FILE.
002060     PERFORM B600-PRINT-GRAND-TOTALS.
002070     CLOSE PAYROLL-INPUT-FILE
002080          CONTROL-BREAK-REPORT.
002090     STOP RUN.
002100*
002110*········································································
002120*    1.  INITIALIZING OF NUMERIC VARIABLES
```

Program 1–2 *(continued)*

```
002130*    2.  SETTING SWITCH TO CONTROL FOR END OF FILE CONDITION.
002140*······················································
002150*
002160 B100-INITIALIZE-VARIABLES.
002170     MOVE ZEROES TO WS-PAGE-NUMBER
002180                   WS-ACCUMULATORS.
002190     MOVE 'NO'  TO WS-EOF-INDICATOR.
002200*
002210*······················································
002220*    THIS MODULE IS EXECUTED ONLY AT THE BEGINNING OF THE
002230*    PROGRAM TO ENSURE THAT A CONTROL BREAK DOES NOT OCCUR ON
002240*    THE FIRST RECORD.
002250*······················································
002260*
002270 B400-INITIAL-RECORD-ROUTINE.
002280     MOVE PI-REGION-NUMBER   TO PR-PREVIOUS-REGION-NUMBER.
002290*
002300*······················································
002310*    1.  EACH RECORD IS TESTED FOR A NEW REGION NUMBER.  IF A NEW
002320*        REGION IS DETECTED, REGION TOTALS ARE PRINTED.
002330*    2.  INDIVIDUAL EMPLOYEE DATA IS PRINTED ON THE REPORT.
002340*    3.  INDIVIDUAL EMPLOYEE VALUES ARE ADDED TO REGION TOTALS.
002350*    4.  SUBSEQUENT EMPLOYEE RECORDS ARE READ.
002360*······················································
002370*
002380 B500-PROCESS-RECORDS.
002390     IF PI-REGION-NUMBER NOT = PR-PREVIOUS-REGION-NUMBER
002400         PERFORM Z300-REGION-TOTAL-ROUTINE.
002410     PERFORM C200-WRITE-DETAIL-LINE.
002420     PERFORM C300-ADD-FIELDS-TO-TOTALS.
002430     PERFORM Z200-READ-PAYROLL-RECORD.
002440*
002450*······················································
002460*    1.  REGION TOTALS FOR THE LAST REGION IN THE COMPANY ARE
002470*        CALCULATED AND PRINTED.
002480*    2.  GRAND TOTALS ARE PRINTED.
002490*······················································
002500*
002510 B600-PRINT-GRAND-TOTALS.
002520     PERFORM Z300-REGION-TOTAL-ROUTINE.
002530     MOVE SPACES                 TO TL-TOTAL-LINE.
002540     MOVE GT-TOT-YTD-GROSS-PAY    TO TL-YTD-GROSS-PAY.
002550     MOVE GT-TOT-YTD-FEDERAL-TAXES TO TL-YTD-FEDERAL-TAXES.
002560     MOVE GT-TOT-YTD-FICA-TAXES   TO TL-YTD-FICA-TAXES.
002570     MOVE GT-TOT-YTD-STATE-TAXES  TO TL-YTD-STATE-TAXES.
002580     MOVE 'GRAND TOTALS'          TO TL-STUB-HEADING-NAME.
002590     MOVE TL-TOTAL-LINE           TO CB-CONTROL-BREAK-RECORD.
002600     WRITE CB-CONTROL-BREAK-RECORD
002610         AFTER 1.
002620/
002630*
002640*······················································
002650*    1.  HEADINGS ARE PRINTED AT THE TOP OF EACH NEW PAGE.
002660*    2.  INDIVIDUAL EMPLOYEE DATA IS PRINTED.
002670*······················································
002680*
002690 C200-WRITE-DETAIL-LINE.
002700     IF WS-LINES-USED > WS-LINES-PER-PAGE
002710         PERFORM Z100-PRINT-HEADINGS.
002720     MOVE PI-EMPLOYEE-NAME       TO DL-EMPLOYEE-NAME.
002730     MOVE PI-DEPARTMENT-NUMBER   TO DL-DEPARTMENT-NUMBER.
002740     MOVE PI-PLANT-NUMBER        TO DL-PLANT-NUMBER.
002750     MOVE PI-REGION-NUMBER       TO DL-REGION-NUMBER.
```

Program 1–2   *(continued)*

```
002760      MOVE PI-YTD-GROSS-PAY          TO DL-YTD-GROSS-PAY.
002770      MOVE PI-YTD-FEDERAL-TAXES      TO DL-YTD-FEDERAL-TAXES.
002780      MOVE PI-YTD-FICA-TAXES         TO DL-YTD-FICA-TAXES.
002790      MOVE PI-YTD-STATE-TAXES        TO DL-YTD-STATE-TAXES.
002800      MOVE DL-DETAIL-LINE TO CB-CONTROL-BREAK-RECORD.
002810      WRITE CB-CONTROL-BREAK-RECORD
002820          AFTER 1.
002830      ADD 1 TO WS-LINES-USED.
002840*
002850**************************************************************
002860*    INDIVIDUAL EMPLOYEE VALUES ARE ADDED TO THE REGION TOTALS.
002870**************************************************************
002880*
002890 C300-ADD-FIELDS-TO-TOTALS.
002900      ADD PI-YTD-GROSS-PAY     TO RT-TOT-YTD-GROSS-PAY.
002910      ADD PI-YTD-FEDERAL-TAXES TO RT-TOT-YTD-FEDERAL-TAXES.
002920      ADD PI-YTD-FICA-TAXES    TO RT-TOT-YTD-FICA-TAXES.
002930      ADD PI-YTD-STATE-TAXES   TO RT-TOT-YTD-STATE-TAXES.
002940/
002950*
002960**************************************************************
002970*    COMMON MODULE TO PRINT THE HEADINGS.  THIS MODULE IS
002980*    PERFORMED FROM THE MAIN MODULE AND FROM
002990*    C200-WRITE-DETAIL-LINE WHEN NECESSARY.
003000**************************************************************
003010*
003020 Z100-PRINT-HEADINGS.
003030      ADD 1                    TO WS-PAGE-NUMBER.
003040      MOVE WS-PAGE-NUMBER      TO HD-PAGE-NUMBER-OUT.
003050      MOVE HD-HEADING-LINE-1   TO CB-CONTROL-BREAK-RECORD.
003060      WRITE CB-CONTROL-BREAK-RECORD
003070          AFTER PAGE.
003080      MOVE HD-HEADING-LINE-2   TO CB-CONTROL-BREAK-RECORD.
003090      WRITE CB-CONTROL-BREAK-RECORD
003100          AFTER 2.
003110      MOVE HD-HEADING-LINE-3   TO CB-CONTROL-BREAK-RECORD.
003120      WRITE CB-CONTROL-BREAK-RECORD
003130          AFTER 1.
003140      MOVE SPACES              TO CB-CONTROL-BREAK-RECORD.
003150      WRITE CB-CONTROL-BREAK-RECORD
003160          AFTER 1.
003170      MOVE 5                   TO WS-LINES-USED.
003180*
003190**************************************************************
003200*    COMMON MODULE TO READ EACH EMPLOYEE RECORD.  THIS MODULE IS
003210*    PERFORMED FROM THE MAIN MODULE AND FROM B500-PROCESS-RECORDS.
003220**************************************************************
003230*
003240 Z200-READ-PAYROLL-RECORD.
003250      READ PAYROLL-INPUT-FILE
003260          AT END MOVE 'END' TO WS-EOF-INDICATOR.
003270*
003280**************************************************************
003290*    COMMON MODULE TO CALCULATE AND PRINT REGION TOTALS.  THIS IS
003300*    PERFORMED FROM B600-PRINT-GRAND-TOTALS FOR THE LAST REGION
003310*    AND FROM B500-PROCESS-RECORDS WHEN A NEW REGION IS DETECTED.
003320**************************************************************
003330*
003340 Z300-REGION-TOTAL-ROUTINE.
003350      MOVE SPACES                TO TL-TOTAL-LINE.
003360      MOVE RT-TOT-YTD-GROSS-PAY      TO TL-YTD-GROSS-PAY.
003370      MOVE RT-TOT-YTD-FEDERAL-TAXES  TO TL-YTD-FEDERAL-TAXES.
003380      MOVE RT-TOT-YTD-FICA-TAXES     TO TL-YTD-FICA-TAXES.
```

Program 1–2 *(concluded)*

```
003390      MOVE RT-TOT-YTD-STATE-TAXES    TO TL-YTD-STATE-TAXES.
003400      MOVE 'REGION TOTALS'           TO TL-STUB-HEADING-NAME.
003410      MOVE PR-PREVIOUS-REGION-NUMBER TO TL-REGION-NUMBER.
003420      MOVE TL-TOTAL-LINE             TO CB-CONTROL-BREAK-RECORD.
003430      WRITE CB-CONTROL-BREAK-RECORD
003440          AFTER 2.
003450      MOVE SPACES                    TO CB-CONTROL-BREAK-RECORD.
003460      WRITE CB-CONTROL-BREAK-RECORD
003470          AFTER 1.
003480      ADD 3                          TO WS-LINES-USED.
003490      ADD RT-TOT-YTD-GROSS-PAY       TO GT-TOT-YTD-GROSS-PAY.
003500      ADD RT-TOT-YTD-FEDERAL-TAXES   TO GT-TOT-YTD-FEDERAL-TAXES.
003510      ADD RT-TOT-YTD-FICA-TAXES      TO GT-TOT-YTD-FICA-TAXES.
003520      ADD RT-TOT-YTD-STATE-TAXES     TO GT-TOT-YTD-STATE-TAXES.
003530      MOVE ZEROES                    TO RT-REGION-TOTAL-ACCUMULATORS.
003540      MOVE PI-REGION-NUMBER          TO PR-PREVIOUS-REGION-NUMBER.
```

DATA Division Standards

1. Vertically align similar clauses. Notice the vertical alignment of both PIC clauses and VALUE clauses throughout the DATA division. This serves to make the statements readable and makes it easier to manually count the number of characters in a record.

2. Use the same form of a statement consistently. Make a decision as to the form used (i.e., PIC, PIC IS, VALUE, VALUE IS) and be consistent throughout.

3. Indent successive levels within records. Successive level numbers are usually indented four spaces and associated data-names separated from the level numbers by two spaces. Also note the indentation of 88-level items, such as at line 860.

4. Use level numbers with successive gaps of 5 (5, 10, 15, and so on).

5. Utilize the RECORD CONTAINS clause. Even though this is an optional statement, it serves the purpose of having the compiler inform the programmer if the number of actual characters is incorrect and can save many problems later.

6. Use significant data-names. COBOL allows up to 30 characters and thus provides the programmer sufficient abilities to be creative. Also use a two- or three-character prefix to identify subdivisions of records. (DL-EMPLOYEE-NAME thus is a part of DL-DETAIL-LINE; PI-EMPLOYEE-NAME is a part of PI-PAYROLL-INPUT-RECORD.)

7. Decide on a general order of records within WORKING-STORAGE. Though any order, consistently applied, is acceptable, the authors generally place switches, flags, and accumulators first, followed by heading lines, detail lines, and total lines. Another convenient method is an alphabetical arrangement.

PROCEDURE Division Standards

1. Use structured design concepts. This is perhaps the most important organizational standard that could be adopted.

2. Provide some sequencing scheme for procedure names. Though the scheme is arbitrary (some programmers use a straight numbering scheme, such as 100– 200–), any program is difficult to follow without some sort of sequencing, particularly when the program is very long. The authors use both a letter (which indicates the level of detail from the structure chart) and a number (which indicates sequence within a detail level).

   One advantage to the lettering is knowing the level of detail. Also if the programmer is ever tempted to perform a module at a higher level of detail, it would be immediately apparent. For example, the programmer should never perform a B-level module from a C-level module.

   Additionally, the authors give common modules (modules that are referenced from more than one place in the program) the letter Z as the detail letter. This gives the programmer immediate knowledge that a common module affects more than one other module, thus leading to extra care when modifying the common module. The labeling scheme is also used on the structure chart to make cross-referencing between the structure chart and the program a fairly simple process.

3. Use significant procedure names. Typically a procedure name is divided into two or three parts for the name itself. An additional sequencing number can also be added. For instance, a common scheme for a three-part name would include a verb, an adjective, and a noun, such as PRINT–DETAIL–RECORDS.

4. Initialize variables in the PROCEDURE division. Most organizations prefer to initialize constant values in the DATA division, while any value that may change during the execution of the program, such as accumulators, are initialized in the PROCEDURE division. Though this choice is arbitrary, be consistent.

5. Vertically align similar statements or clauses. The obvious example is a set of MOVE statements such as in lines 2530 through 2590. Readability is improved, and it is easier to ensure that all necessary fields have been included.

6. Make a decision related to the use of READ/INTO and WRITE/FROM options and be consistent. The same also applies to the form of the AFTER clause of the WRITE statement. Make a decision as to the use of either the integer or the data-name option and be consistent.

7. Make effective use of 88-level condition-names. Condition-names afford the opportunity to make COBOL more English-like and improve readability.

8. Minimize the use of switches. Though switches cannot be totally eliminated, excessive use of switches leads to confusion.

9. Indent IF/ELSE statements by aligning the ELSE clause with its associated IF statement. This is particularly important when using nested IF statements.

10. Minimize the use of nested IF statements. Some organizations ban their use altogether. Others specify a certain level in the depth of nested IF statements that they will allow.

11. Eliminate the use of AND and OR in the same IF statement condition. This is particularly hazardous when using the NOT operator. Also minimize the use of implied subjects and operators in compound IF statements.

12. Choose a sequence of procedures and be consistent. Figure 1–20 provides two alternative methods of ordering the paragraphs in Program 1–2. The location of these procedures, except the main module, has no effect on the actual execution of these procedures when using structured design concepts.

Figure 1–20   *Alternative PROCEDURE Division Module Sequences*

By detail level	By execution sequence
A100	A100
B100	B100
B400	Z100
B500	Z200
B600	B400
C200	B500
C300	Z300
Z100	C200
Z200	C300
Z300	B600

Other Programming Standards

1. Make effective use of internal comments. Well-written COBOL code usually does not suffice. Additional comments help make the program easier to modify. Additionally, internal documentation is more likely to be changed than external documentation.

2. Make effective use of white space (with blank lines or a slash in column 7, for example) to separate parts of a program.

3. Include one and only one statement per line. Additionally, indent subservient clauses on the next line. Examples here include the AT END clause of the READ statement, the VARYING clause of the PERFORM, and the OCCURS clause.

4. Make effective use of structured walkthroughs. This is where teams of programmers, including peers, subordinates, and superiors come together to discuss the structure and design of a program before it is actually written. It is much less costly to catch a design problem in the design phase than when the program is actually put into production.

5. Consider using skeleton COBOL programs. This is particularly useful with current text processing systems, which enable electronic merging of one set of source statements into another. One company with which the authors are familiar uses a series of skeleton programs for all their applications. If a programmer does not wish to use one of these skeletons, the reasons for the departure from the standard must be defended to the structured walkthrough team.

2

Tables

The use of tables in computer programming enables a program to store data in main storage to be used repeatedly. They also minimize the number of data names that are used in a program by utilizing indexes or subscripts to manipulate data in the tables. There are a myriad of applications for the use of tables, such as tables for pay rates, tables for tax rates, tables for print images, tables for names of the months, days of the week, tables for sorting, tables for variable length records and many other examples.

TERMS AND STATEMENTS

Binary search	OCCURS clause	SET statement
Displacement value	OCCURS/	Security
Hard-coding	DEPENDING ON	Single level table
INDEXED BY clause	clause	Subscript
Index	PERFORM	Three level table
Index data item	VARYING	Two level table
Index-name	Statement	USAGE IS INDEX
Input-loading	SEARCH ALL	clause
Linear search	statement	Volatility
Nested looping	SEARCH statement	

Table Concepts

Consider the table of pay rates in Figure 2–1. This table shows five different pay levels and the corresponding pay rates for each level. At payroll time, data are read in from time cards that contain the pay level and number of hours worked for each employee. Then depending on the pay level, the gross pay is computed. For instance, an employee on the third pay level would be paid $8.50 per hour.

Figure 2–1   *Pay Rate Table*

Pay level	Pay rate
1	7.50
2	8.00
3	8.50
4	9.00
5	9.50

Need for Tables

There are two ways to compute gross pay without the use of tables. One alternative is to determine the person's pay rate external to the program and to enter the pay rate into the input record along with the employee's hours worked. This alternative does not make effective use of the computer and may cause additional input data errors. The second alternative is to create data names for each of the pay rates and then select the appropriate pay rate using IF statements. This latter approach is illustrated in Figure 2–2.

Figure 2–2   *Pay Rates Defined without a COBOL Table*

```
WORKING-STORAGE SECTION.
01  PR-PAY-RATE-VALUES.
    05  PAY-RATE-1      PIC 9V99 VALUE 7.50.
    05  PAY-RATE-2      PIC 9V99 VALUE 8.00.
    05  PAY-RATE-3      PIC 9V99 VALUE 8.50.
    05  PAY-RATE-4      PIC 9V99 VALUE 9.00.
    05  PAY-RATE-5      PIC 9V99 VALUE 9.50.

PROCEDURE DIVISION.

    IF IN-PAY-LEVEL = 1
        MOVE PAY-RATE-1 TO WS-PAY-RATE-WORK.
    IF IN-PAY-LEVEL = 2
        MOVE PAY-RATE-2 TO WS-PAY-RATE-WORK.
    IF IN-PAY-LEVEL = 3
        MOVE PAY-RATE-3 TO WS-PAY-RATE-WORK.
    IF IN-PAY-LEVEL = 4
        MOVE PAY-RATE-4 TO WS-PAY-RATE-WORK.
    IF IN-PAY-LEVEL = 5
        MOVE PAY-RATE-5 TO WS-PAY-RATE-WORK.
```

In Figure 2–2, each pay rate is defined with its own programmer-supplied data name and its associated value with a VALUE clause. Then in the PROCEDURE division, the input pay level is tested to determine the appropriate pay rate. In essence, a table of pay rate values has been created in main storage so it can be repeatedly accessed. However, this does not take advantage of COBOL, which allows for the definition and manipulation of tables in a simpler manner. Notice the names that were given to each of the pay rates—PAY-RATE-1, PAY-RATE-2, and so on. It would be simpler if there were a way to indicate to the computer each pay rate's numerical position in the table. This is done in COBOL either through the use of subscripts or indexes. Subscripts are numeric values that are defined and manipulated by the programmer to indicate the value's numerical position in a table. Indexes are compiler-generated values that also are used to determine a value's position in a table. While indexes are compiler-generated, they may be manipulated by the programmer.

Definition and Creation of Tables

Before it can be shown how subscripts and indexes are manipulated, however, it is necessary to first illustrate how a table can be created. A table can be defined as a collection of related entries. To indicate the number of entries in a table, the **OCCURS clause** is used. The format of the OCCURS clause is illustrated in Figure 2–3. Figure 2–4 shows a revision of the COBOL statements in Figure 2–2 to illustrate how the table is defined and accessed.

Figure 2–3 *Format of the OCCURS Clause*

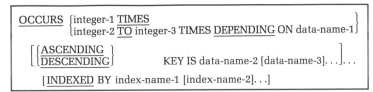

Rules to be aware of when using the OCCURS clause are as follows:

- Integer-1 and integer-2 must be a numeric integer literal greater than zero. Some compilers allow the use of zero for integer-2.
- An OCCURS clause cannot be associated with an 01-, 77-, or 88-level number.
- An OCCURS clause may be used with an elementary item or group data-item.
- An OCCURS clause may not contain a VALUE clause.
- The OCCURS clause must follow the data-name that it describes, such as 05 data-name PIC X(2) OCCURS, or 05 data-name OCCURS PIC X(2).
- When either the INDEXED BY or the KEY clauses are used they must follow the OCCURS clause, such as 05 data-name PIC X(2) OCCURS n TIMES ASCENDING KEY data-name INDEXED BY index-name.
- If used, the INDEXED BY must be the last entry in the OCCURS clause on many systems.
- The DEPENDING option allows the use of a variable number of entries in a table where integer-2 is the smallest number of entries and integer-3 is the maximum number of entries.
- Data-name-1 defines the number of entries to be used in the table and cannot be less than integer-2 or greater than integer-3.
- No type of OCCURS clause can be subordinate to an **OCCURS/DEPENDING ON clause.**
- An OCCURS/DEPENDING ON can only be followed by subordinate items.

The PIC clause can be located anywhere after the data-name, but as a matter of style, it is a good idea to place the PIC clause in its normal location followed by the OCCURS, KEY, and INDEXED BY clauses.

Instead of creating data names for each of the pay rates, it is now possible to use only one data-name, PAY–RATE, that OCCURS 5 TIMES. The OCCURS 5 TIMES entry indicates to the compiler that the data-name PAY–RATE has five possible data values. The programmer is responsible for defining a sufficient number of posi-

Figure 2-4   *OCCURS Clause Example*

```
WORKING-STORAGE SECTION.
01  PR-PAY-RATE-VALUES.
        05  FILLER            PIC 9V99 VALUE 7.50.
        05  FILLER            PIC 9V99 VALUE 8.00.
        05  FILLER            PIC 9V99 VALUE 8.50.
        05  FILLER            PIC 9V99 VALUE 9.00.
        05  FILLER            PIC 9V99 VALUE 9.50.
01  FILLER REDEFINES PR-PAY-RATE-VALUES.
        05  PAY-RATE          PIC 9V99
                OCCURS 5 TIMES.

PROCEDURE DIVISION.
     MOVE PAY-RATE(IN-PAY-LEVEL) TO WS-PAY-RATE-WORK.
```

tions. Notice the use of the REDEFINES clause. This allows the system to initialize the values in the table through the use of VALUE clause in PR–PAY–RATE–VALUES and then assign the data-name PAY–RATE to the same locations through the REDE FINES clause. Notice also that the OCCURS clause appears at the 05 level and that no data-name has been used at the 01 level. For better documentation within the program, the programmer may wish to use a data-name at the 01 level, such as PAY–RATE–TABLE, but in this example, there is no need to access the value at the 01 level. Instead of a data-name, FILLER is used.

Whenever all of the elements in a table may not be used, it is often advantageous to use the DEPENDING ON option of the OCCURS clause. Figure 2–5 shows an example of its use.

Figure 2-5   *DEPENDING ON Option of OCCURS Clause*

```
01  WS-NUMBER-ELEMENTS            PIC 9(4).
01  NA-NAME-ADDRESS-VALUES.
        05  NA-NAME ADDRESS           PIC X(50).
                OCCURS 1 TO 1000 TIMES
                DEPENDING ON WS-NUMBER-ELEMENTS.
```

The value of WS–NUMBER–ELEMENTS is the maximum number of elements in the table, which in this example can be from 1 through 1,000. Flexibility is the advantage of using this option. The program may need only 75 elements the first time it is used but may require 900 elements the next time. The system will always check the subscript or index against the number of elements defined by WS–NUM BER–ELEMENTS. This option will usually cause fewer programming errors when a table is only partially used, and in such cases its use is recommended.

Table Access

Once a table has been defined, any element in the table can be accessed by the use of subscripts or indexes. The format for the access of an element in a table is shown in Figure 2–6.

The entries in the PROCEDURE division in Figure 2–4 are greatly simplified. All that needs to be done is to ensure that the value contained in IN–PAY–LEVEL is an appropriate numeric value indicating a particular pay rate. For instance, if IN–PAY–LEVEL were 3, then 8.50 would be moved to WS–PAY–RATE–WORK. If IN–PAY–LEVEL were 5, then 9.50 would be moved, and so on.

Figure 2–6 *Table Element Access Formats*

```
Format for Access by Subscripts:
        Data-name (subscript[, subscript][, subscript])
        where:
                data-name is any data-name that has been defined with
                        an OCCURS clause, either at the group or
                        elementary level, and
                subscript is any numeric literal or elementary
                        data-name that represents a positive integer.

Format for Access by Indexes:
        Data-name (index[, index][, index])
        where:
                index is either an index-name specified as a
                        part of the OCCURS clause or an index data item
                        defined in WORKING–STORAGE.
```

Table Concepts—Single Level Tables

Creating

A **single level table** is a list of row or column values and is defined by using a single OCCURS clause. The creation of a table can be accomplished by two different methods: (1) hard-coding or (2) input-loading. **Hard-coding**, also known as a compile time table, means that the table is created by the use of VALUE and REDEFINES clauses. **Input-loading**, also referred to as run-time tables, means that the data will be read in from an external device and transferred to the table by means of MOVE statements in the PROCEDURE division. The decision to hard-code or input-load the table depends on two primary factors: security and volatility. **Volatility** refers to how frequently the data change. Input-loading the data from an external device would be appropriate if the data change frequently. **Security** considerations may necessitate making it difficult for others to have access to the table values. In this case, hard-coding the table can make it relatively inaccessible. In a production environment it is normal to compile and store it in an object code form in a cataloged library. Table values stored in object program form are difficult to change. In either case, the table itself is defined in the same way; the difference lies simply in how the table is filled with data.

As is normal in COBOL, there are many ways to define or create tables. For instance, Figure 2–7 shows two ways that could have been used to define the pay rate table. They both produce results equivalent to that shown in Figure 2–4.

Because of the use of the REDEFINES clause, the way the tables are defined is at the discretion of the programmer. In any case data values defined with VALUE clauses are assigned to appropriate positions in the table in sequence from top to bottom or left to right.

To illustrate the concept of input-loading with subscripts, assume that the pay rates have been keyed into input records currently residing on a disk device. The COBOL statements necessary to input-load the sample table are illustrated in Figure 2–8.

In Figure 2–8, WS–PAY–RATE–SUBSCRIPT is defined in WORKING–STORAGE and initialized to 1 in the PROCEDURE division. The first time B200–TABLE–LOAD is performed, the data from the first record will be transferred to PAY–RATE(1). The second record is read and will be transferred to PAY–RATE(2). This procedure continues until all five data records have been input-loaded. After the fifth record has been transferred, WS–PAY–RATE–SUBSCRIPT becomes 6 and the loop is terminated (because the UNTIL is then a true condition). Notice that WS–PAY–RATE–SUBSCRIPT is a single subscript data-name because it is used with a single level

Figure 2–7   *Hard-Coding a Single Level Table*

```
Example A:

      WORKING-STORAGE SECTION.
      01   PR-PAY-RATE-VALUES.
             05   FILLER            PIC X(3) VALUE '750'.
             05   FILLER            PIC X(3) VALUE '800'.
             05   FILLER            PIC X(3) VALUE '850'.
             05   FILLER            PIC X(3) VALUE '900'.
             05   FILLER            PIC X(3) VALUE '950'.
      01   FILLER REDEFINES PR-PAY-RATE-VALUES.
             05   PAY-RATE          PIC 9V99
                    OCCURS 5 TIMES.

Example B:

      WORKING-STORAGE SECTION.
      01   PR-PAY-RATE-VALUES.
             05   FILLER            PIC X(15)
                    VALUE '750800850900950'.
      01   FILLER REDEFINES PR-PAY-RATE-VALUES.
             05   PAY-RATE          PIC 9V99
                    OCCURS 5 TIMES.
```

table. Another way to accomplish the same result is through the use of the VARYING option of the PERFORM. The format for this option is shown in Figure 2–9.

Figure 2–10 illustrates how the **PERFORM/VARYING statement** is used. This statement automatically initializes the subscript or index (FROM 1), increments the subscript or index (BY 1), and tests the loop condition (UNTIL WS–PAY–RATE–SUBSCRIPT > 5).

Accessing

A **subscript** is a positive integer, numeric value that must be defined with an appropriate PICTURE clause. This value, when manipulated by the programmer, readily corresponds to the mathematical concept of subscripting.

Figure 2–8   *Input-Loading a Table with Subscripts*

```
FD   PAY-RATE-TABLE-FILE
       RECORD CONTAINS 3 CHARACTERS
       LABEL RECORDS STANDARD.
01   PR-PAY-RATE-RECORD.
       05   PR-PAY-RATE              PIC 9V99.
     .
WORKING-STORAGE SECTION.
01   FILLER.
       05   PAY-RATE                 PIC 9V99
              OCCURS 5 TIMES.
01   WS-WORK-AREAS.
       05   WS-PAY-RATE-SUBSCRIPT    PIC 9.
     .
PROCEDURE-DIVISION.
     .
     MOVE 1 TO WS-PAY-RATE-SUBSCRIPT.
     PERFORM-B200-TABLE-LOAD
         UNTIL WS-PAY-RATE-SUBSCRIPT > 5.
     .
B200-TABLE-LOAD.
     READ PAY-RATE-TABLE-FILE.
     MOVE PR-PAY-RATE TO PAY-RATE(WS-PAY-RATE-SUBSCRIPT).
     ADD 1              TO WS-PAY-RATE-SUBSCRIPT.
```

Figure 2-9 *Format of the PERFORM/VARYING*

```
PERFORM procedure-name-1 [THRU procedure-name-2]

        VARYING   {index-name-1}   FROM   {index-name-2}
                  {identifier-1}          {literal-1   }
                                          {identifier-2}

        BY   {literal-2   }   UNTIL condition-1
             {identifier-3}

        [AFTER   {index-name-3}   FROM   {index-name-4}
                 {identifier-4}          {literal-3   }
                                         {identifier-5}

        BY   {literal-4   }   UNTIL condition-2]
             {identifier-6}

        [AFTER   {index-name-5}   FROM   {index-name-6}
                 {identifier-7}          {literal-5   }
                                         {identifier-8}

        BY   {literal-6   }   UNTIL condition-3]]
             {identifier-9}
```

Figure 2-10 *Example of the PERFORM/VARYING Statement*

```
PERFORM B200-TABLE-LOAD
    VARYING WS-PAY-RATE-SUBSCRIPT
    FROM 1 BY 1
    UNTIL WS-PAY-RATE-SUBSCRIPT > 5.

B200-TABLE-LOAD
    READ PAY-RATE-TABLE-FILE.
    MOVE IN-PAY-RATE TO PAY-RATE(WS-PAY-RATE-SUBSCRIPT).
```

An **index** is a compiler-generated, internal data-item that does not have a PICTURE clause. The programmer can associate an index with a particular table by specifying as part of the OCCURS clause with an **INDEXED BY clause** and an **index-name.** Figure 2-3 shows the format for these clauses, and Figure 2-12 illustrates how they are used. While the index is specified by the INDEXED BY clause, it must be initialized by a PERFORM/VARYING statement or a **SET statement** before it can be used in a program.

An **index data item** is an elementary item that is not associated with any particular table and can be used to save index-name values for future reference. It is specified by the programmer with a **USAGE IS INDEX clause** without a PICTURE clause. The index data item can receive the index-name value only through a SET statement. It can then be used in place of a subscript or index-name when referencing data elements in a table. An index data item cannot be used in a PERFORM/VARYING statement, nor can it be used for any other purpose than storing index-name values and referencing data elements in a table. Neither an index-name nor an index data item can be the object of a MOVE or any arithmetic statement.

Formats of the SET statement are shown in Figure 2-11.

Rules for the use of the SET statement are:

- All identifiers must be either index data items or numeric, elementary, integer items (except identifier-4 cannot be an index data item).
- When a literal is used, it must be a positive integer.
- SET/DOWN decreases the value represented and SET/UP increases the value represented by the index.

Figure 2-12 illustrates possible alternatives of both an index-name and an index data item when input-loading a table.

Figure 2–11 *Formats of the SET Statement*

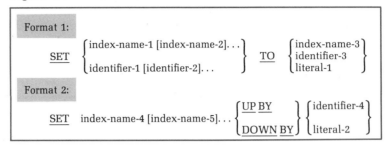

Figure 2–12 *Uses of Index-Names and Index Data Items*

```
FILE SECTION.
FD   PAY-RATE-TABLE-FILE
     RECORD CONTAINS 3 CHARACTERS
     LABEL RECORDS STANDARD.
01   PR-PAY-RATE-RECORD.
     05   PR-PAY-RATE PIC 9V99.
 .
 .
 .
WORKING-STORAGE SECTION.
01   PAY-RATE-TABLE.
     05   PAY-RATE     PIC 9V99
              OCCURS 5 TIMES
              INDEXED BY PAY-RATE-INDEX.
01   WS-WORK-AREAS.
     05   OTHER-INDEX USAGE IS INDEX.
 .
 .
 .
PROCEDURE DIVISION.
A000-INDEXING.
*  SET INDEX OPTION
     OPEN INPUT PAY-RATE-TABLE-FILE.
     SET PAY-RATE-INDEX TO 1.
     PERFORM B200-TABLE-LOAD
         UNTIL PAY-RATE-INDEX > 5.
     CLOSE PAY-RATE-TABLE-FILE.
*  PERFORM VARYING OPTION
     OPEN INPUT PAY-RATE-TABLE-FILE.
     PERFORM B300-TABLE-LOAD
         VARYING PAY-RATE-INDEX
         FROM 1 BY 1
         UNTIL PAY-RATE-INDEX > 5.
     CLOSE PAY-RATE-TABLE-FILE.
*  INDEX OPTION.
     OPEN INPUT PAY-RATE-TABLE-FILE.
     PERFORM B400-TABLE-LOAD
         VARYING PAY-RATE-INDEX
         FROM 1 BY 1
         UNTIL PAY-RATE-INDEX > 5.
     CLOSE PAY-RATE-TABLE-FILE.
     STOP RUN.
B200-TABLE-LOAD.
     READ PAY-RATE-TABLE-FILE.
     MOVE PR-PAY-RATE TO PAY-RATE(PAY-RATE-INDEX).
     SET PAY-RATE-INDEX UP BY 1.
B300-TABLE-LOAD.
     READ PAY-RATE-TABLE-FILE.
     MOVE PR-PAY-RATE TO PAY-RATE(PAY-RATE-INDEX).
B400-TABLE-LOAD.
     READ PAY-RATE-TABLE-FILE.
     SET OTHER-INDEX TO PAY-RATE-INDEX.
     MOVE PR-PAY-RATE TO PAY-RATE(OTHER-INDEX).
```

In this example, PAY–RATE–INDEX is SET to 1 before B200–TABLE–LOAD is performed. In B200–TABLE–LOAD the index is incremented by a SET/UP statement. This logic is equivalent to initializing and incrementing a subscript. The PERFORM/ VARYING is used to perform B300–TABLE–LOAD exactly the same as with subscripts. No initial SET statement is required in this case because the PERFORM/ VARYING initializes the index. B400–TABLE–LOAD shows that an index data item could have been used to reference the data element from the table, but only if the index-name value is SET to the index data item. Notice how the index data item is defined in WORKING–STORAGE with the USAGE IS INDEX clause.

The purpose of using a numeric, elementary item in the SET statement is to convert an index to an occurrence number (which represents a position in a table). This occurrence number can be printed or stored on an external device. An index itself represents an occurrence, but it is actually an internal binary value which represents a displacement value. The **displacement value** indicates how far from the beginning of the table a particular element can be found. This value is calculated when the table is defined, and it is manipulated by either a SET, PERFORM, or SEARCH statement. The system determines the value by subtracting 1 from the occurrence number and multiplying the result by the PICTURE length of the entry that is indexed. Figure 2–13 illustrates the concepts of displacement values and occurrence numbers. When the SET statement is used to set a numeric elementary item to an index, the result is the conversion of the displacement value to an occurrence number. A schematic of the PAY–RATE–TABLE is shown in Figure 2–14.

Figure 2–13 *Indexes as Internal Displacement Values*

05 PAY-RATE PIC 9V99 OCCURS 5 TIMES INDEXED BY PAY-RATE-INDEX.		
Table element	*Displacement value**	*Occurrence number*
PAY-RATE(1)	0	1
PAY-RATE(2)	3	2
PAY-RATE(3)	6	3
PAY-RATE(4)	9	4
PAY-RATE(5)	12	5

* Calculated as: (Occurrence number — 1) times 3.

Figure 2–14 *Schematic of a One Level Table*

Elementary name	PAY-RATE (1)	PAY-RATE (2)	. . .	PAY-RATE (4)
PIC	9V99	9V99		9V99

Searching

Previous sections of this text have shown how to define and load a table and have illustrated how to access a table directly using both subscripts and indexes. Many times, it is not possible to access a table directly; instead elements in the table must be searched to determine the appropriate data element. With the **SEARCH statement** and the PERFORM/VARYING statement, the programmer can accomplish a linear search. With the **SEARCH ALL statement** a binary search is possible. Both SEARCH statements require the use of indexes rather than subscripts. They also require that the INDEXED BY clause be associated with the table that is to be searched. A **linear search** means that the table will be sequentially searched

Figure 2–15   *Formats of the SEARCH Statement*

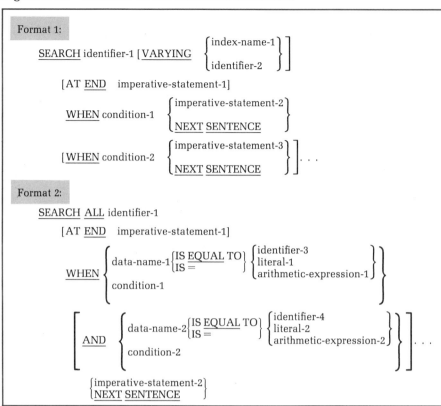

from beginning to end. A **binary search** minimizes the number of searches by continually dividing the table in half to find the appropriate table element. The formats of the SEARCH statement are shown in Figure 2–15.

1. Rules for only the SEARCH are:
   - Any valid COBOL condition may be used in a WHEN to terminate a SEARCH.
   - Any number of WHEN clauses may be used.
   - WHEN conditions are tested in the order in which they appear in the statement.
   - The first WHEN condition that is satisfied terminates the SEARCH.

2. Rules for the use of SEARCH and the SEARCH ALL are:
   - The identifier must be the subject of an OCCURS clause or be subordinate to a subject of an OCCURS clause.
   - An INDEXED BY clause must be associated with the OCCURS clause.
   - Any imperative statement may be used in both the AT END and WHEN clauses, but if any of the imperative statements do not terminate with a GO TO statement, control passes to the next sentence after execution of the imperative statement (which essentially means the next statement in the program).

3. Rules for only the SEARCH ALL are:
   - The SEARCH ALL statement requires the table data to have been sorted in either ascending or descending order.
   - Either an ASCENDING KEY or DESCENDING KEY clause must be specified as a part of the OCCURS clause.
   - The statement must contain only one WHEN clause.
   - The statement may contain as many conditions as needed connected by AND.

- Only the equal condition or a condition-name can be tested.
- The index-name being used in the search must be on the left side of the condition.

Linear Search with SEARCH

In the program example in Figure 2–16, two tables have been hard-coded to provide examples of implementing a linear search.

Figure 2–16 *One Level SEARCH*

	Table 1 Department code	Table 2 Pay rate for department
FU	— Furniture	8.75
HD	— Hardware	9.43
SP	— Sporting goods	8.50
WC	— Women's clothing	9.75

```
DATA DIVISION.
FILE SECTION.
FD  EMPLOYEE-HOUR-FILE
    LABEL RECORDS STANDARD.
01  EH-EMPLOYEE-HOUR-RECORD.
    05  EH-EMPLOYEE-NAME   PIC X(20).
    05  EH-DEPARTMENT-CODE PIC X(2).
    05  EH-HOURS-WORKED    PIC 9(2).
WORKING-STORAGE SECTION.
01  DEPARTMENT-TABLE-VALUES.
    05  FILLER PIC X(2) VALUE 'FU'.
    05  FILLER PIC X(2) VALUE 'HD'.
    05  FILLER PIC X(2) VALUE 'SP'.
    05  FILLER PIC X(2) VALUE 'WC'.
01  FILLER REDEFINES DEPARTMENT-TABLE-VALUES.
    05  TB-DEPARTMENT-CODE PIC X(2).
            OCCURS 4 TIMES.
            INDEXED BY DEPARTMENT-INDEX.
01  PAY-RATE-VALUES.
    05  FILLER PIC 9V99 VALUE 8.75.
    05  FILLER PIC 9V99 VALUE 9.43.
    05  FILLER PIC 9V99 VALUE 8.50.
    05  FILLER PIC 9V99 VALUE 9.75.
01  FILLER REDEFINES PAY-RATE-VALUES.
    05  PAY-RATE          PIC 9V99
            OCCURS 4 TIMES.
01  WS-WORK-AREAS.
    05  PAY-RATE-INDEX USAGE IS INDEX.
    05  WS-END-OF-FILE-INDICATOR PIC X(3) VALUE SPACES.
        88 END-OF-FILE VALUE 'END'.
    05  WS-ENTRY-FOUND-INDICATOR PIC X(3).
        88 ENTRY-FOUND VALUE 'YES'.
    05  WS-GROSS-PAY PIC 9(5)V99.
PROCEDURE DIVISION.
A000-SEARCH-EXAMPLE.
    OPEN INPUT EMPLOYEE-HOUR-FILE.
    PERFORM Z100-READ-EMPLOYEE-FILE.
    PERFORM B200-PROCESS-RECORDS
        UNTIL END-OF-FILE.
    CLOSE EMPLOYEE-HOUR-FILE.
    STOP RUN.
B200-PROCESS-RECORDS.
    PERFORM C100-SEARCH-TABLE.
    IF ENTRY-FOUND
        SET PAY-RATE-INDEX TO DEPARTMENT-INDEX
        COMPUTE WS-GROSS-PAY = EH-HOURS-WORKED *
                            PAY-RATE(PAY-RATE-INDEX)
    ELSE PERFORM C300-ERROR-ROUTINE.
    PERFORM C400-PRINT-EMPLOYEE.
```

Figure 2–16 *(concluded)*

```
        PERFORM Z100-READ-EMPLOYEE-FILE.
C100-SEARCH-TABLE.
    SET DEPARTMENT-INDEX TO 1.
    SEARCH TB-DEPARTMENT-CODE.
        AT END MOVE 'NO' TO WS-ENTRY-FOUND-INDICATOR
        WHEN TB-DEPARTMENT-CODE(DEPARTMENT-INDEX) =
            EH-DEPARTMENT-CODE
            MOVE 'YES' TO WS-ENTRY-FOUND-INDICATOR.
C300-ERROR-ROUTINE.

C400-PRINT-EMPLOYEE.

Z100-READ-EMPLOYEE-FILE.
```

After a record is read, C100–SEARCH–TABLE is performed. Control returns to B200–PROCESS–RECORDS which indicates whether an appropriate department code in the table was found with an appropriately set WS–ENTRY–FOUND–INDICATOR. The imperative statement after the AT END clause is executed only when the entire search has been completed and no equality of TB–DEPARTMENT–CODE(DEPARTMENT–INDEX) to EH–DEPARTMENT–CODE has been satisfied. After DEPARTMENT–INDEX has been set to 1, the SEARCH statement appropriately increments DEPARTMENT–INDEX to accomplish the linear search. When the WHEN condition is satisfied, DEPARTMENT–INDEX contains a displacement value that corresponds to the occurrence number of the appropriate table element. Then when PAY–RATE–INDEX is set to DEPARTMENT–INDEX, the index data item, PAY–RATE–INDEX, is used to access the other table. When the AT END condition is true (meaning no match has been found), DEPARTMENT–INDEX is not usable because it would not correspond to an element in the table.

Binary Search with SEARCH ALL   A binary search requires the addition of either an ASCENDING KEY clause or a DESCENDING KEY clause to the OCCURS clause as indicated in Figure 2–17.

Figure 2–17   *Binary SEARCH Requirements*

```
01  FILLER REDEFINES DEPARTMENT-TABLE-VALUES.
    05  TB-DEPARTMENT-CODE PIC X(2)
        OCCURS 4 TIMES
        ASCENDING KEY TB-DEPARTMENT-CODE
        INDEXED BY DEPARTMENT-INDEX.

    SEARCH ALL TB-DEPARTMENT-CODE
        AT END MOVE 'NO' TO WS-ENTRY-FOUND-INDICATOR
        WHEN TB-DEPARTMENT-CODE(DEPARTMENT-INDEX) =
            EH-DEPARTMENT-CODE
            MOVE 'YES' TO WS-ENTRY-FOUND-INDICATOR.
```

In order to do a binary search, one of the table elements must be either in ascending or descending sequence. An appropriate KEY clause must follow the OCCURS and the SEARCH statement must be changed to a SEARCH ALL statement. The WHEN condition can be any permissible, relational comparison with the SEARCH statement. However, when using the SEARCH ALL, an equal condition must be specified and can only utilize a compound condition with AND as the connective.

Linear Search with PERFORM/ VARYING A linear search can be made with the PERFORM/VARYING statement. Figure 2–18 shows an example.

Figure 2–18 *One Level Search with PERFORM/VARYING*

```
B200-PROCESS
   PERFORM C100-TABLE-SEARCH
      VARYING ROW-SUB FROM 1 BY 1
      UNTIL WS-END-SEARCH = 'END'.

   C100-TABLE-SEARCH.
     IF TABLE-VALUE(ROW-SUB) = PR-INPUT-VALUE
       PERFORM D100-VALUE-FOUND
       MOVE 'END' TO WS-END-SEARCH
     ELSE
       IF ROW-SUB = 5
         PERFORM D200-NO-VALUE-FOUND
         MOVE 'END' TO WS-END-SEARCH.
```

Whenever WS–END–SEARCH contains the value END, the search is terminated. This happens in a table search when the value is not in the table or when IF ROW–SUB = 5 is a true condition.

Combining Two Tables into One

In Figure 2–16 the definition of two separate tables was shown. One was for the department code. The other was for the pay rates that were associated with the department codes. Another way to define this data would have been to combine the two tables into one, as shown in Figure 2–19. This would allow a programmer to use the same index-name (or subscript, if used) for both sets of data.

Figure 2–19 *Two Tables in One*

```
01  DEPARTMENT-PAY-RATE-VALUES.
    05  FILLER PIC X(5) VALUE 'FU875'.
    05  FILLER PIC X(5) VALUE 'HD943'.
    05  FILLER PIC X(5) VALUE 'SP850'.
    05  FILLER PIC X(5) VALUE 'WC975'.
01  FILLER REDEFINES DEPARTMENT-PAY-RATE-VALUES.
    05  DEPARTMENT-PAY-RATES
            OCCURS 4 TIMES
            ASCENDING KEY TB-DEPARTMENT-CODE
            INDEXED BY DEPARTMENT-INDEX.
        10  TB-DEPARTMENT-CODE PIC X(2).
        10  TB-PAY RATE          PIC 9V99.
```

In Figure 2–19 a new group data-name was created called DEPARTMENT–PAY–RATES. It has been subdivided into two elementary items. If DEPARTMENT–PAY–RATES(1) were referenced, 'FU875' would be accessed. If TB–DEPARTMENT–CODE(1) were referenced, 'FU' would be accessed. If TB–PAY–RATE(1) were referenced, '875' would be accessed. Notice that as always, the PIC clause is associated with the elementary item. Figure 2–20 is a schematic of the table illustrated in Figure 2–19.

Figure 2–20   *Schematic of a One Level Table with a Group*

Item				
Group name	DEPARTMENT-PAY-RATES (1)	. . .	DEPARTMENT-PAY-RATES (4)	
Elementary name	DEPT-CODE (1)	PAY-RATE (1)	. . .	DEPT-CODE (4)	PAY-RATE (4)
PIC	X(2)	9V99	. . .	X(2)	9V99

Table Concepts—Two Level Tables

Two level tables are useful in applications where the list contains both rows and columns of data. COBOL allows the definition of a **two level table** by specifying an OCCURS clause that is subordinate to another OCCURS clause. Entries in a two level table are referenced by two values. The first value refers to the row, and the second value refers to the column entry in the table. These values are either subscripts or indexes. Figure 2–21 illustrates a table that has rows and columns and can best be accessed by the use of a two level table. This example is a table of freight rates where the rows indicate the origin of a shipment and the columns are the destinations of a shipment. The appropriate origin-to-destination rate will be selected and multiplied by the weight of the shipment.

Figure 2–21   *Freight Rate Table*

		Destination		
Origin	Denver	Kansas City	Philadelphia	New York
Denver	1.50	4.20	5.10	6.75
Kansas City	4.20	1.75	3.75	4.15
Philadelphia	5.10	3.75	2.50	2.75
New York	6.75	4.15	2.75	3.40

If a programmer were to define this table as a single level table, it could be defined as shown in Example A of Figure 2–22. In order to access the data, both the origin and destination of the data would have to be input. (This would correspond to the appropriate row and column in the table.) This makes the PROCEDURE division statements rather complex. Instead what can be done is to define the table as a two level table, with two OCCURS clauses, and access the data accordingly.

Example B illustrates that entries in the DATA division are simplified because there is not a need to create names for each column. Also the PROCEDURE division entries are simplified because the positions in the table for both rows and columns are determined by the values of the input items SR–ORIGIN and SR– DESTINATION.

Creating

As with one level tables, a programmer has the choice with two level tables of hard-coding or input-loading. If a table is to be hard-coded (as the table shown in Figure 2–21), it would be as defined in either one of the examples in Figure 2–23.

A schematic of a two level table is given in Figure 2–24.

If input-loading of the table is desired it would depend on how the data are stored on the input records. First, assume that the freight rates for each origin (row) are on one input record. The records could be input-loaded according to one of the PROCEDURE division examples shown in Figure 2–25.

Figure 2–22   *Rows and Columns in a One or Two Level Table*

```
         FD   SHIPMENT-FILE
              RECORD CONTAINS 50 CHARACTERS
              LABEL RECORDS ARE STANDARD.
         01   SR-SHIPMENT-RECORD.
              05   SR-ORIGIN           PIC 9.
              05   SR-DESTINATION      PIC 9.
              05   SR-SHIPMENT-WEIGHT  PIC 9(5).
                   .
                   .

   Example A:

              05   SHIPMENT-ORIGIN
                      OCCURS 4 TIMES.
                   10   DENVER        PIC 9V99.
                   10   KANSAS-CITY   PIC 9V99.
                   10   PHILADELPHIA  PIC 9V99.
                   10   NEW-YORK      PIC 9V99.

          PROCEDURE DIVISION.
                   .
              IF SR DESTINATION = 1
                  MOVE DENVER(SR-ORIGIN)         TO WS-RATE.
              IF SR DESTINATION = 2
                  MOVE KANSAS-CITY(SR-ORIGIN)    TO WS-RATE.
              IF SR DESTINATION = 3
                  MOVE PHILADELPHIA(SR-ORIGIN)   TO WS-RATE.
              IF SR DESTINATION = 4
                  MOVE NEW-YORK(SR-ORIGIN)       TO WS-RATE.
   Example B:

              05   SHIPMENT-ORIGIN
                      OCCURS 4 TIMES.
                   10   FREIGHT-RATE  PIC 9V99
                          OCCURS 4 TIMES.
          PROCEDURE DIVISION.
                   .
              MOVE FREIGHT-RATE(SR-ORIGIN, SR-DESTINATION) TO WS-RATE.
```

Notice the definition of RT–RATE–TABLE–VALUE in the DATA division with an OCCURS clause. This allows access to each one of the four individual data elements by using either subscripts or indexes. In this case access can be made to all four of the data values at once by referencing RT–RATE–TABLE–RECORD as shown in B100–LOAD–TABLE in Example A. The four values are moved as a group to SHIPMENT–ORIGIN with ORIGIN–INDEX as the index. Because SHIPMENT–ORIGIN is defined with the first OCCURS clause, reference to SHIPMENT–ORIGIN requires the use of either a single index or a single subscript. SHIPMENT–ORIGIN is also a group item, logically referring to a row in the two level table. SHIPMENT–ORIGIN is further subdivided by one elementary item, FREIGHT–RATE, which, when referenced requires the use of two indexes or two subscripts. Notice that while SHIPMENT–ORIGIN was named to represent the rows in the table, FREIGHT–RATE was named to represent the intersection of rows and columns; it was not given a name to represent the columns, such as SHIPMENT– DESTINATION.

The easiest way to input-load the two level table in Figure 2–25 is shown in Example A. Example B illustrates the ability, however, to fill the table by referencing FREIGHT– RATE with two indexes. For each record read in B100–LOAD–TABLE, C100–MOVE–FREIGHT–RATE is executed four times VARYING DESTINATION–INDEX. Note that WS–FREIGHT–RATE–SUBSCRIPT, used to reference RT–RATE–TABLE–VALUE, changes along with DESTINATION–INDEX because of the SET

Figure 2–23   *Hard-Coding a Two Level Table*

```
Example A:
    01   FREIGHT-TABLE-VALUES.
        05   FILLER PIC 9V99 VALUE 1.50.
        05   FILLER PIC 9V99 VALUE 4.20.
        05   FILLER PIC 9V99 VALUE 5.10.
        05   FILLER PIC 9V99 VALUE 6.75.
        05   FILLER PIC 9V99 VALUE 4.20.
        05   FILLER PIC 9V99 VALUE 1.75.
        05   FILLER PIC 9V99 VALUE 3.75.
        05   FILLER PIC 9V99 VALUE 4.15.
        05   FILLER PIC 9V99 VALUE 5.10.
        05   FILLER PIC 9V99 VALUE 3.75.
        05   FILLER PIC 9V99 VALUE 2.50.
        05   FILLER PIC 9V99 VALUE 2.75.
        05   FILLER PIC 9V99 VALUE 6.75.
        05   FILLER PIC 9V99 VALUE 4.15.
        05   FILLER PIC 9V99 VALUE 2.75.
        05   FILLER PIC 9V99 VALUE 3.40.
    01   FILLER REDEFINES FREIGHT-TABLE-VALUES.
        05   SHIPMENT-ORIGIN
                OCCURS 4 TIMES.
            10   FREIGHT-RATE  PIC 9V99
                    OCCURS 4 TIMES.

Example B:
    01   FREIGHT-TABLE-VALUES.
        05   FILLER PIC X(12) VALUE '150420510675'.
        05   FILLER PIC X(12) VALUE '420175375415'.
        05   FILLER PIC X(12) VALUE '510375250275'.
        05   FILLER PIC X(12) VALUE '675415275340'.
    01   FILLER REDEFINES FREIGHT-TABLE-VALUES.
        05   SHIPMENT-ORIGIN OCCURS 4 TIMES.
            10   FREIGHT-RATE   PIC 9V99.
                    OCCURS 4 TIMES.

  where SHIPMENT-ORIGIN(1) would refer to '150420510675',
        FREIGHT-RATE(1,1) would refer to 1.50,
        FREIGHT-RATE(1,2) would refer to 4.20,

        FREIGHT-RATE(4,4) would refer to 3.40.
```

Figure 2–24   *Schematic of a Two Level Table*

Group name	ORIGIN (1)				. . .	ORIGIN (4)			
Elementary name	RATE				. . .	RATE			
	(1,1)	(1,2)	(1,3)	(1,4)		(4,1)	(4,2)	(4,3)	(4,4)
PIC	9V99	9V99	9V99	9V99	. . .	9V99	9V99	9V99	9V99

statement. The first time C100–MOVE–FREIGHT–RATE is executed, both ORIGIN–INDEX and DESTINATION–INDEX represent an occurrence number of 1. The second time it is executed ORIGIN–INDEX remains 1, while DESTINATION–INDEX becomes 2, representing the data value to be placed in row 1, column 2. This continues UNTIL DESTINATION–INDEX is greater than 4, which terminates the execution of the loop for C100–MOVE–FREIGHT–RATE. ORIGIN–INDEX then is incremented

Figure 2–25 *Input-Loading a Two Level Table*

```
        FD   RATE-TABLE-FILE.
             RECORD CONTAINS 12 CHARACTERS
             LABEL RECORDS STANDARD.
        01   RT-RATE-TABLE-RECORD.
             05   RT-RATE-TABLE-VALUE   PIC 9V99
                     OCCURS 4 TIMES.
        WORKING-STORAGE SECTION
        01   FREIGHT-TABLE.
             05   SHIPMENT-ORIGIN
                     OCCURS 4 TIMES.
                     INDEXED BY ORIGIN-INDEX.
                  10   FREIGHT-RATE      PIC 9V99
                          OCCURS 4 TIMES.
                          INDEXED BY DESTINATION-INDEX.
        01   WS-WORK-AREAS.
             05   WS-FREIGHT-RATE-SUBSCRIPT PIC 9.

 Example A:

        PROCEDURE DIVISION.
        A000-FREIGHT-RATES.
             OPEN INPUT RATE-TABLE-FILE.
             PERFORM B100-LOAD-TABLE
                 VARYING ORIGIN-INDEX
                 FROM 1 BY 1
                 UNTIL ORIGIN-INDEX > 4.

        B100-LOAD-TABLE.
             READ RATE-TABLE-FILE.
             MOVE RT-RATE-TABLE-RECORD TO SHIPMENT-ORIGIN(ORIGIN-INDEX).

 Example B:

        PROCEDURE DIVISION.
        A000-FREIGHT-RATES.
             OPEN INPUT RATE-TABLE-FILE.
             PERFORM B100-LOAD-TABLE
                 VARYING ORIGIN-INDEX
                 FROM 1 TO 1
                 UNTIL ORIGIN-INDEX > 4.

        B100-LOAD-TABLE.
             READ RATE-TABLE-FILE.
             PERFORM C100-MOVE-FREIGHT-RATE
                 VARYING DESTINATION-INDEX
                 FROM 1 BY 1
                 UNTIL DESTINATION-INDEX > 4.
        C100-MOVE-FREIGHT-RATE.
             SET WS-FREIGHT-RATE-SUBSCRIPT TO DESTINATION-INDEX.
             MOVE RT-RATE-TABLE-VALUE(WS-FREIGHT-RATE-SUBSCRIPT)
                 TO FREIGHT-RATE(ORIGIN-INDEX, DESTINATION-INDEX).
```

to 2 and B100–LOAD–TABLE is performed, which reads the next record and begins performing C100–MOVE–FREIGHT–RATE for a second time. During this second performance, DESTINATION–INDEX becomes 1 again and the loop continues. This concept of a performed loop within another performed loop is termed **nested looping.** The nested looping concept shown in Example B would be required if each of the 16 data elements (a 4 by 4 table) were on a separate record in RATE–TABLE–FILE. The only difference in the logic would be the placement of the READ statement and the elimination of the SET statement to refer to RT–RATE–TABLE–VALUE.

Example A of Figure 2–26 illustrates this difference. Regardless of the format of the input data and the definition of the table, the programmer can determine

Figure 2–26   *Input-Loading Individual Elements*

```
Example A:

      FD   RATE-TABLE-FILE
           RECORD CONTAINS 3 CHARACTERS
           LABEL RECORDS STANDARD.
      01   RT-RATE-TABLE-RECORD.
           05   RT-RATE-TABLE-VALUE PIC 9V99.
      WORKING-STORAGE SECTION


      PROCEDURE DIVISION.
      A000-FREIGHT-RATES.
           OPEN INPUT RATE-TABLE-FILE.
           PERFORM B100-LOAD-TABLE
               VARYING ORIGIN-INDEX
               FROM 1 BY 1
               UNTIL ORIGIN-INDEX > 4.


      B100-LOAD-TABLE.
           PERFORM C100-MOVE-FREIGHT-RATE
               VARYING DESTINATION-INDEX
               FROM 1 BY 1
               UNTIL DESTINATION-INDEX > 4.
      C100-MOVE-FREIGHT-RATE.
           READ RATE-TABLE FILE.
           MOVE RT-RATE-TABLE-VALUE
               TO-FREIGHT-RATE(ORIGIN-INDEX, DESTINATION-INDEX).

Example B:

      PROCEDURE DIVISION.
      A000-FREIGHT-RATES.
           OPEN INPUT RATE-TABLE-FILE.
           PERFORM B100-LOAD-TABLE
               VARYING ORIGIN-INDEX
               FROM 1 BY 1
               UNTIL ORIGIN-INDEX > 4.
               AFTER DESTINATION-INDEX
               FROM 1 BY 1
               UNTIL DESTINATION-INDEX > 4.
      B100-LOAD-TABLE.
           READ RATE-TABLE-FILE.
           MOVE RT-RATE-TABLE-VALUE
               TO FREIGHT-RATE(ORIGIN-INDEX, DESTINATION-INDEX).
```

an appropriate means of input-loading a table. Example B shows another way of input-loading individual elements when each of the data elements is on a separate record. In this example, the use of the PERFORM/VARYING statement has been extended for use with two level tables. When the AFTER clause is added to the PERFORM/VARYING statement the index or subscript named in the AFTER clause is incremented first (in this case DESTINATION– INDEX), and then the first subscript or index is incremented next (in this case ORIGIN–INDEX). The first subscript or index is held constant while the second subscript or index is allowed to vary. The first time through B100–LOAD–TABLE in Example B, both ORIGIN–INDEX and DESTINATION–INDEX are equal to 1. The first data element read is placed into FREIGHT–RATE(1, 1). The second time through B100–LOAD–TABLE, ORIGIN–IN DEX remains at 1 while DESTINATION–INDEX is incremented to 2. The second data element read is placed into FREIGHT–RATE(1, 2). This continues until all data elements have been loaded.

Accessing

Once the table has been loaded either by hard-coding or input-loading, it is possible to directly access a data element in the table. Assume that the table has been previously loaded by one of the methods shown in Figure 2–25 and that shipment orders are now ready to be processed to determine the appropriate tariff. The input data records representing the shipment orders contain the customer's name, shipment weight, and two numbers representing the origin and destination. The direct access of the appropriate rate is shown in Figure 2–27.

Figure 2–27   *Direct Access of a Two Level Table*

```
DATA DIVISION.
FILE SECTION.
FD   RATE-TABLE-FILE
     RECORD CONTAINS 12 CHARACTERS
     LABEL RECORDS STANDARD.
01   RT-RATE-TABLE-RECORD.
     05  RT-RATE-TABLE-VALUE PIC 9V99 OCCURS 4 TIMES.
FD   SHIPMENT-FILE
     RECORD CONTAINS 27 CHARACTERS
     LABEL RECORDS STANDARD.
01   SR-SHIPMENT-RECORD.
     05   SR-CUSTOMER-NAME      PIC X(20).
     05   SR-SHIPMENT-WEIGHT    PIC 9(5).
     05   SR-ORIGIN             PIC 9.
          88  VALID-ORIGIN VALUE 1 THRU 4.
     05   SR-DESTINATION        PIC 9.
          88  VALID-DESTINATION VALUE 1 THRU 4.
WORKING-STORAGE SECTION
01   FREIGHT-TABLE.
     05   SHIPMENT-ORIGIN
             OCCURS 4 TIMES
             INDEXED BY ORIGIN-INDEX.
          10  FREIGHT-RATE      PIC 9V99
               OCCURS 4 TIMES
               INDEXED BY DESTINATION-INDEX.
01   WS-WORK-AREAS.
     05   WS-FREIGHT-RATE-SUBSCRIPT PIC 9.
     05   WS-TARIFF                 PIC 9(7)V99.
     05   WS-END-OF-FILE-INDICATOR  PIC X(3).
          88 END-OF-FILE            VALUE 'END'.
PROCEDURE DIVISION.
A000-FREIGHT-RATES.
*  LOAD TABLE
     OPEN INPUT RATE-TABLE-FILE.
     PERFORM B100-LOAD-TABLE
         VARYING ORIGIN-INDEX
         FROM 1 BY 1
         UNTIL ORIGIN-INDEX > 5.
     CLOSE RATE-TABLE-FILE.
*  MAIN PROCESSING
     OPEN INPUT SHIPMENT-FILE.
     PERFORM Z100-READ-SHIPMENT.
     PERFORM B300-PROCESS-SHIPMENT
         UNTIL END-OF-FILE.
     CLOSE SHIPMENT-FILE.
     STOP RUN.
B100-LOAD-TABLE.
     .
     .
B300-PROCESS-SHIPMENT.
     IF NOT VALID-ORIGIN OR
        NOT VALID-DESTINATION
          PERFORM C100-ERROR-ROUTINE
```

Figure 2–27 *(concluded)*

```
        ELSE
            PERFORM C200-CALCULATE-TARIFF.
        PERFORM Z100-READ-SHIPMENT.
C100-ERROR-ROUTINE.
    .
    .
C200-CALCULATE-TARIFF.
    SET ORIGIN-INDEX       TO SR-ORIGIN.
    SET DESTINATION-INDEX TO SR-DESTINATION.
    COMPUTE WS-TARIFF = SR-SHIPMENT-WEIGHT *
                FREIGHT-RATE(ORIGIN INDEX, DESTINATION-INDEX).
    PERFORM D100-PRINT-RESULTS.
    .
    .
    .
Z100-READ-SHIPMENT.
    READ SHIPMENT-FILE.
        AT END MOVE 'END' TO WS-END-OF-FILE INDICATOR.
```

In Figure 2–27 the table is input-loaded and the first shipment record is read. When B300–PROCESS–SHIPMENT is executed, the first thing done is to check the range of the input indicators, SR–ORIGIN and SR–DESTINATION. The appropriate range is from 1 to 4. This checking is done to guard against a subscript or index error. If both of the values are valid, C200–CALCULATE–TARIFF is performed, which uses the SET statements to convert SR–ORIGIN and SR–DESTINATION to their respective indexes. The indexes are then used to access a single data element from FREIGHT–RATE.

Searching

Linear Search with SEARCH

The SEARCH statement can be used to search any level of table. The rules for use of the SEARCH statement are the same for a two level table as for a single level table, but the logic is more complicated. In searching a two level table with the SEARCH statement, the first level must be searched, and a satisfied WHEN condition must be found before the next level can be searched.

To illustrate the ability to use the SEARCH statement, consider the table illustrated in Figure 2–28.

Figure 2–28   *Two Level Search*

Sales month	Week 1	Week 2	Week 3	Week 4
January	11000	22000	13000	14000
February	21000	32000	43000	24000
March	31000	32000	43000	54000
April	41000	42000	53000	44000
May	51000	52000	63000	34000
June	71000	42000	33000	24000
July	21000	42000	33000	44000
August	11000	12000	23000	14000
September	21000	22000	33000	24000
October	21000	22000	23000	35000
November	31000	32000	43000	52000
December	31000	42000	53000	74000

```
DATA DIVISION.
FILE SECTION.
FD  PREVIOUS-YEARS-SALES
    LABEL RECORDS STANDARD.
01  YS-YEARS-SALES-RECORD.
```

Figure 2–28 *(concluded)*

```
      05   YS-MONTH-NAME               PIC X(9).
      05   YS-PREVIOUS-SALES           PIC 9(5).


  WORKING-STORAGE SECTION.
  01   MONTHS-SALES-DATA.
      05   MONTH-TABLE
               OCCURS 12 TIMES.
               INDEXED BY MONTH-INDEX.
          10   MONTH-NAME              PIC X(9).
          10   WEEKS-SALES-DATA        PIC 9(5)
                   OCCURS 4 TIMES
                   INDEXED BY SALES-INDEX.
  01   WS-WORK-INDICATORS.
      05   WS-MONTH-FOUND-INDICATOR    PIC X(3).
          88   MONTH-FOUND             VALUE 'YES'.
      05   WS THIS-YEAR-HIGH-INDICATOR PIC X(3).
          88 THIS-YEARS-SALES-HIGHER   VALUE 'YES'.
      05   WS-END-OF-FILE-INDICATOR    PIC X(3).
          88   END-OF-FILE             VALUE 'END'.
  PROCEDURE DIVISION.
  A000-MONTHS-SALES.


      .

      PERFORM B100-LOAD-TABLE . . .
      .


      OPEN INPUT PREVIOUS-YEARS-SALES.
      PERFORM Z100-READ-SALES.
      PERFORM B300-PROCESS-SALES.
          UNTIL END-OF-FILE.
      CLOSE PREVIOUS-YEARS-SALES.
      STOP RUN.
  B100-LOAD-TABLE.

      .

  B300-PROCESS-SALES.
      PERFORM C100-MONTH-SEARCH.
      IF MONTH-FOUND
          PERFORM C200-SALES-SEARCH
          IF THIS-YEARS-SALES-HIGHER
              PERFORM C300-NEW-SALES-RECORD
          ELSE
              NEXT SENTENCE
      ELSE
          PERFORM C400-ERROR-ROUTINE.
      PERFORM Z100-READ-SALES.
  C100-MONTH-SEARCH.
      SET MONTH-INDEX TO 1.
      SEARCH MONTH-TABLE
          AT END MOVE 'END' TO WS-MONTH-FOUND-INDICATOR
          WHEN YS-MONTH-NAME = MONTH-NAME(MONTH-INDEX)
              MOVE 'YES' TO WS-MONTH-FOUND-INDICATOR.
  C200-SALES-SEARCH.
      SET SALES-INDEX TO 1.
      SEARCH WEEKS-SALES-DATA
          AT END MOVE 'END' TO WS-THIS-YEAR-HIGH-INDICATOR
          WHEN WEEKS-SALES-DATA(MONTH-INDEX, SALES-INDEX) >
              YS-PREVIOUS-SALES
              MOVE 'YES' TO WS-THIS-YEAR-HIGH-INDICATOR.
  C300-NEW-SALES-RECORD.

      .

  C400-ERROR-ROUTINE.

      .

  Z100-READ-SALES.
      READ PREVIOUS-YEARS-SALES
          AT END MOVE 'END' TO WS-END-OF-FILE-INDICATOR.
```

In the table in Figure 2–28, a company has accumulated weekly sales for each of 12 months in the current year. This data will be input-loaded into the table defined in WORKING–STORAGE. The purpose of the skeleton program is to compare this year's data with previous weekly sales records. The input file contains the name of the month and the highest amount of weekly sales in that month from previous years. The program will ascertain if any of the sales in any of the months have surpassed previous sales records, thus setting a new weekly sales record.

In B300–PROCESS–SALES, the logic is to first perform C100–MONTH–SEARCH to determine the appropriate row in the table. If the correct month is found, MONTH–INDEX represents the correct row in the table, and the logic finds the correct column by performing C200–SALES–SEARCH. If the month is not found, there is an error. In C200–SALES–SEARCH, YS–PREVIOUS–SALES is compared to WEEKS–SALES–DATA(MONTH–INDEX, SALES–INDEX). If a positive comparison is made, the WS–THIS–YEAR–HIGH–INDICATOR will be set. At the point at which C200–SALES–SEARCH is entered, MONTH–INDEX has been predetermined. The search in C200–SALES–SEARCH will manipulate only SALES–INDEX.

Actually, Figure 2–28 represents two tables, where MONTH–TABLE is a one level table with 12 rows and WEEKLY–SALES–DATA is a two level table with 12 rows and four columns. This approach becomes necessary when the column data is not all formatted the same. The PIC X(9) for MONTHLY–NAME is not the same as the PIC 9(5) for WEEKLY–SALES–DATA. Note the difference in Figure 2–28 and in Figure 2–27, where the column data are all of the same type.

Binary Search with SEARCH ALL

The rules for using the SEARCH ALL on a two level table are the same as for all other level tables. The data being searched must previously have been placed in either ascending or descending order. Figure 2–29 illustrates a two level binary search.

The data in Figure 2–29 represents product codes and associated quantities on hand at four branch locations and would be input-loaded into PRODUCT–LOCA TION–TABLE. The program is to do a binary search first on the row data (city name) and then on the column data (product code) to determine if sufficient quantities exist for a customer order. The data being searched is in ascending order and the required KEY IS clauses are included in the table specification. The input data used to search the table would consist of a city name, a product code, and the number of units requested.

In B200–PROCESS, a binary search is performed by C100–CITY–NAME–SEARCH to determine the appropriate row in the table. If the city name is not found, the search is terminated and C500–CITY–ERROR–ROUTINE is executed. If the correct row is found, C200–PRODUCT–CODE–SEARCH is performed to find the appropriate column within that row. If a product code is not found, C400–PROD UCT–ERROR–ROUTINE is executed. C300–COMPARE–TO–REQUEST is performed when the appropriate row and column are found. C300–COMPARE–TO–REQUEST utilizes PRODUCT–QUANTITY(CITY–INDEX PRODUCT–INDEX) to compare to the customer request. Notice that the condition names CITY–FOUND and PRODUCT–FOUND control the logic of the search.

Linear Search with PERFORM/ VARYING

Figure 2–30 illustrates some examples using a PERFORM/VARYING for a linear search.

Example A of Figure 2–30 will move zeros into each element of a table with five rows and four columns. When using a PERFORM/VARYING for a two level table, the last-named subscript or index varies the fastest. The order in which zeros would be moved to ACCUMULATOR–TABLE (ROW–INDEX, COL–INDEX) is:

```
ROW–INDEX:   11112222333344445555
COL–INDEX:   12341234123412341234
```

Figure 2–29 *Two Level SEARCH ALL*

City name	Product code	Quantity	Product code	Quantity	Product code	Quantity
Atlanta	123	105	175	047	198	047
Denver	127	157	195	402	250	089
Kansas City	123	205	175	397	195	412
New York	175	089	195	125	198	175

```
01  PRODUCT-LOCATION-TABLE.
    05   PRODUCT-LOCATION              OCCURS 4 TIMES
                                       ASCENDING KEY CITY-NAME
                                       INDEXED BY LOCATION-INDEX.
         10   CITY-NAME               PIC X(20).
         10   PRODUCT-QTY-DATA        OCCURS 3 TIMES
                                      ASCENDING KEY PRODUCT-CODE
                                      INDEXED BY PRODUCT-INDEX.
              15   PRODUCT-CODE       PIC X(3).
              15   PRODUCT-QTY        PIC 9(5).
01  WS-WORK-INDICATORS.
    05   WS-CITY-FOUND-INDICATOR    PIC X(3).
         88   CITY-FOUND            VALUE 'YES'.
    05   WS-PRODUCT-FOUND-INDICATOR PIC X(3).
         88   PRODUCT-FOUND         VALUE 'YES'.


    PERFORM B200-PROCESS
        UNTIL END-OF-FILE.



B200-PROCESS.
    PERFORM C100-CITY-NAME-SEARCH.
    IF CITY-FOUND
        PERFORM C200-PRODUCT-CODE-SEARCH
        IF PRODUCT-FOUND
            PERFORM C300-COMPARE-TO-REQUEST
        ELSE
            PERFORM C400-PRODUCT-ERROR-ROUTINE
    ELSE
            PERFORM C500-CITY-ERROR-ROUTINE.
    PERFORM Z100-READ-DATA.
C100-CITY-NAME-SEARCH.
    SEARCH ALL PRODUCT-LOCATION
        AT END MOVE 'END' TO WS-CITY-FOUND-INDICATOR
        WHEN CITY-NAME(LOCATION-INDEX) = INPUT-CITY-NAME
            MOVE 'YES' TO WS-CITY-FOUND-INDICATOR.
C200-PRODUCT-CODE-SEARCH.
    SEARCH ALL PRODUCT-CODE
        AT END MOVE 'END' TO WS-PRODUCT-FOUND-INDICATOR
        WHEN PRODUCT-CODE(CITY-INDEX PRODUCT-INDEX)
            = INPUT-PRODUCT-CODE
            MOVE 'YES' TO WS-PRODUCT-FOUND INDICATOR.
C300-COMPARE-TO-REQUEST.

C400-PRODUCT-ERROR-ROUTINE.

C500-CITY-ERROR-ROUTINE.

Z100-READ-DATA.
    READ INPUT-DATA-FILE
        AT END MOVE 'END' TO WS-EOJ-INDICATOR.
```

Figure 2–30 *Two Level Access/Search with*
PROGRAM/VARYING

```
Example A:

     PERFORM D200-RESET-ACCUMULATORS
         VARYING ROW-INDEX
             FROM 1 BY 1
             UNTIL ROW-INDEX > 5
         AFTER COL-INDEX
             FROM 1 BY 1
             UNTIL COL-INDEX > 4.


D200-RESET-ACCUMULATORS.
     MOVE ZEROS TO ACCUMULATOR-TABLE(ROW-INDEX, COL-INDEX).

Example B:

     PERFORM D300-TOTAL-COL-VALUES
         VARYING COL-INDEX
             FROM 1 BY 1.
             UNTIL COL-INDEX > 4
         AFTER ROW-INDEX
             FROM 1 BY 1
             UNTIL ROW-INDEX > 5.


D300-TOTAL COL-VALUES.
     ADD ACCUMULATOR-TABLE(ROW-INDEX, COL-INDEX)
         TO WS-COL-TOTALS(COL-INDEX).

Example C:

B200-PROCESS-SALES.
     PERFORM C100-TABLE-SEARCH
         VARYING ROW-SUB
             FROM 1 BY 1
             UNTIL END-OF-SEARCH = 'END'
         AFTER COL-SUB
             FROM 1 BY 1
             UNTIL END-OF-SEARCH OR COL-SUB > 4.


C100-TABLE-SEARCH.
     IF TABLE-VALUE(ROW-SUB, COL-SUB) = PR-INPUT-VALUE
         PERFORM D100-FOUND-VALUE
         MOVE 'END' TO WS-END-SEARCH
     ELSE
         IF ROW-SUB = 5 AND COL-SUB = 4
             PERFORM D200-NO-VALUE-FOUND
             MOVE 'END' TO WS-END-SEARCH.
```

Example B will add all of the individual items in each column and store the sum in the column's location in a table named WS–COL–TOTALS. WS–COL–TO TALS would be a one level table with four elements. Notice the order in which the addition takes place:

ACCUMULATOR–TABLE	ROW–INDEX:	12345123451234512345
	COL–INDEX:	11111222223333344444
WS–ROW–TOTALS	COL–INDEX:	11111222223333344444

Example C assumes the table has five rows and four columns. Each row is searched until the value being searched for is found. If the value is not found in the first row, the second row is searched, and so on. When the value is found or when the entire table is searched and the value is not found, END is moved to WS–END–SEARCH to terminate the search. In this example, subscripts, not indexes, were used.

Table Concepts—Three Level Tables

A **three level table** can be considered as a series of two level tables where each table is on a separate page. To define such a table in COBOL requires three OCCURS clauses, each subordinate to the other. Entries in a three level table are referenced by three values. The first value refers to the page. The second value refers to the row. The third value refers to the column entry in the table. These values may be either subscripts or indexes. Figure 2–31 illustrates a three level table. This example shows a series of rate tables where the pages indicate the method of shipment (refrigerated or nonrefrigerated), the rows indicate the origin of a shipment, and the columns are the destinations of a shipment.

Figure 2–31 *Three Level Rate Table*

	Refrigerated items (1) Destination			
Origin	*Atlanta*	*Chicago*	*Dallas*	*St. Louis*
Atlanta	2.50	5.65	7.05	8.40
Chicago	5.65	2.75	4.90	5.65
Dallas	7.05	4.90	3.20	4.10
St. Louis	8.40	5.65	4.10	3.25
	Nonrefrigerated items (2) Destination			
Origin	*Atlanta*	*Chicago*	*Dallas*	*St. Louis*
Atlanta	1.45	4.15	5.05	6.70
Chicago	4.15	1.70	3.70	4.10
Dallas	5.05	3.70	1.90	2.40
St. Louis	6.70	4.10	2.40	1.95

Figure 2–32 is an example of how the table can be defined.

Figure 2–32 *Three Level Table*

```
WORKING-STORAGE SECTION.
01  FREIGHT-RATE-TABLE.
    05  METHOD                         OCCURS 2 TIMES.
        10  SHIPMENT-ORIGIN            OCCURS 4 TIMES.
            15  FREIGHT-RATE  PIC 9V99 OCCURS 4 TIMES.
```

Creating

Three level tables can be either hard-coded or input-loaded. Figure 2–33 is one example of a hard-coded table.

A schematic of a three level table is given in Figure 2–34.

Input-loading the table depends on how the data is stored on the input records. If the freight rates for each row are on a single input record the records could be input-loaded according to the example in Figure 2–35.

Figure 2–33 *Hard-Coding a Three Level Table*

```
01   FREIGHT-TABLE-VALUES.
     05   REFRIGERATED.
          10   FILLER     PIC X(12)    VALUE   '250565705840'.
          10   FILLER     PIC X(12)    VALUE   '565275490565'.
          10   FILLER     PIC X(12)    VALUE   '705490320410'.
          10   FILLER     PIC X(12)    VALUE   '804565410325'.
     05   NON-REFRIGERATED.
          10   FILLER     PIC X(12)    VALUE   '145415505670'.
          10   FILLER     PIC X(12)    VALUE   '415170370410'.
          10   FILLER     PIC X(12)    VALUE   '505370190240'.
          10   FILLER     PIC X(12)    VALUE   '670410240195'.

01   FREIGHT-RATE-TABLE REDEFINES FREIGHT-TABLE-VALUES.
     05   METHOD                          OCCURS 2 TIMES.
          10   SHIPMENT-ORIGIN            OCCURS 4 TIMES.
               15   FREIGHT-RATE  PIC 9V99 OCCURS 4 TIMES.

where SHIPMENT-ORIGIN(2, 2) would refer to 415170370410,
      FREIGHT-RATE(1, 3, 3) would refer to 3.20 and
      FREIGHT-RATE(2, 4, 1) would refer to 6.70.
```

Figure 2–34 *Schematic of a Three Level Table*

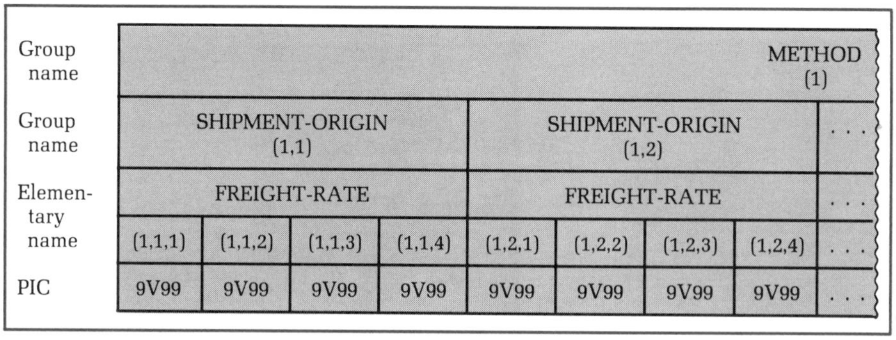

One row of four values is read at a time into the input area. Then the row of values is moved into the page indicated by METHOD–INDEX, and the row of that page is indicated by ORIGIN–INDEX.

Accessing

After a table has been placed in a program, any of its elements can be accessed. Assume that the input data records representing the shipment orders contain the customer's name, shipment weight, and three codes representing the method of shipment, the origin, and the destination. If orders are to be processed to determine the shipment tariff, a direct access can be made to find the appropriate rate in the table as shown by Figure 2–36.

The purpose of B300–PROCESS–SHIPMENT is to ensure that the range of any level of the table is not exceeded; if so, C100–ERROR–ROUTINE is executed. If the range of the table is not exceeded, C200–CALCULATE–TARIFF is performed which converts the codes in the input record to their respective indexes. These three indexes are then used to access a single data element from FREIGHT–RATE by a direct table lookup. This value is multiplied by SR–SHIPMENT–WEIGHT to determine WS–TARIFF, which is the cost of shipping this order.

Figure 2–35 *Input-Loading a Three Level Table*

```
FD   RATE-TABLE-FILE
     RECORD CONTAINS 12 CHARACTERS
     LABEL RECORDS ARE STANDARD.
01   RT-RATE-TABLE-RECORD.
     05   RT-RATE-TABLE-ROW.
          10  RT-RATE-TABLE-VALUES  PIC 9V99 OCCURS 4 TIMES.
WORKING-STORAGE SECTION.
01   FREIGHT-TABLE.
     05   METHOD                          OCCURS 2 TIMES
                                          INDEXED BY METHOD-INDEX.

          10   SHIPMENT-ORIGIN            OCCURS 4 TIMES
                                          INDEXED BY ORIGIN-INDEX.

               15  FREIGHT-RATE    PIC 9V99 OCCURS 4 TIMES
                                          INDEXED BY RATE-INDEX.


PROCEDURE DIVISION.
A100-FREIGHT-RATES.
     OPEN INPUT RATE-TABLE-FILE.
     PERFORM B100-LOAD-TABLE
          VARYING METHOD-INDEX
               FROM 1 BY 1
               UNITL METHOD-INDEX > 2
          AFTER ORIGIN-INDEX
               FROM 1 BY 1
               UNTIL ORIGIN-INDEX > 4.

B100-LOAD-TABLE.
     READ RATE-TABLE-FILE.
     MOVE RT-RATE-TABLE-ROW TO
          SHIPMENT-ORIGIN(METHOD-INDEX, ORIGIN-INDEX).
```

Figure 2–36 *Direct Access of a Three Level Table*

```
DATA DIVISION.
FILE SECTION.
FD   RATE-TABLE-FILE
     RECORD CONTAINS 12 CHARACTERS
     LABEL RECORDS ARE STANDARD.
01   RT-RATE-TABLE-RECORD.
     05   RT-RATE-TABLE-ROW.
          10   RT-RATE-TABLE-VALUES     PIC 9V99  OCCURS 4 TIMES.
FD   SHIPMENT-FILE
     RECORD CONTAINS 28 CHARACTERS
     LABEL RECORDS ARE STANDARD.
01   SR-SHIPMENT-RECORD.
     05   SR-CUSTOMER-NAME         PIC X(20).
     05   SR-SHIPMENT-WEIGHT       PIC 9(5).
     05   SR-METHOD                PIC 9.
          88   VALID-METHOD        VALUE 1 THRU 2.
     05   SR-ORIGIN                PIC 9.
          88   VALID-ORIGIN        VALUE 1 THRU 4.
     05   SR-DESTINATION           PIC 9.
          88   VALID-DESTINATION   VALUE 1 THRU 4.
WORKING-STORAGE SECTION.
01   FREIGHT-TABLE.
     05   METHOD                        OCCURS 2 TIMES
                                        INDEXED BY METHOD-INDEX.

          10   SHIPMENT-ORIGIN          OCCURS 4 TIMES
                                        INDEXED BY ORIGIN-INDEX.
               15  FREIGHT-RATE  PIC 9V99 OCCURS 4 TIMES
                                        INDEXED BY RATE-INDEX.
```

Figure 2–36 *(concluded)*

```
01  WS-WORK-AREAS.
    05  WS-FREIGHT-RATE-SUBSCRIPT      PIC 9.
    05  WS-TARIFF                      PIC 9(7)V99.
    05  WS-END-OF-FILE-INDICATOR       PIC X(3).
        88  END-OF-FILE                VALUE 'END'.
PROCEDURE DIVISION.
A000-FREIGHT-RATES.
*LOAD TABLE**********
    OPEN INPUT RATE-TABLE-FILE.
    PERFORM B100-LOAD-TABLE
        VARYING METHOD-INDEX
            FROM 1 BY 1
                UNTIL METHOD-INDEX > 2
        AFTER ORIGIN-INDEX
            FROM 1 BY 1
                UNTIL ORIGIN-INDEX > 4.
    CLOSE RATE-TABLE-FILE.
*MAIN PROCESSING******
    OPEN INPUT SHIPMENT-FILE.
    PERFORM Z100-READ-SHIPMENT.
    PERFORM B300-PROCESS-SHIPMENT
        UNTIL END-OF-FILE.
    CLOSE SHIPMENT-FILE.
    STOP RUN.
B100-LOAD-TABLE.
    READ RATE-TABLE-FILE.
    MOVE RT-RATE-TABLE-ROW TO
        SHIPMENT-ORIGIN(METHOD-INDEX, ORIGIN-INDEX).
B300-PROCESS-SHIPMENT.
    IF NOT VALID-METHOD
        OR NOT VALID ORIGIN
        OR NOT VALID-DESTINATION
        PERFORM C100-ERROR-ROUTINE
    ELSE
        PERFORM C200-CALCULATE-TARIFF.
    PERFORM Z100-READ-SHIPMENT.
C100-ERROR-ROUTINE.

C200-CALCULATE-TARIFF.
    SET METHOD-INDEX TO SR-METHOD.
    SET ORIGIN-INDEX TO SR-ORIGIN.
    SET DESTINATION-INDEX TO SR-DESTINATION.
    COMPUTE WS-TARIFF = SR-SHIPMENT-WEIGHT *
        FREIGHT-RATE(METHOD-INDEX, ORIGIN-INDEX, DESTINATION-INDEX).
    PERFORM D100-PRINT-RESULTS.

Z100-READ-SHIPMENT.
    READ SHIPMENT-FILE.
        AT END MOVE "END" TO WS-END-OF-FILE-INDICATOR.
```

Searching

Linear Search with SEARCH

Assume a wholesale clothing business and the prices for the merchandise vary according to the particular product, the type of customer, and the quantity of the product purchased. These individual prices per item are stored in a three level table as shown in Figure 2–37.

This table has been input-loaded into the table defined in WORKING–STORAGE in Figure 2–38. The purpose of the skeleton program is to calculate the price for merchandise ordered by one of the customers. The input record contains the account number of the customer, the code for the product ordered, the code for the type

Figure 2–37　*Three Level Price Table*

• Level 1 is the particular product: male swimming suits (MS), female swimming suits (FS).

• Level 2 is the type of customer: wholesaler (W), retailer (R), small retailer (SR).

• Level 3 is the quantity purchased: 1–5, 6–10, over 10.

	FS				*MS*		
	1–5	*6–10*	*Over 10*		*1–5*	*6–10*	*Over 10*
W	20	17	12	W	10	8	6
R	24	21	16	R	12	9	7
SR	28	25	21	SR	15	12	10

Figure 2–38　*Three Level SEARCH*

```
DATA DIVISION.
FD  CUSTOMER-ORDER-FILE
    LABEL RECORDS ARE STANDARD.
01  CO-RECORD.
    05  CO-ACCOUNT-NUMBER          PIC 9(7).
    05  CO-PRODUCT                 PIC X(2).
    05  CO-TYPE-CUSTOMER           PIC X(2).
    05  CO-QUANTITY-ORDERED        PIC 9(2).

WORKING-STORAGE SECTION.
01  PRODUCT-PRICE-DATA.
    05  PRODUCT-NAME               OCCURS 2 TIMES
                                   INDEXED BY PRODUCT-INDEX.
        10  PRODUCT                PIC X(2).
        10  TYPE-CUSTOMER          OCCURS 3 TIMES
                                   INDEXED BY CUSTOMER-INDEX.
            15  CUSTOMER           PIC X(2).
            15  QUANTITY-ORDERED   OCCURS 3 TIMES
                                   INDEXED BY QUANTITY-INDEX.
                20  PRICE          PIC 9(2).
01  WS-WORK-INDICATORS.
    05  WS-PRICE                   PIC 9(2).
    05  WS-PRODUCT-FOUND           PIC X(3).
        88  PRODUCT-FOUND          VALUE 'YES'.
    05  WS-CUSTOMER-FOUND          PIC X(3).
        88  CUSTOMER-FOUND         VALUE 'YES'.
    05  WS-QUANTITY-FOUND          PIC X(3).
        88  QUANTITY-FOUND         VALUE 'YES'.
    05  WS-END-OF-FILE             PIC X(3).
        88  END-OF-FILE            VALUE 'END'.
PROCEDURE DIVISION.
A000-CUSTOMER-ORDERS.
    .
    .
    PERFORM B100-LOAD-TABLE . . .
    .
    .
    OPEN INPUT CUSTOMER-ORDER-FILE.
    PERFORM Z100-READ-ORDERS.
    PERFORM B300-PROCESS-ORDERS
        UNTIL END-OF-FILE.
    .
    STOP RUN.
B100-LOAD-TABLE.
    .
B300-PROCESS-ORDERS.
```

Figure 2–38 *(concluded)*

```
        PERFORM C100-PRODUCT-SEARCH.
        IF PRODUCT-FOUND
            PERFORM C200-CUSTOMER-SEARCH
            IF CUSTOMER-FOUND
                PERFORM C300-QUANTITY-SEARCH
                IF QUANTITY-FOUND
                    PERFORM C400-CALCULATE-COST
                ELSE
                    NEXT SENTENCE
            ELSE
                    PERFORM C600-ERROR-ROUTINE-CUSTOMER
        ELSE
            PERFORM C500-ERROR-ROUTINE-PRODUCT.
        PERFORM Z100-READ-ORDERS.
C100-PRODUCT-SEARCH.
    SET PRODUCT-INDEX TO 1.
    SEARCH PRODUCT-NAME
        AT END MOVE 'END' TO WS-PRODUCT-FOUND
    WHEN PRODUCT(PRODUCT-INDEX) = CO-PRODUCT
        MOVE 'YES' TO WS-PRODUCT-FOUND.
C200-CUSTOMER-SEARCH.
    SET CUSTOMER-INDEX TO 1.
    SEARCH TYPE-CUSTOMER
        AT END MOVE 'END' TO WS-CUSTOMER-FOUND
    WHEN CUSTOMER(PRODUCT-INDEX, CUSTOMER-INDEX) =
        CO-TYPE-CUSTOMER
        MOVE 'YES' TO WS-CUSTOMER FOUND.
C300-QUANTITY-SEARCH.
    SET QUANTITY-INDEX TO 1.
    SEARCH QUANTITY-ORDERED
        AT END MOVE 'END' TO WS-QUANTITY-ORDERED
    WHEN CO-QUANTITY-ORDERED < 6
        MOVE PRICE(PRODUCT-INDEX, CUSTOMER-INDEX,
            QUANTITY-INDEX) TO WS-PRICE
        MOVE 'YES' TO WS-CUSTOMER-FOUND
    WHEN CO-QUANTITY-ORDERED < 10
        MOVE PRICE(PRODUCT-INDEX, CUSTOMER-INDEX,
            QUANTITY-INDEX) TO WS-PRICE
        MOVE 'YES' TO WS-CUSTOMER-FOUND
    WHEN CO-QUANTITY-ORDERED > 9
        MOVE PRICE(PRODUCT-INDEX, CUSTOMER-INDEX,
            QUANTITY-INDEX) TO WS-PRICE
        MOVE 'YES' TO WS-CUSTOMER-FOUND.
C400-CALCULATE-COST.
    .
C500-ERROR-ROUTINE-PRODUCT.
    .
C600-ERROR-ROUTINE-CUSTOMER.
    .
Z100-READ-ORDERS.
    READ CUSTOMER-ORDER-FILE
        AT END MOVE 'END' TO WS-END-OF-FILE.
```

of customer, and the quantity ordered. The program is to do a SEARCH of a table and determine the cost of the order.

B300–PROCESS–ORDERS will first perform C100–PRODUCT–SEARCH to determine the correct page in the table. If the correct page is found, C200–CUSTOMER–SEARCH determines the correct row of the page. If the correct row is found C300–QUANTITY–SEARCH will find the correct column for the row and page already found. In this example it was accomplished by the use of three WHEN options.

This also could have been accomplished using a linear IF statement. If all of the locations in the table have been found C400–CALCULATE–COST is performed to determine the cost of the order by multiplying the value now located at WS–PRICE and CO–QUANTITY–ORDERED. If the PRODUCT–INDEX is outside the range of PRODUCT–NAME, C500–ERROR–ROUTINE–PRODUCT is performed. If CUS TOMER–INDEX is outside the range of TYPE–CUSTOMER, C600–ERROR–ROU TINE–CUSTOMER is performed.

Binary Search with SEARCH ALL

To make a binary search of a three level table requires that the page, row, and column to be searched are in either ascending or descending order. For the most part these would be special kinds of tables, such as a pay rate table for department number, job level, and years at job level; a quantity ordered table such as in Figure 2–37; or an insurance premium table arranged by sex, age, and dollar amount of policy. Most times the data in a table lends itself to a combination of binary and linear searches. That is, the page and the row can be found by a binary search, while the column uses a linear search.

Using the data in Figure 2–37 the program in Figure 2–38 can be modified to do a binary search such as illustrated by Figure 2–39.

Figure 2–39 *Three Level SEARCH ALL*

```
DATA DIVISION.
FD  CUSTOMER-ORDER-FILE
LABEL RECORDS ARE STANDARD.
01  CO-RECORD.
        05  CO-ACCOUNT-NUMBER          PIC 9(7).
        05  CO-PRODUCT                 PIC X(2).
        05  CO-TYPE-CUSTOMER           PIC X(2).
        05  CO QUANTITY-ORDERED        PIC 9(2).

WORKING-STORAGE SECTION.
01  PRODUCT-PRICE-DATA.
        05  PRODUCT-NAME               OCCURS 2 TIMES
                                       ASCENDING KEY PRODUCT-NAME
                                       INDEXED BY PRODUCT-INDEX.

            10  PRODUCT                PIC X(2).
            10  TYPE-CUSTOMER          OCCURS 3 TIMES
                                       ASCENDING KEY TYPE-CUSTOMER
                                       INDEXED BY CUSTOMER-INDEX.

                15  CUSTOMER           PIC X(2).
                15  QUANTITY-ORDERED   OCCURS 3 TIMES
                                       INDEXED BY QUANTITY-INDEX.

                    20  PRICE          PIC 9(2).
01  WS-WORK-INDICATORS.
        05  WS-PRICE                   PIC 9(2).
        05  WS-PRODUCT-FOUND           PIC X(3).
            88  PRODUCT-FOUND          VALUE 'YES'.
        05  WS-CUSTOMER-FOUND          PIC X(3).
            88  CUSTOMER-FOUND         VALUE 'YES'.
        05  WS-QUANTITY-FOUND          PIC X(3).
            88  QUANTITY-FOUND         VALUE 'YES'.
        05  WS-END-OF-FILE             PIC X(3).
            88  END-OF-FILE            VALUE 'END'.
PROCEDURE DIVISION.
A000-CUSTOMER-ORDERS.
    .
    .
    PERFORM B100-LOAD-TABLE . . .
    .
    .
    OPEN INPUT CUSTOMER-ORDER-FILE.
    PERFORM Z100-READ-ORDERS.
```

Figure 2–39 *(concluded)*

```
        PERFORM B300-PROCESS-ORDERS.
            UNTIL END-OF-FILE.


        STOP RUN.
B100-LOAD-TABLE.


B300-PROCESS-ORDERS.
    PERFORM C100-PRODUCT-SEARCH.
    IF PRODUCT-FOUND
        PERFORM C200-CUSTOMER-SEARCH
        IF CUSTOMER-FOUND
            PERFORM C300-QUANTITY-SEARCH
            IF QUANTITY-FOUND
                PERFORM C400-CALCULATE-COST
            ELSE
                NEXT SENTENCE
        ELSE
            PERFORM C600-ERROR-ROUTINE-CUSTOMER
    ELSE
        PERFORM C500-ERROR-ROUTINE-PRODUCT.
    PERFORM Z100-READ-ORDERS.
C100-PRODUCT-SEARCH.
    SEARCH ALL PRODUCT-NAME
        AT END MOVE 'END' TO WS-PRODUCT-FOUND
    WHEN PRODUCT(PRODUCT-INDEX) = CO-PRODUCT
        MOVE 'YES' TO WS-PRODUCT-FOUND.
C200-CUSTOMER-SEARCH.
    SEARCH ALL TYPE-CUSTOMER
        AT END MOVE 'END' TO WS-CUSTOMER-FOUND
    WHEN CUSTOMER(PRODUCT-INDEX, CUSTOMER-INDEX) =
        CO-TYPE-CUSTOMER
        MOVE 'YES' TO WS-CUSTOMER-FOUND.
C300-QUANTITY-SEARCH.
    IF CO-QUANTITY-ORDER < 6
        SET QUANTITY-INDEX TO 1
    ELSE
        IF CO-QUANTITY-ORDER < 10
            SET QUANTITY-INDEX TO 2
        ELSE
            IF CO-QUANTITY-ORDERED > 9
                SET QUANTITY-INDEX TO 3.
    MOVE PRICE(PRODUCT-INDEX, CUSTOMER-INDEX, QUANTITY-INDEX)
        TO WS-PRICE.
    MOVE 'YES' TO WS-QUANTITY-FOUND.
C400-CALCULATE-COST.


C500-ERROR-ROUTINE-PRODUCT.


C600-ERROR-ROUTINE-CUSTOMER.


Z100-READ-ORDERS.
    READ CUSTOMER-ORDER-FILE
        AT END MOVE 'END' TO WS-END-OF-FILE.
```

Linear Search with PERFORM/ VARYING

Figure 2–40 illustrates some examples using a PERFORM/VARYING for a linear search.

Example A of Figure 2–40 will move zeros to each element in a 4 by 5 by 6 three level table. Example B will add all of the individual items in each row and store that sum in the appropriate row of a page in a 5 by 6 two level table named WS–ROW–TOTALS. Example C is a 4 by 5 by 6 three level table. It is searched

Figure 2–40 *Three Level Access/Search with PERFORM/ VARYING*

```
Example A:

      PERFORM E300-ZERO-OUT-FIELDS
          VARYING PAGE-SUB FROM 1 BY 1 UNTIL PAGE-SUB > 4
          AFTER ROW-SUB FROM 1 BY 1 UNTIL ROW-SUB > 5
          AFTER COL-SUB FROM 1 BY 1 UNTIL COL-SUB > 6.

   E300-ZERO-OUT-FIELDS.
       MOVE ZEROS TO TOTALS-TABLE(PAGE-SUB, ROW-SUB, COL-SUB).

Example B:

      PERFORM E400-TOTAL-ROW-VALUES
          VARYING PAGE-SUB FROM 1 BY 1 UNTIL PAGE-SUB > 4
          AFTER ROW-SUB FROM 1 BY 1 UNTIL ROW-SUB > 5
          AFTER COL-SUB FROM 1 BY 1 UNTIL COL-SUB > 6.

   E400-TOTAL-ROW-VALUES.
       ADD TOTALS-TABLE(PAGE-SUB, ROW-SUB, COL-SUB)
           TO WS-ROW-TOTALS(PAGE-SUB, ROW-SUB).

Example C:

   B200-PROCESS-SALES.
       PERFORM C100-TABLE-SEARCH
           VARYING PAGE-SUB FROM 1 BY 1 UNTIL WS-END-SEARCH = 'END'
           AFTER ROW-SUB FROM 1 BY 1 UNTIL WS-END-SEARCH = 'END'
           AFTER COL-SUB FROM 1 BY 1 UNTIL WS-END-SEARCH = 'END'
                                          OR COL-SUB > 6.

   C100-TABLE-SEARCH.
       IF TABLE-VALUE(PAGE-SUB, ROW-SUB, COL-SUB) = PR-INPUT-VALUE
          PERFORM D100-FOUND-VALUE
          MOVE 'END' TO WS-END-SEARCH
       ELSE
          IF PAGE-SUB = 4 AND ROW-SUB = 5 AND COL-SUB = 6
             PERFORM D200-NO-VALUE-FOUND
             MOVE 'END' TO WS-END-SEARCH.
```

for a value equal to PR–INPUT–VALUE. If the value is found D100–FOUND–VALUE is performed, otherwise D200–NO–VALUE–FOUND is performed.

These examples all assume the use of subscripts.

Program Example

Statement of the Problem

This program inputs employee data records that have been stored in random order to:

1. Check for valid department number, valid region number, and valid shift number.
2. Calculate gross pay, overtime pay, and regular pay for each employee based on the pay rate according to the region worked in, the shift worked, and their job level.

3. Calculate summary gross pay for all employees by region worked in, the shift worked, and the job level. This is to be printed beginning on a new page at the end of the report in table form.

Overtime is calculated for any person who has worked more than 80 hours this two-week pay period at the rate of 1.5 times the normal pay rate for those hours over 80. No one works more than 100 hours.

The program will utilize tables to determine each employee's pay rate, to print out department and region names, and to store the final totals. The first table is the pay rate table which is shown in Figure 2–41. It is a three level table with the page being the region; the row, the job level; and the column, the shift worked. This table is to be input-loaded because of the volatility of pay rate tables.

Figure 2–41   *Pay Rate Table*

Job level	Eastern region Shift			Job level	Central region Shift		
	1	2	3		1	2	3
1	7.70	7.90	8.20	1	7.35	7.60	7.85
2	8.00	8.40	8.80	2	7.65	7.95	8.25
3	8.50	8.90	9.30	3	8.15	8.55	8.95
4	9.00	9.50	10.00	4	8.65	9.15	9.65
5	9.75	10.25	11.00	5	9.40	9.90	10.50

Job level	Western region Shift		
	1	2	3
1	7.60	7.75	8.05
2	7.90	8.35	8.70
3	8.40	8.85	9.00
4	8.90	9.45	9.75
5	9.65	10.15	10.80

The second table is a one level table for department names and is shown in Figure 2–42. It forms the basis for printing the department names on the report. Because of the static nature of the data it will be hard-coded.

Figure 2–42
Department Name Table

Department	
Name	Number
Shipping	10
Assembly	15
Receiving	20
Accounting	25
Maintenance	30
Production	35

The third table is the table for the region names and is shown in Figure 2–43. It is used for the same reasons as the second table.

Figure 2–43
Region Name Table

| | Region | |
Name		Number
Eastern		1
Central		2
Western		3

A fourth table is to be created by the program. This is a three level table to store the totals of all employees by region, job level, and shift. Its format is similar to Figure 2–41, except that an employee's gross pay will be accumulated into the proper page, row, and column, replacing the pay rate. The printer spacing chart in Figure 2–45 illustrates its format when printed in the report.

Input

The data records shown in Figure 2–44 are to be used for input. The first 15 records are to be input-loaded into the pay rate table, and the remaining records contain the employee data that are to be used as input to calculate employee gross pay and totals for region, job level, and shift.

Figure 2–44   *Input Data File for Program 2–1*

```
The record definition for the pay rate table is:

1-4  Shift 1 pay rate (two assumed decimal positions)
5-8  Shift 2 pay rate (two assumed decimal positions)
9-12 Shift 3 pay rate (two assumed decimal positions)

============
077007900820
080008400880
085008900930
090009501000
097510251100
073507600785
076507950825
081508550895
086509150965
094009901050
076007750805
079008350870
084008850900
089009450975
096510151080

============
The record definition for the payroll data is:

1- 2  Department number
3      Region number
4- 6  Employee number
8      Job level
10     Shift worked
12-14 Hours worked (no decimals)

============
101022 2 2 075
```

Figure 2-44 *(concluded)*

```
102042 1 1 067
102059 3 3 071
153111 4 1 080
151122 5 2 013
152123 1 2 080
202126 3 1 049
202159 5 3 093
201175 4 2 080
203176 2 3 080
253222 5 1 080
252226 4 2 100
302242 3 3 084
304999 4 4 080
303277 3 2 007
352299 2 1 100
353311 3 1 082
354322 3 2 057
351411 4 1 012
351420 4 2 094
202421 1 1 085
203422 2 2 043
253459 3 1 012
303477 3 2 092
302499 5 1 070
301517 2 2 080
353522 4 2 100
104542 1 3 010
202611 3 2 058
303621 4 3 099
151677 1 3 072
252777 3 2 097
252799 5 3 084
151811 1 2 022
253821 1 3 011
353822 3 3 082
302826 3 5 095
201859 3 1 093
152842 3 1 081
153899 4 2 008
253921 4 1 076
352922 5 1 010
101926 4 1 014
401982 3 2 080
101995 3 3 080
============
```

Output

The output will be a printed report in the format shown in Figure 2-45.

Structure Chart

The structure chart for Program 2-1 is shown in Figure 2-46.

Figure 2-45 Printer Spacing Chart for Program 2-1

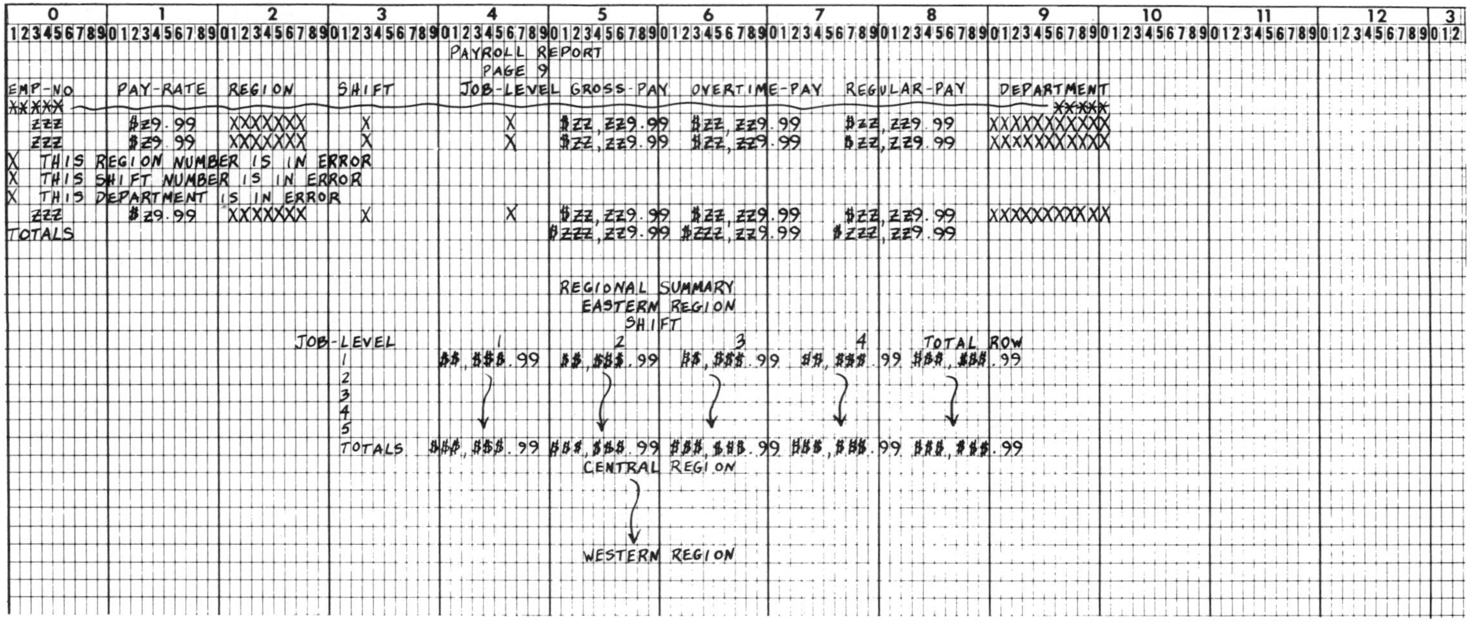

```
                1         2         3         4         5         6         7         8         9        10        11        12        13
      1234567890123456789012345678901234567890123456789012345678901234567890123456789012345678901234567890123456789012345678901234567890123

                                PAYROLL REPORT
                                PAGE 9
EMP-NO    PAY-RATE  REGION   SHIFT    JOB-LEVEL  GROSS-PAY    OVERTIME-PAY   REGULAR-PAY    DEPARTMENT
XX-XXX    $Z9.99    XXXXXX            X          $ZZ,ZZ9.99   $ZZ,ZZ9.99     $ZZ,ZZ9.99     XXXXXXXXX
ZZZ       $Z9.99    XXXXXX            X          $ZZ,ZZ9.99   $ZZ,ZZ9.99     $ZZ,ZZ9.99     XXXXXXXXX
X THIS REGION NUMBER IS IN ERROR
X THIS SHIFT NUMBER IS IN ERROR
X THIS DEPARTMENT IS IN ERROR
ZZZ       $Z9.99    XXXXXXX           X          $ZZ,ZZ9.99   $ZZ,ZZ9.99     $ZZ,ZZ9.99     XXXXXXXXXXX
TOTALS

                         REGIONAL SUMMARY
                         EASTERN REGION
                                        SHIFT
          JOB-LEVEL                 1           2           3           4        TOTAL ROW
              1          $$$,$$$.99  $$,$$$.99   $$,$$$.99   $$,,$$$.99  $$$,$$$.99
              2
              3
              4
              5
          TOTALS         $$$,$$$.99  $$$,$$$.99  $$$,$$$.99  $$$,$$$.99  $$$,$$$.99
                         CENTRAL REGION

                         WESTERN REGION
```

Figure 2-46 *Structure Chart for Program 2-1*

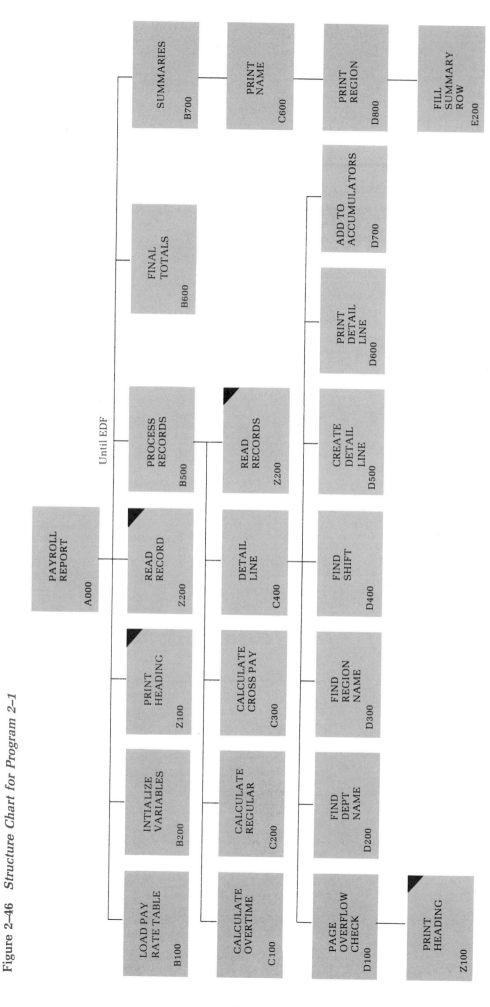

Program

Program 2-1

```
000010 IDENTIFICATION DIVISION.
000020 PROGRAM-ID.  PAYROLL.
000030***************************************************
000040* PROGRAM EXAMPLE 2-1.  THIS PROGRAM USES SEVERAL TABLES      *
000050***************************************************
000060 ENVIRONMENT DIVISION.
000070 CONFIGURATION SECTION.
000080    SOURCE-COMPUTER.  IBM-4341.
000090    OBJECT-COMPUTER.  IBM-4341.
000100 INPUT-OUTPUT SECTION.
000110    FILE-CONTROL.
000120    SELECT PAY-RATE-FILE ASSIGN TO UT-S-RATE.
000130    SELECT PAYROLL-FILE  ASSIGN TO UT-S-PAY.
000140    SELECT REPORT-FILE   ASSIGN TO UT-S-PRINTER.
000150*
000160 DATA DIVISION.
000170 FILE SECTION.
000180 FD  PAY-RATE-FILE
000190    RECORD CONTAINS 12 CHARACTERS
000200    LABEL RECORDS STANDARD.
000210 01  PAY-RATE-RECORD.
000220    05  PAY-RATE-ROW.
000230       10  PAY-RATE-VALUES      PIC 99V99 OCCURS 3 TIMES.
000240 FD  PAYROLL-FILE
000250    RECORD CONTAINS 14 CHARACTERS
000260    LABEL RECORDS STANDARD.
000270 01  PR-PAYROLL-RECORD.
000280    05  PR-DEPARTMENT-NUMBER    PIC 9(2).
000290    05  PR-REGION-NUMBER        PIC 9(1).
000300    05  PR-EMPLOYEE-NUMBER      PIC 9(3).
000310    05  FILLER                  PIC X(1).
000320    05  PR-JOB-LEVEL            PIC 9(1).
000330    05  FILLER                  PIC X(1).
000340    05  PR-SHIFT                PIC 9(1).
000350    05  FILLER                  PIC X(1).
000360    05  PR-HOURS-WORKED         PIC 9(3).
000370 FD  REPORT-FILE
000380    RECORD CONTAINS 132 CHARACTERS
000390    LABEL RECORDS STANDARD.
000400 01  RR-REPORT-RECORD           PIC X(132).
000410 WORKING-STORAGE SECTION.
000420 01  WS-REPORT-INDICATORS.
000430    05  WS-END-OF-FILE-INDICATOR PIC X(3).
000440        88  END-OF-FILE         VALUE 'END'.
000450    05  DEPT-FOUND-INDICATOR    PIC X(3).
000460        88  DEPARTMENT-FOUND    VALUE 'YES'.
000470    05  REGION-FOUND-INDICATOR  PIC X(3).
000480        88  REGION-FOUND        VALUE 'YES'.
000490    05  SHIFT-FOUND-INDICATOR   PIC X(3).
000500        88  SHIFT-FOUND         VALUE 'YES'.
000510    05  WS-LINES-PER-PAGE       PIC 9(2) VALUE 40.
000520    05  MISC-REGION             PIC 9(5).
000530 01  WS-WORK-AREAS.
000540    05  WS-GROSS-PAY            PIC 9(4)V99.
000550    05  WS-OVERTIME-PAY         PIC 9(4)V99.
000560    05  WS-REGULAR-PAY          PIC 9(4)V99.
000570 01  WS-ACCUMULATORS.
000580    05  T-TOTAL-ACCUMULATORS.
000590        10  TOT-GROSS-PAY       PIC 9(6)V99.
000600        10  TOT-OVERTIME-PAY    PIC 9(6)V99.
000610        10  TOT-REGULAR-PAY     PIC 9(6)V99.
000620    05  WS-PAGE-NUMBER          PIC 9(2).
```

Program 2–1   *(continued)*

```
000630        05  WS-LINES-USED           PIC 9(2).
000640        05  WS-JOB-LEVEL-NUMBER     PIC 9(1).
000650 01 PAY-RATE-TABLE.
000660        05  REGION                        OCCURS 3 TIMES
000670                                          INDEXED BY R-INDEX.
000680            10  JOB-LEVEL                 OCCURS 5 TIMES
000690                                          INDEXED BY J-INDEX.
000700                15  SHIFT-RATE PIC 99V99  OCCURS 3 TIMES
000710                                          INDEXED BY S-INDEX.
000720 01 TOTALS-TABLE.
000730        05  REGION-TOTAL                  OCCURS 3 TIMES
000740                                          INDEXED BY REGION-INDEX.
000750            10  JOB-LEVEL-TOTAL           OCCURS 6 TIMES
000760                                          INDEXED BY LEVEL-INDEX.
000770                15  SHIFT-TOTAL PIC 9(6)V99 OCCURS 4 TIMES
000780                                          INDEXED BY SHIFT-INDEX.
000790 01 DEPARTMENT-NAME-VALUES.
000800        05  FILLER          PIC X(13) VALUE 'SHIPPING   10'.
000810        05  FILLER          PIC X(13) VALUE 'ASSEMBLY   15'.
000820        05  FILLER          PIC X(13) VALUE 'RECEIVING  20'.
000830        05  FILLER          PIC X(13) VALUE 'ACCOUNTING 25'.
000840        05  FILLER          PIC X(13) VALUE 'MAINTENANCE30'.
000850        05  FILLER          PIC X(13) VALUE 'PRODUCTION 35'.
000860 01 FILLER REDEFINES DEPARTMENT-NAME-VALUES.
000870        05  DEPARTMENT-TABLE    OCCURS 6 TIMES
000880                               ASCENDING KEY DEPARTMENT-NUMBER
000890                               INDEXED BY DEPARTMENT-INDEX.
000900            10  DEPARTMENT-NAME     PIC X(11).
000910            10  DEPARTMENT-NUMBER   PIC X(2).
000920 01 REGION-NAME-VALUES.
000930        05  FILLER                  PIC X(8) VALUE 'EASTERN1'.
000940        05  FILLER                  PIC X(8) VALUE 'CENTRAL2'.
000950        05  FILLER                  PIC X(8) VALUE 'WESTERN3'.
000960 01 FILLER REDEFINES REGION-NAME-VALUES.
000970        05  REGION-TABLE            OCCURS 3 TIMES
000980                                    ASCENDING KEY REGION-NUMBER
000990                                    INDEXED BY R-TABLE-INDEX.
001000            10  REGION-NAME         PIC X(7).
0G1010            10  REGION-NUMBER       PIC 9(1).
001020 01 SHIFT-NUMBER-VALUES.
001030        05  FILLER                  PIC 9(3) VALUE 123.
001040 01 FILLER REDEFINES SHIFT-NUMBER-VALUES.
001050        05  SHIFT-TABLE             OCCURS 3 TIMES
001060                                    ASCENDING KEY SHIFT-NUMBER
001070                                    INDEXED BY S-WORKED-INDEX.
001080            10  SHIFT-NUMBER        PIC 9(1).
001090 01 DL-DETAIL-LINE.
001100        05  FILLER              PIC X(2) VALUE SPACES.
001110        05  DL-EMPLOYEE-NUMBER  PIC X(3).
001120        05  FILLER              PIC X(6) VALUE SPACES.
001130        05  DL-PAY-RATE         PIC $Z9.99.
001140        05  FILLER              PIC X(3) VALUE SPACES.
001150        05  DL-REGION-NAME      PIC X(7).
001160        05  FILLER              PIC X(5) VALUE SPACES.
001170        05  DL-SHIFT            PIC X(1).
001180        05  FILLER              PIC X(11) VALUE SPACES.
001190        05  DL-JOB-LEVEL        PIC X(1).
001200        05  FILLER              PIC X(5) VALUE SPACES.
001210        05  DL-GROSS-PAY        PIC $ZZ,ZZ9.99.
001220        05  FILLER              PIC X(2) VALUE SPACES.
001230        05  DL-OVERTIME-PAY     PIC $ZZ,ZZ9.99.
001240        05  FILLER              PIC X(4) VALUE SPACES.
001250        05  DL-REGULAR-PAY      PIC $ZZ,ZZ9.99.
```

Program 2–1   *(continued)*

```
001260      05  FILLER                  PIC X(3) VALUE SPACES.
001270      05  DL-DEPARTMENT-NAME      PIC X(11).
001280  01  ER-ERROR-LINE.
001290      05  ER-NUMBER               PIC ZZ9.
001300      05  FILLER                  PIC X(2) VALUE SPACES.
001310      05  ER-MESSAGE              PIC X(50).
001320  01  HD-HEADING-LINE-1.
001330      05  FILLER            .    PIC X(40) VALUE SPACES.
001340      05  FILLER                 PIC X(14) VALUE 'PAYROLL REPORT'.
001350  01  HD-HEADING-LINE-2.
001360      05  FILLER                 PIC X(43) VALUE SPACES.
001370      05  FILLER                 PIC X(5)  VALUE 'PAGE'.
001380      05  HD-PAGE-NUMBER         PIC Z9.
001390  01  HD-HEADING-LINE-3.
001400      05  FILLER                 PIC X(10) VALUE 'EMP-NO'.
001410      05  FILLER                 PIC X(10) VALUE 'PAY-RATE'.
001420      05  FILLER                 PIC X(10) VALUE 'REGION'.
001430      05  FILLER                 PIC X(10) VALUE 'SHIFT'.
001440      05  FILLER                 PIC X(11) VALUE 'JOB-LEVEL'.
001450      05  FILLER                 PIC X(11) VALUE 'GROSS-PAY'.
001460      05  FILLER                 PIC X(14) VALUE 'OVERTIME-PAY'.
001470      05  FILLER                 PIC X(14) VALUE 'REGULAR-PAY'.
001480      05  FILLER                 PIC X(10) VALUE 'DEPARTMENT'.
001490  01  ASTERISK-LINE.
001500      05  FILLER                 PIC X(100) VALUE ALL '*'.
001510  01  TL-TOTAL-LINE.
001520      05  FILLER                 PIC X(49) VALUE 'TOTALS'.
001530      05  TL-GROSS-PAY           PIC $ZZZ,ZZ9.99.
001540      05  FILLER                 PIC X(1)  VALUE SPACES.
001550      05  TL-OVERTIME-PAY        PIC $ZZZ,ZZ9.99.
001560      05  FILLER                 PIC X(3)  VALUE SPACES.
001570      05  TL-REGULAR-PAY         PIC $ZZZ,ZZ9.99.
001580  01  SL-SUMMARY-LINE-1.
001590      05  FILLER                 PIC X(50) VALUE SPACES.
001600      05  FILLER                 PIC X(20) VALUE 'REGIONAL SUMMARY'.
001610  01  SL-SUMMARY-LINE-2.
001620      05  FILLER                 PIC X(52) VALUE SPACES.
001630      05  SL-REGION-NAME         PIC X(8).
001640      05  FILLER                 PIC X(6)  VALUE 'REGION'.
001650  01  SL-SUMMARY-LINE-3.
001660      05  FILLER                 PIC X(56) VALUE SPACES.
001670      05  FILLER                 PIC X(5)  VALUE 'SHIFT'.
001680  01  SL-SUMMARY-LINE-4.
001690      05  FILLER                 PIC X(26) VALUE SPACES.
001700      05  FILLER                 PIC X(15) VALUE 'JOB-LEVEL'.
001710      05  FILLER                 PIC X(49)
001720          VALUE '   1         2         3      TOTAL ROW'.
001730  01  SL-SUMMARY-LINE-5.
001740      05  FILLER                 PIC X(30) VALUE SPACES.
001750      05  SL-JOB-LEVEL           PIC X(7).
001760      05  SL-SHIFT               OCCURS 4 TIMES.
001770          10  SL-SHIFT-VALUE     PIC $$$$,$$$.99.
001780*
001790  PROCEDURE DIVISION.
001800  A000-PAYROLL-REPORT.
001810      OPEN INPUT  PAY-RATE-FILE
001820                  PAYROLL-FILE
001830           OUTPUT REPORT-FILE.
001840      PERFORM B100-LOAD-PAY-RATE-TABLE
001850          VARYING R-INDEX
001860              FROM 1 BY 1
001870                  UNTIL R-INDEX > 3
001880          AFTER J-INDEX
```

Program 2–1   *(continued)*

```
001890          FROM 1 BY 1
001900          UNTIL J-INDEX > 5.
001910      PERFORM B200-INITIALIZE-VARIABLES.
001920      PERFORM Z100-PRINT-REPORT-HEADINGS.
001930      PERFORM Z200-READ-PAYROLL.
001940      PERFORM B500-PROCESS-RECORDS
001950          UNTIL END-OF-FILE.
001960      PERFORM B600-FINAL-TOTALS.
001970      PERFORM B700-SUMMARIES.
001980      CLOSE PAY-RATE-FILE
001990            PAYROLL-FILE
002000            REPORT-FILE.
002010      STOP RUN.
002020 B100-LOAD-PAY-RATE-TABLE.
002030      READ PAY-RATE-FILE.
002040      MOVE PAY-RATE-ROW TO JOB-LEVEL(R-INDEX J-INDEX).
002050 B200-INITIALIZE-VARIABLES.
002060      MOVE 'NO' TO WS-END-OF-FILE-INDICATOR.
002070      MOVE ZEROS TO WS-ACCUMULATORS
002080                    TOTALS-TABLE.
002090 B500-PROCESS-RECORDS.
002100      IF PR-HOURS-WORKED > 80
002110          PERFORM C100-CALCULATE-OVERTIME
002120      ELSE
002130          MOVE ZEROES TO WS-OVERTIME-PAY.
002140      PERFORM C200-CALCULATE-REGULAR.
002150      PERFORM C300-CALCULATE-GROSS-PAY.
002160      PERFORM C400-DETAIL-LINE.
002170      PERFORM Z200-READ-PAYROLL.
002180 B600-FINAL-TOTALS.
002190      MOVE TOT-GROSS-PAY    TO TL-GROSS-PAY.
002200      MOVE TOT-OVERTIME-PAY TO TL-OVERTIME-PAY.
002210      MOVE TOT-REGULAR-PAY  TO TL-REGULAR-PAY.
002220      WRITE RR-REPORT-RECORD FROM TL-TOTAL-LINE
002230          AFTER 2.
002240 B700-SUMMARIES.
002250      WRITE RR-REPORT-RECORD FROM SL-SUMMARY-LINE-1
002260          AFTER PAGE.
002270      PERFORM C600-PRINT-REGION-NAME
002280          VARYING REGION-INDEX
002290          FROM 1 BY 1
002300          UNTIL REGION-INDEX > 3.
002310 C100-CALCULATE-OVERTIME.
002320      COMPUTE WS-OVERTIME-PAY ROUNDED = (PR-HOURS-WORKED - 80) *
002330          SHIFT-RATE(PR-REGION-NUMBER PR-JOB-LEVEL PR-SHIFT)
002340          * 1.5.
002350 C200-CALCULATE-REGULAR.
002360      IF PR-HOURS-WORKED > 80
002370          COMPUTE WS-REGULAR-PAY ROUNDED = 80 *
002380              SHIFT-RATE(PR-REGION-NUMBER PR-JOB-LEVEL PR-SHIFT)
002390      ELSE
002400          COMPUTE WS-REGULAR-PAY ROUNDED = PR-HOURS-WORKED *
002410              SHIFT-RATE(PR-REGION-NUMBER PR-JOB-LEVEL PR-SHIFT).
002420 C300-CALCULATE-GROSS-PAY.
002430      COMPUTE WS-GROSS-PAY = WS-OVERTIME-PAY + WS-REGULAR-PAY.
002440 C400-DETAIL-LINE.
002450      PERFORM D100-PAGE-OVERFLOW-CHECK.
002460      PERFORM D200-FIND-DEPT-NAME.
002470      PERFORM D300-FIND-REGION-NAME.
002480      PERFORM D400-FIND-SHIFT.
002490      IF DEPARTMENT-FOUND
002500         AND REGION-FOUND
002510         AND SHIFT-FOUND
```

Program 2–1   *(continued)*

```
002520          PERFORM D500-CREATE-DETAIL-LINE
002530          PERFORM D600-PRINT-DETAIL-LINE
002540          PERFORM D700-ADD-TO-ACCUMULATORS.
002550 C600-PRINT-REGION-NAME.
002560     SET MISC-REGION                    TO REGION-INDEX.
002570     MOVE REGION-NAME(MISC-REGION) TO SL-REGION-NAME.
002580     WRITE RR-REPORT-RECORD FROM SL-SUMMARY-LINE-2
002590          AFTER 3.
002600     WRITE RR-REPORT-RECORD FROM SL-SUMMARY-LINE-3
002610          AFTER 1.
002620     WRITE RR-REPORT-RECORD FROM SL-SUMMARY-LINE-4
002630          AFTER 1.
002640     MOVE ZERO TO WS-JOB-LEVEL-NUMBER.
002650     PERFORM D800-PRINT-REGION-SUMMARY
002660          VARYING LEVEL-INDEX
002670          FROM 1 BY 1
002680          UNTIL LEVEL-INDEX > 6.
002690 D100-PAGE-OVERFLOW-CHECK.
002700     IF WS-LINES-USED > WS-LINES-PER-PAGE
002710          PERFORM Z100-PRINT-REPORT-HEADINGS.
002720 D200-FIND-DEPT-NAME.
002730     SEARCH ALL DEPARTMENT-TABLE
002740          AT END
002750            MOVE PR-DEPARTMENT-NUMBER TO ER-NUMBER
002760            MOVE 'THIS DEPARTMENT NUMBER IS IN ERROR' TO ER-MESSAGE
002770            WRITE RR-REPORT-RECORD FROM ER-ERROR-LINE
002780              AFTER 1
002790            MOVE 'NO' TO DEPT-FOUND-INDICATOR
002800          WHEN DEPARTMENT-NUMBER(DEPARTMENT-INDEX) =
002810            PR-DEPARTMENT-NUMBER
002820            MOVE 'YES' TO DEPT-FOUND-INDICATOR.
002830 D300-FIND-REGION-NAME.
002840     SEARCH ALL REGION-TABLE
002850          AT END
002860            MOVE PR-REGION-NUMBER TO ER-NUMBER
002870            MOVE 'THIS REGION NUMBER IS IN ERROR' TO ER-MESSAGE
002880            WRITE RR-REPORT-RECORD FROM ER-ERROR-LINE
002890              AFTER 1
002900            MOVE 'NO' TO REGION-FOUND-INDICATOR
002910          WHEN REGION-NUMBER(R-TABLE-INDEX) = PR-REGION-NUMBER
002920            MOVE 'YES' TO REGION-FOUND-INDICATOR.
002930 D400-FIND-SHIFT.
002940     SEARCH ALL SHIFT-TABLE
002950          AT END MOVE PR-SHIFT TO ER-NUMBER
002960            MOVE 'THIS SHIFT NUMBER IS IN ERROR' TO ER-MESSAGE
002970            WRITE RR-REPORT-RECORD FROM ER-ERROR-LINE
002980              AFTER 1
002990            MOVE 'NO' TO SHIFT-FOUND-INDICATOR
003000          WHEN SHIFT-NUMBER(S-WORKED-INDEX) = PR-SHIFT
003010            MOVE 'YES' TO SHIFT-FOUND-INDICATOR.
003020 D500-CREATE-DETAIL-LINE.
003030     MOVE PR-EMPLOYEE-NUMBER TO DL-EMPLOYEE-NUMBER.
003040     MOVE SHIFT-RATE(PR-REGION-NUMBER PR-JOB-LEVEL PR-SHIFT)
003050          TO DL-PAY-RATE.
003060     MOVE REGION-NAME(PR-REGION-NUMBER) TO DL-REGION-NAME.
003070     MOVE PR-SHIFT                      TO DL-SHIFT.
003080     MOVE PR-JOB-LEVEL                  TO DL-JOB-LEVEL.
003090     MOVE WS-GROSS-PAY                  TO DL-GROSS-PAY.
003100     MOVE WS-OVERTIME-PAY               TO DL-OVERTIME-PAY.
003110     MOVE WS-REGULAR-PAY                TO DL-REGULAR-PAY.
003120     MOVE DEPARTMENT-NAME(DEPARTMENT-INDEX)
003130          TO DL-DEPARTMENT-NAME.
003140 D600-PRINT-DETAIL-LINE.
```

Program 2–1 *(concluded)*

```
003150     WRITE RR-REPORT-RECORD FROM DL-DETAIL-LINE
003160         AFTER 1.
003170     ADD 1 TO WS-LINES-USED.
003180 D700-ADD-TO-ACCUMULATORS.
003190     ADD WS-GROSS-PAY TO TOT-GROSS-PAY
003200     ADD WS-GROSS-PAY TO
003210         SHIFT-TOTAL(PR-REGION-NUMBER PR-JOB-LEVEL PR-SHIFT)
003220     ADD WS-GROSS-PAY TO
003230         SHIFT-TOTAL(PR-REGION-NUMBER PR-JOB-LEVEL 4)
003240     ADD WS-GROSS-PAY TO
003250         SHIFT-TOTAL(PR-REGION-NUMBER 6 PR-SHIFT).
003260     ADD WS-GROSS-PAY TO
003270         SHIFT-TOTAL(PR-REGION-NUMBER 6 4).
003280     ADD WS-OVERTIME-PAY TO TOT-OVERTIME-PAY.
003290     ADD WS-REGULAR-PAY  TO  TOT-REGULAR-PAY.
003300 D800-PRINT-REGION-SUMMARY.
003310     ADD 1 TO WS-JOB-LEVEL-NUMBER.
003320     IF WS-JOB-LEVEL-NUMBER = 6
003330         MOVE 'TOTALS' TO SL-JOB-LEVEL
003340     ELSE
003350         MOVE WS-JOB-LEVEL-NUMBER TO SL-JOB-LEVEL.
003360     PERFORM E200-FILL-SUMMARY-ROW
003370         VARYING SHIFT-INDEX
003380         FROM 1 BY 1
003390         UNTIL SHIFT-INDEX > 4.
003400     WRITE RR-REPORT-RECORD FROM SL-SUMMARY-LINE-5
003410         AFTER 1.
003420 E200-FILL-SUMMARY-ROW.
003430     MOVE SHIFT-TOTAL (REGION-INDEX LEVEL-INDEX SHIFT-INDEX)
003440         TO SL-SHIFT-VALUE(SHIFT-INDEX).
003450 Z100-PRINT-REPORT-HEADINGS.
003460     ADD 1            TO WS-PAGE-NUMBER.
003470     MOVE WS-PAGE-NUMBER TO HD-PAGE-NUMBER.
003480     MOVE 5           TO WS-LINES-USED.
003490     WRITE RR-REPORT-RECORD FROM HD-HEADING-LINE-1
003500         AFTER PAGE.
003510     WRITE RR-REPORT-RECORD FROM HD-HEADING-LINE-2
003520         AFTER 1.
003530     WRITE RR-REPORT-RECORD FROM HD-HEADING-LINE-3
003540         AFTER 2.
003550     WRITE RR-REPORT-RECORD FROM ASTERISK-LINE
003560         AFTER 1.
003570 Z200-READ-PAYROLL.
003580     READ PAYROLL-FILE
003590         AT END MOVE 'END' TO WS-END-OF-FILE-INDICATOR.
```

Discussion

In the DATA division the department name table, the region name table, and the shift number table have been hard-coded in lines 790–1080. The table to store the summary gross pay for all employees by region, the shift worked, and the job level are defined in lines 720–780 and the pay rate table in lines 650–710. The department name table, the region name table, and the shift number table will utilize a binary search, while the totals table will utilize a positional lookup. The pay rate table is input-loaded, a row at a time, at lines 1840–1900 and 2020–2040.

After the table is loaded, the first payroll data record is input, and B500–PRO CESS–RECORDS is performed until there are no more payroll data records in the file. Within this procedure the determination is made whether or not overtime pay is to be calculated at line 2100.

C200–CALCULATE–REGULAR will calculate the regular pay. Notice the pay rate is determined by a positional lookup in the pay rate table using as subscripts the numbers for the region, job level, and shift from the payroll input record. This is done at statements 2320–2410.

After the regular pay has been determined C300–CALCULATE–GROSS–PAY will add together any overtime pay and regular pay to arrive at the gross pay. C400–DETAIL–LINE will then check for a page overflow condition at line 2450, use a binary search at lines 2730–2820 to determine if the department number is valid, use a binary search at lines 2840–2920 to determine if the region number is valid, and use a binary search at lines 2940–3010 to determine if the shift number is valid. If any of these are not valid, appropriate switches are set, and error messages are printed. If all of these numbers are valid then the detail line is created at lines 3030–3130. Notice that values from the payroll input record are used to make positional searches for the department name, region name, and shift rate in the appropriate tables. The detail line is printed at lines 3140–3170.

At lines 3180–3290 the totals for gross pay, overtime, and regular pay are accumulated. Also the gross pay is accumulated for the grand total (line 3260), the row total (line 3220), and the column total (line 3240), for the appropriate region. Line 3200 accumulates the gross pay by job level and shift within a region. Again, positional table lookups are made using subscript values from the payroll input record.

After the inputting of the payroll data file is completed B600–FINAL–TOTALS is performed. At lines 2180–2230 the total lines are printed. B700–SUMMARIES prints the summary tables for each region.

Lines 2270–2300 control the printing of these tables with a PERFORM/VARYING statement using indexes. Lines 2550–2640 moves the appropriate region name to the output area and print the table headings. Lines 2650–2680 causes the printing of each row in the table. This is done by lines 3300–3410.

The output for Program 2–1 is shown in Figure 2–47.

Figure 2–47 *Output from Program 2–1*

```
                                  PAYROLL REPORT
                                     PAGE  1

  EMP-NO   PAY-RATE  REGION    SHIFT    JOB-LEVEL   GROSS-PAY   OVERTIME-PAY   REGULAR-PAY   DEPARTMENT
 ........................................................................................................
   022     $ 8.40   EASTERN      2          2      $   630.00  $     0.00    $   630.00    SHIPPING
   042     $ 7.35   CENTRAL      1          1      $   492.45  $     0.00    $   492.45    SHIPPING
   059     $ 8.95   CENTRAL      3          3      $   635.45  $     0.00    $   635.45    SHIPPING
   111     $ 8.90   WESTERN      1          4      $   712.00  $     0.00    $   712.00    ASSEMBLY
   122     $10.25   EASTERN      2          5      $   133.25  $     0.00    $   133.25    ASSEMBLY
   123     $ 7.60   CENTRAL      2          1      $   608.00  $     0.00    $   608.00    ASSEMBLY
   126     $ 8.15   CENTRAL      1          3      $   399.35  $     0.00    $   399.35    RECEIVING
   159     $10.50   CENTRAL      3          5      $ 1,044.75  $   204.75    $   840.00    RECEIVING
   175     $ 9.50   EASTERN      2          4      $   760.00  $     0.00    $   760.00    RECEIVING
   176     $ 8.70   WESTERN      3          2      $   696.00  $     0.00    $   696.00    RECEIVING
   222     $ 9.65   WESTERN      1          5      $   772.00  $     0.00    $   772.00    ACCOUNTING
   226     $ 9.15   CENTRAL      2          4      $ 1,006.50  $   274.50    $   732.00    ACCOUNTING
   242     $ 8.95   CENTRAL      3          3      $   769.70  $    53.70    $   716.00    MAINTENANCE
   4   THIS REGION NUMBER IS IN ERROR
   4   THIS SHIFT NUMBER IS IN ERROR
   277     $ 8.85   WESTERN      2          3      $    61.95  $     0.00    $    61.95    MAINTENANCE
   299     $ 7.65   CENTRAL      1          2      $   841.50  $   299.50    $   612.00    PRODUCTION
   311     $ 8.40   WESTERN      1          3      $   697.20  $    25.20    $   672.00    PRODUCTION
   4   THIS REGION NUMBER IS IN ERROR
   411     $ 9.00   EASTERN      1          4      $   108.00  $     0.00    $   108.00    PRODUCTION
   420     $ 9.50   EASTERN      2          4      $   959.50  $   199.50    $   760.00    PRODUCTION
   421     $ 7.35   CENTRAL      1          1      $   643.13  $    55.13    $   588.00    RECEIVING
   422     $ 8.35   WESTERN      2          2      $   359.05  $     0.00    $   359.05    RECEIVING
```

Figure 2–47 *(concluded)*

```
459    $ 8.40   WESTERN    1         3    $   100.80  $     0.00  $   100.80   ACCOUNTING
477    $ 8.85   WESTERN    2         3    $   867.30  $   159.30  $   708.00   MAINTENANCE
499    $ 9.40   CENTRAL    1         5    $   658.00  $     0.00  $   658.00   MAINTENANCE
517    $ 8.40   EASTERN    2         2    $   672.00  $     0.00  $   672.00   MAINTENANCE
522    $ 9.45   WESTERN    2         4    $ 1,039.50  $   283.50  $   756.00   PRODUCTION
  4  THIS REGION NUMBER IS IN ERROR
611    $ 8.55   CENTRAL    2         3    $   495.90  $     0.00  $   495.90   RECEIVING
621    $ 9.75   WESTERN    3         4    $ 1,057.88  $   277.88  $   780.00   MAINTENANCE
677    $ 8.20   EASTERN    3         1    $   590.40  $     0.00  $   590.40   ASSEMBLY
777    $ 8.55   CENTRAL    2         3    $   902.03  $   218.03  $   684.00   ACCOUNTING
799    $10.50   CENTRAL    3         5    $   903.00  $    63.00  $   840.00   ACCOUNTING
811    $ 7.90   EASTERN    2         1    $   173.80  $     0.00  $   173.80   ASSEMBLY
821    $ 8.05   WESTERN    3         1    $    88.55  $     0.00  $    88.55   ACCOUNTING
822    $ 9.00   WESTERN    3         3    $   747.00  $    27.00  $   720.00   PRODUCTION
  5  THIS SHIFT NUMBER IS IN ERROR
859    $ 8.50   EASTERN    1         3    $   845.75  $   165.75  $   680.00   RECEIVING
842    $ 8.15   CENTRAL    1         3    $   664.23  $    12.23  $   652.00   ASSEMBLY
899    $ 9.45   WESTERN    2         4    $    75.60  $     0.00  $    75.60   ASSEMBLY


                              PAYROLL REPORT
                                 PAGE  2


EMP-NO   PAY-RATE  REGION    SHIFT   JOB-LEVEL  GROSS-PAY  OVERTIME-PAY  REGULAR-PAY  DEPARTMENT
.................................................................................................

921    $ 8.90   WESTERN    1         4    $   676.40  $     0.00  $   676.40   ACCOUNTING
922    $ 9.40   CENTRAL    1         5    $    94.00  $     0.00  $    94.00   PRODUCTION
926    $ 9.00   EASTERN    1         4    $   126.00  $     0.00  $   126.00   SHIPPING
 40  THIS DEPARTMENT NUMBER IS IN ERROR
995    $ 9.30   EASTERN    3         3    $   744.00  $     0.00  $   744.00   SHIPPING

TOTALS                                    $23,851.92  $ 2,248.97  $ 21,602.95


                            REGIONAL SUMMARY


                             EASTERN REGION
                                 SHIFT
              JOB-LEVEL       1           2           3        TOTAL ROW
                  1          $.00     $173.80     $590.40       $764.20
                  2          $.00   $1,302.00        $.00     $1,302.00
                  3       $845.75        $.00     $744.00     $1,589.75
                  4       $234.00   $1,719.50        $.00     $1,953.50
                  5          $.00     $133.25        $.00       $133.25
              TOTALS   $1,079.75   $3,328.55   $1,334.40     $5,742.70


                             CENTRAL REGION
                                 SHIFT
              JOB-LEVEL       1           2           3        TOTAL ROW
                  1     $1,135.58     $608.00        $.00     $1,743.58
                  2       $841.50        $.00        $.00       $841.50
                  3     $1,063.58   $1,397.93   $1,405.15     $3,866.66
                  4          $.00   $1,006.50        $.00     $1,006.50
                  5       $752.00        $.00   $1,947.75     $2,699.75
              TOTALS   $3,792.66   $3,012.43   $3,352.90    $10,157.99


                             WESTERN REGION
                                 SHIFT
              JOB-LEVEL       1           2           3        TOTAL ROW
                  1          $.00        $.00      $88.55        $88.55
                  2          $.00     $359.05     $696.00     $1,055.05
                  3       $798.00     $929.25     $747.00     $2,474.25
                  4     $1,388.40   $1,115.10   $1,057.88     $3,561.38
                  5       $772.00        $.00        $.00       $772.00
              TOTALS   $2,958.40   $2,403.40   $2,589.43     $7,951.23
```

Programming Style

1. Choose from either subscripts or indexes to access tables, and use them consistently throughout the program. Since subscripts cannot be used for the SEARCH statement, and since indexes are compiler-generated (and are, therefore, more efficient), the authors recommend using indexes.

2. When a PIC clause and an OCCURS are both used at the same level number, place the PIC clause immediately following the data-name.

3. Create table and data-item names that are descriptive of the table and data.

4. Hard-code tables that are fairly static and tables that should be as secure as possible.

5. Input-load tables that are volatile by the nature of the data.

6. Use the PERFORM/VARYING statement to input-load tables.

7. Use the SEARCH statement to access table data in a linear search.

8. Use the SEARCH ALL statement to access table data in a binary search.

Common Errors

1. Using a data-name instead of a positive integer number literal for integer-1 in the OCCURS clause.

2. Using an OCCURS clause at the 01 level.

3. Placing the OCCURS clause after the INDEXED BY or ASCENDING KEY clause.

4. Placing the wrong programmer-supplied name after the REDEFINES clause.

5. Trying to initialize an index by statements other than PERFORM/VARYING and SET.

6. Using an index data item in a PERFORM/VARYING statement.

7. Using the SEARCH ALL statement when the table data is not in ascending or descending sequence.

8. Improper termination of the WHEN clause.

9. Loading or accessing tables when the value of the subscript or index is larger than indicated by the OCCURS clause.

10. Testing for an unequal condition after the WHEN in a SEARCH ALL statement.

11. Confusing an index-name with an index data item. The index-name is associated with a particular table and is defined with an INDEXED BY clause where an index data item is not associated with any particular table and is defined with USAGE IS INDEX clause.

12. Attempting to reference a table data entry with an inappropriate number of subscripts or indexes.

13. Failure to appropriately initialize an index prior to its use. Remember, an index is initialized either by the use of the SET command or through the use of a PERFORM/VARYING.

14. Using a numeric data entry as the object of the DEPENDING ON entry. That is, OCCURS 1 TO 100 TIMES DEPENDING ON WS–NUMBER must define WS–NUMBER as numeric. Also, WS–NUMBER cannot be defined within the variable area.

15. Following the DEPENDING ON clause by an item not subordinate to it.

16. Allowing a DEPENDING ON clause to be subordinate to another DEPENDING ON clause.

17. Using more than one WHEN condition for a SEARCH ALL.

Exercises

1. Define both an index-name and an index data item.

2. What is the purpose of the OCCURS clause?

3. Define both a subscript and an index.

4. What is the difference between hard-coding and input-loading a table?

5. Write a COBOL statement that will reserve 10 numeric fields that are each four positions long with two assumed decimal positions.

6. Write a COBOL statement that will reserve storage locations for one table to include 10 fields each in the following order:
   a. A five-position alphanumeric field called F1.
      A six-position numeric field with two decimal positions called F2.
      A four-position numeric field with two decimal positions called F3.
   b. How many positions in storage will be saved for the table?
   c. Illustrate in a diagram the order in which these fields are stored.

7.
   a. How many storage positions (characters) and storage locations will be reserved for each of the following tables:

```
01  TABLE-1.
    05  MONTH-NAME PIC X(10) OCCURS 12 TIMES.
01  TABLE-2.
    05  DEPT-VALUES OCCURS 5 TIMES.
        10  D-ITEM  PIC 9(5).
        10  D-NAME  PIC X(10).
01  TABLE-3.
    05  DEPT-NAMES PIC X(10) OCCURS 12 TIMES.
    05  DEPT-CODES PIC 99 OCCURS 12 TIMES.
01  TABLE-4.
    05  AIRLINE-TO OCCURS 20 TIMES.
        10  AIRLINE-RATE PIC 999V99
                OCCURS 15 TIMES.
01  TABLE-5.
    05  SHIPMENT-ORIGIN OCCURS 10 TIMES.
        10  FREIGHT-OUT OCCURS 5 TIMES.
            15  F1 PIC X(5).
            15  F2 PIC 99.
```

   b. How many subscripts or indexes are needed with the following names from the tables defined in *a* above?

   MONTH–NAME.
   DEPT–VALUES.
   D–ITEM.
   DEPT–NAMES.
   AIRLINE–TO.
   AIRLINE–RATE.
   SHIPMENT–ORIGIN.
   F1.

8. Write a list of the values of ROW and COLUMN and the order in which they occur for each of the following sets of PERFORM statements.

   a.
```
PERFORM B100-RATE-TABLE-1
    VARYING COLUMN
```

```
                    FROM 1 BY 2
                    UNTIL COLUMN > 10.
        b.  PERFORM B200-RATE-TABLE-2
                  VARYING ROW
                        FROM 1 BY 1
                        UNTIL ROW > 3
                  AFTER COLUMN
                       FROM 1 BY 1
                       UNTIL COLUMN > 4.
        c.  PERFORM B300-RATE-TABLE-3
                 VARYING ROW
                 FROM 1 BY 1
                 UNTIL ROW > 4
          B300-RATE-TABLE-3.
            PERFORM B400-RATE-TABLE-4
                VARYING COLUMN
                FROM 2 BY 2
                UNTIL COLUMN > 8.
```

9. Hard-code the following data using an index, and allow for two fields of data. The first is a 2-position numeric field and the second a 10-position alphanumeric field.

```
        10AUTOMOTIVE
        15APPLIANCES
        23TV
        45CLOTHING
        36HARDWARE
```

10. Write the statements necessary to make a linear search for the numeric field in Exercise 9 above to find the table entry defined by IN–DEPT–NUMBER. If the entry is not found PERFORM Z400–ERROR–RTN. If the entry is found PER FORM D500–PROCESS and move the literal YES to a switch called WS–TABLE–SWITCH.

11. Given the following entries correct only those that are in error. Assume all programmer-defined names have been properly defined.

```
    a.  05   AT OCCURS 15 TIMES.
    b.  MOVE PAY-RATE(ROW, COLUMN) TO    WS-AREA.
    c.  01  TABLE-2 REDEFINES TABLE-1.
            05   F1 PIC 99.
            05   F2 PIC XX.
    d.  SET INDEX-1 TO DEPT-INDEX.
    e.  SEARCH ALL TABLE-1
            WHEN TABLE-CODE > IN-TABLE-CODE
            MOVE 'YES' TO WS-SWITCH.
    f.  INDEXED BY 1.
    g.  ASCENDING KEY DEPT-CODE.
    h.  SUBTRACT IN-TOTAL FROM WS-TOTAL(R1, R2)
            GIVING IN-TOTAL(R1, R2).
    i.  05   AMOUNT-IN PIC 99 OCCURS 4 TIMES.
        10   NAME-IN OCCURS 5 TIMES.
```

12. Hard-code the following data which will be used with a SEARCH ALL statement. Allow for a three level table. Each level has fields in the following order: a two-position alphanumeric, a three-position numeric, and two one-position numeric fields.

	Page 1	Page 2
	1231234	1111411
	2451335	2222122
	3642136	3333244

13. Code only the PROCEDURE division statements for the following problems and use PERFORM statements.

   a. Copy a one level table into another one level table where each table contains 10 elements.

   b. Copy the table in *a* above in reverse order.

   c. Find the smallest value in a 10 element one level table.

   d. Search a two level (5 by 6) table to find the value of an element in the table that is equal to the value of B–VALUE. If such a value is found, perform the routine VALUE–FOUND and exit the table. Otherwise, perform VALUE–NOT–FOUND and exit the table. Do not use the SEARCH statement.

14. Use the SEARCH statement to search a one level table for the conditions: If the table element's value is less than 10, move that value to A, or if the value is equal to 10 move that value to B.

15. Use SEARCH statements to solve problem 13*d* above. Code only the statements necessary in the PROCEDURE division.

16. How many times will ROUTINE–A be executed in the following statement:

```
PERFORM ROUTINE-A
VARYING A1
    FROM 1 BY 1
    UNTIL A1 > 20
AFTER B1
    FROM 3 BY 3
    UNTIL B1 > 21
AFTER C1
FROM 10 BY -1
UNTIL C1 < 3.
```

Problems

1. Modify Program 2–1 so that summary totals are accumulated for each region for:

   a. Accumulated gross pay by department (print out the department name) by shift (a three level table).

   b. Total the accumulated pay by shift for each department in step *a* above.

   c. Total the accumulated pay by department for each shift in step *a* above.

   d. Add a check for an invalid job level. If job level is invalid, do not process the record but print out the value of the invalid job level number and the message THIS JOB LEVEL IS IN ERROR.

   e. Input load the tables for department names and region names as well as the pay rate table.

   f. Use the tables and data from Program 2–1.

2. Modify Program 2–1 so that summary tables are printed for the number of employees in each region by shift within job level. Also print a final summary table for the number of employees in the company by shift within job level. Produce a grand total for each row and each column in this final summary. Use the data in Program 2–1.

3. Modify Program 2–1 to print a two level table totaling the number of employees

by job class and region for the company. Produce a grand total for each row and each column in this table. Use the tables and data from Program 2–1.

4. Write a program to create a report to do the following:
   a. Start the program at the top of a new page.
   b. Hard-code the following table:

	Department		
Number	*Name*	*Number*	*Name*
1	Accounting	6	Personnel
2	Legal	7	Research
3	Maintenance	8	Sales
4	Manufacturing	9	Transportation
5	Marketing	10	Warehouse

   c. Input-load the following plant name and region name tables and allow fields for totals:

	Plant		Region
Number	Name	Number	Name
1	Personal computer	1	Western
2	Desk top computer	2	Southern
3	Main frame computer	3	Northern
4	Super computer	4	Eastern

   d. Use data set A of Appendix C as the input data after the tables have been created.
   e. Edit output fields appropriately.
   f. Summarize year-to-date gross pay for each region:
      Totals for department by plant.
      Grand totals for all departments in each plant.
      Grand totals for all plants by department.

3

Sorting and Merging Files

There are many times when it is necessary to arrange data records in a file in a prescribed manner that is different than the original order of the file. Control break processing requires data to be grouped according to major, intermediate, and minor control groups. For instance, in an employee file it may be necessary to initially create the file in employee number order (perhaps the social security number), but then rearrange the data records by the department in which the employee works, by the branch location of the employee, by region, and so forth. At other times it may be desirable to have the data records in alphabetical order, in order by ZIP code, in order by pay rate, or other arrangements depending on the application.

TERMS AND STATEMENTS

ASCENDING KEY clause	Internal programmed sort	SD entry
Bubble sort	MERGE statement	Shell sort
DESCENDING KEY clause	OUTPUT PROCEDURE	SORT statement
EXIT statement	Post-processing	Sort description
External utility program sort	Pre-processing	Sort keys
INPUT PROCEDURE	RELEASE statement	USING/GIVING option
	RETURN statement	Variable length records

Sorting Concepts

To illustrate the concepts of sorting, consider the inventory data records listed in Figure 3–1. The records are currently in department number order, but there is no apparent order relative to two other columns of data, part number and store number. What are some other orders that may be of benefit to a user? One other sequence would be in ascending (from low to high) part number sequence that could be used to prepare a part number listing. This listing could be used to look up the price and quantity on hand of a particular part. If the data records were sorted in this sequence, they would appear as illustrated in Figure 3–2.

Figure 3–1   *Inventory Records—Original Order*

Department number	Part number	Unit price	Store number	Quantity on hand
01	2243	86.20	2	100
01	1752	92.75	1	300
05	1892	42.97	1	40
05	2575	55.20	2	10
07	1876	45.75	2	40
07	1215	19.20	1	150
07	5542	75.67	1	200

Figure 3–2   *Inventory Records—Part Number Order*

Department number	Part number	Unit price	Store number	Quantity on hand
07	1215	19.20	1	150
01	1752	92.75	1	300
05	1892	42.97	1	40
07	1876	45.75	2	40
01	2243	86.20	2	100
05	2575	55.20	2	10
07	5542	75.67	1	200

Perhaps it is important to produce a listing of the file that considers both the part number and the department number. That way the program would provide a listing for each separate department, and the data records within each department would be in ascending order, as shown in Figure 3–3.

Figure 3–3   *Inventory Records—Part Number within Department Number Order*

Department number	Part number	Unit price	Store number	Quantity on hand
01	1752	92.75	1	300
01	2243	86.20	2	100
05	1892	42.97	1	40
05	2575	55.20	2	10
07	1215	19.20	1	150
07	1876	45.75	2	40
07	5542	75.67	1	200

Another variation could sort the data so the program provides for each store a separate listing by ascending department number and ascending part number within each department. The data would be arranged in the order prescribed as shown in Figure 3–4.

Figure 3–4   *Inventory Records—Part Number within Department Number within Store Number Order*

Department number	Part number	Unit price	Store number	Quantity on hand
01	1752	92.75	1	300
05	1892	42.97	1	40
07	1215	19.20	1	150
07	5542	75.67	1	200
01	2243	86.20	2	100
05	2575	55.20	2	10
07	1876	45.75	2	40

At this point realize that the sequence has been from minor to intermediate and then to major in prescribing the order of the data. Remember the concept of within processing.

Sorting of data records may consider just one data field when rearranging data, and these sorts are relatively simple. When it is necessary to consider two or more fields, it becomes more complex. The programmer must be able to identify major, intermediate, and minor sort fields. The first step is to determine those major, intermediate, and minor sort fields, referred to as **sort keys.**

Sorting Alternatives

To sort data records it is necessary to choose one of three essential alternatives: (1) an **internal programmed sort,** (2) the use of the SORT statement in COBOL, or (3) an **external utility program sort** supplied by the computer vendor. The internal programmed sort requires the use of tables. This method normally is used when neither the COBOL SORT statement or an external utility program is available. The external utility program, while probably the most efficient way to sort data files, varies so widely among vendors that it is beyond the scope of this text. The internal programmed sort and the SORT statement then will be used and illustrated in this chapter. Additionally, the MERGE statement will be illustrated, which provides the ability to merge two or more files that have already been sorted.

Internal Programmed Sort

To illustrate the concept of the internal sort, two methods of internal sorting will be shown, both of which are considered to be exchange sorts. That is, a comparison is made between values in the sort field and if necessary, an exchange of records is made. The first sort method is called the **bubble sort,** and the second method is called the **shell sort.**

Bubble Sort

Assume that a table has been defined as shown in Figure 3–5 for the previously shown inventory data and it is desired to sort this data in ascending order by part number.

Figure 3–5 *COBOL Table Definition for Inventory Data*

```
01   INVENTORY-TABLE-DATA.
     05   FILLER              PIC X(14) VALUE '01224386202100'.
     05   FILLER              PIC X(14) VALUE '01175292751300'.
     05   FILLER              PIC X(14) VALUE '05189242971040'.
     05   FILLER              PIC X(14) VALUE '05257555202010'.
     05   FILLER              PIC X(14) VALUE '07187625752040'.
     05   FILLER              PIC X(14) VALUE '07121519201150'.
     05   FILLER              PIC X(14) VALUE '07554275671200'.
01   FILLER REDEFINES INVENTORY-TABLE-DATA.
     05   INVENTORY-ITEM
          OCCURS 7 TIMES.
          10   DEPT-NUMBER     PIC X(2).
          10   PART-NUMBER     PIC X(4).
          10   UNIT-PRICE      PIC 9(2)V99.
          10   STORE-NUMBER    PIC X(1).
          10   QUANTITY        PIC 9(3).
```

The data records in the table can be envisioned to reside in seven different positions in memory as shown by the original order of the data in Figure 3–6.

The bubble sort begins at the top of the table and compares the value of the part number in position 1 with the value of the part number in position 2. In this case the part number in the first position is larger than the part number in the second position, so the record in the first position is exchanged with the record in the second position. When the part numbers in the second and third positions are compared, an exchange is necessary. The third comparison requires no change. The fourth and fifth comparisons result in part number 2575 being pushed down to position 6; no exchange is necessary when comparing 2575 to the last part number because it is already in its proper position. The first pass through a table will always result in the largest value being pushed down to the bottom or last position in the table. Concurrently smaller values are bubbling up to the top, which gives the bubble sort its name.

The second pass requires the same kinds of comparisons. However, it is now not necessary to make a comparison to the last position in the table, since the first pass through the table pushes the largest value to the bottom.

This process continues through five passes, by the time the final exchange is made and all the data records have been sorted. At most it is necessary to make one less pass than the number of positions in the table (in this case 7 − 1 = 6) in order to assure that it will be sorted. Each pass through the table requires one less comparison than the number of records that remain out of order. This number decreases after each pass, since each pass results in another value being placed in its proper position in the sort sequence. Therefore, at most, an internal bubble sort requires $(n-1) + (n-1)-1 + \ldots 1$ comparisons or $n(n-1)$ divided by 2. (In this case $6 + 5 + 4 + 3 + 2 + 1 = 21$ or 7 times 6 = 42 divided by 2 = 21. For a table that has 100 entries, this would require $100 \times 99 / 2$ or 4,950 comparisons. It should be obvious why the internal programmed sort should be used only for small data sets.

To illustrate the COBOL logic necessary to accomplish a bubble sort refer to Figure 3–7.

In the DATA division several data-items are necessary in addition to the table itself. A TABLE–FLAG is defined to control whether or not the table is sorted. When TABLE–FLAG = 'YES' the table is sorted. When TABLE–FLAG = 'NO' the table is not sorted. TABLE–SUBSCRIPT and TABLE–SUBSCRIPT–PLUS are defined and are manipulated in order to make each pass through the table. SAVE–AREA is used to store a record temporarily during an exchange.

In the PROCEDURE division the number of table entries, in this case 7, is moved

Figure 3–6   *Comparisons Made during Bubble Sort*

First pass through the table:

Position	Original order	Compare 1 to 2	Compare 2 to 3	Compare 3 to 4	Compare 4 to 5	Compare 5 to 6	Compare 6 to 7
1	2243	1752	1752	1752	1752	1752	1752
2	1752	2243	1892	1892	1892	1892	1892
3	1892	1892	2243	2243	2243	2243	2243
4	2575	2575	2575	2575	1876	1876	1876
5	1876	1876	1876	1876	2575	1215	1215
6	1215	1215	1215	1215	1215	2575	2575
7	5542	5542	5542	5542	5542	5542	5542*

Second pass through the table:

Position		Compare 1 to 2	Compare 2 to 3	Compare 3 to 4	Compare 4 to 5	Compare 5 to 6
1	1752	1752	1752	1752	1752	1752
2	1892	1892	1892	1892	1892	1892
3	2243	2243	2243	1876	1876	1876
4	1876	1876	1876	2243	1215	1215
5	1215	1215	1215	1215	2243	2243
6	2575	2575	2575	2575	2575	2575*
7	5542	5542	5542	5542	5542	5542*

Third pass through the table:

Position		Compare 1 to 2	Compare 2 to 3	Compare 3 to 4	Compare 4 to 5
1	1752	1752	1752	1752	1752
2	1892	1892	1876	1876	1876
3	1876	1876	1892	1215	1215
4	1215	1215	1215	1892	1892
5	2243	2243	2243	2243	2243*
6	2575	2575	2575	2575	2575*
7	5542	5542	5542	5542	5542*

Fourth pass through the table:

Position		Compare 1 to 2	Compare 2 to 3	Compare 3 to 4
1	1752	1752	1752	1752
2	1876	1876	1215	1215
3	1215	1215	1876	1876
4	1892	1892	1892	1892*
5	2243	2243	2243	2243*
6	2575	2575	2575	2575*
7	5542	5542	5542	5542*

Fifth pass through the table:

Position		Compare 1 to 2	Compare 2 to 3
1	1752	1215	1215
2	1215	1752	1752
3	1876	1876	1876*
4	1892	1892	1892*
5	2243	2243	2243*
6	2575	2575	2575*
7	5542	5542	5542*

* Automatically in the correct position after this pass is completed.

Figure 3–7 *COBOL Logic for Bubble Sort*

```
DATA DIVISION.
WORKING-STORAGE SECTION.
01   TABLE-WORK-AREAS.
     05   TABLE-FLAG                   PIC X(3).
          88  TABLE-IS-SORTED VALUE 'YES'.
     05   TABLE-SUBSCRIPT              PIC 9(1).
     05   TABLE-SUBSCRIPT-PLUS         PIC 9(1).
     05   NUMBER-OF-ENTRIES-IN-TABLE   PIC 9(1).
     05   SAVE-AREA                    PIC X(14).
01   INVENTORY-TABLE-DATA.
     05   FILLER              PIC X(14) VALUE '01224386202100'.
     05   FILLER              PIC X(14) VALUE '01175292751300'.
     05   FILLER              PIC X(14) VALUE '05189242971040'.
     05   FILLER              PIC X(14) VALUE '05257555202010'.
     05   FILLER              PIC X(14) VALUE '07187625752040'.
     05   FILLER              PIC X(14) VALUE '07121519201150'.
     05   FILLER              PIC X(14) VALUE '07554275671200'.
01   FILLER REDEFINES INVENTORY-TABLE-DATA.
     05   INVENTORY-ITEM
          OCCURS 7 TIMES.
          10   DEPT-NUMBER     PIC X(2).
          10   PART-NUMBER     PIC X(4).
          10   UNIT-PRICE      PIC 9(2)V99.
          10   STORE-NUMBER    PIC X(1).
          10   QUANTITY        PIC 9(3).
PROCEDURE DIVISION.
     *

     MOVE 'NO' TO TABLE-FLAG.
     MOVE 7 TO NUMBER-OF-ENTRIES-IN-TABLE.
     PERFORM TABLE-SORT
         UNTIL TABLE-IS-SORTED.
     .
     .
TABLE-SORT.
     MOVE 'YES' TO TABLE-FLAG.
     PERFORM TABLE-SWAP
         VARYING TABLE-SUBSCRIPT
         FROM 1 BY 1
         UNTIL TABLE-SUBSCRIPT = NUMBER-OF-ENTRIES-IN-TABLE.
     SUBTRACT 1 FROM NUMBER-OF-ENTRIES-IN-TABLE.
TABLE-SWAP.
     COMPUTE TABLE-SUBSCRIPT-PLUS = TABLE-SUBSCRIPT + 1.
     IF PART-NUMBER(TABLE-SUBSCRIPT) >
         PART-NUMBER(TABLE-SUBSCRIPT-PLUS)
         MOVE INVENTORY-ITEM(TABLE-SUBSCRIPT) TO SAVE-AREA
         MOVE INVENTORY-ITEM(TABLE-SUBSCRIPT-PLUS) TO
             INVENTORY-ITEM(TABLE-SUBSCRIPT)
         MOVE SAVE-AREA TO INVENTORY-ITEM(TABLE-SUBSCRIPT-PLUS)
         MOVE 'NO' TO TABLE-FLAG.
```

to NUMBER–OF–ENTRIES–IN–TABLE. Next TABLE–SORT is performed UNTIL TABLE–IS–SORTED. The first statement in TABLE–SORT sets TABLE–FLAG to 'YES', which essentially makes the assumption that the records are in order at the beginning of each pass. If no change is made to TABLE–FLAG during the iterations of TABLE–SWAP, TABLE–SORT will not be entered again.

The PERFORM/VARYING statement causes the repeated loop of TABLE–SWAP until TABLE–SUBSCRIPT becomes equal to NUMBER–OF–ENTRIES–IN–TABLE. Initially this will cause six iterations of TABLE–SWAP. After the first pass NUMBER–OF–ENTRIES–IN–TABLE is decremented by 1, because it is not necessary to again compare to the last position in the table.

In TABLE–SWAP TABLE–SUBSCRIPT–PLUS is defined as TABLE–SUBSCRIPT plus 1. In the first iteration, TABLE–SUBSCRIPT is 1 so TABLE–SUBSCRIPT–PLUS

Figure 3–8 *Shell Sort Comparisons*

Shell Sort—Find highest value and place at bottom of table.

First pass through the table:

Position	Original order	Compare 1 to 2	Compare 1 to 3	Compare 1 to 4	Compare 4 to 5	Compare 4 to 6	Compare 4 to 7
1	2243	High	High				
2	1752						
3	1892						
4	2575			High	High	High	
5	1876						
6	1215						
7	5542						High

Second pass through the table:

Position		Compare 1 to 2	Compare 1 to 3	Compare 1 to 4	Compare 4 to 5	Compare 4 to 6	New Order
1	2243	High	High				2243
2	1752						1752
3	1892						1892
4	2575			High	High	High	1215
5	1876						1876
6	1215						2575*
7	5542						5542*

Third pass through the table:

Position		Compare 1 to 2	Compare 1 to 3	Compare 1 to 4	Compare 1 to 5	New Order
1	2243	High	High	High	High	1876
2	1752					1752
3	1892					1892
4	1215					1215
5	1876					2243*
6	2575					2575*
7	5542					5542*

Fourth pass through the table:

Position		Compare 1 to 2	Compare 1 to 3	Compare 3 to 4	New Order
1	1876	High			1876
2	1752				1752
3	1892		High	High	1215
4	1215				1892*
5	2243				2243*
6	2575				2575*
7	5542				5542*

Fifth pass through the table:

Position		Compare 1 to 2	Compare 1 to 3	New Order
1	1876	High	High	1215
2	1752			1752
3	1215			1876*
4	1892			1892*
5	2243			2243*
6	2575			2575*
7	5542			5542*

* Automatically in the correct position after this pass is completed.

becomes 2. In the second iteration TABLE–SUBSCRIPT is 2, and TABLE–SUB
SCRIPT–PLUS becomes 3, and so on to cause the appropriate comparisons.

The IF statement determines whether an exchange is necessary. If no exchange
is necessary, control returns to the PERFORM/VARYING statement. If an exchange
is necessary both records involved are exchanged using SAVE–AREA as a tem-
porary storage location. Also TABLE–FLAG is set to 'NO' whenever an exchange
is made. At least one more pass through the table will be made following any
exchange.

Shell Sort

The shell sort, named for its creator, D. L. Shell, is similar to the bubble sort in
that it is an exchange sort. In the shell sort, the number of required exchanges is
minimized, since the only time an exchange is made is when the largest value
(smallest if descending order is required) of the remaining unsorted values is found.
When that value is found it is exchanged with the value that currently is at the
bottom position of the unsorted values. Figure 3–8 illustrates the concept of the
shell sort, and Figure 3–9 shows the necessary COBOL logic.

Figure 3–9 *Shell Sort COBOL Logic*

```
DATA DIVISION.
WORKING-STORAGE SECTION.
01   TABLE-WORK-AREAS.
     05   TABLE-FLAG                    PIC X(3).
          88  TABLE-IS-SORTED  VALUE 'YES'.
          88  TABLE-NOT-SORTED VALUE 'NO'.
     05   TABLE-SUBSCRIPT               PIC 9(1).
     05   TABLE-SUBSCRIPT-PLUS          PIC 9(1).
     05   NUMBER-OF-ENTRIES-IN-TABLE    PIC 9(1).
     05   SAVE-AREA                     PIC X(14).
     05   HIGHEST-POSITION-VALUE        PIC 9(1).
01   INVENTORY-TABLE-DATA.
     05   FILLER             PIC X(14) VALUE '01224386202100'.
     05   FILLER             PIC X(14) VALUE '01175292751300'.
     05   FILLER             PIC X(14) VALUE '05189242971040'.
     05   FILLER             PIC X(14) VALUE '05257555202010'.
     05   FILLER             PIC X(14) VALUE '07187625752040'.
     05   FILLER             PIC X(14) VALUE '07121519201150'.
     05   FILLER             PIC X(14) VALUE '07554275671200'.
01   FILLER REDEFINES INVENTORY-TABLE-DATA.
     05   INVENTORY-ITEM
          OCCURS 7 TIMES.
          10   DEPT-NUMBER       PIC X(2).
          10   PART-NUMBER       PIC X(4).
          10   UNIT-PRICE        PIC 9(2)V99.
          10   STORE-NUMBER      PIC X(1).
          10   QUANTITY          PIC X(3).
PROCEDURE DIVISION.
     *
     MOVE 'NO' TO TABLE-FLAG.
     MOVE 7 TO NUMBER-OF-ENTRIES-IN-TABLE.
     PERFORM TABLE-SORT
         UNTIL TABLE-IS-SORTED.

TABLE-SORT.
     MOVE 'YES' TO TABLE-FLAG.
     MOVE 1 TO HIGHEST-POSITION-VALUE.
     PERFORM TABLE-SWAP
         VARYING TABLE-SUBSCRIPT
         FROM 1 BY 1
         UNTIL TABLE-SUBSCRIPT = NUMBER-OF-ENTRIES-IN-TABLE.
```

Figure 3–9 *(concluded)*

```
IF TABLE-NOT-SORTED
    MOVE INVENTORY-ITEM(HIGHEST-POSITION-VALUE) TO SAVE-AREA
    MOVE INVENTORY-ITEM(TABLE-SUBSCRIPT-PLUS) TO
        INVENTORY-ITEM(HIGHEST-POSITION-VALUE)
    MOVE SAVE-AREA
        TO INVENTORY-ITEM(NUMBER-OF-ENTRIES-IN-TABLE).
    SUBTRACT 1 FROM NUMBER-OF-ENTRIES-IN-TABLE.
TABLE-SWAP.
    COMPUTE TABLE-SUBSCRIPT-PLUS = TABLE-SUBSCRIPT + 1.
    IF PART-NUMBER(HIGHEST-POSITION-VALUE) >
        PART-NUMBER(TABLE-SUBSCRIPT-PLUS)
        MOVE 'NO' TO TABLE-FLAG
    ELSE
        MOVE TABLE-SUBSCRIPT-PLUS TO HIGHEST-POSITION-VALUE.
```

The first pass through the table requires no exchange, since the largest value in this case is found to be in the proper location. The second pass finds the value in the fourth position to be the highest, so it is exchanged with the record in the sixth position. This process continues until the data records are sorted. It is easy to see that the advantage of the shell sort results from fewer exchanges.

The COBOL logic for a shell sort differs only slightly from the bubble sort. The highest position value is always assumed to be the first position. The actual comparison uses a different subscript (HIGHEST–POSITION–VALUE). Also the actual exchange of records occurs only when necessary and only after a completed pass through the table.

Use of the SORT Statement

Main Storage During Use of SORT Statement

Under normal processing conditions, processing in main storage of the computer takes place as shown in the chart depicted in Figure 3–10. Data are entered from an external device, such as a disk, tape, or terminal and is placed in input storage in the CPU. Data are then manipulated (usually by moving to a WORKING–STORAGE record), processed, and then transferred to output storage, still in the CPU. WRITE statements then transfer the data to an internal buffer area and subsequently to an output device.

During the execution of the SORT statement, however, additional external storage is needed as shown in Figure 3–11. In this chart, it is evident that after the data are entered into the system, they are then transferred to an external disk device for the actual sorting. The data are then reentered into main storage for eventual output to another external device, perhaps in the form of a sorted listing.

Figure 3–10   *Main Storage—Normal Processing Conditions*

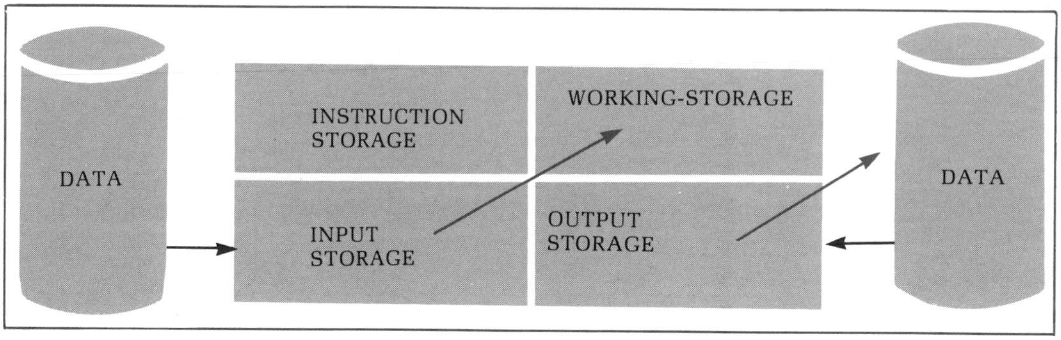

Figure 3–11   *Main Storage—Sort Processing Conditions*

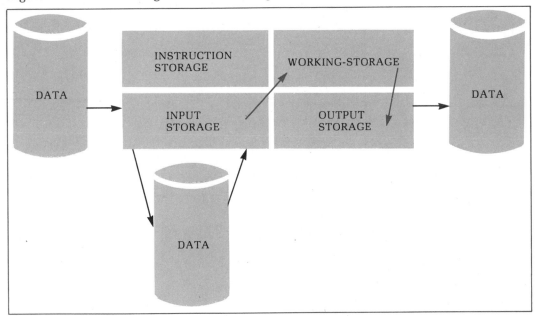

Sort Components

In order to utilize the SORT statement, it is normal to SELECT and define three data files to accomplish the sort: (1) an unsorted input file, (2) a sort work file to be used by the SORT verb, and (3) a sorted output file. A skeleton of a COBOL program is shown in Figure 3–12 which illustrates the major components necessary to utilize the COBOL SORT statement.

Figure 3–12   *Necessary Sort Components*

```
.
INPUT-OUTPUT SECTION.
    SELECT UNSORTED-FILE ASSIGN ...
    SELECT SORT-WORK-FILE ASSIGN ..
    SELECT SORTED-FILE ASSIGN ...
DATA DIVISION.
FILE SECTION.
FD   UNSORTED-FILE...
.
FD   SORTED-FILE...
.
SD   SORT-WORK-FILE...
.
PROCEDURE DIVISION.
.
    SORT SORT-WORK-FILE ...
```

Once a file has been selected, it must also be defined with an FD (file description) entry in the DATA division. This is not true for a sort work file; instead a **sort description (SD entry)** is required for a sort work file. The format of the SD entry is essentially the same as for an FD entry with only minor differences, such as the restriction against specifying any blocking factor.

The format of the SORT statement is shown in Figure 3–13. Some examples of the alternative combinations of the SORT statement are shown in Figure 3–14. Example A uses an ascending sequence for all keys. Example B uses a descending

Figure 3–13   *Format of the SORT Statement*

SORT sort-work-file

    ON $\left\{ \begin{array}{l} \underline{\text{ASCENDING}} \\ \underline{\text{DESCENDING}} \end{array} \right\}$ <u>KEY</u> sort-key(s)

    $\left[\text{ON} \left\{ \begin{array}{l} \underline{\text{ASCENDING}} \\ \underline{\text{DESCENDING}} \end{array} \right\} \quad \underline{\text{KEY}} \text{ sort-key(s)} \right]$

    [COLLATING <u>SEQUENCE</u> IS alphabet-name]

    $\left\{ \begin{array}{l} \underline{\text{USING}} \text{ input-file-name} \\ \underline{\text{INPUT}} \underline{\text{PROCEDURE}} \text{ IS section-name } [\underline{\text{THRU}} \text{ section-name}] \end{array} \right\}$

    $\left\{ \begin{array}{l} \underline{\text{GIVING}} \text{ output-file-name} \\ \underline{\text{OUTPUT}} \underline{\text{PROCEDURE}} \text{ IS section-name } [\underline{\text{THRU}} \text{ section-name}] \end{array} \right\}$

Figure 3–14   *Examples of the SORT Statement*

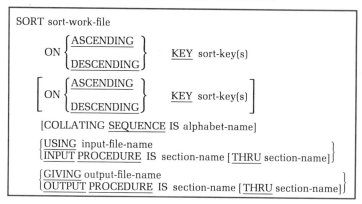

```
Example A:

              SORT SORT-WORK-FILE
                  ASCENDING KEY SW-ACCOUNT-NUMBER
                               SW-TRANSACTION-DATE
                               SW-TRANSACTION-TYPE
                  USING  UNSORTED-FILE
                  GIVING SORTED-FILE.

Example B:

              SORT SORT-WORK-FILE
                  DESCENDING KEY SW-ACCOUNT-NUMBER
                                SW-TRANSACTION-DATE
                                SW-TRANSACTION-TYPE
                  INPUT PROCEDURE B400-VALIDATION-RTN
                  GIVING SORTED-FILE.

Example C:

              SORT SORT-WORK-FILE
                  ASCENDING KEY  SW-ACCOUNT-NUMBER
                  DESCENDING KEY SW-TRANSACTION-DATE
                  ASCENDING KEY  SW-TRANSACTION-TYPE
                  USING UNSORTED-FILE
                  OUTPUT PROCEDURE B500-CONTROL-BREAK-ROUTINE.

Example D:

              SORT SORT-WORK-FILE
                  ASCENDING KEY  SW-ACCOUNT-NUMBER
                                SW-TRANSACTION-DATE
                  DESCENDING KEY SW-TRANSACTION-TYPE
                  INPUT PROCEDURE B400-VALIDATION-RTN
                  OUTPUT PROCEDURE B500-CONTROL-BREAK-ROUTINE.
```

sequence for all keys. Examples C and D illustrate the ability to assign different sequences for multiple keys.

Options of the SORT Statement

SORT USING/
GIVING Option
To illustrate the use of the SORT statement, the data file shown in Figure 3–15 will be used as the input data set. These data represent transactions by customers

Figure 3–15   *Input Data Set*

```
Bank Data:

The record layout is:

Columns 1-7    Customer account number
Columns 9-16   Transaction date
Column  18     Transaction type
               1 = Deposit
               2 = Cleared check
               3 = Credit memo
               4 = Debit memo
Columns 20-25  Amount of transaction
=========================
61-5472 87/04/01 2 005225
63-5478 87/04/01 2 025000
63-5478 87/04/02 2 045000
62-6476 87/04/02 3 100500
61-5472 87/04/03 2 090000
62-6476 87/04/04 1 525000
63-5478 87/04/05 1 025000
61-5472 87/04/05 2 100000
62-6476 87/04/08 2 040000
63-5478 87/04/10 2 025000
62-6476 87/04/10 4 010000
61-5472 87/04/13 2 005200
61-5472 87/04/14 2 002550
63-5478 87/04/15 2 250000
63-5478 87/04/18 2 042552
63-5478 87/04/21 1 040000
61-5472 87/04/21 2 001000
61-5472 87/04/23 2 007500
63-5478 87/04/23 2 012500
62-6476 87/04/23 2 062300
63-5478 87/04/25 2 037500
62-6476 87/04/29 2 057525

=========================
```

of a bank and are currently in order by date, representing the sequence that the transactions are received by the bank. The data will need to be sorted by transaction type within transaction date within account number. Notice that the format of the date is year, month, and day. The reason for this order is to ensure an appropriate sort if data from more than one year is present.

In Example A of Figure 3–14 the unsorted data file will be sorted in the desired order by using UNSORTED–FILE as the input file. The SORT statement is the only PROCEDURE division statement necessary to sort the file, and it results in the sorted data being transferred to SORTED–FILE in the prescribed order.

Consider the source statements in Program 3–1, which would accomplish the desired sort on this data.

The **USING/GIVING option** of the SORT statement is useful under two conditions: (1) when both the input file and the output file are defined exactly the same and (2) when there is to be no pre-processing or post-processing of the data. **Pre-processing** means that some processing is to take place before the sort, and **post-processing** means some processing is to take place after the sort. The SORT statement has the option of combining the sort procedure itself with either pre- or post-processing or a combination of both.

Note in Program 3–1 that the input file, output file, and the sort work file have exactly the same record description in terms of total number of characters, but that only the sort work file has been subdivided. When implementing the USING/GIVING option, no subdivisions are absolutely necessary for either the input or

Program 3–1

```
000010 IDENTIFICATION DIVISION.
000020 PROGRAM-ID.    CUSTSORT.
000030.............................................................
000040*          PROGRAM 3-1 SORT WITH USING/GIVING OPTION          *
000050.............................................................
000060 ENVIRONMENT DIVISION.
000070 CONFIGURATION SECTION.
000080    SOURCE-COMPUTER.   IBM-4341.
000090    OBJECT-COMPUTER.   IBM-4341.
000100 INPUT-OUTPUT SECTION.
000110 FILE-CONTROL.
000120      SELECT UNSORTED-CUSTOMER
000130          ASSIGN TO UT-S-UNSORT.
000140      SELECT SORTED-CUSTOMER
000150          ASSIGN TO UT-S-SORTED.
000160      SELECT SORT-WORK-FILE
000170          ASSIGN TO UT-S-SORTWK1.
000180*
000190 DATA DIVISION.
000200 FILE SECTION.
000210 FD  UNSORTED-CUSTOMER
000220      RECORD CONTAINS 25 CHARACTERS
000230      LABEL RECORDS ARE STANDARD.
000240 01  UC-UNSORTED-CUSTOMER-RECORD      PIC X(25).
000250 FD  SORTED-CUSTOMER
000260      RECORD CONTAINS 25 CHARACTERS
000270      LABEL RECORDS ARE STANDARD.
000280 01  SC-SORTED-CUSTOMER-RECORD        PIC X(25).
000290 SD  SORT-WORK-FILE.
000300 01  SW-SORT-WORK-RECORD.
000310      05  SW-ACCOUNT-NUMBER           PIC X(7).
000320      05  FILLER                      PIC X(1).
000330      05  SW-TRANSACTION-DATE         PIC X(8).
000340      05  FILLER                      PIC X(1).
000350      05  SW-TRANSACTION-TYPE         PIC X(1).
000360      05  FILLER                      PIC X(1).
000370      05  SW-TRANSACTION-AMOUNT       PIC 9(4)V99.
000380 PROCEDURE DIVISION.
000390 A000-NUM-DATE-TYPE-ORDER.
000400      SORT SORT-WORK-FILE
000410          ASCENDING KEY SW-ACCOUNT-NUMBER
000420                        SW-TRANSACTION-DATE
000430                        SW-TRANSACTION-TYPE
000440          USING UNSORTED-CUSTOMER
000450          GIVING SORTED-CUSTOMER.
000460      STOP RUN.
```

the output file because the SORT statement itself directs all necessary MOVE operations. Figure 3–16 illustrates the concept of what physically occurs during the execution of the single SORT statement when choosing the USING/GIVING option. The SORT statement causes the following:

- Directs the opening of the input file named in the USING clause.
- Reads and releases each of the input records to the sort work file to be sorted by the sort control system.
- Sorts the data records and returns control to the SORT statement.
- Opens the output file.
- Returns the sorted data records, one at a time, from the sort work file.
- Writes the sorted data records onto the file named in GIVING clause.
- Closes both the input file and the output file.

Figure 3–16 *System Flowchart of the SORT USING/GIVING*

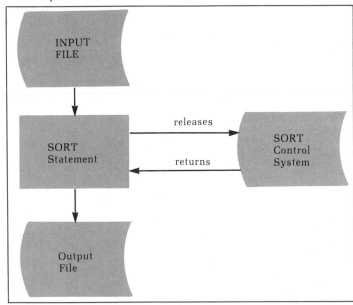

If a programmer desires to then use the sorted disk file for some other processing, such as the printing of the report, it would be necessary to follow the SORT statement with a procedure to open the sorted disk file as input and then proceed with normal processing.

Four other items are important to note from Program 3–1. (1) The sort description entry does not contain the LABEL RECORDS STANDARD entry even though the work file is a disk file. Most systems require the LABEL RECORDS clause to be left out. (2) No blocking can be specified on the sort work file since the sort control system accomplishes all necessary data operations on the sort work file. (3) The KEY or keys referenced in the SORT statement must be defined as a part of the sort work record. (4) The only elementary items that absolutely must be defined in the sort work record are those referenced as keys in the SORT statement; the remaining fields could be defined with FILLERS to maintain record structure. The other records, input and output, may or may not be subdivided depending on the application.

SORT INPUT PROCEDURE/ GIVING Option

Example B of Figure 3–14 illustrates how an INPUT PROCEDURE can be used in place of the USING option. Multiple keys are always specified in major to minor order. If all fields are to be sorted in the same sequence (ascending or descending), they do not have to be specified separately. If, however, one of the two fields was to be sorted in a different order, then it would be necessary to have both an **ASCENDING KEY clause** and a **DESCENDING KEY clause.** An **INPUT PROCEDURE** will allow pre-processing of the data before the sort takes place. Pre-processing may be necessary for several reasons. One reason may be that the unsorted data file may need to be validated. Another reason may be that the input data file is not defined in the same manner as the output data file. Whatever the reason, the pre-processing takes place in the INPUT PROCEDURE. Figure 3–17 illustrates the concept of what actually occurs during the SORT with an INPUT PROCEDURE. The SORT statement does the following:

- Transfers control to the named INPUT PROCEDURE, which opens the input file.
- The programmer directs the INPUT PROCEDURE to read, move, and release each of the input records to the sort work file to be sorted by the sort control system.

- The sort control system sorts the data records and returns control to the SORT statement.
- The output file is opened.
- The sorted data records are returned, one at a time, from the sort work file.
- The sorted data records are written onto the file named in GIVING clause.
- The output file is closed. It is the responsibility of the programmer to close the input file. This is normally done in the INPUT PROCEDURE.

Figure 3–17   *System Flowchart of the SORT INPUT PROCEDURE/GIVING*

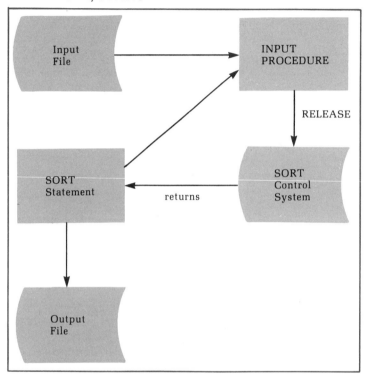

Program 3–2 illustrates the necessary logic when the input and the output file have their elementary fields in a different format.

Program 3–2

```
000010 IDENTIFICATION DIVISION.
000020 PROGRAM-ID.    CUSTSORT.
000030*************************************************
000040* PROGRAM 3-2 SORT WITH INPUT PROCEDURE AND GIVING OPTION    *
000050*************************************************
000060 ENVIRONMENT DIVISION.
000070 CONFIGURATION SECTION.
000080    SOURCE-COMPUTER.    IBM-4341.
000090    OBJECT-COMPUTER.    IBM-4341.
000100 INPUT-OUTPUT SECTION.
000110 FILE-CONTROL.
000120    SELECT UNSORTED-CUSTOMER
000130        ASSIGN TO UT-S-UNSORT.
000140    SELECT SORTED-CUSTOMER
000150        ASSIGN TO UT-S-SORTED.
000160    SELECT SORT-WORK-FILE
000170        ASSIGN TO UT-S-SORTWK1.
000180*
```

Program 3–2 *(concluded)*

```
000190 DATA DIVISION.
000200 FILE SECTION.
000210 FD  UNSORTED-CUSTOMER
000220     RECORD CONTAINS 25 CHARACTERS
000230     LABEL RECORDS ARE STANDARD.
000240 01  UC-UNSORTED-CUSTOMER-RECORD.
000250     05  UC-ACCOUNT-NUMBER          PIC X(7).
000260     05  FILLER                     PIC X(1).
000270     05  UC-TRANSACTION-DATE        PIC X(8).
000280     05  FILLER                     PIC X(1).
000290     05  UC-TRANSACTION-TYPE        PIC X(1).
000300     05  FILLER                     PIC X(1).
000310     05  UC-TRANSACTION-AMOUNT      PIC 9(4)V99.
000320 FD  SORTED-CUSTOMER
000330     RECORD CONTAINS 22 CHARACTERS
000340     LABEL RECORDS ARE STANDARD.
000350 01  SC-SORTED-CUSTOMER-RECORD      PIC X(22).
000360 SD  SORT-WORK-FILE.
000370 01  SW-SORT-WORK-RECORD.
000380     05  SW-ACCOUNT-NUMBER          PIC X(7).
000390     05  SW-TRANSACTION-DATE        PIC X(8).
000400     05  SW-TRANSACTION-TYPE        PIC X(1).
000410     05  SW-TRANSACTION-AMOUNT      PIC 9(4)V99.
000420 WORKING-STORAGE SECTION.
000430 01  WS-RECORD-INDICATORS.
000440     05  WS-END-OF-FILE-INDICATOR   PIC X(3).
000450         88  END-OF-FILE VALUE 'END'.
000460 PROCEDURE DIVISION.
000470 MAIN-LINE SECTION.
000480 A000-NUM-DATE-TYPE-ORDER.
000490     SORT SORT-WORK-FILE
000500         ASCENDING KEY SW-ACCOUNT-NUMBER
000510                       SW-TRANSACTION-DATE
000520                       SW-TRANSACTION-TYPE
000530         INPUT PROCEDURE B100-REFORMAT-DATA
000540         GIVING SORTED-CUSTOMER.
000550     STOP RUN.
000560 B100-REFORMAT-DATA SECTION.
000570 B100-REFORMAT-DATA-PARA.
000580     OPEN INPUT UNSORTED-CUSTOMER.
000590     PERFORM C100-INITIALIZE-VARIABLES.
000600     PERFORM Z100-READ-RECORD.
000610     PERFORM C300-READ-UNSORTED
000620         UNTIL END-OF-FILE.
000630     CLOSE UNSORTED-CUSTOMER.
000640     GO TO B100-REFORMAT-EXIT.
000650 C100-INITIALIZE-VARIABLES.
000660     MOVE SPACES                TO WS-END-OF-FILE-INDICATOR.
000670 C300-READ-UNSORTED.
000680     MOVE UC-ACCOUNT-NUMBER     TO SW-ACCOUNT-NUMBER.
000690     MOVE UC-TRANSACTION-DATE   TO SW-TRANSACTION-DATE.
000700     MOVE UC-TRANSACTION-TYPE   TO SW-TRANSACTION-TYPE.
000710     MOVE UC-TRANSACTION-AMOUNT TO SW-TRANSACTION-AMOUNT.
000720     RELEASE SW-SORT-WORK-RECORD.
000730     PERFORM Z100-READ-RECORD.
000740 Z100-READ-RECORD.
000750     READ UNSORTED-CUSTOMER
000760         AT END MOVE 'END' TO WS-END-OF-FILE-INDICATOR.
000770 B100-REFORMAT-EXIT.
000780     EXIT.
```

The first thing to note in Program 3–2 is the use of the **RELEASE statement** at line 720. The format of the RELEASE statement is the same format as a WRITE statement to a disk device, including the optional FROM clause. However, the WRITE statement is not used because the COBOL program does not have actual physical control of the sorting device. The sorting device is controlled by the sort control system, so a RELEASE is necessary even though it is logically the equivalent of the WRITE statement. Note that before the RELEASE is executed, the input fields are moved to the fields in the sort work record.

When utilizing either an INPUT PROCEDURE or an **OUTPUT PROCEDURE,** syntax requires that the named procedure be a section name rather than a paragraph name. Difficulties with using sections in the PROCEDURE division were discussed in Chapter 1. However, in this case, there is no alternative. Notice first of all that a section in the PROCEDURE division must have a section header with the word SECTION. A SECTION in the PROCEDURE division may contain several paragraphs. In Program 3–2, the B100–REFORMAT–DATA section begins at line 560 and ends at line 780. When a PERFORM is used to control the execution of a paragraph, the compiler knows when the end of the paragraph is reached when another paragraph name is detected or when the end of the source statements is reached. Similarly, the end of a performed section is detected when either another section name is detected, the end of the source statements is reached, or a paragraph with the single entry EXIT is found prior to another section or the end of the program. When specifying either an INPUT PROCEDURE or an OUTPUT PROCEDURE, it is the same as controlling the execution of a section with a PERFORM statement and the same considerations apply.

Two syntactical requirements of standard COBOL cause specific problems when using either an INPUT or an OUTPUT PROCEDURE. First, standard COBOL requires that when even one section is used in the PROCEDURE division, then the entire division must be organized into sections. That causes the need to insert a section header at line 470. Secondly, when either an INPUT or an OUTPUT PROCEDURE is specified, all procedures referenced during that procedure's execution must be located within that section. It is not permissible to reference with a PERFORM statement any procedure that is outside the section named in the SORT statement. This requires all statements to be contained within the named section, B100–REFOR MAT–DATA. No reference can be made to any statements outside the section.

Consider what would happen if the GO TO statement were not present in line 640. When the SORT statement references B100–REFORMAT–DATA, control is transferred to that section. UNSORTED–INVENTORY is opened, variables are initialized, the first record is read, and the PERFORM statement at line 610 then transfers control to the paragraph labeled C300–READ–UNSORTED. This paragraph will be executed in an iterative process until all the data records have been read, then control passes to the CLOSE at line 630. Without the GO TO statement, program execution would be at the end of a paragraph but not at the end of the section. Thus, control would fall through to lines 650 through 760 erroneously. The purpose of the GO TO statement is to bypass the execution of paragraphs C100 through Z100 and to transfer control to the paragraph at line 770, which is still in the B100–REFORMAT–DATA section. This paragraph contains only one entry, the **EXIT statement,** the purpose of which is to specifically state where the end of the section is located. The EXIT statement, when used, must be placed in a paragraph by itself as the last statement in the section. This necessitates the use of the GO TO statement. The programmer can guard against fall-through logic by using the GO TO statement to bypass a paragraph or set of paragraphs.

Remember that in structured programming a procedure must have only one entry point and only one exit point. When using paragraphs as procedures, no violations of this single-entry, single-exit requirement are possible so long as the paragraph is only referenced with a PERFORM statement. When sections are used, however, the programmer must ensure that exiting from a section occurs only at the end of the section as has been illustrated in Program 3–2. The one-entry, one-exit concept has not been violated.

Some COBOL compilers allow the reference to procedures outside an INPUT or an OUTPUT PROCEDURE section. When this is true, the GO TO statement is not necessary. For instance, consider the abbreviated PROCEDURE division in Figure 3–18. Notice that the section designated as the INPUT PROCEDURE terminates with the EXIT paragraph, while the PERFORM statement at line 610 refers to a paragraph outside the INPUT PROCEDURE.

Figure 3–18 *Reference to a Procedure Outside a Section*

```
000460 PROCEDURE DIVISION.
000470 MAIN-LINE SECTION.
000480 A000-NUM-DATE-TYPE-ORDER.
000490     SORT SORT-WORK-FILE
000500         ASCENDING KEY SW-ACCOUNT-NUMBER
000510                       SW-TRANSACTION-DATE
000520                       SW-TRANSACTION-TYPE
000530         INPUT PROCEDURE B100-REFORMAT-DATA
000540         GIVING SORTED-CUSTOMER.
000550     STOP RUN.
000560 B100-REFORMAT-DATA SECTION.
000570 B100-REFORMAT-DATA-PARA.
000580     OPEN INPUT UNSORTED-CUSTOMER.
000590     PERFORM C100-INITIALIZE-VARIABLES.
000600     PERFORM Z100-READ-RECORD.
000610     PERFORM C300-READ-UNSORTED
000620         UNTIL END-OF-FILE.
000630     CLOSE UNSORTED-CUSTOMER.
000640 B100-REFORMAT-EXIT.
000650     EXIT.
000660 C100-INITIALIZE-VARIABLES SECTION.
000670     MOVE SPACES              TO WS-END-OF-FILE-INDICATOR.
000680 C300-READ-UNSORTED SECTION.
000690     MOVE UC-ACCOUNT-NUMBER   TO SW-ACCOUNT-NUMBER.
000710     MOVE UC-TRANSACTION-DATE TO SW-TRANSACTION-DATE.
000720     MOVE UC-TRANSACTION-TYPE TO SW-TRANSACTION-TYPE.
000730     MOVE UC-TRANSACTION-AMOUNT TO SW-TRANSACTION-AMOUNT.
000740     RELEASE SW-SORT-WORK-RECORD.
000750     PERFORM Z100-READ-RECORD.
000760 Z100-READ-RECORD SECTION.
000770     READ UNSORTED-CUSTOMER
000780         AT END MOVE 'END' TO WS-END-OF-FILE-INDICATOR.
```

SORT USING/ OUTPUT PROCEDURE Option

Example C of Figure 3–14 shows the option of implementing the SORT USING/ OUTPUT PROCEDURE to accomplish post-processing. The concept of what physically occurs during this process is shown in Figure 3–19. In this option the SORT statement causes:

- The opening of the input file named in the USING clause.
- The reads, moves, and releases for each of the input records to the sort work file to be sorted by the sort control system.
- The sort control system to sort the data records and return control to the SORT statement.
- Control to be passed to the OUTPUT PROCEDURE, which opens the output file.
- The OUTPUT PROCEDURE to return the sorted data records, one at a time, from the sort control system.
- The writing of the sorted data records onto the output file and returning of

Figure 3–19 *System Flowchart of the SORT USING/OUTPUT PROCEDURE*

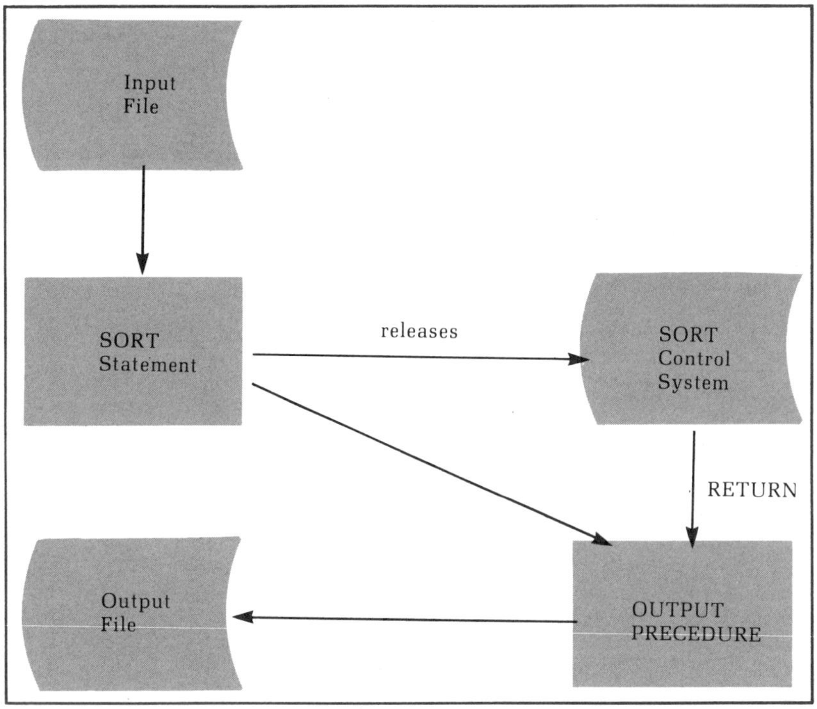

control to the SORT statement. The SORT statement then closes the input file, but the programmer must close the output file.

Program 3–3 illustrates the concept of the SORT USING/OUTPUT PROCEDURE, when the input file is a disk file and the output file is a printed report. Note the use of sections previously described for the INPUT PROCEDURE. Note also the use of the **RETURN statement** at line 820. This is the logical equivalent of the READ statement and has exactly the same format as the READ, including the optional INTO clause. The arguments for using a RETURN are the same as for using the RELEASE in an INPUT PROCEDURE. The printed output for Program 3–3 is shown in Figure 3–20.

Program 3–3

```
000010 IDENTIFICATION DIVISION.
000020 PROGRAM-ID.   CUSTSORT.
000030**********************************************************
000040* PROGRAM 3-3 SORT WITH USING AND AN OUTPUT PROCEDURE OPTION   *
000050**********************************************************
000060 ENVIRONMENT DIVISION.
000070 CONFIGURATION SECTION.
000080    SOURCE-COMPUTER.  IBM-4341.
000090    OBJECT-COMPUTER.  IBM-4341.
000100 INPUT-OUTPUT SECTION.
000110 FILE-CONTROL.
000120    SELECT UNSORTED-CUSTOMER
000130        ASSIGN TO UT-S-UNSORT.
000140    SELECT SORTED-CUSTOMER
000150        ASSIGN TO UT-S-SORTED.
000160    SELECT SORT-WORK-FILE
000170        ASSIGN TO UT-S-SORTWK1.
000180*
000190 DATA DIVISION.
000200 FILE SECTION.
```

Program 3–3 *(concluded)*

```
000210 FD   UNSORTED-CUSTOMER
000220      RECORD CONTAINS 25 CHARACTERS
000230      LABEL RECORDS ARE STANDARD.
000240 01   UC-UNSORTED-CUSTOMER-RECORD       PIC X(25).
000250 FD   SORTED-CUSTOMER
000260      RECORD CONTAINS 132 CHARACTERS
000270      LABEL RECORDS ARE OMITTED.
000280 01   SI-SORTED-CUSTOMER-RECORD.
000290      05  FILLER                        PIC X(3).
000300      05  SI-ACCOUNT-NUMBER             PIC X(7).
000310      05  FILLER                        PIC X(3).
000320      05  SI-TRANSACTION-DATE           PIC X(8).
000330      05  FILLER                        PIC X(3).
000340      05  SI-TRANSACTION-TYPE           PIC X(1).
000350      05  FILLER                        PIC X(3).
000360      05  SI-TRANSACTION-AMOUNT         PIC $Z,ZZ9.99.
000370      05  FILLER                        PIC X(95).
000380 SD   SORT-WORK-FILE.
000390 01   SW-SORT-WORK-RECORD.
000400      05  SW-ACCOUNT-NUMBER             PIC X(7).
000410      05  FILLER                        PIC X(1).
000420      05  SW-TRANSACTION-DATE           PIC X(8).
000430      05  FILLER                        PIC X(1).
000440      05  SW-TRANSACTION-TYPE           PIC X(1).
000450      05  FILLER                        PIC X(1).
000460      05  SW-TRANSACTION-AMOUNT         PIC 9(4)V99.
000470 WORKING-STORAGE SECTION.
000480 01   WS-RECORD-INDICATORS.
000490      05  WS-END-OF-FILE-INDICATOR      PIC X(3).
000500          88  END-OF-FILE VALUE 'END'.
000510 PROCEDURE DIVISION.
000520 MAIN-LINE SECTION.
000530 A000-NUM-DATE-TYPE-ORDER.
000540      SORT SORT-WORK-FILE
000550          ASCENDING KEY SW-ACCOUNT-NUMBER
000560                        SW-TRANSACTION-DATE
000570                        SW-TRANSACTION-TYPE
000580          USING UNSORTED-CUSTOMER
000590          OUTPUT PROCEDURE B100-PRINT-REPORT.
000600      STOP RUN.
000610 B100-PRINT-REPORT SECTION.
000620 B100-PRINT-REPORT-PARA.
000630      OPEN OUTPUT SORTED-CUSTOMER.
000640      PERFORM C100-INITIALIZE-VARIABLES.
000650      PERFORM Z100-RETURN-RECORD.
000660      PERFORM C300-PRINT-DETAIL
000670          UNTIL END-OF-FILE.
000680      CLOSE SORTED-CUSTOMER.
000690      GO TO B100-PRINT-EXIT.
000700 C100-INITIALIZE-VARIABLES.
000710      MOVE SPACES               TO WS-END-OF-FILE-INDICATOR.
000720 C300-PRINT-DETAIL.
000730      MOVE SPACES               TO SI-SORTED-CUSTOMER-RECORD.
000740      MOVE SW-ACCOUNT-NUMBER    TO SI-ACCOUNT-NUMBER.
000750      MOVE SW-TRANSACTION-DATE  TO SI-TRANSACTION-DATE.
000760      MOVE SW-TRANSACTION-TYPE  TO SI-TRANSACTION-TYPE.
000770      MOVE SW-TRANSACTION-AMOUNT TO SI-TRANSACTION-AMOUNT.
000780      WRITE SI-SORTED-CUSTOMER-RECORD
000790          AFTER 1.
000800      PERFORM Z100-RETURN-RECORD.
000810 Z100-RETURN-RECORD.
000820      RETURN SORT-WORK-FILE
000830          AT END MOVE 'END' TO WS-END-OF-FILE-INDICATOR.
000840 B100-PRINT-EXIT.
000850      EXIT.
```

Figure 3–20   *Output from*
Program 3–3

61–5472	87/04/01	2	$ 52.25
61–5472	87/04/03	2	$ 900.00
61–5472	87/04/05	2	$1,000.00
61–5472	87/04/13	2	$ 52.00
61–5472	87/04/14	2	$ 25.50
61–5472	87/04/21	2	$ 10.00
61–5472	87/04/23	2	$ 75.00
62–6476	87/04/02	3	$1,005.00
62–6476	87/04/04	1	$5,250.00
62–6476	87/04/08	2	$ 400.00
62–6476	87/04/10	4	$ 100.00
62–6476	87/04/23	2	$ 623.00
62–6476	87/04/29	2	$ 575.25
63–5478	87/04/01	2	$ 250.00
63–5478	87/04/02	2	$ 450.00
63–5478	87/04/05	1	$ 250.00
63–5478	87/04/10	2	$ 250.00
63–5478	87/04/15	2	$2,500.00
63–5478	87/04/18	2	$ 425.52
63–5478	87/04/21	1	$ 400.00
63–5478	87/04/23	2	$ 125.00
63–5478	87/04/25	2	$ 375.00

SORT INPUT PROCEDURE/ OUTPUT PROCEDURE Option

Example D of Figure 3–14 shows the fourth option of the SORT statement, which is the combination of both an INPUT PROCEDURE and an OUTPUT PROCEDURE. This concept is shown in Figure 3–21, where the sort statement causes:

■ The transfer of control to the INPUT PROCEDURE, which directs the opening of the input file.
■ The INPUT PROCEDURE to read, move, and release each of the input records to the sort work file to be sorted by the sort control system.

Figure 3–21   *System Flowchart of the SORT INPUT PROCEDURE/OUTPUT PROCEDURE*

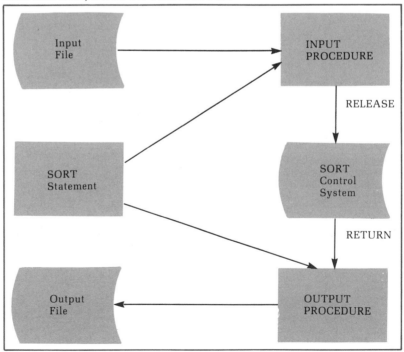

- The sort control system to sort the data records and to return control to the SORT statement.
- Control to be passed to the OUTPUT PROCEDURE, which opens the output file.
- The OUTPUT PROCEDURE to return the sorted data records, one at a time, from the sort control system.
- The writing the sorted data records onto the file. Realize that this output file may be a disk file or it may be some other device, such as a line printer. It is the responsibility of the programmer to close both the input file and the output file.

Program 3–4 is a combination of the Program 3–2 and 3–3, the output of which is shown in Figure 3–22.

Program 3–4

```
000010 IDENTIFICATION DIVISION.
000020 PROGRAM-ID.    CUSTSORT.
000030****************************************************************
000040* PROGRAM 3-4 SORT WITH INPUT AND OUTPUT PROCEDURES            *
000050****************************************************************
000060 ENVIRONMENT DIVISION.
000070 CONFIGURATION SECTION.
000080   SOURCE-COMPUTER.  IBM-4341.
000090   OBJECT-COMPUTER.  IBM-4341.
000100 INPUT-OUTPUT SECTION.
000110 FILE-CONTROL.
000120     SELECT UNSORTED-CUSTOMER
000130         ASSIGN TO UT-S-UNSORT.
000140     SELECT SORTED-CUSTOMER
000150         ASSIGN TO UT-S-SORTED.
000160     SELECT SORT-WORK-FILE
000170         ASSIGN TO UT-S-SORTWK1.
000180*
000190 DATA DIVISION.
000200 FILE SECTION.
000210 FD  UNSORTED-CUSTOMER
000220     RECORD CONTAINS 25 CHARACTERS
000230     LABEL RECORDS ARE STANDARD.
000240 01  UC-UNSORTED-CUSTOMER-RECORD.
000250     05  UC-ACCOUNT-NUMBER        PIC X(7).
000260     05  FILLER                   PIC X(1).
000270     05  UC-TRANSACTION-DATE      PIC X(8).
000280     05  FILLER                   PIC X(1).
000290     05  UC-TRANSACTION-TYPE      PIC X(1).
000300     05  FILLER                   PIC X(1).
000310     05  UC-TRANSACTION-AMOUNT    PIC 9(4)V99.
000320 FD  SORTED-CUSTOMER
000330     RECORD CONTAINS 132 CHARACTERS
000340     LABEL RECORDS ARE OMITTED.
000350 01  SC-SORTED-CUSTOMER-RECORD.
000360     05  FILLER                   PIC X(3).
000370     05  SC-ACCOUNT-NUMBER        PIC X(7).
000380     05  FILLER                   PIC X(3).
000390     05  SC-TRANSACTION-DATE      PIC X(8).
000400     05  FILLER                   PIC X(3).
000410     05  SC-TRANSACTION-TYPE      PIC X(1).
000420     05  FILLER                   PIC X(3).
000430     05  SC-TRANSACTION-AMOUNT    PIC $Z,ZZ9.99.
000440     05  FILLER                   PIC X(95).
000450 SD  SORT-WORK-FILE.
000460 01  SW-SORT-WORK-RECORD.
000470     05  SW-ACCOUNT-NUMBER        PIC X(7).
```

Program 3–4   *(concluded)*

```
000480       05  SW-TRANSACTION-DATE          PIC X(8).
000490       05  SW-TRANSACTION-TYPE          PIC X(1).
000500       05  SW-TRANSACTION-AMOUNT        PIC 9(4)V99.
000510 WORKING-STORAGE SECTION.
000520 01  WS-RECORD-INDICATORS.
000530       05  WS-END-OF-FILE-INDICATOR       PIC X(3).
000540           88  END-OF-FILE VALUE 'END'.
000550 PROCEDURE DIVISION.
000560 MAIN-LINE SECTION.
000570 A000-NUM-DATE-TYPE-ORDER.
000580     SORT SORT-WORK-FILE
000590         ASCENDING KEY SW-ACCOUNT-NUMBER
000600                       SW-TRANSACTION-DATE
000610                       SW-TRANSACTION-TYPE
000620         INPUT PROCEDURE B100-REFORMAT-DATA
000630         OUTPUT PROCEDURE B200-PRINT-REPORT.
000640     STOP RUN.
000650 B100-REFORMAT-DATA SECTION.
000660 B100-REFORMAT-DATA-PARA.
000670     OPEN INPUT UNSORTED-CUSTOMER.
000680     PERFORM C100-INITIALIZE-VARIABLES.
000690     PERFORM Z100-READ-RECORD.
000700     PERFORM C300-READ-UNSORTED
000710         UNTIL END-OF-FILE.
000720     CLOSE UNSORTED-CUSTOMER.
000730     GO TO B100-REFORMAT-EXIT.
000740 C100-INITIALIZE-VARIABLES.
000750     MOVE SPACES              TO WS-END-OF-FILE-INDICATOR.
000760 C300-READ-UNSORTED.
000770     MOVE UC-ACCOUNT-NUMBER     TO SW-ACCOUNT-NUMBER.
000780     MOVE UC-TRANSACTION-DATE   TO SW-TRANSACTION-DATE.
000790     MOVE UC-TRANSACTION-TYPE   TO SW-TRANSACTION-TYPE.
000800     MOVE UC-TRANSACTION-AMOUNT TO SW-TRANSACTION-AMOUNT.
000810     RELEASE SW-SORT-WORK-RECORD.
000820     PERFORM Z100-READ-RECORD.
000830 Z100-READ-RECORD.
000840     READ UNSORTED-CUSTOMER
000850         AT END MOVE 'END' TO WS-END-OF-FILE-INDICATOR.
000860 B100-REFORMAT-EXIT.
000870     EXIT.
000880 B200-PRINT-REPORT SECTION.
000890 B200-PRINT-REPORT-PARA.
000900     OPEN OUTPUT SORTED-CUSTOMER.
000910     PERFORM C400-INITIALIZE-VARIABLES.
000920     PERFORM Z200-RETURN-RECORD.
000930     PERFORM C600-PRINT-DETAIL
000940         UNTIL END-OF-FILE.
000950     CLOSE SORTED-CUSTOMER.
000960     GO TO B200-PRINT-EXIT.
000970 C400-INITIALIZE-VARIABLES.
000980     MOVE SPACES              TO WS-END-OF-FILE-INDICATOR.
000990 C600-PRINT-DETAIL.
001000     MOVE SPACES              TO SC-SORTED-CUSTOMER-RECORD.
001010     MOVE SW-ACCOUNT-NUMBER     TO SC-ACCOUNT-NUMBER.
001020     MOVE SW-TRANSACTION-DATE   TO SC-TRANSACTION-DATE.
001030     MOVE SW-TRANSACTION-TYPE   TO SC-TRANSACTION-TYPE.
001040     MOVE SW-TRANSACTION-AMOUNT TO SC-TRANSACTION-AMOUNT.
001050     WRITE SC-SORTED-CUSTOMER-RECORD
001060         AFTER 1.
001070     PERFORM Z200-RETURN-RECORD.
001080 Z200-RETURN-RECORD.
001090     RETURN SORT-WORK-FILE
001100         AT END MOVE 'END' TO WS-END-OF-FILE-INDICATOR.
001110 B200-PRINT-EXIT.
001120     EXIT.
```

Figure 3–22 *Output from Program 3–4*

```
61-5472    87/04/01    2    $      52.25
61-5472    87/04/03    2    $     900.00
61-5472    87/04/05    2    $1,000.00
61-5472    87/04/13    2    $      52.00
61-5472    87/04/14    2    $      25.50
61-5472    87/04/21    2    $      10.00
61-5472    87/04/23    2    $      75.00
62-6476    87/04/02    2    $1,005.00
62-6476    87/04/04    1    $5,250.00
62-6476    87/04/08    2    $     400.00
62-6476    87/04/10    4    $     100.00
62-6476    87/04/23    2    $     623.00
62-6476    87/04/29    2    $     575.25
63-5478    87/04/01    2    $     250.00
63-5478    87/04/02    2    $     450.00
63-5478    87/04/05    1    $     250.00
63-5478    87/04/10    2    $     250.00
63-5478    87/04/15    2    $2,500.00
63-5478    87/04/18    2    $     425.52
63-5478    87/04/21    1    $     400.00
63-5478    87/04/23    2    $     125.00
63-5478    87/04/25    2    $     375.00
```

The MERGE Statement

The **MERGE statement** allows a program to merge two or more files. Each of the files must have been previously sorted in the desired sequence and each must be defined in precisely the same manner. The MERGE statement is used mainly to combine several smaller files into a larger file. As an example, the customer data used in the previous programs may be sorted on a daily basis and stored on a tape file. The MERGE statement could then combine the daily files into a monthly file that could be used to produce monthly bank statements.

The format of the MERGE statement is shown in Figure 3–23. Note that an INPUT PROCEDURE cannot be specified. This requires all input files to the MERGE and the merge work file to be defined with exactly the same total number of characters. Since the programmer cannot reference records in the input files, there is no reason to subdivide those records. The MERGE may utilize either a GIVING or an OUTPUT PROCEDURE depending on the application. The MERGE may also use multiple keys.

Figure 3–23 *Format of the MERGE Statement*

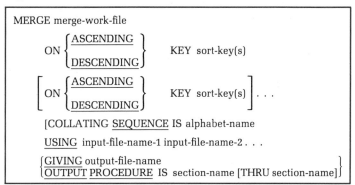

To illustrate the MERGE capabilities assume that the bank data has been sorted and stored in two 15-day files as shown in Figure 3–24. Program 3–5 shows the

merging of these two files into a report, the output from which is shown in Figure
3–25. The output from this two-file program is identical to the output shown in
Figure 3–22 that resulted from the SORT with one file.

Figure 3–24   *Bank*
Data as Two Separate
Files

```
First 15 days:

61-547287/04/012005225
61-547287/04/032090000
61-547287/04/052100000
61-547287/04/132005200
61-547287/04/142002550
62-647687/04/023100500
62-647687/04/041525000
62-647687/04/082040000
62-647687/04/104010000
63-547887/04/012025000
63-547887/04/022045000
63-547887/04/051025000
63-547887/04/102025000
63-547887/04/152250000

Second 15 days:

61-547287/04/212001000
61-547287/04/232007500
62-647687/04/232062300
62-647687/04/292057525
63-547887/04/182042552
63-547887/04/211040000
63-547887/04/232012500
63-547887/04/252037500
```

Program 3–5

```
000010 IDENTIFICATION DIVISION.
000020 PROGRAM-ID.    CUSTMERG.
000030*****************************************************************
000040* PROGRAM 3-5 MERGE WITH OUTPUT PROCEDURE                       *
000050*****************************************************************
000060 ENVIRONMENT DIVISION.
000070 CONFIGURATION SECTION.
000080    SOURCE-COMPUTER.  IBM-4341.
000090    OBJECT-COMPUTER.  IBM-4341.
000100 INPUT-OUTPUT SECTION.
000110 FILE-CONTROL.
000120    SELECT UNMERGED-CUSTOMER-A
000130       ASSIGN TO UT-S-UNMERGA.
000140    SELECT UNMERGED-CUSTOMER-B
000150       ASSIGN TO UT-S-UNMERGB.
000160    SELECT MERGED-CUSTOMER
000170       ASSIGN TO UT-S-MERGED.
000180    SELECT MERGE-WORK-FILE
000190       ASSIGN TO UT-S-SORTWK1.
000200*
000210 DATA DIVISION.
000220 FILE SECTION.
000230 FD  UNMERGED-CUSTOMER-A
000240    RECORD CONTAINS 22 CHARACTERS
000250    LABEL RECORDS ARE STANDARD.
000260 01  UC-UNMERGED-CUSTOMER-RECORD-A    PIC X(22).
000270 FD  UNMERGED-CUSTOMER-B
000280    RECORD CONTAINS 22 CHARACTERS
```

Program 3–5 *(concluded)*

```
000290      LABEL RECORDS ARE STANDARD.
000300 01   UC-UNMERGED-CUSTOMER-RECORD-B      PIC X(22).
000310 FD   MERGED-CUSTOMER
000320      RECORD CONTAINS 132 CHARACTERS
000330      LABEL RECORDS ARE OMITTED.
000340 01   MC-MERGED-CUSTOMER-RECORD.
000350      05  FILLER                         PIC X(3).
000360      05  MC-ACCOUNT-NUMBER              PIC X(7).
000370      05  FILLER                         PIC X(3).
000380      05  MC-TRANSACTION-DATE            PIC X(8).
000390      05  FILLER                         PIC X(3).
000400      05  MC-TRANSACTION-TYPE            PIC X(1).
000410      05  FILLER                         PIC X(3).
000420      05  MC-TRANSACTION-AMOUNT          PIC $Z,ZZ9.99.
000430      05  FILLER                         PIC X(95).
000440 SD   MERGE-WORK-FILE.
000450 01   MW-MERGE-WORK-RECORD.
000460      05  MW-ACCOUNT-NUMBER              PIC X(7).
000470      05  MW-TRANSACTION-DATE            PIC X(8).
000480      05  MW-TRANSACTION-TYPE            PIC X(1).
000490      05  MW-TRANSACTION-AMOUNT          PIC 9(4)V99.
000500 WORKING-STORAGE SECTION.
000510 01   WS-RECORD-INDICATORS.
000520      05  WS-END-OF-FILE-INDICATOR       PIC X(3).
000530          88  END-OF-FILE VALUE 'END'.
000540 PROCEDURE DIVISION.
000550 MAIN-LINE SECTION.
000560 A000-NUM-DATE-TYPE-ORDER.
000570      MERGE MERGE-WORK-FILE
000580          ASCENDING KEY MW-ACCOUNT-NUMBER
000590                        MW-TRANSACTION-DATE
000600                        MW-TRANSACTION-TYPE
000610          USING UNMERGED-CUSTOMER-A
000620                UNMERGED-CUSTOMER-B
000630          OUTPUT PROCEDURE B100-PRINT-REPORT.
000640      STOP RUN.
000650 B100-PRINT-REPORT SECTION.
000660 B100-PRINT-REPORT-PARA.
000670      OPEN OUTPUT MERGED-CUSTOMER.
000680      PERFORM C100-INITIALIZE-VARIABLES.
000690      PERFORM Z100-RETURN-RECORD.
000700      PERFORM C300-PRINT-DETAIL
000710          UNTIL END-OF-FILE.
000720      CLOSE MERGED-CUSTOMER.
000730      GO TO B100-PRINT-EXIT.
000740 C100-INITIALIZE-VARIABLES.
000750      MOVE SPACES                TO WS-END-OF-FILE-INDICATOR.
000760 C300-PRINT-DETAIL.
000770      MOVE SPACES                TO MC-MERGED-CUSTOMER-RECORD.
000780      MOVE MW-ACCOUNT-NUMBER     TO MC-ACCOUNT-NUMBER.
000790      MOVE MW-TRANSACTION-DATE   TO MC-TRANSACTION-DATE.
000800      MOVE MW-TRANSACTION-TYPE   TO MC-TRANSACTION-TYPE.
000810      MOVE MW-TRANSACTION-AMOUNT TO MC-TRANSACTION-AMOUNT.
000820      WRITE MC-MERGED-CUSTOMER-RECORD
000830          AFTER 1.
000840      PERFORM Z100-RETURN-RECORD.
000850 Z100-RETURN-RECORD.
000860      RETURN MERGE-WORK-FILE
000870          AT END MOVE 'END' TO WS-END-OF-FILE-INDICATOR.
000880 B100-PRINT-EXIT.
000890      EXIT.
```

Figure 3–25 *Output from Program 3–5*

61-5472	87/04/01	2	$ 52.25
61-5472	87/04/03	2	$ 900.00
61-5472	87/04/05	2	$1,000.00
61-5472	87/04/13	2	$ 52.00
61-5472	87/04/14	2	$ 25.50
61-5472	87/04/21	2	$ 10.00
61-5472	87/04/23	2	$ 75.00
62-6476	87/04/02	3	$1,005.00
62-6476	87/04/04	1	$5,250.00
62-6476	87/04/08	2	$ 400.00
62-6476	87/04/10	4	$ 100.00
62-6476	87/04/23	2	$ 623.00
62-6476	87/04/29	2	$ 575.25
63-5478	87/04/01	2	$ 250.00
63-5478	87/04/02	2	$ 450.00
63-5478	87/04/05	1	$ 250.00
63-5478	87/04/10	2	$ 250.00
63-5478	87/04/15	2	$2,500.00
63-5478	87/04/18	2	$ 425.52
63-5478	87/04/21	1	$ 400.00
63-5478	87/04/23	2	$ 125.00
63-5478	87/04/25	2	$ 375.00

Sorting Variable Length Records

All discussion thus far has centered on sorting of fixed length records. Sorting of **variable length records** poses additional problems.

Both magnetic tape and magnetic disk allow the existence of variable length records in a file. The main reason to utilize variable length records is to conserve physical space. However, the operating system requirements for variable length records are significant (particularly when sorting). The use of variable length records should be undertaken with caution.

There are three different types of variable length records as shown in Figures 3–26, 3–27, and 3–28.

Figure 3–26 *Variable Number of Fixed-Length Segments*

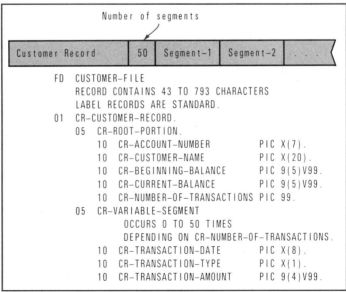

```
           FD   CUSTOMER-FILE
                RECORD CONTAINS 43 TO 793 CHARACTERS
                LABEL RECORDS ARE STANDARD.
           01   CR-CUSTOMER-RECORD.
                05  CR-ROOT-PORTION.
                    10  CR-ACCOUNT-NUMBER         PIC X(7).
                    10  CR-CUSTOMER-NAME          PIC X(20).
                    10  CR-BEGINNING-BALANCE      PIC 9(5)V99.
                    10  CR-CURRENT-BALANCE        PIC 9(5)V99.
                    10  CR-NUMBER-OF-TRANSACTIONS PIC 99.
                05  CR-VARIABLE-SEGMENT
                        OCCURS 0 TO 50 TIMES
                        DEPENDING ON CR-NUMBER-OF-TRANSACTIONS.
                    10  CR-TRANSACTION-DATE       PIC X(8).
                    10  CR-TRANSACTION-TYPE       PIC X(1).
                    10  CR-TRANSACTION-AMOUNT     PIC 9(4)V99.
```

Figure 3–27   *Variable Length Field*

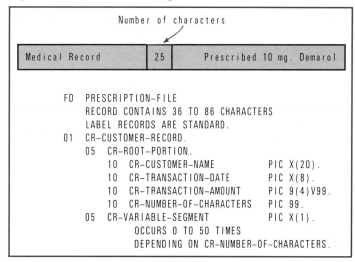

```
                          Number of characters

 Medical Record          25          Prescribed 10 mg. Demarol


        FD   PRESCRIPTION-FILE
             RECORD CONTAINS 36 TO 86 CHARACTERS
             LABEL RECORDS ARE STANDARD.
        01   CR-CUSTOMER-RECORD.
             05   CR-ROOT-PORTION.
                  10   CR-CUSTOMER-NAME         PIC X(20).
                  10   CR-TRANSACTION-DATE      PIC X(8).
                  10   CR-TRANSACTION-AMOUNT    PIC 9(4)V99.
                  10   CR-NUMBER-OF-CHARACTERS  PIC 99.
             05   CR-VARIABLE-SEGMENT           PIC X(1).
                  OCCURS 0 TO 50 TIMES
                  DEPENDING ON CR-NUMBER-OF-CHARACTERS.
```

Figure 3–28   *Fixed-Length Records of Different Lengths*

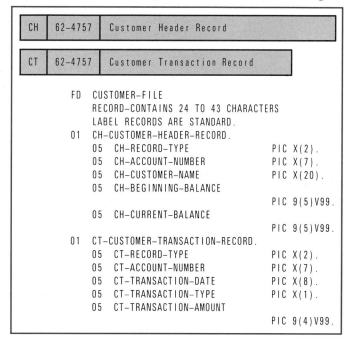

```
 CH   62-4757   Customer Header Record

 CT   62-4757   Customer Transaction Record


        FD   CUSTOMER-FILE
             RECORD-CONTAINS 24 TO 43 CHARACTERS
             LABEL RECORDS ARE STANDARD.
        01   CH-CUSTOMER-HEADER-RECORD.
             05   CH-RECORD-TYPE          PIC X(2).
             05   CH-ACCOUNT-NUMBER       PIC X(7).
             05   CH-CUSTOMER-NAME        PIC X(20).
             05   CH-BEGINNING-BALANCE

                                          PIC 9(5)V99.
             05   CH-CURRENT-BALANCE

                                          PIC 9(5)V99.
        01   CT-CUSTOMER-TRANSACTION-RECORD.
             05   CT-RECORD-TYPE          PIC X(2).
             05   CT-ACCOUNT-NUMBER       PIC X(7).
             05   CT-TRANSACTION-DATE     PIC X(8).
             05   CT-TRANSACTION-TYPE     PIC X(1).
             05   CT-TRANSACTION-AMOUNT

                                          PIC 9(4)V99.
```

Applications that use either of the methods of variable length records shown in Figure 3–26 or Figure 3–27 pose essentially the same concerns. Both types of records are divided into a fixed-length root portion and a variable portion that changes in length dependent on a numeric value in the root portion. Note that some compilers do not allow the use of the numeric literal '0' to be used in the OCCURS/DEPENDING ON clause. The SORT verb can reference only keys that are in the root portion of the record. If it is necessary to sort the variable portion, either an internal programmed sort must be used or the variable portion would have to be placed in a separate file to use the SORT verb.

To provide an illustration, consider the data file shown in Figure 3–29, which is a file that contains a variable number of fixed-length segments.

Figure 3–29 *Data File with Variable Length Records*

```
63-5478FRANK  JAMES  C        0050000     0987/04/01  2 025000
                                            87/04/02  2 045000
                                            87/04/05  1 025000
                                            87/04/10  2 025000
                                            87/04/15  2 250000
                                            87/04/18  2 042552
                                            87/04/21  1 040000
                                            87/04/23  2 012500
                                            87/04/25  2 037500
62-6476BALDWIN  ROBERT  D     0125000     0687/04/02  3 100500
                                            87/04/04  1 525000
                                            87/04/08  2 040000
                                            87/04/10  4 010000
                                            87/04/23  2 062300
                                            87/04/29  2 057525
61-5472GARDNER  PAULINE  F    0175000     078//04/01  2 005225
                                            87/04/03  2 090000
                                            87/04/05  2 100000
                                            87/04/13  2 005200
                                            87/04/14  2 002550
                                            87/04/21  2 001000
                                            87/04/23  2 007500
```

Program 3–6 illustrates the COBOL logic to sort the data file in Figure 3–29. Figure 3–30 lists the output from the sort, including both the root portion and the variable segments. Notice the need to move the root portion and the variable portion separately. This is because the movement of the root portion includes the movement of the number of transactions, which is needed in the receiving record to define the number of characters being moved. Remember, it is always the size of the receiving field that determines the number of characters that are moved.

Program 3–6

```
000010 IDENTIFICATION DIVISION.
000020 PROGRAM-ID.    CUSTSORT.
000030*·············································································
000040* PROGRAM 3-6 SORTING VARIABLE LENGTH RECORDS                          *
000050*·············································································
000060 ENVIRONMENT DIVISION.
000070 CONFIGURATION SECTION.
000080    SOURCE-COMPUTER.  IBM-4341.
000090    OBJECT-COMPUTER.  IBM-4341.
000100 INPUT-OUTPUT SECTION.
000110 FILE-CONTROL.
000120    SELECT UNSORTED-CUSTOMER
000130       ASSIGN TO SYS054-UT-3375-CUST.
000140    SELECT SORTED-CUSTOMER
000150       ASSIGN TO SYS018-UR-3203-S.
000160    SELECT SORT-WORK-FILE
000170       ASSIGN TO SYS001-UT-3375-SORTWK1.
000180*
000190 DATA DIVISION.
000200 FILE SECTION.
000210 FD  UNSORTED-CUSTOMER
000220     RECORD CONTAINS 43 TO 793 CHARACTERS
000230     LABEL RECORDS ARE STANDARD.
000240 01  UC-UNSORTED-CUSTOMER-RECORD.
000250     05  UC-ROOT-PORTION.
000260         10  UC-ACCOUNT-NUMBER          PIC X(7).
```

Program 3–6 *(continued)*

```
000270            10  UC-CUSTOMER-NAME          PIC X(20).
000280            10  UC-BEGINNING-BALANCE      PIC S9(5)V99.
000290            10  UC-CURRENT-BALANCE        PIC S9(5)V99.
000300            10  UC-NUMBER-OF-TRANSACTIONS PIC 9(2).
000310        05  UC-VARIABLE-PORTION.
000320            10  UC-VARIABLE-SEGMENT
000330                    OCCURS 0 TO 50 TIMES
000340                    DEPENDING ON UC-NUMBER-OF-TRANSACTIONS.
000350                15  UC-TRANSACTION-DATE   PIC X(8).
000360                15  UC-TRANSACTION-TYPE   PIC X(1).
000370                15  UC-TRANSACTION-AMOUNT PIC 9(4)V99.
000380 FD  SORTED-CUSTOMER
000390     RECORD CONTAINS 132 CHARACTERS
000400     LABEL RECORDS ARE OMITTED.
000410 01  SC-SORTED-CUSTOMER-RECORD.
000420     05  FILLER                       PIC X(3).
000430     05  SC-ACCOUNT-NUMBER            PIC X(7).
000440     05  FILLER                       PIC X(3).
000450     05  SC-CUSTOMER-NAME             PIC X(20).
000460     05  FILLER                       PIC X(3).
000470     05  SC-BEGINNING-BALANCE         PIC $ZZ,ZZ9.99-.
000480     05  FILLER                       PIC X(3).
000490     05  SC-CURRENT-BALANCE           PIC $ZZ,ZZ9.99-.
000500     05  FILLER                       PIC X(3).
000510     05  SC-NUMBER-OF-TRANSACTIONS    PIC Z9.
000520     05  FILLER                       PIC X(3).
000530     05  SC-TRANSACTION-DATE          PIC X(8).
000540     05  FILLER                       PIC X(3).
000550     05  SC-TRANSACTION-TYPE          PIC X(1).
000560     05  FILLER                       PIC X(3).
000570     05  SC-TRANSACTION-AMOUNT        PIC $Z,ZZ9.99.
000580     05  FILLER                       PIC X(39).
000590 SD  SORT-WORK-FILE.
000600 01  SW-SORT-WORK-RECORD.
000610     05  SW-ROOT-PORTION.
000620         10  SW-ACCOUNT-NUMBER         PIC X(7).
000630         10  SW-CUSTOMER-NAME          PIC X(20).
000640         10  SW-BEGINNING-BALANCE      PIC S9(5)V99.
000650         10  SW-CURRENT-BALANCE        PIC S9(5)V99.
000660         10  SW-NUMBER-OF-TRANSACTIONS PIC 9(2).
000670     05  SW-VARIABLE-PORTION.
000680         10  SW-VARIABLE-SEGMENT
000690                 OCCURS 0 TO 50 TIMES
000700                 DEPENDING ON SW-NUMBER-OF-TRANSACTIONS
000710                 INDEXED BY SORT-INDEX.
000720             15  SW-TRANSACTION-DATE   PIC X(8).
000730             15  SW-TRANSACTION-TYPE   PIC X(1).
000740             15  SW-TRANSACTION-AMOUNT PIC 9(4)V99.
000750 WORKING-STORAGE SECTION.
000760 01  WS-RECORD-INDICATORS.
000770     05  WS-END-OF-FILE-INDICATOR     PIC X(3).
000780         88  END-OF-FILE VALUE 'END'.
000790 PROCEDURE DIVISION.
000800 MAIN-LINE SECTION.
000810 A000-NUM-DATE-TYPE-ORDER.
000820     SORT SORT-WORK-FILE
000830         ASCENDING KEY SW-ACCOUNT-NUMBER
000840         INPUT PROCEDURE B100-REFORMAT-DATA
000850         OUTPUT PROCEDURE B200-PRINT-REPORT.
000860     STOP RUN.
000870 B100-REFORMAT-DATA SECTION.
000880 B100-REFORMAT-DATA-PARA.
000890     OPEN INPUT UNSORTED-CUSTOMER.
```

Program 3–6 *(concluded)*

```
000900      PERFORM C100-INITIALIZE-VARIABLES.
000910      PERFORM Z100-READ-RECORD.
000920      PERFORM C300-READ-UNSORTED
000930          UNTIL END-OF-FILE.
000940      CLOSE UNSORTED-CUSTOMER.
000950      GO TO B100-REFORMAT-EXIT.
000960 C100-INITIALIZE-VARIABLES.
000970      MOVE SPACES              TO WS-END-OF-FILE-INDICATOR.
000980 C300-READ-UNSORTED.
000990      MOVE UC-ROOT-PORTION     TO SW-ROOT-PORTION.
001000      MOVE UC-VARIABLE-PORTION TO SW-VARIABLE-PORTION.
001010      RELEASE SW-SORT-WORK-RECORD.
001020      PERFORM Z100-READ-RECORD.
001030 Z100-READ-RECORD.
001040      READ UNSORTED-CUSTOMER
001050          AT END MOVE 'END' TO WS-END-OF-FILE-INDICATOR.
001060 B100-REFORMAT-EXIT.
001070      EXIT.
001080 B200-PRINT-REPORT SECTION.
001090 B200-PRINT-REPORT-PARA.
001100      OPEN OUTPUT SORTED-CUSTOMER.
001110      PERFORM C400-INITIALIZE-VARIABLES.
001120      PERFORM Z100-RETURN-RECORD.
001130      PERFORM C600-PRINT-DETAIL
001140          UNTIL END-OF-FILE.
001150      CLOSE SORTED-CUSTOMER.
001160      GO TO B200-PRINT-EXIT.
001170 C400-INITIALIZE-VARIABLES.
001180      MOVE SPACES                 TO WS-END-OF-FILE-INDICATOR.
001190 C600-PRINT-DETAIL.
001200      MOVE SPACES                 TO SC-SORTED-CUSTOMER-RECORD.
001210      MOVE SW-ACCOUNT-NUMBER       TO SC-ACCOUNT-NUMBER.
001220      MOVE SW-CUSTOMER-NAME        TO SC-CUSTOMER-NAME.
001230      MOVE SW-BEGINNING-BALANCE    TO SC-BEGINNING-BALANCE.
001240      MOVE SW-CURRENT-BALANCE      TO SC-CURRENT-BALANCE.
001250      MOVE SW-NUMBER-OF-TRANSACTIONS TO SC-NUMBER-OF-TRANSACTIONS.
001260      MOVE SW-TRANSACTION-DATE(1)  TO SC-TRANSACTION-DATE.
001270      MOVE SW-TRANSACTION-TYPE(1)  TO SC-TRANSACTION-TYPE.
001280      MOVE SW-TRANSACTION-AMOUNT(1) TO SC-TRANSACTION-AMOUNT.
001290      WRITE SC-SORTED-CUSTOMER-RECORD
001300          AFTER 1.
001310      PERFORM D100-PRINT-REMAINING-SEGMENTS
001320          VARYING SORT-INDEX
001330          FROM 2 BY 1
001340          UNTIL SORT-INDEX > SW-NUMBER-OF-TRANSACTIONS.
001350      PERFORM Z100-RETURN-RECORD.
001360 D100-PRINT-REMAINING-SEGMENTS.
001370      MOVE SPACES TO SC-SORTED-CUSTOMER-RECORD.
001380      MOVE SW-TRANSACTION-DATE(SORT-INDEX)
001390          TO SC-TRANSACTION-DATE.
001400      MOVE SW-TRANSACTION-TYPE(SORT-INDEX)
001410          TO SC-TRANSACTION-TYPE.
001420      MOVE SW-TRANSACTION-AMOUNT(SORT-INDEX)
001430          TO SC-TRANSACTION-AMOUNT.
001440      WRITE SC-SORTED-CUSTOMER-RECORD
001450          AFTER 1.
001460 Z100-RETURN-RECORD.
001470      RETURN SORT-WORK-FILE
001480          AT END MOVE 'END' TO WS-END-OF-FILE-INDICATOR.
001490 B200-PRINT-EXIT.
001500      EXIT.
```

Figure 3–30   *Output from Program 3–6*

```
61-5472   GARDNER PAULINE F    $ 2,250.00   $ 124.48      7   87/04/01   2   $     52.25
                                                              87/04/03   2   $    900.00
                                                              87/04/05   2   $1,000.00
                                                              87/04/13   2   $     52.00
                                                              87/04/14   2   $     25.50
                                                              87/04/21   2   $     10.00
                                                              87/04/23   2   $     75.00
62-6476   BALDWIN ROBERT D     $ 1,250.00   $ 5,806.75    6   87/04/02   3   $1,005.00
                                                              87/04/04   1   $5,250.00
                                                              87/04/08   2   $    400.00
                                                              87/04/10   4   $    100.00
                                                              87/04/23   2   $    623.00
                                                              87/04/29   2   $    575.25
63-5478   FRANK JAMES C        $ 3,850.00   $ 135.25      9   87/04/01   2   $    250.00
                                                              87/04/02   2   $    450.00
                                                              87/04/05   1   $    250.00
                                                              87/04/10   2   $    250.00
                                                              87/04/15   2   $2,500.00
                                                              87/04/18   2   $    425.52
                                                              87/04/21   1   $    400.00
                                                              87/04/23   2   $    125.00
                                                              87/04/25   2   $    375.00
```

Program 3–7 illustrates the COBOL logic necessary to sort the data file in Figure 3–31, in which there are fixed-length records of different sizes in the file. The output from Program 3–7 is included in Figure 3–32.

Figure 3–31   *Data File with Different Size Records*

```
CH63-5478FRANK JAMES C        03850000013525
CT63-547887/04/012025000
CT63-547887/04/022045000
CT63-547887/04/051025000
CT63-547887/04/102025000
CT63-547887/04/152250000
CT63-547887/04/182042552
CT63-547887/04/211040000
CT63-547887/04/232012500
CT63-547887/04/252037500
CH62-6476BALDWIN ROBERT D     01250000580675
CT62-647687/04/023100500
CT62-647687/04/041525000
CT62-647687/04/082040000
CT62-647687/04/104010000
CT62-647687/04/232062300
CT62-647687/04/292057525
CH61-5472GARDNER PAULINE F    02250000012448
CT61-547287/04/012005225
CT61-547287/04/032090000
CT61-547287/04/052100000
CT61-547287/04/132005200
CT61-547287/04/142002550
CT61-547287/04/212001000
CT61-547287/04/232007500
```

Program 3–7

```
000010 IDENTIFICATION DIVISION.
000020 PROGRAM-ID.    CUSTSORT.
000030*....................................................
000040* PROGRAM 3-7 SORTING VARIABLE LENGTH RECORDS          *
000050*....................................................
000060 ENVIRONMENT DIVISION.
000070 CONFIGURATION SECTION.
000080   SOURCE-COMPUTER.  IBM-4341.
000090   OBJECT-COMPUTER.  IBM-4341.
000100 INPUT-OUTPUT SECTION.
000110 FILE-CONTROL.
000120     SELECT UNSORTED-CUSTOMER
000130         ASSIGN TO SYS054-UT-3375-UNSORT.
000140     SELECT SORTED-CUSTOMER
000150         ASSIGN TO SYS018-UR-3203-S.
000160     SELECT SORT-WORK-FILE
000170         ASSIGN TO SYS001-UT-3375-SORTWK1.
000180*
000190 DATA DIVISION.
000200 FILE SECTION.
000210 FD  UNSORTED-CUSTOMER
000220     RECORD CONTAINS 24 TO 43 CHARACTERS
000230     LABEL RECORDS ARE STANDARD.
000240 01  UH-UNSORTED-HEADER.
000250     05  UH-RECORD-TYPE              PIC X(2).
000260         88  UH-HEADER-RECORD VALUE 'CH'.
000270     05  UH-ACCOUNT-NUMBER           PIC X(7).
000280     05  UH-CUSTOMER-NAME            PIC X(20).
000290     05  UH-BEGINNING-BALANCE        PIC S9(5)V99.
000300     05  UH-CURRENT-BALANCE          PIC S9(5)V99.
000310 01  UT-UNSORTED-TRANSACTION.
000320     05  UT-RECORD-TYPE              PIC X(2).
000330         88  UT-TRANSACTION-RECORD VALUE 'CT'.
000340     05  UT-ACCOUNT-NUMBER           PIC X(7).
000350     05  UT-TRANSACTION-DATE         PIC X(8).
000360     05  UT-TRANSACTION-TYPE         PIC X(1).
000370     05  UT-TRANSACTION-AMOUNT       PIC 9(4)V99.
000380 FD  SORTED-CUSTOMER
000390     RECORD CONTAINS 132 CHARACTERS
000400     LABEL RECORDS ARE OMITTED.
000410 01  SH-SORTED-HEADER.
000420     05  FILLER                      PIC X(3).
000430     05  SH-ACCOUNT-NUMBER           PIC X(7).
000440     05  FILLER                      PIC X(3).
000450     05  SH-CUSTOMER-NAME            PIC X(20).
000460     05  FILLER                      PIC X(3).
000470     05  SH-BEGINNING-BALANCE        PIC $ZZ,ZZ9.99-.
000480     05  FILLER           ·          PIC X(3).
000490     05  SH-CURRENT-BALANCE          PIC $ZZ,ZZ9.99-.
000500     05  FILLER                      PIC X(64).
000510 01  ST-SORTED-TRANSACTION.
000520     05  FILLER                      PIC X(3).
000530     05  ST-ACCOUNT-NUMBER           PIC X(7).
000540     05  FILLER                      PIC X(3).
000550     05  ST-TRANSACTION-DATE         PIC X(8).
000560     05  FILLER                      PIC X(3).
000570     05  ST-TRANSACTION-TYPE         PIC X(1).
000580     05  FILLER                      PIC X(3).
000590     05  ST-TRANSACTION-AMOUNT       PIC $Z,ZZ9.99.
000600     05  FILLER                      PIC X(95).
000610 SD  SORT-WORK-FILE.
000620 01  SWH-SORT-WORK-HEADER.
000630     05  SWH-RECORD-TYPE             PIC X(2).
000640         88  SWH-HEADER-RECORD VALUE 'CH'.
000650     05  SWH-ACCOUNT-NUMBER          PIC X(7).
```

Program 3–7   *(continued)*

```
000660        05  SWH-CUSTOMER-NAME              PIC X(20).
000670        05  SWH-BEGINNING-BALANCE          PIC S9(5)V99.
000680        05  SWH-CURRENT-BALANCE            PIC S9(5)V99.
000690 01  SWT-SORT-WORK-TRANSACTION.
000700        05  SWT-RECORD-TYPE                PIC X(2).
000710           88  SWH-TRANSACTION-RECORD VALUE 'CT'.
000720        05  SWT-ACCOUNT-NUMBER             PIC X(7).
000730        05  SWT-TRANSACTION-DATE           PIC X(8).
000740        05  SWT-TRANSACTION-TYPE           PIC X(1).
000750        05  SWT-TRANSACTION-AMOUNT         PIC 9(4)V99.
000760 WORKING-STORAGE SECTION.
000770 01  WS-RECORD-INDICATORS.
000780        05  WS-END-OF-FILE-INDICATOR       PIC X(3).
000790           88  END-OF-FILE VALUE 'END'.
000800 PROCEDURE DIVISION.
000810 MAIN-LINE SECTION.
000820 A000-NUM-DATE-TYPE-ORDER.
000830        SORT SORT-WORK-FILE
000840           ASCENDING KEY SWH-ACCOUNT-NUMBER
000850                         SWH-RECORD-TYPE
000860                         SWT-TRANSACTION-DATE
000870                         SWT-TRANSACTION-TYPE
000880           INPUT PROCEDURE B100-REFORMAT-DATA
000890           OUTPUT PROCEDURE B200-PRINT-REPORT.
000900        STOP RUN.
000910 B100-REFORMAT-DATA SECTION.
000920 B100-REFORMAT-DATA-PARA.
000930        OPEN INPUT UNSORTED-CUSTOMER.
000940        PERFORM C100-INITIALIZE-VARIABLES.
000950        PERFORM Z100-READ-RECORD.
000960        PERFORM C300-READ-UNSORTED
000970           UNTIL END-OF-FILE.
000980        CLOSE UNSORTED-CUSTOMER.
000990        GO TO B100-REFORMAT-EXIT.
001000 C100-INITIALIZE-VARIABLES.
001010        MOVE SPACES                 TO WS-END-OF-FILE-INDICATOR.
001020 C300-READ-UNSORTED.
001030        IF UH-HEADER-RECORD
001040           MOVE UH-UNSORTED-HEADER TO SWH-SORT-WORK-HEADER
001050           RELEASE SWH-SORT-WORK-HEADER
001060        ELSE
001070           MOVE UT-UNSORTED-TRANSACTION
001080              TO SWT-SORT-WORK-TRANSACTION
001090           RELEASE SWT-SORT-WORK-TRANSACTION.
001100        PERFORM Z100-READ-RECORD.
001110 Z100-READ-RECORD.
001120        READ UNSORTED-CUSTOMER
001130           AT END MOVE 'END' TO WS-END-OF-FILE-INDICATOR.
001140 B100-REFORMAT-EXIT.
001150        EXIT.
001160 B200-PRINT-REPORT SECTION.
001170 B200-PRINT-REPORT-PARA.
001180        OPEN OUTPUT SORTED-CUSTOMER.
001190        PERFORM C400-INITIALIZE-VARIABLES.
001200        PERFORM Z100-RETURN-RECORD.
001210        PERFORM C600-PRINT-DETAIL
001220           UNTIL END-OF-FILE.
001230        CLOSE SORTED-CUSTOMER.
001240        GO TO B200-PRINT-EXIT.
001250 C400-INITIALIZE-VARIABLES.
001260        MOVE SPACES                 TO WS-END-OF-FILE-INDICATOR.
001270 C600-PRINT-DETAIL.
001280        IF SWH-HEADER-RECORD
```

Program 3–7   *(concluded)*

```
001290          MOVE SPACES                TO SH-SORTED-HEADER
001300          MOVE SWH-ACCOUNT-NUMBER     TO SH-ACCOUNT-NUMBER
001310          MOVE SWH-CUSTOMER-NAME       TO SH-CUSTOMER-NAME
001320          MOVE SWH-BEGINNING-BALANCE   TO SH-BEGINNING-BALANCE
001330          MOVE SWH-CURRENT-BALANCE     TO SH-CURRENT-BALANCE
001340          WRITE SH-SORTED-HEADER
001350              AFTER 1
001360      ELSE
001370          MOVE SPACES                TO ST-SORTED-TRANSACTION
001380          MOVE SWT-ACCOUNT-NUMBER     TO ST-ACCOUNT-NUMBER
001390          MOVE SWT-TRANSACTION-DATE    TO ST-TRANSACTION-DATE
001400          MOVE SWT-TRANSACTION-TYPE    TO ST-TRANSACTION-TYPE
001410          MOVE SWT-TRANSACTION-AMOUNT TO ST-TRANSACTION-AMOUNT
001420          WRITE ST-SORTED-TRANSACTION
001430              AFTER 1.
001440      PERFORM Z100-RETURN-RECORD.
001450  Z100-RETURN-RECORD.
001460      RETURN SORT-WORK-FILE
001470          AT END MOVE 'END' TO WS-END-OF-FILE-INDICATOR.
001480  B200-PRINT-EXIT.
001490      EXIT.
```

When sorting records of different lengths any sort keys used must be in the same relative position in each of the different records. In this example, both the account number and the record type are in the same location, even though they have different names in each of the two records. The sort keys used are both the names in SWH–SORT–WORK–HEADER, yet when SWT–SORT–WORK–TRANS ACTION is released the same position in the record is used as the sort field.

Neither the transaction date nor the transaction type exist in SWH–SORT–WORK–HEADER, so when those fields are sorted while SWH–SORT–WORK–HEADER is released, the system will actually be sorting a portion of SWH–CUS

Figure 3–32   *Output from Program 3–7*

```
61-5472   GARDNER PAULINE F       $ 2,250.00   $   124.48
61-5472   87/04/01   2   $    52.25
61-5472   87/04/03   2   $   900.00
61-5472   87/04/05   2   $1,000.00
61-5472   87/04/13   2   $    52.00
61-5472   87/04/14   2   $    25.50
61-5472   87/04/21   2   $    10.00
61-5472   87/04/23   2   $    75.00
62-6476   BALDWIN ROBERT D        $ 1,250.00   $ 5,806.75
62-6476   87/04/02   3   $1,005.00
62-6476   87/04/04   1   $5,250.00
62-6476   87/04/08   2   $   400.00
62-6476   87/04/10   4   $   100.00
62-6476   87/04/23   2   $   623.00
62-6476   87/04/29   2   $   575.25
63-5478   FRANK JAMES C           $ 3,850.00   $   135.25
63-5478   87/04/01   2   $   250.00
63-5478   87/04/02   2   $   450.00
63-5478   87/04/05   1   $   250.00
63-5478   87/04/10   2   $   250.00
63-5478   87/04/15   2   $2,500.00
63-5478   87/04/18   2   $   425.52
63-5478   87/04/21   1   $   400.00
63-5478   87/04/23   2   $   125.00
63-5478   87/04/25   2   $   375.00
```

TOMER–NAME. This does not cause an incorrect sort because both SWT–TRANS ACTION–TYPE and SWT–TRANSACTION–DATE are specified as minor sort keys with respect to both SWH–ACCOUNT–NUMBER and SWH–RECORD–TYPE.

In the PROCEDURE division the only difference between sorting fixed-length records and sorting records with different lengths exist in lines 1030 through 1090 and lines 1280 through 1430. A decision must be made as to which type of record is in memory, either a header record or a transaction record. Separate RELEASE statements are required in the INPUT PROCEDURE and separate WRITE statements are required in the OUTPUT PROCEDURE.

Common Errors

1. Attempting to open or close a file that has been opened and closed by the SORT statement with a USING/GIVING option.

2. Failure to properly open and close files when using either an INPUT PROCEDURE or an OUTPUT PROCEDURE.

3. Improper use of sections when implementing either an INPUT PROCEDURE or an OUTPUT PROCEDURE.

4. Failure to properly specify major, intermediate, and minor sort fields in the SORT statement.

5. Identifying a sort key that has not been defined as a part of the record in the SD (sort description) entry.

6. Inappropriate use of the RELEASE or RETURN statement. Remember, the RELEASE is the equivalent of the WRITE statement; the RETURN is the equivalent of a READ statement.

7. During an INPUT PROCEDURE, failure to move data records from an input file to the sort work file before the RELEASE statement is executed.

8. During an OUTPUT PROCEDURE, failure to move data records from the sort work file to the output file after the RETURN statement.

9. When using both an INPUT PROCEDURE and an OUTPUT PROCEDURE, failure to reinitialize the end-of-file indicator after the end of the INPUT PROCEDURE. It would probably be best to use two different indicators; one to test for the end of the input file and one to test for the end of the sort work file.

10. Inappropriate use of the GO TO statement when using sections in either an INPUT PROCEDURE or an OUTPUT PROCEDURE. Remember, the EXIT statement must be in a paragraph by itself at the physical end of the section, and intervening paragraphs must be bypassed.

11. Attempting to use an INPUT PROCEDURE with the MERGE statement.

12. Attempting to merge files that are not in the same sequence.

13. Defining record sizes incorrectly when using the SORT or MERGE statements. This is a particularly common problem when using variable length records. Remember to use the RECORD CONTAINS clause.

14. Incorrectly specifying sort keys when sorting files with different length records.

15. Attempting to implement variable length records with the OCCURS/DEPENDING ON clause when the total record size exceeds the amount of available input memory.

16. Allowing an insufficient number of segments with the OCCURS/DEPENDING ON clause.

Exercises

1. Define the following:
   a. Sort key.
   b. Major sort field.
   c. SD
   d. ASCENDING KEY clause.

2. For each of the following sets of SORT statements, describe what else a programmer would expect to see specified in the ENVIRONMENT, DATA, and PROCEDURE division:

   a.
   ```
   SORT SORT-FILE
        ASCENDING  KEY EMPLOYEE-NAME
        USING EMPLOYEE-FILE
        GIVING OUTPUT-FILE.
   ```

   b.
   ```
   SORT SORT-FILE
        ASCENDING KEY DEPT-NUMBER
        DESCENDING KEY YTD-SALES
        INPUT PROCEDURE IN-ROUTINE
        GIVING DEPT-FILE.
   ```

   c.
   ```
   SORT SORT-FILE
        ASCENDING KEY PAYROLL-NUMBER
        INPUT PROCEDURE IN-ROUTINE
        OUTPUT PROCEDURE OUT-REPORT.
   ```

3. The following skeleton COBOL program was designed to validate an input file and prepare a listing of all valid data records including totals of year-to-date sales. The program, however, does not work. Indicate what would need to be added to the program and what changes would need to be made to the program to make it work.

```
INPUT-OUTPUT SECTION.
FILE-CONTROL.
     SELECT UNSORTED-SALES ASSIGN TO UNSORT.
     SELECT REPORT-FILE    ASSIGN TO SYSPRINT.
DATA DIVISION.
FILE SECTION.
FD  UNSORTED-SALES
     RECORD CONTAINS 14 CHARACTERS
     LABEL RECORDS ARE OMITTED.
01  UI-UNSORTED-SALES-RECORD.
     05  UI-SALES-NUMBER            PIC X(2).
     05  UI-YTD-SALES               PIC 99V99.
FD  REPORT-FILE
     RECORD CONTAINS 133 CHARACTERS
     LABEL RECORDS ARE OMITTED.
01  REPORT-RECORD                   PIC X(133).
WORKING-STORAGE SECTION.
PROCEDURE DIVISION.
A000-MAINLINE SECTION.
A000-NUMBER-ORDER.
     SORT SORT-WORK-FILE
          ASCENDING KEY SW-SALES-NUMBER
          INPUT PROCEDURE B100-REFORMAT-DATA
          OUTPUT PROCEDURE B200-PRINT-REPORT.
     STOP RUN.
B100-REFORMAT-DATA SECTION.
```

```
B100-REFORMAT-DATA-PARA.
    OPEN INPUT UNSORTED-SALES
        OUTPUT REPORT-FILE.
    READ UNSORTED-SALES
        AT END MOVE 'END' TO WS-END-OF-FILE-INDICATOR.
    PERFORM B100-READ-UNSORTED
        UNTIL END-OF-FILE.
    CLOSE UNSORTED-SALES.
B100-READ-UNSORTED.
    MOVE 'NO' TO WS-INVALID-RECORD-INDICATOR.
    PERFORM B100-VALIDATE-ROUTINE.
    IF RECORD-NOT-VALID
        PERFORM B100-PRINT-ERROR-MESSAGE
    ELSE MOVE UI-SALES-NUMBER   TO SW-SALES-NUMBER
        MOVE UI-YTD-SALES        TO SW-UNIT-PRICE
        RETURN SW-SORT-WORK-RECORD.
    READ UNSORTED-SALES
        AT END MOVE 'END' TO WS-END-OF-FILE-INDICATOR.
B100-VALIDATE-ROUTINE.


B100-REFORMAT-EXIT.
    EXIT.
B200-PRINT-REPORT SECTION.
B200-PRINT-REPORT-PARA.
    RETURN SORT-WORK-FILE
        AT END MOVE 'END' TO WS-END-OF-FILE-INDICATOR.
    PERFORM B200-INITIALIZE-VARIABLES.
    PERFORM B200-PRINT-DETAIL
        UNTIL END-OF-FILE.
    PERFORM B200-GRAND-TOTAL-ROUTINE.
    CLOSE REPORT-FILE.
    GO TO B200-PRINT-EXIT.
B200-INITIALIZE-VARIABLES.


B200-PRINT-DETAIL.


    RETURN SORT-WORK-FILE
        AT END MOVE 'END' TO WS-END-OF-FILE-INDICATOR.
B200-PRINT-EXIT.
    EXIT.
```

4. For the following sets of conditions, prepare the SORT statement that would direct the achievement of the desired results. Also indicate what else would need to be specified in the program to make the SORT statement work.

   a. An input file, named SALESPERSON-FILE, is to be sorted on social security number in ascending sequence and stored on a file named SSN-ORDER in exactly the same format as the input file.

   b. An input file, named INVENTORY-FILE, is to be sorted on STORE-NUMBER (in descending sequence) and PRODUCT-NUMBER (in ascending sequence) and a printed report is to be created of the input records.

   c. An input file, named ACCOUNTS-PAYABLE, is to be validated and stored on a disk file called VALID-ACCOUNTS-PAYABLE. The file is to be sorted on VENDOR-NUMBER in ascending sequence.

   d. An input file on tape, named CUSTOMER-TAPE-FILE, is to be validated and sorted on REGION-NUMBER and CUSTOMER-NUMBER, both in ascending sequence. REGION–NUMBER is the major sort field. After the file is sorted, it is to be printed in appropriate format on a line printer, including control breaks on REGION–NUMBER.

Problems

Use Data Set F in Appendix C for Problems 3–1 and 3–2.

1. Prepare printer listings of the data set using an appropriate printer format to display each data field into one or more of the following prescribed orders. Use a USING/GIVING to get the data in the prescribed order; then read the sorted file to create the report.
   a. Alphabetical ascending sequence.
   b. Store number ascending sequence.
   c. Department mnemonic descending sequence.
   d. Employee code ascending sequence.
   e. Commission rate descending sequence.
   f. Employee code within department (both ascending).
   g. Employee code within department within store number (all ascending sequence).

2. Modify Problem 3–1 to utilize a USING/OUTPUT PROCEDURE to create the desired listings.

Use Data Set G in Appendix C for Problems 3–3 and 3–4.

3. Prepare printer listings of the data set using an appropriate printer format to display each data field into one or more of the following prescribed orders. Use a USING/GIVING to get the data in the prescribed order; then read the sorted file to create the report.
   a. Alphabetic descending sequence.
   b. Item number ascending sequence.
   c. Department mnemonic ascending sequence.
   d. Store number ascending sequence.
   e. Sales price descending sequence.
   f. Item number within department (both ascending).
   g. Item number within department within store number (all ascending sequence).

4. Modify Problem 3–3 to utilize a USING/OUTPUT PROCEDURE to create the desired listings.

5. Using the two data sets in Figure 3–24, sort each file in descending transaction amount order, creating two separate files. Then combine them into one file using the MERGE statement, creating a report that will list the contents of the combined data file, including total increase or decrease to the customer accounts.

6. Using Data Set L in Appendix C, sort and combine the header and transaction records so that the records are in sequence by department within store number (both ascending sequence). The transaction records should also be sorted by date. The resultant file will have a header record and all of the transaction records together for each employee. Prepare a report that will list the sorted data file using an appropriate format.

7. Using Data Set M in Appendix C, sort and combine the header and transaction records so that the records are in sequence by item number within department within store number (all ascending sequence). The transaction records should also be sorted by date. The resultant file will have a header record and all of the transaction records together for each inventory item. Prepare a report that will list the sorted data file using an appropriate format.

4

Debugging

The purpose of this chapter is to discuss program debugging where **debugging** is the job of removing errors. Seldom does a program execute successfully on the first attempt. Because this is such a time-consuming activity most systems provide special debugging statements or techniques to help with this process.

TERMS AND STATEMENTS

ABEND	Desk check	Overflow condition
D	END	Program interruption
Data exception	DECLARATIVES	Syntax
DEBUG–ITEM	EXHIBIT statement	TRACE statement
Debug module	Load program	USE FOR
Debugging	Monitoring a field	DEBUGGING
Debugging lines	Monitoring a file	sentence
Debugging section	Monitoring a	
DECLARATIVES	procedure	

Program Compilation

For most COBOL programs three steps are involved in running a program. The first step is to compile (translate) the source program that was coded by the programmer into an object program (machine language). This process checks the grammar (**syntax**) of the program. The second step is the link edit process where the object program and any system programs necessary to execute this program are brought together into a **load program**. The third step, the execution of the load program, is only attempted if the first two steps are error free. In many computer centers, these steps in running a program are referred to as compile, link, and go.

When the computer attempts to compile and execute the program, a listing of the source program will be made along with other listings such as job control language statements, system messages, memory maps, dictionaries, and diagnostics. If an error occurs during compilation, one or more syntax errors have occurred. Usually on the last page of the output there will be a list of errors which will need to be debugged. If during execution, logic or data errors occur in the program, it is terminated. If the programmer requests it, a listing will be produced of the current contents of memory for debugging purposes. The program may successfully execute but the output may be different from what was expected. If so, usually logic or data errors have occurred. When a program is abnormally terminated it is typically referred to as an **ABEND**.

Types of Errors

There are many types of errors that can cause a program to ABEND or give incorrect results. The most common of these errors is called a **data exception**. This occurs when an attempt is made to use nonnumeric data in a numeric operation. An example would be when the input description of the data in the DATA division is different from the data being input. Sometimes when moving data from one location to another or doing arithmetic on two or more fields, the receiving field is shorter in length than the sending field. This results in an **overflow condition,** which will truncate the excess data positions in the receiving field. Other common errors occur when an attempt is made to execute an invalid operation (referred to as a **program interruption).** Some examples are:

- Attempting to READ or WRITE a file before it was opened or after it was closed.
- Attempting to divide a field by zero.
- Referring to a field in the input area after the AT END was executed.
- Attempting to STOP RUN before all the files are closed.
- Incorrectly using the ASSIGN clause.
- Missing job control statements for a file.

Error Correction

Desk Check

The programmer should try to spot and correct program errors before an attempt is made to execute the program. A technique used by many programmers is referred to as a **desk check**. Carefully go through the source code and look for such things as:

- Spelling of reserved words.
- Misuse of reserved words.
- Invalid or missing punctuation.
- PROCEDURE division, programmer-supplied names that have not previously been defined in the DATA division.

- Correcting spacing on a line where the correction leads to another spacing error.
- Statements out of order.
- Invalid duplication of programmer-supplied names.
- Obvious logic problems.

Although this is far from a complete list of things that may go wrong, they are common errors and occur often. It is worth the time to make these checks.

In addition to a desk check it is often necessary to have the system itself check for errors. All systems can detect syntactical errors in the program during compile attempts. These errors are flagged by various error messages, depending upon what vendor's hardware and operating system are being used. It would be prudent to consult a manual for the system being used to determine what these error messages mean.

Even though a program may have had all syntax errors removed, it can still have logic errors which could result in incorrect output when the program is executed. Various vendors provide COBOL statements to help the programmer examine a program and aid in detecting errors. Some of these statements are unique to a particular system, and others are standard COBOL statements. Several of these statements are discussed in this chapter.

The DISPLAY Statement

In developing or modifying a program the programmer may want to produce some output that will help in debugging the program. The DISPLAY statement is a simple way to do this. The general format is shown in Figure 4–1.

Figure 4–1   *The DISPLAY Statement*

The identifier(s) may be elementary or group items previously defined in the DATA division, or these identifiers may be literal(s). Any number of identifiers or literals can be used with each DISPLAY statement. Output from a DISPLAY statement normally prints on a device described by the system when the UPON clause is omitted. To do this printing, however, may require a job control statement for the program. The DISPLAY output can be printed and interspersed with other output from the program in the same report, printed separately after all other output in the same report, or printed separately on another device. This text shows examples with the results of the DISPLAY interspersed with other output from the program. After debugging has been completed the appropriate DISPLAY statements should be deleted from the program.

Program 4–1

```
000001 IDENTIFICATION DIVISION.
000002   PROGRAM-ID.  CHAP4.
000003*************************************************
000004* THE PROGRAM WILL INPUT DATA RECORDS, RE-ARRANGE *
000005* THE FIELDS, PRINT A LISTING OF THE RECORDS AND  *
000006* USE THE DISPLAY STATEMENT FOR DEBUGGING.        *
000007*************************************************
000008 ENVIRONMENT DIVISION.
000009 CONFIGURATION SECTION.
```

Program 4–1   *(continued)*

```
000010    SOURCE-COMPUTER.   NCR.
000011    OBJECT-COMPUTER.   NCR.
000012 INPUT-OUTPUT SECTION.
000013 FILE-CONTROL.
000014     SELECT EMPLOYEE-FILE    ASSIGN TO READER.
000015     SELECT EMPLOYEE-REPORT ASSIGN TO PRINTER.
000016*
000017 DATA DIVISION.
000018 FILE SECTION.
000019 FD   EMPLOYEE-FILE
000020     RECORD CONTAINS 50 CHARACTERS
000021     LABEL RECORDS ARE OMITTED.
000022 01   ER-EMPLOYEE-RECORD.
000023     05  ER-DATE.
000024         10  ER-DAY              PIC X(2).
000025         10  ER-MONTH            PIC X(2).
000026         10  ER-YEAR             PIC X(2).
000027     05  ER-SSN                  PIC X(9).
000028     05  FILLER                  PIC X(5).
000029     05  ER-NAME.
000030         10  ER-LAST             PIC X(10).
000031         10  ER-FIRST            PIC X(10).
000032     05  FILLER                  PIC X(5).
000033     05  ER-STORE                PIC 9(3).
000034     05  ER-STATE                PIC 9(2).
000035 FD   EMPLOYEE-REPORT
000036     RECORD CONTAINS 133 CHARACTERS
000037     LABEL RECORDS ARE OMITTED.
000038 01   PR-RECORD-OUT              PIC X(133).
000039*
000040 WORKING-STORAGE SECTION.
000041 01   WS-PROCESSING-INDICATORS.
000042     05  WS-END-OF-FILE-INDICATOR PIC X(3).
000043         88  END-OF-FILE         VALUE 'END'.
000044 01   DL-DETAIL-LINE.
000045     05  FILLER                  PIC X(1).
000046     05  FILLER                  PIC X(20).
000047     05  DL-DAY                  PIC X(2).
000048     05  FILLER                  PIC X(1).
000049     05  DL-MONTH                PIC X(2).
000050     05  FILLER                  PIC X(1).
000051     05  DL-YEAR                 PIC X(2).
000052     05  FILLER                  PIC X(7).
000053     05  DL-SSN                  PIC X(9).
000054     05  FILLER                  PIC X(11).
000055     05  DL-LAST                 PIC X(10).
000056     05  FILLER                  PIC X(2).
000057     05  DL-FIRST                PIC X(10).
000058     05  FILLER                  PIC X(10).
000059     05  DL-STORE                PIC 9(3).
000060     05  FILLER                  PIC X(7).
000061     05  DL-STATE                PIC 9(2).
000062     05  FILLER                  PIC X(33).
000063*
000064 PROCEDURE DIVISION.
000065 A000-EMPLOYEE-LISTING.
000066     OPEN INPUT EMPLOYEE-FILE
000067          OUTPUT EMPLOYEE-REPORT.
000068     DISPLAY 'VALUE OF WS-END-OF-FILE-INDICATOR: '
000069             WS-END-OF-FILE-INDICATOR.
000070     PERFORM B100-INITIALIZE-VARIABLES.
000071     PERFORM Z100-READ-EMPLOYEE-RECORD.
000072     PERFORM B300-PROCESS-RECORDS
```

Program 4–1 *(concluded)*

```
000073            UNTIL END-OF-FILE.
000074      CLOSE EMPLOYEE-FILE
000075            EMPLOYEE-REPORT.
000076      STOP RUN.
000077 B100-INITIALIZE-VARIABLES.
000078      MOVE SPACES TO WS-END-OF-FILE-INDICATOR.
000079      DISPLAY 'NEW VALUE OF WS-END-OF-FILE-INDICATOR: '
000080            WS-END-OF-FILE-INDICATOR.
000081      MOVE SPACES TO DL-DETAIL-LINE.
000082 B300-PROCESS-RECORDS.
000083      DISPLAY 'RECORD JUST INPUT IS: ' ER-EMPLOYEE-RECORD.
000084      PERFORM C100-CREATE-OUTPUT-RECORD.
000085      WRITE PR-RECORD-OUT
000086            AFTER ADVANCING 1 LINE.
000087      PERFORM Z100-READ-EMPLOYEE-RECORD.
000088 C100-CREATE-OUTPUT-RECORD.
000089      MOVE ER-DAY        TO DL-DAY.
000090      MOVE ER-MONTH      TO DL-MONTH.
000091      MOVE ER-YEAR       TO DL-YEAR.
000092      MOVE ER-SSN        TO DL-SSN.
000093      MOVE ER-LAST       TO DL-LAST.
000094      MOVE ER-FIRST      TO DL-FIRST.
000095      MOVE ER-STORE      TO DL-STORE.
000096      MOVE ER-STATE      TO DL-STATE.
000097      MOVE DL-DETAIL-LINE TO PR-RECORD-OUT.
000098 Z100-READ-EMPLOYEE-RECORD.
000099      READ EMPLOYEE-FILE
000100        AT END MOVE 'END' TO WS-END-OF-FILE-INDICATOR
000101            DISPLAY 'LAST VALUE OF WS-END-OF-FILE-INDICATOR: '
000102                WS-END-OF-FILE-INDICATOR.
```

DISPLAY statements have been placed at lines 68, 79, 83, and 101 in Program 4–1. These statements will output a message and the current contents of the WS–END–OF–FILE–INDICATOR each time the statement is executed, except for line 83. That statement will output the current contents of the record just input into the program. The data records in Figure 4–2 have been used as input to all of the programs in this chapter.

The first line of output in Figure 4–3 displays the contents of WS–END–OF–FILE–INDICATOR before any processing is done. Since this field has not yet been given a value by the program, undefined values (in this case * ^) reside there. Notice the second line of output displays spaces at this location because line 78 moved them there when it was executed. The execution of line 83 will display the record

Figure 4–2 *Input for Chapter Programs*

```
1-6    Date
7-15   Social security number
21-30  Last name
31-40  First name
46-48  Store number
49-50  State number


=================================================
251049654781264    SANTOS    ALFONSO    01540
160155275416280    MARKS     SUSAN      16522
010963411235112    LEE       NA-QUAN    09903
091260332678462    ZULOFF    ADOLF      11637
300651541936294    BROWN     LEROY      15017
=================================================
```

Figure 4–3   *Output from Program 4–1*

```
VALUE OF WS-END-OF-FILE-INDICATOR: ·^
NEW VALUE OF WS-END-OF-FILE-INDICATOR:
RECORD JUST INPUT IS: 251049654781264      SANTOS      ALFONSO      01540
                      25 10 49      654781264            SANTOS      ALFONSO      015      40
RECORD JUST INPUT IS: 160155275416280      MARKS       SUSAN        16522
                      16 01 55      275416280            MARKS       SUSAN        165      22
RECORD JUST INPUT IS: 010963411235112      LEE         NA-QUAN      09903
                      01 09 63      411235112            LEE         NA-QUAN      099      03
RECORD JUST INPUT IS: 091260332678462      ZULOFF      ADOLF        11637
                      09 12 60      332678462            ZULOFF      ADOLF        116      37
RECORD JUST INPUT IS: 300651541936294      BROWN       LEROY        15017
                      30 06 51      541936294            BROWN       LEROY        150      17
LAST VALUE OF WS-END-OF-FILE-INDICATOR: END
```

just input. This data can be checked against the next line of data written, which is the normal output from the program. Observe that all five records that were input are displayed first in the format of the ER–EMPLOYEE–RECORD and then by the format of the PR–RECORD–OUT. The last line is displayed when the AT END clause is true and END is moved to WS–END–OF–FILE–INDICATOR.

The EXHIBIT Statement

Some versions of COBOL allow for the use of the **EXHIBIT statement** whose format is given in Figure 4–4.

Figure 4–4   *The EXHIBIT Statement*

EXHIBIT NAMED prints out the name of the data item and its value whenever the statement is executed. EXHIBIT CHANGED NAMED will print the data item's name and value only if the value of the data item has changed since a previous execution of the statement. If no change has taken place, the contents of the data item are not printed. EXHIBIT CHANGED is just like EXHIBIT CHANGED NAMED, except the name of the data item is never printed. Each execution of an EXHIBIT statement causes the printer to begin a new line. Again, many systems require the use of a job control statement when using the EXHIBIT. EXHIBIT statements should be deleted from the program after debugging is completed.

Program 4–2 is a partial copy of Program 4–1 omitting the DISPLAY statements and replacing them with EXHIBIT statements.

The statement EXHIBIT CHANGED NAMED WS–END–OF–FILE–INDICATOR has been placed at line 68, 78, and 99; and EXHIBIT NAMED RD–RECORD–OUT, at line 81. Notice in Figure 4–5 that the output format is very much like that for the DISPLAY statement. The format for output with the EXHIBIT is: programmer-supplied name = data-value.

When WS–END–OF–FILE–INDICATOR is exhibited for the first time in Figure 4–5, the value of the field is undefined (notice the @A). The second time it has the value spaces, which is what it should have contained because of the MOVE SPACES at line 77. At line 98, when AT END is a true condition, END is moved into the field and is exhibited in the last line of output. Since the data changes in WS–END–OF–FILE–INDICATOR each time an EXHIBIT statement is executed at

Program 4–2

```
000001 IDENTIFICATION DIVISION.
000002   PROGRAM-ID.  CHAP4.
000003************************************************
000004* THE PROGRAM WILL INPUT DATA RECORDS, RE-ARRANGE *
000005* THE FIELDS, PRINT A LISTING OF THE RECORDS AND  *
000006* USE THE EXHIBIT STATEMENT FOR DEBUGGING.        *
000007************************************************
            .
            .
            .
000063*
000064 PROCEDURE DIVISION.
000065 A000-EMPLOYEE-LISTING.
000066     OPEN INPUT EMPLOYEE-FILE
000067          OUTPUT EMPLOYEE-REPORT.
000068     EXHIBIT CHANGED NAMED WS-END-OF-FILE-INDICATOR.
000069     PERFORM B100-INITIALIZE-VARIABLES.
000070     PERFORM Z100-READ-EMPLOYEE-RECORD.
000071     PERFORM B300-PROCESS-RECORDS
000072          UNTIL END-OF-FILE.
000073     CLOSE EMPLOYEE-FILE
000074          EMPLOYEE-REPORT.
000075     STOP RUN.
000076 B100-INITIALIZE-VARIABLES.
000077     MOVE SPACES TO WS-END-OF-FILE-INDICATOR.
000078     EXHIBIT CHANGED NAMED WS-END-OF-FILE-INDICATOR.
000079     MOVE SPACES TO DL-DETAIL-LINE.
000080 B300-PROCESS-RECORDS.
000081     EXHIBIT NAMED ER-EMPLOYEE-RECORD.
000082     PERFORM C100-CREATE-OUTPUT-RECORD.
000083     WRITE PR-RECORD-OUT
000084          AFTER ADVANCING 1 LINE.
000085     PERFORM Z100-READ-EMPLOYEE-RECORD.
000086 C100-CREATE-OUTPUT-RECORD.
000087     MOVE ER-DAY      TO DL-DAY.
000088     MOVE ER-MONTH    TO DL-MONTH.
000089     MOVE ER-YEAR     TO DL-YEAR.
000090     MOVE ER-SSN      TO DL-SSN.
000091     MOVE ER-LAST     TO DL-LAST.
000092     MOVE ER-FIRST    TO DL-FIRST.
000093     MOVE ER-STORE    TO DL-STORE.
000094     MOVE ER-STATE    TO DL-STATE.
000095     MOVE DL-DETAIL-LINE TO PR-RECORD-OUT.
000096 Z100-READ-EMPLOYEE-RECORD.
000097     READ EMPLOYEE-FILE
000098          AT END MOVE 'END' TO WS-END-OF-FILE-INDICATOR
000099               EXHIBIT CHANGED NAMED WS-END-OF-FILE-INDICATOR.
```

Figure 4–5 *Output from Program 4–2*

```
WS-END-OF-FILE-INDICATOR = @A
WS-END-OF-FILE-INDICATOR =
ER-EMPLOYEE-RECORD = 251049654781264    SANTOS   ALFONSO    01540
                     25 10 49    654781264      SANTOS     ALFONSO     015    40
ER-EMPLOYEE-RECORD = 160155275416280    MARKS    SUSAN      16522
                     16 01 55    275416280      MARKS      SUSAN       165    22
ER-EMPLOYEE-RECORD = 010963411235112    LEE      NA-QUAN    09903
                     01 09 63    411235112      LEE        NA-QUAN     099    03
ER-EMPLOYEE-RECORD = 091260332678462    ZULOFF   ADOLF      11637
                     09 12 60    332678462      ZULOFF     ADOLF       116    37
ER-EMPLOYEE-RECORD = 300651541936294    BROWN    LEROY      15017
                     30 06 51    541936294      BROWN      LEROY       150    17
WS-END-OF-FILE-INDICATOR = END
```

lines 68, 78, and 99, the data-item's name and value are always exhibited in this program. At line 81 the input record is always exhibited, followed by the actual data record to be output by the program.

The TRACE Statement

Another debugging statement used by some systems is the **TRACE statement.** Its format is shown in Figure 4–6.

Figure 4–6 *The TRACE Statement*

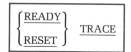

Program 4–3

```
000001 IDENTIFICATION DIVISION.
000002   PROGRAM-ID.  CHAP4.
000003***************************************************
000004* THE PROGRAM WILL INPUT DATA RECORDS, RE-ARRANGE *
000005* THE FIELDS, PRINT A LISTING OF THE RECORDS AND  *
000006* USE THE TRACE STATEMENT FOR DEBUGGING.          *
000007***************************************************
           .
           .
000063*
000064 PROCEDURE DIVISION.
000065 A000-EMPLOYEE-LISTING.
000066     READY TRACE.
000067     OPEN INPUT EMPLOYEE-FILE
000068          OUTPUT EMPLOYEE-REPORT.
000069     PERFORM B100-INITIALIZE-VARIABLES.
000070     PERFORM Z100-READ-EMPLOYEE-RECORD.
000071     PERFORM B300-PROCESS-RECORDS
000072          UNTIL END-OF-FILE.
000073     CLOSE EMPLOYEE-FILE
000074          EMPLOYEE-REPORT.
000075     STOP RUN.
000076 B100-INITIALIZE-VARIABLES.
000077     MOVE SPACES TO WS-END-OF-FILE-INDICATOR.
000078     MOVE SPACES TO DL-DETAIL-LINE.
000079 B300-PROCESS-RECORDS.
000080     PERFORM C100-CREATE-OUTPUT-RECORD.
000081     WRITE PR-RECORD-OUT
000082          AFTER ADVANCING 1 LINE.
000083     PERFORM Z100-READ-EMPLOYEE-RECORD.
000084 C100-CREATE-OUTPUT-RECORD.
000085     MOVE ER-DAY        TO DL-DAY.
000086     MOVE ER-MONTH      TO DL-MONTH.
000087     MOVE ER-YEAR       TO DL-YEAR.
000088     MOVE ER-SSN        TO DL-SSN.
000089     MOVE ER-LAST       TO DL-LAST.
000090     MOVE ER-FIRST      TO DL-FIRST.
000091     MOVE ER-STORE      TO DL-STORE.
000092     MOVE ER-STATE      TO DL-STATE.
000093     MOVE DL-DETAIL-LINE TO PR-RECORD-OUT.
000094 Z100-READ-EMPLOYEE-RECORD.
000095     READ EMPLOYEE-FILE
000096          AT END MOVE 'END' TO WS-END-OF-FILE-INDICATOR.
```

The TRACE statement can be used to determine the flow of control during the execution of procedures in a program. To initialize the statement, enter READY TRACE at the point in the PROCEDURE division where the trace is to begin. When this statement is encountered, each procedure named to which control is transferred as the program is being executed is listed on the output. A programmer can use just one READY TRACE to print the complete flow of control throughout the program or to select only certain segments of the program for observation. Enter RESET TRACE at any point in the program where the TRACE is to stop. Like the EXHIBIT, a job control statement is sometimes necessary to use the TRACE statement. Always delete all READY TRACE and RESET TRACE statements at the completion of debugging a program.

Program 4–3 is a copy of Program 4–2 where the EXHIBIT statements have been deleted and a READY TRACE statement included at line 66.

Figure 4–7   *Output from Program 4–3*

```
B100-INITIALIZE-VARIABLES
Z100-READ-EMPLOYEE-RECORD
B300-PROCESS-RECORDS
C100-CREATE-OUTPUT-RECORD
                25 10 49     654781264    SANTOS    ALFONSO    015    40
Z100-READ-EMPLOYEE-RECORD
B300-PROCESS-RECORDS
C100-CREATE-OUTPUT-RECORD
                16 01 55     275416280    MARKS     SUSAN      165    22
Z100-READ-EMPLOYEE-RECORD
B300-PROCESS-RECORDS
C100-CREATE-OUTPUT-RECORD
                01 09 63     411235112    LEE       NA-QUAN    099    03
Z100-READ-EMPLOYEE-RECORD
B300-PROCESS-RECORDS
C100-CREATE-OUTPUT-RECORD
                09 12 60     332678462    ZULOFF    ADOLF      116    37
Z100-READ-EMPLOYEE-RECORD
B300-PROCESS-RECORDS
C100-CREATE-OUTPUT-RECORD
                30 06 51     541936294    BROWN     LEROY      150    17
Z100-READ-EMPLOYEE-RECORD
```

Notice the flow of control throughout the execution of the program. Procedures B100, Z100, and B300 are executed at lines 69, 70, and 71. While in procedure B300–PROCESS–RECORDS (starting at line 79), procedure C100 is executed, a data record is output, and Z100 is executed. B300–PROCESS–RECORDS will continue to execute until the end of the data file is reached. So the cycle (B300, C100, output data record, Z100) is executed until the AT END at line 96 is a true condition. This occurs the sixth time Z100 is executed. Since there were no errors to alter or ABEND the execution of the program, the flow of control is what was expected from the logic of the program.

The Debugging Module

Standard COBOL provides another method of debugging programs by the use of the **debug module.** It provides two different types of debugging aids: **debugging lines** and **debugging sections.**

Debugging Lines

The basic components of COBOL used in the debugging lines option of the debug module are:

- A compile time switch when using the WITH DEBUGGING MODE clause.
- An object time switch.
- The debugging lines component.

When using debugging lines all of the lines of program code to be used for debugging must have a **D** in column 7. The D indicates that these lines are not part of the normal program but are lines to be used for debugging only. If a debugging statement uses more than one line, each line must have a D in column 7. Debugging lines may be written anywhere after the OBJECT–COMPUTER paragraph.

The WITH DEBUGGING MODE Clause

The general format for the WITH DEBUGGING MODE clause is shown in Figure 4–8.

Figure 4–8   *The WITH DEBUGGING MODE Clause*

```
SOURCE-COMPUTER.
    Computer-name [WITH DEBUGGING MODE].
```

When this clause is omitted from the program during a program compilation the compile time switch is left off, and all lines in the program that have a D in column 7 (called debug lines) are treated as comments. They will not have any effect on the program. When the clause is included as part of the SOURCE–COM PUTER paragraph the compile time switch is turned on by the system, and all of the debug lines are compiled as regular statements.

The object time switch is activated by the system, not by a COBOL statement. During the execution of a program when the WITH DEBUGGING MODE clause has been compiled, the object time switch is turned on, and all of the debug lines are executed along with the program. If the WITH DEBUGGING MODE clause is not compiled with the program, both the compile time and object time switches are left off by the system, and the debug lines are ignored as the program is executed.

The advantage of using these debug lines is that they assist in analyzing data values and operations during execution of a program. After the program has been debugged, these lines can stay in the program permanently and can be changed into comment lines by removing the WITH DEBUGGING MODE clause. When some future change is made to the program, the debug lines are already in the program and can be activated simply.

Although this advantage is useful in some situations, the debugging lines left in the program may cause the program to become difficult to read. In addition, future program changes may warrant the use of debugging lines different from the lines in the initial program. Making these changes can be a laborious task. (The use of debugging sections eliminates this potential problem.)

Program 4–4 is a copy of Program 4–3 and illustrates the use of the debug lines feature.

The TRACE, EXHIBIT, and DISPLAY statements for debugging have been added to illustrate the many options available to the programmer. The D in column 7 makes use of the debug line feature. The WITH DEBUGGING MODE clause at line 12 activates the compile time switch during compilation and the object time switch during execution. The READY TRACE at line 68, EXHIBIT at lines 71, 81, and 102, and the DISPLAY at line 84 will all be executed and used for debugging.

In Figure 4–9 the entire flow of control for the program is listed along with the output for each EXHIBIT and DISPLAY statement and the normal output from the program. The line number of the program that causes each line of output has been added by the authors to the left of each printed line for ease in following the interpretation of the output. These lines, of course, would not normally be a part of this output.

Program 4–4

```
000001 IDENTIFICATION DIVISION.
000002  PROGRAM-ID.  CHAP4.
000003********************************************************
000004* THE PROGRAM WILL INPUT DATA RECORDS, RE-ARRANGE *
000005* THE FIELDS, PRINT A LISTING OF THE RECORDS AND  *
000006* USE THE DEBUG LINES FEATURE ALONG WITH THE      *
000007* DISPLAY, EXHIBIT AND TRACE STATEMENTS FOR       *
000008* DEBUGGING.                                      *
000009********************************************************
000010 ENVIRONMENT DIVISION.
000011 CONFIGURATION SECTION.
000012  SOURCE-COMPUTER.  HP WITH DEBUGGING MODE.
000013  OBJECT-COMPUTER.  HP.
           .
           .
000065*
000066 PROCEDURE DIVISION.
000067 A000-EMPLOYEE-LISTING.
000068D    READY TRACE.
000069     OPEN INPUT EMPLOYEE-FILE
000070          OUTPUT EMPLOYEE-REPORT.
000071D    EXHIBIT CHANGED NAMED WS-END-OF-FILE-INDICATOR.
000072     PERFORM B100-INITIALIZE-VARIABLES.
000073     PERFORM Z100-READ-EMPLOYEE-RECORD.
000074     PERFORM B300-PROCESS-RECORDS
000075          UNTIL END-OF-FILE.
000076     CLOSE EMPLOYEE-FILE
000077           EMPLOYEE-REPORT.
000078     STOP RUN.
000079 B100-INITIALIZE-VARIABLES.
000080     MOVE SPACES TO WS-END-OF-FILE-INDICATOR.
000081D    EXHIBIT CHANGED-NAMED WS-END-OF-FILE-INDICATOR.
000082     MOVE SPACES TO DL-DETAIL-LINE.
000083 B300-PROCESS-RECORDS.
000084D    DISPLAY 'RECORD JUST INPUT IS: ' ER-EMPLOYEE-RECORD.
000085     PERFORM C100-CREATE-OUTPUT-RECORD.
000086     WRITE PR-RECORD-OUT
000087          AFTER ADVANCING 1 LINE.
000088     PERFORM Z100-READ-EMPLOYEE-RECORD.
000089 C100-CREATE-OUTPUT-RECORD.
000090     MOVE ER-DAY        TO DL-DAY.
000091     MOVE ER-MONTH      TO DL-MONTH.
000092     MOVE ER-YEAR       TO DL-YEAR.
000093     MOVE ER-SSN        TO DL-SSN.
000094     MOVE ER-LAST       TO DL-LAST.
000095     MOVE ER-FIRST      TO DL-FIRST.
000096     MOVE ER-STORE      TO DL-STORE.
000097     MOVE ER-STATE      TO DL-STATE.
000098     MOVE DL-DETAIL-LINE TO PR-RECORD-OUT.
000099 Z100-READ-EMPLOYEE-RECORD.
000100     READ EMPLOYEE-FILE
000101          AT END MOVE 'END' TO WS-END-OF-FILE-INDICATOR
000102D           EXHIBIT CHANGED NAMED WS-END-OF-FILE-INDICATOR.
```

If the WITH DEBUGGING MODE clause is deleted from the program so that all of the D lines are deactivated, the normal output from executing the program will be as shown in Figure 4–10.

Program 4–5 is a copy of Program 4–4 with the D statements deleted. Line 85 was added to single space between output lines at this point in the program. The DISPLAY statement has no means of vertically controlling the carriage on the printer. The remaining DISPLAY statements added at lines 90, 94, and 96 are to compare

Figure 4–9   *Output from Program 4–4*

```
Statement
number      Actual output

  71      WS-END-OF-FILE-INDICATOR = 00
  72      B100-INITIALIZE-VARIABLES
  81      WS-END-OF-FILE-INDICATOR =
  73      Z100-READ-EMPLOYEE-RECORD
  74      B300-PROCESS-RECORDS
  84      RECORD JUST INPUT IS: 251049654781264    SANTOS    ALFONSO    01540
  85      C100-CREATE-OUTPUT-RECORD
  86                    25 10 49      654781264         SANTOS    ALFONSO    015    40
  88      Z100-READ-EMPLOYEE-RECORD
  74      B300-PROCESS-RECORDS
  84      RECORD JUST INPUT IS: 160155275416280    MARKS     SUSAN      16522
  85      C100-CREATE-OUTPUT-RECORD
  86                    16 01 55      275416280         MARKS     SUSAN      165    22
  88      Z100-READ-EMPLOYEE-RECORD
  74      B300-PROCESS-RECORDS
  84      RECORD JUST INPUT IS: 010963411235112    LEE       NA-QUAN    09903
  85      C100-CREATE-OUTPUT-RECORD
  86                    01 09 63      411235112         LEE       NA-QUAN    099    03
  88      Z100-READ-EMPLOYEE-RECORD
  74      B300-PROCESS-RECORDS
  84      RECORD JUST INPUT IS: 091260332678462    ZULOFF    ADOLF      11637
  85      C100-CREATE-OUTPUT-RECORD
  86                    09 12 60      332678462         ZULOFF    ADOLF      116    37
  88      Z100-READ-EMPLOYEE-RECORD
  74      B300-PROCESS-RECORDS
  84      RECORD JUST INPUT IS: 300651541936294    BROWN     LEROY      15017
  85      C100-CREATE-OUTPUT-RECORD
  86                    30 06 51      541936294         BROWN     LEROY      150    17
  88      Z100-READ-EMPLOYEE-RECORD
 102      WS-END-OF-FILE-INDICATOR = END
```

Figure 4–10   *Normal Output from Program without the WITH DEBUGGING Clause*

```
25 10 49     654781264     SANTOS    ALFONSO    015    40
16 01 55     275416280     MARKS     SUSAN      165    22
01 09 63     411235112     LEE       NA-QUAN    099    03
09 12 60     332678462     ZULOFF    ADOLF      116    37
30 06 51     541936294     BROWN     LEROY      150    17
```

a field input into the program to the field that will eventually be output. When the program logic is correct these values will be the same.

In Figure 4–11 the output has a line of spaces between each group of four lines displayed. The fields ER–SSN, DL–SSN, ER–STORE, DL–STORE, ER–STATE and DL–STATE are displayed in the first three lines of each group. These values are to verify that the input and output fields contain the same data. The fourth line in each group is the normal output of the program.

The Debugging Section

The compile time and object time switches are also used with the debugging section feature of the debug module. When the WITH DEBUGGING MODE is specified, all debugging sections are compiled and executed as specified by the program. If

Program 4–5

```
000001 IDENTIFICATION DIVISION.
000002   PROGRAM-ID.  CHAP4.
000003*************************************************
000004* THE PROGRAM WILL INPUT DATA RECORDS, RE-ARRANGE *
000005* THE FIELDS, PRINT A LISTING OF THE RECORDS AND   *
000006* USE THE DISPLAY STATEMENT WITH THE DEBUG LINE    *
000007* FEATURE.                                         *
000008*************************************************
000009 ENVIRONMENT DIVISION.
000010 CONFIGURATION SECTION.
000011   SOURCE-COMPUTER.  NCR WITH DEBUGGING MODE.
000012   OBJECT-COMPUTER.  NCR.
             .
             .
             .
000064*
000065 PROCEDURE DIVISION.
000066 A000-EMPLOYEE-LISTING.
000067     OPEN INPUT EMPLOYEE-FILE
000068          OUTPUT EMPLOYEE-REPORT.
000069     PERFORM B100-INITIALIZE-VARIABLES.
000070     PERFORM Z100-READ-EMPLOYEE-RECORD.
000071     PERFORM B300-PROCESS-RECORDS
000072          UNTIL END-OF-FILE.
000073     CLOSE EMPLOYEE-FILE
000074           EMPLOYEE-REPORT.
000075     STOP RUN.
000076 B100-INITIALIZE-VARIABLES.
000077     MOVE SPACES TO WS-END-OF-FILE-INDICATOR.
000078     MOVE SPACES TO DL-DETAIL-LINE.
000079 B300-PROCESS-RECORDS.
000080     PERFORM C100-CREATE-OUTPUT-RECORD.
000081     WRITE PR-RECORD-OUT
000082          AFTER ADVANCING 1 LINE.
000083     PERFORM Z100-READ-EMPLOYEE-RECORD.
000084 C100-CREATE-OUTPUT-RECORD.
000085D    DISPLAY SPACES.
000086     MOVE ER-DAY        TO DL-DAY.
000087     MOVE ER-MONTH      TO DL-MONTH.
000088     MOVE ER-YEAR       TO DL-YEAR.
000089     MOVE ER-SSN        TO DL-SSN.
000090D    DISPLAY 'ER-SSN ' ER-SSN ' DL-SSN ' DL-SSN.
000091     MOVE ER-LAST       TO DL-LAST.
000092     MOVE ER-FIRST      TO DL-FIRST.
000093     MOVE ER-STORE      TO DL-STORE.
000094D    DISPLAY 'ER-STORE ' ER-STORE ' DL-STORE ' DL-STORE.
000095     MOVE ER-STATE      TO DL-STATE.
000096D    DISPLAY 'ER-STATE ' ER-STATE ' DL-STATE ' DL-STATE.
000097     MOVE DL-DETAIL-LINE TO PR-RECORD-OUT.
000098 Z100-READ-EMPLOYEE-RECORD.
000099     READ EMPLOYEE-FILE
000100          AT END MOVE 'END' TO WS-END-OF-FILE-INDICATOR.
```

the clause is omitted, debugging sections are treated as documentation. Both debugging sections and debugging lines can be used in the same program. The debugging section does not require that position 7 of the record contain a D, although it may be more efficient to do so when both sections and lines are to be deactivated.

When debugging sections are used, all such sections must be written together at the beginning of the program. The reserved word **DECLARATIVES** followed by a period on a line by itself indicates that the debugging sections are to follow. The reserved words **END DECLARATIVES** followed by a period on a line by itself indicates the end of the debugging sections.

Figure 4–11   *Output from Program 4–5*

```
ER-SSN  654781264  DL-SSN  654781264
ER-STORE  015  DL-STORE  015
ER-STATE  40  DL-STATE  40
                    25 10 49        654781264     SANTOS    ALFONSO    015   40

ER-SSN  275416280  DL-SSN  275416280
ER-STORE  165  DL-STORE  165
ER-STATE  22  DL-STATE  22
                    16 01 55        275416280     MARKS     SUSAN      165   22

ER-SSN  411235112  DL-SSN  411235112
ER-STORE  099  DL-STORE  099
ER-STATE  03  DL-STATE  03
                    01 09 63        411235112     LEE       NA-QUAN    099   03

ER-SSN  332678462  DL-SSN  332678462
ER-STORE  116  DL-STORE  116
ER-STATE  37  DL-STATE  37
                    09 12 60        332678462     ZULOFF    ADOLF      116   37

ER-SSN  541936294  DL-SSN  541936294
ER-STORE  150  DL-STORE  150
ER-STATE  17  DL-STATE  17
                    30 06 51        541936294     BROWN     LEROY      150   17
```

The USE FOR DEBUGGING Sentence

The **USE FOR DEBUGGING sentence** must be used for each section in the declaratives portion of the program to identify all of the items in the program that are to be monitored by the debugging section. The general format for this sentence is given in Figure 4–12.

Figure 4–12   *The USE FOR DEBUGGING Sentence*

```
Programmer-supplied-section-name SECTION.
    USE FOR DEBUGGING ON

        ⎧ cd-name-1                        ⎫
        ⎪ [ALL REFERENCES OF] identifier-1 ⎪
        ⎨ identifier-2                      ⎬
        ⎪ ALL PROCEDURES                   ⎪
        ⎪ procedure-name-1                 ⎪
        ⎩ file-name-1                      ⎭

        ⎡ cd-name-2                        ⎤
        ⎢ [ALL REFERENCES OF] identifier-3 ⎥
        ⎢ identifier-4                     ⎥ . . .
        ⎢ procedure-name-2                 ⎥
        ⎣ file-name-2                      ⎦
```

Rules for the use of the USE FOR DEBUGGING sentence are:

- Programmer-supplied names in one USE statement cannot be used in another USE statement or in any other way in the debugging section.
- There may be any number of debugging sections in a program each with its own USE statement.
- Paragraphs in one section can be referenced in another section by the use of a PERFORM.
- Procedures in the nondeclarative portion of the program cannot contain statements that refer to any procedures within the declarative portion.

■ Programmer-supplied names that contain an OCCURS clause or that are subordinate to an OCCURS clause can only be specified in a USE statement without a subscript or index.

Some examples of violations of these rules are shown in Figure 4–13.

Figure 4–13 *Invalid Examples of USE FOR DEBUGGING Rules*

```
Example A:

PROCEDURE DIVISION.
DECLARATIVES.
USING-DEBUG-1 SECTION.
        USE FOR DEBUGGING ON
            TOTAL-1  TOTAL-2
        ALL PROCEDURES
X100-DEBUG.
    PERFORM B300-PROCESS.
    DISPLAY TOTAL-1.
END DECLARATIVES.


Example B:


    05  RATE-TABLE          PIC 99V99
                            OCCURS 10 TIMES
                            INDEXED BY RATE-INDEX.




PROCEDURE DIVISION.
DECLARATIVES.
USING-DEBUG-1 SECTION.
        USE FOR DEBUGGING ON
            RATE-TABLE
            EMPLOYEE-FILE.
X100-DEBUG.
    DISPLAY SPACES.
    DISPLAY . . . .
USING-DEBUG-2 SECTION.
        USE FOR DEBUGGING ON
            ALL PROCEDURES.
X200-DEBUG.
    DISPLAY . . . .
USING-DEBUG-3 SECTION.
    USE FOR DEBUGGING ON
    EMPLOYEE-FILE.
X300-DEBUG.
    PERFORM X100-DEBUG.
END DECLARATIVES.
```

Example A of Figure 4–13 is an illustration of using one section and one paragraph within that section. Only one USE statement is required. The debugging section is started with the word DECLARATIVES and ended with the phrase END DECLARATIVES. There are two errors in this example. The name TOTAL–1 is permissible in the USE sentence, but since it is a name used in the nondeclarative portion of the program, it is an error to use it anywhere else in the debugging section. B300–PROCESS is another name that is invalid because it is not the name of a paragraph within the declaratives portion of the paragraph.

Example B has multiple sections and multiple paragraphs within a section. PERFORM X100–DEBUG is valid because, although X100–DEBUG is in another section, it is contained in the declarative portion. Notice that RATE–TABLE has been defined as a table. Therefore, when used in a USE sentence, it cannot contain a subscript or an index. EMPLOYEE–FILE can only be used once in a particular USE statement. In this example it is invalid, since it appears twice. Since ALL PROCEDURES is used in a USE statement, it automatically monitors all procedures. Therefore, no procedure can be specified by its name. That would result in an error because it would be considered a duplication of names.

The DEBUG–ITEM Special Register

Whenever one or more debugging sections are used, a program COBOL establishes a special register called a **DEBUG–ITEM.** This register provides information about the conditions causing the execution of debugging sections. The format for this register is given in Figure 4–14.

Figure 4–14   *Format for the DEBUG-ITEM Special Register*

```
01    DEBUG-ITEM.
      05    DEBUG-LINE       PICTURE IS X(6).
      05    FILLER           PICTURE IS X VALUE IS SPACE.
      05    DEBUG-NAME       PICTURE IS X(30).
      05    FILLER           PICTURE IS X VALUE IS SPACE.
      05    DEBUG-SUB-1      PICTURE IS S9999
                            SIGN IS LEADING SEPARATE CHARACTER.
      05    FILLER           PICTURE IS X VALUE IS SPACE.
      05    DEBUG-SUB-2      PICTURE IS S9999
                            SIGN IS LEADING SEPARATE CHARACTER.
      05    FILLER           PICTURE IS X VALUE IS SPACE.
      05    DEBUG-SUB-3      PICTURE IS S9999
                            SIGN IS LEADING SEPARATE CHARACTER.
      05    FILLER           PICTURE IS X VALUE IS SPACE.
      05    DEBUG-CONTENTS   PICTURE IS X(n).
```

Rules for the use of DEBUG–ITEM are:

- The special register DEBUG–ITEM is defined by COBOL for use only in the debugging section of a program.
- Only one special register DEBUG–ITEM is defined regardless of the number of debug sections in the program.
- Data are assigned to the fields in this register everytime the programmer-supplied name in the USE statement is encountered in the nondeclarative portion of the program.
- It is up to the programmer to use the data in the various fields of the register, as necessary, in the debugging sections. All of the names in the special register are reserved words and can be used by the programmer.
- The size of DEBUG–CONTENTS is adjusted by COBOL to fit the size of the data it receives.
- The special register DEBUG–ITEM will not appear in a program listing.
- An SD file cannot be monitored.

Monitoring a File

The process of **monitoring a file** is activated when the file name in a USE statement is encountered in a statement in the nondeclarative portion of the program. At that time the statement is executed and data are assigned to the DEBUG–ITEM as follows:

1. The sequence number of the COBOL statement is assigned to DEBUG–LINE.
2. The name of the file is assigned to DEBUG–NAME.
3. The contents of the input record are assigned to DEBUG–CONTENTS if the executed statement is a READ. Otherwise, spaces are assigned.
4. The remaining fields are all assigned spaces.

The declarative portion of the program is then executed causing the file to be monitored and control to be transferred back to the next statement in the program.

If the statement executed is a READ with an end-of-file or INVALID KEY condition, no debugging takes place, and the program continues as normal. Program 4–6 is an example of this process.

Program 4–6

```
000010 IDENTIFICATION DIVISION.
000020   PROGRAM-ID.  CHAP4.
000030*****************************************************************
000040* PROGRAM EXAMPLE 4-6 USING THE DEBUG SECTION TO MONITOR A FILE  *
000050*****************************************************************
000060 ENVIRONMENT DIVISION.
000070 CONFIGURATION SECTION.
000080   SOURCE-COMPUTER.  IBM WITH DEBUGGING MODE.
000090   OBJECT-COMPUTER.  IBM.
000100 INPUT-OUTPUT SECTION.
000110 FILE-CONTROL.
000120     SELECT EMPLOYEE-FILE   ASSIGN TO UT-S-EMPLOY.
000130     SELECT EMPLOYEE-REPORT ASSIGN TO UT-S-PRINTER.
000140*
000150 DATA DIVISION.
000160 FILE SECTION.
000170 FD  EMPLOYEE-FILE
000180     RECORD CONTAINS 50 CHARACTERS
000190     LABEL RECORDS ARE STANDARD.
000200 01  ER-EMPLOYEE-RECORD.
000210     05  ER-DATE.
000220         10  ER-DAY            PIC X(2).
000230         10  ER-MONTH          PIC X(2).
000240         10  ER-YEAR           PIC X(2).
000250     05  ER-SSN                PIC X(9).
000260     05  FILLER                PIC X(5).
000270     05  ER-NAME.
000280         10  ER-LAST           PIC X(10).
000290         10  ER-FIRST          PIC X(10).
000300     05  FILLER                PIC X(5).
000310     05  ER-STORE              PIC 9(3).
000320     05  ER-STATE              PIC 9(2).
000330 FD  EMPLOYEE-REPORT
000340     RECORD CONTAINS 132 CHARACTERS
000350     LABEL RECORDS ARE OMITTED.
000360 01  PR-RECORD-OUT             PIC X(132).
000370*
000380 WORKING-STORAGE SECTION.
000390 01  WS-PROCESSING-INDICATORS.
000400     05  WS-END-OF-FILE-INDICATOR PIC X(3).
000410         88  END-OF-FILE          VALUE 'END'.
000420 01  DL-DETAIL-LINE.
000430     05  FILLER                PIC X(20).
000440     05  DL-DAY                PIC X(2).
000450     05  FILLER                PIC X(1).
000460     05  DL-MONTH              PIC X(2).
000470     05  FILLER                PIC X(1).
000480     05  DL-YEAR               PIC X(2).
000490     05  FILLER                PIC X(7).
000500     05  DL-SSN                PIC X(9).
000510     05  FILLER                PIC X(11).
000520     05  DL-LAST               PIC X(10).
000530     05  FILLER                PIC X(2).
000540     05  DL-FIRST              PIC X(10).
000550     05  FILLER                PIC X(10).
000560     05  DL-STORE              PIC 9(3).
```

Program 4–6   *(concluded)*

```
000570      05  FILLER                  PIC X(7).
000580      05  DL-STATE                PIC 9(2).
000590*
000600 PROCEDURE DIVISION.
000610 DECLARATIVES.
000620 USING-DEBUG-1 SECTION.
000630     USE FOR DEBUGGING ON  EMPLOYEE-FILE.
000640 X100-DEBUG.
000650     DISPLAY SPACES.
000660     DISPLAY 'DEBUG-LINE IS '      DEBUG-LINE
000670             ' INPUT-RECORD IS ' DEBUG-CONTENTS.
000680 END DECLARATIVES.
000690 A000-EMPLOYEE-LISTING SECTION.
000700     OPEN INPUT EMPLOYEE-FILE
000710          OUTPUT EMPLOYEE-REPORT.
000720     PERFORM B100-INITIALIZE-VARIABLES.
000730     PERFORM Z100-READ-EMPLOYEE-RECORD.
000740     PERFORM B300-PROCESS-RECORDS
000750          UNTIL END-OF-FILE.
000760     CLOSE EMPLOYEE-FILE
000770           EMPLOYEE-REPORT.
000780     STOP RUN.
000790 B100-INITIALIZE-VARIABLES.
000800     MOVE SPACES TO WS-END-OF-FILE-INDICATOR.
000810     MOVE SPACES TO DL-DETAIL-LINE.
000820 B300-PROCESS-RECORDS.
000830     PERFORM C100-CREATE-OUTPUT-RECORD.
000840     WRITE PR-RECORD-OUT
000850          AFTER 1.
000860     PERFORM Z100-READ-EMPLOYEE-RECORD.
000870 C100-CREATE-OUTPUT-RECORD.
000880     MOVE ER-DAY       TO DL-DAY.
000890     MOVE ER-MONTH     TO DL-MONTH.
000900     MOVE ER-YEAR      TO DL-YEAR.
000910     MOVE ER-SSN       TO DL-SSN.
000920     MOVE ER-LAST      TO DL-LAST.
000930     MOVE ER-FIRST     TO DL-FIRST.
000940     MOVE ER-STORE     TO DL-STORE.
000950     MOVE ER-STATE     TO DL-STATE.
000960     MOVE DL-DETAIL-LINE TO PR-RECORD-OUT.
000970 Z100-READ-EMPLOYEE-RECORD.
000980     READ EMPLOYEE-FILE
000990          AT END MOVE 'END' TO WS-END-OF-FILE-INDICATOR.
```

The declarative portion of the Program 4–6 is specified from line 610 through line 680. The file name EMPLOYEE–FILE is to be monitored. The OPEN statement at line 700 is the first encounter of the file being monitored. The name EMPLOYEE–FILE causes the declarative portion of the program to be activated and lines 650, 660, and 670 are executed. Control is then transferred back to line 710.

Line 730 causes line 980 to be executed, which in turn activates the declarative portion of the program. Lines 650, 660, and 670 are executed, and control is returned to line 740. Since this was a READ and it did not have an end-of-file or INVALID KEY condition, the contents of the record were moved to DEBUG–CONTENTS and displayed. The WRITE at line 840 displays the contents of PR–RECORD–OUT as normal. Looping continues in the program until an at end-of-file condition occurs. This causes the debugging to be omitted and control is transferred to line 760. The CLOSE statement activates the declarative portion for the last time and the program is terminated.

Figure 4–15 displays the output from Program 4–6. The reader may notice an

Figure 4–15   *Output from Program 4–6*

```
┌─────────────────────────────────────────────────────────────────────────────┐
│  DEBUG-LINE IS 000070   INPUT-RECORD IS                                       │
│                                                                               │
│  DEBUG-LINE IS 000098   INPUT-RECORD IS 251049654781264    SANTOS   ALFONSO  01540      │
│                         25 10 49        654781264           SANTOS   ALFONSO  015    40  │
│                                                                               │
│  DEBUG-LINE IS 000098   INPUT-RECORD IS 160155275416280    MARKS    SUSAN    16522      │
│                         16 01 55        275416280           MARKS    SUSAN    165    22  │
│                                                                               │
│  DEBUG-LINE IS 000098   INPUT-RECORD IS 010963411235112    LEE      NA-QUAN  09903      │
│                         01 09 63        411235112           LEE      NA-QUAN  099    03  │
│                                                                               │
│  DEBUG-LINE IS 000098   INPUT-RECORD IS 091260332678462    ZULOFF   ADOLF    11637      │
│                         09 12 60        332678462           ZULOFF   ADOLF    116    37  │
│                                                                               │
│  DEBUG-LINE IS 000098   INPUT-RECORD IS 300651541936294    BROWN    LEROY    15017      │
│                         30 06 51        541936294           BROWN    LEROY    150    17  │
│                                                                               │
│  DEBUG-LINE IS 000076   INPUT-RECORD IS                                       │
└─────────────────────────────────────────────────────────────────────────────┘
```

apparent conflict of line numbers between the output from Program 4–6 and the statement numbers in the source COBOL program. When the programs were initially created with a text editor, the sequence numbers in columns 1 through 6 were incremented by 10 to allow for additional statements to be inserted without renumbering. Compiler output, such as that associated with debugging, always normalizes the statement numbers irrespective of the source sequence numbers. Therefore, statement number 000990 in Program 4–6 would be referenced by the compiler as statement number 000099. Statement normalizing also occurs when the compiler gives the programmer a listing of syntax errors.

Notice that the first and last lines did not display the contents of the input record. This is because an OPEN caused the first debug line, and a CLOSE caused the last debug line. Printed lines 2, 4, 6, 8, and 10 were caused by the READ; and 3, 5, 7, 9, and 11 were caused by the normal WRITE statement.

Monitoring a Field   Either the ALL REFERENCES clause or reference to a specific field can be used to **monitor a field**. ALL REFERENCES will cause the declarative portion of a program to execute each time an explicit reference is made to that data field in the nondeclarative portion. If just the data-name is used in the USE statement, the declarative portion is activated only when the named field is referenced and its value changed in the nondeclarative portion. Although only sum-counter data fields in a REPORT SECTION can be monitored (this is discussed in a later chapter) all other data fields in a program can be monitored.

The process of monitoring a field is activated when the data name that appears in a USE statement is referenced in the nondeclarative portion of a program. After the name is referenced, data are assigned to DEBUG–ITEM as follows:

1.   The sequence number of the COBOL statement is assigned to DEBUG–LINE.
2.   The name of the field is assigned to DEBUG–NAME. Be careful if qualified names are being used. Only 30 positions of the qualifying name and its qualifiers can be assigned to DEBUG–NAME. If a name contains a subscript or index they are ignored.
3.   When the subscript or index of a field is ignored, its value is placed in DEBUG–SUB–1 through DEBUG–SUB–3, accordingly.
4.   The value of the field is assigned to DEBUG–CONTENTS.

The declarative portion of the program is then executed causing the field to be monitored, and control is transferred to the next statement in the program. Program 4–7 is an example of this process.

Program 4–7

```
000010 IDENTIFICATION DIVISION.
000020    PROGRAM-ID.  CHAP4.
000030*******************************************************
000040* PROGRAM EXAMPLE 4-7 USING THE DEBUG SECTION TO MONITOR FIELDS  *
000050*******************************************************
000060 ENVIRONMENT DIVISION.
000070 CONFIGURATION SECTION.
000080    SOURCE-COMPUTER.  IBM WITH DEBUGGING MODE.
000090    OBJECT-COMPUTER.  IBM.
000100 INPUT-OUTPUT SECTION.
000110 FILE-CONTROL.
000120    SELECT EMPLOYEE-FILE    ASSIGN TO UT-S-EMPLOY.
000130    SELECT EMPLOYEE-REPORT ASSIGN TO UT-S-PRINTER.
000140*
000150 DATA DIVISION.
000160 FILE SECTION.
000170 FD  EMPLOYEE-FILE
000180     RECORD CONTAINS 50 CHARACTERS
000190     LABEL RECORDS ARE STANDARD.
000200 01  ER-EMPLOYEE-RECORD.
000210    05  ER-DATE.
000220       10  ER-DAY            PIC X(2).
000230       10  ER-MONTH          PIC X(2).
000240       10  ER-YEAR           PIC X(2).
000250    05  ER-SSN               PIC X(9).
000260    05  FILLER               PIC X(5).
000270    05  ER-NAME.
000280       10  ER-LAST           PIC X(10).
000290       10  ER-FIRST          PIC X(10).
000300    05  FILLER               PIC X(5).
000310    05  ER-STORE             PIC 9(3).
000320    05  ER-STATE             PIC 9(2).
000330 FD  EMPLOYEE-REPORT
000340     RECORD CONTAINS 132 CHARACTERS
000350     LABEL RECORDS ARE OMITTED.
000360 01  PR-RECORD-OUT           PIC X(132).
000370*
000380 WORKING-STORAGE SECTION.
000390 01  WS-PROCESSING-INDICATORS.
000400    05  WS-END-OF-FILE-INDICATOR PIC X(3).
000410       88  END-OF-FILE            VALUE  'END'.
000420 01  DL-DETAIL-LINE.
000430    05  FILLER               PIC X(20).
000440    05  DL-DAY               PIC X(2).
000450    05  FILLER               PIC X(1).
000460    05  DL-MONTH             PIC X(2).
000470    05  FILLER               PIC X(1).
000480    05  DL-YEAR              PIC X(2).
000490    05  FILLER               PIC X(7).
000500    05  DL-SSN               PIC X(9).
000510    05  FILLER               PIC X(11).
000520    05  DL-LAST              PIC X(10).
000530    05  FILLER               PIC X(2).
000540    05  DL-FIRST             PIC X(10).
000550    05  FILLER               PIC X(10).
000560    05  DL-STORE             PIC 9(3).
000570    05  FILLER               PIC X(7).
000580    05  DL-STATE             PIC 9(2).
000590 01  DEBUG-ITEM-RECORD       PIC X(132).
000600*
000610 PROCEDURE DIVISION.
000620 DECLARATIVES.
000630 USING-DEBUG-1 SECTION.
000640     USE FOR DEBUGGING ON DL-SSN
000650                         DL-LAST.
```

Program 4–7 *(concluded)*

```
000660 X100-DEBUG.
000670     MOVE DEBUG-ITEM TO DEBUG-ITEM-RECORD.
000680     WRITE PR-RECORD-OUT FROM DEBUG-ITEM-RECORD
000690         AFTER 1.
000700 END DECLARATIVES.
000710 A000-EMPLOYEE-LISTING SECTION.
000720     OPEN INPUT  EMPLOYEE-FILE
000730          OUTPUT EMPLOYEE-REPORT.
000740     PERFORM B100-INITIALIZE-VARIABLES.
000750     PERFORM Z100-READ-EMPLOYEE-RECORD.
000760     PERFORM B300-PROCESS-RECORDS
000770        UNTIL END-OF-FILE.
000780     CLOSE EMPLOYEE-FILE
000790           EMPLOYEE-REPORT.
000800     STOP RUN.
000810 B100-INITIALIZE-VARIABLES.
000820     MOVE SPACES TO WS-END-OF-FILE-INDICATOR.
000830     MOVE SPACES TO DL-DETAIL-LINE.
000840 B300-PROCESS-RECORDS.
000850     PERFORM C100-CREATE-OUTPUT-RECORD.
000860     WRITE PR-RECORD-OUT
000870         AFTER 1.
000880     PERFORM Z100-READ-EMPLOYEE-RECORD.
000890 C100-CREATE-OUTPUT-RECORD.
000900     MOVE ER-DAY        TO DL-DAY.
000910     MOVE ER-MONTH      TO DL-MONTH.
000920     MOVE ER-YEAR       TO DL-YEAR.
000930     MOVE ER-SSN        TO DL-SSN.
000940     MOVE ER-LAST       TO DL-LAST.
000950     MOVE ER-FIRST      TO DL-FIRST.
000960     MOVE ER-STORE      TO DL-STORE.
000970     MOVE ER-STATE      TO DL-STATE.
000980     MOVE DL-DETAIL-LINE TO PR-RECORD-OUT.
000990 Z100-READ-EMPLOYEE-RECORD.
001000     READ EMPLOYEE-FILE
001010        AT END MOVE 'END' TO WS-END-OF-FILE-INDICATOR.
```

Lines 640 and 650 of Program 4–7 indicate that the fields DL–SSN and DL–LAST are to be monitored. Because each of these fields appears only once in the PROCEDURE division, the clauses ALL REFERENCES DL–SSN and ALL REFERENCES DL–LAST would give the same debugging results.

DL–SSN in line 930 causes lines 670 through 690 of the declaratives portion to be executed and to return control to line 940. DL–LAST now causes the same lines in the declaratives portion to be executed a second time and control is returned to line 950. Both DL–SSN and DL–LAST cause their line numbers and values to be displayed. The WRITE at line 860 displays the contents of PR–RECORD–OUT as normal. This process continues until the program is terminated.

Figure 4–16 shows the results of the monitoring. Lines 1, 4, 7, 10, and 13 were caused by the execution of MOVE ER-SSN TO DL-SSN. Lines 2, 5, 8, 11, and 14 were caused by the execution of MOVE ER-LAST TO DL-LAST. WRITE PR-RECORD-OUT caused the display of lines 3, 6, 9, 12, and 15.

Monitoring a Procedure

Individual procedure names can be monitored by naming the procedure in a USE statement, or all procedures in the program can be monitored by the use of ALL PROCEDURES. The process of **monitoring a procedure** is activated when the procedure name in the USE statement is executed in the nondeclarative portion of a program. After the procedure is executed, data are assigned to DEBUG–ITEM as follows:

Figure 4–16 *Output from Program 4–7*

```
000093 DL-SSN                            654781264
000094 DL-LAST                           SANTOS
               25 10 49    654781264     SANTOS      ALFONSO     015     40
000093 DL-SSN                            275416280
000094 DL-LAST                           MARKS
               16 01 55    275416280     MARKS       SUSAN       165     22
000093 DL-SSN                            411235112
000094 DL-LAST                           LEE
               01 09 63    411235112     LEE         NA-QUAN     099     03
000093 DL-SSN                            332678462
000094 DL-LAST                           ZULOFF
               09 12 60    332678462     ZULOFF      ADOLF       116     37
000093 DL-SSN                            541936294
000094 DL-LAST                           BROWN
               30 06 51    541936294     BROWN       LEROY       150     17
```

1. The sequence number of the COBOL statement is assigned to DEBUG–LINE.
2. The name of the procedure is assigned to DEBUG–NAME.
3. The phrase PERFORM LOOP is assigned to DEBUG–CONTENTS if the procedure is being executed under control of a PERFORM, and the sequence number of the PERFORM statement is assigned to DEBUG–LINE.
4. The phrase START PROGRAM is assigned to DEBUG–CONTENTS if this is the first statement in the nondeclarative portion and it has a procedure name. The sequence number of the procedure is assigned to DEBUG–LINE.
5. One of the phrases SORT INPUT, SORT OUTPUT, or MERGE OUTPUT is assigned to DEBUG–CONTENTS depending on whether an INPUT/OUTPUT SORT procedure or a MERGE has been executed. The sequence number of that statement is assigned to DEBUG–LINE.
6. The phrase FALL THROUGH is assigned to DEBUG–CONTENTS if this paragraph is preceded by a section name and control was passed through the section. The sequence number of the section, not the paragraph, is assigned to DEBUG–LINE.
7. The remaining fields are all assigned spaces.
8. If any other phrase is assigned to DEBUG–CONTENTS, the programmer will need to consult the systems manual. Only under special circumstances can a paragraph or section in the declaratives portion be monitored.

The declarative portion of the program is then executed causing the procedure to be monitored, and control is transferred back to the next statement in the program. Program 4–8 is an example of monitoring a procedure.

Lines 640 and 650 of Program 4–8 indicate that the procedures B100–INITIALIZE–VARIABLES and C100–CREATE–OUTPUT–RECORD are to be monitored. The PERFORM statements at lines 740 and 850 cause the declarative portion of the program to be activated and lines 670, 680, and 690 to be executed. Control is then transferred back to either line 750 or 860. Notice that a WRITE, instead of a DISPLAY statement, is used at line 680. The program could have been designed to use a DISPLAY statement, if desired.

Figure 4–17 is the output of Program 4–8. B100–INITIALIZE–VARIABLES was monitored only once. Its results are displayed in the printed line. C100–CREATE–OUTPUT–RECORD was monitored five times as shown by lines 2, 4, 6, 8, and 10. Lines 3, 5, 7, 9, and 11 are the normal output from the DISPLAY PR–RECORD–OUT statement in the nondeclaratives portion of the program.

Program 4–8

```
000010 IDENTIFICATION DIVISION.
000020    PROGRAM-ID.  CHAP4.
000030**************************************************************
000040* PROGRAM EXAMPLE 4-8 USING DEBUG SECTION TO MONITOR PROCEDURES  *
000050**************************************************************
000060 ENVIRONMENT DIVISION.
000070 CONFIGURATION SECTION.
000080    SOURCE-COMPUTER.  IBM WITH DEBUGGING MODE.
000090    OBJECT-COMPUTER.  IBM.
000100 INPUT-OUTPUT SECTION.
000110 FILE-CONTROL.
000120    SELECT EMPLOYEE-FILE   ASSIGN TO UT-S-EMPLOY.
000130    SELECT EMPLOYEE-REPORT ASSIGN TO UT-S-PRINTER.
000140*
000150 DATA DIVISION.
000160 FILE SECTION.
000170 FD  EMPLOYEE-FILE
000180     RECORD CONTAINS 50 CHARACTERS
000190     LABEL RECORDS ARE STANDARD.
000200 01  ER-EMPLOYEE-RECORD.
000210     05  ER-DATE.
000220         10  ER-DAY          PIC X(2).
000230         10  ER-MONTH        PIC X(2).
000240         10  ER-YEAR         PIC X(2).
000250     05  ER-SSN              PIC X(9).
000260     05  FILLER              PIC X(5).
000270     05  ER-NAME.
000280         10  ER-LAST         PIC X(10).
000290         10  ER-FIRST        PIC X(10).
000300     05  FILLER              PIC X(5).
000310     05  ER-STORE            PIC 9(3).
000320     05  ER-STATE            PIC 9(2).
000330 FD  EMPLOYEE-REPORT
000340     RECORD CONTAINS 132 CHARACTERS
000350     LABEL RECORDS ARE OMITTED.
000360 01  PR-RECORD-OUT           PIC X(132).
000370*
000380 WORKING-STORAGE SECTION.
000390 01  WS-PROCESSING-INDICATORS.
000400     05  WS-END-OF-FILE-INDICATOR PIC X(3).
000410         88  END-OF-FILE         VALUE 'END'.
000420 01  DL-DETAIL-LINE.
000430     05  FILLER              PIC X(20).
000440     05  DL-DAY              PIC X(2).
000450     05  FILLER              PIC X(1).
000460     05  DL-MONTH            PIC X(2).
000470     05  FILLER              PIC X(1).
000480     05  DL-YEAR             PIC X(2).
000490     05  FILLER              PIC X(7).
000500     05  DL-SSN              PIC X(9).
000510     05  FILLER              PIC X(11).
000520     05  DL-LAST             PIC X(10).
000530     05  FILLER              PIC X(2).
000540     05  DL-FIRST            PIC X(10).
000550     05  FILLER              PIC X(10).
000560     05  DL-STORE            PIC 9(3).
000570     05  FILLER              PIC X(7).
000580     05  DL-STATE            PIC 9(2).
000590 01  DEBUG-ITEM-RECORD       PIC X(132).
000600*
000610 PROCEDURE DIVISION.
000620 DECLARATIVES.
000630 USING-DEBUG-1 SECTION.
000640     USE FOR DEBUGGING ON B100-INITIALIZE-VARIABLES
000650                         C100-CREATE-OUTPUT-RECORD.
```

Program 4–8 *(concluded)*

```
000660 X100-DEBUG.
000670     MOVE DEBUG-ITEM TO DEBUG-ITEM-RECORD.
000680     WRITE PR-RECORD-OUT FROM DEBUG-ITEM-RECORD
000690         AFTER 1.
000700 END DECLARATIVES.
000710 A000-EMPLOYEE-LISTING SECTION.
000720     OPEN INPUT  EMPLOYEE-FILE
000730          OUTPUT EMPLOYEE-REPORT.
000740     PERFORM B100-INITIALIZE-VARIABLES.
000750     PERFORM Z100-READ-EMPLOYEE-RECORD.
000760     PERFORM B300-PROCESS-RECORDS
000770         UNTIL END-OF-FILE.
000780     CLOSE EMPLOYEE-FILE
000790           EMPLOYEE-REPORT.
000800     STOP RUN.
000810 B100-INITIALIZE-VARIABLES.
000820     MOVE SPACES TO WS-END-OF-FILE-INDICATOR.
000830     MOVE SPACES TO DL-DETAIL-LINE.
000840 B300-PROCESS-RECORDS.
000850     PERFORM C100-CREATE-OUTPUT-RECORD.
000860     WRITE PR-RECORD-OUT
000870         AFTER 1.
000880     PERFORM Z100-READ-EMPLOYEE-RECORD.
000890 C100-CREATE-OUTPUT-RECORD.
000900     MOVE ER-DAY        TO DL-DAY.
000910     MOVE ER-MONTH      TO DL-MONTH.
000920     MOVE ER-YEAR       TO DL-YEAR.
000930     MOVE ER-SSN        TO DL-SSN.
000940     MOVE ER-LAST       TO DL-LAST.
000950     MOVE ER-FIRST      TO DL-FIRST.
000960     MOVE ER-STORE      TO DL-STORE.
000970     MOVE ER-STATE      TO DL-STATE.
000980     MOVE DL-DETAIL-LINE TO PR-RECORD-OUT.
000990 Z100-READ-EMPLOYEE-RECORD.
001000     READ EMPLOYEE-FILE
001010         AT END MOVE 'END' TO WS-END-OF-FILE-INDICATOR.
```

Figure 4–17 *Output from Program 4–8*

```
000074 B100-INITIALIZE-VARIABLES                    PERFORM LOOP
000085 C100-CREATE-OUTPUT-RECORD                    PERFORM LOOP
            25 10 49      654781264    SANTOS      ALFONSO   015   40
000085 C100-CREATE-OUTPUT-RECORD                    PERFORM LOOP
            16 01 55      275416280    MARKS       SUSAN     165   22
000085 C100-CREATE-OUTPUT-RECORD                    PERFORM LOOP
            01 09 63      411235112    LEE         NA-QUAN   099   03
000085 C100-CREATE-OUTPUT-RECORD                    PERFORM LOOP
            09 12 60      332678462    ZULOFF      ADOLF     116   37
000085 C100-CREATE-OUTPUT-RECORD                    PERFORM LOOP
            30 06 51      541936294    BROWN       LEROY     150   17
```

Mixed Monitoring

Program 4–9 shows the ability to monitor more than one item in the same program. The program uses the debug module to monitor the execution of the input file (named EMPLOYEE–FILE), the data field DL–LAST, and the main processing procedure B300–PROCESS–RECORDS.

Program 4–9

```
000010 IDENTIFICATION DIVISION.
000020   PROGRAM-ID.  CHAP4.
000030********************************************************************
000040* PROGRAM EXAMPLE 4-9 USING DEBUG SECTION TO MONITOR MIXED ITEMS *
000050********************************************************************
000060 ENVIRONMENT DIVISION.
000070 CONFIGURATION SECTION.
000080   SOURCE-COMPUTER.  IBM WITH DEBUGGING MODE.
000090   OBJECT-COMPUTER.  IBM.
000100 INPUT-OUTPUT SECTION.
000110 FILE-CONTROL.
000120   SELECT EMPLOYEE-FILE   ASSIGN TO UT-S-EMPLOY.
000130   SELECT EMPLOYEE-REPORT ASSIGN TO UT-S-PRINTER.
000140*
000150 DATA DIVISION.
000160 FILE SECTION.
000170 FD  EMPLOYEE-FILE
000180     RECORD CONTAINS 50 CHARACTERS
000190     LABEL RECORDS ARE STANDARD.
000200 01  ER-EMPLOYEE-RECORD.
000210     05  ER-DATE.
000220         10  ER-DAY             PIC X(2).
000230         10  ER-MONTH           PIC X(2).
000240         10  ER-YEAR            PIC X(2).
000250     05  ER-SSN                 PIC X(9).
000260     05  FILLER                 PIC X(5).
000270     05  ER-NAME.
000280         10  ER-LAST            PIC X(10).
000290         10  ER-FIRST           PIC X(10).
000300     05  FILLER                 PIC X(5).
000310     05  ER-STORE               PIC 9(3).
000320     05  ER-STATE               PIC 9(2).
000330 FD  EMPLOYEE-REPORT
000340     RECORD CONTAINS 132 CHARACTERS
000350     LABEL RECORDS ARE OMITTED.
000360 01  PR-RECORD-OUT              PIC X(132).
000370*
000380 WORKING-STORAGE SECTION.
000390 01  WS-PROCESSING-INDICATORS.
000400     05  WS-END-OF-FILE-INDICATOR PIC X(3).
000410         88  END-OF-FILE          VALUE  'END'.
000420 01  DL-DETAIL-LINE.
000430     05  FILLER                 PIC X(20).
000440     05  DL-DAY                 PIC X(2).
000450     05  FILLER                 PIC X(1).
000460     05  DL-MONTH               PIC X(2).
000470     05  FILLER                 PIC X(1).
000480     05  DL-YEAR                PIC X(2).
000490     05  FILLER                 PIC X(7).
000500     05  DL-SSN                 PIC X(9).
000510     05  FILLER                 PIC X(11).
000520     05  DL-LAST                PIC X(10).
000530     05  FILLER                 PIC X(2).
000540     05  DL-FIRST               PIC X(10).
000550     05  FILLER                 PIC X(10).
000560     05  DL-STORE               PIC 9(3).
000570     05  FILLER                 PIC X(7).
000580     05  DL-STATE               PIC 9(2).
000590 01  DEBUG-ITEM-RECORD          PIC X(132).
000600*
000610 PROCEDURE DIVISION.
000620 DECLARATIVES.
000630 USING-DEBUG-1 SECTION.
000640     USE FOR DEBUGGING ON EMPLOYEE-FILE
000650                       B300-PROCESS-RECORDS
```

Program 4–9   *(concluded)*

```
000660                        DL-LAST.
000670 X100-DEBUG.
000680     MOVE DEBUG-ITEM TO DEBUG-ITEM-RECORD.
000690     WRITE PR-RECORD-OUT FROM DEBUG-ITEM-RECORD
000700         AFTER 1.
000710 END DECLARATIVES.
000720 A000-EMPLOYEE-LISTING SECTION.
000730     OPEN INPUT  EMPLOYEE-FILE
000740          OUTPUT EMPLOYEE-REPORT.
000750     PERFORM B100-INITIALIZE-VARIABLES.
000760     PERFORM Z100-READ-EMPLOYEE-RECORD.
000770     PERFORM B300-PROCESS-RECORDS
000780         UNTIL END-OF-FILE.
000790     CLOSE EMPLOYEE-FILE.
000800     CLOSE EMPLOYEE-REPORT.
000810     STOP RUN.
000820 B100-INITIALIZE-VARIABLES.
000830     MOVE SPACES TO WS-END-OF-FILE-INDICATOR.
000840     MOVE SPACES TO DL-DETAIL-LINE.
000850 B300-PROCESS-RECORDS.
000860     PERFORM C100-CREATE-OUTPUT-RECORD.
000870     WRITE PR-RECORD-OUT
000880         AFTER 1.
000890     PERFORM Z100-READ-EMPLOYEE-RECORD.
000900 C100-CREATE-OUTPUT-RECORD.
000910     MOVE ER-DAY        TO DL-DAY.
000920     MOVE ER-MONTH      TO DL-MONTH.
000930     MOVE ER-YEAR       TO DL-YEAR.
000940     MOVE ER-SSN        TO DL-SSN.
000950     MOVE ER-LAST       TO DL-LAST.
000960     MOVE ER-FIRST      TO DL-FIRST.
000970     MOVE ER-STORE      TO DL-STORE.
000980     MOVE ER-STATE      TO DL-STATE.
000990     MOVE DL-DETAIL-LINE TO PR-RECORD-OUT.
001000 Z100-READ-EMPLOYEE-RECORD.
001010     READ EMPLOYEE-FILE
001020         AT END MOVE 'END' TO WS-END-OF-FILE-INDICATOR.
```

Figure 4–18   *Output from Program 4–9*

```
000073 EMPLOYEE-FILE
000101 EMPLOYEE-FILE                    251049654781264   SANTOS   ALFONSO      01540
000077 B300-PROCESS-RECORDS             PERFORM LOOP
000095 DL-LAST                          SANTOS
           25 10 49   654781264   SANTOS      ALFONSO           015      40
000101 EMPLOYEE-FILE                    160155275416280   MARKS    SUSAN        16522
000077 B300-PROCESS-RECORDS             PERFORM LOOP
000095 DL-LAST                          MARKS
           16 01 55   275416280   MARKS       SUSAN             165      22
000101 EMPLOYEE-FILE                    010963411235112   LEE      NA-QUAN      09903
000077 B300-PROCESS-RECORDS             PERFORM LOOP
000095 DL-LAST                          LEE
           01 09 63   411235112   LEE         NA-QUAN           099      03
000101 EMPLOYEE-FILE                    091260332678462   ZULOFF   ADOLF        11637
000077 B300-PROCESS-RECORDS             PERFORM LOOP
000095 DL-LAST                          ZULOFF
           09 12 60   332678462   ZULOFF      ADOLF             116      37
000101 EMPLOYEE-FILE                    300651541936294   BROWN    LEROY        15017
000077 B300-PROCESS-RECORDS             PERFORM LOOP
000095 DL-LAST                          BROWN
           30 06 51   541936294   BROWN       LEROY             150      17
000079 EMPLOYEE-FILE
```

The files are opened, and B100-INITIALIZE-VARIABLES sets the end-of-file indicator switch and clears out any unwanted characters in the area where the output record will be built. The first data record is brought into the program by performing Z100–READ–EMPLOYEE–RECORD where EMPLOYEE–FILE is monitored.

Next the main processing statement B300–PROCESS–RECORD is executed until an end-of-file condition is reached. During the processing, this procedure is monitored. In order to process the data record residing in the input area, C100–CREATE–OUTPUT–RECORD is performed. This procedure moves the input fields, one at a time, to the record being built. The output field DL–LAST is monitored. When the end-of-file condition occurs control is transferred to the CLOSE statement. Note that the files are closed separately to allow for the monitoring of EMPLOYEE–FILE with the WRITE statement.

The declarative portion of the program is from line 620 through line 710. The OPEN statement at line 730 causes EMPLOYEE–FILE to be monitored. Program lines 670 through 700 are executed, and control is transferred to line 750. At line 760 execution of this statement transfers control to line 1000. The READ at line 1010 causes EMPLOYEE–FILE to be monitored. Lines 670 through 700 are executed, and control is transferred to line 770. Here, PERFORM B300–PROCESS–RECORDS causes the procedure to be monitored, lines 670 through 700 are executed again, control is transferred to line 850, and the output record is created. At line 950 the monitoring of DL–LAST takes place, and transfer of control is made to line 960.

PERFORM B300–PROCESS–RECORDS continues looping until an end-of-file condition exists. The CLOSE statement causes the monitoring process to occur for the final time with EMPLOYEE– FILE. Figure 4–18 are the results of executing Program 4–9.

Make a special note of the statement MOVE ER–LAST TO DL–LAST at line 950 in Program 4–9. If ER–LAST was also to be monitored, there would be two data fields in the same monitored operation. This would cause a problem in the DECLARATIVES portion. The end result would be that the monitoring of DL–LAST would overlap that of ER–LAST, and ER–LAST monitored results would be lost.

Programming Style

1. When using the DISPLAY for debugging, use the debug lines feature. A program can be tested for correct results without taking out the debugging lines.

2. Unless your system has non-standard COBOL debugging features that are superior to the DISPLAY or the debug module, use standard COBOL statements for a more universal understanding of the program.

3. When using the debugging section, use comment statements such as a row of asterisks at the beginning and end of the DECLARATIVES portion.

4. When using the debugging section use as few sections as possible. They tend to complicate the debugging logic.

Common Errors

1. Forgetting to remove debugging statements from the program when not using the debug module.

2. Misuse of the EXHIBIT statement.

3. Forgetting to turn the READY statement off with a RESET TRACE.

4. Forgetting to include the WITH DEBUGGING MODE clause when using the debug module.

5. Forgetting to place a D in column 7 of a debugging line.

6. Referencing names or procedures in the nondeclarative portion from the declarative portion.

7. Using DEBUG–ITEM names in the nondeclarative portion instead of the declarative portion.

8. Monitoring a file with the WRITE statement and having the files closed.

Exercises

1. Define debugging.

2. Explain the process programmers should go through in doing a desk check for errors.

3. What is the difference between the following three statements:
   a. EXHIBIT NAMED WS–TOTAL.
   b. EXHIBIT CHANGED NAMED WS–TOTAL.
   c. EXHIBIT CHANGED WS–TOTAL.

4. What are the basic COBOL components used in the debugging lines options of the debug module.

5. What happens when the WITH DEBUGGING MODE clause is omitted from a program?

6. Explain the use of DECLARATIVES when using debugging sections.

7. Correct any logic and syntax errors in the following:

```
a.  DECLARATIVES.
    FIRST SECTION.
        USE FOR DEBUGGING ON B600-TOTALS.
    FIRST-PARAGRAPH.
        MOVE DEBUG-LINE TO WS-OUT-PUT.
        DISPLAY WS-OUTPUT.
    END-DECLARATIVES.
b.  DECLARATIVES.
    ONE SECTION.
        USE FOR DEBUGGING ON IN-FILE IN-FIELD.
    ONE PARAGRAPH.
        IF WS-CODE = 2
            MOVE DEBUG-ITEM TO OUT-RECORD.
            WRITE PR-RECORD-OUT AFTER ADVANCING 1 LINE.
c.  DECLARATIVES.
    FIRST SECTION.
        USE FOR DEBUGGING ON D-400-PROCESS.
    ONE PARAGRAPH.
        IF A = 1 DISPLAY DEBUG-ITEM
            ELSE DISPLAY DEBUG-CONTENTS.
    TWO PARAGRAPH.
        ADD 1 TO WS-COUNTER.
    TWO SECTION.
        USE FOR DEBUGGING ON WS-COUNTER.
    THREE PARAGRAPH.
        IF B = 1 PERFORM ONE-PARAGRAPH.
        PERFORM TWO-PARAGRAPH.
    FOUR PARAGRAPH.
        PERFORM D500-TOTALS.
    END DECLARATIVES.
```

8. Given the following entries, correct only those that are in error. Assume programmer-supplied names have been properly defined.

    a. `OBJECT-COMPUTER. ABC DEBUGGING MODE.`
    b. `D      ADD 1 TO N.`
    c. `USE FOR DEBUGGING ALL FIELDS.`
    d. `USE FOR DEBUGGING ON WS-TOTAL, PROCEDURES, FILE-1.`
    e. `END DECLARATIVE.`
                     `DISPLAY DEBUG-CONTENTS.`
    f. `MOVE 1 TO DEBUG-SUB-1.`
    g. `D      USE FOR DEBUGGING WS-TOTAL.`
    h. `EXHIBIT CHANGED NAMED.`

Problems

1. Modify Program 4–1 to be debugged as a separate program for each of the following:
   a. When the WITH DEBUGGING MODE clause is omitted, code the declarative portion of the program to be ignored when a program is executed.
   b. Write a debugging section to monitor all of the procedures in the program and output the contents of DEBUG–ITEM.
   c. Write three debugging sections. The first should monitor all of the DL fields. The second should monitor WS–END–OF–FILE–INDICATOR. The third should monitor EMPLOYEE–REPORT. Use either a DISPLAY or a WRITE statement in each section to output the entire contents of DEBUG–ITEM.
   d. Rewrite the debugging sections in *c* above so that only one DISPLAY or WRITE statement is used in the entire declarative portion to display what is being monitored in the three debugging sections.

2. Modify Program 2–1 to be debugged as a separate program for each of the following:
   a. Write a debugging section to monitor C600–PRINT–REGION–NAME when printing summaries.
   b. Write three debugging sections. The first should monitor the field WS–OVERTIME–PAY. The second should monitor the execution of the procedure C400–DETAIL–LINE. The third should monitor reading the PAY–RATE–FILE at line 179. Write out the entire contents of DEBUG–ITEM.
   c. Write a debugging section to monitor the input and output of each file in the program.

3. Modify Program 3–4 to be debugged as follows:
   a. Write only one debugging section.
   b. Monitor WS–END–OF–FILE–INDICATOR for all references.
   c. Monitor UC–TRANSACTION–DATE and SC–TRANSACTION–DATE.
   d. Monitor B100–REFORMAT–EXIT.
   e. Write a discussion of exactly what has happened during this debugging process.

4. Modify Program 3–6 to be debugged as follows:
   a. Use whatever number of debugging sections desired by the programmer.
   b. Monitor UC–ROOT–PORTION and UC–VARIABLE–SEGMENT.
   c. Monitor the procedures B200–PRINT–REPORT–SECTION and C600–PRINT–DETAIL.
   d. Write a discussion of exactly what has happened during the bebugging process.

5

Validation of Input Data

If data that are invalid or incorrect are allowed to enter the system, then every future access to these data elements is apt to cause problems. For instance, if a field that is supposed to contain numeric characters actually contains nonnumeric characters, any reference to that field in an arithmetic statement will cause abnormal termination of the program. The value of an arithmetic field must be checked for a reasonable limit. Otherwise, any total using that field will be unreasonable. For instance, it is not uncommon to hear about someone receiving an abnormally large check from a government agency—so large that it is unreasonable. The headlines usually tell of a computer malfunction; it is really programmer malfunction. To guard against input data errors, it is imperative that the systems analyst and programmer determine the validity of the data as soon as the data are entered into the system.

TERMS AND
STATEMENTS

Alphabetic test	Limit test	REPLACING
Check digit	Modulus-11	LEADING option
Class test	Numeric test	Reasonableness test
Consistency test	REDEFINES clause	Sign test
Existence test	REPLACING ALL	Transaction
INSPECT statement	option	validation
Inter-file test	REPLACING FIRST	
Justification test	option	

Types of Data Validation

There are many different types of data validation that should be considered when data enter into the computer system. Much of what needs to be considered depends on the data being entered. The design approach to data validation also depends on whether the data are entering into the system in a batch mode or in an interactive mode. The basic difference between the two modes is one of response or what is done when an error is detected. In a batch mode all fields in an entire record are checked for errors. Generally, if any errors are detected the entire record will be rejected. In an interactive mode each field is checked upon entry into the computer. If an error is detected, the individual field is rejected, and the user is prompted to reenter the data until it is acceptable.

Required Fields (Existence Test)

In most cases data must be contained in all fields in a given record. For instance, in an inventory record, the record would not be of much value if it did not have data in an inventory number field. In a payroll record, it would be difficult to pay an employee if the employee's name were missing. For these and many other fields, it is important to determine if there are any data in the field. In COBOL this **existence test** is relatively simple, as the following example in Figure 5–1 shows.

Figure 5–1   *Existence Test Syntax and Example*

```
        IF alphanumeric-data-field = SPACES
              imperative statement(s)

Example:

          05   ITEM-NUMBER          PIC X(5).
          .
          .
          IF ITEM-NUMBER = SPACES
             PERFORM Z200-ERROR-PROCEDURE.
```

ITEM-NUMBER Data field contents	Result of IF statement
`1`	False, Z200 module not performed.
`1 4 7 6 4`	False, Z200 module not performed.
`1`	False, Z200 module not performed.
(blank)	True, Z200 module is performed.

Justification Tests

Another important test is the **justification test,** which is made to ensure that the data in a field are appropriately aligned. A left-justification test will often be necessary for an alphanumeric field that must be left-justified. Examples of fields that normally would be left-justified include a person's name, an inventory description field, and an address field. In order to accomplish a left-justification test, it is necessary to define the field into group and elementary fields and to test for the existence of a space in the first position of the field being tested. The field can be accessed normally by using the group name. The entries shown in Figure 5–2 for the DATA division and the PROCEDURE division will illustrate.

In addition to testing for left-justification, it is sometimes appropriate to correct a field if it is not left-justified. This can be accomplished by the use of table processing as shown in Figure 5–3.

Figure 5–2 *Left-Justification Test Syntax and Example*

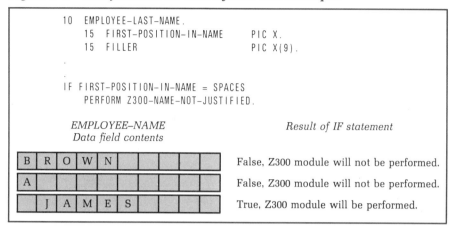

```
     10   EMPLOYEE-LAST-NAME.
          15   FIRST-POSITION-IN-NAME      PIC X.
          15   FILLER                      PIC X(9).


     IF FIRST-POSITION-IN-NAME = SPACES
          PERFORM Z300-NAME-NOT-JUSTIFIED.
```

EMPLOYEE–NAME Data field contents	Result of IF statement
B R O W N	False, Z300 module will not be performed.
A	False, Z300 module will not be performed.
J A M E S	True, Z300 module will be performed.

Figure 5–3 *Left-Justification Correction and Example*

```
     10   EMPLOYEE-LAST-NAME.
          15   FIRST-POSITION-IN-NAME      PIC X.
          15   FILLER                      PIC X(9).
     10   EMPLOYEE-LAST-NAME-TABLE
               REDEFINES EMPLOYEE-LAST-NAME.
          15   EMPLOYEE-CHARACTER          PIC X(1)
               OCCURS 10 TIMES.


     IF EMPLOYEE-LAST-NAME = SPACES
          PERFORM C100-NAME-DOES-NOT-EXIST
     ELSE
          IF FIRST-POSITION-IN-NAME = SPACES
               MOVE 10 TO WS-LENGTH-SUBSCRIPT
               PERFORM C200-JUSTIFY-NAME
                    UNTIL FIRST-POSITION-IN-NAME NOT = SPACES
          ELSE


 C200-JUSTIFY-NAME.
     PERFORM D100-MOVE-FIELD-TO LEFT
          VARYING WS-CHARACTER-SUBSCRIPT
               FROM 1 BY 1
                    UNTIL WS-CHARACTER-SUBSCRIPT = WS-LENGTH-SUBSCRIPT.
     MOVE SPACE TO EMPLOYEE-CHARACTER(WS-LENGTH-SUBSCRIPT).
     SUBTRACT 1 FROM WS-LENGTH-SUBSCRIPT.
 D100-MOVE-FIELD-TO-LEFT.
     COMPUTE WS-NEXT-CHARACTER = WS-CHARACTER-SUBSCRIPT + 1.
     MOVE EMPLOYEE-CHARACTER(WS-NEXT-CHARACTER)
          TO EMPLOYEE-CHARACTER(WS-CHARACTER-SUBSCRIPT).
```

In Figure 5–3, EMPLOYEE–LAST–NAME–TABLE is defined to subdivide the name into 10 separate characters so that each character can be moved to the left. The justification test is made only after the field has been tested for existence. If the field does not exist, the entire field contains spaces, so a left justification correction would be inappropriate.

Next, if the field is not justified, C200–JUSTIFY–NAME is performed and continues until the first character contains some nonblank character. WS–LENGTH–SUB SCRIPT is used to contain the length of the table to be justified, which is initially 10. Each time the table is moved to the left, WS–LENGTH–SUBSCRIPT is decremented. This decrementing decreases the number of characters that has to be moved each time, since the rightmost character in the table will be filled with a space after each movement of characters to the left.

WS–NEXT–CHARACTER is defined as one more than WS–LENGTH–SUB SCRIPT, which allows the movement of a character from one position to the next. The first time that D100–MOVE–FIELD–TO–LEFT is performed, WS–CHARACTER– SUBSCRIPT is equal to 1 and WS–NEXT–CHARACTER is equal to 2. The character in the second position is moved to the character in the first position. The next iteration of D100–MOVE–FIELD–TO–LEFT causes the movement of the third character to the second position, and so on until all of the characters have been moved and the PERFORM/VARYING is terminated. Then a space is moved to the last position in the table, and the size of the table that needs to be moved to the left is decremented.

If the first character position contains a nonblank character after the first movement to the left, then the justification is discontinued. If the first character still contains a space, additional shifting will occur, but on fewer characters. A right-justification correction could take place in a similar manner.

The REDEFINES Clause

While it is possible to accomplish both existence and left-justification tests on alphanumeric fields, the movement of a numeric field to a report field would cause a data exception, resulting in abnormal termination of the program. The **REDEFINES clause,** which has been previously illustrated with table processing, eliminates this problem.

Consider the data fields defined in Figure 5–4 and the corresponding IF statements to test for existence and right-justification on a numeric field.

Figure 5–4 *Examples of the REDEFINES Clause*

```
05   YTD-SALES                          PIC 9(5)V99.
05   YTD-SALES-X REDEFINES YTD-SALES PIC X(7).
05   YTD-SALES-J REDEFINES YTD-SALES.
     10   FILLER                        PIC X(6).
     10   LAST-POSITION-IN-YTD-SALES  PIC X(1).
     .
     .
IF YTD-SALES-X = SPACES
     PERFORM Z300-SALES-NOT-EXISTENT
ELSE
        IF LAST-POSITION-IN-YTD-SALES = SPACES
              PERFORM Z400-SALES-NOT-JUSTIFIED.
```

The REDEFINES clause is used to assign a different PICTURE clause to the same data field. In the case of YTD–SALES–X, the REDEFINES clause assigns a PIC X(7) so the field can be compared to SPACES. YTD–SALES–J also REDEFINES YTD–SALES so it can be subdivided into two elementary items for the right-justification test.

Numeric or Alphabetic Tests

A **numeric test** or **alphabetic test,** often termed **class tests,** can be performed to ascertain whether a data field contains appropriate characters. The format for the class test is shown in Figure 5–5. A numeric test can be performed on a field defined as numeric or alphanumeric. An alphabetic test is performed normally only on a field defined as alphabetic but can be performed on an alphanumeric field.

Figure 5–5   *Format of the Class Tests*

The essential purpose for performing a numeric test on a numeric field is to preclude the possibility of a data exception when completing calculations with a numeric field. If the programmer does not ensure that a numeric field has only valid digits and a possible sign, abnormal termination will occur when referencing that field in an arithmetic statement or in a MOVE statement when moving the nonnumeric characters to a numeric or a numeric edit-field. A numeric test can also be performed on alphanumeric fields such as zip code, inventory part numbers, and telephone numbers (assuming that parentheses and hyphens are not used).

Alphabetic tests have more limited uses than numeric tests. For instance, would an alphabetic test on a name field be appropriate? Only if the name field does not allow any characters other than the letters A through Z and blanks. Many name fields contain commas, periods, apostrophes, and hyphens. When that is the case an alphabetic test would not produce the desired results.

The class test may be used either with an IF statement such as IF YTD–SALES IS NUMERIC PERFORM FURTHER–TESTS or with a PERFORM statement such as PERFORM READ–ROUTINE UNTIL FIELD–A IS NUMERIC. In either case the NOT may be used to allow for a different wording of the same test. See Figure 5–6.

Inspection

Many times during the input phase, it is just as easy for the COBOL program itself to change the data rather than making the data entry process more difficult. A case in point is the input of numeric fields into a fixed-length numeric field. The digits in the field must be right-justified in the field to properly align with the assumed decimal point, and all characters must be numeric digits. When the number represented requires fewer digits than the number of characters in the field, the field must be padded on the left with zeros. This makes data entry difficult to accomplish and difficult to read, particularly when many numeric data fields follow each other on the record. The INSPECT statement can overcome this obstacle by providing the capability of padding with zeros during the validation process. The relevant formats of the **INSPECT statement** to pad with zeros are shown in Figure 5–7.

Figure 5–6   *Example of the Class Test*

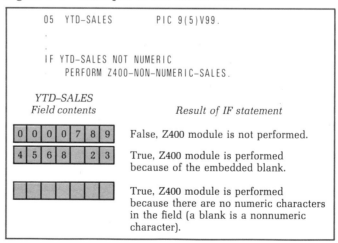

Figure 5–7 *Format of the INSPECT Statement*

Examples A through C in Figure 5–8 show the results of using this form of the INSPECT statement. Particularly note the effect of the INSPECT statements on each of the data fields.

Figure 5–8 *Examples of the INSPECT Statement*

	INSPECT statement	Field before INSPECT	Field after INSPECT
Example A:	INSPECT YTD-SALES REPLACING LEADING SPACES BY ZEROS.	b b b 7 5 0 0 0	0 0 0 7 5 0 0 0
Example B:	INSPECT YTD-SALES REPLACING ALL SPACES BY ZEROS.	b b 7 5 b 0 0 0	0 0 7 5 0 0 0 0
Example C:	INSPECT YTD-SALES REPLACING FIRST SPACE BY ZERO.	b b b 7 5 0 0 0	0 b b 7 5 0 0 0

b — denotes a blank character

Note that the correct padding of zeros occurs with the **REPLACING LEADING option** in Example A, not with the **REPLACING ALL option** in Example B or with the **REPLACING FIRST option** in Example C. The REPLACING ALL option would replace any positions that were left blank, even blanks that were embedded between two digits. The REPLACING FIRST option would replace only the first position.

The result of the INSPECT/REPLACING LEADING statement appropriately pads each field with zeros, but its use requires some planning with respect to the sequencing of validation tests. Looking again at Figure 5–8, it should be obvious that a numeric test would cause all fields to be invalid if done before the INSPECT. Also if padding with zeros occurs before an existence test, the program would never detect a missing numeric field. The best sequence then would be (1) existence, (2) justification, (3) pad with zeros with the INSPECT, and (4) a numeric test.

Sign Tests

The **sign test** can be used to determine whether a numeric field is positive, negative, or zero. The format of the sign test is shown in Figure 5–9. Examples of the sign test are shown in Figure 5–10. A sign test on a nonnumeric field does not make sense, and it could yield unpredictable results. The field being tested must be defined with a signed, numeric PICTURE clause. Like the class tests, the sign test can be used either with an IF statement or with a PERFORM statement. The NOT provides a means of wording the tested condition in different terms. Note also that relation

Figure 5–9 *Format of the Sign Test*

tests could take the place of sign tests; for example, IF YTD–SALES > ZERO would be the same as IF YTD–SALES IS POSITIVE. The choice of either form depends simply on which form is more readable. Remember, though, a sign test is valid only on a signed, numeric field.

Figure 5–10   *Examples of the Sign Test*

```
Example A:

      IF SALES-AMOUNT IS ZERO
          PERFORM ZERO-AMOUNT-ROUTINE.

Example B:

      IF EOQ IS NEGATIVE
          COMPUTE EOQ = EOQ * (-1)
          PERFORM SQR-ROOT-ROUTINE.

Example C:

      IF FEDERAL-TAXES IS POSITIVE
          PERFORM W-2-ROUTINE.

Example D:

      PERFORM ADDITION-ROUTINE
          UNTIL SALES-AMOUNT IS ZERO.
```

Limit and Reasonableness Tests

A **limit test** is designed to place an absolute limit on a numeric value, while a **reasonableness test** only flags a field for being outside a specified range. One example of where a limit test would be applied would be in the case of the total accumulated FICA tax withheld from an employee's pay. FICA tax is calculated using a percentage of gross pay subject to the tax. However, that percentage applies only to a set amount of pay; beyond that amount no tax is to be withheld. A limit test would be used to determine whether the maximum has been reached.

Figure 5–11   *Modulus-11 Method to Create and Test Codes*

```
Existing code        = 4    3    2    1    0
Multiplied by weight = 6    5    4    3    2
Sum of multiplication = 24 + 15 +  8 +  3 +  0 = 50
```
Divide the sum of the multiplication by 11 and obtain the remainder: $50/11 = 4$ with a remainder of 6.
Subtract the remainder from 11. The result is the check digit. $(11 - 6 = 5)$. The account number would become 432105.

If the account number were to be entered as 432150 a transposition error has occurred. The above procedure would be repeated on the entire code, including the check digit to determine if the code is valid. Since the check digit has been included in the code checking procedure; the remainder should be zero if no input error has occurred.

```
Existing code        = 4    3    2    1    5    0
Multiplied by weight = 6    5    4    3    2    1
Sum of multiplication = 24 + 15 +  8 +  3 + 10 +  0 = 60
```

$60/11 = 5$ with a remainder of 5.

The calculated remainder is 5, not zero. Therefore, the code is invalid and would be rejected.

```
      DIVIDE 11 INTO SUM-OF-MULTIPLY
          GIVING DIVIDE-RESULT
          REMAINDER CHECK-DIGIT-REMAINDER.
      IF CHECK-DIGIT-REMAINDER NOT = ZERO
          PERFORM Z300-ERROR-ROUTINE.
```

An example of a reasonableness test could be applied to a sales quota system. Management may set a given sales quota for each employee and then set a range of reasonable values above and below the quota. If an employee's sales are outside the range, it is not an error in the absolute sense; it just warrants further investigation.

Code Checking

Quite frequently companies will perform tests on codes, particularly customer codes, to ensure their validity and to guard against input error, such as transposition (the reversal of digits in a numeric field). The most common method is to attach a digit to the existing account number. This digit, called a **check digit,** will have been mathematically derived from the existing digits. Thus, if an error occurs during data entry, the error will be detected by performing the same mathematical derivation to see if the check digit is correct for this data field.

One method for performing this mathematical derivation is called **Modulus-11.** To see how this works, consider the example of determining a check digit for the five-digit code shown in Figure 5–11.

The remainder can be determined in COBOL by using the REMAINDER option of the DIVIDE statement, as shown at the bottom of Figure 5–11.

Date Checking

Dates are frequently a part of input records and should also be validated. For instance, the month can be validated for the values 1 through 12, and the day of the month can be validated if the month is known. The date of the input data can also be compared to the current date to ascertain if it is equal to or less than the current date.

In order to compare an input date to the current date, it is necessary to obtain the date from the system. The ACCEPT statement allows the retrieval of the current date or time. However, data retrieved by the ACCEPT statement are not always in the desired format. It is often necessary to reformat the dates. A commonly used technique to reformat the date and time into different forms is through the use of the REDEFINES clause. The source statements in Figure 5–12 show an example of defining each of the three formats of the ACCEPT statement. After they are defined, it is simply a matter of accepting them into the right area and then moving them to the appropriate output fields. Another method of reformatting the Gregorian date for appropriate output is shown in Program 2–1.

Consistency Tests

The **consistency tests** may also be called an interfield test. Its purpose is to test the interrelationships among fields within a given logical record. For instance, it is typical to establish a commission rate scheme for sales personnel, where each salesperson receives a commission on sales depending on the type of employee. Management may set a certain commission rate for field sales personnel, a different rate for district sales managers, and a still different rate for regional sales managers. The internal consistency within a salesperson's record could then be tested by comparing an employee type code with a known commission rate for that particular employee type.

Inter-file Tests

Quite frequently validation takes place during an update procedure and a master file is to be updated if the validation is successful. After all fields in the transaction record are appropriately validated, it is advisable to make relevant comparisons between fields in the transaction file and fields in the master file. Suppose a credit customer has successfully applied for an increase in his/her credit limit. To update

Figure 5–12   *Examples of the REDEFINES Clause for Dates*

```
DATA DIVISION.
WORKING-STORAGE SECTION.
01  DT-DATE-AND-TIME-AREA.
     05  DT-GREGORIAN-DATE                PIC 9(6).
     05  DT-GREGORIAN-DATE-X REDEFINES DT-GREGORIAN-DATE.
         10   DT-GREGORIAN-YEAR           PIC X(2).
         10   DT-GREGORIAN-MONTH          PIC X(2).
         10   DT-GREGORIAN-DAY            PIC X(2).
     05  DT-JULIAN-DATE                   PIC 9(5).
     05  DT-JULIAN-DATE-X REDEFINES DT-JULIAN-DATE.
         10   DT-JULIAN-YEAR              PIC X(2).
         10   DT-JULIAN-DAYS              PIC X(3).
     05  DT-TIME                          PIC 9(8).
     05  DT-TIME-X REDEFINES DT-TIME.
         10   DT-HOURS                    PIC X(2).
         10   DT-MINUTES                  PIC X(2).
         10   DT-SECONDS                  PIC X(2).
         10   DT-HUNDREDTHS               PIC X(2).
01  HD-DATE-HEADING.
     05  FILLER                           PIC X(1).
     05  HD-GREGORIAN-DATE.
         10   HD-GREGORIAN-MONTH          PIC X(2).
         10   FILLER                      PIC X(1) VALUE '/'.
         10   HD-GREGORIAN-DAY            PIC X(2).
         10   FILLER                      PIC X(1) VALUE '/'.
         10   HD-GREGORIAN-YEAR           PIC X(2).
     05  FILLER                           PIC X(5) VALUE SPACES.
     05  HD-JULIAN-DATE.
         10   HD-JULIAN-YEAR              PIC X(2).
         10   FILLER                      PIC X(1) VALUE SPACES.
         10   HD-JULIAN-DAYS              PIC X(3).
     05  FILLER                           PIC X(5) VALUE SPACES.
     05  HD-TIME.
         10   HD-HOURS                    PIC X(2).
         10   FILLER                      PIC X(1) VALUE ':'.
         10   HD-MINUTES                  PIC X(2).
         10   FILLER                      PIC X(1) VALUE ':'.
         10   HD-SECONDS                  PIC X(2).
         10   FILLER                      PIC X(1) VALUE '.'.
         10   HD-HUNDREDTHS               PIC X(2).
```

the credit records with the company, it is necessary to create a transaction record that would include as fields the account number, name, new credit limit, and a transaction code to indicate that this transaction is a credit-limit increase.

One **inter-file test** is mandatory; the comparison of the account number stored in the master file to the account number entered on the transaction record. While the account number could have been tested for validity using a technique like Modulus-11, it still must be compared to the master account number to ensure that a customer exists with that account number. Two other inter-file checks are advisable in this case to ensure that the change is being made to the correct customer account. One test would be to compare the previously stored credit limit with the new credit limit. The new credit limit should be higher since this was an application for an increase in credit limit. Of equal or more importance would be the comparison of names on both the transaction and the master records. If the names are not the same, the posting of the transaction should not take place.

Program Example

To illustrate data-validation concepts, consider the implementation of a computerized system for an employee sales file. Assume that a master file of existing employ-

Figure 5–13 *System Flowchart for Payroll Validation*

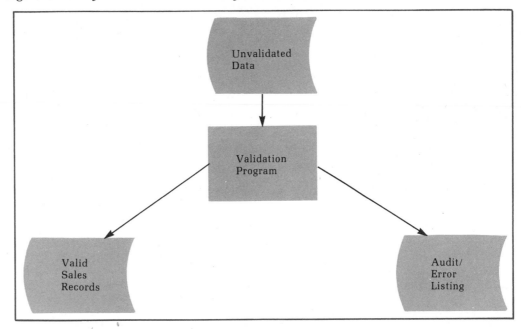

ees is to be created. The process has previously been a manual procedure, but now it is desired to capture this data and store it onto a disk device for future access. Obviously, the first time that the data enters into the system, it must be valid data. Erroneous data must not be allowed to enter into the computer system, so it is necessary to have the computer look at the data to detect any errors before the data are stored on disk. The concept of what is to be accomplished is illustrated in the systems flowchart in Figure 5–13.

Statement of the Problem

Consider the following programming specifications for this program. Realize it is the responsibility of the systems analyst or programmer to develop and define these required operations for each and every application.

Program Description:

This program is used to create an initial master file on disk for the implementation of a computerized system. Other programs will have to be developed to maintain the file and produce other required operations such as sales analysis, updating procedures, and so forth. All reasonable data-validation procedures must be completed in order to ensure data accuracy. These procedures are defined later as a part of this document.

An audit/error listing will be produced providing a listing of all input records. If errors are detected, an appropriate message will be displayed indicating the type of error. If a record passes all validation tests, the record will be transferred to a disk file. Appropriate validation totals will be printed at the end of the audit/error listing.

Required Operations:

1. Read each sales record.
2. For each input record, display the input record image on the audit/error list for documentation purposes. Fields will need to be separated for readability purposes.
3. For each input record, complete the data-validation procedures that are described later in this document.
4. For each error detected on a record, print an error message indicating the type of error found. If a record has more than one error, print the input record image only once; print each indicated error on a separate line.
5. For each record that passes ALL validation tests, transfer the record to a disk file. This becomes the master sales file.

6. During the validation process accumulate the following totals:
   a. Total number of input records.
   b. Total number of valid records.
   c. Total number of invalid records.
   d. Total number of errors.
   e. Total dollar value of all numeric fields for all records placed on the master file. (These totals will be compared to current general ledger totals.)
7. Appropriate headings should be printed on the top of each page of the report and should include the following:
   a. Page numbering.
   b. Current date.
   c. Column headings for each field of input data and for detected error messages.
8. The following data-validation procedures need to be undertaken for each input record:

Field	Validation procedure
Salesperson number	Existence, sequence
Employee name	Existence, left-justification. (If either the last name or first name is not left-justified, the program is to make the correction.)
Year-to-date sales	Existence, fill leading zeros, numeric, maximum $3,500 at the time of the program.
Year-to-date returns	Existence, fill leading zeros, numeric, maximum $875 at the time of the program.
Commission rate	Existence, fill leading zeros, numeric, maximum 30 percent at the time of the program.

Input

The data set that is to be validated before placing on disk is shown in Figure 5–14.

Structure Chart

Figure 5–15 presents the structure chart for the validation program and will assist the discussion of Program 5–1. In a validation program there are two basic design alternatives. One alternative is to group types of validation such as to do all existence tests first, then proceed to all numeric tests, and so on. The second alternative is to accomplish all tests on a given field and then proceed to subsequent fields. The latter generally is preferred because of its greater ease of program modification. If additional tests on a field are necessary, those tests can be added easily.

Study the structure chart for the five modules called by B400–VALIDATE–RECORDS. For each record all field validations will be performed and then test whether or not the record has passed all tests. If the record is invalid, the number of invalid records will be incremented. If the record is valid, a valid record procedure will be performed. After either case, the next employee record will then be read. In the valid-record procedure the record will be written to the disk file, the number of valid records will be incremented, the numeric fields will be accumulated, and the detail line will be printed.

For each of the fields tested, the logic will be essentially the same as shown for the name tests. Validation checks will be undertaken, and if an error is detected, appropriate error procedures will be performed. The detail blocks for fields other than name tests are not shown in the structure chart, but they follow the same essential logic.

The structure chart lacks the ability to adequately explain the logic at the point where it is necessary to design the instructions for the field validation procedures. It is often necessary to move to a more detailed form of documentation and planning

Figure 5–14 *Data Set for Input Data Validation*

```
The following are sales records. The record definition is:

 1– 4  Salesperson number
 6–16  Last name
17–26  First name
27–33  Year-to-date sales
35–41  Year-to-date returns
43–44  Commission rate

================================================
0017 PAYNE       MAX          98700     5673  5
0125 LISHER      JANET F.     50000        0 15
     BROCKETT    JANE R.      75000    90000  5
0356 GOLTMAN     LINDA S.    109877     1000 10
0396 VOLSKY      CHRIS        32680     5847  8
0401 OWENS       GEORGE                 3957 35
0479 WETZEL      ROBERT D.   208876     5877 15
0529 PEACOCK     BARBARA      67330    15664  8
0580 DUPREE      KELLY L.    357888    27582
0635 HUNT        ROBERT       45320           10
0746 JACKSON     JASON        78450     8478 15
0859 HUTCHENS    JEFF         57630     4857 14
0927 BARCLAY     RICHARD     198740    48563 11
1001 DILL        JEFF         58640    28456 20
1000 UNLAND      KIM L.       47564    39585 25
0999 GOODMAN     EVE          64542    23847 10
1634 VAUGHN                   47899    45678 20
1805 KIMBERLING  CARLA K.     50000    10000 30
1856 LOVELAND    GEORGE       46275    27656 10
1867 STEWARD     KEVIN J.    115000    17500 15
1938 DWYER       JOHN D.      23175     4000 10
2157 YOUNG       KAREN L.    112359     3575 30
2186 SMITH       DOUGLAS      18345    37758 20
2269 THOMPSON    LISA S.      50000    10000 20
2294 HERMAN      JACK         48465     8747  5
2341 ADAMS       ROBYN A.     23175     4000 10
2395 MATNEY      DELORES      79574    85746  5
2485 PHILLIPS    TRACY L.     50000    10000 30
2487 HUME        LETA         48353    28437 20
2575 CROSS       CHERYL       38563    38250 10
================================================
```

tool such as a structured flowchart. Figure 5–16 illustrates the logic necessary for two of the fields.

The validation of the salesperson number field is fairly simple since there are only three tests—one for existence, one for the appropriate range, and one for a sequence check. In the flowchart, if an error is detected, two procedures are programmed: (1) moving the appropriate error message and (2) moving YES to a field-error indicator. The field-error indicator is tested after the name check is completed to determine whether the error procedures should be performed. Notice that the range test will be executed only if the number passes the existence test. This logic follows throughout each field validation and reinforces the point made earlier in this chapter about the importance of determining the appropriate sequence of validation checks. Only if a field passes one type of test is another type of test undertaken.

The validation of the last name field is more involved. If the field passes the existence test, a left-justification test is performed. If it is determined that the field is not left-justified it is corrected by using the procedures previously discussed. Note that whenever a field fails a test, the flow of logic returns to the module that has called this particular field check; no further checks are made on the data field.

Figure 5–15 Structure Chart for Program 5–1

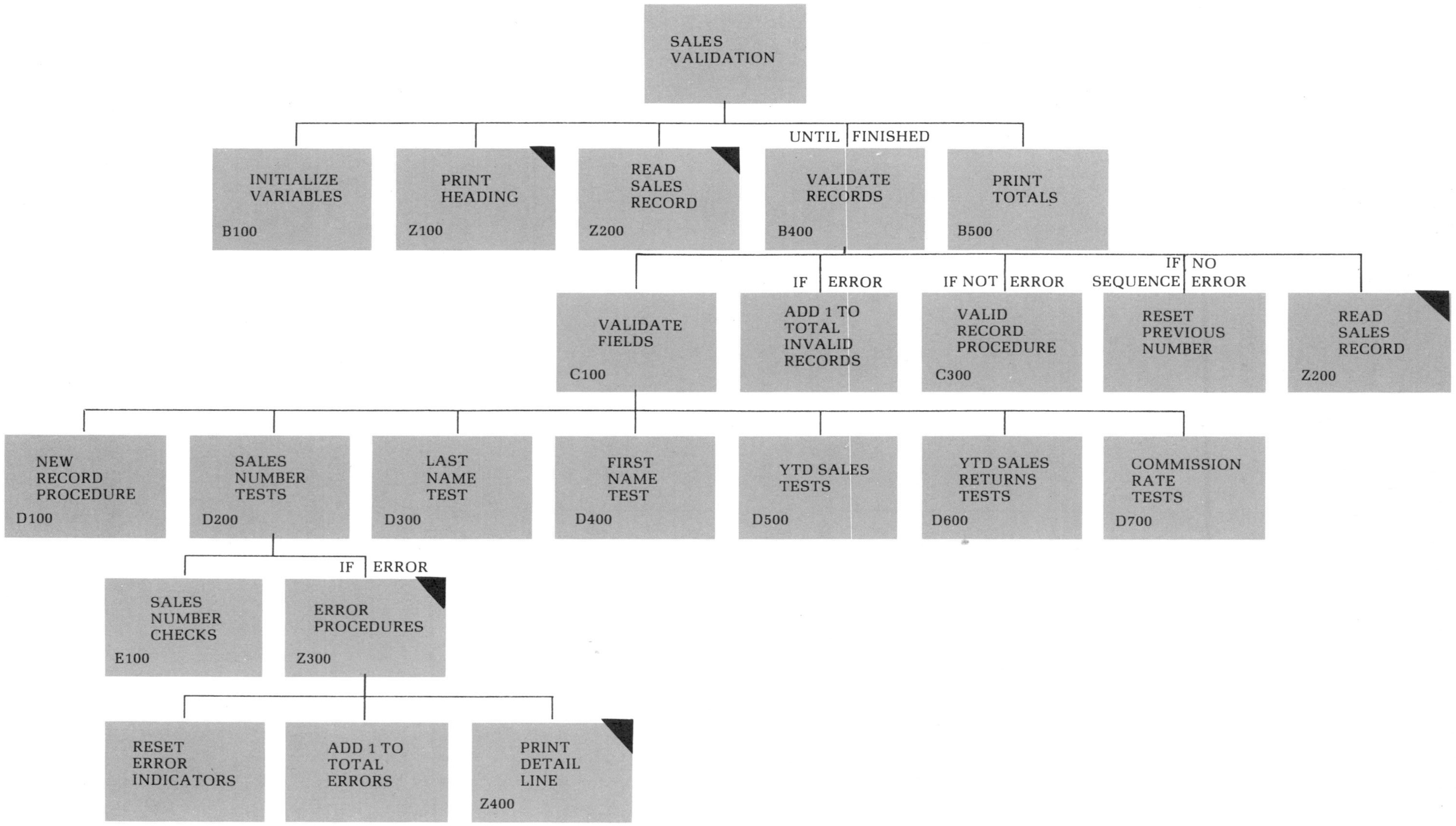

```
                                        SALES
                                      VALIDATION
                                          |
       +-----------------+----------------+-----------------+
       |                 |                |                 |
  INITIALIZE        PRINT           READ SALES          VALIDATE         PRINT
  VARIABLES         HEADING          RECORD             RECORDS         TOTALS
                                                     UNTIL FINISHED
    B100             Z100             Z200              B400             B500

                                                          |
                        +-------------------+-------------+------------------+
                        |                   |        IF NOT ERROR      IF NO  |
                     VALIDATE          ADD 1 TO        VALID RECORD   SEQUENCE ERROR
                     FIELDS          TOTAL INVALID     PROCEDURE      RESET PREVIOUS   READ SALES
                                       RECORDS                         NUMBER         RECORD
                      C100          IF ERROR            C300                           Z200
                        |
    +---------+---------+---------+---------+---------+---------+
    |         |         |         |         |         |
  SALES     LAST      FIRST     YTD SALES  YTD SALES  COMMISSION
  NUMBER    NAME      NAME      TESTS      RETURNS    RATE
  TESTS     TEST      TEST                 TESTS      TESTS
  D200      D300      D400      D500       D600       D700
    |
    +---------+---------+
    |         |
  NEW       SALES     ERROR
  RECORD    NUMBER    PROCEDURES
  PROCEDURE CHECKS
  D100      E100      Z300
                    IF ERROR
                        |
            +-----------+-----------+
            |           |           |
          RESET       ADD 1 TO    PRINT
          ERROR       TOTAL       DETAIL
          INDICATORS  ERRORS      LINE
                                  Z400
```

Figure 5–16 *Partial Flowchart of Program 5–1*

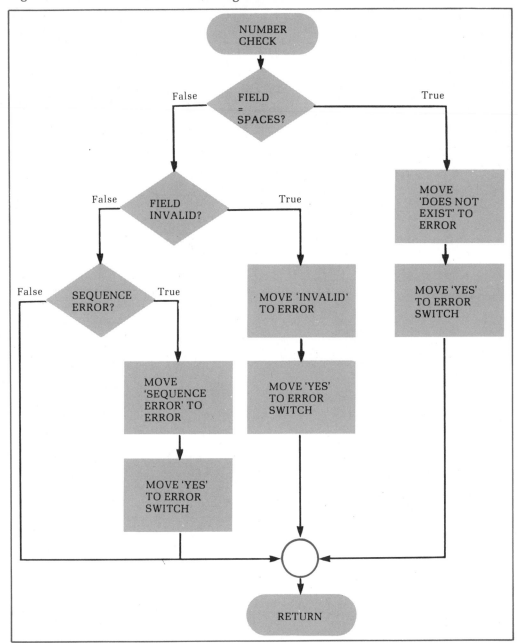

Figure 5–16   *(concluded)*

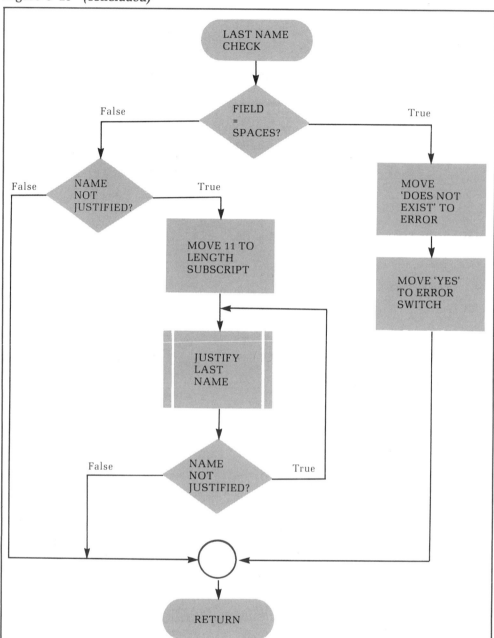

Program

_____

Program 5–1

```
000010 IDENTIFICATION DIVISION.
000020 PROGRAM-ID.    SLSVAL.
000030**************************************************
000040* PROGRAM EXAMPLE 5-1 SALES FILE VALIDATION        *
000050**************************************************
000060 ENVIRONMENT DIVISION.
000070 CONFIGURATION SECTION.
000080    SOURCE-COMPUTER.  IBM-4341.
000090    OBJECT-COMPUTER.  IBM-4341.
000100 INPUT-OUTPUT SECTION.
000110 FILE-CONTROL.
000120    SELECT VALID-SALES-FILE
000130       ASSIGN TO UT-S-SALES.
000140    SELECT AUDIT-ERROR-LISTING
000150       ASSIGN TO UT-S-PRINTER.
000160    SELECT SALES-INPUT-FILE
000170       ASSIGN TO UT-S-SALESIN.
000180*
000190 DATA DIVISION.
000200 FILE SECTION.
000210 FD  VALID-SALES-FILE
000220     RECORD CONTAINS 41 CHARACTERS
000230     LABEL RECORDS STANDARD.
000240 01  VS-VALID-SALES-RECORD.
000250     05  VS-SALESPERSON-NUMBER      PIC X(4).
000260     05  VS-LAST-NAME               PIC X(11).
000270     05  VS-FIRST-NAME              PIC X(10).
000280     05  VS-YEAR-TO-DATE-SALES      PIC 9(5)V99.
000290     05  VS-YEAR-TO-DATE-SALES-RETURNS PIC 9(5)V99.
000300     05  VS-COMMISSION-RATE         PIC V99.
000310 FD  SALES-INPUT-FILE
000320     RECORD CONTAINS 44 CHARACTERS
000330     LABEL RECORDS ARE STANDARD.
000340 01  SI-SALES-INPUT-RECORD.
000350     05  SI-SALESPERSON-NUMBER      PIC X(4).
000360         88  VALID-SALESPERSON-NUMBER VALUE '0001' THRU '2500'.
000370     05  FILLER                     PIC X(1).
000380     05  SI-LAST-NAME               PIC X(11).
000390     05  SI-LAST-NAME-TABLE
000400         REDEFINES SI-LAST-NAME.
000410         10  SI-LAST-NAME-CHARACTER  PIC X(1)
000420             OCCURS 11 TIMES.
000430     05  SI-FIRST-NAME              PIC X(10).
000440     05  SI-FIRST-NAME-TABLE
000450         REDEFINES SI-FIRST-NAME.
000460         10  SI-FIRST-NAME-CHARACTER PIC X(1)
000470             OCCURS 10 TIMES.
000480     05  SI-YEAR-TO-DATE-SALES      PIC 9(5)V99.
000490     05  SI-YEAR-TO-DATE-SALES-X
000500         REDEFINES SI-YEAR-TO-DATE-SALES PIC X(7).
000510         88  VALID-YTD-SALES VALUE '0000000' THRU '0350000'.
000520     05  FILLER                     PIC X(1).
000530     05  SI-YEAR-TO-DATE-SALES-RETURNS PIC 9(5)V99.
000540     05  SI-YEAR-TO-DATE-SALES-RETNS-X
000550         REDEFINES SI-YEAR-TO-DATE-SALES-RETURNS
000560                                    PIC X(7).
000570         88  VALID-YTD-SALES-RETURNS
000580             VALUE '0000000' THRU '0087500'.
000590     05  FILLER                     PIC X(1).
000600     05  SI-COMMISSION-RATE         PIC V99.
000610     05  SI-COMMISSION-RATE-X
000620         REDEFINES SI-COMMISSION-RATE  PIC X(2).
000630         88  VALID-COMMISSION-RATE VALUE '05' THRU '30'.
000640 FD  AUDIT-ERROR-LISTING
000650     RECORD CONTAINS 132 CHARACTERS
```

Program 5–1 *(continued)*

```
000660      LABEL RECORDS ARE OMITTED.
000670 01  AE-AUDIT-ERROR-RECORD          PIC X(132).
000680*
000690 WORKING-STORAGE SECTION.
000700 01  WS-REPORT-CONTROLS.
000710     05  WS-PAGE-NUMBER             PIC 9(4).
000720     05  WS-LINES-PER-PAGE          PIC 9(4)
000730                                    VALUE 55.
000740     05  WS-LINES-USED              PIC 9(4).
000750 01  DW-DATE-WORK-AREA.
000760     05  DW-DATE-AREA               PIC 9(6).
000770     05  DW-DATE-AREA-X
000780         REDEFINES DW-DATE-AREA     PIC X(6).
000790 01  TOT-ACCUMULATORS.
000800     05  TOT-RECORDS-READ           PIC 9(4).
000810     05  TOT-VALID-RECORDS          PIC 9(4).
000820     05  TOT-INVALID-RECORDS        PIC 9(4).
000830     05  TOT-NUMBER-OF-ERRORS       PIC 9(4).
000840     05  TOT-YTD-SALES              PIC 9(6)V99.
000850     05  TOT-YTD-SALES-RETURNS      PIC 9(6)V99.
000860 01  RI-RECORD-INDICATORS.
000870     05  FIRST-ERROR-INDICATOR      PIC X(3).
000880         88  RECORD-ALREADY-BAD     VALUE 'YES'.
000890     05  RECORD-ERROR-INDICATOR     PIC X(3).
000900         88  RECORD-IS-IN-ERROR     VALUE 'YES'.
000910     05  FIELD-ERROR-INDICATOR      PIC X(3).
000920         88  FIELD-IS-IN-ERROR      VALUE 'YES'.
000930     05  LENGTH-SUBSCRIPT           PIC 9(2).
000940     05  CHARACTER-SUBSCRIPT        PIC 9(2).
000950     05  NEXT-CHARACTER             PIC 9(2).
000960     05  PREVIOUS-NUMBER            PIC X(4).
000970     05  EOF-INDICATOR              PIC X(3).
000980         88 END-OF-SALES-FILE       VALUE 'END'.
000990 01  HD-HEADING-LINE-1.
001000     05  HD-DATE-OUT                PIC XX/XX/XX.
001010     05  FILLER                     PIC X(25) VALUE SPACES.
001020     05  FILLER                     PIC X(25)
001030         VALUE 'SALES VALIDATION REPORT'.
001040     05  FILLER                     PIC X(20) VALUE SPACES.
001050     05  FILLER                     PIC X(5)
001060         VALUE 'PAGE '.
001070     05  HD-PAGE-NUMBER-OUT         PIC ZZZ9.
001080 01  HD-HEADING-LINE-2.
001090     05  FILLER           PIC X(6)  VALUE 'NUMBER'.
001100     05  FILLER           PIC X(2)  VALUE SPACES.
001110     05  FILLER           PIC X(9)  VALUE 'LAST NAME'.
001120     05  FILLER           PIC X(6)  VALUE SPACES.
001130     05  FILLER           PIC X(10) VALUE 'FIRST NAME'.
001140     05  FILLER           PIC X(4)  VALUE SPACES.
001150     05  FILLER           PIC X(5)  VALUE 'SALES'.
001160     05  FILLER           PIC X(6)  VALUE SPACES.
001170     05  FILLER           PIC X(7)  VALUE 'RETURNS'.
001180     05  FILLER           PIC X(3)  VALUE SPACES.
001190     05  FILLER           PIC X(4)  VALUE 'RATE'.
001200     05  FILLER           PIC X(3)  VALUE SPACES.
001210     05  FILLER           PIC X(13) VALUE 'ERROR MESSAGE'.
001220 01  DL-DETAIL-LINE.
001230     05  DL-OUTPUT-AREA.
001240         10  DL-SALESPERSON-NUMBER  PIC X(4).
001250         10  FILLER                 PIC X(4) VALUE SPACES.
001260         10  DL-LAST-NAME           PIC X(11).
001270         10  FILLER                 PIC X(4) VALUE SPACES.
001280         10  DL-FIRST-NAME          PIC X(10).
001290         10  FILLER                 PIC X(4) VALUE SPACES.
```

Program 5–1 *(continued)*

```
001300          10  DL-YEAR-TO-DATE-SALES      PIC X(7).
001310          10  FILLER                     PIC X(4) VALUE SPACES.
001320          10  DL-YEAR-TO-DATE-SALES-RETURNS PIC X(7).
001330          10  FILLER                     PIC X(4) VALUE SPACES.
001340          10  DL-COMMISSION-RATE         PIC X(2).
001350          10  FILLER                     PIC X(4) VALUE SPACES.
001360       05  DL-FOUND-ERROR                PIC X(40).
001370 01  TL-TOTAL-LINE-1.
001380       05  FILLER                        PIC X(40)
001390           VALUE 'TOTAL NUMBER OF RECORDS READ'.
001400       05  TL-RECORDS-READ-OUT           PIC ZZ9.
001410 01  TL-TOTAL-LINE-2.
001420       05  FILLER                        PIC X(40)
001430           VALUE 'TOTAL NUMBER OF RECORDS VALID'.
001440       05  TL-VALID-RECORDS-OUT          PIC ZZ9.
001450 01  TL-TOTAL-LINE-3.
001460       05  FILLER                        PIC X(40)
001470           VALUE 'TOTAL NUMBER OF RECORDS INVALID'.
001480       05  TL-INVALID-RECORDS-OUT        PIC ZZ9.
001490 01  TL-TOTAL-LINE-4.
001500       05  FILLER                        PIC X(40)
001510           VALUE 'TOTAL NUMBER OF ERRORS'.
001520       05  TL-ERRORS-OUT                 PIC ZZ9.
001530 01  TL-TOTAL-LINE-5.
001540       05  FILLER                        PIC X(40)
001550           VALUE 'TOTAL YTD SALES OF VALID RECORDS'.
001560       05  TL-YTD-SALES-OUT              PIC $Z,ZZZ,ZZZ.99.
001570 01  TL-TOTAL-LINE-6.
001580       05  FILLER                        PIC X(40)
001590           VALUE 'TOTAL YTD RETURNS OF VALID RECORDS'.
001600       05  TL-YTD-RETURNS-OUT            PIC $Z,ZZZ,ZZZ.99.
001610*
001620 PROCEDURE DIVISION.
001630 A000-SALES-VALIDATE.
001640     OPEN INPUT SALES-INPUT-FILE
001650          OUTPUT VALID-SALES-FILE
001660                 AUDIT-ERROR-LISTING.
001670     PERFORM B100-INITIALIZE-VARIABLES.
001680     PERFORM Z100-PRINT-HEADINGS.
001690     PERFORM Z200-READ-SALES-RECORD.
001700     PERFORM B400-VALIDATE-RECORDS
001710         UNTIL END-OF-SALES-FILE.
001720     PERFORM B500-PRINT-TOTALS.
001730     CLOSE SALES-INPUT-FILE
001740           VALID-SALES-FILE
001750           AUDIT-ERROR-LISTING.
001760     STOP RUN.
001770 B100-INITIALIZE-VARIABLES.
001780     MOVE ZEROS          TO TOT-ACCUMULATORS
001790                            WS-PAGE-NUMBER.
001800     MOVE 'NO'           TO EOF-INDICATOR.
001810     MOVE LOW-VALUES     TO PREVIOUS-NUMBER.
001820     ACCEPT DW-DATE-AREA FROM DATE.
001830     MULTIPLY 100.0001   BY DW-DATE-AREA.
001840     MOVE DW-DATE-AREA-X TO HD-DATE-OUT.
001850 B400-VALIDATE-RECORDS.
001860     PERFORM C100-VALIDATE-FIELDS.
001870     IF RECORD-IS-IN-ERROR
001880         ADD 1 TO TOT-INVALID-RECORDS
001890     ELSE
001900         PERFORM C300-VALID-RECORD-PROCEDURE.
001910     IF SI-SALESPERSON-NUMBER > PREVIOUS-NUMBER
001920         MOVE SI-SALESPERSON-NUMBER TO PREVIOUS-NUMBER.
001930     PERFORM Z200-READ-SALES-RECORD.
```

Program 5–1   *(continued)*

```
001940 B500-PRINT-TOTALS.
001950     MOVE TOT-RECORDS-READ        TO TL-RECORDS-READ-OUT.
001960     MOVE TOT-VALID-RECORDS       TO TL-VALID-RECORDS-OUT.
001970     MOVE TOT-INVALID-RECORDS     TO TL-INVALID-RECORDS-OUT.
001980     MOVE TOT-NUMBER-OF-ERRORS    TO TL-ERRORS-OUT.
001990     MOVE TOT-YTD-SALES           TO TL-YTD-SALES-OUT.
002000     MOVE TOT-YTD-SALES-RETURNS   TO TL-YTD-RETURNS-OUT.
002010     WRITE AE-AUDIT-ERROR-RECORD  FROM TL-TOTAL-LINE-1
002020         AFTER 2.
002030     WRITE AE-AUDIT-ERROR-RECORD  FROM TL-TOTAL-LINE-2
002040         AFTER 1.
002050     WRITE AE-AUDIT-ERROR-RECORD  FROM TL-TOTAL-LINE-3
002060         AFTER 1.
002070     WRITE AE-AUDIT-ERROR-RECORD  FROM TL-TOTAL-LINE-4
002080         AFTER 1.
002090     WRITE AE-AUDIT-ERROR-RECORD  FROM TL-TOTAL-LINE-5
002100         AFTER 1.
002110     WRITE AE-AUDIT-ERROR-RECORD  FROM TL-TOTAL-LINE-6
002120         AFTER 1.
002130 C100-VALIDATE-FIELDS.
002140     PERFORM D100-NEW-RECORD-PROCEDURE.
002150     PERFORM D200-SALESPERSON-NUMBER-TESTS.
002160     PERFORM D300-LAST-NAME-TESTS.
002170     PERFORM D400-FIRST-NAME-TESTS.
002180     PERFORM D500-YEAR-TO-DATE-SALES-TESTS.
002190     PERFORM D600-YTD-SALES-RETURNS-TESTS.
002200     PERFORM D700-COMMISSION-RATE-TESTS.
002210 C300-VALID-RECORD-PROCEDURE.
002220     MOVE SI-SALESPERSON-NUMBER         TO VS-SALESPERSON-NUMBER.
002230     MOVE SI-LAST-NAME                  TO VS-LAST-NAME.
002240     MOVE SI-FIRST-NAME                 TO VS-FIRST-NAME.
002250     MOVE SI-YEAR-TO-DATE-SALES         TO VS-YEAR-TO-DATE-SALES.
002260     MOVE SI-YEAR-TO-DATE-SALES-RETURNS
002270         TO VS-YEAR-TO-DATE-SALES-RETURNS.
002280     MOVE SI-COMMISSION-RATE            TO VS-COMMISSION-RATE.
002290     WRITE VS-VALID-SALES-RECORD.
002300     ADD 1 TO TOT-VALID-RECORDS.
002310     ADD SI-YEAR-TO-DATE-SALES          TO TOT-YTD-SALES.
002320     ADD SI-YEAR-TO-DATE-SALES-RETURNS TO TOT-YTD-SALES-RETURNS.
002330     PERFORM Z400-PRINT-DETAIL-LINE.
002340 D100-NEW-RECORD-PROCEDURE.
002350     ADD 1      TO TOT-RECORDS-READ.
002360     MOVE 'NO'  TO FIRST-ERROR-INDICATOR
002370                   RECORD-ERROR-INDICATOR
002380                   FIELD-ERROR-INDICATOR.
002390     MOVE SPACES TO DL-FOUND-ERROR.
002400     PERFORM E400-MOVE-TO-DETAIL-LINE.
002410 D200-SALESPERSON-NUMBER-TESTS.
002420     PERFORM E500-SALESPERSON-NUMBER-CHECK.
002430     IF FIELD-IS-IN-ERROR
002440         PERFORM Z300-ERROR-PROCEDURES.
002450 D300-LAST-NAME-TESTS.
002460     PERFORM E600-LAST-NAME-CHECK.
002470     IF FIELD-IS-IN-ERROR
002480         PERFORM Z300-ERROR-PROCEDURES.
002490 D400-FIRST-NAME-TESTS.
002500     PERFORM E700-FIRST-NAME-CHECK.
002510     IF FIELD-IS-IN-ERROR
002520         PERFORM Z300-ERROR-PROCEDURES.
002530 D500-YEAR-TO-DATE-SALES-TESTS.
002540     PERFORM E800-YEAR-TO-DATE-SALES-CHECK.
002550     IF FIELD-IS-IN-ERROR
002560         PERFORM Z300-ERROR-PROCEDURES.
002570 D600-YTD-SALES-RETURNS-TESTS.
```

Program 5–1 *(continued)*

```
002580      PERFORM E900-YTD-SALES-RETURNS-CHECK.
002590      IF FIELD-IS-IN-ERROR
002600          PERFORM Z300-ERROR-PROCEDURES.
002610 D700-COMMISSION-RATE-TESTS.
002620      PERFORM E1000-COMMISSION-RATE-CHECK.
002630      IF FIELD-IS-IN-ERROR
002640          PERFORM Z300-ERROR-PROCEDURES.
002650 E400-MOVE-TO-DETAIL-LINE.
002660      MOVE SI-SALESPERSON-NUMBER     TO DL-SALESPERSON-NUMBER.
002670      MOVE SI-LAST-NAME              TO DL-LAST-NAME.
002680      MOVE SI-FIRST-NAME             TO DL-FIRST-NAME.
002690      MOVE SI-YEAR-TO-DATE-SALES-X TO DL-YEAR-TO-DATE-SALES.
002700      MOVE SI-YEAR-TO-DATE-SALES-RETNS-X
002710          TO DL-YEAR-TO-DATE-SALES-RETURNS.
002720      MOVE SI-COMMISSION-RATE-X      TO DL-COMMISSION-RATE.
002730 E500-SALESPERSON-NUMBER-CHECK.
002740      IF SI-SALESPERSON-NUMBER = SPACES
002750          MOVE 'NUMBER DOES NOT EXIST' TO DL-FOUND-ERROR
002760          MOVE 'YES' TO FIELD-ERROR-INDICATOR
002770      ELSE
002780          IF NOT VALID-SALESPERSON-NUMBER
002790              MOVE 'SALES NUMBER NOT VALID' TO DL-FOUND-ERROR
002800              MOVE 'YES' TO FIELD-ERROR-INDICATOR
002810          ELSE
002820              IF SI-SALESPERSON-NUMBER NOT > PREVIOUS-NUMBER
002830                  MOVE 'SEQUENCE ERROR' TO DL-FOUND-ERROR
002840                  MOVE 'YES' TO FIELD-ERROR-INDICATOR.
002850 E600-LAST-NAME-CHECK.
002860      IF SI-LAST-NAME = SPACES
002870          MOVE 'LAST NAME DOES NOT EXIST' TO DL-FOUND-ERROR
002880          MOVE 'YES' TO FIELD-ERROR-INDICATOR
002890      ELSE
002900          IF SI-LAST-NAME-CHARACTER(1) = SPACES
002910              MOVE 11 TO LENGTH-SUBSCRIPT
002920              PERFORM F100-JUSTIFY-LAST-NAME
002930                  UNTIL SI-LAST-NAME-CHARACTER(1) NOT = SPACES.
002940 E700-FIRST-NAME-CHECK.
002950      IF SI-FIRST-NAME = SPACES
002960          MOVE 'FIRST NAME DOES NOT EXIST' TO DL-FOUND-ERROR
002970          MOVE 'YES' TO FIELD-ERROR-INDICATOR
002980      ELSE
002990          IF SI-FIRST-NAME-CHARACTER(1) = SPACES
003000              MOVE 10 TO LENGTH-SUBSCRIPT
003010              PERFORM F200-JUSTIFY-FIRST-NAME
003020                  UNTIL SI-FIRST-NAME-CHARACTER(1) NOT = SPACES.
003030 E800-YEAR-TO-DATE-SALES-CHECK.
003040      IF SI-YEAR-TO-DATE-SALES-X = SPACES
003050          MOVE 'YTD SALES DOES NOT EXIST' TO DL-FOUND-ERROR
003060          MOVE 'YES' TO FIELD-ERROR-INDICATOR
003070      ELSE
003080          INSPECT SI-YEAR-TO-DATE-SALES
003090              REPLACING LEADING SPACES BY ZEROES
003100          IF SI-YEAR-TO-DATE-SALES NOT NUMERIC
003110              MOVE 'YTD SALES NOT NUMERIC' TO DL-FOUND-ERROR
003120              MOVE 'YES' TO FIELD-ERROR-INDICATOR
003130          ELSE
003140              IF NOT VALID-YTD-SALES
003150                  MOVE 'YTD SALES NOT VALID' TO DL-FOUND-ERROR
003160                  MOVE 'YES' TO FIELD-ERROR-INDICATOR.
003170 E900-YTD-SALES-RETURNS-CHECK.
003180      IF SI-YEAR-TO-DATE-SALES-RETNS-X = SPACES
003190          MOVE 'YTD RETURNS DOES NOT EXIST' TO DL-FOUND-ERROR
003200          MOVE 'YES' TO FIELD-ERROR-INDICATOR
003210      ELSE
```

Program 5–1   *(continued)*

```
003220          INSPECT SI-YEAR-TO-DATE-SALES-RETURNS
003230              REPLACING LEADING SPACES BY ZEROES
003240          IF SI-YEAR-TO-DATE-SALES-RETURNS NOT NUMERIC
003250              MOVE 'YTD RETURNS NOT NUMERIC' TO DL-FOUND-ERROR
003260              MOVE 'YES' TO FIELD-ERROR-INDICATOR
003270          ELSE
003280              IF NOT VALID-YTD-SALES-RETURNS
003290                  MOVE 'YTD RETURNS TOO HIGH' TO DL-FOUND-ERROR
003300                  MOVE 'YES' TO FIELD-ERROR-INDICATOR.
003310 E1000-COMMISSION-RATE-CHECK.
003320      IF SI-COMMISSION-RATE-X = SPACES
003330          MOVE 'COMMISSION DOES NOT EXIST' TO DL-FOUND-ERROR
003340          MOVE 'YES' TO FIELD-ERROR-INDICATOR
003350      ELSE
003360          INSPECT SI-COMMISSION-RATE
003370              REPLACING LEADING SPACES BY ZEROES
003380          IF SI-COMMISSION-RATE NOT NUMERIC
003390              MOVE 'COMMISSION NOT NUMERIC' TO DL-FOUND-ERROR
003400              MOVE 'YES' TO FIELD-ERROR-INDICATOR
003410          ELSE
003420              IF NOT VALID-COMMISSION-RATE
003430                  MOVE 'COMMISSION OUT OF RANGE'
003440                      TO DL-FOUND-ERROR
003450                  MOVE 'YES' TO FIELD-ERROR-INDICATOR.
003460 F100-JUSTIFY-LAST-NAME.
003470      PERFORM G100-MOVE-LAST-NAME-TO-LEFT
003480          VARYING CHARACTER-SUBSCRIPT
003490          FROM 1 BY 1
003500          UNTIL CHARACTER-SUBSCRIPT = LENGTH-SUBSCRIPT.
003510      MOVE SPACE TO SI-LAST-NAME-CHARACTER(LENGTH-SUBSCRIPT).
003520      SUBTRACT 1 FROM LENGTH-SUBSCRIPT.
003530 F200-JUSTIFY-FIRST-NAME.
003540      PERFORM G200-MOVE-FIRST-NAME-TO-LEFT
003550          VARYING CHARACTER-SUBSCRIPT
003560          FROM 1 BY 1
003570          UNTIL CHARACTER-SUBSCRIPT = LENGTH-SUBSCRIPT.
003580      MOVE SPACE TO SI-FIRST-NAME-CHARACTER(LENGTH-SUBSCRIPT).
003590      SUBTRACT 1 FROM LENGTH-SUBSCRIPT.
003600 G100-MOVE-LAST-NAME-TO-LEFT.
003610      COMPUTE NEXT-CHARACTER = CHARACTER-SUBSCRIPT + 1.
003620      MOVE SI-LAST-NAME-CHARACTER(NEXT-CHARACTER)
003630          TO SI-LAST-NAME-CHARACTER(CHARACTER-SUBSCRIPT).
003640 G200-MOVE-FIRST-NAME-TO-LEFT.
003650      COMPUTE NEXT-CHARACTER = CHARACTER-SUBSCRIPT + 1.
003660      MOVE SI-FIRST-NAME-CHARACTER(NEXT-CHARACTER)
003670          TO SI-FIRST-NAME-CHARACTER(CHARACTER-SUBSCRIPT).
003680 Z100-PRINT-HEADINGS.
003690      ADD 1 TO WS-PAGE-NUMBER.
003700      MOVE WS-PAGE-NUMBER         TO HD-PAGE-NUMBER-OUT.
003710      WRITE AE-AUDIT-ERROR-RECORD FROM HD-HEADING-LINE-1
003720          AFTER PAGE.
003730      WRITE AE-AUDIT-ERROR-RECORD FROM HD-HEADING-LINE-2
003740          AFTER 2.
003750      MOVE 3 TO WS-LINES-USED.
003760 Z200-READ-SALES-RECORD.
003770      READ SALES-INPUT-FILE
003780          AT END MOVE 'END' TO EOF-INDICATOR.
003790 Z300-ERROR-PROCEDURES.
003800      MOVE 'YES' TO RECORD-ERROR-INDICATOR.
003810      MOVE 'NO'  TO FIELD-ERROR-INDICATOR.
003820      ADD 1 TO TOT-NUMBER-OF-ERRORS.
003830      PERFORM Z400-PRINT-DETAIL-LINE.
003840 Z400-PRINT-DETAIL-LINE.
003850      IF RECORD-ALREADY-BAD
```

Program 5-1   *(concluded)*

```
003860          MOVE SPACES TO DL-OUTPUT-AREA
003870      ELSE
003880          MOVE 'YES' TO FIRST-ERROR-INDICATOR.
003890      MOVE DL-DETAIL-LINE TO AE-AUDIT-ERROR-RECORD.
003900      WRITE AE-AUDIT-ERROR-RECORD
003910          AFTER 1.
003920      ADD 1 TO WS-LINES-USED.
003930      IF WS-LINES-USED > WS-LINES-PER-PAGE
003940          PERFORM Z100-PRINT-HEADINGS.
```

Discussion

Referring to the source program listing of Program 5-1, notice that each of the input fields is defined in SI-SALES-INPUT-RECORD with an alphanumeric PICTURE clause. A data exception would occur if a numeric field containing nonnumeric characters were moved to a numeric report item. When such fields are moved to DL-DETAIL-LINE, the receiving fields must be defined as alphanumeric. Another reason to define the receiving fields, as well as the sending fields, as alphanumeric is because it is important to prepare the report with exact images of the fields as they were input. Since there can be no assumptions as to the validity of input numeric fields, it is necessary to define them with alphanumeric PICTURE clauses. REDEFINES clauses are then necessary in statements 500 and 550, since these data fields must be added to accumulators when a record passes all tests.

Note that the use of 88-level condition-names simplifies the logic of several tests. The use of the THRU option eliminates the necessity of a compound IF statement and makes the IF statement sound more like English. The problems of program modification are also minimized when using 88-level condition-names. The only modification necessary would be in the DATA division. No entries in the PROCE DURE division would be affected.

Figure 5-17 contains the output from Program 5-1 and will be helpful in following the logic of the program.

After the files are opened in lines 1640-1660, B100-INITIALIZE-VARIABLES is performed to initialize the accumulators, page number, end of file indicator, and set PREVIOUS-NUMBER to LOW-VALUES. PREVIOUS-NUMBER is set to LOW-VALUES initially so that the first record will not be detected as being out of sequence. Also, the current date is determined. Then the first record is read, and B400-VALI DATE-RECORDS is performed.

Statement 1860 causes the execution of C100-VALIDATE-FIELDS, which in turn performs D100-NEW-RECORD-PROCEDURE. For each new record this procedure is executed to count the number of records read, initialize record indicators, clear DL-FOUND-ERROR on the detail line, and move the input record image to the detail line. Notice that RECORD-ERROR-INDICATOR, FIELD-ERROR-INDICA TOR, and FIRST-ERROR-INDICATOR are initialized to 'NO' to make the initial assumption that the record is valid. If errors are detected, these indicators will be used to determine whether to perform Z300-ERROR-PROCEDURES.

Next D200-SALESPERSON-NUMBER-TESTS is performed, which in turn per forms E500-SALESPERSON-NUMBER-CHECK. The third employee's record does not pass the existence test accomplished in statement 2740. Thus an appropriate error message is moved to the detail line, FIELD-ERROR-INDICATOR is set to 'YES', and control returns to statement 2430.

Since the FIELD-ERROR-INDICATOR has been set to 'YES' the condition FIELD-IS-IN-ERROR is true, which causes Z300-ERROR-PROCEDURES to be per formed. RECORD-ERROR-INDICATOR is set to 'YES' in statement 3800. This indica-

Figure 5–17 *Output from Program 5–1*

```
01/25/87                                  SALES VALIDATION REPORT              PAGE    1

NUMBER  LAST NAME    FIRST NAME    SALES     RETURNS   RATE   ERROR MESSAGE
0017    PAYNE        MAX           98700      5673      5
0125    LISHER       JANET F.      50000         0     15
        BROCKETT     JANE R.       75000     90000      5     NUMBER DOES NOT EXIST
                                                              YTD RETURNS TOO HIGH

0356    GOLTMAN      LINDA S.     109877      1000     10
0396    VOLSKY       CHRIS         32680      5847      8
0401    OWENS        GEORGE                   3957     35     YTD SALES DOES NOT EXIST
                                                              COMMISSION OUT OF RANGE

0479    WETZEL       ROBERT D.    208876      5877     15
0529    PEACOCK      BARBARA       67330     15664      8
0580    DUPREE       KELLY L.     357888     27582            YTD SALES NOT VALID
                                                              COMMISSION DOES NOT EXIST

0635    HUNT         ROBERT        45320               10     YTD RETURNS DOES NOT EXIST
0746    JACKSON      JASON         78450      8478     15
0859    HUTCHENS     JEFF          57630      4857     14
0927    BARCLAY      RICHARD      198740     48563     11
1001    DILL         JEFF          58640     28456     20
1000    UNLAND       KIM L.        47564     39585     25     SEQUENCE ERROR
0999    GOODMAN      EVE           64542     23847     10     SEQUENCE ERROR
1634    VAUGHN                     47899     45678     20     FIRST NAME DOES NOT EXIST
1805    KIMBERLING   CARLA K.      50000     10000     30
1856    LOVELAND     GEORGE        46275     27656     10
1867    STEWARD      KEVIN J.     115000     17500     15
1938    DWYER        JOHN D.       23175      4000     10
2157    YOUNG        KAREN L.     112359      3575     30
2186    SMITH        DOUGLAS       18345     37758     20
2269    THOMPSON     LISA S.       50000     10000     20
2294    HERMAN       JACK          48465      8747      5
2341    ADAMS        ROBYN A.      23175      4000     10
2395    MATNEY       DELORES       79574     85746      5
2485    PHILLIPS     TRACY L.      50000     10000     30
2487    HUME         LETA          48353     28437     20
2575    CROSS        CHERYL        38563     38250     10     SALES NUMBER NOT VALID

TOTAL NUMBER OF RECORDS READ          30
TOTAL NUMBER OF RECORDS VALID         22
TOTAL NUMBER OF RECORDS INVALID        8
TOTAL NUMBER OF ERRORS                11
TOTAL YTD SALES OF VALID RECORDS    $   16,256.44
TOTAL YTD RETURNS OF VALID RECORDS  $    3,718.34
```

tor flags the record as containing at least one error, which means it will be rejected because it is invalid. FIELD–ERROR–INDICATOR is reset to 'NO', which is necessary for subsequent field tests. The TOT–NUMBER–OF–ERRORS is accumulated and Z400–PRINT–DETAIL–LINE is performed. The IF statement at statement 3850 tests to determine whether this is the first error that has been detected, so that the input record image is printed only for the first error and not printed for subsequent errors. Notice the results in the output in Figure 5–17 for employee Brockett. The input record image is printed for the first error but not for the second.

After the error has been printed for the third employee, control returns to statement 2160, which will in turn perform additional field tests. Control eventually returns to statement 1870. An error was detected for the third employee record, so RECORD–IS–IN–ERROR is a true condition causing the execution of statement 1880 and the reading of the next record. The cycle then continues for each employee. The IF statement at line 1910 is used to reset the PREVIOUS–NUMBER when appropriate.

Figure 5–18 is a file dump of the valid file that was created as a result of the running of Program 5–1. Notice that all numeric fields have been appropriately pad-

Figure 5–18 *Listing of Valid File from Disk*

```
0017PAYNE        MAX          0098700000567305
0125LISHER       JANET F.     0050000000000015
0356GOLTMAN      LINDA S.     0109877000100010
0396VOLSKY       CHRIS        0032680000584708
0479WETZEL       ROBERT D.    0208876000587715
0529PEACOCK      BARBARA      0067330001566408
0746JACKSON      JASON        0078450000847815
0859HUTCHENS     JEFF         0057630000485714
0927BARCLAY      RICHARD      0198740004856311
1001DILL         JEFF         0058640002845620
1805KIMBERLING   CARLA K.     0050000001000030
1856LOVELAND     GEORGE       0046275002765610
1867STEWARD      KEVIN J.     0115000001750015
1938DWYER        JOHN D.      0023175000400010
2157YOUNG        KAREN L.     0112359000357530
2186SMITH        DOUGLAS      0018345003775820
2269THOMPSON     LISA S.      0050000001000020
2294HERMAN       JACK         0048465000874705
2341ADAMS        ROBYN A.     0023175000400010
2395MATNEY       DELORES      0079574008574605
2485PHILLIPS     TRACY L.     0050000001000030
2487HUME         LETA         0048353002843720
```

ded on the left with zeros and that the records in which the names were not justified have been corrected.

Transaction Validation

Transaction validation concepts are slightly different than validation of data that is to be placed directly into a new file, as was the case with the previous example. To effectively validate transactions that are going to be used to update existing records in files, the programmer must make a basic decision. The decision centers around the two types of transaction validation that occur. The first type of validation is dependent on the type of transaction being validated. This type of validation can be undertaken without concurrently accessing the file being updated. The second type of transaction validation consists of the tests that were previously defined as inter-file tests. These tests must, of course, be undertaken only when both the input transactions and the file to be updated are accessed concurrently.

The reason a decision must be made is simply because the first level of validation can be undertaken in a program that is separate from the actual updating procedure. In other words, a fairly standard validation program can be used to validate transactions, and the result will be a valid transaction file. This valid transaction file is then used as input to an update program (either immediately after the validation run or many days later).

The major difference in this situation is that not all tests are performed on every record. Figure 5–19 shows the COBOL statements that could be used to replace C100–VALIDATE–FIELDS that was previously used in Program 5–1.

Programming Style

1. Define input fields with an alphanumeric PICTURE clause when preparing a validation program. Use the REDEFINES clause for numeric fields, when necessary.
2. Make effective use of 88-level condition-names to simplify IF statements and to make them more readable.

Figure 5–19 *Transaction Validation*

```
002180 C100-VALIDATE-FIELDS.
002190     PERFORM D100-NEW-RECORD-PROCEDURE.
           IF NOT VALID-TRANSACTION-CODE
               MOVE 'TRANS CODE NOT VALID' TO DL-FOUND-ERROR
               PERFORM Z300-ERROR-PROCEDURES
           ELSE
               PERFORM D200-SALESPERSON-NUMBER-TESTS
               IF ADDITION-OF-SALESPERSON
                   PERFORM D300-LAST-NAME-TESTS
                   PERFORM D400-FIRST-NAME-TESTS
                   PERFORM D700-COMMISSION-RATE-TESTS
               ELSE
                   IF DELETION-OF-SALESPERSON
                       NEXT SENTENCE
                   ELSE
                       IF NAME-CHANGE
                           PERFORM D300-LAST-NAME-TESTS
                           PERFORM D400-FIRST-NAME-TESTS
                       ELSE
                           IF UPDATE-YTD-SALES
                               PERFORM D500-YEAR-TO-DATE-SALES-TESTS
                           ELSE
                               IF UPDATE-YTD-SALES-RETURNS
                                   PERFORM D600-YTD-SALES-RETURNS-TESTS
                               ELSE
                                   PERFORM D700-COMMISSION-RATE-TESTS.
002260 C300-VALID-RECORD-PROCEDURE.
```

3. Appropriately indent subclauses or statements to clearly delineate the intended logic in the PROCEDURE division.

4. Line up PICTURE clauses and multiple MOVE statements for easier reading of the source listing.

Common Errors

1. Counting a REDEFINES PICTURE clause towards the character count in a record.

2. Relying on compound IF statements instead of 88-level condition-names.

3. Inappropriately using the INSPECT/REPLACING ALL statement when attempting to pad with zeros.

4. Confusing limit checks with reasonableness checks.

5. Inappropriate sequencing of validation tests.

6. Using nondescriptive error messages; be concise but specific. The user needs to know what was wrong with the data.

7. Failing to consider necessary interfield relationships.

8. Misplacing a period in a long IF statement.

9. Failing to appropriately accumulate control totals, including record counts and error counts.

Exercises

1. List five different types of data-validation tests.

2. For the following data fields in an inventory record, list the appropriate validation tests that should be performed, and indicate the correct sequence of data validation.

a. Store number.
b. Department code, alphabetic.
c. Vendor number.
d. Item description.
e. Quantity on hand.
f. Sales price per unit.
g. Cost per unit.
h. Year-to-date quantity sold.
i. Year-to-date quantity purchased.

3. For the following data fields in a salesperson record, list the appropriate validation tests that should be performed, and indicate the correct sequence of data validation.
a. Salesperson number.
b. Salesperson name.
c. Store number.
d. Department code.
e. Employee code.
f. Year-to-date sales.
g. Year-to-date sales returns.
h. Commission rate.

4. For the data fields listed in Figure 5–20, indicate the results of the related INSPECT statements on the field contents and the result in the TALLY field.

Figure 5–20 *INSPECT Results*

Field contents before INSPECT	INSPECT statement	Field contents after INSPECT	Contents of COUNT
b b b 4 , 2 1 3 0 0	INSPECT FIELD REPLACING ALL SPACES BY '*'.		
b b b 4 , 2 1 3 0 0	INSPECT FIELD REPLACING FIRST SPACES BY '*'.		
b b b 4 , 2 1 3 0 0	INSPECT FIELD REPLACING LEADING SPACES BY '*'.		

5. For each of the following data fields explain what the results of the related IF statements will be. What message will be prepared when the IF statement is executed, if any?

```
Data field              IF statement
contents
b b b 7 5 0 0    IF FIELD = SPACES
                     MOVE 'FIELD DOES NOT EXIST' TO MESSAGE
                 ELSE
                     INSPECT FIELD
                        REPLACING LEADING SPACES BY ZEROES
                     IF FIELD NOT NUMERIC
                        MOVE 'FIELD NOT NUMERIC' TO MESSAGE
                     ELSE
                        IF FIELD > 8000
                            MOVE 'FIELD > 8000' TO MESSAGE.
b b b 7 5 b 0    IF FIELD = SPACES
                     MOVE 'FIELD DOES NOT EXIST' TO MESSAGE
                 ELSE
```

```
                              INSPECT FIELD
                                  REPLACING LEADING SPACES BY ZEROS
                              IF FIELD NOT NUMERIC
                                  MOVE 'FIELD NOT NUMERIC' TO MESSAGE
                              ELSE
                                  IF FIELD > 8000
                                      MOVE 'FIELD > 8000' TO MESSAGE.
b b b 8 0 0 1   IF FIELD = SPACES
                    MOVE 'FIELD DOES NOT EXIST' TO MESSAGE
                ELSE
                    INSPECT FIELD
                        REPLACING LEADING SPACES BY ZEROS
                    IF FIELD NOT NUMERIC
                        MOVE 'FIELD NOT NUMERIC' TO MESSAGE
                    ELSE
                        IF FIELD > 8000
                            MOVE 'FIELD > 8000' TO MESSAGE.
b b b b b b b   IF FIELD = SPACES
                    MOVE 'FIELD DOES NOT EXIST' TO MESSAGE
                ELSE
                    INSPECT FIELD
                        REPLACING LEADING SPACES BY ZEROS
                    IF FIELD NOT NUMERIC
                        MOVE 'FIELD NOT NUMERIC' TO MESSAGE
                    ELSE
                        IF FIELD > 8000
                            MOVE 'FIELD > 8000' TO MESSAGE.
B R O W N b b   IF FIELD = SPACES
                    MOVE 'FIELD DOES NOT EXIST' TO MESSAGE
                ELSE
                    IF FIRST-POS-IN-FIELD = SPACES
                        MOVE 'FIELD NOT JUSTIFIED' TO MESSAGE
                    IF FIELD NOT ALPHABETIC
                        MOVE 'FIELD NOT ALPHABETIC' TO MESSAGE.
b b b b b b b   IF FIELD = SPACES
                    MOVE 'FIELD DOES NOT EXIST' TO MESSAGE
                ELSE
                    IF FIRST-POS-IN-FIELD = SPACES
                        MOVE 'FIELD NOT JUSTIFIED' TO MESSAGE
                    IF FIELD NOT ALPHABETIC
                        MOVE 'FIELD NOT ALPHABETIC' TO MESSAGE.
b B R O W N b   IF FIELD = SPACES
                    MOVE 'FIELD DOES NOT EXIST' TO MESSAGE
                ELSE
                    IF FIRST-POS-IN-FIELD = SPACES
                        MOVE 'FIELD NOT JUSTIFIED' TO MESSAGE
                    IF FIELD NOT ALPHABETIC
                        MOVE 'FIELD NOT ALPHABETIC' TO MESSAGE.
B R O 2 N b     IF FIELD = SPACES
                    MOVE 'FIELD DOES NOT EXIST' TO MESSAGE
                ELSE
                    IF FIRST-POS-IN-FIELD = SPACES
                        MOVE 'FIELD NOT JUSTIFIED' TO MESSAGE
                    IF FIELD NOT ALPHABETIC
                        MOVE 'FIELD NOT ALPHABETIC' TO MESSAGE.
```

Figure 5–21 *Printer Spacing Chart for Problem 5–1*

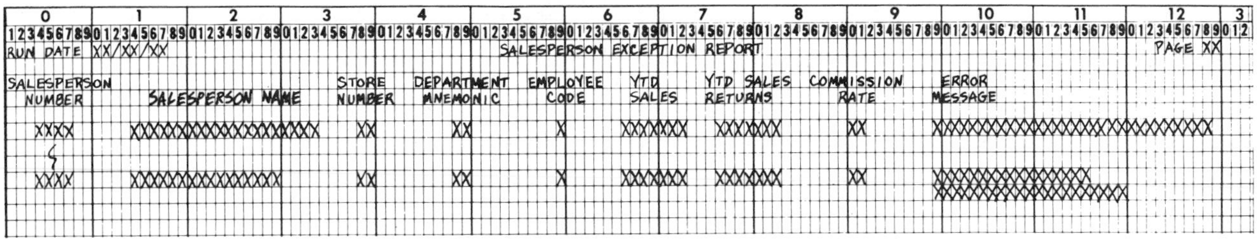

Problems

Use Data Set B in Appendix C for Problems 5–1 through 5–3.

1. Write a COBOL program to produce a listing of all invalid data records in the Data Set B in Appendix C. The required output is illustrated in the printer spacing chart in Figure 5–21. Complete all reasonable validation procedures on the data set with the following items provided to assist in determining appropriate validation procedures. For any record determined to be invalid, print an error message that appropriately informs the user of the type of error. If a record has more than one error, do not repeat the display of the input record image. Simply ignore all records that are found to be valid—do not print valid records on the printer.

   a. The highest salesperson number that has been issued so far is 9025.
   b. Valid store numbers are 10 through 50.
   c. Valid employee codes range from 1 through 5.
   d. Department mnemonics should be alphabetic.
   e. Commission rates may range up to 25 percent.
   f. Year-to-date sales must be equal to or greater than year-to-date sales returns.
   g. Every salesperson has had sales, though not everyone has had sales returns.
   h. If the salesperson name is not left-justified, correct it.

2. Modify the program created for Problem 5–1 or write a program from scratch according to the printer spacing chart shown in Figure 5–22 (note that valid records are listed) with the following additional requirements:
   a. Transfer all valid records to a disk file.
   b. Accumulate the following totals:
      (1) Total number of records read.
      (2) Total number of valid records.
      (3) Total number of invalid records.
      (4) Total year-to-date sales of valid records.
      (5) Total year-to-date sales returns of valid records.
      (6) Total year-to-date net sales of valid records. (Net sales are calculated by subtracting year-to-date sales returns from year-to-date sales.)

3. From the data file created in Problem 5–2, which contains valid data records, provide a listing according to the printer spacing chart illustrated in Figure 5–23. Note that the totals of year-to-date sales, year-to-date sales returns, and net year-to-date sales on this report should be the same as determined from the program developed and tested for Problem 5– 2. The commission is calculated by multiplying net year-to-date sales times the commission rate. The

Figure 5–22   *Printer Spacing Chart for Problem 5–2*

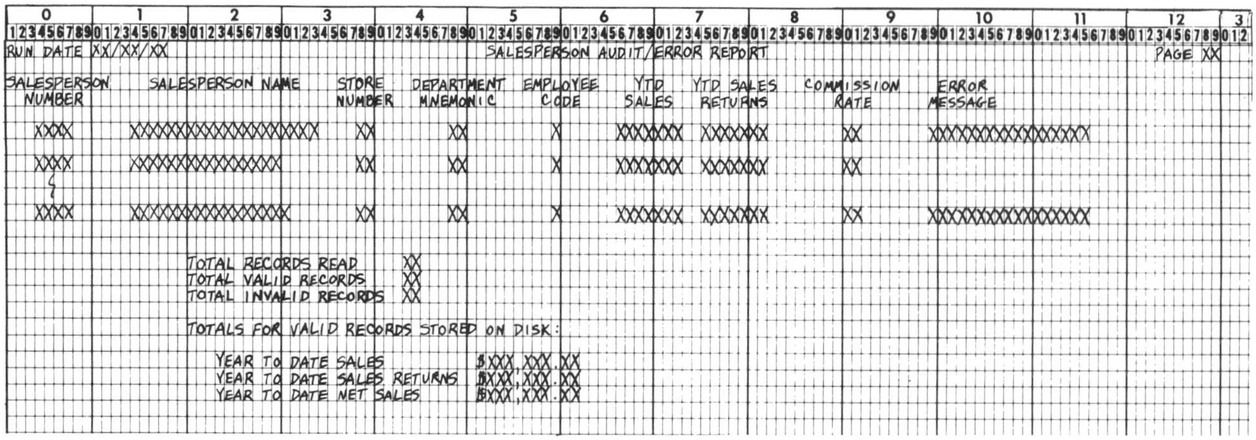

```
RUN DATE XX/XX/XX                    SALESPERSON AUDIT/ERROR REPORT                    PAGE XX

SALESPERSON   SALESPERSON NAME      STORE    DEPARTMENT  EMPLOYEE   YTD      YTD SALES   COMMISSION   ERROR
  NUMBER                            NUMBER    MNEMONIC     CODE     SALES     RETURNS      RATE       MESSAGE

   XXXX    XXXXXXXXXXXXXXXXXX        XX         XX          X      XXXXXXX   XXXXXXX       XX      XXXXXXXXXXXXXXXXXX
   XXXX    XXXXXXXXXXXXXX            XX         XX          X      XXXXXXX   XXXXXXX       XX
   XXXX    XXXXXXXXXXXXX             XX         XX          X      XXXXXXX   XXXXXXX       XX      XXXXXXXXXXXXXXXXXX

               TOTAL RECORDS READ     XX
               TOTAL VALID RECORDS    XX
               TOTAL INVALID RECORDS  XX

               TOTALS FOR VALID RECORDS STORED ON DISK:

                   YEAR TO DATE SALES          $XXX,XXX.XX
                   YEAR TO DATE SALES RETURNS  $XXX,XXX.XX
                   YEAR TO DATE NET SALES      $XXX,XXX.XX
```

procedures described in Problem 5–2 and Problem 5–3 may be combined into one program, or they may be written as two separate programs.

Use Data Set C in Appendix C for Problems 5–4 through 5–6.

4. Write a COBOL program to produce a listing of all invalid data records in the Data Set C according to the printer spacing chart shown in Figure 5–24. Complete all reasonable validation procedures on the data set with the following items provided to assist in determining appropriate validation procedures. For any record determined to be invalid, print an error message that appropriately informs the user of the type of error. If a record has more than one error, do not repeat the display of the input record image. Simply ignore all records that are found to be valid—do not print valid records on the printer.

   a. Valid store numbers are 10 and 20.
   b. Department mnemonics should be alphabetic and must be AU or AP for automotive and appliances.
   c. Valid item numbers range up through 890.
   d. The highest sales price per unit in the automotive department is $75.
   e. The highest sales price per unit in the appliance department is $795.
   f. All fields should exist.
   g. If the item description is not left-justified, correct it.

Figure 5–23   *Printer Spacing Chart for Problem 5–3*

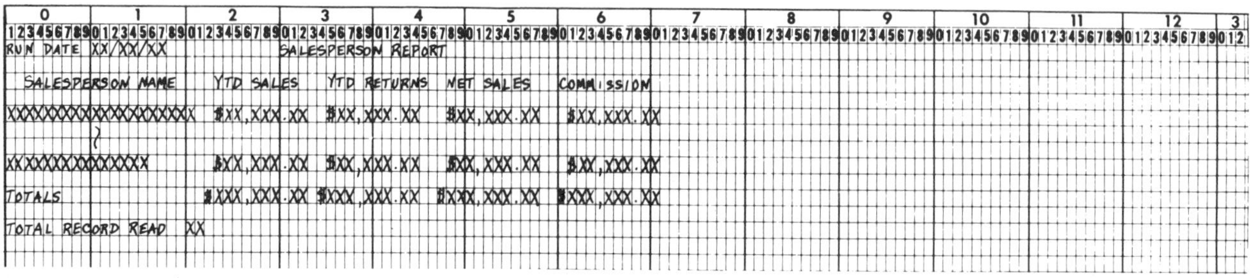

```
RUN DATE XX/XX/XX        SALESPERSON REPORT

   SALESPERSON NAME      YTD SALES     YTD RETURNS    NET SALES     COMMISSION

XXXXXXXXXXXXXXXXXXX      $XX,XXX.XX    $XX,XXX.XX    $XX,XXX.XX    $XX,XXX.XX

XXXXXXXXXXXXX           $XX,XXX.XX    $XX,XXX.XX    $XX,XXX.XX    $XX,XXX.XX
TOTALS                  $XXX,XXX.XX   $XXX,XXX.XX   $XXX,XXX.XX   $XXX,XXX.XX
TOTAL RECORD READ  XX
```

5. Modify the program created for Problem 5–4, or write a program from scratch according to the printer spacing chart shown in Figure 5–25 (note that valid records are listed) with the following additional requirements:
   a. Transfer all valid records to a disk file.
   b. Accumulate the following totals:
      (1) Total number of records read.
      (2) Total number of valid records.
      (3) Total number of invalid records.
      (4) Total year-to-date sales quantities of valid records.
      (5) Total year-to-date quantities purchased of valid records.
      (6) Total year-to-date sales dollars (price times quantity).
      (7) Total year-to-date purchase dollars (cost times quantity purchased).

6. From the data file created in Problem 5–5, which contains valid data records, provide a listing according to the printer spacing chart illustrated in Figure 5–26. Note that the totals of year-to-date sales quantities, year-to-date sales purchases, year-to-date sales dollars, and year-to-date purchase dollars on this report should be the same as determined from the program developed and tested for Problem 5–5. The procedures described in Problem 5–5 and Problem 5–6 may be combined into one program, or they may be written as two separate programs.

Figure 5–24 *Printer Spacing Chart for Problem 5–4*

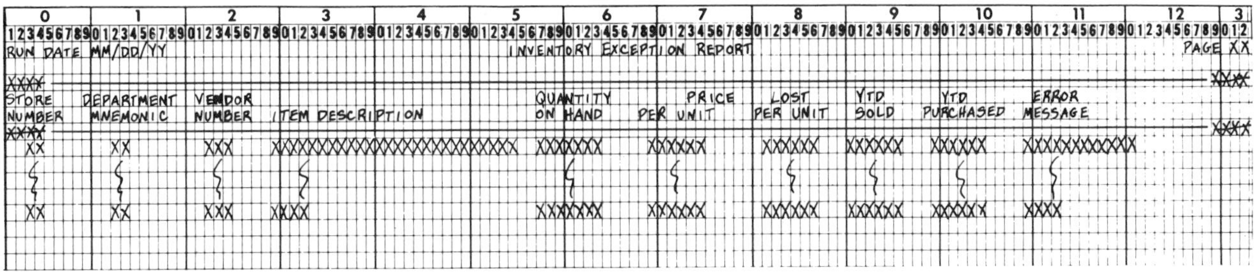

Figure 5–25 *Printer Spacing Chart for Problem 5–5*

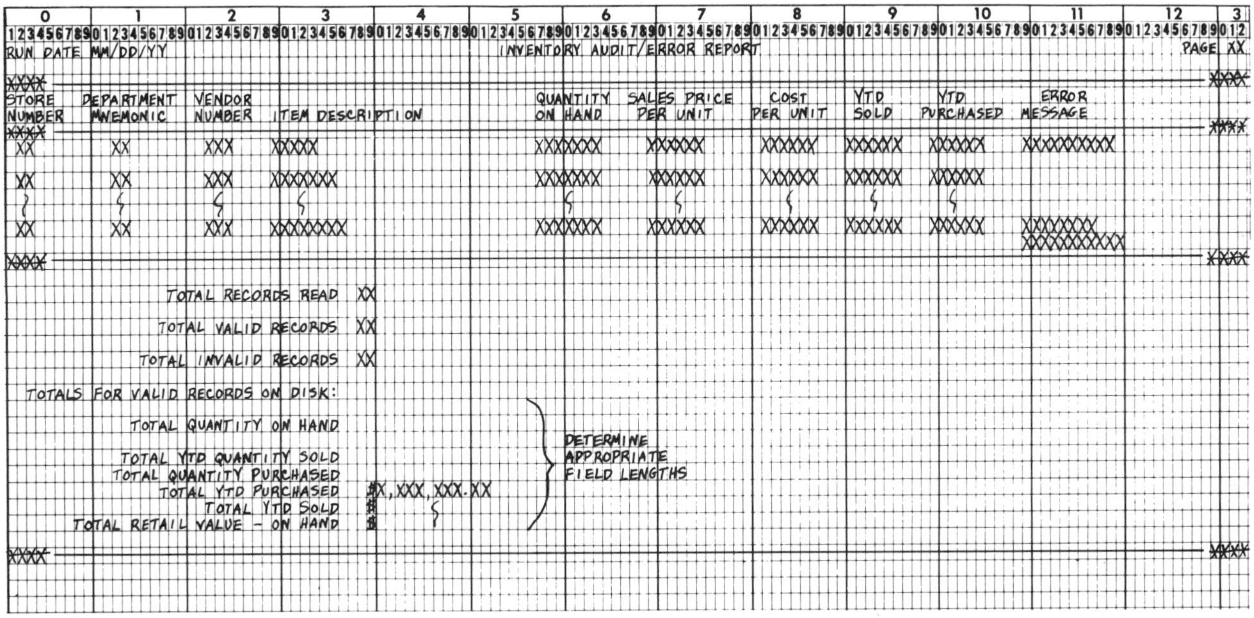

Figure 5–26   *Printer Spacing Chart for Problem 5–6*

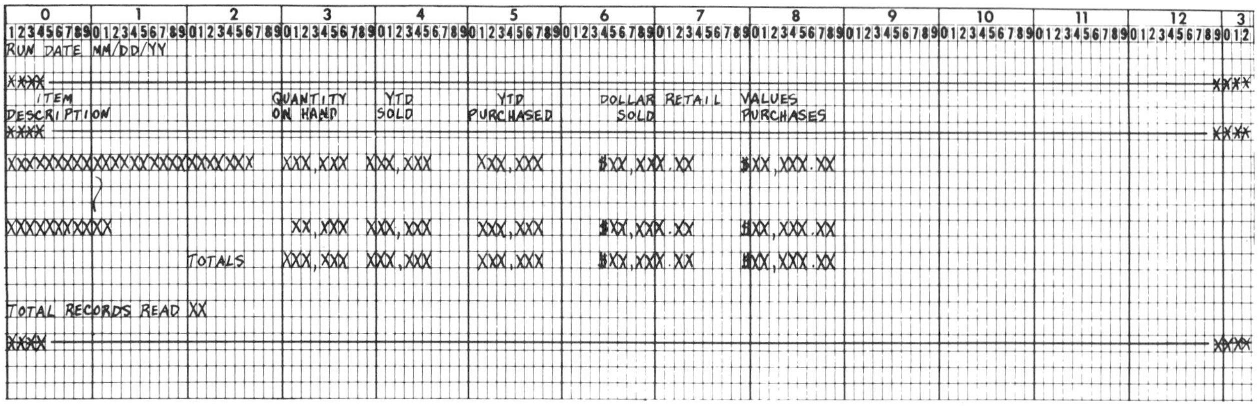

```
RUN DATE MM/DD/YY
XXXX                                                              XXXX
         ITEM            QUANTITY  YTD      YTD        DOLLAR RETAIL  VALUES
DESCRIPTION             ON HAND   SOLD    PURCHASED      SOLD        PURCHASES
XXXX                                                              XXXX
XXXXXXXXXXXXXXXXXXXXXXX  XXX,XXX  XXX,XXX   XXX,XXX    $XX,XXX.XX  $XX,XXX.XX

XXXXXXXXXXX               XX,XXX  XXX,XXX   XXX,XXX    $XX,XXX.XX  $XX,XXX.XX
              TOTALS     XXX,XXX  XXX,XXX   XXX,XXX    $XX,XXX.XX  $XX,XXX.XX

TOTAL RECORDS READ XX
XXXX                                                              XXXX
```

Use Data Set H in Appendix C for Problems 5–7 and 5–9.

7. Use an INPUT PROCEDURE/GIVING to validate the data file, and sort the valid data using employee code as the minor sort key; department mnemonic as the intermediate key, and store number as the major sort key. The results of the program will be a validated sales file (on disk) in the prescribed order and an exception report listing all invalid data records. Utilize the printer spacing chart illustrated for Problem 5–1. Also use the information in Problem 5–1 to help determine reasonable data-validation procedures. You may wish to include a procedure in the program to print the contents of the sorted file to ensure that it was created in the proper sequence.

Use Data Set I in Appendix C for Problems 5–8 and 5–10.

8. Use an INPUT PROCEDURE/GIVING to validate the data file and sort the valid data using item number as the minor sort key, department mnemonic as the intermediate key, and store number as the major sort key. The results of the program will be a validated inventory file (on disk) in the prescribed order and an exception report listing all invalid data records. Utilize the printer spacing chart illustrated for Problem 5–4. Also use the information in Problem 5–4 to determine reasonable data-validation procedures. You may wish to include a procedure in the program to print the contents of the sorted file to ensure that it was created in the proper sequence.

Figure 5–27   *Printer Spacing Chart for Problem 5–9*

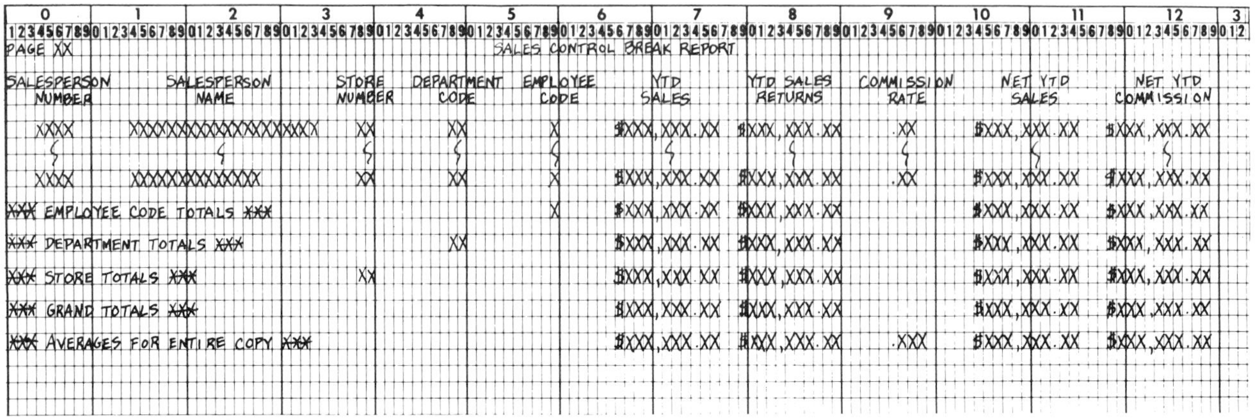

```
PAGE XX                               SALES CONTROL BREAK REPORT
SALESPERSON   SALESPERSON      STORE   DEPARTMENT  EMPLOYEE   YTD        YTD SALES   COMMISSION   NET YTD     NET YTD
  NUMBER        NAME           NUMBER    CODE        CODE     SALES      RETURNS       RATE       SALES       COMMISSION
   XXXX     XXXXXXXXXXXXXXXXX    XX        XX          X    $XXX,XXX.XX $XXX,XXX.XX    .XX    $XXX,XXX.XX  $XXX,XXX.XX

   XXXX     XXXXXXXXXXXX         XX        XX          X    $XXX,XXX.XX $XXX,XXX.XX    .XX    $XXX,XXX.XX  $XXX,XXX.XX
XXX EMPLOYEE CODE TOTALS XXX                           X    $XXX,XXX.XX $XXX,XXX.XX           $XXX,XXX.XX  $XXX,XXX.XX
XXX DEPARTMENT TOTALS XXX                   XX              $XXX,XXX.XX $XXX,XXX.XX           $XXX,XXX.XX  $XXX,XXX.XX
XXX STORE TOTALS XXX               XX                       $XXX,XXX.XX $XXX,XXX.XX           $XXX,XXX.XX  $XXX,XXX.XX
XXX GRAND TOTALS XXX                                        $XXX,XXX.XX $XXX,XXX.XX           $XXX,XXX.XX  $XXX,XXX.XX
XXX AVERAGES FOR ENTIRE COPY XXX                            $XXX,XXX.XX $XXX,XXX.XX    .XXX   $XXX,XXX.XX  $XXX,XXX.XX
```

9. Combine the procedures in Problems 5–2 and 5–7 utilizing an INPUT PROCE DURE and an OUTPUT PROCEDURE to produce both the validation report and a control break report, the format of which is shown in Figure 5–27.

10. Combine the procedures in Problems 5–5 and 5–6 utilizing an INPUT PROCE DURE and an OUTPUT PROCEDURE to produce both the validation report and a control break report, the format of which is shown in Figure 5–28.

Figure 5–28 *Printer Spacing Chart for Problem 5–10*

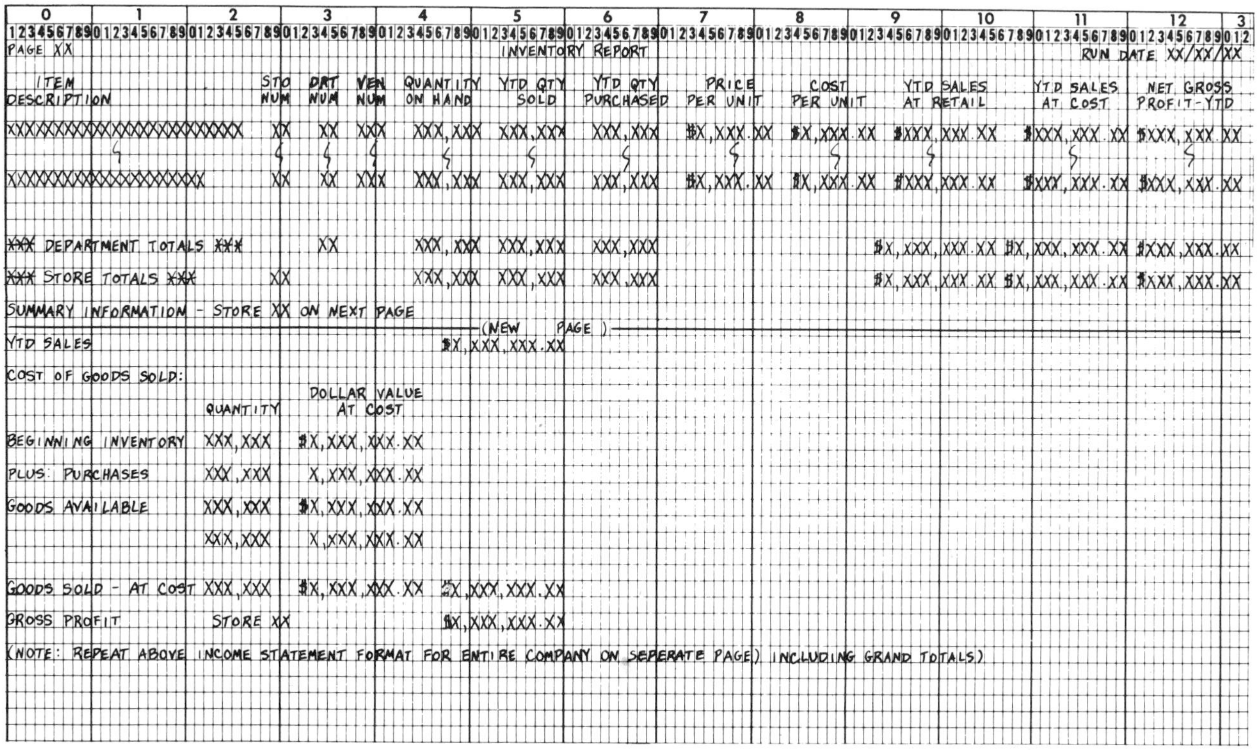

```
PAGE XX                                    INVENTORY REPORT                                    RUN DATE XX/XX/XX
  ITEM                STO DRT VEN QUANTITY YTD QTY  YTD QTY   PRICE      COST     YTD SALES    YTD SALES    NET GROSS
DESCRIPTION           NUM NUM NUM ON HAND   SOLD   PURCHASED PER UNIT  PER UNIT   AT RETAIL    AT COST     PROFIT-YTD
XXXXXXXXXXXXXXXXXXXXXX  XX  XX  XXX XXX,XXX XXX,XXX  XXX,XXX  $X,XXX.XX $X,XXX.XX $XXX,XXX.XX $XXX,XXX.XX $XXX,XXX.XX

XXXXXXXXXXXXXXXXXX      XX  XX  XXX XXX,XXX XXX,XXX  XXX,XXX  $X,XXX.XX $X,XXX.XX $XXX,XXX.XX $XXX,XXX.XX $XXX,XXX.XX


XXX DEPARTMENT TOTALS XXX   XX       XXX,XXX XXX,XXX  XXX,XXX           $X,XXX,XXX.XX $X,XXX,XXX.XX $XXX,XXX.XX
XXX STORE TOTALS XXX        XX       XXX,XXX XXX,XXX  XXX,XXX           $X,XXX,XXX.XX $X,XXX,XXX.XX $XXX,XXX.XX
SUMMARY INFORMATION - STORE XX ON NEXT PAGE
                                     ──(NEW    PAGE )────────────────────────────────────
YTD SALES                      $X,XXX,XXX.XX
COST OF GOODS SOLD:
                                 DOLLAR VALUE
                    QUANTITY       AT COST
BEGINNING INVENTORY XXX,XXX    $X,XXX,XXX.XX
PLUS PURCHASES      XXX,XXX     X,XXX,XXX.XX
GOODS AVAILABLE     XXX,XXX    $X,XXX,XXX.XX
                    XXX,XXX     X,XXX,XXX.XX

GOODS SOLD - AT COST XXX,XXX  $X,XXX,XXX.XX  $X,XXX,XXX.XX
GROSS PROFIT        STORE XX    $X,XXX,XXX.XX
(NOTE: REPEAT ABOVE INCOME STATEMENT FORMAT FOR ENTIRE COMPANY ON SEPERATE PAGE) INCLUDING GRAND TOTALS)
```

Sequential File Processing

⫴ Files that are organized sequentially may be physically stored on one of several different devices. Some of these devices such as punched cards and magnetic tapes will allow only files that are organized sequentially. Other devices, such as magnetic disk, can accept files that are organized as sequential, indexed, or relative files. Indexed files are covered in Chapter 7, and relative files are the subject of Chapter 8. This chapter covers the topics of sequential processing as it relates to either magnetic tape or disk.

TERMS AND STATEMENTS

Abeyance file	File reporting	Record counts
Adds, deletes, and changes	File updating	REWRITE statement
	HIGH-VALUES	Sequential organization
Audit trail	Hash totals	Transaction counts
Batch totals	In-place updating	Transaction file
Control files	Master file	Transaction register
File backup	Numeric totals	
File control	Pre-numbered documents	
File creation		

Sequential File Concepts

Files that use **sequential organization** must always be accessed sequentially; they cannot be accessed randomly. This method is dictated either by the predominant use for the data file or the storage media used. As transactions are recorded over a period of time they can be grouped at particular points in time and processed in a batch mode. When a high percentage of records in a file are accessed, sequential processing is most efficient. When a file is only to be accessed in this manner, sequential organization is dictated.

Magnetic tape requires files to be organized sequentially. Magnetic disk can also accept sequentially organized files. Data records stored on a tape file must contain a field (or multiple fields), the contents of which enable the data records to be placed in sequence (usually ascending sequence). Candidates for the sequence fields include items such as social security number, inventory part number, customer account number, general ledger account number, or some combination of two or more fields. In order for a file to be placed on a magnetic device, the data then must be validated and sorted. This process is normally termed **file creation** and results in the creation of a **master file.** Once a master file has been initially created, the data fields in those records are kept current and up-to-date by a **file updating** process. In order to efficiently process the data records that represent any changes, those data records must be in the same sequential order as the data records in the master file. The set of records that represents changes to an existing master file is called a **transaction file.** At any time a file may also be accessed for a report. **File reporting** constitutes the third major process when working with files, sequential or otherwise. The overall process of file creation, file updating, and file reporting is depicted in the system flowchart in Figure 6–1.

As stated in the chapter on data validation, when a file is first entered into the system, no assumption can be made as to its validity. Therefore, it is necessary to validate a newly created master file. Also since the file must be in sequence, sorting must be accomplished. During the sort and validation processes it is necessary to produce an audit trail of the results. This trail includes a printed listing of any validation errors that have been detected and the control totals, which will be discussed shortly. The creation process results in a master file on tape or disk that has been validated and is in the correct sequential order.

The updating process uses this newly created master file (now called the old master file) and the transaction file as input. The records in the two files are compared in sequential order. Any changes that are indicated are placed into a new master file. When using magnetic tape, this new master file is a separate tape volume. When using magnetic disk, it may be on the same disk volume as the old master file, but it is still in a different location. The old master file becomes a backup file, and if anything happens to the new master file during or after the update, the new file could be recreated using the backup file. Organizations normally keep at least three generations of a file at any one time.

Audit Trail and File Control

Audit Trail

To satisfy internal and external auditing requirements, and to satisfy many different external governmental requirements, it is imperative that both an **audit trail** and **file control** be considered.

An audit trail is a collection of evidence which allows the ability to track an occurrence (sometimes called a transaction) completely through the system. As an example, consider the receipt of an order for merchandise from a customer. An audit trail should evidence each movement of this order through the system. The essential steps through this hypothetical system are depicted in Figure 6–2.

Figure 6-1 *File Creation, Updating, and Reporting*

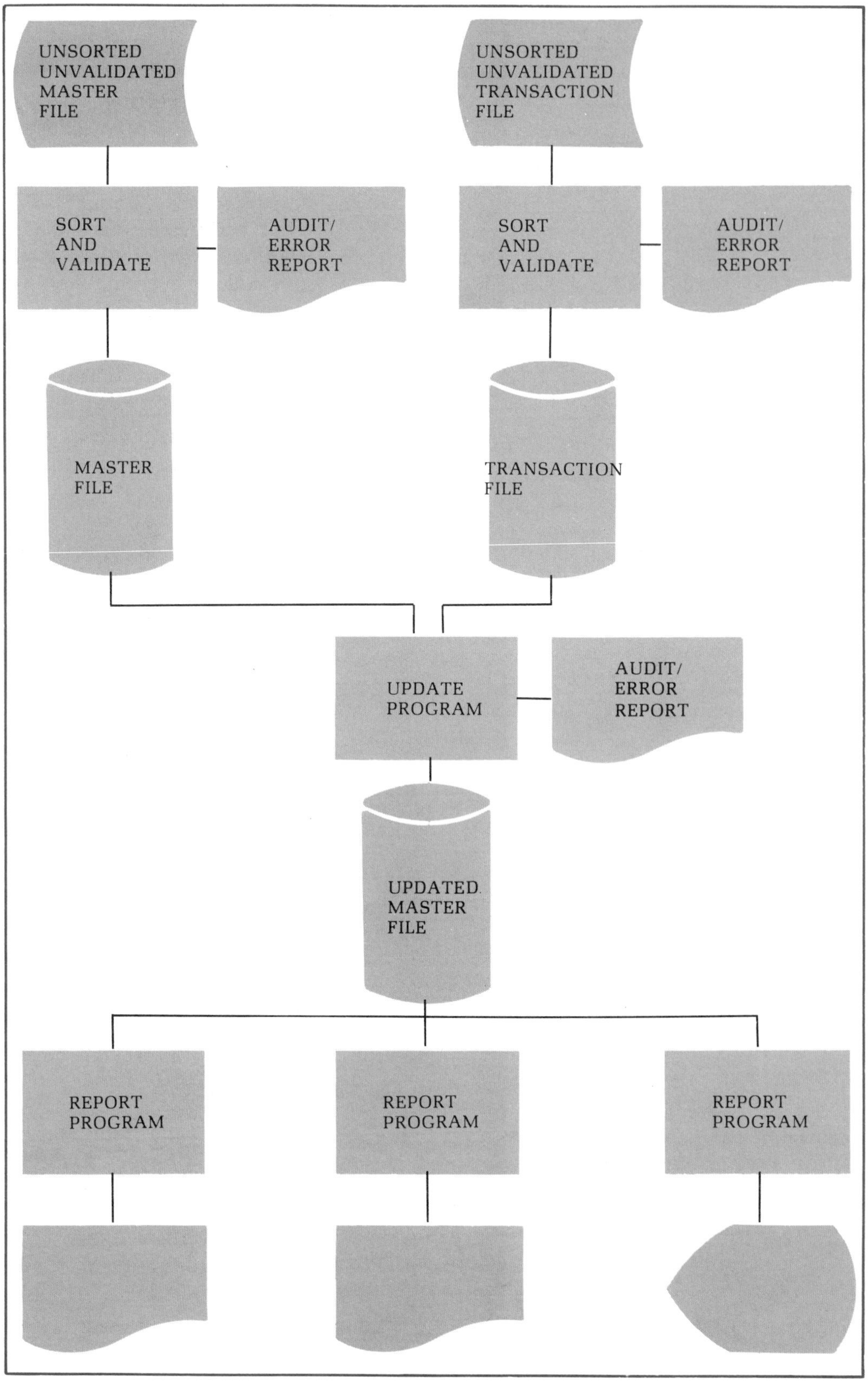

Figure 6–2 *Audit Trail*

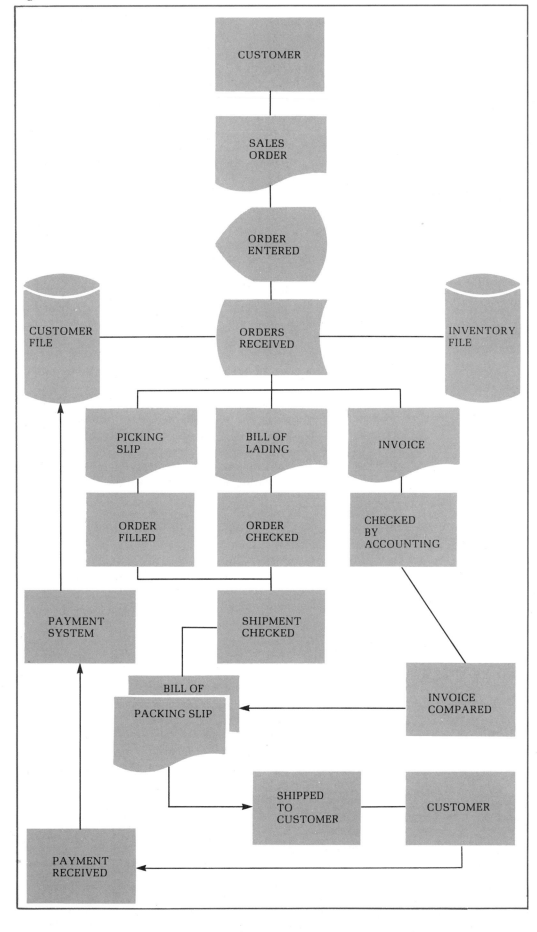

In this example a system flowchart assists in depicting movement through the order entry and invoicing process. Each process point should create some type of evidence in the computer system. For instance, when the orders are initially entered into the system, a record of each order should be created in the form of a stored file of orders and perhaps a printed listing of each day's orders. These transactions are then used to update both the inventory file and the customer file, and an appropriate **transaction register** should be created, either on magnetic media, printer, or both.

Other movement points would have similar needs to create evidence in the system, such as evidence of filled orders, shipped orders, and invoices sent to customers. The main point simply is that the created trail of computer evidence (listings or stored files) provides a means of following a sales order from its initial receipt to the final payment from the customer.

File Control

File control helps ensure the integrity of the data in a file as well as the integrity of the programs that access a file. File control ensures that records are not lost, misplaced, or erroneously recorded. File control also helps ensure that the interrelationships among files in the system are kept intact. A simple example of the latter would be that the balance of the accounts receivable account in the general ledger must be equal to the total of all customer balances in the accounts receivable subsidiary file.

Some of the more important file control procedures include record and transaction counts, numeric and hash totals, batch totals, pre-numbered documents, backup, and the use of control files.

Record counts ensure that a program has not inadvertently lost or added records. When records are added or deleted, an update program should keep track of those changes and provide the effect of the change on the beginning number of records in the file. If the actual number of records in the file disagrees with the computed number of records, the error can be detected immediately. **Transaction counts** have a similar purpose, providing evidence of the different type of transactions including any transactions that are rejected.

Numeric totals and **hash totals** provide another means of ensuring that records have not been lost or added erroneously. Additionally, they provide evidence that is used for audit trail considerations and many times become numeric values that are used in other files. Numeric totals are calculated on values, such as current sales, payments received, credit limit, and quantity on hand. Hash totals are used on values that would not normally be added together, such as account numbers or part numbers. The calculated total has no meaning in itself; it is used only for control purposes.

Batch totals are calculated external to the system in question and compared to other calculated totals. For example, a manual procedure could be used to calculate a total of sales orders for a day, both in terms of number of sales orders and in dollar amounts. The same figures calculated by the program could be compared to the batch totals. If a difference exists, an immediate investigation should occur.

Pre-numbered documents, such as invoices and checks, should be used and controlled by the computer system. For instance, when getting ready to produce payroll checks, the computer system could inform the operator of the next expected payroll check number. The operator would then ensure that the number was correct before proceeding with the check printing operation.

File backup, the creation of an extra copy of a file, should be accomplished immediately after a file has been created or changed. In a batch mode, the backup procedure could occur as a part of the update procedure. In an online mode (where a file is continually updated), backup files should be created after a reasonable period of time, perhaps weekly, daily, or several times each day, depending on the volatility of the file.

The purpose of **control files** is to provide the ability to store record counts, hash counts, numeric totals, and document numbers, which may be stored in at least three different locations. One location for a control file is in a record of the file being controlled. For instance, a control record could be placed as the last record in a sequential file. Another method is to create a separate control file for each updated file. Or all control records for all files could be collected together in one file. A third method stores control information related to a file in another master file. For example, when controlling any file that is a subsidiary file to a general ledger account, the control information can be placed as a record in the general ledger file, co-located with the appropriate account.

The choice of which method to use is dependent on many factors of systems design, and no method is generally preferred over another. The authors have arbitrarily chosen to create a separate control file for each file being controlled.

Figure 6–3 *File Creation in a Batch Mode*

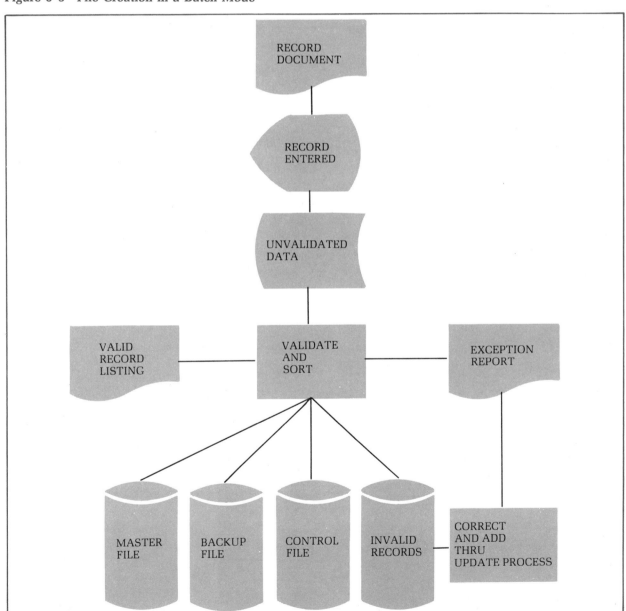

Sequential File Creation

Figure 6–3 depicts the creation process as it normally occurs in a batch mode and Figure 6–4 illustrates the slight difference when implementing an online system.

In a batch mode all records are placed in any order from source documents onto some input medium, such as tape or disk. The sequential creation process (maybe one or more programs) must sort and validate the entire batch of records during one execution. The audit trail may consist of a valid record listing, an exception report, the transfer of valid records to the master file, the transfer of invalid records to another file, and the creation of the control file. The master file must contain only valid records and must be in the appropriate sequence. The file of invalid records (called an **abeyance file**) would have to be corrected using the information from the exception report. After the corrections are made, these records must be entered into the file during the later execution of an update program.

In an online system, data are entered into the system and are immediately validated. The personnel who are entering the data are informed as to the error made and allowed to reenter the data. Only valid records are allowed entry to the system.

In either case, it is important to realize that file creation occurs only once at the inception of system automation. Thereafter, the file is updated, and backups are created repeatedly throughout the life of the file. Also any records that are not loaded into the file during the creation process will have to be added through the updating process.

Figure 6–4   *File Creation in an Online Mode*

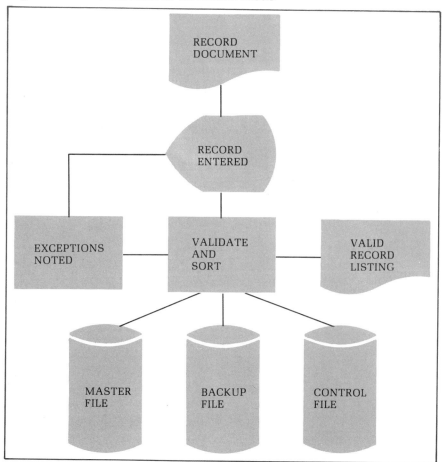

Program Example

The processes of sorting and validating the original file are not discussed in this chapter, since they were the subjects of previous chapters. It will simply be assumed that the file has been sorted and validated. The creation program example will be concerned with only the creation process itself, regardless of whether the system is online or batch.

Input

The input to the creation program is a sorted and validated data set that contains information on salespersons. This data set, including the record layout, is shown in Figure 6–5. (This data set will also be used in the following chapters on indexed and relative files.)

Figure 6–5   *Sorted and Validated Sales File*

```
The sales records are 44 characters in length. The
record layout is as follows:

1 – 4  Salesperson number
6 –16  Last name
17–26  First name
27–33  Year-to-date sales
35–41  Year-to-date sales returns
43–44  Commission rate


==============================================
0017 PAYNE       MAX        0098700 0005673 05
0125 LISHER      JANET F.   0050000 0000000 15
0243 BROCKETT    JANE R.    0075000 0090000 05
0356 GOLTMAN     LINDA S.   0109877 0001000 10
0396 VOLSKY      CHRIS      0032680 0005847 08
0401 OWENS       GEORGE     0036220 0003957 09
0479 WETZEL      ROBERT D.  0208876 0005877 15
0529 PEACOCK     BARBARA    0067330 0015664 08
0580 DUPREE      KELLY L.   0357888 0027582 10
0635 HUNT        ROBERT     0045320 0047534 10
0746 JACKSON     JASON      0078450 0008478 15
0859 HUTCHENS    JEFF       0057630 0004857 14
0927 BARCLAY     RICHARD    0198740 0048563 11
1001 DILL        JEFF       0058640 0028456 20
1132 UNLAND      KIM L.     0047564 0039585 25
1415 GOODMAN     EVE        0064542 0023847 10
1634 VAUGHN      SYLVIA A.  0047899 0045678 20
1805 KIMBERLING  CARLA K.   0050000 0010000 30
1856 LOVELAND    GEORGE*    0046275 0027656 10
1867 STEWARD     KEVIN J.   0115000 0017500 15
1938 DWYER       JOHN D.    0023175 0004000 10
2157 YOUNG       KAREN L.   0112359 0003575 30
2186 SMITH       DOUGLAS    0018345 0037758 20
2269 THOMPSON    LISA S.    0050000 0010000 20
2294 HERMAN      JACK       0048465 0008747 05
2341 ADAMS       ROBYN A.   0023175 0004000 10
2395 MATNEY      DELORES    0079574 0085746 05
2485 PHILLIPS    TRACY L.   0050000 0010000 30
2487 HUME        LETA       0048353 0028437 20
2575 CROSS       CHERYL     0038563 0038250 10
==============================================
```

Output

The major output from this program will be a newly created sales file that evidences a salesperson's number, name, year-to-date sales and returns, commission rate, and fields to accumulate current sales and returns during a one-month period. It is quite common during file creation to add additional fields to allow the storing of data during the update process.

Another output is a sales control file and a printed report evidencing the records that were placed into the file, including totals and a backup file.

Structure Chart   The structure chart for this program is illustrated in Figure 6–6. From the structure chart, it is easy to see that this is not a difficult program, since it follows a structure similar to a simple report program.

Figure 6–6   *Structure Chart for Program 6–1*

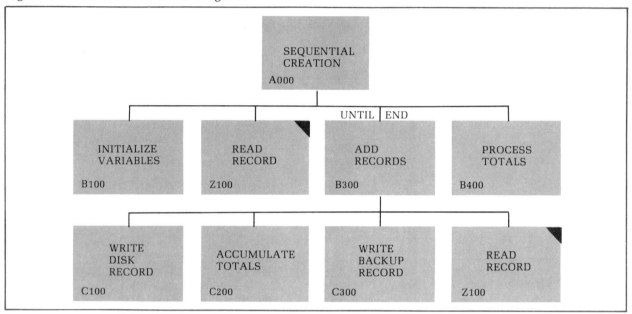

Program

Program 6–1

```
000010 IDENTIFICATION DIVISION.
000020 PROGRAM-ID.    SEQCREAT.
000030*................................................
000040* PROGRAM EXAMPLE 6-1 SEQUENTIAL FILE CREATION          *
000050*................................................
000060 ENVIRONMENT DIVISION.
000070 CONFIGURATION SECTION.
000080    SOURCE-COMPUTER.  IBM-4341.
000090    OBJECT-COMPUTER.  IBM-4341.
000100 INPUT-OUTPUT SECTION.
000110 FILE-CONTROL.
000120    SELECT OLD-SALES-FILE
000130       ASSIGN TO UT-S-SLSOLD.
000140    SELECT SALES-BACKUP-FILE
000150       ASSIGN TO UT-S-SBACK.
000160    SELECT SALES-REPORT
000170       ASSIGN TO UT-S-PRINTER.
000180    SELECT SALES-INPUT-FILE
000190       ASSIGN TO UT-S-SALESIN.
000200    SELECT SALES-CONTROL-FILE
000210       ASSIGN TO UT-S-SALESCT.
000220*
000230 DATA DIVISION.
000240 FILE SECTION.
000250 FD  OLD-SALES-FILE
000260     RECORD CONTAINS 55 CHARACTERS
000270     LABEL RECORDS STANDARD.
000280 01  OS-OLD-SALES-RECORD.
```

Program 6–1 *(continued)*

```
000290       05  OS-SALESPERSON-NUMBER         PIC X(4).
000300       05  OS-LAST-NAME                  PIC X(11).
000310       05  OS-FIRST-NAME                 PIC X(10).
000320       05  OS-YEAR-TO-DATE-SALES         PIC 9(5)V99.
000330       05  OS-YEAR-TO-DATE-SALES-RETURNS PIC 9(5)V99.
000340       05  OS-CURRENT-SALES              PIC 9(5)V99.
000350       05  OS-CURRENT-SALES-RETURNS      PIC 9(5)V99.
000360       05  OS-COMMISSION-RATE            PIC V99.
000370 FD  SALES-BACKUP-FILE
000380      RECORD CONTAINS 55 CHARACTERS
000390      LABEL RECORDS STANDARD.
000400 01  SB-SALES-BACKUP-RECORD             PIC X(55).
000410 FD  SALES-INPUT-FILE
000420      RECORD CONTAINS 44 CHARACTERS
000430      LABEL RECORDS ARE STANDARD.
000440 01  SI-SALES-INPUT-RECORD.
000450       05  SI-SALESPERSON-NUMBER         PIC X(4).
000460       05  SI-HASH-NUMBER REDEFINES
000470           SI-SALESPERSON-NUMBER         PIC 9(4).
000480       05  FILLER                        PIC X(1).
000490       05  SI-LAST-NAME                  PIC X(11).
000500       05  SI-FIRST-NAME                 PIC X(10).
000510       05  SI-YEAR-TO-DATE-SALES         PIC 9(5)V99.
000520       05  FILLER                        PIC X(1).
000530       05  SI-YEAR-TO-DATE-SALES-RETURNS PIC 9(5)V99.
000540       05  FILLER                        PIC X(1).
000550       05  SI-COMMISSION-RATE            PIC V99.
000560 FD  SALES-REPORT
000570      RECORD CONTAINS 132 CHARACTERS
000580      LABEL RECORDS ARE OMITTED.
000590 01  SR-SALES-REPORT-LINE               PIC X(132).
000600 FD  SALES-CONTROL-FILE
000610      RECORD CONTAINS 84 CHARACTERS
000620      LABEL RECORDS ARE STANDARD.
000630 01  SC-SALES-CONTROL-RECORD.
000640       05  SC-BEG-TOT-FIELDS.
000650           10  SC-BEG-TOT-RECORDS-STORED    PIC S9(4).
000660           10  SC-BEG-TOT-HASH-NUMBER       PIC S9(6).
000670           10  SC-BEG-TOT-YTD-SALES         PIC S9(6)V99.
000680           10  SC-BEG-TOT-YTD-SALES-RETURNS PIC S9(6)V99.
000690           10  SC-BEG-TOT-CURRENT-SALES     PIC S9(6)V99.
000700           10  SC-BEG-TOT-CURRENT-RETURNS   PIC S9(6)V99.
000710       05  SC-CHG-TOT-FIELDS.
000720           10  SC-CHG-TOT-RECORDS-STORED    PIC S9(4).
000730           10  SC-CHG-TOT-HASH-NUMBER       PIC S9(6).
000740           10  SC-CHG-TOT-YTD-SALES         PIC S9(6)V99.
000750           10  SC-CHG-TOT-YTD-SALES-RETURNS PIC S9(6)V99.
000760           10  SC-CHG-TOT-CURRENT-SALES     PIC S9(6)V99.
000770           10  SC-CHG-TOT-CURRENT-RETURNS   PIC S9(6)V99.
000780*
000790 WORKING-STORAGE SECTION.
000800 01  WS-WORK-AREAS.
000810       05  WS-EOF-INDICATOR              PIC X(3).
000820           88  END-OF-INPUT-FILE         VALUE 'END'.
000830 01  WS-ACCUMULATORS.
000840       05  WS-TOT-RECORDS-STORED         PIC S9(4).
000850       05  WS-TOT-HASH-NUMBER            PIC S9(6).
000860       05  WS-TOT-YTD-SALES              PIC S9(6)V99.
000870       05  WS-TOT-YTD-SALES-RETURNS      PIC S9(6)V99.
000880 01  HD-HEADING-LINE.
000890       05  FILLER                        PIC X(28)
000900                                         VALUE 'SEQUENTIAL SALES FILE TOTALS'.
000910 01  CH-COLUMN-HEADING-LINE.
000920       05  FILLER                        PIC X(20) VALUE SPACES.
```

Program 6–1   *(continued)*

```
000930        05  FILLER                    PIC X(8) VALUE 'RECORDS'.
000940        05  FILLER                    PIC X(11) VALUE SPACES.
000950        05  FILLER                    PIC X(5) VALUE 'SALES'.
000960        05  FILLER                    PIC X(8) VALUE SPACES.
000970        05  FILLER                    PIC X(8) VALUE 'RETURNS'.
000980        05  FILLER                    PIC X(1) VALUE SPACES.
000990        05  FILLER                    PIC X(11)
001000                                          VALUE 'HASH NUMBER'.
001010 01  TL-TOTAL-LINE.
001020        05  TL-STUB-HEADING           PIC X(20)
001030                                      VALUE 'BEGINNING TOTALS'.
001040        05  TL-TOT-RECORDS-STORED     PIC Z,ZZ9.
001050        05  FILLER                    PIC X(11) VALUE SPACES.
001060        05  TL-TOT-YTD-SALES          PIC ZZZ,ZZZ.99-.
001070        05  FILLER                    PIC X(2) VALUE SPACES.
001080        05  TL-TOT-YTD-SALES-RETURNS  PIC ZZZ,ZZZ.99-.
001090        05  FILLER                    PIC X(2) VALUE SPACES.
001100        05  TL-TOT-HASH-NUMBER          PIC ZZZ,ZZ9-.
001110*
001120 PROCEDURE DIVISION.
001130 A000-CREATE.
001140        OPEN INPUT SALES-INPUT-FILE
001150             OUTPUT OLD-SALES-FILE
001160                    SALES-BACKUP-FILE
001170                    SALES-REPORT
001180                    SALES-CONTROL-FILE.
001190        PERFORM B100-INITIALIZE-VARIABLES.
001200        PERFORM Z100-READ-NEW-RECORD.
001210        PERFORM B300-ADD-RECORDS
001220             UNTIL END-OF-INPUT-FILE.
001230        PERFORM B400-PROCESS-TOTALS.
001240        CLOSE SALES-INPUT-FILE
001250              OLD-SALES-FILE
001260              SALES-BACKUP-FILE
001270              SALES-REPORT
001280              SALES-CONTROL-FILE.
001290        STOP RUN.
001300 B100-INITIALIZE-VARIABLES.
001310        MOVE 'NO'  TO WS-EOF-INDICATOR.
001320        MOVE ZEROES TO WS-ACCUMULATORS.
001330 B300-ADD-RECORDS.
001340        PERFORM C100-WRITE-SALES-RECORD.
001350        PERFORM C200-ACCUMULATE-TOTALS.
001360        WRITE SB-SALES-BACKUP-RECORD
001370             FROM OS-OLD-SALES-RECORD.
001380        PERFORM Z100-READ-NEW-RECORD.
001390 B400-PROCESS-TOTALS.
001400        MOVE WS-TOT-RECORDS-STORED  TO SC-BEG-TOT-RECORDS-STORED
001410                                       TL-TOT-RECORDS-STORED.
001420        MOVE WS-TOT-HASH-NUMBER     TO SC-BEG-TOT-HASH-NUMBER
001430                                       TL-TOT-HASH-NUMBER.
001440        MOVE WS-TOT-YTD-SALES       TO SC-BEG-TOT-YTD-SALES
001450                                       TL-TOT-YTD-SALES.
001460        MOVE WS-TOT-YTD-SALES-RETURNS TO TL-TOT-YTD-SALES-RETURNS
001470                                         SC-BEG-TOT-YTD-SALES-RETURNS.
001480        MOVE ZEROES                 TO SC-BEG-TOT-CURRENT-SALES
001490                                       SC-BEG-TOT-CURRENT-RETURNS
001500                                       SC-CHG-TOT-FIELDS.
001510        WRITE SC-SALES-CONTROL-RECORD.
001520        WRITE SR-SALES-REPORT-LINE FROM HD-HEADING-LINE
001530             AFTER PAGE.
001540        WRITE SR-SALES-REPORT-LINE FROM CH-COLUMN-HEADING-LINE
001550             AFTER 2.
001560        WRITE SR-SALES-REPORT-LINE FROM TL-TOTAL-LINE
```

Program 6–1   *(concluded)*

```
001570          AFTER 2.
001580 C100-WRITE-SALES-RECORD.
001590     MOVE SI-SALESPERSON-NUMBER  TO OS-SALESPERSON-NUMBER.
001600     MOVE SI-LAST-NAME           TO OS-LAST-NAME.
001610     MOVE SI-FIRST-NAME          TO OS-FIRST-NAME.
001620     MOVE SI-YEAR-TO-DATE-SALES  TO OS-YEAR-TO-DATE-SALES.
001630     MOVE SI-YEAR-TO-DATE-SALES-RETURNS
001640          TO OS-YEAR-TO-DATE-SALES-RETURNS.
001650     MOVE ZEROS                  TO OS-CURRENT-SALES
001660                                    OS-CURRENT-SALES-RETURNS.
001670     MOVE SI-COMMISSION-RATE     TO OS-COMMISSION-RATE.
001680     WRITE OS-OLD-SALES-RECORD.
001690 C200-ACCUMULATE-TOTALS.
001700     ADD 1                       TO WS-TOT-RECORDS-STORED.
001710     ADD SI-HASH-NUMBER          TO WS-TOT-HASH-NUMBER.
001720     ADD SI-YEAR-TO-DATE-SALES   TO WS-TOT-YTD-SALES.
001730     ADD SI-YEAR-TO-DATE-SALES-RETURNS
001740          TO WS-TOT-YTD-SALES-RETURNS.
001750 Z100-READ-NEW-RECORD.
001760     READ SALES-INPUT-FILE
001770          AT END MOVE 'END' TO WS-EOF-INDICATOR.
```

Discussion

First, notice the different files that are selected. The file called OLD–SALES–FILE is actually the newly created master file, a copy of which is duplicated on SALES–BACKUP–FILE. SALES–CONTROL–FILE and SALES–REPORT are then used to serve audit trail and control purposes. It would have been a simple matter to have also included in SALES–REPORT a detailed listing of each newly created record in OLD–SALES–FILE.

The SC–BEG–TOT–FIELDS in SC–SALES–CONTROL–RECORD are used to store control totals related to the creation process. The SC–CHG–TOT–FIELDS are to be used in later report and update programs. During the creation program these fields are initially set to zero.

In the PROCEDURE division notice the movement of zeros to OS–CURRENT–SALES and OS–CURRENT–SALES–RETURNS. These fields are to be used later during the update process to contain an accumulation of sales throughout the month. Each record in the backup file is created by the WRITE statement at lines 1360–1370. The printed report, which evidences the results of this creation program, is shown in Figure 6–7. These totals are also placed in the control file record for future control purposes.

Figure 6–7   *Output from Program 6–1–Audit Trail Report*

```
SEQUENTIAL SALES FILE TOTALS

                  RECORDS         SALES      RETURNS   HASH NUMBER
BEGINNING TOTALS     30        23,386.40    6,882.67     40,130
```

It is also possible to add additional records at the end of an existing sequential file. To do so, the file must be opened EXTEND instead of OUTPUT. Refer to Appendix A or G for the format of this alternative.

Sequential File Reporting

The programmer should be very familiar with the file reporting phase. Most beginning COBOL texts are dominated by reports from existing files on tape, disk, or cards.

When the entire sequential file is accessed, it is possible and advisable to compare the actual number of records in the file to the number of records that are stored in the control file. Additionally, numeric and hash totals can be compared.

Program Example

Program 6–2 illustrates the concept of reporting and control and initially uses the newly created file from Program 6–1 as input. This program will also be run after the file has been updated.

Structure Chart

Since the programmer is familiar with the structure of a report program, only that portion of the structure chart that relates to the control process has been changed. Figure 6–8 illustrates this concept. The control processes are shaded on the structure chart.

Actual totals are calculated in the process labeled C200 as each record is read from the master file. In the process labeled B400, the control record, is read from the control file and beginning control totals are printed. Since the file was just created, these totals should agree with the totals from the creation Program 6–1. Any changes to the file (there should not be any yet) are then printed. These change totals are then added to the beginning totals, and the results are printed for the ending totals as evidenced by the data in the control file. Actual totals (calculated in C200) are then printed, enabling a comparison between control totals and actual totals.

Program

Program 6–2

```
000010 IDENTIFICATION DIVISION.
000020 PROGRAM-ID.    SEQREPT.
000030**********************************************************
000040* PROGRAM EXAMPLE 6-2 SEQUENTIAL REPORT                  *
000050**********************************************************
000060 ENVIRONMENT DIVISION.
000070 CONFIGURATION SECTION.
000080   SOURCE-COMPUTER.   IBM-4341.
000090   OBJECT-COMPUTER.   IBM-4341.
000100 INPUT-OUTPUT SECTION.
000110 FILE-CONTROL.
000120     SELECT OLD-SALES-FILE
000130         ASSIGN TO UT-S-SLSOLD.
000140     SELECT SALES-REPORT
000150         ASSIGN TO UT-S-PRINTER.
000160     SELECT SALES-CONTROL-FILE
000170         ASSIGN TO UT-S-SALESCT.
000180*
000190 DATA DIVISION.
000200 FILE SECTION.
000210 FD   OLD-SALES-FILE
000220      RECORD CONTAINS 55 CHARACTERS
000230      LABEL RECORDS STANDARD.
000240 01   OS-OLD-SALES-RECORD.
000250      05  OS-SALESPERSON-NUMBER        PIC X(4).
000260      05  OS-HASH-NUMBER REDEFINES
000270          OS-SALESPERSON-NUMBER        PIC 9(4).
000280      05  OS-LAST-NAME                 PIC X(11).
000290      05  OS-FIRST-NAME                PIC X(10).
000300      05  OS-YEAR-TO-DATE-SALES        PIC 9(5)V99.
000310      05  OS-YEAR-TO-DATE-SALES-RETURNS PIC 9(5)V99.
000320      05  OS-CURRENT-SALES             PIC 9(5)V99.
000330      05  OS-CURRENT-SALES-RETURNS     PIC 9(5)V99.
000340      05  OS-COMMISSION-RATE           PIC V99.
000350 FD   SALES-REPORT
```

Program 6–2 *(continued)*

```
000360     RECORD CONTAINS 132 CHARACTERS
000370     LABEL RECORDS ARE OMITTED.
000380 01  SR-SALES-LINE                      PIC X(132).
000390 FD  SALES-CONTROL-FILE
000400     RECORD CONTAINS 84 CHARACTERS
000410     LABEL RECORDS ARE STANDARD.
000420 01  SC-SALES-CONTROL-RECORD.
000430     05  SC-BEG-TOT-FIELDS.
000440         10  SC-BEG-TOT-RECORDS-STORED    PIC S9(4).
000450         10  SC-BEG-TOT-HASH-NUMBER       PIC S9(6).
000460         10  SC-BEG-TOT-YTD-SALES         PIC S9(6)V99.
000470         10  SC-BEG-TOT-YTD-SALES-RETURNS PIC S9(6)V99.
000480         10  SC-BEG-TOT-CURRENT-SALES     PIC S9(6)V99.
000490         10  SC-BEG-TOT-CURRENT-RETURNS   PIC S9(6)V99.
000500     05  SC-CHG-TOT-FIELDS.
000510         10  SC-CHG-TOT-RECORDS-STORED    PIC S9(4).
000520         10  SC-CHG-TOT-HASH-NUMBER       PIC S9(6).
000530         10  SC-CHG-TOT-YTD-SALES         PIC S9(6)V99.
000540         10  SC-CHG-TOT-YTD-SALES-RETURNS PIC S9(6)V99.
000550         10  SC-CHG-TOT-CURRENT-SALES     PIC S9(6)V99.
000560         10  SC-CHG-TOT-CURRENT-RETURNS   PIC S9(6)V99.
000570*
000580 WORKING-STORAGE SECTION.
000590 01  WS-RECORD-INDICATORS.
000600     05  WS-END-OF-FILE-INDICATOR     PIC X(3).
000610         88  END-OF-SALES-FILE        VALUE 'YES'.
000620 01  WS-ACCUMULATORS.
000630     05  WS-TOT-RECORDS-STORED        PIC S9(4).
000640     05  WS-TOT-HASH-NUMBER           PIC S9(6).
000650     05  WS-TOT-YTD-SALES             PIC S9(6)V99.
000660     05  WS-TOT-YTD-SALES-RETURNS     PIC S9(6)V99.
000670     05  WS-TOT-CURRENT-SALES         PIC S9(6)V99.
000680     05  WS-TOT-CURRENT-RETURNS       PIC S9(6)V99.
000690     05  WS-END-TOT-RECORDS-STORED    PIC S9(4).
000700     05  WS-END-TOT-HASH-NUMBER       PIC S9(6).
000710     05  WS-END-TOT-YTD-SALES         PIC S9(6)V99.
000720     05  WS-END-TOT-YTD-SALES-RETURNS PIC S9(6)V99.
000730     05  WS-END-TOT-CURRENT-SALES     PIC S9(6)V99.
000740     05  WS-END-TOT-CURRENT-RETURNS   PIC S9(6)V99.
000750 01  HD-HEADING-LINE.
000760     05  FILLER                       PIC X(12)
000770                                      VALUE 'SALES REPORT'.
000780 01  CH-COLUMN-HEADING-LINE.
000790     05  FILLER                       PIC X(20) VALUE SPACES.
000800     05  FILLER                       PIC X(8)  VALUE 'RECORDS'.
000810     05  FILLER                       PIC X(2)  VALUE SPACES.
000820     05  FILLER                       PIC X(4)  VALUE 'HASH'.
000830     05  FILLER                       PIC X(5)  VALUE SPACES.
000840     05  FILLER                       PIC X(5)  VALUE 'SALES'.
000850     05  FILLER                       PIC X(8)  VALUE SPACES.
000860     05  FILLER                       PIC X(8)  VALUE 'RETURNS'.
000870     05  FILLER                       PIC X(5)  VALUE SPACES.
000880     05  FILLER                       PIC X(5)  VALUE 'SALES'.
000890     05  FILLER                       PIC X(5)  VALUE SPACES.
000900     05  FILLER                       PIC X(8)  VALUE 'RETURNS'.
000910 01  DL-DETAIL-LINE.
000920     05  DL-SALESPERSON-NUMBER        PIC Z(4).
000930     05  FILLER                       PIC X(4) VALUE SPACES.
000940     05  DL-LAST-NAME                 PIC X(11).
000950     05  FILLER                       PIC X(4) VALUE SPACES.
000960     05  DL-FIRST-NAME                PIC X(10).
000970     05  FILLER                       PIC X(4) VALUE SPACES.
000980     05  DL-YEAR-TO-DATE-SALES        PIC ZZ,ZZZ.99.
000990     05  FILLER                       PIC X(4) VALUE SPACES.
001000     05  DL-YEAR-TO-DATE-SALES-RETURNS PIC ZZ,ZZZ.99.
```

Program 6–2   *(continued)*

```
001010      05  FILLER                      PIC X(4) VALUE SPACES.
001020      05  DL-CURRENT-SALES            PIC ZZ,ZZZ.99.
001030      05  FILLER                      PIC X(4) VALUE SPACES.
001040      05  DL-CURRENT-SALES-RETURNS    PIC ZZ,ZZZ.99.
001050      05  FILLER                      PIC X(4) VALUE SPACES.
001060      05  DL-COMMISSION-RATE          PIC .99.
001070 01  TL-TOTAL-LINE.
001080      05  TL-STUB-HEADING             PIC X(20).
001090      05  TL-TOT-RECORDS-STORED       PIC Z,ZZ9-.
001100      05  FILLER                      PIC X(1) VALUE SPACES.
001110      05  TL-TOT-HASH-NUMBER          PIC ZZZ,ZZ9-.
001120      05  FILLER                      PIC X(2) VALUE SPACES.
001130      05  TL-TOT-YTD-SALES            PIC ZZZ,ZZZ.99-.
001140      05  FILLER                      PIC X(2) VALUE SPACES.
001150      05  TL-TOT-YTD-SALES-RETURNS    PIC ZZZ,ZZZ.99-.
001160      05  FILLER                      PIC X(2) VALUE SPACES.
001170      05  TL-TOT-CURRENT-SALES        PIC ZZ,ZZZ.99.
001180      05  FILLER                      PIC X(2) VALUE SPACES.
001190      05  TL-TOT-CURRENT-RETURNS      PIC ZZ,ZZZ.99.
001200*
001210 PROCEDURE DIVISION.
001220 A000-SEQ-REPORT.
001230      OPEN INPUT OLD-SALES-FILE
001240                 SALES-CONTROL-FILE
001250           OUTPUT SALES-REPORT.
001260      WRITE SR-SALES-LINE FROM HD-HEADING-LINE
001270           AFTER PAGE.
001280      PERFORM B100-INITIALIZE-VARIABLES.
001290      PERFORM Z100-READ-RECORD.
001300      PERFORM B300-PRINT-RECORDS
001310          UNTIL END-OF-SALES-FILE.
001320      PERFORM B400-PROCESS-TOTALS.
001330      CLOSE OLD-SALES-FILE
001340            SALES-CONTROL-FILE
001350            SALES-REPORT.
001360      STOP RUN.
001370 B100-INITIALIZE-VARIABLES.
001380      MOVE 'NO'  TO WS-END-OF-FILE-INDICATOR.
001390      MOVE ZEROES TO WS-ACCUMULATORS.
001400 B300-PRINT-RECORDS.
001410      PERFORM C100-WRITE-DETAIL-LINE.
001420      PERFORM C200-ACCUMULATE-TOTALS.
001430      PERFORM Z100-READ-RECORD.
001440 B400-PROCESS-TOTALS.
001450      READ SALES-CONTROL-FILE
001460          AT END MOVE 'YES' TO WS-END-OF-FILE-INDICATOR.
001470      PERFORM C400-PRINT-BEG-TOTALS.
001480      PERFORM C500-PRINT-CHG-TOTALS.
001490      PERFORM C600-PRINT-END-TOTALS.
001500      PERFORM C700-PRINT-ACTUAL-TOTALS.
001510 C100-WRITE-DETAIL-LINE.
001520      MOVE OS-SALESPERSON-NUMBER    TO DL-SALESPERSON-NUMBER.
001530      MOVE OS-LAST-NAME             TO DL-LAST-NAME.
001540      MOVE OS-FIRST-NAME            TO DL-FIRST-NAME.
001550      MOVE OS-YEAR-TO-DATE-SALES    TO DL-YEAR-TO-DATE-SALES.
001560      MOVE OS-YEAR-TO-DATE-SALES-RETURNS
001570           TO DL-YEAR-TO-DATE-SALES-RETURNS.
001580      MOVE OS-CURRENT-SALES         TO DL-CURRENT-SALES.
001590      MOVE OS-CURRENT-SALES-RETURNS TO DL-CURRENT-SALES-RETURNS.
001600      MOVE OS-COMMISSION-RATE       TO DL-COMMISSION-RATE.
001610      WRITE SR-SALES-LINE FROM DL-DETAIL-LINE
001620           AFTER 1.
001630 C200-ACCUMULATE-TOTALS.
001640      ADD 1                        TO WS-TOT-RECORDS-STORED.
001650      ADD OS-HASH-NUMBER           TO WS-TOT-HASH-NUMBER.
```

Program 6–2 *(concluded)*

```
001660    ADD OS-YEAR-TO-DATE-SALES        TO WS-TOT-YTD-SALES.
001670    ADD OS-YEAR-TO-DATE-SALES-RETURNS
001680        TO WS-TOT-YTD-SALES-RETURNS.
001690    ADD OS-CURRENT-SALES             TO WS-TOT-CURRENT-SALES.
001700    ADD OS-CURRENT-SALES-RETURNS TO WS-TOT-CURRENT-RETURNS.
001710 C400-PRINT-BEG-TOTALS.
001720    WRITE SR-SALES-LINE FROM CH-COLUMN-HEADING-LINE
001730        AFTER 2.
001740    MOVE 'BEGINNING  - CONTROL'      TO TL-STUB-HEADING.
001750    MOVE SC-BEG-TOT-RECORDS-STORED  TO TL-TOT-RECORDS-STORED.
001760    MOVE SC-BEG-TOT-HASH-NUMBER     TO TL-TOT-HASH-NUMBER.
001770    MOVE SC-BEG-TOT-YTD-SALES        TO TL-TOT-YTD-SALES.
001780    MOVE SC-BEG-TOT-YTD-SALES-RETURNS
001790        TO TL-TOT-YTD-SALES-RETURNS.
001800    MOVE SC-BEG-TOT-CURRENT-SALES    TO TL-TOT-CURRENT-SALES.
001810    MOVE SC-BEG-TOT-CURRENT-RETURNS TO TL-TOT-CURRENT-RETURNS.
001820    WRITE SR-SALES-LINE FROM TL-TOTAL-LINE
001830        AFTER 2.
001840 C500-PRINT-CHG-TOTALS.
001850    MOVE 'NET CHANGE - CONTROL'      TO TL-STUB-HEADING.
001860    MOVE SC-CHG-TOT-RECORDS-STORED TO TL-TOT-RECORDS-STORED.
001870    MOVE SC-CHG-TOT-HASH-NUMBER     TO TL-TOT-HASH-NUMBER.
001880    MOVE SC-CHG-TOT-YTD-SALES        TO TL-TOT-YTD-SALES.
001890    MOVE SC-CHG-TOT-YTD-SALES-RETURNS
001900        TO TL-TOT-YTD-SALES-RETURNS.
001910    MOVE SC-CHG-TOT-CURRENT-SALES    TO TL-TOT-CURRENT-SALES.
001920    MOVE SC-CHG-TOT-CURRENT-RETURNS TO TL-TOT-CURRENT-RETURNS.
001930    WRITE SR-SALES-LINE FROM TL-TOTAL-LINE
001940        AFTER 2.
001950 C600-PRINT-END-TOTALS.
001960    MOVE 'ENDING - CONTROL'          TO TL-STUB-HEADING.
001970    ADD SC-BEG-TOT-RECORDS-STORED SC-CHG-TOT-RECORDS-STORED
001980        GIVING WS-END-TOT-RECORDS-STORED
001990              TL-TOT-RECORDS-STORED.
002000    ADD SC-BEG-TOT-HASH-NUMBER SC-CHG-TOT-HASH-NUMBER
002010        GIVING WS-END-TOT-HASH-NUMBER
002020              TL-TOT-HASH-NUMBER.
002030    ADD SC-BEG-TOT-YTD-SALES SC-CHG-TOT-YTD-SALES
002040        GIVING WS-END-TOT-YTD-SALES
002050              TL-TOT-YTD-SALES.
002060    ADD SC-BEG-TOT-YTD-SALES-RETURNS SC-CHG-TOT-YTD-SALES-RETURNS
002070        GIVING WS-END-TOT-YTD-SALES-RETURNS
002080              TL-TOT-YTD-SALES-RETURNS.
002090    ADD SC-BEG-TOT-CURRENT-SALES SC-CHG-TOT-CURRENT-SALES
002100        GIVING WS-END-TOT-CURRENT-SALES
002110              TL-TOT-CURRENT-SALES.
002120    ADD SC-BEG-TOT-CURRENT-RETURNS SC-CHG-TOT-CURRENT-RETURNS
002130        GIVING WS-END-TOT-CURRENT-RETURNS
002140              TL-TOT-CURRENT-RETURNS.
002150    WRITE SR-SALES-LINE FROM TL-TOTAL-LINE
002160        AFTER 2.
002170 C700-PRINT-ACTUAL-TOTALS.
002180    MOVE 'ENDING - ACTUAL'           TO TL-STUB-HEADING.
002190    MOVE WS-TOT-RECORDS-STORED       TO TL-TOT-RECORDS-STORED.
002200    MOVE WS-TOT-HASH-NUMBER          TO TL-TOT-HASH-NUMBER.
002210    MOVE WS-TOT-YTD-SALES            TO TL-TOT-YTD-SALES.
002220    MOVE WS-TOT-YTD-SALES-RETURNS TO TL-TOT-YTD-SALES-RETURNS.
002230    MOVE WS-TOT-CURRENT-SALES        TO TL-TOT-CURRENT-SALES.
002240    MOVE WS-TOT-CURRENT-RETURNS
002250        TO TL-TOT-CURRENT-RETURNS.
002260    WRITE SR-SALES-LINE FROM TL-TOTAL-LINE
002270        AFTER 2.
002280 Z100-READ-RECORD.
002290    READ OLD-SALES-FILE
002300        AT END MOVE 'YES' TO WS-END-OF-FILE-INDICATOR.
```

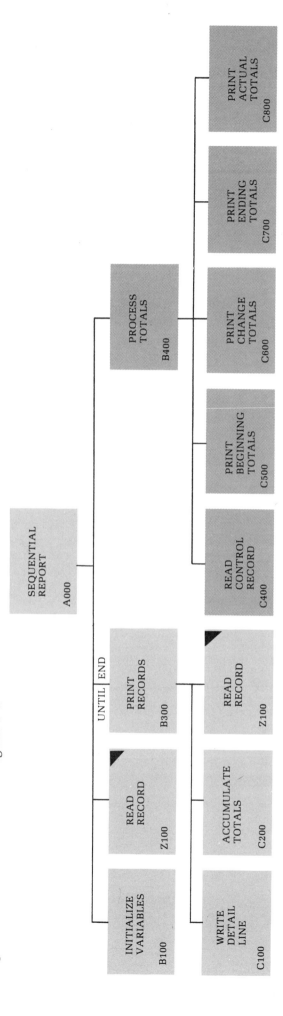

Figure 6–8 Structure Chart for Program 6–2

Figure 6–9   *Output from Program 6–2 after Creation*

```
     SALES REPORT
       17    PAYNE       MAX            987.00         56.73         .00      .00    .05
      125    LISHER      JANET F.       500.00           .00         .00      .00    .15
      243    BROCKETT    JANE R.        750.00        900.00         .00      .00    .05
      356    GOLTMAN     LINDA S.     1,098.77         10.00         .00      .00    .10
      396    VOLSKY      CHRIS          326.80         58.47         .00      .00    .08
      401    OWENS       GEORGE         362.20         39.57         .00      .00    .09
      479    WETZEL      ROBERT D.    2,088.76         58.77         .00      .00    .15
      529    PEACOCK     BARBARA        673.30        156.64         .00      .00    .08
      580    DUPREE      KELLY L.     3,578.88        275.82         .00      .00    .10
      635    HUNT        ROBERT         453.20        475.34         .00      .00    .10
      746    JACKSON     JASON          784.50         84.78         .00      .00    .15
      859    HUTCHENS    JEFF           576.30         48.57         .00      .00    .14
      927    BARCLAY     RICHARD      1,987.40        485.63         .00      .00    .11
     1001    DILL        JEFF           586.40        284.56         .00      .00    .20
     1132    UNLAND      KIM L.         475.64        395.85         .00      .00    .25
     1415    GOODMAN     EVE            645.42        238.47         .00      .00    .10
     1634    VAUGHN      SYLVIA A.      478.99        456.78         .00      .00    .20
     1805    KIMBERLING  CARLA K.       500.00        100.00         .00      .00    .30
     1856    LOVELAND    GEORGE         462.75        276.56         .00      .00    .10
     1867    STEWARD     KEVIN J.     1,150.00        175.00         .00      .00    .15
     1938    DWYER       JOHN D.        231.75         40.00         .00      .00    .10
     2157    YOUNG       KAREN L.     1,123.59         35.75         .00      .00    .30
     2186    SMITH       DOUGLAS        183.45        377.58         .00      .00    .20
     2269    THOMPSON    LISA S.        500.00        100.00         .00      .00    .20
     2294    HERMAN      JACK           484.65         87.47         .00      .00    .05
     2341    ADAMS       ROBYN A.       231.75         40.00         .00      .00    .10
     2395    MATNEY      DELORES        795.74        857.46         .00      .00    .05
     2485    PHILLIPS    TRACY L.       500.00        100.00         .00      .00    .30
     2487    HUME        LETA           483.53        284.37         .00      .00    .20
     2575    CROSS       CHERYL         385.63        382.50         .00      .00    .10

                      RECORDS   HASH     SALES      RETURNS      SALES    RETURNS

 BEGINNING - CONTROL      30    40,130   23,386.40   6,882.67      .00      .00

 NET CHANGE - CONTROL      0         0         .00        .00      .00      .00

 ENDING - CONTROL         30    40,130   23,386.40   6,882.67      .00      .00

 ENDING - ACTUAL          30    40,130   23,386.40   6,882.67      .00      .00
```

Discussion

C200–ACCUMULATE–TOTALS is almost an exact duplicate of the parallel module in Program 6–1. The only difference is the added necessity to accumulate current sales and current returns. Later when the update program is run, both current sales and current returns will become larger. This report program could then be used at any time to print the contents of the file and to determine if the file is still in control.

B400–PROCESS–TOTALS prints out the contents of the control record and the actual totals. Though no actual comparison is made by the program, it would be a simple matter to add a module labeled C900–COMPARE–ACTUAL–TO–CONTROL.

Figure 6–9 lists the output from executing Program 6–2 immediately after the file has been initially created. Note that all current sales figures are zero and that the control figures agree with the totals calculated during the run of the creation program. Note also that the control totals and the actual totals are in agreement.

Sequential File Updating

File updating is an ongoing activity with both sequential and nonsequential files. The frequency with which updating occurs varies with the application and may occur daily, weekly, monthly, or continually as would be the case in an online application. The assumption made in the current application is that the update program will be run on a daily basis each business day throughout a one-month period. Therefore, current sales and returns figures will become increasingly larger

Figure 6–10   *Sequential File Updating*

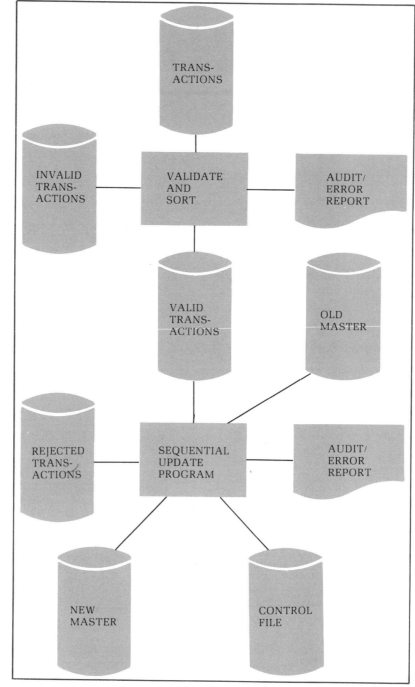

throughout the month. The year-to-date values, which will also become larger, represent all sales and returns from the beginning of the current fiscal year to the current date. At the end of a month, a separate update program will be necessary to update the beginning totals and zero out the current sales and returns.

Sequential Updating Concepts

The system concept of a sequential update is illustrated in Figure 6–10. The essential process is a merging of the old master file with a validated and sorted transaction file. Both an old master record and a transaction record will be compared to determine the appropriate action to be taken.

Figure 6–10 makes a particular assumption about the sorting and validating

Figure 6-11 *Sequential File Updating Alternative*

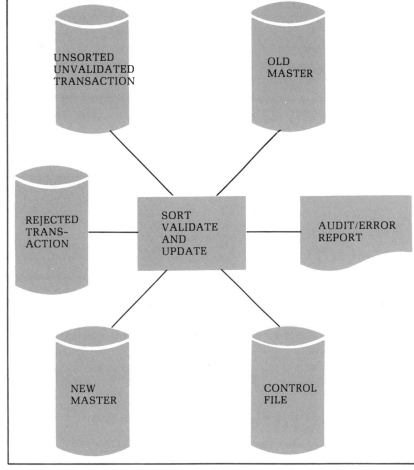

processes. The assumption is that a separate program or programs accomplish the sort and validation of the transaction file. This program would validate the transactions, based on the type of transaction and would reject any transactions that were in error. However, the validation process can only detect errors, such as invalid transaction codes, missing fields, nonnumeric characters in numeric fields, wrong field alignment, and so on. Other errors cannot be detected until the transactions are compared to the old master file. Inter-file validation procedures, then, will still have to be conducted within the update program. For example, a transaction record may indicate that a new record is to be added to the file, but the record may already exist in the master file. Other types of inter-file errors that are found during the update process will be shown when the sequential updating logic is developed.

An alternative to the structure previously described is illustrated in Figure 6-11. The assumption made here is that all sorting, transaction validation, and updating logic are contained in one program.

While the process may look simpler, it actually has the effect of changing two or three simple programs into one complex program. Whenever simplicity and complexity are the alternatives, it is best to opt for simplicity. Just because a program does contain many different processes does not mean that it should contain them. If a program can be broken down into smaller modular programs, doing so is at least worth considering.

The programmer might ask the question: Could a program be written that would include not only the sorting and validation of transactions during an update but also the entire creation and reporting phases as well? The answer is yes. However, it would be ludicrous to consider. The authors contend that simplicity is the rule, thereby eliminating many added problems.

Adds, Deletes, and Changes

In any update there is the possibility of three types of transactions, which include **adds, deletes,** and **changes.** A record may be added to the file, a record may be deleted from the file; and a change may occur to any field in any record of the file. A sequential update requires the correct sequencing of both transactions and master file to ensure that changes are made to the correct record, additions are placed on the new file in the correct sequence, and deletions cause the removal of the correct record.

Consider the records in an old master file that have sequence numbers as indicated in Figure 6–12.

Figure 6–12 *File Sequence for Update*

Old master file records	Transaction file records
123	123
146	123
185	127
200	185
257	

A sequential update program contains a major loop just like any other program. The number of times the loop is executed is generally equal to the number of transactions that exist. The process will include a comparison of a transaction record to an old master record, and an action will take place as a result of this comparison. Figure 6–13 illustrates the results of this sequential comparison.

Figure 6–13 *Sequential Update Procedures*

Old master record read	Results of comparison	Transaction record read	Action	Results placed on new master
123	Equal	123	Old updated	
123	Equal	123	Old updated	
123	Master <	127	Old transferred	123 as changed
146	Master >	127	New transferred	127 added
146	Master <	185	Old transferred	146 no change
185	Equal	185	Old updated	
185	Master <	End-of-file	Old transferred	185 as changed
200	Master <	End-of-file	Old transferred	200 no change
257	Master <	End-of-file	Old transferred	257 no change
End-of-file		End-of-file	Program ended	

When the first records are read from both the transaction file and the old master file, the two identifying numbers are equal. This would dictate either a change or a delete. Assuming a change has been indicated by a transaction code, the change is made to the old master record. However, the old master record is not transferred to the new file since it is assumed that there may be multiple changes to a record. When the next transaction is entered, it is also an update to record 123, so the old record is changed again.

When transaction 127 is read, the master record 123 is less than the transaction. The old master record that has been changed twice is then transferred to the new file, and another master record is input.

At this point the next transaction (number 127) and the next master (number 146) are compared. Since the master is greater than the transaction, the situation dictates that the transaction should be an addition. Assuming that the transaction code does indicate an addition, it is added to the new file and another transaction (number 185) is input. This process continues until the entire transaction file is read.

When the end of the transaction file is detected, remaining old master records will be transferred to the new master file. The reader may have two additional questions. What if the end of the master file is encountered first? What if a newly added record also has subsequent updates? The answers to those questions will be discussed shortly. At this point it is important to understand only the general process of sequential updating.

Program Example

It is important to remember that the sorting and validating of the transaction file is assumed to have already taken place prior to the update. With this in mind, a programmer can concentrate on the update logic.

Input

Input to this program is an existing old master file, a control file for control purposes, and a sorted, validated transaction file. The data set to be used as the transaction file is shown in Figure 6–14. Shown are two sets of transactions that will be used to update the file, which represents two days' transactions.

Figure 6–14 *Sorted and Validated Transaction File Data Sets*

```
The transaction records are 46 characters in length.
The record layout is as follows:

1 – 4  Salesperson number
6 –16  Last name
17–26  First name
27–33  Current sales
35–41  Current sales returns
43–44  Commission rate
46     Transaction code
       1 = Addition
       2 = Deletion
       3 = Name change
       4 = Sales update
       5 = Sales returns update
       6 = Commission rate change

Transaction Set 1:

==============================================
0017                      0020000          4
0020  DOUGLAS     BRENT                 05 1
0020                      0072500          4
0125  LISHER      JANET F.                 1
0243                                        2
0356                                        2
0396  VOLSKI      CHRIS                    3
0401                      0075000          4
0479                               0010000 5
0590  DUPREE      KELLY J.                 3
0635  HUNT        ROBERT                10 1
1805                                        2
1867                               0015000 5
2485                               0005000 5
2485                                  25 6

==============================================

Transaction Set 2:

==============================================
0017                      0052523          4
0125  LISHER      JANET F. 0022500          4
0396  VOLSKI      JAMES                    3
0529                      0050000          4
0746                               0010000 5

==============================================
```

Figure 6–15   *Structure Chart for Program 6–3*

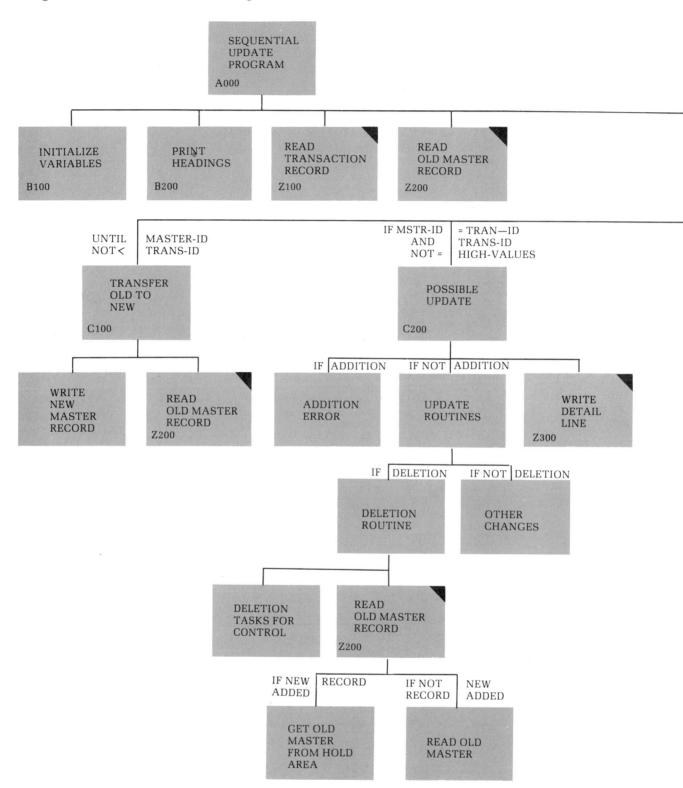

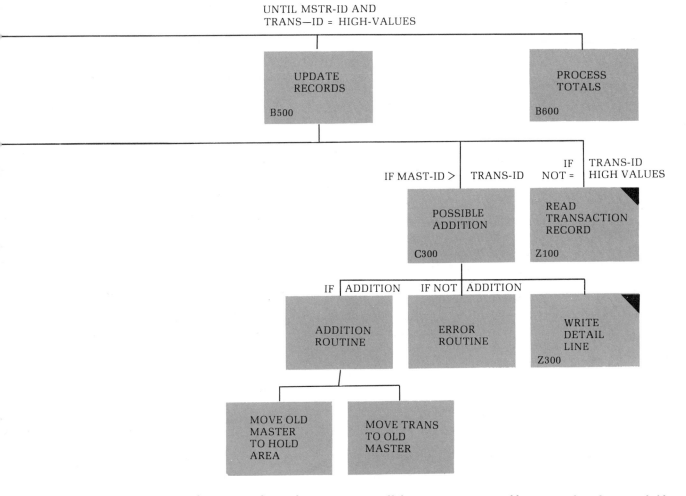

UNTIL MSTR-ID AND
TRANS—ID = HIGH-VALUES

Output

The output from this program will be a new master file, an updated control file, and an audit/error listing. The detail of the audit/error listing will include an image of each transaction, an indication of the action taken as a result of the transaction, and an error message for any rejected transaction.

Additionally, summary totals will be prepared to indicate the number and type of transactions, an accumulation of current changes, and the effect of those changes on the control file.

Structure Chart

The structure chart for Program 6–3 is shown in Figure 6–15. Note that the first level in the structure chart shows a priming read for both a transaction record and an old master record.

When processing data in a file, a program normally has one major loop that tests for and detects the end-of-file condition by using a program switch. However, when accomplishing an update program, two files are involved, and there is no previous knowledge of when the end-of-file condition will be reached for either file. It is necessary to continue the loop until both files have reached their respective ends. Thus, it would be possible to define and control an end-of-file switch for both the master file and the transaction file. The iteration of the major loop labeled B500 on the structure chart has the condition of until master-identifier is equal to HIGH–VALUES and transaction-identifier is equal to HIGH–VALUES. **HIGH–VAL**

UES, the largest value in the collating sequence of any particular computer, is used as the end-of-file switch for both files. When the end-of-file is detected, the AT END clause will move HIGH–VALUES to the respective master-identifier and the transaction-identifier. HIGH–VALUES is used because any other value compared to it will be lower. Consequently, HIGH–VALUES serves not only as an end-of-file indicator but also serves to automatically result in a proper comparison during the update process. Note that HIGH–VALUES may be moved only to a field that is defined as alphanumeric.

To illustrate the sequential update process, consider the three possible results of the comparison between the master-identifier and the transaction-identifier. Module C100 will be iterated until the master is not less than the transaction, meaning that it will be executed at least once if the master is less than the transaction. When a master is less than a transaction it is necessary to transfer the old master record to the new master file and obtain another old master record. The effect of this logic is to transfer as many old master records to the new file as necessary until an old master record is obtained that is equal to or greater than the current transaction.

At any time that the transaction and master records are equal, possible updating is dictated. The reason that it is only possible is because the transaction code may indicate that the transaction is not an update, but an addition instead. This, of course, would be an error. If it is not an addition, then deletion or change routines will be executed. In either case, the results of entering the possible update routine will be printed.

When a master is greater than a transaction, a possible addition is dictated. The transaction code is tested to ensure that an addition was desired. If not, an error is printed. If an addition was desired then the addition routine is executed.

After each transaction has been processed, then another transaction record is read. At the C level of detail, two additional conditions are placed on the Z100–READ–TRANS–RECORD and C200–POSSIBLE–UPDATE related to whether the transaction-identifier is equal to HIGH–VALUES. When the end of the transaction file has been reached, another transaction record cannot be read, necessitating the test for HIGH–VALUES before executing Z100–READ–TRANS–RECORD. Also at the point that both the master file and the transaction have reached their ends, both identifiers would contain HIGH–VALUES and C200–POSSIBLE–UPDATE would be entered erroneously. Thus, the test for HIGH–VALUES is also necessary for module C200–POSSIBLE–UPDATE.

To understand the special case of an added record, study the module labeled C300–POSSIBLE–ADDITION. If the transaction is an addition, the addition routine would be performed, which includes moving the existing old master record to a holding area and moving the newly added record to the old master. (Realize that this movement of the record to the old master is only a movement in main storage, not a movement to the old physical file.) Though not shown it would also include the setting of a switch to indicate that a new record was added.

The reason for doing this is twofold. First, this module was entered because the old master record was greater than the transaction, and the newly added record must be placed on the new file in sequence before the previously read old master record. Second, it is possible to have an added record followed by additional transactions, making it necessary to place the newly added record in the position of the previous old master. This would then allow appropriate subsequent updates to occur. This newly added record would not be transferred to the new file until a subsequent transaction was greater than the added record. This procedure works even if there are not additional transactions to an added record.

Why set a switch when a new record is added? The answer is in Z200–READ–MASTER. If a new record has been previously added, the old master record that was placed in a hold area must now be brought in as the next old record to be processed. When a new record has not been added, the next old master is obtained by reading the record from the file.

Another question remains. What change to this structure is necessary if the transaction validation process does occur during the update program? All that is necessary is for the validation module to be added as C050–VALIDATE–RECORDS and a condition to be placed on modules C100, C200, and C300 so that these would not be entered if the record did not pass the validation tests. The complexity added is not apparent at this level in the structure chart. The complexity would be in all of the validation routines necessary in C050–VALIDATE–RECORDS.

Program

Program 6–3

```
000010 IDENTIFICATION DIVISION.
000020 PROGRAM-ID.    SEQUPDT.
000030*·············································································
000040* PROGRAM EXAMPLE 6-3 SEQUENTIAL UPDATE                                 *
000050*·············································································
000060 ENVIRONMENT DIVISION.
000070 CONFIGURATION SECTION.
000080    SOURCE-COMPUTER.  IBM-4341.
000090    OBJECT-COMPUTER.  IBM-4341.
000100 INPUT-OUTPUT SECTION.
000110 FILE-CONTROL.
000120    SELECT OLD-SALES-FILE
000130       ASSIGN TO UT-S-SLSOLD.
000140    SELECT NEW-SALES-FILE
000150       ASSIGN TO UT-S-SLSNEW.
000160    SELECT SALES-CONTROL-FILE
000170       ASSIGN TO UT-S-SALESCT.
000180    SELECT SALES-REPORT-FILE
000190       ASSIGN TO PRINTER.
000200    SELECT SALES-TRANSACTION-FILE
000210       ASSIGN TO UT-S-TRANS.
000220*
000230 DATA DIVISION.
000240 FILE SECTION.
000250 FD  OLD-SALES-FILE
000260     RECORD CONTAINS 55 CHARACTERS
000270     LABEL RECORDS STANDARD.
000280 01  OS-OLD-SALES-RECORD.
000290     05  OS-SALESPERSON-NUMBER         PIC X(4).
000300     05  OS-HASH-NUMBER
000310         REDEFINES OS-SALESPERSON-NUMBER PIC 9(4).
000320     05  OS-LAST-NAME                  PIC X(11).
000330     05  OS-FIRST-NAME                 PIC X(10).
000340     05  OS-YEAR-TO-DATE-SALES         PIC 9(5)V99.
000350     05  OS-YEAR-TO-DATE-SALES-RETURNS PIC 9(5)V99.
000360     05  OS-CURRENT-SALES              PIC 9(5)V99.
000370     05  OS-CURRENT-SALES-RETURNS      PIC 9(5)V99.
000380     05  OS-COMMISSION-RATE            PIC V99.
000390 FD  NEW-SALES-FILE
000400     RECORD CONTAINS 55 CHARACTERS
000410     LABEL RECORDS STANDARD.
000420 01  NS-NEW-SALES-RECORD.
000430     05  NS-SALESPERSON-NUMBER         PIC X(4).
000440     05  NS-LAST-NAME                  PIC X(11).
000450     05  NS-FIRST-NAME                 PIC X(10).
000460     05  NS-YEAR-TO-DATE-SALES         PIC 9(5)V99.
000470     05  NS-YEAR-TO-DATE-SALES-RETURNS PIC 9(5)V99.
000480     05  NS-CURRENT-SALES              PIC 9(5)V99.
000490     05  NS-CURRENT-SALES-RETURNS      PIC 9(5)V99.
000500     05  NS-COMMISSION-RATE            PIC V99.
000510 FD  SALES-CONTROL-FILE
000520     RECORD CONTAINS 84 CHARACTERS
000530     LABEL RECORDS ARE STANDARD.
```

Program 6–3 *(continued)*

```
000540 01  SC-SALES-CONTROL-RECORD.
000550     05   SC-BEG-TOT-FIELDS.
000560          10   SC-BEG-TOT-RECORDS-STORED    PIC S9(4).
000570          10   SC-BEG-TOT-HASH-NUMBER       PIC S9(6).
000580          10   SC-BEG-TOT-YTD-SALES         PIC S9(6)V99.
000590          10   SC-BEG-TOT-YTD-SALES-RETURNS PIC S9(6)V99.
000600          10   SC-BEG-TOT-CURRENT-SALES     PIC S9(6)V99.
000610          10   SC-BEG-TOT-CURRENT-RETURNS   PIC S9(6)V99.
000620     05   SC-CHG-TOT-FIELDS.
000630          10   SC-CHG-TOT-RECORDS-STORED    PIC S9(4).
000640          10   SC-CHG-TOT-HASH-NUMBER       PIC S9(6).
000650          10   SC-CHG-TOT-YTD-SALES         PIC S9(6)V99.
000660          10   SC-CHG-TOT-YTD-SALES-RETURNS PIC S9(6)V99.
000670          10   SC-CHG-TOT-CURRENT-SALES     PIC S9(6)V99.
000680          10   SC-CHG-TOT-CURRENT-RETURNS   PIC S9(6)V99.
000690 FD  SALES-TRANSACTION-FILE
000700     RECORD CONTAINS 46 CHARACTERS
000710     LABEL RECORDS ARE STANDARD.
000720 01  ST-SALES-TRANS-RECORD.
000730     05   ST-SALESPERSON-NUMBER          PIC X(4).
000740     05   ST-HASH-NUMBER
000750          REDEFINES ST-SALESPERSON-NUMBER PIC 9(4).
000760     05   FILLER                         PIC X(1).
000770     05   ST-LAST-NAME                   PIC X(11).
000780     05   ST-FIRST-NAME                  PIC X(10).
000790     05   ST-CURRENT-SALES               PIC 9(5)V99.
000800     05   FILLER                         PIC X(1).
000810     05   ST-CURRENT-SALES-RETURNS       PIC 9(5)V99.
000820     05   FILLER                         PIC X(1).
000830     05   ST-COMMISSION-RATE             PIC V99.
000840     05   FILLER                         PIC X(1).
000850     05   ST-TRANSACTION-CODE            PIC X(1).
000860          88   ADDITION-OF-SALESPERSON    VALUE '1'.
000870          88   DELETION-OF-SALESPERSON    VALUE '2'.
000880          88   NAME-CHANGE                VALUE '3'.
000890          88   UPDATE-CURRENT-SALES       VALUE '4'.
000900          88   UPDATE-CURRENT-SALES-RETURNS VALUE '5'.
000910          88   UPDATE-COMMISSION-RATE     VALUE '6'.
000920 FD  SALES-REPORT-FILE
000930     RECORD CONTAINS 132 CHARACTERS
000940     LABEL RECORDS ARE OMITTED.
000950 01  SR-SALES-REPORT-LINE               PIC X(132).
000960*
000970 WORKING-STORAGE SECTION.
000980 01  WS-ACCUMULATORS.
000990     05   WS-CHG-TOT-RECORDS-STORED      PIC S9(4).
001000     05   WS-CHG-TOT-HASH-NUMBER         PIC S9(6).
001010     05   WS-CHG-YTD-SALES               PIC S9(6)V99.
001020     05   WS-CHG-YTD-SALES-RETURNS       PIC S9(6)V99.
001030     05   WS-CHG-CURRENT-SALES           PIC S9(6)V99.
001040     05   WS-CHG-CURRENT-RETURNS         PIC S9(6)V99.
001050 01  UC-UPDATE-CONTROL-AREAS.
001060     05   UC-MASTER-PENDING-SWITCH       PIC X(3).
001070          88   MASTER-IS-PENDING         VALUE 'YES'.
001080     05   UC-COUNT-SUB                   PIC 9(4).
001090     05   UC-MASTER-HOLD-AREA            PIC X(55).
001100     05   UC-HEADING-CONTROL-VALUES.
001110          10   FILLER     PIC X(20) VALUE 'ADDITIONS'.
001120          10   FILLER     PIC X(20) VALUE 'DELETIONS'.
001130          10   FILLER     PIC X(20) VALUE 'NAME CHANGES'.
001140          10   FILLER     PIC X(20) VALUE 'SALES CHANGES'.
001150          10   FILLER     PIC X(20) VALUE 'RETURNS CHANGES'.
001160          10   FILLER     PIC X(20) VALUE 'COM RATE CHANGES'.
001170          10   FILLER     PIC X(20) VALUE 'REJECTIONS'.
```

Program 6–3   *(continued)*

```
001180          10  FILLER          PIC X(20) VALUE 'TOTAL TRANSACTIONS'.
001190      05  FILLER REDEFINES UC-HEADING-CONTROL-VALUES.
001200          10  UC-HEADING-LINE         PIC X(20)
001210              OCCURS 8 TIMES.
001220      05  UC-RECORD-CONTROL-TOTALS.
001230          10  UC-NUM-OF-ADDS          PIC 9(4).
001240          10  UC-NUM-OF-DELETES       PIC 9(4).
001250          10  UC-NUM-OF-CHG-NAME      PIC 9(4).
001260          10  UC-NUM-OF-CHG-SALES     PIC 9(4).
001270          10  UC-NUM-OF-CHG-RTNS      PIC 9(4).
001280          10  UC-NUM-OF-CHG-COM-RATE  PIC 9(4).
001290          10  UC-NUM-OF-REJECTIONS    PIC 9(4).
001300          10  UC-NUM-OF-TRANSACTIONS  PIC 9(4).
001310      05  FILLER REDEFINES UC-RECORD-CONTROL-TOTALS.
001320          10  UC-RECORD-COUNT         PIC 9(4)
001330              OCCURS 8 TIMES.
001340 01  HD-HEADING-LINE.
001350      05  FILLER                      PIC X(13)
001360                                      VALUE 'UPDATE REPORT'.
001370 01  CH-COLUMN-HEADING-LINE-1.
001380      05  FILLER                      PIC X(52)
001390                                      VALUE 'RECORD IMAGE'.
001400      05  FILLER                      PIC X(25)
001410                                      VALUE 'UPDATE ACTION'.
001420      05  FILLER                      PIC X(30)
001430                                      VALUE 'ERROR MESSAGE'.
001440 01  CH-COLUMN-HEADING-LINE-2.
001450      05  FILLER              PIC X(20) VALUE SPACES.
001460      05  FILLER              PIC X(8) VALUE 'RECORDS'.
001470      05  FILLER              PIC X(2)  VALUE SPACES.
001480      05  FILLER              PIC X(4) VALUE 'HASH'.
001490      05  FILLER              PIC X(5) VALUE SPACES.
001500      05  FILLER              PIC X(5) VALUE 'SALES'.
001510      05  FILLER              PIC X(8) VALUE SPACES.
001520      05  FILLER              PIC X(8) VALUE 'RETURNS'.
001530      05  FILLER              PIC X(5) VALUE SPACES.
001540      05  FILLER              PIC X(5) VALUE 'SALES'.
001550      05  FILLER              PIC X(8) VALUE SPACES.
001560      05  FILLER              PIC X(8) VALUE 'RETURNS'.
001570 01  DL-DETAIL-LINE.
001580      05  DL-RECORD-IMAGE             PIC X(50).
001590      05  FILLER                      PIC X(2) VALUE SPACES.
001600      05  DL-UPDATE-ACTION            PIC X(25).
001610      05  DL-ERROR-MESSAGE            PIC X(30).
001620 01  TL-TOTAL-LINE-1.
001630      05  TL-STUB-HEADING             PIC X(20).
001640      05  TL-TOT-RECORDS-STORED       PIC Z,ZZ9-.
001650      05  FILLER                      PIC X(2) VALUE SPACES.
001660      05  TL-TOT-HASH-NUMBER          PIC ZZZ,ZZ9-.
001670      05  FILLER                      PIC X(2) VALUE SPACES.
001680      05  TL-TOT-YTD-SALES            PIC ZZZ,ZZZ.99-.
001690      05  FILLER                      PIC X(2) VALUE SPACES.
001700      05  TL-TOT-YTD-SALES-RETURNS    PIC ZZZ,ZZZ.99-.
001710      05  FILLER                      PIC X(2) VALUE SPACES.
001720      05  TL-TOT-CURRENT-SALES        PIC ZZZ,ZZZ.99-.
001730      05  FILLER                      PIC X(2) VALUE SPACES.
001740      05  TL-TOT-CURRENT-RETURNS      PIC ZZZ,ZZZ.99-.
001750 01  TL-TOTAL-LINE-2.
001760      05  TL-HEADING                  PIC X(30).
001770      05  TL-COUNT                    PIC Z,ZZ9.
001780*
001790 PROCEDURE DIVISION.
001800 A000-UPDATE.
001810     OPEN INPUT OLD-SALES-FILE
```

Program 6–3 *(continued)*

```
001820              SALES-TRANSACTION-FILE
001830         I-0    SALES-CONTROL-FILE
001840       OUTPUT NEW-SALES-FILE
001850              SALES-REPORT-FILE.
001860     PERFORM B100-INITIALIZE-VARIABLES.
001870     PERFORM B200-PRINT-HEADINGS.
001880     PERFORM Z100-READ-TRANS-RECORD.
001890     PERFORM Z200-READ-MASTER-RECORD.
001900     PERFORM B500-UPDATE-RECORDS
001910         UNTIL ST-SALESPERSON-NUMBER = HIGH-VALUES
001920             AND OS-SALESPERSON-NUMBER = HIGH-VALUES.
001930     PERFORM B600-PROCESS-TOTALS.
001940     CLOSE OLD-SALES-FILE
001950           SALES-TRANSACTION-FILE
001960           SALES-CONTROL-FILE
001970           NEW-SALES-FILE
001980           SALES-REPORT-FILE.
001990     STOP RUN.
002000 B100-INITIALIZE-VARIABLES.
002010     MOVE ZEROES TO WS-ACCUMULATORS
002020                    UC-RECORD-CONTROL-TOTALS.
002030     MOVE 'NO'  TO UC-MASTER-PENDING-SWITCH.
002040 B200-PRINT-HEADINGS.
002050     WRITE SR-SALES-REPORT-LINE FROM HD-HEADING-LINE
002060         AFTER PAGE.
002070     WRITE SR-SALES-REPORT-LINE FROM CH-COLUMN-HEADING-LINE-1
002080         AFTER 1.
002090 B500-UPDATE-RECORDS.
002100     MOVE SPACES TO DL-DETAIL-LINE.
002110     PERFORM C100-TRANSFER-OLD-TO-NEW
002120         UNTIL OS-SALESPERSON-NUMBER NOT < ST-SALESPERSON-NUMBER.
002130     IF OS-SALESPERSON-NUMBER = ST-SALESPERSON-NUMBER
002140         IF OS-SALESPERSON-NUMBER NOT = HIGH-VALUES
002150             PERFORM C200-POSSIBLE-UPDATE
002160         ELSE
002170             NEXT SENTENCE
002180     ELSE
002190         IF OS-SALESPERSON-NUMBER > ST-SALESPERSON-NUMBER
002200             PERFORM C300-POSSIBLE-ADDITION.
002210     IF ST-SALESPERSON-NUMBER NOT = HIGH-VALUES
002220         PERFORM Z100-READ-TRANS-RECORD.
002230 B600-PROCESS-TOTALS.
002240     READ SALES-CONTROL-FILE
002250         AT END MOVE HIGH-VALUES TO SC-SALES-CONTROL-RECORD.
002260     PERFORM C500-PRINT-BEG-TOTALS.
002270     PERFORM C600-PRINT-CHG-TOTALS.
002280     PERFORM C700-PRINT-END-TOTALS.
002290     PERFORM C800-PRINT-COUNT-SUMMARY
002300         VARYING UC-COUNT-SUB
002310         FROM 1 BY 1
002320         UNTIL UC-COUNT-SUB > 8.
002330     REWRITE SC-SALES-CONTROL-RECORD.
002340 C100-TRANSFER-OLD-TO-NEW.
002350     MOVE OS-OLD-SALES-RECORD TO NS-NEW-SALES-RECORD.
002360     WRITE NS-NEW-SALES-RECORD.
002370     PERFORM Z200-READ-MASTER-RECORD.
002380 C200-POSSIBLE-UPDATE.
002390     IF ADDITION-OF-SALESPERSON
002400         MOVE 'REJECTED'            TO DL-UPDATE-ACTION
002410         MOVE 'RECORD ALREADY EXISTS' TO DL-ERROR-MESSAGE
002420         ADD 1 TO UC-NUM-OF-REJECTIONS
002430     ELSE
002440         PERFORM D200-UPDATE-RECORD.
002450     PERFORM Z300-WRITE-DETAIL-LINE.
```

Program 6-3 *(continued)*

```
002460 C300-POSSIBLE-ADDITION.
002470     IF ADDITION-OF-SALESPERSON
002480        ADD ST-HASH-NUMBER           TO WS-CHG-TOT-HASH-NUMBER
002490        PERFORM D300-MOVE-TRANS-TO-OLD
002500     ELSE
002510        MOVE 'REJECTED'              TO DL-UPDATE-ACTION
002520        MOVE 'TRANS NOT ADDITION'    TO DL-ERROR-MESSAGE
002530        ADD 1                        TO UC-NUM-OF-REJECTIONS.
002540     PERFORM Z300-WRITE-DETAIL-LINE.
002550 C500-PRINT-BEG-TOTALS.
002560     WRITE SR-SALES-REPORT-LINE FROM CH-COLUMN-HEADING-LINE-2
002570        AFTER 2.
002580     MOVE 'BEGINNING - CONTROL'      TO TL-STUB-HEADING.
002590     MOVE SC-BEG-TOT-RECORDS-STORED  TO TL-TOT-RECORDS-STORED.
002600     MOVE SC-BEG-TOT-HASH-NUMBER     TO TL-TOT-HASH-NUMBER.
002610     MOVE SC-BEG-TOT-YTD-SALES       TO TL-TOT-YTD-SALES.
002620     MOVE SC-BEG-TOT-YTD-SALES-RETURNS
002630        TO TL-TOT-YTD-SALES-RETURNS.
002640     MOVE SC-BEG-TOT-CURRENT-SALES   TO TL-TOT-CURRENT-SALES.
002650     MOVE SC-BEG-TOT-CURRENT-RETURNS
002660        TO TL-TOT-CURRENT-RETURNS.
002670     WRITE SR-SALES-REPORT-LINE FROM TL-TOTAL-LINE-1
002680        AFTER 2.
002690 C600-PRINT-CHG-TOTALS.
002700     MOVE 'PREVIOUS CHANGES'         TO TL-STUB-HEADING.
002710     MOVE SC-CHG-TOT-RECORDS-STORED  TO TL-TOT-RECORDS-STORED.
002720     MOVE SC-CHG-TOT-HASH-NUMBER     TO TL-TOT-HASH-NUMBER.
002730     MOVE SC-CHG-TOT-YTD-SALES       TO TL-TOT-YTD-SALES.
002740     MOVE SC-CHG-TOT-YTD-SALES-RETURNS
002750        TO TL-TOT-YTD-SALES-RETURNS.
002760     MOVE SC-CHG-TOT-CURRENT-SALES   TO TL-TOT-CURRENT-SALES.
002770     MOVE SC-CHG-TOT-CURRENT-RETURNS TO TL-TOT-CURRENT-RETURNS.
002780     WRITE SR-SALES-REPORT-LINE FROM TL-TOTAL-LINE-1
002790        AFTER 2.
002800     MOVE 'CURRENT CHANGES'          TO TL-STUB-HEADING.
002810     MOVE WS-CHG-TOT-RECORDS-STORED  TO TL-TOT-RECORDS-STORED.
002820     MOVE WS-CHG-TOT-HASH-NUMBER     TO TL-TOT-HASH-NUMBER.
002830     MOVE WS-CHG-YTD-SALES           TO TL-TOT-YTD-SALES.
002840     MOVE WS-CHG-CURRENT-SALES       TO TL-TOT-CURRENT-SALES.
002850     MOVE WS-CHG-YTD-SALES-RETURNS   TO TL-TOT-YTD-SALES-RETURNS.
002860     MOVE WS-CHG-CURRENT-RETURNS     TO TL-TOT-CURRENT-RETURNS.
002870     WRITE SR-SALES-REPORT-LINE FROM TL-TOTAL-LINE-1
002880        AFTER 2.
002890 C700-PRINT-END-TOTALS.
002900     MOVE 'ENDING - CONTROL'         TO TL-STUB-HEADING.
002910     ADD WS-CHG-TOT-RECORDS-STORED TO SC-CHG-TOT-RECORDS-STORED.
002920     ADD WS-CHG-TOT-HASH-NUMBER    TO SC-CHG-TOT-HASH-NUMBER.
002930     ADD WS-CHG-YTD-SALES          TO SC-CHG-TOT-YTD-SALES.
002940     ADD WS-CHG-CURRENT-SALES      TO SC-CHG-TOT-CURRENT-SALES.
002950     ADD WS-CHG-YTD-SALES-RETURNS  TO SC-CHG-TOT-YTD-SALES-RETURNS
002960     ADD WS-CHG-CURRENT-RETURNS    TO SC-CHG-TOT-CURRENT-RETURNS.
002970     ADD SC-BEG-TOT-RECORDS-STORED SC-CHG-TOT-RECORDS-STORED
002980        GIVING TL-TOT-RECORDS-STORED.
002990     ADD SC-BEG-TOT-HASH-NUMBER SC-CHG-TOT-HASH-NUMBER
003000        GIVING TL-TOT-HASH-NUMBER.
003010     ADD SC-BEG-TOT-YTD-SALES SC-CHG-TOT-YTD-SALES
003020        GIVING TL-TOT-YTD-SALES.
003030     ADD SC-BEG-TOT-YTD-SALES-RETURNS SC-CHG-TOT-YTD-SALES-RETURNS
003040        GIVING TL-TOT-YTD-SALES-RETURNS.
003050     ADD SC-BEG-TOT-CURRENT-SALES SC-CHG-TOT-CURRENT-SALES
003060        GIVING TL-TOT-CURRENT-SALES.
003070     ADD SC-BEG-TOT-CURRENT-RETURNS SC-CHG-TOT-CURRENT-RETURNS
003080        GIVING TL-TOT-CURRENT-RETURNS.
003090     WRITE SR-SALES-REPORT-LINE FROM TL-TOTAL-LINE-1
```

Program 6-3 *(continued)*

```
003100          AFTER 2.
003110 C800-PRINT-COUNT-SUMMARY.
003120     MOVE UC-HEADING-LINE(UC-COUNT-SUB) TO TL-HEADING.
003130     MOVE UC-RECORD-COUNT(UC-COUNT-SUB) TO TL-COUNT.
003140     WRITE SR-SALES-REPORT-LINE FROM TL-TOTAL-LINE-2
003150          AFTER 2.
003160 D200-UPDATE-RECORD.
003170     IF DELETION-OF-SALESPERSON
003180         MOVE 'RECORD DELETED'          TO DL-UPDATE-ACTION
003190         SUBTRACT 1                     FROM WS-CHG-TOT-RECORDS-STORED
003200         SUBTRACT ST-HASH-NUMBER        FROM WS-CHG-TOT-HASH-NUMBER
003210         SUBTRACT OS-YEAR-TO-DATE-SALES FROM WS-CHG-YTD-SALES
003220         SUBTRACT OS-YEAR-TO-DATE-SALES-RETURNS
003230             FROM WS-CHG-YTD-SALES-RETURNS
003240         SUBTRACT OS-CURRENT-SALES FROM WS-CHG-CURRENT-SALES
003250         SUBTRACT OS-CURRENT-SALES-RETURNS
003260             FROM WS-CHG-CURRENT-RETURNS
003270         ADD 1 TO UC-NUM-OF-DELETES
003280         PERFORM Z200-READ-MASTER-RECORD.
003290     IF NAME-CHANGE
003300         MOVE 'NAME CHANGED'       TO DL-UPDATE-ACTION
003310         MOVE ST-LAST-NAME         TO OS-LAST-NAME
003320         MOVE ST-FIRST-NAME        TO OS-FIRST-NAME
003330         ADD 1                     TO UC-NUM-OF-CHG-NAME.
003340     IF UPDATE-CURRENT-SALES
003350         MOVE 'YTD SALES UPDATED'  TO DL-UPDATE-ACTION
003360         ADD ST-CURRENT-SALES      TO OS-YEAR-TO-DATE-SALES
003370                                      OS-CURRENT-SALES
003380                                      WS-CHG-YTD-SALES
003390                                      WS-CHG-CURRENT-SALES
003400         ADD 1                     TO UC-NUM-OF-CHG-SALES.
003410     IF UPDATE-CURRENT-SALES-RETURNS
003420         MOVE 'YTD SALES RETURNS UPDATED' TO DL-UPDATE-ACTION
003430         ADD ST-CURRENT-SALES-RETURNS
003440             TO OS-YEAR-TO-DATE-SALES-RETURNS
003450                OS-CURRENT-SALES-RETURNS
003460                WS-CHG-YTD-SALES-RETURNS
003470                WS-CHG-CURRENT-RETURNS
003480         ADD 1 TO UC-NUM-OF-CHG-RTNS.
003490     IF UPDATE-COMMISSION-RATE
003500         MOVE 'COMMISSION RATE UPDATED' TO DL-UPDATE-ACTION
003510         MOVE ST-COMMISSION-RATE        TO OS-COMMISSION-RATE
003520         ADD 1 TO UC-NUM-OF-CHG-COM-RATE.
003530 D300-MOVE-TRANS-TO-OLD.
003540     MOVE OS-OLD-SALES-RECORD    TO UC-MASTER-HOLD-AREA.
003550     MOVE 'RECORD ADDED'         TO DL-UPDATE-ACTION.
003560     MOVE ST-SALESPERSON-NUMBER  TO OS-SALESPERSON-NUMBER.
003570     MOVE ST-LAST-NAME           TO OS-LAST-NAME.
003580     MOVE ST-FIRST-NAME          TO OS-FIRST-NAME.
003590     MOVE ZEROES                 TO OS-YEAR-TO-DATE-SALES
003600                                    OS-YEAR-TO-DATE-SALES-RETURNS
003610                                    OS-CURRENT-SALES
003620                                    OS-CURRENT-SALES-RETURNS.
003630     MOVE ST-COMMISSION-RATE     TO OS-COMMISSION-RATE.
003640     MOVE 'YES'                  TO UC-MASTER-PENDING-SWITCH.
003650     ADD 1                       TO WS-CHG-TOT-RECORDS-STORED
003660                                    UC-NUM-OF-ADDS.
003670 Z100-READ-TRANS-RECORD.
003680     READ SALES-TRANSACTION-FILE
003690         AT END MOVE HIGH-VALUES TO ST-SALESPERSON-NUMBER.
003700     IF ST-SALESPERSON-NUMBER NOT = HIGH-VALUES
003710         ADD 1 TO UC-NUM-OF-TRANSACTIONS.
003720 Z200-READ-MASTER-RECORD.
003730     IF MASTER-IS-PENDING
```

Program 6-3   *(concluded)*

```
003740          MOVE UC-MASTER-HOLD-AREA TO OS-OLD-SALES-RECORD
003750          MOVE 'NO'                 TO UC-MASTER-PENDING-SWITCH
003760      ELSE
003770          READ OLD-SALES-FILE
003780              AT END MOVE HIGH-VALUES TO OS-SALESPERSON-NUMBER.
003790 Z300-WRITE-DETAIL-LINE.
003800      MOVE ST-SALES-TRANS-RECORD TO DL-RECORD-IMAGE.
003810      WRITE SR-SALES-REPORT-LINE FROM DL-DETAIL-LINE
003820          AFTER 1.
```

Discussion

Since the logic was well developed with the structure chart, it is left to the programmer to study the major logic of the actual program. Note particularly the setting of the switch for an added record at line 3640, the testing of that switch in the IF statement at line 3730, and the resetting of the switch at line 3750. Also study the various control tasks throughout the program to accumulate changes in record counts, hash totals, numeric totals, and transaction counts. The output from the execution of Program 6-3 immediately after the file was initially created is shown in Figure 6-16 with the first transaction data set. Figure 6-17 contains the output from running Program 6-2, the report program, using the updated file as input. The programmer would be well-advised to compare the file before and after the update.

All subsequent update runs will work the same as the first. Figure 6-18 illustrates the output from the update program using the second transaction set. The only essential difference is noted in the printing of the control totals. Since this run is the second in the month, the printing of the control totals includes printing of all

Figure 6-16   *Output from Program 6-3 with First Transactions*

```
UPDATE REPORT
RECORD IMAGE                                   UPDATE ACTION           ERROR MESSAGE
0017                    0020000            4   YTD SALES UPDATE
0020    DOUGLAS BRENT                 05   1   RECORD ADDED
0020                    0072500            4   YTD SALES UPDATED
0125    LISHER  JANET F.                   1   REJECTED                RECORD ALREADY EXISTS
0243                                       2   RECORD DELETED
0356                                       2   RECORD DELETED
0396    VOLSKI  CHRIS                      3   NAME CHANGED
0401                    0075000            4   YTD SALES UPDATED
0479                            0010000    5   YTD SALES RETURNS UPDATED
0590    DUPREE  KELLY J.                   3   REJECTED                TRANS NOT ADDITION
0635    HUNT    ROBERT                10   1   REJECTED                RECORD ALREADY EXISTS
1805                                       2   RECORD DELETED
1867                    0015000            5   YTD SALES RETURNS UPDATED
2485                    0005000            5   YTD SALES RETURNS UPDATED
2485                               25  6   COMMISSION RATE UPDATED


                   RECORDS   HASH      SALES      RETURNS     SALES     RETURNS

BEGINNING-CONTROL    30     40,130   23,386.40   6,882.67       .00        .00
PREVIOUS CHANGES      0          0         .00        .00       .00        .00
CURRENT CHANGES       2-     2,384-     673.77-    710.00-  1,675.00    300.00
ENDING-CONTROL       28     37,746   22,712.63   6,172.67   1,675.00    300.00
ADDITIONS                        1
DELETIONS                        3
NAME CHANGES                     1
SALES CHANGES                    3
RETURNS CHANGES                  3
COM RATE CHANGES                 1
REJECTIONS                       3
TOTAL TRANSACTIONS              15
```

Figure 6–17   *Output from Program 6–2 after First Update*

```
        SALES REPORT
           17    PAYNE        MAX            1,187.00     56.73    200.00        .00    .05
           20    DOUGLAS      BRENT            725.00       .00    725.00        .00    .05
          125    LISHER       JANET F.         500.00       .00       .00        .00    .15
          396    VOLSKI       CHRIS            326.80     58.47       .00        .00    .08
          401    OWENS        GEORGE         1,112.20     39.57    750.00        .00    .09
          479    WETZEL       ROBERT D.      2,088.76    158.77       .00     100.00    .15
          529    PEACOCK      BARBARA          673.30    156.64       .00        .00    .08
          580    DUPREE       KELLY L.       3,578.88    275.82       .00        .00    .10
          635    HUNT         ROBERT           453.20    475.34       .00        .00    .10
          746    JACKSON      JASON            784.50     84.78       .00        .00    .15
          859    HUTCHENS     JEFF             576.30     48.57       .00        .00    .14
          927    BARCLAY      RICHARD        1,987.40    485.63       .00        .00    .11
         1001    DILL         JEFF             586.40    284.56       .00        .00    .20
         1132    UNLAND       KIM L.           475.64    395.85       .00        .00    .25
         1415    GOODMAN      EVE              645.42    238.47       .00        .00    .10
         1634    VAUGHN       SYLVIA A.        478.99    456.78       .00        .00    .20
         1856    LOVELAND     GEORGE           462.75    276.56       .00        .00    .10
         1867    STEWARD      KEVIN J.       1,150.00    325.00       .00     150.00    .15
         1938    DWYER        JOHN D.          231.75     40.00       .00        .00    .10
         2157    YOUNG        KAREN L.       1,123.59     35.75       .00        .00    .30
         2186    SMITH        DOUGLAS          183.45    377.58       .00        .00    .20
         2269    THOMPSON     LISA S.          500.00    100.00       .00        .00    .20
         2294    HERMAN       JACK             484.65     87.47       .00        .00    .05
         2341    ADAMS        ROBYN A.         231.75     40.00       .00        .00    .10
         2395    MATNEY       DELORES          795.74    857.46       .00        .00    .05
         2485    PHILLIPS     TRACY L.         500.00    150.00       .00      50.00    .25
         2487    HUME         LETA             483.53    284.37       .00        .00    .20
         2575    CROSS        CHERYL           385.63    382.50       .00        .00    .10

                              RECORDS   HASH      SALES      RETURNS      SALES    RETURNS

        BEGINNING - CONTROL      30    40,130   23,386.40   6,882.67        .00        .00
        NET CHANGE - CONTROL      2-    2,384-      673.77-    710.00-   1,675.00    300.00
        ENDING - CONTROL         28    37,746   22,712.63   6,172.67   1,675.00    300.00
        ENDING - ACTUAL          28    37,746   22,712.63   6,172.67   1,675.00    300.00
```

Figure 6–18   *Output from Program 6–3 with Second Transactions*

```
    UPDATE REPORT
    RECORD IMAGE                                 UPDATE ACTION            ERROR MESSAGE
    0017                           0052523       4   YTD SALES UPDATED
    0125   LISHER    JANET F.      0022500       4   YTD SALES UPDATED
    0396   VOLSKI    JAMES                       3   NAME CHANGED
    0529                           0050000       4   YTD SALES UPDATED
    0746                                0010000   5   YTD SALES RETURNS UPDATED

                          RECORDS   HASH      SALES      RETURNS      SALES    RETURNS

    BEGINNING - CONTROL      30    40,130   23,386.40   6,882.67        .00        .00
    PREVIOUS CHANGES          2-    2,384-      673.77-    710.00-   1,675.00    300.00
    CURRENT CHANGES           0         0    1,250.23     100.00   1,250.23    100.00
    ENDING - CONTROL         28    37,746   23,962.86   6,272.67   2,925.23    400.00
    ADDITIONS                 0
    DELETIONS                 0
    NAME CHANGES              1
    SALES CHANGES             3
    RETURNS CHANGES           1
    COM RATE CHANGES          0
    REJECTIONS                0
    TOTAL TRANSACTIONS        5
```

accumulated previous changes. Compare these previous totals to the current changes in the output in Figures 6–16 and 6–17. Figure 6–19 contains the output of the report program after the second update.

Figure 6–19   *Output from Program 6–2 after Second Update*

```
    SALES REPORT
      17    PAYNE      MAX          1,712.23     56.73    725.23       .00    .05
      20    DOUGLAS    BRENT          725.00       .00    725.00       .00    .05
     125    LISHER     JANET F.       725.00       .00    225.00       .00    .15
     396    VOLSKI     JAMES          326.80     58.47       .00       .00    .08
     401    OWENS      GEORGE       1,112.20     39.57    750.00       .00    .09
     479    WETZEL     ROBERT D.    2,088.76    158.77       .00    100.00    .15
     529    PEACOCK    BARBARA      1,173.30    156.64    500.00       .00    .08
     580    DUPREE     KELLY L.     3,578.88    275.82       .00       .00    .10
     635    HUNT       ROBERT         453.20    475.34       .00       .00    .10
     746    JACKSON    JASON          784.50    184.78       .00    100.00    .15
     859    HUTCHENS   JEFF           576.30     48.57       .00       .00    .14
     927    BARCLAY    RICHARD      1,987.40    485.63       .00       .00    .11
    1001    DILL       JEFF           586.40    284.56       .00       .00    .20
    1132    UNLAND     KIM L.         475.64    395.85       .00       .00    .25
    1415    GOODMAN    EVE            645.42    238.47       .00       .00    .10
    1634    VAUGHN     SYLVIA A.      478.99    456.78       .00       .00    .20
    1856    LOVELAND   GEORGE         462.75    276.56       .00       .00    .10
    1867    STEWARD    KEVIN J.     1,150.00    325.00       .00    150.00    .15
    1938    DWYER      JOHN D.        231.75     40.00       .00       .00    .10
    2157    YOUNG      KAREN L.     1,123.59     35.75       .00       .00    .30
    2186    SMITH      DOUGLAS        183.45    377.58       .00       .00    .20
    2269    THOMPSON   LISA S.        500.00    100.00       .00       .00    .20
    2294    HERMAN     JACK           484.65     87.47       .00       .00    .05
    2341    ADAMS      ROBYN A.       231.75     40.00       .00       .00    .10
    2395    MATNEY     DELORES        795.74    857.46       .00       .00    .05
    2485    PHILLIPS   TRACY L.       500.00    150.00       .00     50.00    .25
    2487    HUME       LETA           483.53    284.37       .00       .00    .20
    2575    CROSS      CHERYL         385.63    382.50       .00       .00    .10

                      RECORDS    HASH       SALES      RETURNS       SALES    RETURNS
    BEGINNING - CONTROL    30   40,130   23,386.40   6,882.67         .00        .00
    NET CHANGE - CONTROL    2-   2,384-      576.46     610.00-   2,925.23     400.00
    ENDING - CONTROL       28   37,746   23,962.86   6,272.67    2,925.23     400.00
    ENDING - ACTUAL        28   37,746   23,962.86   6,272.67    2,925.23     400.00
```

In-place Sequential Updating

The updating that took place on the old master file resulted in a new master file being created. This type of old-new processing is mandatory when working with tape files, because a tape file can be opened for input or output but not both. However, when a sequential file is placed on disk, it is possible to update the records in place. **In-place updating** allows the appropriate change to be made to an old record and then the record is rewritten in the same location. In-place updating did take place on the control file. Notice that the file was opened as I–O in the statement at line 1830 in Program 6–3. A file opened as I–O can be used for both input and output to accomplish an in-place update. Note that the assumption made for the control file was that it was to be stored on magnetic disk. If only tape were to be used, the control record would probably have been placed as the last record in each of the master files.

The control record was input by the READ statement at line 2240, and appropriately updated and rewritten in the REWRITE statement at line 2330. The format for the REWRITE statement for a sequential file is the same as for a WRITE statement, including the optional FROM clause.

In-place sequential updating may also occur on a master file if the file is stored on magnetic disk. However, additions may not be accommodated because there is no way to insert records in the proper sequence.

Deletions can be accommodated without physically deleting the record. Adding a field would be required in each record to indicate when a record has been logically deleted. If, during an in-place update run, a record was to be deleted, the extra field could be changed to indicate logical deletion. The next time a report program or an update program was run against the file, it would be necessary to test the delete field to determine if the record was active. Eventually, it would be advisable to transfer all active records to the new file.

Changes to any records can be easily accommodated by utilizing an in-place update program. All that is required is to obtain the record to be updated, make the change, and then REWRITE the record in place.

Program Example

In order to illustrate this concept, consider Program 6–4, which uses an in-place update for the month-end procedures. It was previously mentioned that the old-new update runs would occur on every business day and that it would be necessary at the end of the month to place zeros in the current sales and current returns fields. Additionally, it would be necessary to prepare the control record to begin another month. Program 6–4 accomplishes all of these tasks.

The input to this program is the last version of the month of the new master file. The output from this program is the first version of the old master file for the next month. An additional output from this program is a backup file of the changed and re-created file.

Program

Program 6–4

```
000010 IDENTIFICATION DIVISION.
000020 PROGRAM-ID.    SEQMOEND.
000030**************************************************************
000040* PROGRAM EXAMPLE 6-4 SEQUENTIAL FILE MONTH END IN-PLACE UPDATE  *
000050**************************************************************
000060 ENVIRONMENT DIVISION.
000070 CONFIGURATION SECTION.
000080    SOURCE-COMPUTER.   IBM-4341.
000090    OBJECT-COMPUTER.   IBM-4341.
000100 INPUT-OUTPUT SECTION.
000110 FILE-CONTROL.
000120    SELECT OLD-SALES-FILE
000130       ASSIGN TO UT-S-SLSOLD.
000140    SELECT SALES-BACKUP-FILE
000150       ASSIGN TO UT-S-SBACK.
000160    SELECT SALES-CONTROL-FILE
000170       ASSIGN TO UT-S-SALESCT.
000180*
000190 DATA DIVISION.
000200 FILE SECTION.
000210 FD  OLD-SALES-FILE
000220     RECORD CONTAINS 55 CHARACTERS
000230     LABEL RECORDS STANDARD.
000240 01  OS-OLD-SALES-RECORD.
000250     05  OS-SALESPERSON-NUMBER      PIC X(4).
000260     05  OS-LAST-NAME               PIC X(11).
000270     05  OS-FIRST-NAME              PIC X(10).
000280     05  OS-YEAR-TO-DATE-SALES      PIC 9(5)V99.
000290     05  OS-YEAR-TO-DATE-SALES-RETURNS PIC 9(5)V99.
```

Program 6–4   *(continued)*

```
000300        05   OS-CURRENT-SALES              PIC 9(5)V99.
000310        05   OS-CURRENT-SALES-RETURNS      PIC 9(5)V99.
000320        05   OS-COMMISSION-RATE            PIC V99.
000330 FD  SALES-BACKUP-FILE
000340     RECORD CONTAINS 55 CHARACTERS
000350     LABEL RECORDS STANDARD.
000360 01  SB-SALES-BACKUP-RECORD               PIC X(55).
000370 FD  SALES-CONTROL-FILE
000380     RECORD CONTAINS 84 CHARACTERS
000390     LABEL RECORDS ARE STANDARD.
000400 01  SC-SALES-CONTROL-RECORD.
000410     05   SC-BEG-TOT-FIELDS.
000420          10   SC-BEG-TOT-RECORDS-STORED    PIC S9(4).
000430          10   SC-BEG-TOT-HASH-NUMBER       PIC S9(6).
000440          10   SC-BEG-TOT-YTD-SALES         PIC S9(6)V99.
000450          10   SC-BEG-TOT-YTD-SALES-RETURNS PIC S9(6)V99.
000460          10   SC-BEG-TOT-CURRENT-SALES     PIC S9(6)V99.
000470          10   SC-BEG-TOT-CURRENT-RETURNS   PIC S9(6)V99.
000480     05   SC-CHG-TOT-FIELDS.
000490          10   SC-CHG-TOT-RECORDS-STORED    PIC S9(4).
000500          10   SC-CHG-TOT-HASH-NUMBER       PIC S9(6).
000510          10   SC-CHG-TOT-YTD-SALES         PIC S9(6)V99.
000520          10   SC-CHG-TOT-YTD-SALES-RETURNS PIC S9(6)V99.
000530          10   SC-CHG-TOT-CURRENT-SALES     PIC S9(6)V99.
000540          10   SC-CHG-TOT-CURRENT-RETURNS   PIC S9(6)V99.
000550*
000560 WORKING-STORAGE SECTION.
000570 01  WS-WORK-AREAS.
000580     05   WS-EOF-INDICATOR                 PIC X(3).
000590          88 END-OF-INPUT-FILE             VALUE 'END'.
000600*
000610 PROCEDURE DIVISION.
000620 A000-CREATE.
000630     OPEN I-O    OLD-SALES-FILE
000640                 SALES-CONTROL-FILE
000650          OUTPUT SALES-BACKUP-FILE.
000660     PERFORM B100-INITIALIZE-VARIABLES.
000670     PERFORM Z100-READ-SALES-RECORD.
000680     PERFORM B300-PROCESS-RECORDS
000690          UNTIL END-OF-INPUT-FILE.
000700     PERFORM B400-REWRITE-CONTROL-RECORD.
000710     CLOSE OLD-SALES-FILE
000720           SALES-CONTROL-FILE
000730           SALES-BACKUP-FILE.
000740     STOP RUN.
000750 B100-INITIALIZE-VARIABLES.
000760     MOVE 'NO'  TO WS-EOF-INDICATOR.
000770 B300-PROCESS-RECORDS.
000780     PERFORM C100-UPDATE-SALES-RECORD.
000790     WRITE SB-SALES-BACKUP-RECORD
000800           FROM OS-OLD-SALES-RECORD.
000810     PERFORM Z100-READ-SALES-RECORD.
000820 B400-REWRITE-CONTROL-RECORD.
000830     READ SALES-CONTROL-FILE.
000840     ADD SC-CHG-TOT-RECORDS-STORED TO SC-BEG-TOT-RECORDS-STORED.
000850     ADD SC-CHG-TOT-HASH-NUMBER    TO SC-BEG-TOT-HASH-NUMBER.
000860     ADD SC-CHG-TOT-YTD-SALES      TO SC-BEG-TOT-YTD-SALES.
000870     ADD SC-CHG-TOT-YTD-SALES-RETURNS
000880         TO SC-BEG-TOT-YTD-SALES-RETURNS.
000890     MOVE ZEROES                   TO SC-BEG-TOT-CURRENT-SALES
000900                                      SC-BEG-TOT-CURRENT-RETURNS
000910                                      SC-CHG-TOT-FIELDS.
000920     REWRITE SC-SALES-CONTROL-RECORD.
000930 C100-UPDATE-SALES-RECORD.
```

Program 6–4   *(concluded)*

```
000940        MOVE ZEROES TO OS-CURRENT-SALES
000950                       OS-CURRENT-SALES-RETURNS.
000960        REWRITE OS-OLD-SALES-RECORD.
000970  Z100-READ-SALES-RECORD.
000980        READ OLD-SALES-FILE
000990           AT END MOVE 'END' TO WS-EOF-INDICATOR.
```

Processing Variable Length Records

The sequential processing of variable length records poses some additional problems. If the structure of the file contains a variable number of different length records for each logical entity, it is necessary during the update process to input the header record and then load each of the other records into a table. At that point, an old master record has been read. Additional transactions would then have to be placed into the end of the table for each updated record. The transferring of the old master record to the new file would necessitate the writing of the header record and the unloading of the changed table onto the new file. The process is further complicated when a new record is added. The previous old master record will need to be moved to a hold area that has been defined as including a table for the additional physical records.

Processing variable length records that contain a variable number of segments is similar, except there is no need to load a table; the table is already part of the record. Program 6–5, abbreviated to show only those changes relevant to the use of variable length records, illustrates the sequential update logic (similar to Program 6–3), which would update a file that contains records with a variable number of segments. Since the structure is essentially the same as the previous programs, suffice it to say that it is necessary to change the creation process demonstrated by Program 6–1 to include the initializing of the table. The result of this program is to place in a table along with the record itself all transactions that resulted in changes in sales and returns. This detail would then be available at a later time when reporting from the file.

Program Example

Program 6–5

```
000010 IDENTIFICATION DIVISION.
000020 PROGRAM-ID.     SEQUPDT.
000030***************************************************************
000040* PROGRAM EXAMPLE 6-5 SEQUENTIAL UPDATE - VARIABLE LENGTH RECORDS*
000050***************************************************************
                .
000230 DATA DIVISION.
000240 FILE SECTION.
000250 FD  OLD-SALES-FILE
000260     RECORD CONTAINS 57 TO 217 CHARACTERS
000270     LABEL RECORDS STANDARD.
000280 01  OS-OLD-SALES-RECORD.
000290     05  OS-ROOT-PORTION.
000300         10  OS-SALESPERSON-NUMBER        PIC X(4).
000310         10  OS-HASH-NUMBER REDEFINES
000320             OS-SALESPERSON-NUMBER        PIC 9(4).
000330         10  OS-LAST-NAME                 PIC X(11).
000340         10  OS-FIRST-NAME                PIC X(10).
000350         10  OS-YEAR-TO-DATE-SALES        PIC 9(5)V99.
```

Program 6–5   *(continued)*

```
000360            10   OS-YEAR-TO-DATE-SALES-RETURNS PIC 9(5)V99.
000370            10   OS-CURRENT-SALES             PIC 9(5)V99.
000380            10   OS-CURRENT-SALES-RETURNS     PIC 9(5)V99.
000390            10   OS-COMMISSION-RATE           PIC V99.
000400            10   OS-NUMBER-OF-CHANGES         PIC 99.
000410        05  OS-VARIABLE-PORTION.
000420            10   OS-SEGMENT
000430                 OCCURS 0 TO 20 TIMES
000440                 DEPENDING ON OS-NUMBER-OF-CHANGES.
000450                 15  OS-TRANSACTION-TYPE      PIC X(1).
000460                 15  OS-SALE-OR-RETURN-AMOUNT PIC 9(5)V99.
000470 FD  NEW-SALES-FILE
000480     RECORD CONTAINS 57 TO 217 CHARACTERS
000490     LABEL RECORDS STANDARD.
000500 01  NS-NEW-SALES-RECORD.
000510        05  NS-ROOT-PORTION.
000520            10   NS-SALESPERSON-NUMBER        PIC X(4).
000530            10   NS-LAST-NAME                 PIC X(11).
000540            10   NS-FIRST-NAME                PIC X(10).
000550            10   NS-YEAR-TO-DATE-SALES        PIC 9(5)V99.
000560            10   NS-YEAR-TO-DATE-SALES-RETURNS PIC 9(5)V99.
000570            10   NS-CURRENT-SALES             PIC 9(5)V99.
000580            10   NS-CURRENT-SALES-RETURNS     PIC 9(5)V99.
000590            10   NS-COMMISSION-RATE           PIC V99.
000600            10   NS-NUMBER-OF-CHANGES         PIC 99.
000610        05  NS-VARIABLE-PORTION.
000620            10   NS-SEGMENT
000630                 OCCURS 0 TO 20 TIMES
000640                 DEPENDING ON NS-NUMBER-OF-CHANGES.
000650                 15  NS-TRANSACTION-TYPE      PIC X(1).
000660                 15  NS-SALE-OR-RETURN-AMOUNT PIC 9(5)V99.


001120*
001130 WORKING-STORAGE SECTION.

001210 01  MH-MASTER-HOLD-AREA.
001220        05  MH-ROOT-PORTION.
001230            10   FILLER                       PIC X(55).
001240            10   MH-NUMBER-OF-CHANGES         PIC 99.
001250        05  MH-VARIABLE-PORTION.
001260            10   MH-SEGMENT
001270                 OCCURS 0 TO 20 TIMES
001280                 DEPENDING ON MH-NUMBER-OF-CHANGES PIC X(8).

002000 PROCEDURE DIVISION.
002010 A000-UPDATE.
002020     OPEN INPUT OLD-SALES-FILE

002550 C100-TRANSFER-OLD-TO-NEW.
002560     MOVE OS-ROOT-PORTION      TO NS-ROOT-PORTION.
002570     MOVE OS-VARIABLE-PORTION TO NS-VARIABLE-PORTION.
002580     WRITE NS-NEW-SALES-RECORD.
002590     PERFORM Z200-READ-MASTER-RECORD.
002600 C200-POSSIBLE-UPDATE.

003380 D200-UPDATE-RECORD.
003390     IF DELETION-OF-SALESPERSON

003560     IF UPDATE-CURRENT-SALES
003570         MOVE 'YTD SALES UPDATED' TO DL-UPDATE-ACTION
003580         ADD ST-CURRENT-SALES      TO OS-YEAR-TO-DATE-SALES
003590                                      OS-CURRENT-SALES
003600                                      WS-CHG-YTD-SALES
003610                                      WS-CHG-CURRENT-SALES
```

Program 6–5 *(concluded)*

```
003620          ADD 1 TO UC-NUM-OF-CHG-SALES
003630                 OS-NUMBER-OF-CHANGES
003640          MOVE ST-TRANSACTION-CODE
003650               TO OS-TRANSACTION-TYPE(OS-NUMBER-OF-CHANGES)
003660          MOVE ST-CURRENT-SALES
003670               TO OS-SALE-OR-RETURN-AMOUNT(OS-NUMBER-OF-CHANGES).
003680      IF UPDATE-CURRENT-SALES-RETURNS
003690          MOVE 'YTD SALES RETURNS UPDATED' TO DL-UPDATE-ACTION
003700          ADD ST-CURRENT-SALES-RETURNS
003710              TO OS-YEAR-TO-DATE-SALES-RETURNS
003720                 OS-CURRENT-SALES-RETURNS
003730                 WS-CHG-YTD-SALES-RETURNS
003740                 WS-CHG-CURRENT-RETURNS
003750          ADD 1 TO UC-NUM-OF-CHG-RTNS
003760                 OS-NUMBER-OF-CHANGES
003770          MOVE ST-TRANSACTION-CODE
003780               TO OS-TRANSACTION-TYPE(OS-NUMBER-OF-CHANGES)
003790          MOVE ST-CURRENT-SALES-RETURNS
003800               TO OS-SALE-OR-RETURN-AMOUNT(OS-NUMBER-OF-CHANGES).


003850  D300-MOVE-TRANS-TO-OLD.
003860      MOVE OS-ROOT-PORTION          TO MH-ROOT-PORTION.
003870      MOVE OS-VARIABLE-PORTION      TO MH-VARIABLE-PORTION.
003880      MOVE 'RECORD ADDED'           TO DL-UPDATE-ACTION.
003890      MOVE ST-SALESPERSON-NUMBER    TO OS-SALESPERSON-NUMBER.
003900      MOVE ST-LAST-NAME             TO OS-LAST-NAME.
003910      MOVE ST-FIRST-NAME            TO OS-FIRST-NAME.
003920      MOVE ZEROES                   TO OS-YEAR-TO-DATE-SALES
003930                                       OS-YEAR-TO-DATE-SALES-RETURNS
003940                                       OS-CURRENT-SALES
003950                                       OS-CURRENT-SALES-RETURNS
003960                                       OS-NUMBER-OF-CHANGES.
003970      MOVE ST-COMMISSION-RATE       TO OS-COMMISSION-RATE.
003980      MOVE 'YES'                    TO UC-MASTER-PENDING-SWITCH.
003990      ADD 1                         TO WS-CHG-TOT-RECORDS-STORED
004000                                       UC-NUM-OF-ADDS.


004060  Z200-READ-MASTER-RECORD.
004070      IF MASTER-IS-PENDING
004080          MOVE MH-ROOT-PORTION      TO OS-OLD-SALES-RECORD
004090          MOVE MH-VARIABLE-PORTION  TO OS-VARIABLE-PORTION
004100          MOVE 'NO'                 TO UC-MASTER-PENDING-SWITCH
004110      ELSE
004120          READ OLD-SALES-FILE
004130              AT END MOVE HIGH-VALUES TO OS-SALESPERSON-NUMBER.
```

Discussion

Note the changes in definitions for the old sales file, the new sales file, and the holding area that is used to temporarily store an old master when a new record is to be added. Because this is a file with variable length records using table segments, it is necessary when moving the record to move it in two parts. First the root portion is moved, and then the variable portion (the table) is moved. The only other change should be noted in the MOVE statements to store the transaction when a current sales or current returns update occurs. More illustrations using variable length records will be given in the next chapter on indexed files, which are normally better candidates for variable length records.

Programming Style

1. Always use the comparison of old master and transaction identifiers to dictate the transfer of old to new, possible updating, or possible additions.

2. Though not used in the text example, all programs should make use of available storage-saving features of the particular compiler in use. For instance, on magnetic tape or disk one should use packed-decimal format (USAGE COMP–3) for all real numeric fields and binary (USAGE COMP) for integer numeric fields when they are available.

Common Errors

1. Using too many switches in a sequential update program.

2. Making the sequential update program too complicated by adding sorting and validating procedures on the transaction file.

3. Incorrectly defining the records in an existing master file. This is a particularly acute problem when using binary or packed-decimal fields.

4. Attempting to have the transaction type dictate the update logic.

5. Failing to consider audit trail, backup, and control procedures.

6. Using inadequate or illogical control procedures.

Exercises

1. Define file creation, file updating, and file reporting.

2. What function does an audit trail serve?

3. What is the purpose of file control?

4. What is the purpose of batch totals? Hash totals?

5. Given the following transaction codes:
   A = Addition of new record
   D = Deletion of old record
   C = Change of address field and the following:

	Old master tape record	Transaction tape record	
	ID	ID	Transaction code
Set A:	1	1	C
	2	2	C
	3	3	C
	5	4	A
	6	6	D
Set B:	1	1	C
	2	2	D
	3	4	A
	5	5	D
	6	6	A
		8	A
		9	D

   answer the following questions:
   a. What is the sequence of records placed on the new master file for Set A?

b.   Are there any invalid update conditions in Set A? If so, explain.

c.   What is the sequence of records placed on the new master file for Set B?

d.   Are there any invalid update conditions in Set B? If so, explain.

e.   What happens when the master file in Set B is finished processing before the transaction file is finished?

6.   Given that M is the control code a master file and T is the control code for a transaction record, answer the following questions for a sequential update:

a.   If M > T what should the program logic do for a change transaction?

b.   If M = T what should the program logic do for a change transaction?

c.   If M < T what should the program logic do?

d.   If M = T what should the program logic do for an add transaction?

7.   What is the function of HIGH–VALUES in a sequential update?

8.   Given the following entries, correct only those that are in error. Assume all programmer-defined names have been properly defined.

a.   `OPEN I-O FI.`

b.   `05  WS-SWITCH    PIC 999.`
        `MOVE HIGH-VALUES  TO WS-SWITCH.`

c.   `RECORD CONTAINS 50 TO 100 CHARACTERS.`

d.   `REWRITE CR-CONTROL-RECORD.`

Problems

1.   For a sales file, use Data Set F to create an old master file. (The file is sorted and validated.) Using Program 6–1 as a model, add both current sales and current returns fields for subsequent update procedures. Include the creation of a control file that is adequate to include the following:

a.   Number of records

b.   Hash totals on:
   (1)   Salesperson number.
   (2)   Store number.
   (3)   Employee code.
   (4)   Commission rate.

c.   Other reasonable numeric totals.

2.   Using Data Set B, modify the program requirements for Problem 6–1 to include validation and sorting requirements in order to create the master file. The sort procedure should use the salesperson number as the sort key. The validation procedure should utilize the following considerations, reproduced here from Problem 5–1.

a.   The highest salesperson number that has been issued so far is 9025.

b.   Valid store numbers are 10 through 50.

c.   Valid employee codes range from 1 through 5.

d.   Department mnemonics should be alphabetic.

e.   Commission rates may range up to 25 percent.

f.   Year-to-date sales must be equal to or greater than year-to-date sales returns.

g.   Every salesperson has had sales, though not everyone has had sales returns.

h.   If the salesperson's name is not left-justified, correct it.

3.   For an inventory file, use Data Set E to create an old master file. (The file is sorted and validated.) Using Program 6–1 as a model, add fields for both current quantity sold and current quantity purchased for subsequent update procedures. Include the creation of a control file that is adequate to include the following:

    a. Number of records.

    b. Hash totals on:

        (1) Store number.

        (2) Item number.

        (3) Sales price per unit.

        (4) Cost per unit.

    c. Other reasonable numeric totals.

4. Using Data Set I, modify the program requirements for Problem 6–3 to include validation and sorting requirements in order to create the master file. The sort procedure should use the item number, department mnemonic, and the store number as the sort keys. The validation procedure should utilize the following considerations, reproduced here from Problem 5–4.

    a. Valid store numbers are 10 and 20.

    b. Department mnemonics should be alphabetic and must be AU or AP for automotive and appliances.

    c. Valid item numbers range up through 898.

    d. The highest sales price per unit in the automotive department is $75.

    e. The highest sales price per unit in the appliance department is $795.

    f. All fields should exist.

    g. If the item description is not left-justified, correct it.

5. Using Program 6–2 as a model, write a report program that will list the contents of the file and adequately consider control totals. Use either the file created in Problem 6–1, 6–2, 6–3, or 6–4. The program written for this assignment can also be used to report from the relevant file after an update procedure.

6. Write a sequential update program for one of the sales files previously created in Problem 6–1 or 6–2. Use Data Set N in Appendix C for the transactions. Notice that the transactions are unvalidated and unsorted. Use the same validation considerations as listed for Problem 6–2. You may write a separate program to accomplish the sort and validation procedures or combine them into the update program. Make sure to adequately control the file that is being updated. After successful testing of the update program, run the report program against the updated file.

7. Write a sequential update program for one of the inventory files previously created in Problem 6–3 or 6–4. Use Data Set O in Appendix C for the transactions. Notice that the transactions are unvalidated and unsorted. Use the same validation considerations as listed for Problem 6–4. You may write a separate program to accomplish the sort and validation procedures or combine them into the update program. Make sure to adequately control the file that is being updated. After successful testing of the update program, run the report program against the updated file.

8. Modify any combination of the previous procedures for the sales file so that variable length records are utilized. Assume that the concept of a variable number of segments is to be used so that current changes to the dollar values of current sales or current returns are the types of transactions that will be placed in the file.

9. Modify any combination of the previous procedures for the inventory file so that variable length records are utilized. Assume that the concept of a variable number of segments is to be used so that current changes to the values of current quantity sold or current quantity purchased are the types of transactions that will be placed in the file.

10. Write a month-end update program to get the sales file ready for the next month. Remember to also consider the control file.

11. Write a month-end update program to get the inventory file ready for the next month. Remember to also consider the control file.

7

Indexed Files

The importance of magnetic disk cannot be overestimated with respect to administrative and business information systems. Files stored on disk are more flexible than files stored on magnetic tape. Disk files can be organized sequentially and also on a relative or indexed basis. Indexed files constitute a large portion of file organizations used in administrative systems, particularly those systems that require not only random access to data records such as is necessary in online information systems but also sequential access for administrative reporting purposes.

TERMS AND STATEMENTS

ACCESS MODE clause	INVALID KEY clause	RECORD KEY clause
ALTERNATE RECORD KEY clause	In-place updating	REWRITE statement
	Indexed-sequential access method	Random organization
DECLARATIVES	KEY IS clause	Random update
DELETE statement	LOW–VALUES	Record pointer
EXCEPTION/ ERROR procedure	Master file	SELECT statement
	Multiple file processing	START statement
FILE STATUS clause		USE statement
File creation	ORGANIZATION IS INDEXED	Variable length records
File reporting		
File updating	Primary Key	WITH DUPLICATES clause
I–O	READ statement	WRITE statement

Indexed File Concepts

A good example for the use of indexed files is a checking account system in a bank. Throughout the business day, random access is needed to accommodate online inquiries and updates for transactions, such as balance inquiries for check cashing and automatic teller processing. Cleared checks and deposits would be batched and processed efficiently by utilizing a sequential method to update the accounts at the end of the business day and to provide management reports. Bank statements provided to the customer at month end would also be accomplished by sequential access. Indexed files can readily accommodate both random and sequential modes of access. Other common applications of the use of indexed files occur in credit card systems and hotel accounting systems.

Though the methods vary widely by vendor, the **indexed-sequential access method** utilizes at least one index (a table of pointers to records within a file) that is created and stored separately from the actual data file. This enables access to the file in either a sequential or a random mode. An index for an indexed file can be thought of in much the same way as a card catalog index in a public library. To access the data (or book) randomly, first the index is accessed to determine the actual physical location of the record (or book). Then using the knowledge gained from the index, the actual record (book) is located. As with sequential file processing, indexed file processing includes **file creation, file updating,** and **file reporting.**

Several requirements are necessary to create the file and index. (The COBOL program loads only the records into the file; the index is actually created by a utility program supplied by the vendor.) One requirement is that each record contain a unique identifier that can be used as the entry in the index. This unique identifier, called the **primary key,** is the equivalent to the Library of Congress number assigned to books in a library. The index will contain the actual physical location of the data record along with the primary key. The data file itself must be in ascending sequence, which allows a program to access a data record randomly or in ascending sequence.

When an indexed file is initially created in sequence, the records are loaded into a primary data area. Since **in-place updating** normally occurs on an indexed file, any additions to the file are placed in an overflow data area. Deletions from the file are either physically removed or are flagged as being logically deleted. Because of the added records, the indexed file may no longer be in sequence after a period of time and may have to be periodically reorganized. This reorganization is accomplished either by a COBOL program or by a utility program supplied by the vendor. Figure 7–1 illustrates the need to reorganize an indexed file periodically.

In Figure 7–1 notice that the file after initial creation and before being updated,

Figure 7–1   *Indexed File Organization and Reorganization*

Primary data file space		Overflow data file space		Assumed transactions	
Before update	*After update*	*Before update*	*After update*	*Key*	*Type of transaction*
123	123		196	196	Addition
146	146		127	127	Addition
185	185			185	Update
200	Deleted			200	Deletion
257	257				
Reorganized file					
123					
127					
146					
185					
196					
257					

is in sequential order. Additionally, since there have been no additions, there are no records that have been placed in the overflow area. Transactions used to accomplish an in-place update of the indexed file include additions, changes, and deletions; and these transactions do not come to the file in any known sequence. Not all records in the master file are affected by an update. For instance, in Figure 7–1, records with primary keys 123, 196, and 257 do not have transactions that affect these records.

Any changes to the file will be handled just as with an in-place update on a sequential file. That is, the appropriate change will take place and the changed record will replace the previous contents of the record.

However, additions are placed in the overflow area and are not in physical sequence. At least a portion of the file then is out of sequence. Therefore, software that actually accesses the data must keep track of both the logical sequence and the physical sequence of the file. The COBOL program does not concern itself with the physical sequence of the data. Access software is supplied by the vendor so that the actual access to the data records in the file is transparent to the programmer.

Similarly, deletions cause unused space to be interspersed with active records, both in the primary data area and in the overflow area if previously added records are later deleted. The end result is that access to the file using any mode becomes slower and slower when more records are added and deleted.

Reorganization will eventually become desirable in order to resequence the data file in physical order and to reclaim the unused space caused by deletions. The reorganized file is shown in Figure 7–1.

Input/Output Statements for Indexed Files

There are many input and output statements that will be discussed in this chapter. To provide the reader with an initial overview and to have the format of these statements in one place in the chapter, their formats are presented in Figure 7–2.

Figure 7–2   *Input and Output Formats for Indexed Files*

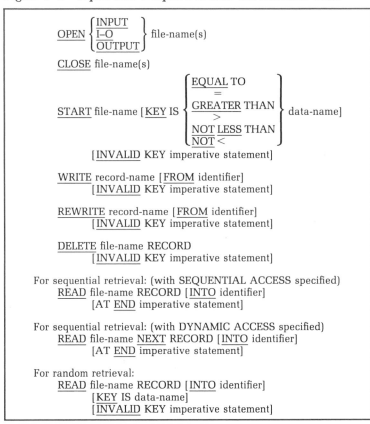

Discussion of these statements and their use in particular situations will occur in the context of actual examples.

Indexed File Creation

The SELECT Statement

The first COBOL consideration with respect to indexed files is the **SELECT statement,** the format of which is shown in Figure 7–3. In this format of the SELECT statement both the **ORGANIZATION IS INDEXED** and the RECORD KEY clauses are required; all others are optional and may appear in any order.

Figure 7–3 *SELECT Statement Format for Indexed Files*

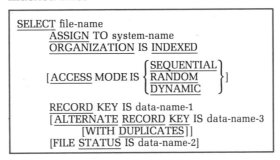

```
SELECT file-name
     ASSIGN TO system-name
     ORGANIZATION IS INDEXED

                      ⎧SEQUENTIAL⎫
     [ACCESS MODE IS  ⎨RANDOM    ⎬]
                      ⎩DYNAMIC   ⎭

     RECORD KEY IS data-name-1
     [ALTERNATE RECORD KEY IS data-name-3
          [WITH DUPLICATES]]
     [FILE STATUS IS data-name-2]
```

ACCESS MODE Clause

The **ACCESS MODE clause** specifies the type of access that is used. If this clause is omitted, the system assumes sequential access, which is used either for the creation of the file or for a sequential access of the file after creation.

Specifying RANDOM as an access mode indicates that the key will be used to randomly access data records. This mode cannot be used for the creation of an indexed file. If DYNAMIC is specified, the nature of the I/O request is used by the compiler to determine whether the file is being accessed randomly or sequentially.

If the file is opened as either INPUT or OUTPUT, the system allows reading or writing either sequentially or randomly. If the file is opened I–O the system allows reading, writing, and rewriting of the file either sequentially or randomly. When DYNAMIC is specified all forms of the I/O statements assume that the current contents of the RECORD KEY are to be used to access the record randomly through the index. If sequential access is desired the reserved word NEXT must be added to the READ statement. DYNAMIC is not a mode in itself; it simply allows the specification of the access mode by the nature of the I/O request and allows the programmer to access an indexed file both sequentially and randomly in the same program.

The format for the OPEN I–O statement is given in Figure 7–4.

Figure 7–4 *Format of the OPEN I–O Statement*

```
OPEN [I–O file-name]
```

Rules for the use of the OPEN I–O are:

- The file name for an indexed file must have a SELECT statement with an associated ORGANIZATION IS INDEXED clause.
- The file name must have an ACCESS MODE clause that specifies either RANDOM or DYNAMIC to effect random access; SEQUENTIAL or DYNAMIC to effect sequential access.

RECORD KEY Clause

The **RECORD KEY clause** specifies a data-name which is the unique, primary key used to create and access the index. The data-name specified must be defined as an elementary or group item within the record description that is associated with the FD for the named file.

ALTERNATE RECORD KEY Clause

Access to the data files may also be done by using a key other than the primary key. This is accomplished by using the **ALTERNATE RECORD KEY clause.** Some COBOL compilers allow the creation of alternate indexes at the same time that the original primary index is created. If this is true and alternate key access is desired, specification of the **ALTERNATE RECORD KEY clause** will be necessary. Specification of the **WITH DUPLICATES clause** enables the field named in the ALTERNATE KEY clause to contain nonunique values. If the WITH DUPLICATES clause is omitted, the field named by the ALTERNATE KEY clause must contain unique values. Notice again that this is not possible with the primary key, which absolutely must be unique. As will be shown in Program 7–3, alternate keys enable access to a file by using a different key and are important tools for data access.

FILE STATUS Clause

The **FILE STATUS clause** invokes an operating system utility that assists working with indexed files. (FILE STATUS can also be used with sequential files.) The data-name specified must be defined as a two-position alphanumeric item, usually in WORKING–STORAGE. The contents of the data-name specified are updated by the operating system after each and every input or output operation on a file that uses the FILE STATUS clause. The data-name can then be tested by the programmer in the PROCEDURE division to determine the result of the input or output operation. The possible values that will be placed in the named FILE STATUS data-name are listed in Figure 7–5 along with their meanings.

Figure 7–5   *FILE STATUS Values and Meanings*

Data-name contents	Meaning
00	Successful completion.
02	Duplicate alternate key (may or may not be an error depending on whether WITH DUPLICATES was specified)—relates to either a READ or WRITE.
10	End-of-file was detected during a READ.
21	Sequence error—primary key is lower than previously written primary key.
22	Duplicate primary key during a WRITE.
23	No record found during a READ.
24	Boundary error (indexed file)—attempt to WRITE past the end of the file.
30	Permanent data error (hardware problem).
34	Boundary error (sequential file).
9x	Additional implementor errors—consult the COBOL manual for details.

The use of FILE STATUS depends on the program being implemented. For example, a creation program will need to test for successful completion (a FILE STATUS of '00') and should also test for either a sequence error or a duplicate primary key. Other values tested are at the discretion of the programmer. However, the failure to test for a specific error does not mean that the error does not exist. It only means that the programmer does not know that it exists. Later program examples will solidify the concept of the use of FILE STATUS.

Since the FILE STATUS is used for both reading and writing with a file, it is helpful to create a simple way to utilize the FILE STATUS codes in COBOL. Figure 7–6 shows the creation of a DATA division entry that can be used in all programs with appropriate condition-names assigned to the various FILE STATUS values.

Values that are used for 9X and above are supplied by the vendor who supplies your particular compiler. Consult the COBOL manual for their meanings; it would be wise to create additional condition-names for the entire set for the compiler in use, including the 9X series, which are those supplied by the vendor.

Figure 7–6 *Condition-Names and FILE STATUS Values*

```
05  WS-FILE-STATUS-FLAG              PIC X(2).
    88  SUCCESSFUL-COMPLETION             VALUE '00'.
    88  DUPLICATE-ALTERNATE-KEY           VALUE '02'.
    88  END-OF-FILE                       VALUE '10'.
    88  SEQUENCE-ERROR                    VALUE '21'.
    88  DUPLICATE-KEY                     VALUE '22'.
    88  NO-RECORD-FOUND                   VALUE '23'.
    88  BOUNDARY-VIOLATION-INV-KEY        VALUE '24'.
    88  PERMANENT-I-O-DATA-ERROR          VALUE '30'.
    88  BOUNDARY-VIOLATION-I-O            VALUE '34'.
    88  IMPLEMENTOR-ERROR                 VALUE '9X'.
```

The WRITE Statement

The format for the WRITE statement for indexed files is shown in Figure 7–7. Notice the optional INVALID KEY clause.

Figure 7–7 *Format of the WRITE Statement for Indexed Files*

```
WRITE record-name [FROM identifier]
        [INVALID KEY imperative-statement(s)]
```

The **INVALID KEY clause** allows an optional method for detecting errors during an attempt to WRITE a record to or READ a record from an indexed file. The types of errors detected depends on how the file has been opened and how the file is being accessed. When initially loading data records into a file, the file is specified as ACCESS IS SEQUENTIAL and is opened as OUTPUT. Under these conditions the INVALID KEY will be true if one of several conditions have occurred. Two of these conditions occur if the prime key of the record that is being written is not higher than the prime key of the previously stored record. This causes either a sequence error or a duplicate prime key error, because the records must be created in sequence and no duplicates of the primary key may occur. Another situation that would cause the INVALID KEY to be true during a sequential WRITE is when a duplicate alternate key was detected and the WITH DUPLICATES clause was not specified.

Error Detection

While the INVALID KEY is useful for either a READ or WRITE statement (the REWRITE and START statements may also use the INVALID KEY clause), there is no corresponding way to test for an error that may occur during an OPEN or CLOSE operation. Additionally, there is not a way to test for other types of errors that are identified by the vendor software, unless the FILE STATUS is tested. Testing the FILE STATUS is a more comprehensive method because it includes all possible errors that can be detected by the INVALID KEY *and* can detect additional types of errors.

The testing of the FILE STATUS instead of using the INVALID KEY is becoming a common standard when working with indexed files. However, one restriction remains. Standard COBOL requires either the use of the INVALID KEY clause or an EXCEPTION/ERROR procedure. In order to eliminate the use of the INVALID KEY clause an EXCEPTION/ERROR procedure must be included in the program, even if it is not used in the logic.

An **EXCEPTION/ERROR procedure** must be placed in a DECLARATIVES section, which is placed as the first type of procedure in the PROCEDURE division. The formats of **DECLARATIVES** and the EXCEPTION/ERROR procedure are shown in Figure 7–8.

Figure 7–8   *Format of DECLARATIVES and the EXCEPTION/ERROR Procedure*

```
DECLARATIVES Format:
    DECLARATIVES.
section-name SECTION.
    USE sentence
[paragraph-name.
    [sentence]. . .]
    END DECLARATIVE.

EXCEPTION/ERROR PROCEDURE Format:

    USE AFTER STANDARD {EXCEPTION}  PROCEDURE
                       {ERROR    }

              ┌ file-name-1 [file-name-2]. . . ┐
              │ INPUT                          │
        ON   ┤ OUTPUT                          ├
              │ I–O                            │
              └ EXTEND                         ┘
```

The EXCEPTION/ERROR procedure may specify error handling to be undertaken in addition to the system procedures provided by the vendor. The EXCEPTION/ERROR procedure must be specified when the INVALID KEY clause is omitted. Whenever any error is detected, the procedures in the appropriate DECLARATIVES section are invoked. Any sentences in the section are then executed, and control returns to the statement following the statement that causes the error to be detected.

All FILE STATUS testing could be undertaken with the DECLARATIVES procedure. However, the authors prefer to keep the testing of the FILE STATUS within the logic of the program. Therefore, a dummy EXCEPTION/ERROR procedure will be used throughout the program examples. The dummy procedure satisfies the requirement that the EXCEPTION/ERROR procedure must exist when omitting the INVALID KEY clause, but the actual FILE STATUS testing will take place within the main body of the program.

Program Example

Statement of the Problem

Program 7–1 creates an indexed-sequential file using the same sales file that was used in Chapter 6 for sequential files. The indexed file will use salesperson number as the primary key and last name, year-to-date sales, and commission rate as alternate keys. All alternate keys may have duplicates. Appropriate control and audit trail considerations will apply as with sequential files. The data file is presumed to be previously validated and sorted using salesperson number as the sort key.

Program

Program 7–1

```
000010 IDENTIFICATION DIVISION.
000020 PROGRAM-ID.    INDCREAT.
000030*·······················································
000040* PROGRAM EXAMPLE 7-1 INDEXED SALES CREATION          *
000050*·······················································
000060 ENVIRONMENT DIVISION.
000070 CONFIGURATION SECTION.
000080   SOURCE-COMPUTER.  IBM-4341.
000090   OBJECT-COMPUTER.  IBM-4341.
000100 INPUT-OUTPUT SECTION.
000110 FILE-CONTROL.
000120     SELECT INDEXED-SALES-FILE
000130         ASSIGN TO SYS042-DA-3375-SALES
000140         ORGANIZATION IS INDEXED
000150         ACCESS IS DYNAMIC
000160         RECORD KEY IS IS-SALESPERSON-NUMBER
000170         FILE STATUS IS EL-STATUS-ERROR.
000180     SELECT SALES-BACKUP-FILE
000190         ASSIGN TO SYS055-UT-3375-SBACK.
000200     SELECT SALES-REPORT
000210         ASSIGN TO SYS018-UR-3203-S.
000220     SELECT SALES-INPUT-FILE
000230         ASSIGN TO SYS016-UR-2501-S.
000240     SELECT SALES-CONTROL-FILE
000250         ASSIGN TO SYS025-UT-3375-SALESCT.
000260*
000270 DATA DIVISION.
000280 FILE SECTION.
000290 FD  INDEXED-SALES-FILE
000300     RECORD CONTAINS 55 CHARACTERS
000310     LABEL RECORDS STANDARD.
000320 01  IS-INDEXED-SALES-RECORD.
000330     05  IS-SALESPERSON-NUMBER       PIC 9(4).
000340     05  IS-LAST-NAME                PIC X(11).
000350     05  IS-FIRST-NAME               PIC X(10).
000360     05  IS-YEAR-TO-DATE-SALES       PIC 9(5)V99.
000370     05  IS-YEAR-TO-DATE-SALES-RETURNS PIC 9(5)V99.
000380     05  IS-CURRENT-SALES            PIC 9(5)V99.
000390     05  IS-CURRENT-SALES-RETURNS    PIC 9(5)V99.
000400     05  IS-COMMISSION-RATE          PIC V99.
000410 FD  SALES-BACKUP-FILE
000420     RECORD CONTAINS 55 CHARACTERS
000430     LABEL RECORDS STANDARD.
000440 01  SB-SALES-BACKUP-RECORD          PIC X(55).
000450 FD  SALES-INPUT-FILE
000460     RECORD CONTAINS 44 CHARACTERS
000470     LABEL RECORDS ARE STANDARD.
000480 01  SI-SALES-TRANS-RECORD.
000490     05  SI-SALESPERSON-NUMBER       PIC X(4).
000500     05  SI-HASH-NUMBER
000510         REDEFINES SI-SALESPERSON-NUMBER PIC 9(4).
000520     05  FILLER                      PIC X(1).
000530     05  SI-LAST-NAME                PIC X(11).
000540     05  SI-FIRST-NAME               PIC X(10).
000550     05  SI-YEAR-TO-DATE-SALES       PIC 9(5)V99.
000560     05  FILLER                      PIC X(1).
000570     05  SI-YEAR-TO-DATE-SALES-RETURNS PIC 9(5)V99.
000580     05  FILLER                      PIC X(1).
000590     05  SI-COMMISSION-RATE          PIC V99.
000600 FD  SALES-REPORT
000610     RECORD CONTAINS 133 CHARACTERS
```

Program 7–1 *(continued)*

```
000620      LABEL RECORDS ARE OMITTED.
000630 01 SR-SALES-REPORT-LINE                    PIC X(133).
000640 FD SALES-CONTROL-FILE
000650      RECORD CONTAINS 84 CHARACTERS
000660      LABEL RECORDS ARE STANDARD.
000670 01 SC-SALES-CONTROL-RECORD.
000680      05  SC-BEG-TOT-FIELDS.
000690          10  SC-BEG-TOT-RECORDS-STORED    PIC S9(4).
000700          10  SC-BEG-TOT-HASH-NUMBER       PIC S9(6).
000710          10  SC-BEG-TOT-YTD-SALES         PIC S9(6)V99.
000720          10  SC-BEG-TOT-YTD-SALES-RETURNS PIC S9(6)V99.
000730          10  SC-BEG-TOT-CURRENT-SALES     PIC S9(6)V99.
000740          10  SC-BEG-TOT-CURRENT-RETURNS   PIC S9(6)V99.
000750      05  SC-CHG-TOT-FIELDS.
000760          10  SC-CHG-TOT-RECORDS-STORED    PIC S9(4).
000770          10  SC-CHG-TOT-HASH-NUMBER       PIC S9(6).
000780          10  SC-CHG-TOT-YTD-SALES         PIC S9(6)V99.
000790          10  SC-CHG-TOT-YTD-SALES-RETURNS PIC S9(6)V99.
000800          10  SC-CHG-TOT-CURRENT-SALES     PIC S9(6)V99.
000810          10  SC-CHG-TOT-CURRENT-RETURNS   PIC S9(6)V99.
000820*
000830 WORKING-STORAGE SECTION.
000840 01 WS-ACCUMULATORS.
000850      05  WS-TOT-RECORDS-STORED            PIC S9(4).
000860      05  WS-TOT-HASH-NUMBER               PIC S9(6).
000870      05  WS-TOT-YTD-SALES                 PIC S9(6)V99.
000880      05  WS-TOT-YTD-SALES-RETURNS         PIC S9(6)V99.
000890 01 WS-WORK-AREAS.
000900      05  WS-EOF-INDICATOR                 PIC X(3).
000910          88  END-OF-INPUT-FILE            VALUE 'END'.
000920 01 HD-HEADING-LINE.
000930      05  FILLER                           PIC X(1).
000940      05  FILLER                           PIC X(28)
000950                          VALUE 'INDEXED SALES FILE TOTALS'.
000960 01 CH-COLUMN-HEADING-LINE.
000970      05  FILLER                           PIC X(20) VALUE SPACES.
000980      05  FILLER                           PIC X(8) VALUE 'RECORDS'.
000990      05  FILLER                           PIC X(11) VALUE SPACES.
001000      05  FILLER                           PIC X(5) VALUE 'SALES'.
001010      05  FILLER                           PIC X(8) VALUE SPACES.
001020      05  FILLER                           PIC X(8) VALUE 'RETURNS'.
001030      05  FILLER                           PIC X(1) VALUE SPACES.
001040      05  FILLER                           PIC X(11)
001050                          VALUE 'HASH NUMBER'.
001060 01 TL-TOTAL-LINE.
001070      05  FILLER                           PIC X(1).
001080      05  TL-STUB-HEADING                  PIC X(20)
001090                          VALUE 'BEGINNING TOTALS'.
001100      05  TL-TOT-RECORDS-STORED            PIC Z,ZZ9.
001110      05  FILLER                           PIC X(11) VALUE SPACES.
001120      05  TL-TOT-YTD-SALES                 PIC ZZZ,ZZZ.99-.
001130      05  FILLER                           PIC X(2) VALUE SPACES.
001140      05  TL-TOT-YTD-SALES-RETURNS         PIC ZZZ,ZZZ.99-.
001150      05  FILLER                           PIC X(2) VALUE SPACES.
001160      05  TL-TOT-HASH-NUMBER               PIC ZZZ,ZZ9-.
001170 01 EL-ERROR-LINE.
001180      05  FILLER                           PIC X(1).
001190      05  EL-ERROR-OPERATION               PIC X(30).
001200      05  FILLER                           PIC X(5) VALUE SPACES.
001210      05  EL-STATUS-ERROR                  PIC XX.
001220          88  SUCCESSFUL-COMPLETION        VALUE '00'.
001230          88  SEQUENCE-ERROR               VALUE '21'.
001240          88  DUPLICATE-RECORD             VALUE '22'.
001250*
```

Program 7–1 *(continued)*

```
001260 PROCEDURE DIVISION.
001270 DECLARATIVES.
001280 DUMMY-ERROR-PROCEDURE SECTION.
001290     USE AFTER ERROR PROCEDURE ON INDEXED-SALES-FILE.
001300 END DECLARATIVES.
001310 A000-CREATE.
001320     PERFORM B100-INITIALIZE-VARIABLES.
001330     PERFORM B200-OPEN-TO-LOAD.
001340     PERFORM Z100-READ-NEW-RECORD.
001350     PERFORM B400-ADD-RECORDS
001360         UNTIL END-OF-INPUT-FILE.
001370     PERFORM B500-PROCESS-TOTALS.
001380     CLOSE SALES-REPORT
001390           SALES-CONTROL-FILE
001400           SALES-BACKUP-FILE
001410           SALES-INPUT-FILE
001420           INDEXED-SALES-FILE.
001430     STOP RUN.
001440 B100-INITIALIZE-VARIABLES.
001450     MOVE 'NO'   TO WS-EOF-INDICATOR.
001460     MOVE ZEROES TO WS-ACCUMULATORS.
001470 B200-OPEN-TO-LOAD.
001480     OPEN INPUT  SALES-INPUT-FILE
001490          OUTPUT INDEXED-SALES-FILE
001500                 SALES-REPORT
001510                 SALES-BACKUP-FILE
001520                 SALES-CONTROL-FILE.
001530     IF NOT SUCCESSFUL-COMPLETION
001540         MOVE 'LOAD OPENING' TO EL-ERROR-OPERATION
001550         PERFORM C100-ABORT-RUN
001560         STOP RUN.
001570 B400-ADD-RECORDS.
001580     PERFORM C200-WRITE-INDEXED-RECORD.
001590     IF DUPLICATE-RECORD
001600        OR SEQUENCE-ERROR
001610            MOVE 'DUPLICATE OR OUT OF SEQUENCE'
001620                TO EL-ERROR-OPERATION
001630            WRITE SR-SALES-REPORT-LINE FROM EL-ERROR-LINE
001640                AFTER 1
001650     ELSE
001660         PERFORM C400-ACCUMULATE-TOTALS
001670         WRITE SB-SALES-BACKUP-RECORD
001680             FROM IS-INDEXED-SALES-RECORD.
001690     PERFORM Z100-READ-NEW-RECORD.
001700 B500-PROCESS-TOTALS.
001710     MOVE WS-TOT-RECORDS-STORED    TO SC-BEG-TOT-RECORDS-STORED
001720                                      TL-TOT-RECORDS-STORED.
001730     MOVE WS-TOT-HASH-NUMBER       TO SC-BEG-TOT-HASH-NUMBER
001740                                      TL-TOT-HASH-NUMBER.
001750     MOVE WS-TOT-YTD-SALES         TO SC-BEG-TOT-YTD-SALES
001760                                      TL-TOT-YTD-SALES.
001770     MOVE WS-TOT-YTD-SALES-RETURNS TO TL-TOT-YTD-SALES-RETURNS
001780                                      SC-BEG-TOT-YTD-SALES-RETURNS.
001790     MOVE ZEROES                   TO SC-BEG-TOT-CURRENT-SALES
001800                                      SC-BEG-TOT-CURRENT-RETURNS
001810                                      SC-CHG-TOT-FIELDS.
001820     WRITE SC-SALES-CONTROL-RECORD.
001830     WRITE SR-SALES-REPORT-LINE FROM HD-HEADING-LINE
001840         AFTER PAGE.
001850     WRITE SR-SALES-REPORT-LINE FROM CH-COLUMN-HEADING-LINE
001860         AFTER 2.
001870     WRITE SR-SALES-REPORT-LINE FROM TL-TOTAL-LINE
001880         AFTER 2.
001890 C100-ABORT-RUN.
```

Program 7–1 *(concluded)*

```
001900     WRITE SR-SALES-REPORT-LINE FROM EL-ERROR-LINE
.001910         AFTER 1.
 001920     CLOSE INDEXED-SALES-FILE
 001930           SALES-REPORT
 001940           SALES-CONTROL-FILE
 001950           SALES-BACKUP-FILE
 001960           SALES-INPUT-FILE.
 001970 C200-WRITE-INDEXED-RECORD.
 001980     MOVE SI-SALESPERSON-NUMBER TO IS-SALESPERSON-NUMBER.
 001990     MOVE SI-LAST-NAME         TO IS-LAST-NAME.
 002000     MOVE SI-FIRST-NAME        TO IS-FIRST-NAME.
 002010     MOVE SI-YEAR-TO-DATE-SALES TO IS-YEAR-TO-DATE-SALES.
 002020     MOVE SI-YEAR-TO-DATE-SALES-RETURNS
 002030         TO IS-YEAR-TO-DATE-SALES-RETURNS.
 002040     MOVE ZEROS               TO IS-CURRENT-SALES
 002050                                 IS-CURRENT-SALES-RETURNS.
 002060     MOVE SI-COMMISSION-RATE   TO IS-COMMISSION-RATE.
 002070     WRITE IS-INDEXED-SALES-RECORD.
 002080 C400-ACCUMULATE-TOTALS.
 002090     ADD 1                    TO WS-TOT-RECORDS-STORED.
 002100     ADD SI-HASH-NUMBER        TO WS-TOT-HASH-NUMBER.
 002110     ADD SI-YEAR-TO-DATE-SALES TO WS-TOT-YTD-SALES.
 002120     ADD SI-YEAR-TO-DATE-SALES-RETURNS
 002130         TO WS-TOT-YTD-SALES-RETURNS.
 002140 Z100-READ-NEW-RECORD.
 002150     READ SALES-INPUT-FILE
 002160         AT END MOVE 'END' TO WS-EOF-INDICATOR.
```

Discussion

Some systems allow the creation of alternate indexes to coincide with the creation of an indexed file. The system used by the authors does not allow this. Therefore, no ALTERNATE KEY clauses are included in Program 7–1. The system used by the authors builds alternate indexes by using a vendor-supplied utility program, which is used after the original file has been created. If the system in use does allow the creation of alternate indexes to coincide with initial file creation, all that is necessary is to include appropriate ALTERNATE KEY clauses in the SELECT statement. If, at a later time, it is necessary to add additional alternate keys, it may be necessary to use an existing indexed file as input to another program that will create additional alternate indexes.

Notice the definition of EL–STATUS–ERROR in lines 1210 through 1240. The reason it has been included in EL–ERROR–LINE is to expedite the printing of an error, should an error be detected, by printing out the contents of the FILE STATUS. During the creation of an indexed file both a sequence error and a duplicate key should be tested. Realistically, however, a sequence error should never occur if file creation has been preceded with an appropriate sorting phase. But just because a process should have been completed does not mean that it has been done. Approach the testing of the FILE STATUS as an opportunity to discover problems with the data, not a programming drudgery. The actual testing of the FILE STATUS occurs in lines 1590 and 1600.

Note that the RECORD KEY clause specifies IS–SALESPERSON–NUMBER, which is required to be defined as a part of IS–INDEXED–SALES–RECORD at line 330. Notice also that at line 150 access has been specified as DYNAMIC and the file has been opened for OUTPUT. The purpose of DYNAMIC access is to allow the program to be able to access the same file in either random or sequential order. When DYNAMIC is specified the program uses the current contents of the RECORD KEY to determine the required location of the record to be stored. The file could also have been specified as ACCESS SEQUENTIAL.

Notice the USE statement at line 1290 and the testing of the FILE STATUS in line 1530 immediately after the file is opened. If the file is, for any reason, unable to be opened for OUTPUT the program will be terminated immediately by performing C100–ABORT–RUN.

The only other item to particularly note is the fact that SI–SALESPERSON–NUMBER from the transaction file has been moved to IS–SALESPERSON–NUMBER, the primary key, in line 1980. The current value of IS–SALESPERSON–NUMBER is used by the WRITE IS–INDEXED–SALES–RECORD statement at line 2070 to transfer the data record to the indexed file. Failure to appropriately move the correct value to the primary key will cause unpredictable results. The WRITE in this case is not like a WRITE to a printer. When a WRITE to a printer is executed, so long as the printer has been opened for output, the programmer can be confident that the WRITE actually takes place. However, a WRITE to an indexed file is a *request* to WRITE, not necessarily resulting in an actual physical transfer of data to the file.

For the physical transfer of data to actually occur, both the index and the data file must receive contents appropriately. That is why the FILE STATUS must be checked. The program, in essence, is asking the system to indicate what happened as a result of the request. If the WRITE occurred as intended, C400–ACCUMULATE–TOTALS is performed; if not, an error message is printed on the printer. No errors were encountered during the execution of this program and resulted in the same control totals being calculated and placed in the control file as during the creation of the sequential file in Chapter 6. Figure 7–9 lists the output from Program 7–1.

Figure 7–9 *Output from Program 7–1*

```
INDEXED SALES FILE TOTALS
                     RECORDS           SALES      RETURNS  HASH NUMBER
BEGINNING TOTALS        30          23,386.40    6,882.67    40,130
```

Indexed File Reporting

In order to report from an indexed file a programmer must decide whether access to the file is to be random or sequential. It is also important to consider whether access will be by primary key or alternate key.

Random Reporting—Primary or Alternate Key

Consider the program statements in Figure 7–10, which illustrate the ability to randomly access an indexed file by primary or alternate key.

In Figure 7–10 first notice that the SELECT statement includes the clause ACCESS IS RANDOM and that some alternate keys have been specified. In the PROCEDURE division REQUEST–FILE has been opened as INPUT. This file would contain the primary or alternate key of the desired records. INDEXED–SALES–FILE has been opened as I–O, which enables updating.

Example A illustrates necessary logic for access by primary key. Note that IS–SALESPERSON–NUMBER has received the contents of a requested number in a MOVE statement. The effect of this move followed by READ INDEXED–SALES–FILE is that IS–SALESPERSON–NUMBER acts as a **record pointer** which points to the expected physical location of the requested record in the indexed file. After the READ has been attempted the FILE STATUS is checked to determine whether the READ has been successful. If NO–RECORD–FOUND is true (EL–STATUS–ERROR = '23'), C200–NO–RECORD–RTN is performed, which would probably print an appropriate error message. If SUCCESSFUL–COMPLETION is true (EL–STATUS–

Figure 7–10 *Random Access by Primary or Alternate Key*

```
            SELECT INDEXED-SALES-FILE
                ASSIGN TO SYS025-DA-3375-PAYROL
                ORGANIZATION IS INDEXED
                ACCESS IS RANDOM
                FILE STATUS IS EL-STATUS-ERROR
                RECORD KEY IS IS-SALESPERSON-NUMBER
                ALTERNATE RECORD KEY IS-LAST-NAME
                    WITH DUPLICATES
                ALTERNATE RECORD KEY IS-YEAR-TO-DATE-SALES
                    WITH DUPLICATES
                ALTERNATE RECORD KEY IS-COMMISSION-RATE
                    WITH DUPLICATES.

    01  WS-RECORD-INDICATORS.
        05  EL-STATUS-ERROR              PIC X(2).
            88  SUCCESSFUL-COMPLETION     VALUE '00'.
            88  DUPLICATE-ALTERNATE-KEY   VALUE '02'.
            88  END-OF-SALES-FILE         VALUE '10'.
            88  NO-RECORD-FOUND           VALUE '23'.

    PROCEDURE DIVISION.
    A000-INDEXED-SALES.
        OPEN INPUT   REQUEST-FILE
             I-0     INDEXED-SALES-FILE
             OUTPUT REPORT-FILE.
        PERFORM Z100-READ-REQUEST.
        PERFORM B200-PROCESS-REQUESTS
            UNTIL END-OF-REQUEST-FILE.
        CLOSE REQUEST-FILE
              SALES-INDEXED-FILE
              REPORT-FILE.
```

Example A:

```
    B200-PROCESS-REQUESTS.
        MOVE RQ-SALESPERSON-NUMBER TO IS-SALESPERSON-NUMBER.
        READ INDEXED-SALES-FILE.
        IF NO-RECORD-FOUND
            PERFORM C200-NO-RECORD-RTN
        ELSE
            IF SUCCESSFUL-COMPLETION
                PERFORM C300-MOVE-RECORD-TO-PRINTER
            ELSE
                PERFORM Z200-UNEXPECTED-ERROR.
```

Example B:

```
    B200-PROCESS-REQUESTS.
        MOVE RQ-LAST-NAME TO IS-LAST-NAME.
        READ INDEXED-PAYROLL-FILE
            KEY IS IP-LAST-NAME
        IF NO-RECORD-FOUND
            PERFORM C200-NO-RECORD-RTN
        ELSE
            IF SUCCESSFUL-COMPLETION
                PERFORM C300-MOVE-RECORD-TO-PRINTER
            ELSE
                IF DUPLICATE-ALTERNATE-KEY
                    PERFORM C400-COMPARE-FIRST-NAME
                ELSE
                    PERFORM Z200-UNEXPECTED-ERROR.
```

ERROR = '00'), C300–MOVE–RECORD–TO–PRINTER is executed. If neither is true a general error routine is executed.

Example B illustrates access by an alternate key, IS–LAST–NAME. The logic of Example A is modified slightly here to allow for the possibility of DUPLICATE–ALTERNATE–KEY (EL–STATUS–ERROR = '02') being true. The other difference is that a name request has been moved to IS–LAST–NAME, the alternate key being used, and the READ statement has been modified to include the **KEY IS clause.** The KEY IS clause simply tells the system that the named alternate key is to be used for random access rather than the primary key. The key named in the KEY IS clause must have a valid key that can be found in the indexed file so control is still needed for NO–RECORD–FOUND.

Sequential Reporting—Primary or Alternate Key

Sequential reporting from an indexed sequential file by primary key is similar to reporting from a standard sequential file. The only difference is the SELECT statement and the advisability of testing the FILE STATUS immediately after opening the file. Actually, however, the same can be done on a sequential file. Reporting from an indexed file using either the primary or alternate indexes is illustrated in Program 7–2.

Program Example

Program 7–2

```
000010 IDENTIFICATION DIVISION.
000020 PROGRAM-ID.    INDALT.
000030********************************************************
000040* PROGRAM EXAMPLE 7-2 INDEXED REPORT - ALTERNATE INDEXES    *
000050********************************************************
000060 ENVIRONMENT DIVISION.
000070 CONFIGURATION SECTION.
000080    SOURCE-COMPUTER.  IBM-4341.
000090    OBJECT-COMPUTER.  IBM-4341.
000100 INPUT-OUTPUT SECTION.
000110 FILE-CONTROL.
000120    SELECT INDEXED-SALES-FILE
000130        ASSIGN TO SYS042-DA-3375-SALES
000140        ORGANIZATION IS INDEXED
000150        ACCESS IS SEQUENTIAL
000160        RECORD KEY IS IS-SALESPERSON-NUMBER
000170        ALTERNATE RECORD KEY IS IS-LAST-NAME
000180            WITH DUPLICATES
000190        ALTERNATE RECORD KEY IS IS-YEAR-TO-DATE-SALES
000200            WITH DUPLICATES
000210        ALTERNATE RECORD KEY IS IS-COMMISSION-RATE
000220            WITH DUPLICATES
000230        FILE STATUS IS EL-STATUS-ERROR.
000240    SELECT SALES-CONTROL-FILE
000250        ASSIGN TO SYS025-UT-3375-SALESCT.
000260    SELECT SALES-REPORT
000270        ASSIGN TO SYS018-UR-3203-S.
000280    SELECT REPORT-REQUEST-FILE
000290        ASSIGN TO SYS016-UR-2501-S.
000300*
000310 DATA DIVISION.
000320 FILE SECTION.
000330 FD  INDEXED-SALES-FILE
000340     RECORD CONTAINS 55 CHARACTERS
000350     LABEL RECORDS STANDARD.
000360 01  IS-INDEXED-SALES-RECORD.
000370     05  IS-SALESPERSON-NUMBER         PIC X(4).
```

Program 7-2 *(continued)*

```
000380      05  IS-HASH-NUMBER REDEFINES
000390          IS-SALESPERSON-NUMBER       PIC 9(4).
000400      05  IS-LAST-NAME                PIC X(11).
000410      05  IS-FIRST-NAME              PIC X(10).
000420      05  IS-YEAR-TO-DATE-SALES       PIC 9(5)V99.
000430      05  IS-YEAR-TO-DATE-SALES-RETURNS PIC 9(5)V99.
000440      05  IS-CURRENT-SALES            PIC 9(5)V99.
000450      05  IS-CURRENT-SALES-RETURNS    PIC 9(5)V99.
000460      05  IS-COMMISSION-RATE          PIC V99.
000470 FD  SALES-CONTROL-FILE
000480     RECORD CONTAINS 84 CHARACTERS
000490     LABEL RECORDS ARE STANDARD.
000500 01  SC-SALES-CONTROL-RECORD.
000510      05  SC-BEG-TOT-FIELDS.
000520          10  SC-BEG-TOT-RECORDS-STORED     PIC S9(4).
000530          10  SC-BEG-TOT-HASH-NUMBER        PIC S9(6).
000540          10  SC-BEG-TOT-YTD-SALES          PIC S9(6)V99.
000550          10  SC-BEG-TOT-YTD-SALES-RETURNS  PIC S9(6)V99.
000560          10  SC-BEG-TOT-CURRENT-SALES      PIC S9(6)V99.
000570          10  SC-BEG-TOT-CURRENT-RETURNS    PIC S9(6)V99.
000580      05  SC-CHG-TOT-FIELDS.
000590          10  SC-CHG-TOT-RECORDS-STORED     PIC S9(4).
000600          10  SC-CHG-TOT-HASH-NUMBER        PIC S9(6).
000610          10  SC-CHG-TOT-YTD-SALES          PIC S9(6)V99.
000620          10  SC-CHG-TOT-YTD-SALES-RETURNS  PIC S9(6)V99.
000630          10  SC-CHG-TOT-CURRENT-SALES      PIC S9(6)V99.
000640          10  SC-CHG-TOT-CURRENT-RETURNS    PIC S9(6)V99.
000650 FD  SALES-REPORT
000660     RECORD CONTAINS 133 CHARACTERS
000670     LABEL RECORDS ARE OMITTED.
000680 01  SR-SALES-LINE                    PIC X(133).
000690 FD  REPORT-REQUEST-FILE
000700     RECORD CONTAINS 1 CHARACTERS
000710     LABEL RECORDS ARE STANDARD.
000720 01  RR-REPORT-REQUEST-RECORD.
000730      05  RR-REQUESTED-SEQUENCE         PIC X(1).
000740          88  PRIMARY-SEQUENCE          VALUE '1'.
000750          88  LAST-NAME-SEQUENCE        VALUE '2'.
000760          88  YEAR-TO-DATE-SEQUENCE     VALUE '3'.
000770          88  COMMISSION-RATE-SEQUENCE  VALUE '4'.
000780*
000790 WORKING-STORAGE SECTION.
000800 01  WS-RECORD-INDICATORS.
000810      05  WS-END-OF-REQUEST-FILE        PIC X(3).
000820          88  END-OF-REQUEST-FILE       VALUE 'END'.
000830 01  WS-ACCUMULATORS.
000840      05  WS-TOT-RECORDS-STORED         PIC S9(4).
000850      05  WS-TOT-HASH-NUMBER            PIC S9(6).
000860      05  WS-TOT-YTD-SALES              PIC S9(6)V99.
000870      05  WS-TOT-YTD-SALES-RETURNS      PIC S9(6)V99.
000880      05  WS-TOT-CURRENT-SALES          PIC S9(6)V99.
000890      05  WS-TOT-CURRENT-RETURNS        PIC S9(6)V99.
000900      05  WS-END-TOT-RECORDS-STORED     PIC S9(4).
000910      05  WS-END-TOT-HASH-NUMBER        PIC S9(6).
000920      05  WS-END-TOT-YTD-SALES          PIC S9(6)V99.
000930      05  WS-END-TOT-YTD-SALES-RETURNS  PIC S9(6)V99.
000940      05  WS-END-TOT-CURRENT-SALES      PIC S9(6)V99.
000950      05  WS-END-TOT-CURRENT-RETURNS    PIC S9(6)V99.
000960 01  HD-HEADING-LINE.
000970      05  FILLER                        PIC X(1).
000980      05  FILLER                        PIC X(12)
000990                                        VALUE 'SALES REPORT'.
001000      05  FILLER                        PIC X(3) VALUE ' -- '.
001010      05  HD-SEQUENCE-TYPE              PIC X(25).
```

Program 7–2 *(continued)*

```
001020 01  CH-COLUMN-HEADING-LINE.
001030     05  FILLER                       PIC X(1).
001040     05  FILLER                       PIC X(20) VALUE SPACES.
001050     05  FILLER                       PIC X(8)  VALUE 'RECORDS'.
001060     05  FILLER                       PIC X(2)  VALUE SPACES.
001070     05  FILLER                       PIC X(4)  VALUE 'HASH'.
001080     05  FILLER                       PIC X(5)  VALUE SPACES.
001090     05  FILLER                       PIC X(5)  VALUE 'SALES'.
001100     05  FILLER                       PIC X(8)  VALUE SPACES.
001110     05  FILLER                       PIC X(8)  VALUE 'RETURNS'.
001120     05  FILLER                       PIC X(5)  VALUE SPACES.
001130     05  FILLER                       PIC X(5)  VALUE 'SALES'.
001140     05  FILLER                       PIC X(5)  VALUE SPACES.
001150     05  FILLER                       PIC X(8)  VALUE 'RETURNS'.
001160 01  DL-DETAIL-LINE.
001170     05  FILLER                       PIC X(1).
001180     05  DL-SALESPERSON-NUMBER        PIC Z(4).
001190     05  FILLER                       PIC X(4) VALUE SPACES.
001200     05  DL-LAST-NAME                 PIC X(11).
001210     05  FILLER                       PIC X(4) VALUE SPACES.
001220     05  DL-FIRST-NAME                PIC X(10).
001230     05  FILLER                       PIC X(4) VALUE SPACES.
001240     05  DL-YEAR-TO-DATE-SALES        PIC ZZ,ZZZ.99.
001250     05  FILLER                       PIC X(4) VALUE SPACES.
001260     05  DL-YEAR-TO-DATE-SALES-RETURNS PIC ZZ,ZZZ.99.
001270     05  FILLER                       PIC X(4) VALUE SPACES.
001280     05  DL-CURRENT-SALES             PIC ZZ,ZZZ.99.
001290     05  FILLER                       PIC X(4) VALUE SPACES.
001300     05  DL-CURRENT-SALES-RETURNS     PIC ZZ,ZZZ.99.
001310     05  FILLER                       PIC X(4) VALUE SPACES.
001320     05  DL-COMMISSION-RATE           PIC .99.
001330     05  FILLER                       PIC X(4) VALUE SPACES.
001340     05  DL-FILE-STATUS               PIC XX.
001350 01  EL-ERROR-LINE.
001360     05  FILLER                       PIC X(1).
001370     05  EL-ERROR-OPERATION           PIC X(30).
001380     05  FILLER                       PIC X(5) VALUE SPACES.
001390     05  EL-STATUS-ERROR              PIC X(2).
001400         88  SUCCESSFUL-COMPLETION    VALUE '00'.
001410         88  END-OF-SALES-FILE        VALUE '10'.
001420 01  TL-TOTAL-LINE.
001430     05  FILLER                       PIC X(1).
001440     05  TL-STUB-HEADING              PIC X(20).
001450     05  TL-TOT-RECORDS-STORED        PIC Z,ZZ9-.
001460     05  FILLER                       PIC X(1) VALUE SPACES.
001470     05  TL-TOT-HASH-NUMBER           PIC ZZZ,ZZ9-.
001480     05  FILLER                       PIC X(2) VALUE SPACES.
001490     05  TL-TOT-YTD-SALES             PIC ZZZ,ZZZ.99-.
001500     05  FILLER                       PIC X(2) VALUE SPACES.
001510     05  TL-TOT-YTD-SALES-RETURNS     PIC ZZZ,ZZZ.99-.
001520     05  FILLER                       PIC X(2) VALUE SPACES.
001530     05  TL-TOT-CURRENT-SALES         PIC ZZ,ZZZ.99.
001540     05  FILLER                       PIC X(2) VALUE SPACES.
001550     05  TL-TOT-CURRENT-RETURNS       PIC ZZ,ZZZ.99.
001560*
001570 PROCEDURE DIVISION.
001580 DECLARATIVES.
001590 DUMMY-ERROR-PROCEDURE SECTION.
001600     USE AFTER ERROR PROCEDURE ON INDEXED-SALES-FILE.
001610 END DECLARATIVES.
001620 A000-SEQ-REPORT.
001630     OPEN INPUT REPORT-REQUEST-FILE.
001640     READ REPORT-REQUEST-FILE
001650         AT END MOVE 'END' TO WS-END-OF-REQUEST-FILE.
```

Program 7–2 *(continued)*

```
001660      PERFORM B200-PRINT-REPORTS
001670          UNTIL END-OF-REQUEST-FILE.
001680      CLOSE REPORT-REQUEST-FILE.
001690      STOP RUN.
001700 B200-PRINT-REPORTS.
001710      PERFORM C100-INITIALIZE-VARIABLES.
001720      PERFORM C200-OPEN-FOR-REPORT.
001730      PERFORM Z200-READ-RECORD.
001740      PERFORM C400-PRINT-RECORDS
001750          UNTIL END-OF-SALES-FILE.
001760      PERFORM C500-PROCESS-TOTALS.
001770      CLOSE INDEXED-SALES-FILE
001780            SALES-CONTROL-FILE
001790            SALES-REPORT.
001800      READ REPORT-REQUEST-FILE
001810          AT END MOVE 'END' TO WS-END-OF-REQUEST-FILE.
001820 C100-INITIALIZE-VARIABLES.
001830      MOVE ZEROS TO WS-ACCUMULATORS.
001840 C200-OPEN-FOR-REPORT.
001850      OPEN INPUT INDEXED-SALES-FILE
001860                 SALES-CONTROL-FILE
001870           OUTPUT SALES-REPORT.
001880      IF NOT SUCCESSFUL-COMPLETION
001890          MOVE 'REPORT OPENING' TO EL-ERROR-OPERATION
001900          PERFORM Z100-ABORT-RUN
001910          STOP RUN.
001920      IF PRIMARY-SEQUENCE
001930          MOVE 'PRIMARY SEQUENCE'        TO HD-SEQUENCE-TYPE.
001940      IF LAST-NAME-SEQUENCE
001950          MOVE 'LAST NAME SEQUENCE'      TO HD-SEQUENCE-TYPE
001960          MOVE LOW-VALUES                TO IS-LAST-NAME
001970          START INDEXED-SALES-FILE
001980              KEY NOT < IS-LAST-NAME.
001990      IF YEAR-TO-DATE-SEQUENCE
002000          MOVE 'YTD SALES SEQUENCE'      TO HD-SEQUENCE-TYPE
002010          MOVE ZEROS                     TO IS-YEAR-TO-DATE-SALES
002020          START INDEXED-SALES-FILE
002030              KEY NOT < IS-YEAR-TO-DATE-SALES.
002040      IF COMMISSION-RATE-SEQUENCE
002050          MOVE 'COMMISSION RATE SEQUENCE' TO HD-SEQUENCE-TYPE
002060          MOVE ZEROS                      TO IS-COMMISSION-RATE
002070          START INDEXED-SALES-FILE
002080              KEY NOT < IS-COMMISSION-RATE.
002090      WRITE SR-SALES-LINE FROM HD-HEADING-LINE
002100          AFTER PAGE.
002110      IF NOT SUCCESSFUL-COMPLETION
002120          MOVE 'START OPENING' TO EL-ERROR-OPERATION
002130          PERFORM Z100-ABORT-RUN
002140          STOP RUN.
002150 C400-PRINT-RECORDS.
002160      PERFORM D200-ACCUMULATE-TOTALS.
002170      MOVE IS-SALESPERSON-NUMBER TO DL-SALESPERSON-NUMBER.
002180      MOVE IS-LAST-NAME          TO DL-LAST-NAME.
002190      MOVE IS-FIRST-NAME         TO DL-FIRST-NAME.
002200      MOVE IS-YEAR-TO-DATE-SALES TO DL-YEAR-TO-DATE-SALES.
002210      MOVE IS-YEAR-TO-DATE-SALES-RETURNS
002220          TO DL-YEAR-TO-DATE-SALES-RETURNS.
002230      MOVE IS-CURRENT-SALES      TO DL-CURRENT-SALES.
002240      MOVE IS-CURRENT-SALES-RETURNS TO DL-CURRENT-SALES-RETURNS.
002250      MOVE IS-COMMISSION-RATE    TO DL-COMMISSION-RATE.
002260      MOVE EL-STATUS-ERROR       TO DL-FILE-STATUS.
002270      WRITE SR-SALES-LINE FROM DL-DETAIL-LINE
002280          AFTER 1.
002290      PERFORM Z200-READ-RECORD.
```

Program 7–2 *(continued)*

```
002300 C500-PROCESS-TOTALS.
002310     READ SALES-CONTROL-FILE.
002320     PERFORM C400-PRINT-BEG-TOTALS.
002330     PERFORM C500-PRINT-CHG-TOTALS.
002340     PERFORM C600-PRINT-END-TOTALS.
002350     PERFORM C700-PRINT-ACTUAL-TOTALS.
002360 D200-ACCUMULATE-TOTALS.
002370     ADD 1                       TO WS-TOT-RECORDS-STORED.
002380     ADD IS-HASH-NUMBER          TO WS-TOT-HASH-NUMBER.
002390     ADD IS-YEAR-TO-DATE-SALES   TO WS-TOT-YTD-SALES.
002400     ADD IS-YEAR-TO-DATE-SALES-RETURNS
002410         TO WS-TOT-YTD-SALES-RETURNS.
002420     ADD IS-CURRENT-SALES        TO WS-TOT-CURRENT-SALES.
002430     ADD IS-CURRENT-SALES-RETURNS TO WS-TOT-CURRENT-RETURNS.
002440 C400-PRINT-BEG-TOTALS.
002450     WRITE SR-SALES-LINE FROM CH-COLUMN-HEADING-LINE
002460         AFTER 2.
002470     MOVE 'BEGINNING - CONTROL'     TO TL-STUB-HEADING.
002480     MOVE SC-BEG-TOT-RECORDS-STORED  TO TL-TOT-RECORDS-STORED.
002490     MOVE SC-BEG-TOT-HASH-NUMBER     TO TL-TOT-HASH-NUMBER.
002500     MOVE SC-BEG-TOT-YTD-SALES       TO TL-TOT-YTD-SALES.
002510     MOVE SC-BEG-TOT-YTD-SALES-RETURNS
002520         TO TL-TOT-YTD-SALES-RETURNS.
002530     MOVE SC-BEG-TOT-CURRENT-SALES   TO TL-TOT-CURRENT-SALES.
002540     MOVE SC-BEG-TOT-CURRENT-RETURNS TO TL-TOT-CURRENT-RETURNS.
002550     WRITE SR-SALES-LINE FROM TL-TOTAL-LINE
002560         AFTER 2.
002570 C500-PRINT-CHG-TOTALS.
002580     MOVE 'NET CHANGE - CONTROL'    TO TL-STUB-HEADING.
002590     MOVE SC-CHG-TOT-RECORDS-STORED  TO TL-TOT-RECORDS-STORED.
002600     MOVE SC-CHG-TOT-HASH-NUMBER     TO TL-TOT-HASH-NUMBER.
002610     MOVE SC-CHG-TOT-YTD-SALES       TO TL-TOT-YTD-SALES.
002620     MOVE SC-CHG-TOT-YTD-SALES-RETURNS
002630         TO TL-TOT-YTD-SALES-RETURNS.
002640     MOVE SC-CHG-TOT-CURRENT-SALES   TO TL-TOT-CURRENT-SALES.
002650     MOVE SC-CHG-TOT-CURRENT-RETURNS TO TL-TOT-CURRENT-RETURNS.
002660     WRITE SR-SALES-LINE FROM TL-TOTAL-LINE
002670         AFTER 2.
002680 C600-PRINT-END-TOTALS.
002690     MOVE 'ENDING - CONTROL'        TO TL-STUB-HEADING.
002700     ADD SC-BEG-TOT-RECORDS-STORED SC-CHG-TOT-RECORDS-STORED
002710         GIVING WS-END-TOT-RECORDS-STORED
002720                TL-TOT-RECORDS-STORED.
002730     ADD SC-BEG-TOT-HASH-NUMBER SC-CHG-TOT-HASH-NUMBER
002740         GIVING WS-END-TOT-HASH-NUMBER
002750                TL-TOT-HASH-NUMBER.
002760     ADD SC-BEG-TOT-YTD-SALES SC-CHG-TOT-YTD-SALES
002770         GIVING WS-END-TOT-YTD-SALES
002780                TL-TOT-YTD-SALES.
002790     ADD SC-BEG-TOT-YTD-SALES-RETURNS SC-CHG-TOT-YTD-SALES-RETURNS
002800         GIVING WS-END-TOT-YTD-SALES-RETURNS
002810                TL-TOT-YTD-SALES-RETURNS.
002820     ADD SC-BEG-TOT-CURRENT-SALES SC-CHG-TOT-CURRENT-SALES
002830         GIVING WS-END-TOT-CURRENT-SALES
002840                TL-TOT-CURRENT-SALES.
002850     ADD SC-BEG-TOT-CURRENT-RETURNS SC-CHG-TOT-CURRENT-RETURNS
002860         GIVING WS-END-TOT-CURRENT-RETURNS
002870                TL-TOT-CURRENT-RETURNS.
002880     WRITE SR-SALES-LINE FROM TL-TOTAL-LINE
002890         AFTER 2.
002900 C700-PRINT-ACTUAL-TOTALS.
002910     MOVE 'ENDING - ACTUAL'         TO TL-STUB-HEADING.
002920     MOVE WS-TOT-RECORDS-STORED     TO TL-TOT-RECORDS-STORED.
002930     MOVE WS-TOT-HASH-NUMBER        TO TL-TOT-HASH-NUMBER.
```

Program 7–2 *(concluded)*

```
002940      MOVE WS-TOT-YTD-SALES          TO TL-TOT-YTD-SALES.
002950      MOVE WS-TOT-YTD-SALES-RETURNS  TO TL-TOT-YTD-SALES-RETURNS.
002960      MOVE WS-TOT-CURRENT-SALES      TO TL-TOT-CURRENT-SALES.
002970      MOVE WS-TOT-CURRENT-RETURNS    TO TL-TOT-CURRENT-RETURNS.
002980      WRITE SR-SALES-LINE FROM TL-TOTAL-LINE
002990          AFTER 2.
003000 Z100-ABORT-RUN.
003010      WRITE SR-SALES-LINE FROM EL-ERROR-LINE
003020          AFTER 1.
003030      CLOSE INDEXED-SALES-FILE
003040            SALES-CONTROL-FILE
003050            REPORT-REQUEST-FILE
003060            SALES-REPORT.
003070 Z200-READ-RECORD.
003080      READ INDEXED-SALES-FILE.
```

Discussion

Note the controlling module B200–PRINT–RECORDS in lines 1700 through 1810. This module is the same as any main module that has been used in previous programs. In C200–OPEN–FOR–REPORT, the RR–REQUESTED–SEQUENCE is tested to determine the type of sequence that is desired. Following the logic back to B200–PRINT–REPORTS when PRIMARY–SEQUENCE is true, the file has been opened and the first record is read by the PERFORM statement at line 1730. Since access has been defined as SEQUENTIAL and nothing else has been indicated, the file will be accessed by the primary key, IS–SALESPERSON–NUMBER. The subsequent reporting process follows any standard sequential reporting program. If the ACCESS had been specified as DYNAMIC, the READ statement would have been modified to READ INDEXED–SALES–FILE NEXT. The READ statement must contain the reserved word NEXT so that the system can distinguish a sequential READ from a random READ. This is true irrespective of the form of the OPEN statement.

In Figure 7–11 the results of requesting prime sequence is evident in the first portion of the abbreviated output. Notice the sequence of the data in the first column which is IS–SALESPERSON–NUMBER. Note also that the printed control totals evidence agreement with the totals when the file was initially created.

Sequential reporting using alternate keys is a little more complex because it is necessary to (1) inform the compiler which alternate key to use, (2) inform the compiler as to the beginning alternate key value, and (3) control properly for duplicates in the alternate key (inherent in the WITH DUPLICATES clause). This concept is shown in lines 2040 through 2080 in Program 7–2. This module is used to initiate the printing of the entire file using IS–COMMISSION–RATE as the alternate key.

What remains is to inform the compiler which key to use and the starting point for the key. Both of the requirements are inherent in the **START statement** at lines 2070 and 2080. The START statement's purpose is to initialize the record pointer at the appropriate location. The START statement also allows the specification of an alternate key.

In this case ZEROS has been previously moved to IS–COMMISSION–RATE to ensure that the entire file is accessed. Notice also that **LOW–VALUES** can be used for alphanumeric fields, such as the statement at line 1960 for IS–LAST–NAME. The contents of IS–COMMISSION–RATE (zeros) are then compared in the KEY NOT LESS THAN clause and will cause access to begin with the first commission rate that has a value equal to or higher than zeros. Since no value would be lower than zeros, access will begin with the person that has the lowest commission rate in the file.

The entire file does not have to be accessed when sequentially accessing a file with alternate keys. It is possible to select only a portion of the file. For example,

Figure 7–11 *Abbreviated Output from Program 7–2 before Updating*

```
SALES REPORT - PRIMARY SEQUENCE
    17    PAYNE         MAX              987.00        56.73          .00        .00    .05    00
   125    LISHER        JANET F.         500.00          .00          .00        .00    .15    00
   243    BROCKETT      JANE R.          750.00       900.00          .00        .00    .05    00
      .
  2487    HUME          LETA             483.53       284.37          .00        .00    .20    00
  2575    CROSS         CHERYL           385.63       382.50          .00        .00    .10    00
                        RECORDS   HASH    SALES       RETURNS        SALES     RETURNS

BEGINNING  - CONTROL      30    40,130  23,386.40    6,882.67         .00        .00

NET CHANGE - CONTROL       0         0       .00          .00         .00        .00

ENDING - CONTROL          30    40,130  23,386.40    6,882.67         .00        .00

ENDING - ACTUAL           30    40,130  23,386.40    6,882.67         .00        .00

SALES REPORT - COMMISSION RATE SEQUENCE
    17    PAYNE         MAX              987.00        56.73          .00        .00    .05    02
   243    BROCKETT      JANE R.          750.00       900.00          .00        .00    .05    02
  2294    HERMAN        JACK             484.65        87.47          .00        .00    .05    02
  2395    MATNEY        DELORES          795.74       857.46          .00        .00    .05    00
      .
  2157    YOUNG         KAREN L.       1,123.59        35.75          .00        .00    .30    02
  2485    PHILLIPS      TRACY L.         500.00       100.00          .00        .00    .30    00
                        RECORDS   HASH    SALES       RETURNS        SALES     RETURNS

BEGINNING  - CONTROL.     30    40,130  23,386.40    6,882.67         .00        .00

NET CHANGE - CONTROL       0         0       .00          .00         .00        .00

ENDING - CONTROL          30    40,130  23,386.40    6,882.67         .00        .00

ENDING - ACTUAL           30    40,130  23,386.40    6,882.67         .00        .00
```

should the programmer desire to access only those persons who had commission rates starting with .10 and above, line 2060 would be changed to be MOVE .10 TO IS–COMMISSION–RATE.

Refer to the listing of the data in commission rate sequence in Figure 7–11, particularly noting the contents of the last two columns. The next to the last column contains the commission rates, which are in appropriate sequence. Also note the sequence of the primary keys for any given commission rate. They are in sequence from low to high.

The rightmost column is the FILE STATUS. FILE STATUS = '02' indicates that the READ statement detected that the particular record read contained an alternate key that was duplicated by at least one additional indexed record. Note that this is true for the first three employees that have a commission rate of .05. However, when the fourth record is read the FILE STATUS = '00', SUCCESSFUL–COMPLE TION.

In this context, SUCCESSFUL–COMPLETION means that this record contains an alternate key but that it is not duplicated by any record that has a higher primary key. If IS–COMMISSION–RATE had not been defined WITH DUPLICATES, program termination would have occurred as a result of FILE STATUS indicating DUPLI CATE–ALTERNATE–KEY.

Other variations of the START statement are possible, as shown by the format in Figure 7–12.

The knowledge of what the file status means can be used to access only those records that have a single alternate key. Figure 7–13 illustrates the logic necessary for printing a subset of the data file using IS–COMMISSION–RATE of .05.

First, .05 is moved to IS–COMMISSION–RATE because only those records with a commission rate of .05 are to be printed (any valid commission rate would work),

Figure 7–12   *Format of the START Statement*

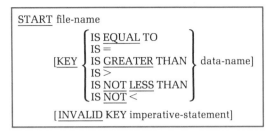

Figure 7–13   *Accessing a Subset of Alternate Key Values*

```
    MOVE .05 TO IS-COMMISSION-RATE.
    START INDEXED-SALES-FILE
        KEY = IS-COMMISSION-RATE.
    IF NOT SUCCESSFUL-COMPLETION
        PERFORM Z100-START-ERROR
    ELSE
        PERFORM Z200-READ-RECORD
        PERFORM Z300-MOVE-TO-DETAIL-LINE.
    PERFORM C400-PRINT-SUBSET
        UNTIL END-OF-FILE
            OR END-OF-SET.


C400-PRINT-SUBSET.
    PERFORM Z200-READ-RECORD.
    PERFORM Z300-MOVE-TO-DETAIL-LINE.
    IF SUCCESSFUL-COMPLETION
        MOVE 'YES' TO END-OF-SET-SWITCH.
```

and the START statement utilizes a KEY = clause rather than a KEY NOT LESS THAN used in previous modules. These statements together set the record pointer at the first record in the file that contains a commission rate of .05. Z300–MOVE–TO–DETAIL–LINE is then performed to ensure that even if the first record read is the only record in the subset, it will be printed. Then the PERFORM statement is modified to include UNTIL END–OF–SET, which would have to be defined in WORK ING–STORAGE. Then in C400–PRINT–SUBSET, when SUCCESSFUL–COMPLE TION is true, the END–OF–SET–SWITCH is reset, indicating that the end of the subset has been reached. The programmer may notice that testing for END–OF– FILE is not really necessary, because if the last subset of commission rates were to be accessed the END–OF–SUBSET would be reached before END–OF–FILE would be reached.

Indexed File Maintenance

File maintenance is a major, ongoing activity designed to ensure that the data in the files are accurate and up to date. To update files there must be a choice made between a **sequential update** and a **random update.** An indexed file can be updated using either approach, depending on the application.

Random updating of an indexed file is much easier than sequential updating. It has also become a more common procedure because of the expansion of online information systems. The essential tasks in random updating simply involve (1) having the system find the record to update, (2) accomplishing the update procedure, and (3) putting the changed record back in its previous location. This process is termed **in-place updating** just as it was for sequential files.

COBOL Statements Necessary for Random Updating

The four major statements necessary for a random update are the READ, WRITE, DELETE, and REWRITE statements, the formats of which are illustrated in Figure 7–15 through 7–18.

In all cases the programmer may use the optional **INVALID KEY clause** to test the file status. As previously defined, FILE STATUS can be tested for various types of errors. The INVALID KEY clause can be used to test for possible errors, but *only* when one of these four statements or the START statement is used. In previous examples, specifically in Figure 7–10 in the examples of random reporting, the ability to test for a specific FILE STATUS value was shown. The exact nature of the error can be pinpointed and appropriate processing can be undertaken depending on the value of FILE STATUS.

When the INVALID KEY clause is used, all that is known is that some problem exists, not what the specific error is. For instance, during indexed file creation, a WRITE statement is used to physically place data onto a file. If the INVALID KEY condition is true (which means that an error has occurred) the only thing that is known for certain is that FILE STATUS is not '00' (SUCCESSFUL–COMPLETION). A WRITE statement may result in a SEQUENCE–ERROR, a DUPLICATE–KEY, a DUPLICATE–ALTERNATE–KEY, or one of several implementor errors.

Testing the FILE STATUS is superior to using the INVALID KEY clause because of the ability to ascertain exact error sources and because the testing can be accomplished independently of the actual placement of the input or output statements in the program. In fact, the FILE STATUS can be tested anywhere in the program that logically follows an input or output procedure including an OPEN statement. Processing similar to that shown in Figure 7–14 should be undertaken immediately after an indexed file has been opened. If this is not accomplished and an OPEN error occurs, any subsequent processing is meaningless and possibly dangerous, so the program is terminated immediately.

Figure 7–14   *Use of FILE STATUS after OPEN*

```
OPEN INPUT   TRANSACTION-FILE
     I-O     MASTER-INDEX-FILE
     OUTPUT  REPORT-FILE.
IF NOT SUCCESSFUL-COMPLETION
    PERFORM Z100-ABORT-RUN
    STOP RUN.


Z100-ABORT-RUN.
    MOVE WS-FILE-STATUS-FLAG TO EL-ERROR-FLAG.
    MOVE 'OPEN ERROR ON MASTER FILE - RUN ABORTED' TO
        EL-ERROR-TYPE.
    MOVE EL-ERROR-LINE TO PR-PRINT-RECORD.
    WRITE PR-PRINT-RECORD
        AFTER ADVANCING PAGE.
    CLOSE TRANSACTION-FILE
          MASTER-INDEX-FILE
          REPORT-FILE.
```

The READ Statement

The format of the **READ statement** when processing an indexed file randomly is shown in Figure 7–15. Before issuing a READ the record pointer needs to be set properly by moving a value to the primary key field.

Figure 7–15   *Format of a Random READ*

```
READ file-name RECORD [INTO identifier]
    [KEY IS data-name]
    [INVALID KEY imperative-statement(s)]
```

Rules related to a random READ statement are:

- If the READ is unsuccessful, the contents of the associated record are unavailable, and the record pointer is undefined.
- The file status is updated only if the FILE STATUS clause is specified for that file.
- The record associated with file-name must contain the primary key and alternate key, if specified, named in the SELECT statement.
- The READ must be preceded by a value moved to the primary or alternate key to set the record pointer.
- If alternate keys are specified WITH DUPLICATES and the KEY IS clause is used, a successful read results in obtaining the first record in the subset. If the record obtained is the only record, SUCCESSFUL–COMPLETION will be true. If not, DUPLICATE–ALTERNATE–KEY will be true.

The WRITE Statement

The format of the **WRITE statement** for a random write to an indexed file is shown in Figure 7–16. The WRITE must be preceded by a valid READ, attempting to see if a record exists with the current primary key. The purpose of a random WRITE is to add a record to the file.

Figure 7–16   *Format of a Random WRITE*

```
WRITE record-name [FROM identifier]
    [INVALID KEY imperative-statement(s)]
```

Rules related to a random WRITE are:

- The file status is updated only if the FILE STATUS clause is specified for that file.
- The record associated with record-name must contain the primary and alternate keys named in the SELECT statement.
- The record pointer must have been previously set by attempting a READ using the relevant primary or alternate key.
- The record pointer is unchanged by the WRITE statement, successful or not.

The DELETE Statement

The format of the DELETE statement is shown in Figure 7–17. The purpose of the **DELETE statement** is to delete a record from an indexed file. The major concern related to a DELETE statement is to ensure that the record pointer has been set with an appropriate READ statement before the DELETE is executed.

Figure 7–17   *Format of a Random DELETE*

```
DELETE file-name RECORD
    [INVALID KEY imperative-statement(s)]
```

Rules related to a DELETE statement are:

- The file status is updated only if the FILE STATUS clause is specified for that file.
- The record associated with file-name must contain the primary and alternate keys named in the SELECT statement.
- The record pointer must have been previously set by attempting a READ using the relevant primary or alternate key.
- After a successful DELETE, the physical record is unavailable from the file but is still in the record area.

■ Some systems do not physically delete the record until the file is reorganized using a utility program even though the record is logically deleted.

The REWRITE Statement

The format of the **REWRITE statement** is shown in Figure 7–18. The purpose of the REWRITE statement is to place the updated contents of a record back in its original location (in place updating). It can be used only on a preexisting record that has been input by a READ statement.

Figure 7–18 *Format of a Random REWRITE*

```
REWRITE record-name [FROM identifier]
        [INVALID KEY imperative-statement(s)]
```

Rules related to the REWRITE statement are:

■ The file status is updated only if the FILE STATUS clause is specified for that file.
■ The record associated with record-name must contain the primary and alternate keys named in the SELECT statement.
■ The record pointer must have been previously set by attempting a READ using the relevant primary or alternate key.
■ The current record pointer is not affected by execution of a REWRITE statement.

Program Example

Statement of the Problem

The program will accomplish a random update of an existing indexed sales file. Evidence of the appropriate update procedures will include a detailed listing of all transactions indicating errors if they exist, record counts, and other appropriate control totals. It is assumed that the transaction file has been previously validated.

Input

Input to Program 7–3 is the transaction file shown in Figure 7–19 and the indexed master sales file that was created by Program 7–1. The programmer may notice that these are the same transaction records that were used to update the sequential file in Chapter 6. Control totals, therefore, should be the same, since the original file and the transaction files are identical.

Program

Program 7–3

```
000010 IDENTIFICATION DIVISION.
000020 PROGRAM-ID.    INDUPDT.
000030****************************************************************
000040* PROGRAM EXAMPLE 7-3 INDEXED RANDOM UPDATE                    *
000050****************************************************************
000060 ENVIRONMENT DIVISION.
000070 CONFIGURATION SECTION.
000080    SOURCE-COMPUTER.  IBM-4341.
000090    OBJECT-COMPUTER.  IBM-4341.
000100 INPUT-OUTPUT SECTION.
000110 FILE-CONTROL.
000120    SELECT INDEXED-SALES-FILE
000130        ASSIGN TO SYS042-DA-3375-SALES
000140        ORGANIZATION IS INDEXED
000150        ACCESS IS DYNAMIC
000160        RECORD KEY IS IS-SALESPERSON-NUMBER
000170        ALTERNATE RECORD KEY IS IS-LAST-NAME
000180            WITH DUPLICATES
000190        ALTERNATE RECORD KEY IS IS-YEAR-TO-DATE-SALES
```

Program 7–3 *(continued)*

```
000200              WITH DUPLICATES
000210              ALTERNATE RECORD KEY IS IS-COMMISSION-RATE
000220              WITH DUPLICATES
000230              FILE STATUS IS EL-STATUS-ERROR.
000240          SELECT SALES-REPORT-FILE
000250              ASSIGN TO SYS018-UR-3203-S.
000260          SELECT SALES-TRANSACTION-FILE
000270              ASSIGN TO SYS016-UR-2501-S.
000280          SELECT SALES-CONTROL-FILE
000290              ASSIGN TO SYS025-UT-3375-SALESCT.
000300*
000310 DATA DIVISION.
000320 FILE SECTION.
000330 FD  INDEXED-SALES-FILE
000340      RECORD CONTAINS 55 CHARACTERS
000350      LABEL RECORDS STANDARD.
000360 01  IS-INDEXED-SALES-RECORD.
000370      05  IS-SALESPERSON-NUMBER            PIC X(4).
000380      05  IS-HASH-NUMBER
000390          REDEFINES IS-SALESPERSON-NUMBER  PIC 9(4).
000400      05  IS-LAST-NAME                     PIC X(11).
000410      05  IS-FIRST-NAME                    PIC X(10).
000420      05  IS-YEAR-TO-DATE-SALES            PIC 9(5)V99.
000430      05  IS-YEAR-TO-DATE-SALES-RETURNS    PIC 9(5)V99.
000440      05  IS-CURRENT-SALES                 PIC 9(5)V99.
000450      05  IS-CURRENT-SALES-RETURNS         PIC 9(5)V99.
000460      05  IS-COMMISSION-RATE               PIC V99.
000470 FD  SALES-TRANSACTION-FILE
000480      RECORD CONTAINS 46 CHARACTERS
000490      LABEL RECORDS ARE STANDARD.
000500 01  ST-SALES-TRANS-RECORD.
000510      05  ST-SALESPERSON-NUMBER            PIC X(4).
000520      05  ST-HASH-NUMBER
000530          REDEFINES ST-SALESPERSON-NUMBER  PIC 9(4).
000540      05  FILLER                           PIC X(1).
000550      05  ST-LAST-NAME                     PIC X(11).
000560      05  ST-FIRST-NAME                    PIC X(10).
000570      05  ST-CURRENT-SALES                 PIC 9(5)V99.
000580      05  FILLER                           PIC X(1).
000590      05  ST-CURRENT-SALES-RETURNS         PIC 9(5)V99.
000600      05  FILLER                           PIC X(1).
000610      05  ST-COMMISSION-RATE               PIC V99.
000620      05  FILLER                           PIC X(1).
000630      05  ST-TRANSACTION-CODE              PIC X(1).
000640          88  ADDITION-OF-SALESPERSON          VALUE '1'.
000650          88  DELETION-OF-SALESPERSON          VALUE '2'.
000660          88  NAME-CHANGE                      VALUE '3'.
000670          88  UPDATE-CURRENT-SALES             VALUE '4'.
000680          88  UPDATE-CURRENT-SALES-RETURNS VALUE '5'.
000690          88  UPDATE-COMMISSION-RATE           VALUE '6'.
000700 FD  SALES-CONTROL-FILE
000710      RECORD CONTAINS 84 CHARACTERS
000720      LABEL RECORDS ARE STANDARD.
000730 01  SC-SALES-CONTROL-RECORD.
000740      05  SC-BEG-TOT-FIELDS.
000750          10  SC-BEG-TOT-RECORDS-STORED    PIC S9(4).
000760          10  SC-BEG-TOT-HASH-NUMBER       PIC S9(6).
000770          10  SC-BEG-TOT-YTD-SALES         PIC S9(6)V99.
000780          10  SC-BEG-TOT-YTD-SALES-RETURNS PIC S9(6)V99.
000790          10  SC-BEG-TOT-CURRENT-SALES     PIC S9(6)V99.
000800          10  SC-BEG-TOT-CURRENT-RETURNS   PIC S9(6)V99.
000810      05  SC-CHG-TOT-FIELDS.
000820          10  SC-CHG-TOT-RECORDS-STORED    PIC S9(4).
000830          10  SC-CHG-TOT-HASH-NUMBER       PIC S9(6).
```

Program 7–3   *(continued)*

```
000840          10  SC-CHG-TOT-YTD-SALES          PIC S9(6)V99.
000850          10  SC-CHG-TOT-YTD-SALES-RETURNS PIC S9(6)V99.
000860          10  SC-CHG-TOT-CURRENT-SALES      PIC S9(6)V99.
000870          10  SC-CHG-TOT-CURRENT-RETURNS    PIC S9(6)V99.
000880 FD  SALES-REPORT-FILE
000890     RECORD CONTAINS 133 CHARACTERS
000900     LABEL RECORDS ARE OMITTED.
000910 01  SR-SALES-REPORT-LINE                   PIC X(133).
000920*
000930 WORKING-STORAGE SECTION.
000940 01  WS-ACCUMULATORS.
000950     05  WS-CHG-TOT-RECORDS-STORED          PIC S9(4).
000960     05  WS-CHG-TOT-HASH-NUMBER             PIC S9(6).
000970     05  WS-CHG-YTD-SALES                   PIC S9(6)V99.
000980     05  WS-CHG-YTD-SALES-RETURNS           PIC S9(6)V99.
000990     05  WS-CHG-CURRENT-SALES               PIC S9(6)V99.
001000     05  WS-CHG-CURRENT-RETURNS             PIC S9(6)V99.
001010 01  WS-WORK-AREAS.
001020     05  WS-EOF-INDICATOR                   PIC X(3).
001030         88 END-OF-TRANSACTION-FILE         VALUE 'END'.
001040 01  UC-UPDATE-CONTROL-AREAS.
001050     05  UC-COUNT-SUB                       PIC 9(4).
001060     05  UC-HEADING-CONTROL-VALUES.
001070         10  FILLER      PIC X(20) VALUE 'ADDITIONS'.
001080         10  FILLER      PIC X(20) VALUE 'DELETIONS'.
001090         10  FILLER      PIC X(20) VALUE 'NAME CHANGES'.
001100         10  FILLER      PIC X(20) VALUE 'YTD SALES CHANGES'.
001110         10  FILLER      PIC X(20) VALUE 'YTD RTNS CHANGES'.
001120         10  FILLER      PIC X(20) VALUE 'COM RATE CHANGES'.
001130         10  FILLER      PIC X(20) VALUE 'REJECTIONS'.
001140         10  FILLER      PIC X(20) VALUE 'TOTAL TRANSACTIONS'.
001150     05  FILLER REDEFINES UC-HEADING-CONTROL-VALUES.
001160         10  UC-HEADING-LINE                PIC X(20)
001170             OCCURS 8 TIMES.
001180     05  UC-RECORD-CONTROL-TOTALS.
001190         10  UC-NUM-OF-ADDS                 PIC 9(4).
001200         10  UC-NUM-OF-DELETES              PIC 9(4).
001210         10  UC-NUM-OF-CHG-NAME             PIC 9(4).
001220         10  UC-NUM-OF-CHG-SALES            PIC 9(4).
001230         10  UC-NUM-OF-CHG-RTNS             PIC 9(4).
001240         10  UC-NUM-OF-CHG-COM-RATE         PIC 9(4).
001250         10  UC-NUM-OF-REJECTIONS           PIC 9(4).
001260         10  UC-NUM-OF-TRANSACTIONS         PIC 9(4).
001270     05  FILLER REDEFINES UC-RECORD-CONTROL-TOTALS.
001280         10  UC-RECORD-COUNT                PIC 9(4)
001290             OCCURS 8 TIMES.
001300 01  HD-HEADING-LINE.
001310     05  FILLER                             PIC X(1).
001320     05  FILLER                             PIC X(13)
001330                                            VALUE 'UPDATE REPORT'.
001340 01  CH-COLUMN-HEADING-LINE.
001350     05  FILLER                             PIC X(1).
001360     05  FILLER                             PIC X(56)
001370                                            VALUE 'RECORD IMAGE'.
001380     05  FILLER                             PIC X(25)
001390                                            VALUE 'UPDATE ACTION'.
001400     05  FILLER                             PIC X(30)
001410                                            VALUE 'ERROR MESSAGE'.
001420 01  CH-COLUMN-HEADING-LINE-2.
001430     05  FILLER                             PIC X(1).
001440     05  FILLER                             PIC X(20) VALUE SPACES.
001450     05  FILLER                             PIC X(8) VALUE 'RECORDS'.
001460     05  FILLER                             PIC X(2) VALUE SPACES.
001470     05  FILLER                             PIC X(4) VALUE 'HASH'.
```

Program 7–3   *(continued)*

```
001480        05  FILLER                        PIC X(5) VALUE SPACES.
001490        05  FILLER                        PIC X(5) VALUE 'SALES'.
001500        05  FILLER                        PIC X(8) VALUE SPACES.
001510        05  FILLER                        PIC X(8) VALUE 'RETURNS'.
001520        05  FILLER                        PIC X(5) VALUE SPACES.
001530        05  FILLER                        PIC X(5) VALUE 'SALES'.
001540        05  FILLER                        PIC X(8) VALUE SPACES.
001550        05  FILLER                        PIC X(8) VALUE 'RETURNS'.
001560 01  DL-DETAIL-LINE.
001570        05  FILLER                        PIC X(1).
001580        05  DL-RECORD-IMAGE               PIC X(50).
001590        05  FILLER                        PIC X(6) VALUE SPACES.
001600        05  DL-UPDATE-ACTION              PIC X(25).
001610        05  DL-ERROR-MESSAGE              PIC X(30).
001620 01  EL-ERROR-LINE.
001630        05  FILLER                        PIC X(1).
001640        05  EL-ERROR-OPERATION            PIC X(30).
001650        05  FILLER                        PIC X(5) VALUE SPACES.
001660        05  EL-STATUS-ERROR               PIC X(2).
001670            88  SUCCESSFUL-COMPLETION     VALUE '00'.
001680            88  DUPLICATE-ALTERNATE-KEY   VALUE '02'.
001690            88  NO-RECORD-FOUND           VALUE '23'.
001700 01  TL-TOTAL-LINE-1.
001710        05  FILLER                        PIC X(1).
001720        05  TL-STUB-HEADING               PIC X(20).
001730        05  TL-TOT-RECORDS-STORED         PIC Z,ZZ9-.
001740        05  FILLER                        PIC X(2) VALUE SPACES.
001750        05  TL-TOT-HASH-NUMBER            PIC ZZZ,ZZ9-.
001760        05  FILLER                        PIC X(2) VALUE SPACES.
001770        05  TL-TOT-YTD-SALES              PIC ZZZ,ZZZ.99-.
001780        05  FILLER                        PIC X(2) VALUE SPACES.
001790        05  TL-TOT-YTD-SALES-RETURNS      PIC ZZZ,ZZZ.99-.
001800        05  FILLER                        PIC X(2) VALUE SPACES.
001810        05  TL-TOT-CURRENT-SALES          PIC ZZZ,ZZZ.99-.
001820        05  FILLER                        PIC X(2) VALUE SPACES.
001830        05  TL-TOT-CURRENT-RETURNS        PIC ZZZ,ZZZ.99-.
001840 01  TL-TOTAL-LINE-2.
001850        05  FILLER                        PIC X(1).
001860        05  TL-HEADING                    PIC X(30).
001870        05  TL-COUNT                      PIC Z,ZZ9.
001880*
001890 PROCEDURE DIVISION.
001900 DECLARATIVES.
001910 DUMMY-ERROR-PROCEDURE SECTION.
001920     USE AFTER ERROR PROCEDURE ON INDEXED-SALES-FILE.
001930 END DECLARATIVES.
001940 A000-UPDATE.
001950     PERFORM B100-OPEN-TO-UPDATE.
001960     PERFORM B200-INITIALIZE-VARIABLES.
001970     PERFORM B300-PRINT-HEADINGS.
001980     PERFORM Z100-READ-RECORD.
001990     PERFORM B500-UPDATE-RECORDS
002000         UNTIL END-OF-TRANSACTION-FILE.
002010     PERFORM B600-PROCESS-TOTALS.
002020     CLOSE INDEXED-SALES-FILE
002030           SALES-TRANSACTION-FILE
002040           SALES-CONTROL-FILE
002050           SALES-REPORT-FILE.
002060     STOP RUN.
002070 B100-OPEN-TO-UPDATE.
002080     OPEN INPUT  SALES-TRANSACTION-FILE
002090          I-O    INDEXED-SALES-FILE
002100                 SALES-CONTROL-FILE
002110          OUTPUT SALES-REPORT-FILE.
```

Program 7–3 *(continued)*

```
002120     IF NOT SUCCESSFUL-COMPLETION
002130         MOVE 'OPENING' TO EL-ERROR-OPERATION
002140         PERFORM Z300-ABORT-RUN
002150         STOP RUN.
002160 B200-INITIALIZE-VARIABLES.
002170     MOVE 'NO'   TO WS-EOF-INDICATOR.
002180     MOVE ZEROS TO WS-ACCUMULATORS
002190                   UC-RECORD-CONTROL-TOTALS.
002200 B300-PRINT-HEADINGS.
002210     WRITE SR-SALES-REPORT-LINE FROM HD-HEADING-LINE
002220         AFTER PAGE.
002230     WRITE SR-SALES-REPORT-LINE FROM CH-COLUMN-HEADING-LINE
002240         AFTER 1.
002250 B500-UPDATE-RECORDS.
002260     MOVE SPACES                  TO DL-DETAIL-LINE.
002270     MOVE ST-SALESPERSON-NUMBER TO IS-SALESPERSON-NUMBER.
002280     PERFORM Z200-READ-INDEXED-RECORD.
002290     IF ADDITION-OF-SALESPERSON
002300         PERFORM C300-POSSIBLE-ADDITION
002310     ELSE
002320         PERFORM C400-POSSIBLE-UPDATE.
002330     PERFORM C500-WRITE-DETAIL-LINE.
002340     PERFORM Z100-READ-RECORD.
002350 B600-PROCESS-TOTALS.
002360     READ SALES-CONTROL-FILE.
002370     PERFORM C700-PRINT-BEG-TOTALS.
002380     PERFORM C800-PRINT-CHG-TOTALS.
002390     PERFORM C900-PRINT-END-TOTALS.
002400     PERFORM C1000-PRINT-COUNT-SUMMARY
002410         VARYING UC-COUNT-SUB
002420         FROM 1 BY 1
002430         UNTIL UC-COUNT-SUB > 8.
002440     REWRITE SC-SALES-CONTROL-RECORD.
002450 C300-POSSIBLE-ADDITION.
002460     IF SUCCESSFUL-COMPLETION
002470         MOVE 'REJECTED'            TO DL-UPDATE-ACTION
002480         MOVE 'RECORD ALREADY EXISTS' TO DL-ERROR-MESSAGE
002490         ADD 1                      TO UC-NUM-OF-REJECTIONS
002500     ELSE
002510         PERFORM D200-ADD-RECORD.
002520 C400-POSSIBLE-UPDATE.
002530     IF NO-RECORD-FOUND
002540         MOVE 'REJECTED'        TO DL-UPDATE-ACTION
002550         MOVE 'RECORD NOT FOUND' TO DL-ERROR-MESSAGE
002560         ADD 1                  TO UC-NUM-OF-REJECTIONS
002570     ELSE
002580         PERFORM D400-UPDATE-RECORD.
002590 C500-WRITE-DETAIL-LINE.
002600     MOVE ST-SALES-TRANS-RECORD TO DL-RECORD-IMAGE.
002610     WRITE SR-SALES-REPORT-LINE FROM DL-DETAIL-LINE
002620         AFTER 1.
002630 C700-PRINT-BEG-TOTALS.
002640     WRITE SR-SALES-REPORT-LINE FROM CH-COLUMN-HEADING-LINE-2
002650         AFTER 2.
002660     MOVE 'BEGINNING - CONTROL'   TO TL-STUB-HEADING.
002670     MOVE SC-BEG-TOT-RECORDS-STORED TO TL-TOT-RECORDS-STORED.
002680     MOVE SC-BEG-TOT-HASH-NUMBER   TO TL-TOT-HASH-NUMBER.
002690     MOVE SC-BEG-TOT-YTD-SALES     TO TL-TOT-YTD-SALES.
002700     MOVE SC-BEG-TOT-YTD-SALES-RETURNS
002710         TO TL-TOT-YTD-SALES-RETURNS.
002720     MOVE SC-BEG-TOT-CURRENT-SALES  TO TL-TOT-CURRENT-SALES.
002730     MOVE SC-BEG-TOT-CURRENT-RETURNS
002740         TO TL-TOT-CURRENT-RETURNS.
002750     WRITE SR-SALES-REPORT-LINE FROM TL-TOTAL-LINE-1
```

Program 7–3 *(continued)*

```
002760        AFTER 2.
002770 C800-PRINT-CHG-TOTALS.
002780    MOVE 'PREVIOUS CHANGES'        TO TL-STUB-HEADING.
002790    MOVE SC-CHG-TOT-RECORDS-STORED TO TL-TOT-RECORDS-STORED.
002800    MOVE SC-CHG-TOT-HASH-NUMBER    TO TL-TOT-HASH-NUMBER.
002810    MOVE SC-CHG-TOT-YTD-SALES      TO TL-TOT-YTD-SALES.
002820    MOVE SC-CHG-TOT-YTD-SALES-RETURNS
002830        TO TL-TOT-YTD-SALES-RETURNS.
002840    MOVE SC-CHG-TOT-CURRENT-SALES    TO TL-TOT-CURRENT-SALES.
002850    MOVE SC-CHG-TOT-CURRENT-RETURNS TO TL-TOT-CURRENT-RETURNS.
002860    WRITE SR-SALES-REPORT-LINE FROM TL-TOTAL-LINE-1
002870        AFTER 2.
002880    MOVE 'CURRENT CHANGES'         TO TL-STUB-HEADING.
002890    MOVE WS-CHG-TOT-RECORDS-STORED TO TL-TOT-RECORDS-STORED.
002900    MOVE WS-CHG-TOT-HASH-NUMBER    TO TL-TOT-HASH-NUMBER.
002910    MOVE WS-CHG-YTD-SALES          TO TL-TOT-YTD-SALES.
002920    MOVE WS-CHG-CURRENT-SALES      TO TL-TOT-CURRENT-SALES.
002930    MOVE WS-CHG-YTD-SALES-RETURNS
002940        TO TL-TOT-YTD-SALES-RETURNS.
002950    MOVE WS-CHG-YTD-SALES-RETURNS  TO TL-TOT-YTD-SALES-RETURNS.
002960    MOVE WS-CHG-CURRENT-RETURNS    TO TL-TOT-CURRENT-RETURNS.
002970    WRITE SR-SALES-REPORT-LINE FROM TL-TOTAL-LINE-1
002980        AFTER 2.
002990 C900-PRINT-END-TOTALS.
003000    MOVE 'ENDING - CONTROL'        TO TL-STUB-HEADING.
003010    ADD WS-CHG-TOT-RECORDS-STORED TO SC-CHG-TOT-RECORDS-STORED
003020    ADD WS-CHG-TOT-HASH-NUMBER    TO SC-CHG-TOT-HASH-NUMBER.
003030    ADD WS-CHG-YTD-SALES          TO SC-CHG-TOT-YTD-SALES.
003040    ADD WS-CHG-CURRENT-SALES      TO SC-CHG-TOT-CURRENT-SALES.
003050    ADD WS-CHG-YTD-SALES-RETURNS TO SC-CHG-TOT-YTD-SALES-RETURNS.
003060    ADD WS-CHG-CURRENT-RETURNS    TO SC-CHG-TOT-CURRENT-RETURNS.
003070    ADD SC-BEG-TOT-RECORDS-STORED SC-CHG-TOT-RECORDS-STORED
003080        GIVING TL-TOT-RECORDS-STORED.
003090    ADD SC-BEG-TOT-HASH-NUMBER SC-CHG-TOT-HASH-NUMBER
003100        GIVING TL-TOT-HASH-NUMBER.
003110    ADD SC-BEG-TOT-YTD-SALES SC-CHG-TOT-YTD-SALES
003120        GIVING TL-TOT-YTD-SALES.
003130    ADD SC-BEG-TOT-YTD-SALES-RETURNS SC-CHG-TOT-YTD-SALES-RETURNS
003140        GIVING TL-TOT-YTD-SALES-RETURNS.
003150    ADD SC-BEG-TOT-CURRENT-SALES SC-CHG-TOT-CURRENT-SALES
003160        GIVING TL-TOT-CURRENT-SALES.
003170    ADD SC-BEG-TOT-CURRENT-RETURNS SC-CHG-TOT-CURRENT-RETURNS
003180        GIVING TL-TOT-CURRENT-RETURNS.
003190    WRITE SR-SALES-REPORT-LINE FROM TL-TOTAL-LINE-1
003200        AFTER 2.
003210 C1000-PRINT-COUNT-SUMMARY.
003220    MOVE UC-HEADING-LINE(UC-COUNT-SUB) TO TL-HEADING.
003230    MOVE UC-RECORD-COUNT(UC-COUNT-SUB) TO TL-COUNT.
003240    WRITE SR-SALES-REPORT-LINE FROM TL-TOTAL-LINE-2
003250        AFTER 2.
003260 D200-ADD-RECORD.
003270    ADD 1                         TO WS-CHG-TOT-RECORDS-STORED
003280                                     UC-NUM-OF-ADDS.
003290    ADD ST-HASH-NUMBER            TO WS-CHG-TOT-HASH-NUMBER.
003300    MOVE 'RECORD ADDED'           TO DL-UPDATE-ACTION.
003310    MOVE ST-SALESPERSON-NUMBER    TO IS-SALESPERSON-NUMBER.
003320    MOVE ST-LAST-NAME             TO IS-LAST-NAME.
003330    MOVE ST-FIRST-NAME            TO IS-FIRST-NAME.
003340    MOVE ZEROES                   TO IS-YEAR-TO-DATE-SALES
003350                                     IS-YEAR-TO-DATE-SALES-RETURNS
003360                                     IS-CURRENT-SALES
003370                                     IS-CURRENT-SALES-RETURNS.
003380    MOVE ST-COMMISSION-RATE       TO IS-COMMISSION-RATE.
003390    WRITE IS-INDEXED-SALES-RECORD.
```

Program 7–3 *(concluded)*

```
003400 D400-UPDATE-RECORD.
003410     IF DELETION-OF-SALESPERSON
003420         MOVE 'RECORD DELETED'    TO DL-UPDATE-ACTION
003430         SUBTRACT 1                FROM WS-CHG-TOT-RECORDS-STORED
003440         SUBTRACT ST-HASH-NUMBER FROM WS-CHG-TOT-HASH-NUMBER
003450         SUBTRACT IS-YEAR-TO-DATE-SALES FROM WS-CHG-YTD-SALES
003460         SUBTRACT IS-YEAR-TO-DATE-SALES-RETURNS
003470             FROM WS-CHG-YTD-SALES-RETURNS
003480         SUBTRACT IS-CURRENT-SALES FROM WS-CHG-CURRENT-SALES
003490         SUBTRACT IS-CURRENT-SALES-RETURNS
003500             FROM WS-CHG-CURRENT-RETURNS
003510         ADD 1 TO UC-NUM-OF-DELETES.
003520     IF NAME-CHANGE
003530         MOVE 'NAME CHANGED'      TO DL-UPDATE-ACTION
003540         MOVE ST-LAST-NAME        TO IS-LAST-NAME
003550         MOVE ST-FIRST-NAME       TO IS-FIRST-NAME
003560         ADD 1                    TO UC-NUM-OF-CHG-NAME.
003570     IF UPDATE-CURRENT-SALES
003580         MOVE 'YTD SALES UPDATED' TO DL-UPDATE-ACTION
003590         ADD ST-CURRENT-SALES     TO IS-YEAR-TO-DATE-SALES
003600                                     IS-CURRENT-SALES
003610                                     WS-CHG-YTD-SALES
003620                                     WS-CHG-CURRENT-SALES
003630         ADD 1                    TO UC-NUM-OF-CHG-SALES.
003640     IF UPDATE-CURRENT-SALES-RETURNS
003650         MOVE 'YTD SALES RETURNS UPDATED' TO DL-UPDATE-ACTION
003660         ADD ST-CURRENT-SALES-RETURNS
003670             TO IS-YEAR-TO-DATE-SALES-RETURNS
003680                IS-CURRENT-SALES-RETURNS
003690                WS-CHG-YTD-SALES-RETURNS
003700                WS-CHG-CURRENT-RETURNS
003710         ADD 1 TO UC-NUM-OF-CHG-RTNS.
003720     IF UPDATE-COMMISSION-RATE
003730         MOVE 'COMMISSION RATE UPDATED' TO DL-UPDATE-ACTION
003740         MOVE ST-COMMISSION-RATE       TO IS-COMMISSION-RATE
003750         ADD 1                         TO UC-NUM-OF-CHG-COM-RATE.
003760     IF DELETION-OF-SALESPERSON
003770         DELETE INDEXED-SALES-FILE RECORD
003780     ELSE
003790         REWRITE IS-INDEXED-SALES-RECORD.
003800     IF NOT SUCCESSFUL-COMPLETION
003810         IF NOT DUPLICATE-ALTERNATE-KEY
003820             DISPLAY EL-STATUS-ERROR
003830             MOVE 'UPDATING' TO EL-ERROR-OPERATION
003840             PERFORM Z300-ABORT-RUN
003850             STOP RUN.
003860 Z100-READ-RECORD.
003870     READ SALES-TRANSACTION-FILE
003880         AT END MOVE 'END' TO WS-EOF-INDICATOR.
003890     IF NOT END-OF-TRANSACTION-FILE
003900         ADD 1 TO UC-NUM-OF-TRANSACTIONS.
003910 Z200-READ-INDEXED-RECORD.
003920     READ INDEXED-SALES-FILE.
003930 Z300-ABORT-RUN.
003940     WRITE SR-SALES-REPORT-LINE FROM EL-ERROR-LINE
003950         AFTER 1.
003960     CLOSE INDEXED-SALES-FILE
003970           SALES-TRANSACTION-FILE
003980           SALES-REPORT-FILE.
```

Figure 7–19 *Sales Transactions Used for Random Update*

```
0020 DOUGLAS    BRENT                           05 1
0125 LISHER     JANET F.                           1
0243                                                2
0356                                                2
2485                                             25 6
0396 VOLSKI     CHRIS                              3
0401                         0075000               4
0479                                 0010000        5
0590 DUPREE     KELLY L.                           3
0635 HUNT       ROBERT                          10 1
0017                         0020000               4
0020                         0072500               4
2485                                 0005000        5
1867                                 0015000        5
1805                                                2
```

Discussion

First, notice the specification of the alternate keys in the SELECT statement for the sales file. This is necessary only because alternate keys have been previously built for the file. This would not be the case if alternate keys were not being used. Once alternate keys are built, all programs accessing that file (particularly update programs) must contain the specification of the alternate keys, when the alternate keys have a chance of being changed.

Next notice the logic in B500–UPDATE–RECORDS beginning at line 2250, which moves the ST–SALESPERSON–NUMBER to IS–SALESPERSON–NUMBER (the setting of the record pointer). This is followed by an attempted READ by the PERFORM statement, which performs Z200–READ–INDEXED–RECORD. If ADDITION–OF–SALESPERSON is true, C300–POSSIBLE–ADDITION is executed. In this module a test is then made to determine whether an addition is appropriate. An addition is not appropriate when a record already exists with the same primary key. Referring to the output in Figure 7–20, employees DOUGLAS, LISHER, and HUNT were processed by C300–POSSIBLE–ADDITION.

In B500–UPDATE–RECORD, if the transaction does not specify an addition, C400–POSSIBLE–UPDATE is performed. In this case one of the valid transaction codes (other than for an addition) is appropriate. These include deletes and all changes. If NO–RECORD–FOUND is true, an update is inappropriate, thus necessitating the test at line 2530. This occurred with employee DUPREE. All other employees either had changes to fields or were deleted.

Appropriate updates occur in D400–UPDATE–RECORD, including relevant control procedures. After one of the procedures is selected, the record is either deleted in line 3770 or rewritten in line 3790.

Notice lines 3800 through 3850, which allow for the possibility of an unexpected file status during detail processing. Also notice lines 2120 through 2150 and 3930 through 3980, which abort the program if an OPEN error occurs.

Figure 7–21 also lists the output of Program 7–2, the sequential reporting program, in primary key sequence after the file was updated. The reader will notice that the control totals are the same as when the identical sequential file was updated in Chapter 6.

Sequential Updating of Indexed Files

At the end of the month the previously updated indexed file should be sequentially updated to begin the file for a new month. This is a process similar to that done on sequential files as illustrated in Chapter 6. In the case of indexed files, ACCESS would be SEQUENTIAL and the file would be opened I–O. The appropriate updating

Figure 7–20   *Output from Program 7–3*

```
UPDATE REPORT
RECORD IMAGE                                        UPDATE ACTION              ERROR MESSAGE
0020 DOUGLAS     BRENT              05 1            RECORD ADDED
0125 LISHER      JANET F.              1            REJECTED                   RECORD ALREADY EXISTS
0243                                   2            RECORD DELETED
0356                                   2            RECORD DELETED
2485                               25 6            COMMISSION RATE UPDATED
0396 VOLSKI      CHRIS                 3            NAME CHANGED
0401                    0075000        4            YTD SALES UPDATED
0479                          0010000  5            YTD SALES RETURNS UPDATED
0590 DUPREE      KELLY L.              3            REJECTED                   RECORD NOT FOUND
0635 HUNT        ROBERT            10 1            REJECTED                   RECORD ALREADY EXISTS
0017                    0020000        4            YTD SALES UPDATED
0020                    0072500        4            YTD SALES UPDATED
2485                          0005000  5            YTD SALES RETURNS UPDATED
1867                          0015000  5            YTD SALES RETURNS UPDATED
1805                                   2            RECORD DELETED
```

	RECORDS	HASH	SALES	RETURNS	SALES	RETURNS
BEGINNING – CONTROL	30	40,130	23,386.40	6,882.67	.00	.00
PREVIOUS CHANGES	0	0	.00	.00	.00	.00
CURRENT CHANGES	2–	2,384–	673.77–	710.00–	1,675.00	300.00
ENDING – CONTROL	28	37,746	22,712.63	6,172.67	1,675.00	300.00
ADDITIONS	1					
DELETIONS	3					
NAME CHANGES	1					
YTD SALES CHANGES	3					
YTD RTNS CHANGES	3					
COM RATE CHANGES	1					
REJECTIONS	3					
TOTAL TRANSACTIONS	15					

would occur (moving zeros to current fields), and the record would be rewritten. Appropriate updating of any control files would also occur to begin a new month.

Multiple File Processing and Variable Length Records

It is quite common when recording transactions to access and update multiple files in the same program. For instance, when a credit sale of merchandise takes place, several files may be involved. The inventory file could be accessed to determine the price, and the inventory on hand could be reduced. The customer accounts receivable file could be updated to reflect current balance and then could compare the current balance to the credit limit. A sales file could be updated for subsequent analysis, and an employee file could be updated for subsequent payment of commission on sales. The general ledger may also be involved to record the results of the transaction to an income account and to the accounts receivable account. Needless to say, an update program or series of update programs may be quite complex in either a batch or online mode.

Updating Program Example

Statement of the Problem

To illustrate a multiple file update and to illustrate the use of variable length records with indexed files, three files will be involved. An employee sales file will be used

Figure 7–21 *Output from Program 7–2 after Update*

```
SALES REPORT - PRIMARY SEQUENCE
   17   PAYNE      MAX          1,187.00      56.73     200.00        .00   .05   02
   20   DOUGLAS    BRENT          725.00        .00     725.00        .00   .05   00
  125   LISHER     JANET F.       500.00        .00        .00        .00   .15   02
  396   VOLSKI     CHRIS          326.80      58.47        .00        .00   .08   02
  479   WETZEL     ROBERT D.    2,088.76     158.77        .00     100.00   .15   02
  529   PEACOCK    BARBARA        673.30     156.64        .00        .00   .08   00
  401   OWENS      GEORGE       1,112.20      39.57     750.00        .00   .09   00
  580   DUPREE     KELLY L.     3,578.88     275.82        .00        .00   .10   02
  635   HUNT       ROBERT         453.20     475.34        .00        .00   .10   02
  746   JACKSON    JASON          784.50      84.78        .00        .00   .15   02
  859   HUTCHENS   JEFF           576.30      48.57        .00        .00   .14   00
  927   BARCLAY    RICHARD      1,987.40     485.63        .00        .00   .11   00
 1001   DILL       JEFF           586.40     284.56        .00        .00   .20   02
 1132   UNLAND     KIM L.         475.64     395.85        .00        .00   .25   02
 1415   GOODMAN    EVE            645.42     238.47        .00        .00   .10   02
 1634   VAUGHN     SYLVIA A.      478.99     456.78        .00        .00   .20   02
 1856   LOVELAND   GEORGE         462.75     276.56        .00        .00   .10   02
 1867   STEWARD    KEVIN J.     1,150.00     325.00        .00     150.00   .15   00
 1938   DWYER      JOHN D.        231.75      40.00        .00        .00   .10   02
 2157   YOUNG      KAREN L.     1,123.59      35.75        .00        .00   .30   00
 2186   SMITH      DOUGLAS        183.45     377.58        .00        .00   .20   02
 2269   THOMPSON   LISA S.        500.00     100.00        .00        .00   .20   02
 2294   HERMAN     JACK           484.65      87.47        .00        .00   .05   02
 2395   MATNEY     DELORES        795.74     857.46        .00        .00   .05   02
 2341   ADAMS      ROBYN A.       231.75      40.00        .00        .00   .10   02
 2485   PHILLIPS   TRACY L.       500.00     150.00        .00      50.00   .25   00
 2487   HUME       LETA           483.53     284.37        .00        .00   .20   00
 2575   CROSS      CHERYL         385.63     382.50        .00        .00   .10   00

                      RECORDS  HASH      SALES     RETURNS    SALES    RETURNS

BEGINNING - CONTROL     30    40,130   23,386.40   6,882.67      .00       .00

NET CHANGE - CONTROL     2-    2,384-     673.77-    710.00-  1,675.00   300.00

ENDING - CONTROL        28    37,746   22,712.63   6,172.67  1,675.00   300.00

ENDING - ACTUAL         28    37,746   22,712.63   6,172.67  1,675.00   300.00
```

to accumulate sales and returns for subsequent analysis; an inventory file will be used to access the price and description of the item sold or returned; and an accounts receivable file will be used to keep track of the customer's balance. Additionally, detailed evidence of each transaction will be stored in the customer file so that

Figure 7–22 *Inventory File Layout*

```
The following records contain inventory price data and are
37 characters long.
The record layout is:

1–4    Item number (used as the primary key)
5–10   Item price per unit (i.e., $150)
11–37  Item description

========================================
1001015000SPREADSHEET SOFTWARE
1002002500BOX OF 10 FLOPPIES
10030032009 1/2 × 11 CONTINUOUS PAPER
1004005700STATIC MAT
1005003250PLASTIC FLOPPY HOLDER
1006001680ANTI-STATIC SPRAY
1007001250MAILING LABELS
1008057500COBOL COMPILER
1009230000HAL PC - 2 FLOPPIES
========================================
```

an itemized list of transactions can be provided to the customer when the customer is billed at the end of each billing cycle.

Input

One input to this program is an existing indexed salesperson file that is identical to the file used in Programs 7–1 through 7–3. The same updating procedures will be used.

The second file is an indexed inventory price file, the layout of which is shown in Figure 7–22. The inventory file will only be accessed; it will not be updated in this program.

The third file is an indexed customer file, the layout of which is shown in Figure 7–23. When this file was originally created, zeros were moved to the transaction

Figure 7–23   *Indexed Customer File*

These header records contain customer data and are 62 characters long. The record layout is:

1–2	Record type, CH = customer header
3–10	Record key
	3–6 Customer number
	7–10 Transaction number
11–30	Customer name
31–37	Beginning balance
38–44	Credit limit
45–51	Total amount of debits to account, this month
52–58	Total amount of credits to account, this month
59–62	Total number of transactions recorded, initially zero at the beginning of the month

```
=====================================================
CH10570000ABC CO.              0065075008000000000000000000000
CH10920000XYZ CO.              0010019089000000000000000000000
CH11590000HILLDEBRAND          0021975002000000000000000000000
CH13470000MASTER MECHANICS     0042400007500000000000000000000
CH15960000PLUMBERS UNION       0097800010000000000000000000000
CH16780000SEVEN ELEVEN         0027600010000000000000000000000
CH19900000TENTH STR. TEXACO    0005000001000000000000000000000
CH20030000BATTLEFIELD MALL     0090000020000000000000000000000
CH24170000MUMFORD              0102709011000000000000000000000
CH29230000SMSU                 0042250010000000000000000000000
CH30750000NHPG                 0150000019000000000000000000000
CH41390000SPRINGFIELD DINER    0010500008000000000000000000000
CH47650000EDWARDS CHEVROLET    0232011025000000000000000000000
CH49830000BUNTING TRASH        0458700050000000000000000000000
CH52170000WARDS                1000000200000000000000000000000
CH60820000BARCLAY PAINT        0010219009000000000000000000000
CH61530000ALLEN PLUMBING       0022975005000000000000000000000
CH61570000ACME MANUFACTURING   0055075010000000000000000000000
CH65470000JUNIOR'S DINER       0152400020000000000000000000000
=====================================================
```

The transaction records that will be stored in the customer file are 29 characters long. The record layout is:

1–2	Record type, CT = customer transaction
3–10	Record key
	3–6 Customer number
	7–10 Transaction number
11–17	Debit or credit amount
18	Transaction type
19–21	Quantity of transaction
22–25	Inventory item number sold or returned
26–29	Number of salesperson that handled the transaction

Example Only (no transactions exist at beginning of month)

```
=========================
CT10570001001500010021007 0125
=========================
```

number in the header record. Updates will be stored in the file, but any WRITE to the file requires a unique primary record key. The first transaction recorded will use not only the customer number but also the transaction number. For instance, ABC CO would have a header record which uses 10570000 as the primary key and the first transaction recorded for ABC would have 10570001 as the primary key. This will allow the storage of fixed-length records of two different lengths, one for the header record and one for the transaction record.

The transactions used as input to Program 7–4 are listed in Figure 7–24. The transaction file includes the customer number, salesperson number, and item number. Each of these values is used as a primary key to access each of the respective files.

Figure 7–24 *Transaction File for Multiple File Update*

The following records contain transaction data to concurrently update the sales and customer files. Each record is 20 characters long. The record layout is:

1–4	Customer number
6–9	Salesperson number
11–14	Item number
16–18	Quantity sold or returned
20	Transaction type
	4 = Current sale
	5 = Current sales return

```
================
1057 0017 1001 001 4
5216 2575 1001 002 4
4983 1634 1003 002 4
1596 2487 1008 001 5
6157 2186 1009 001 4
4983 2186 1009 002 4
4983 2186 1005 005 4
6547 1001 1007 010 4
1159 0017 1001 001 5
1092 0017 1003 011 4
================
```

Program

Program 7–4

```
000010 IDENTIFICATION DIVISION.
000020 PROGRAM-ID.    INDUPDT.
000030*··············································································
000040* PROGRAM EXAMPLE 7-4 CONCURRENT INDEXED RANDOM UPDATE              *
000050*··············································································
000060 ENVIRONMENT DIVISION.
000070 CONFIGURATION SECTION.
000080    SOURCE-COMPUTER.   IBM-4341.
000090    OBJECT-COMPUTER.   IBM-4341.
000100 INPUT-OUTPUT SECTION.
000110 FILE-CONTROL.
000120    SELECT INDEXED-SALES-FILE
000130       ASSIGN TO SYS042-DA-3375-SALES
000140       ORGANIZATION IS INDEXED
000150       ACCESS IS RANDOM
000160       RECORD KEY IS IS-SALESPERSON-NUMBER
000170       FILE STATUS IS EL-SALES-ERROR.
000180    SELECT CUSTOMER-INDEXED-FILE
000190       ASSIGN TO SYS041-DA-3375-CUST
000200       ORGANIZATION IS INDEXED
000210       ACCESS IS RANDOM
000220       RECORD KEY IS CH-RECORD-KEY
```

Program 7–4   *(continued)*

```
000230        FILE STATUS IS EL-CUSTOMER-ERROR.
000240    SELECT INVENTORY-INDEXED-FILE
000250        ASSIGN TO SYS043-DA-3375-INVEN
000260        ORGANIZATION IS INDEXED
000270        ACCESS IS RANDOM
000280        RECORD KEY IS II-ITEM-NUMBER
000290        FILE STATUS IS EL-INVENTORY-ERROR.
000300    SELECT SALES-REPORT-FILE
000310        ASSIGN TO SYS018-UR-3203-S.
000320    SELECT SALES-TRANSACTION-FILE
000330        ASSIGN TO SYS016-UR-2501-S.
000340*
000350 DATA DIVISION.
000360 FILE SECTION.
000370 FD  INDEXED-SALES-FILE
000380     RECORD CONTAINS 55 CHARACTERS
000390     LABEL RECORDS STANDARD.
000400 01  IS-INDEXED-SALES-RECORD.
000410     05  IS-SALESPERSON-NUMBER        PIC X(4).
000420     05  IS-LAST-NAME                 PIC X(11).
000430     05  IS-FIRST-NAME                PIC X(10).
000440     05  IS-YEAR-TO-DATE-SALES        PIC 9(5)V99.
000450     05  IS-YEAR-TO-DATE-SALES-RETURNS PIC 9(5)V99.
000460     05  IS-CURRENT-SALES             PIC 9(5)V99.
000470     05  IS-CURRENT-SALES-RETURNS     PIC 9(5)V99.
000480     05  IS-COMMISSION-RATE           PIC V99.
000490 FD  CUSTOMER-INDEXED-FILE
000500     RECORD CONTAINS 29 TO 62 CHARACTERS
000510     LABEL RECORDS ARE STANDARD.
000520 01  CUSTOMER-HEADER-RECORD.
000530     05  CH-RECORD-TYPE               PIC X(2).
000540         88  CUSTOMER-HEADER          VALUE 'CH'.
000550     05  CH-RECORD-KEY.
000560         10  CH-CUSTOMER-NUMBER        PIC X(4).
000570         10  CH-TRANSACTION-NUMBER     PIC 9(4).
000580     05  CH-CUSTOMER-NAME             PIC X(20).
000590     05  CH-BEGINNING-BALANCE         PIC S9(5)V99.
000600     05  CH-CREDIT-LIMIT              PIC 9(5)V99.
000610     05  CH-CURRENT-DEBITS            PIC 9(5)V99.
000620     05  CH-CURRENT-CREDITS           PIC 9(5)V99.
000630     05  CH-NO-OF-DEBITS-OR-CREDITS   PIC 9(4).
000640 01  CUSTOMER-TRANSACTION-RECORD.
000650     05  CT-RECORD-TYPE               PIC X(2).
000660         88  CUSTOMER-TRANSACTION     VALUE 'CT'.
000670     05  CT-RECORD-KEY.
000680         10  CT-CUSTOMER-NUMBER        PIC X(4).
000690         10  CT-TRANSACTION-NUMBER     PIC 9(4).
000700     05  CT-DEBIT-OR-CREDIT-AMOUNT    PIC 9(5)V99.
000710     05  CT-TRANSACTION-TYPE          PIC X(1).
000720     05  CT-QUANTITY-INVOLVED         PIC 9(3).
000730     05  CT-ITEM-NUMBER               PIC X(4).
000740     05  CT-SALESPERSON-NUMBER        PIC X(4).
000750 FD  INVENTORY-INDEXED-FILE
000760     RECORD CONTAINS 37 CHARACTERS
000770     LABEL RECORDS ARE STANDARD.
000780 01  INVENTORY-INDEXED-RECORD.
000790     05  II-ITEM-NUMBER               PIC X(4).
000800     05  II-PRICE-OF-ITEM             PIC 9(4)V99.
000810     05  II-ITEM-DESCRIPTION          PIC X(27).
000820 FD  SALES-TRANSACTION-FILE
000830     RECORD CONTAINS 20 CHARACTERS
000840     LABEL RECORDS ARE STANDARD.
000850 01  TR-TRANSACTION-RECORD.
000860     05  TR-CUSTOMER-NUMBER           PIC X(4).
```

Program 7–4 *(continued)*

```
000870      05    FILLER                      PIC X(1).
000880      05    TR-SALESPERSON-NUMBER       PIC X(4).
000890      05    FILLER                      PIC X(1).
000900      05    TR-ITEM-NUMBER              PIC X(4).
000910      05    FILLER                      PIC X(1).
000920      05    TR-QUANTITY-INVOLVED        PIC 9(3).
000930      05    FILLER                      PIC X(1).
000940      05    TR-TRANSACTION-TYPE         PIC X(1).
000950          88  UPDATE-CURRENT-SALES         VALUE '4'.
000960          88  UPDATE-CURRENT-SALES-RETURNS VALUE '5'.
000970 FD  SALES-REPORT-FILE
000980      RECORD CONTAINS 133 CHARACTERS
000990      LABEL RECORDS ARE OMITTED.
001000 01  SR-SALES-REPORT-LINE               PIC X(133).
001010*
001020 WORKING-STORAGE SECTION.
001030 01  WS-WORK-AREAS.
001040      05    WS-EOF-INDICATOR            PIC X(3).
001050          88  END-OF-TRANSACTION-FILE      VALUE 'END'.
001060      05    WS-TRANSACTION-AMOUNT       PIC 9(6)V99.
001070 01  HD-HEADING-LINE.
001080      05    FILLER                      PIC X(1).
001090      05    FILLER                      PIC X(13)
001100                                        VALUE 'UPDATE REPORT'.
001110 01  CH-COLUMN-HEADING-LINE.
001120      05    FILLER                      PIC X(1).
001130      05    FILLER                      PIC X(56)
001140                                        VALUE 'RECORD IMAGE'.
001150      05    FILLER                      PIC X(25)
001160                                        VALUE 'UPDATE ACTION'.
001170      05    FILLER                      PIC X(30)
001180                                        VALUE 'ERROR MESSAGE'.
001190 01  DL-DETAIL-LINE.
001200      05    FILLER                      PIC X(1).
001210      05    DL-RECORD-IMAGE             PIC X(50).
001220      05    FILLER                      PIC X(6) VALUE SPACES.
001230      05    DL-UPDATE-ACTION            PIC X(25).
001240      05    DL-ERROR-MESSAGE            PIC X(30).
001250 01  EL-ERROR-LINE.
001260      05    FILLER                      PIC X(1).
001270      05    EL-ERROR-OPERATION          PIC X(30).
001280      05    FILLER                      PIC X(5) VALUE SPACES.
001290      05    FILLER                      PIC X(5) VALUE 'SALES'.
001300      05    FILLER                      PIC X(5) VALUE SPACES.
001310      05    EL-SALES-ERROR              PIC X(2).
001320          88  SUCCESSFUL-SALES-COMPLETION VALUE '00'.
001330          88  NO-SALES-RECORD-FOUND       VALUE '23'.
001340      05    FILLER                      PIC X(5) VALUE SPACES.
001350      05    FILLER                      PIC X(5) VALUE 'CUST'.
001360      05    FILLER                      PIC X(5) VALUE SPACES.
001370      05    EL-CUSTOMER-ERROR           PIC X(2).
001380          88  SUCCESSFUL-CUSTOMER-COMPLETION VALUE '00'.
001390          88  NO-CUSTOMER-RECORD-FOUND    VALUE '23'.
001400      05    FILLER                      PIC X(5) VALUE SPACES.
001410      05    FILLER                      PIC X(5) VALUE 'INVEN'.
001420      05    FILLER                      PIC X(5) VALUE SPACES.
001430      05    EL-INVENTORY-ERROR          PIC X(2).
001440          88  SUCCESSFUL-INVEN-COMPLETION VALUE '00'.
001450          88  NO-INVENTORY-RECORD-FOUND   VALUE '23'.
001460*
001470 PROCEDURE DIVISION.
001480 DECLARATIVES.
001490 DUMMY-SALES-ERROR SECTION.
001500      USE AFTER ERROR PROCEDURE ON INDEXED-SALES-FILE.
```

Program 7–4 *(continued)*

```
001510 DUMMY-CUSTOMER-ERROR SECTION.
001520     USE AFTER ERROR PROCEDURE ON CUSTOMER-INDEXED-FILE.
001530 DUMMY-INVENTORY-ERROR SECTION.
001540     USE AFTER ERROR PROCEDURE ON INVENTORY-INDEXED-FILE.
001550 END DECLARATIVES.
001560 A000-UPDATE.
001570     PERFORM B100-OPEN-TO-UPDATE.
001580     PERFORM B200-INITIALIZE-VARIABLES.
001590     PERFORM B300-PRINT-HEADINGS.
001600     PERFORM Z100-READ-TRANSACTION-RECORD.
001610     PERFORM B500-UPDATE-RECORDS
001620         UNTIL END-OF-TRANSACTION-FILE.
001630     CLOSE INDEXED-SALES-FILE
001640         CUSTOMER-INDEXED-FILE
001650         INVENTORY-INDEXED-FILE
001660         SALES-TRANSACTION-FILE
001670         SALES-REPORT-FILE.
001680     STOP RUN.
001690 B100-OPEN-TO-UPDATE.
001700     OPEN INPUT  SALES-TRANSACTION-FILE
001710         OUTPUT SALES-REPORT-FILE
001720         I-0    INDEXED-SALES-FILE
001730                CUSTOMER-INDEXED-FILE
001740                INVENTORY-INDEXED-FILE.
001750     IF NOT SUCCESSFUL-SALES-COMPLETION
001760         OR NOT SUCCESSFUL-CUSTOMER-COMPLETION
001770         OR NOT SUCCESSFUL-INVEN-COMPLETION
001780             MOVE 'OPENING ERROR' TO EL-ERROR-OPERATION
001790             PERFORM Z200-ABORT-RUN
001800                 STOP RUN.
001810 B200-INITIALIZE-VARIABLES.
001820     MOVE 'NO'  TO WS-EOF-INDICATOR.
001830 B300-PRINT-HEADINGS.
001840     WRITE SR-SALES-REPORT-LINE FROM HD-HEADING-LINE
001850         AFTER PAGE.
001860     WRITE SR-SALES-REPORT-LINE FROM CH-COLUMN-HEADING-LINE
001870         AFTER 1.
001880 B500-UPDATE-RECORDS.
001890     MOVE SPACES            TO DL-DETAIL-LINE.
001900     PERFORM Z300-READ-INDEXED-RECORDS.
001910     IF NO-SALES-RECORD-FOUND
001920         OR NO-CUSTOMER-RECORD-FOUND
001930         OR NO-INVENTORY-RECORD-FOUND
001940             MOVE 'REJECTED'         TO DL-UPDATE-ACTION
001950             MOVE 'RECORD NOT FOUND' TO EL-ERROR-OPERATION
001960                                        DL-ERROR-MESSAGE
001970             WRITE SR-SALES-REPORT-LINE FROM EL-ERROR-LINE
001980                 AFTER 1
001990         ELSE
002000             PERFORM C400-UPDATE-RECORD.
002010     PERFORM C500-WRITE-DETAIL-LINE.
002020     PERFORM Z100-READ-TRANSACTION-RECORD.
002030 C400-UPDATE-RECORD.
002040     COMPUTE WS-TRANSACTION-AMOUNT = TR-QUANTITY-INVOLVED *
002050                                      II-PRICE-OF-ITEM.
002060     IF UPDATE-CURRENT-SALES
002070         PERFORM D200-UPDATE-CURRENT-SALES.
002080     IF UPDATE-CURRENT-SALES-RETURNS
002090         PERFORM D300-UPDATE-CURRENT-RETURNS.
002100 C500-WRITE-DETAIL-LINE.
002110     MOVE TR-TRANSACTION-RECORD TO DL-RECORD-IMAGE.
002120     WRITE SR-SALES-REPORT-LINE FROM DL-DETAIL-LINE
002130         AFTER 1.
002140 D200-UPDATE-CURRENT-SALES.
```

Program 7–4 *(concluded)*

```
002150      MOVE 'SALES RECORDED'      TO DL-UPDATE-ACTION.
002160      ADD WS-TRANSACTION-AMOUNT  TO IS-YEAR-TO-DATE-SALES
002170                                    IS-CURRENT-SALES
002180                                    CH-CURRENT-DEBITS.
002190      REWRITE IS-INDEXED-SALES-RECORD.
002200      ADD 1                      TO CH-NO-OF-DEBITS-OR-CREDITS.
002210      REWRITE CUSTOMER-HEADER-RECORD.
002220      MOVE 'CT'                  TO CT-RECORD-TYPE.
002230      MOVE CH-NO-OF-DEBITS-OR-CREDITS TO CH-TRANSACTION-NUMBER.
002240      READ CUSTOMER-INDEXED-FILE.
002250      IF NO-CUSTOMER-RECORD-FOUND
002260          MOVE WS-TRANSACTION-AMOUNT TO CT-DEBIT-OR-CREDIT-AMOUNT
002270          MOVE TR-TRANSACTION-TYPE   TO CT-TRANSACTION-TYPE
002280          MOVE TR-QUANTITY-INVOLVED  TO CT-QUANTITY-INVOLVED
002290          MOVE TR-ITEM-NUMBER        TO CT-ITEM-NUMBER
002300          MOVE IS-SALESPERSON-NUMBER TO CT-SALESPERSON-NUMBER
002310          WRITE CUSTOMER-TRANSACTION-RECORD
002320      ELSE
002330          MOVE 'TRANSACTION NOT WRITTEN' TO DL-ERROR-MESSAGE.
002340 D300-UPDATE-CURRENT-RETURNS.
002350      MOVE 'RETURNS RECORDED'    TO DL-UPDATE-ACTION.
002360      ADD WS-TRANSACTION-AMOUNT  TO IS-YEAR-TO-DATE-SALES-RETURNS
002370                                    IS-CURRENT-SALES-RETURNS
002380                                    CH-CURRENT-CREDITS.
002390      REWRITE IS-INDEXED-SALES-RECORD.
002400      ADD 1                      TO CH-NO-OF-DEBITS-OR-CREDITS.
002410      REWRITE CUSTOMER-HEADER-RECORD.
002420      MOVE 'CT'                  TO CT-RECORD-TYPE.
002430      MOVE CH-NO-OF-DEBITS-OR-CREDITS TO CH-TRANSACTION-NUMBER.
002440      READ CUSTOMER-INDEXED-FILE.
002450      IF NO-CUSTOMER-RECORD-FOUND
002460          MOVE WS-TRANSACTION-AMOUNT TO CT-DEBIT-OR-CREDIT-AMOUNT
002470          MOVE TR-TRANSACTION-TYPE   TO CT-TRANSACTION-TYPE
002480          MOVE TR-QUANTITY-INVOLVED  TO CT-QUANTITY-INVOLVED
002490          MOVE TR-ITEM-NUMBER        TO CT-ITEM-NUMBER
002500          MOVE IS-SALESPERSON-NUMBER TO CT-SALESPERSON-NUMBER
002510          WRITE CUSTOMER-TRANSACTION-RECORD
002520      ELSE
002530          MOVE 'TRANSACTION NOT WRITTEN' TO DL-ERROR-MESSAGE.
002540 Z100-READ-TRANSACTION-RECORD.
002550      READ SALES-TRANSACTION-FILE
002560          AT END MOVE 'END' TO WS-EOF-INDICATOR.
002570 Z200-ABORT-RUN.
002580      WRITE SR-SALES-REPORT-LINE FROM EL-ERROR-LINE
002590          AFTER 1.
002600      CLOSE INDEXED-SALES-FILE
002610            CUSTOMER-INDEXED-FILE
002620            INVENTORY-INDEXED-FILE
002630            SALES-TRANSACTION-FILE
002640            SALES-REPORT-FILE.
002650 Z300-READ-INDEXED-RECORDS.
002660      MOVE TR-SALESPERSON-NUMBER TO IS-SALESPERSON-NUMBER.
002670      MOVE TR-CUSTOMER-NUMBER    TO CH-CUSTOMER-NUMBER.
002680      MOVE ZEROS                 TO CH-TRANSACTION-NUMBER.
002690      MOVE TR-ITEM-NUMBER        TO II-ITEM-NUMBER.
002700      READ INDEXED-SALES-FILE.
002710      READ CUSTOMER-INDEXED-FILE.
002720      READ INVENTORY-INDEXED-FILE.
```

Discussion

The reader will notice that no control totals of any kind are included in this program. This has been done only to allow concentration on the multiple file logic. It should not be construed to mean that control should be eliminated. Quite the contrary is true. When updating multiple files, the control process is just more complex.

In Program 7–4, notice the SELECT statements for each of the files. Each file can be accessed by its respective primary key (no alternates exist for any file, in this case), and each file has been specified as having a separate FILE STATUS. The FILE STATUS values, defined in EL–ERROR–LINE, are tested after the files are opened in lines 1750 through 1770. If any of the files are not available, program termination occurs immediately and since the EL–ERROR–LINE separates each FILE STATUS, the file or files that are causing the problem will be easily detected.

After a priming READ for the SALES–TRANSACTION–FILE, B500–UPDATE–RECORDS is performed. At line 1900, Z300–READ–INDEXED–RECORDS is performed, which causes each of the three keys to be set and a READ to be attempted in lines 2650 through 2720. Note that ZEROS are moved to CH–TRANSACTION–NUMBER so that the header record is appropriately read and not an existing transaction record. If one or more attempts to read a record from each file is not successful an error is printed in lines 1910 through 1980. Referring to the output in Figure 7–25, this happened on the second transaction. That transaction was rejected because the customer record with a key of 52160000 could not be found. Notice the 23 in the printing of EL–ERROR–LINE, which indicates that no record was found in the customer file.

If a record from each file is successfully read, C400–UPDATE–RECORD is performed. In this module, the WS–TRANSACTION–AMOUNT is calculated by multiplying the TR–QUANTITY–INVOLVED from the transaction record by the II–PRICE–OF–TEM obtained from the inventory record just input. This amount is used later to update both the sales file and the customer file.

Assuming a sale, follow the logic to D200–UPDATE–CURRENT–SALES. The transaction amount is added to both year-to-date and current sales in the sales file and to the current debits in the customer file, providing appropriate accumulations in all three fields. The sales record is then rewritten.

Before rewriting the customer header record, the CH–NO–OF–DEBITS–OR–CREDITS is incremented by 1 to indicate that one more transaction for this customer is going to be recorded. CH–NO–OF–DEBITS–OR–CREDITS is then moved to CH–TRANSACTION–NUMBER, and a READ is attempted. Remember, this would make the CH–RECORD–KEY for customer 1057 be equal to 10570001 for the first transaction of the month, 10570002 for second transaction, and so on. The reason for the attempted READ is to ensure that no record exists for that record key.

If the READ is successful, it would indicate that a transaction with that key already exists and would have to be rejected. If no record exists with that particular key, the transaction record to be stored in the customer file is then created and written at line 2310. D300–UPDATE–CURRENT–RETURNS follows parallel logic.

Figure 7–25 *Output from Program 7–4*

```
UPDATE REPORT
RECORD IMAGE                                UPDATE ACTION        ERROR MESSAGE
1057 0017 1001 001 4                        SALES RECORDED
RECORD NOT FOUND           SALES   00   CUST    .23   INVEN   00
5216 2575 1001 002 4                        REJECTED             RECORD NOT FOUND
4983 1634 1003 002 4                        SALES RECORDED
1596 2487 1008 001 5                        RETURNS RECORDED
6157 2186 1009 001 4                        SALES RECORDED
4983 2186 1009 002 4                        SALES RECORDED
4983 2186 1005 005 4                        SALES RECORDED
6547 1001 1007 010 4                        SALES RECORDED
1159 0017 1001 001 5                        RETURNS RECORDED
1092 0017 1003 011 4                        SALES RECORDED
```

Reporting Program Example

To assist the programmer in following the results of Program 7–4, Program 7–5 illustrates the concept of multiple file reporting. In this example, a listing is to be produced of the entire customer file, including an itemized list of all transactions. This should illustrate that the previous update program worked correctly. Additionally, the inventory file will be accessed randomly to obtain the price and the item description, and the sales file will be accessed to obtain the name of the salesperson who completed the transaction.

Program

Program 7–5

```
000010 IDENTIFICATION DIVISION.
000020 PROGRAM-ID.     INDREPT.
000030*·······················································
000040* PROGRAM EXAMPLE 7-5 MULTIPLE FILE REPORT                  *
000050*·······················································
000060 ENVIRONMENT DIVISION.
000070 CONFIGURATION SECTION.
000080    SOURCE-COMPUTER.   IBM-4341.
000090    OBJECT-COMPUTER.   IBM-4341.
000100 INPUT-OUTPUT SECTION.
000110 FILE-CONTROL.
000120    SELECT INDEXED-SALES-FILE
000130        ASSIGN TO SYS042-DA-3375-SALES
000140        ORGANIZATION IS INDEXED
000150        ACCESS IS RANDOM
000160        RECORD KEY IS IS-SALESPERSON-NUMBER
000170        FILE STATUS IS EL-SALES-ERROR.
000180    SELECT CUSTOMER-INDEXED-FILE
000190        ASSIGN TO SYS041-DA-3375-CUST
000200        ORGANIZATION IS INDEXED
000210        ACCESS IS SEQUENTIAL
000220        RECORD KEY IS CH-RECORD-KEY
000230        FILE STATUS IS EL-CUSTOMER-ERROR.
000240    SELECT INVENTORY-INDEXED-FILE
000250        ASSIGN TO SYS043-DA-3375-INVEN
000260        ORGANIZATION IS INDEXED
000270        ACCESS IS RANDOM
000280        RECORD KEY IS II-ITEM-NUMBER
000290        FILE STATUS IS EL-INVENTORY-ERROR.
000300    SELECT CUSTOMER-REPORT-FILE
000310        ASSIGN TO SYS018-UR-3203-S.
000320*
000330 DATA DIVISION.
000340 FILE SECTION.
000350 FD  INDEXED-SALES-FILE
000360     RECORD CONTAINS 55 CHARACTERS
000370     LABEL RECORDS STANDARD.
000380 01  IS-INDEXED-SALES-RECORD.
000390     05  IS-SALESPERSON-NUMBER          PIC X(4).
000400     05  IS-SALESPERSON-NAME.
000410         10  IS-LAST-NAME               PIC X(11).
000420         10  IS-FIRST-NAME              PIC X(10).
000430     05  IS-YEAR-TO-DATE-SALES          PIC 9(5)V99.
000440     05  IS-YEAR-TO-DATE-SALES-RETURNS  PIC 9(5)V99.
000450     05  IS-CURRENT-SALES               PIC 9(5)V99.
000460     05  IS-CURRENT-SALES-RETURNS       PIC 9(5)V99.
000470     05  IS-COMMISSION-RATE             PIC V99.
000480 FD  CUSTOMER-INDEXED-FILE
000490     RECORD CONTAINS 29 TO 62 CHARACTERS
000500     LABEL RECORDS ARE STANDARD.
000510 01  CUSTOMER-HEADER-RECORD.
```

Program 7–5 *(continued)*

```
000520      05   CH-RECORD-TYPE                        PIC X(2).
000530           88   CUSTOMER-HEADER                  VALUE 'CH'.
000540      05   CH-RECORD-KEY.
000550           10   CH-CUSTOMER-NUMBER               PIC X(4).
000560           10   CH-TRANSACTION-NUMBER            PIC 9(4).
000570      05   CH-CUSTOMER-NAME                      PIC X(20).
000580      05   CH-BEGINNING-BALANCE                  PIC S9(5)V99.
000590      05   CH-CREDIT-LIMIT                       PIC 9(5)V99.
000600      05   CH-CURRENT-DEBITS                     PIC 9(5)V99.
000610      05   CH-CURRENT-CREDITS                    PIC 9(5)V99.
000620      05   CH-NO-OF-DEBITS-OR-CREDITS            PIC 9(4).
000630 01  CUSTOMER-TRANSACTION-RECORD.
000640      05   CT-RECORD-TYPE                        PIC X(2).
000650           88   CUSTOMER-TRANSACTION             VALUE 'CT'.
000660      05   CT-RECORD-KEY.
000670           10   CT-CUSTOMER-NUMBER               PIC X(4).
000680           10   CT-TRANSACTION-NUMBER            PIC 9(4).
000690      05   CT-DEBIT-OR-CREDIT-AMOUNT             PIC 9(5)V99.
000700      05   CT-TRANSACTION-TYPE                   PIC X(1).
000710           88   CURRENT-SALE                     VALUE '4'.
000720           88   CURRENT-SALE-RETURN              VALUE '5'.
000730      05   CT-QUANTITY-INVOLVED                  PIC 9(3).
000740      05   CT-ITEM-NUMBER                        PIC X(4).
000750      05   CT-SALESPERSON-NUMBER                 PIC X(4).
000760 FD  INVENTORY-INDEXED-FILE
000770     RECORD CONTAINS 37 CHARACTERS
000780     LABEL RECORDS ARE STANDARD.
000790 01  INVENTORY-INDEXED-RECORD.
000800      05   II-ITEM-NUMBER                        PIC X(4).
000810      05   II-PRICE-OF-ITEM                      PIC 9(4)V99.
000820      05   II-ITEM-DESCRIPTION                   PIC X(27).
000830 FD  CUSTOMER-REPORT-FILE
000840     RECORD CONTAINS 133 CHARACTERS
000850     LABEL RECORDS ARE OMITTED.
000860 01  CR-CUSTOMER-REPORT-LINE                     PIC X(133).
000870*
000880 WORKING-STORAGE SECTION.
000890 01  WS-WORK-AREAS.
000900      05   WS-TRANSACTION-AMOUNT                 PIC 9(6)V99.
000910 01  HD-HEADING-LINE.
000920      05   FILLER                                PIC X(1).
000930      05   FILLER                                PIC X(15)
000940                                                 VALUE 'CUSTOMER REPORT'.
000950 01  CH-COLUMN-HEADING-LINE.
000960      05   FILLER                          PIC X(1).
000970      05   FILLER                          PIC X(8) VALUE 'NUMBER'.
000980      05   FILLER                          PIC X(24) VALUE 'NAME'.
000990      05   FILLER                          PIC X(11) VALUE 'BEGINNING'.
001000      05   FILLER                          PIC X(4) VALUE SPACES.
001010      05   FILLER                          PIC X(10) VALUE 'CREDIT'.
001020      05   FILLER                          PIC X(4) VALUE SPACES.
001030      05   FILLER                          PIC X(10) VALUE 'DEBITS'.
001040      05   FILLER                          PIC X(4) VALUE SPACES.
001050      05   FILLER                          PIC X(10) VALUE 'CREDITS'.
001060      05   FILLER                          PIC X(4) VALUE SPACES.
001070      05   FILLER                          PIC X(5) VALUE 'TRANS'.
001080      05   FILLER                          PIC X(4) VALUE SPACES.
001090      05   FILLER                          PIC X(11) VALUE 'ENDING'.
001100 01  DL-DETAIL-LINE-HEADER.
001110      05   FILLER                                PIC X(1).
001120      05   DL-CUSTOMER-NUMBER                    PIC X(4).
001130      05   FILLER                                PIC X(4) VALUE SPACES.
001140      05   DL-CUSTOMER-NAME                      PIC X(20).
001150      05   FILLER                                PIC X(4) VALUE SPACES.
```

Program 7–5   *(continued)*

```
001160        05   DL-BEGINNING-BALANCE              PIC $ZZ,ZZZ.99-.
001170        05   FILLER                           PIC X(4) VALUE SPACES.
001180        05   DL-CREDIT-LIMIT                   PIC $ZZ,ZZZ.99.
001190        05   FILLER                           PIC X(4) VALUE SPACES.
001200        05   DL-CURRENT-DEBITS                 PIC $ZZ,ZZZ.99.
001210        05   FILLER                           PIC X(4) VALUE SPACES.
001220        05   DL-CURRENT-CREDITS                PIC $ZZ,ZZZ.99.
001230        05   FILLER                           PIC X(4) VALUE SPACES.
001240        05   DL-NO-OF-DEBITS-OR-CREDITS        PIC Z,ZZ9.
001250        05   FILLER                           PIC X(4) VALUE SPACES.
001260        05   DL-ENDING-BALANCE                 PIC $ZZ,ZZZ.99-.
001270 01   DL-DETAIL-LINE-TRANSACTION.
001280        05   FILLER                           PIC X(1).
001290        05   DL-DEBIT-OR-CREDIT-AMOUNT         PIC $ZZ,ZZZ.99-.
001300        05   FILLER                           PIC X(4) VALUE SPACES.
001310        05   DL-QUANTITY-INVOLVED              PIC ZZ9.
001320        05   FILLER                           PIC X(4) VALUE SPACES.
001330        05   DL-PRICE-OF-ITEM                  PIC $Z,ZZ9.99.
001340        05   FILLER                           PIC X(4) VALUE SPACES.
001350        05   DL-TRANSACTION-TYPE               PIC X(6).
001360        05   FILLER                           PIC X(4) VALUE SPACES.
001370        05   DL-ITEM-DESCRIPTION               PIC X(27).
001380        05   FILLER                           PIC X(4) VALUE SPACES.
001390        05   DL-SALESPERSON-NAME               PIC X(20).
001400 01   EL-ERROR-LINE.
001410        05   FILLER                           PIC X(1).
001420        05   EL-ERROR-OPERATION                PIC X(30).
001430        05   FILLER                           PIC X(5) VALUE SPACES.
001440        05   FILLER                           PIC X(5) VALUE 'SALES'.
001450        05   FILLER                           PIC X(5) VALUE SPACES.
001460        05   EL-SALES-ERROR                    PIC X(2).
001470            88   SUCCESSFUL-SALES-COMPLETION VALUE '00'.
001480            88   NO-SALES-RECORD-FOUND        VALUE '23'.
001490        05   FILLER                           PIC X(5) VALUE SPACES.
001500        05   FILLER                           PIC X(5) VALUE 'CUST'.
001510        05   FILLER                           PIC X(5) VALUE SPACES.
001520        05   EL-CUSTOMER-ERROR                 PIC X(2).
001530            88   SUCCESSFUL-CUSTOMER-COMPLETION VALUE '00'.
001540            88   END-OF-CUSTOMER-FILE          VALUE '10'.
001550            88   NO-CUSTOMER-RECORD-FOUND      VALUE '23'.
001560        05   FILLER                           PIC X(5) VALUE SPACES.
001570        05   FILLER                           PIC X(5) VALUE 'INVEN'.
001580        05   FILLER                           PIC X(5) VALUE SPACES.
001590        05   EL-INVENTORY-ERROR                PIC X(2).
001600            88   SUCCESSFUL-INVEN-COMPLETION VALUE '00'.
001610            88   NO-INVENTORY-RECORD-FOUND   VALUE '23'.
001620*
001630 PROCEDURE DIVISION.
001640 DECLARATIVES.
001650 DUMMY-SALES-ERROR SECTION.
001660     USE AFTER ERROR PROCEDURE ON INDEXED-SALES-FILE.
001670 DUMMY-CUSTOMER-ERROR SECTION.
001680     USE AFTER ERROR PROCEDURE ON CUSTOMER-INDEXED-FILE.
001690 DUMMY-INVENTORY-ERROR SECTION.
001700     USE AFTER ERROR PROCEDURE ON INVENTORY-INDEXED-FILE.
001710 END DECLARATIVES.
001720 A000-UPDATE.
001730     PERFORM B100-OPEN-TO-REPORT.
001740     PERFORM B200-PRINT-HEADINGS.
001750     PERFORM Z200-READ-CUSTOMER-RECORD.
001760     PERFORM B400-PRINT-RECORDS
001770        UNTIL END-OF-CUSTOMER-FILE.
001780     CLOSE INDEXED-SALES-FILE
001790            CUSTOMER-INDEXED-FILE
```

Program 7–5 *(continued)*

```
001800            INVENTORY-INDEXED-FILE
001810            CUSTOMER-REPORT-FILE.
001820       STOP RUN.
001830 B100-OPEN-TO-REPORT.
001840       OPEN INPUT  CUSTOMER-INDEXED-FILE
001850            OUTPUT CUSTOMER-REPORT-FILE
001860            I-O    INDEXED-SALES-FILE
001870                   INVENTORY-INDEXED-FILE.
001880       IF NOT SUCCESSFUL-SALES-COMPLETION
001890          OR NOT SUCCESSFUL-CUSTOMER-COMPLETION
001900          OR NOT SUCCESSFUL-INVEN-COMPLETION
001910             MOVE 'OPENING ERROR' TO EL-ERROR-OPERATION
001920             PERFORM Z100-ABORT-RUN
001930             STOP RUN.
001940 B200-PRINT-HEADINGS.
001950       WRITE CR-CUSTOMER-REPORT-LINE FROM HD-HEADING-LINE
001960            AFTER PAGE.
001970       WRITE CR-CUSTOMER-REPORT-LINE FROM CH-COLUMN-HEADING-LINE
001980            AFTER 1.
001990 B400-PRINT-RECORDS.
002000       IF CUSTOMER-HEADER
002010            PERFORM C300-CREATE-HEADER-LINE
002020       ELSE
002030            PERFORM C400-CREATE-TRANSACTION-LINE.
002040       WRITE CR-CUSTOMER-REPORT-LINE
002050            AFTER 1.
002060       PERFORM Z200-READ-CUSTOMER-RECORD.
002070 C300-CREATE-HEADER-LINE.
002080       MOVE CH-CUSTOMER-NUMBER    TO DL-CUSTOMER-NUMBER.
002090       MOVE CH-CUSTOMER-NAME      TO DL-CUSTOMER-NAME.
002100       MOVE CH-BEGINNING-BALANCE  TO DL-BEGINNING-BALANCE.
002110       MOVE CH-CREDIT-LIMIT       TO DL-CREDIT-LIMIT.
002120       MOVE CH-CURRENT-DEBITS     TO DL-CURRENT-DEBITS.
002130       MOVE CH-CURRENT-CREDITS    TO DL-CURRENT-CREDITS.
002140       MOVE CH-NO-OF-DEBITS-OR-CREDITS
002150            TO DL-NO-OF-DEBITS-OR-CREDITS.
002160       COMPUTE DL-ENDING-BALANCE = CH-BEGINNING-BALANCE +
002170                        CH-CURRENT-DEBITS -
002180                        CH-CURRENT-CREDITS.
002190       MOVE DL-DETAIL-LINE-HEADER TO CR-CUSTOMER-REPORT-LINE.
002200 C400-CREATE-TRANSACTION-LINE.
002210       PERFORM Z300-READ-INDEXED-RECORDS.
002220       MOVE CT-DEBIT-OR-CREDIT-AMOUNT  TO DL-DEBIT-OR-CREDIT-AMOUNT.
002230       IF CURRENT-SALE
002240            MOVE 'SALE'               TO DL-TRANSACTION-TYPE
002250       ELSE
002260            MOVE 'RETURN'             TO DL-TRANSACTION-TYPE.
002270       MOVE CT-QUANTITY-INVOLVED      TO DL-QUANTITY-INVOLVED.
002280       IF NO-INVENTORY-RECORD-FOUND
002290            MOVE 'NOT FOUND'          TO DL-ITEM-DESCRIPTION
002300       ELSE
002310            MOVE II-PRICE-OF-ITEM     TO DL-PRICE-OF-ITEM
002320            MOVE II-ITEM-DESCRIPTION  TO DL-ITEM-DESCRIPTION.
002330       IF NO-SALES-RECORD-FOUND
002340            MOVE 'NOT FOUND'          TO DL-SALESPERSON-NAME
002350       ELSE
002360            MOVE IS-SALESPERSON-NAME  TO DL-SALESPERSON-NAME.
002370       MOVE DL-DETAIL-LINE-TRANSACTION TO CR-CUSTOMER-REPORT-LINE.
002380 Z100-ABORT-RUN.
002390       WRITE CR-CUSTOMER-REPORT-LINE FROM EL-ERROR-LINE
002400            AFTER 1.
002410       CLOSE INDEXED-SALES-FILE
002420             CUSTOMER-INDEXED-FILE
002430             INVENTORY-INDEXED-FILE
```

Program 7-5 *(concluded)*

```
002440              CUSTOMER-REPORT-FILE.
002450 Z200-READ-CUSTOMER-RECORD.
002460     READ CUSTOMER-INDEXED-FILE.
002470 Z300-READ-INDEXED-RECORDS.
002480     MOVE CT-SALESPERSON-NUMBER TO IS-SALESPERSON-NUMBER.
002490     MOVE CT-ITEM-NUMBER        TO II-ITEM-NUMBER.
002500     READ INDEXED-SALES-FILE.
002510     READ INVENTORY-INDEXED-FILE.
```

Discussion

First, notice that the CUSTOMER-INDEXED-FILE has been specified for SEQUENTIAL ACCESS, and the file has been opened as INPUT. Therefore, either a READ/ AT END or a READ and a testing of the FILE STATUS being equal to 10 must be used. If the programmer were to forget to change the ACCESS from RANDOM to SEQUENTIAL or DYNAMIC, an infinite loop would probably be the result. Failure to appropriately align access mode, the type of OPEN and the READ, WRITE, or REWRITE statements, will cause various kinds of problems.

In B400-PRINT-RECORDS a test is made to determine whether a transaction or a header record has been read. If a transaction record has been read C400-CREATE-TRANSACTION-LINE is performed, which immediately causes the attempted reading of a record from both the sales file and the inventory file. This allows the ability to use a stored value in one file to point to a record in another file. Thus, it is possible to obtain the item price, item description, and salesperson name randomly, while sequentially accessing the entire customer file. Refer to the output in Figure 7-26 and compare this output from Program 7-5 back to the output from Program 7-4, the update program.

Figure 7-26 *Output from Program 7-5*

```
CUSTOMER REPORT
NUMBER   NAME                    BEGINNING      CREDIT       DEBITS       CREDITS     TRANS    ENDING
1057     ABC CO.              $    650.75    $   800.00   $   150.00   $     .00      1    $    800.75
$    150.00       1    $   150.00    SALE      SPREADSHEET SOFTWARE          PAYNE    MAX
1092     XYZ CO.              $    100.19    $ 8,900.00   $   352.00   $     .00      1    $    452.19
$    352.00      11    $    32.00    SALE      9 1/2 X 11 CONTINUOUS PAPER   PAYNE    MAX
1159     HILLDEBRAND          $    219.75    $   200.00   $     .00    $  150.00      1    $     69.75
$    150.00       1    $   150.00    RETURN    SPREADSHEET SOFTWARE          PAYNE    MAX
1347     MASTER MECHANICS     $    424.00    $   750.00   $     .00    $     .00      0    $    424.00
1596     PLUMBERS UNION       $    978.00    $ 1,000.00   $     .00    $  575.00      1    $    403.00
$    575.00       1    $   575.00    RETURN    COBOL COMPILER                HUME     LETA
1678     SEVEN ELEVEN         $    276.00    $ 1,000.00   $     .00    $     .00      0    $    276.00
1990     TENTH STR. TEXACO    $     50.00    $   100.00   $     .00    $     .00      0    $     50.00
2003     BATTLEFIELD MALL     $    900.00    $ 2,000.00   $     .00    $     .00      0    $    900.00
2417     MUMFORD              $  1,027.09    $ 1,100.00   $     .00    $     .00      0    $  1,027.09
2923     SMSU                 $    422.50    $ 1,000.00   $     .00    $     .00      0    $    422.50
3075     NHPG                 $  1,500.00    $ 1,900.00   $     .00    $     .00      0    $  1,500.00
4139     SPRINGFIELD DINER    $    105.00    $   800.00   $     .00    $     .00      0    $    105.00
4765     EDWARDS CHEVROLET    $  2,320.11    $ 2,500.00   $     .00    $     .00      0    $  2,320.11
4983     BUNTING TRASH        $  4,587.00    $ 5,000.00   $ 4,826.50   $     .00      3    $  9,413.50
$     64.00       2    $    32.00    SALE      9 1/2 X 11 CONTINUOUS PAPER   VAUGHN   SYLVIA A.
$  4,600.00       2    $2,300.00    SALE      HAL PC - 2 FLOPPIES           SMITH    DOUGLAS
$    162.50       5    $    32.50    SALE      PLASTIC FLOPPY HOLDER         SMITH    DOUGLAS
5217     WARDS               $10,000.00    $20,000.00   $     .00    $     .00      0    $10,000.00
6082     BARCLAY PAINT        $    102.19    $   900.00   $     .00    $     .00      0    $    102.19
6153     ALLEN PLUMBING       $    229.75    $   500.00   $     .00    $     .00      0    $    229.75
6157     ACME MANUFACTURING   $    550.75    $ 1,000.00   $ 2,300.00   $     .00      1    $  2,850.75
$  2,300.00       1    $2,300.00    SALE      HAL PC - 2 FLOPPIES           SMITH    DOUGLAS
6547     JUNIOR'S DINER       $  1,524.00    $ 2,000.00   $   125.00   $     .00      1    $  1,649.00
$    125.00      10    $    12.50    SALE      MAILING LABELS                DILL     JEFF
```

Programming Style

1. Make a decision whether to test the FILE STATUS rather than use the IN VALID KEY for all input or output operations. The decision is an organizational decision, which when made should be applied consistently. The authors contend that the testing of the FILE STATUS is more appropriate.
2. Use appropriate control and audit trail procedures.
3. Test the FILE STATUS after an OPEN for an indexed file, and if not successful abort the program. Make sure to CLOSE all opened files.
4. Precede any attempt at a random update with an attempt to READ a record with a relevant primary or alternate key. Make the result of the READ control the subsequent logic of the update.
5. Precede any attempt to update a record with adequate validation of the transaction file, including the transaction code and each relevant field. Make a decision related to completing the validation in a separate program, or write a validation module in the update program.
6. Precede any indexed file creation with appropriate validation and sorting procedures.

Common Errors

1. Failure to adequately control data files. Adequate control should include validation, record counts, and numeric totals, at minimum.
2. Failure to consider necessary record description changes when moving data from other media to disk files.
3. Attempting to use a field that is not unique as the primary key for an indexed file.
4. Attempting to use a nonunique alternate key without specifying the WITH DUPLICATES clause.
5. Failure to use the FILE STATUS to control indexed files.
6. Failure to include appropriate clauses on a SELECT statement for an indexed file.
7. Failure to abort the program when an OPEN error occurs and failure to CLOSE all files when an abort is accomplished.
8. Failure to understand when alternate indexes can be built in your particular system.
9. Failure to specify alternate indexes in the SELECT statement after alternate keys have been built for a file.
10. Failure to correctly set the record pointer which is required by several input and output statements.
11. Invalid use of the START statement. Remember to initialize the alternate key to a relevant value.
12. Failure to understand the meaning of a duplicate alternate key.
13. Failure to precede the creation of an indexed file with adequate validation and sorting procedures.
14. Failure to precede a random READ with a MOVE statement, which will set the record pointer to the relevant primary or alternate key.
15. Failure to define the RECORD KEY or ALTERNATE KEY as a part of the record associated with the FD for that particular file.
16. Failure to align ACCESS, OPEN, and input/output statements correctly.

Exercises

1. What are logical and physical records?

2. What is the purpose of the DELETE statement?

3. Explain the three basic procedures in updating most files.

4. What are the four major statements necessary in the random update of an indexed sequential file and their purposes?

5. No matter which file organization is used, what is included in file processing?

6. Explain the purpose of each of the possible clauses that can be used in the SELECT statement with respect to indexed files. Which are optional or required?

7. Given the following entries correct only those that are in error. Assume all programmer-supplied names have been properly defined.
   - *a.* ACCESS RANDOM.
   - *b.* FILE STATUS IS SEQUENTIAL.
   - *c.* OPEN INPUT I–O UPDATE–FILE.
   - *d.* RECORD KEY IS IP–NUMBER.
   - *e.* ALTERNATE KEY IS WS–NUMBER WITH DUPLICATES.
   - *f.* START INDEXED–FILE KEY AT ALTERNATE KEY.
   - *g.* READ INDEXED–FILE INVALID KEY PERFORM H100–RTN.
   - *h.* WRITE INDEXED–RECORD INVALID KEY STOP RUN.
   - *i.* REWRITE NEW–RECORD.

8. What is the purpose of DYNAMIC access?

Problems

1. For a sales file, use Data Set F (the file is sorted and validated) to create an indexed salesperson file using salesperson number as the primary key. Possible alternate keys that may be used include the following. (If alternate keys are used, determine whether alternate keys can be built when creating the original file.)

   Salesperson name.
   Store number.
   Department mnemonic.
   Employee code.
   Commission rate.

   Using Program 7–1 as a model, add both current sales and current returns fields for subsequent update procedures. Include the creation of a control file that is adequate to include the following:
   - *a.* Number of records.
   - *b.* Hash totals on:
     - (1) Salesperson number.
     - (2) Store number.
     - (3) Employee code.
     - (4) Commission rate.
   - *c.* Other reasonable numeric totals.

2. Using Data Set B, modify the program requirements for Problem 7–1 to include validation and sorting requirements in order to create the master file. The sort procedure should use the salesperson number as the sort key. The validation procedure should utilize the following considerations, reproduced here from Problem 6–2.
   - *a.* The highest salesperson number that has been issued so far is 9025.
   - *b.* Valid store numbers are 10 through 50.

  c. Valid employee codes range from 1 through 5.

  d. Department mnemonics should be alphabetic.

  e. Commission rates may range up to 25 percent.

  f. Year-to-date sales must be equal to or greater than year-to-date sales returns.

  g. Every salesperson has had sales, though not everyone has had sales returns.

  h. If the salesperson name is not left-justified, correct it.

3. For an inventory file, use Data Set E to create an indexed inventory master file using store number, department mnemonic, and item number in combination for the primary key. (The file is sorted and validated.) Possible alternate keys that may be used include the following. (If alternate keys are used, determine whether alternate keys can be built when creating the original file.)

  Store number.

  Department mnemonic.

  Item number.

  Item description.

  Quantity on hand.

  Sales price.

  Cost.

Using Program 7–1 as a model, add both current quantity sold and current quantity purchased fields for subsequent update procedures. Include the creation of a control file that is adequate to include the following:

  a. Number of records.

  b. Hash totals on:

    (1) Store number.

    (2) Item number.

    (3) Sales price per unit.

    (4) Cost per unit.

  c. Other reasonable numeric totals.

4. Using Data Set G, modify the program requirements for Problem 7–3 to include validation and sorting requirements in order to create the master file. The sort procedure should use the item number, department mnemonic, and the store number as the sort keys. The validation procedure should utilize the following considerations, reproduced here from Problem 6–4.

  a. Valid store numbers are 10 and 20.

  b. Department mnemonics should be alphabetic and must be AU or AP for automotive and appliances.

  c. Valid item numbers range up through 898.

  d. The highest sales price per unit in the automotive department is $75.

  e. The highest sales price per unit in the appliance department is $795.

  f. All fields should exist.

  g. If the item description is not left-justified, correct it.

5. Using Program 7–2 as a model, write a report program that will list the contents of the file and adequately consider control totals. Use either the file created in Problem 7–1, 7–2, 7–3, or 7–4. The program written for this assignment can also be used to report from the relevant file after an update procedure. The report written may use one or more of the following keys for the order of the data for the sales file.

  Salesperson number.

  Salesperson name.

  Store number.

  Department mnemonic.

  Employee code.

  Commission rate.

The report written may use one or more of the following keys for the order of the data for the inventory file.

Store number.

Department mnemonic.

Item number.

Item description.

Quantity on hand.

Sales price.

Cost.

6. Write a random update program for one of the sales files previously created in Problem 7–1 or 7–2. Use Data Set N in Appendix C for the transactions. Notice that the transactions are unvalidated and do not have to be sorted. Use the same validation considerations as listed for Problem 7–2 and consider validation necessary on the transaction code and date. You may write a separate program to accomplish the validation procedures or combine them into the update program. Make sure to adequately control the file that is being updated. After successful testing of the update program, run the report program against the updated file.

7. Write a random update program for one of the inventory files previously created in Problem 7–3 or 7–4. Use Data Set O in Appendix C for the transactions. Notice that the transactions are unvalidated and do not have to be sorted. Use the same validation considerations as listed for Problem 7–4. You may write a separate program to accomplish the validation procedures or combine them into the update program. Make sure to adequately control the file that is being updated. After successful testing of the update program, run the report program against the updated file.

8. Modify any combination of the previous procedures for the sales file so that variable length records are utilized. Use either the concept of a variable number of segments or fixed-length records of varying lengths so that current changes to the dollar values of current sales or current returns are the types of transactions that will be placed in the file.

9. Modify any combination of the previous procedures for the inventory file so that variable length records are utilized. Use either the concept of a variable number of segments or fixed-length records of varying lengths so that current changes to the values of current quantity sold or current quantity purchased are the types of transactions that will be placed in the file.

10. Write a month-end update program to get the sales file ready for the next month. Remember to consider the control file also.

11. Write a month-end update program to get the inventory file ready for the next month. Remember to consider the control file also.

12. This assignment involves a random update of three files. Using Programs 7–4 and 7–5 as models, write a system that will accomplish a concurrent random update, including all appropriate control procedures. The files that will be used are:

Sales file (created in Problem 7–1).

Inventory file (created in Problem 7–3, except add both current and year-to-date quantity returns fields).

Accounts receivable file (created from Data Set P in Appendix C). Assume that the data is valid and add appropriate current fields and allow for the transactions to be stored either as a part of the accounts receivable file or as a separate standard sequential file. The following activities are required:

   a. Create each file as an indexed file.

b. Complete the concurrent random update using the transactions in Data Set Q in Appendix C. Use appropriate audit trail and control procedures. No assumptions can be made as to the validity of the transactions.

c. Prepare report listings from each of the files after they are updated. Relevant totals can be compared to the control files as well as totals from the other two files.

d. Prepare detailed billing statements to customers.

Note: This system is installed for the appliance (AP) and automotive (AU) departments only for the inventory. However, payments on account can be received in any department. The process of updating should be to (1) validate the transaction, depending on the type of transaction, (2) access needed files, depending on the type of transaction (a sale on account will need to access all three files, including obtaining the price from the inventory file), and (3) perform appropriate updates. (A sale on account would increase the customer's current sales and balance, increase the salesperson's current and year-to-date sales, and reduce inventory.) Do not perform any update if anything is wrong with the transaction. That is, if any of the fields in the transaction do not align with relevant fields in the associated file. Assume that the sale has already occurred. Do not complete a credit check.

Since the inventory file has been created only for stores 10 and 20, several salespeople have been temporarily reassigned to these stores and to the appliance and automotive departments. It will be necessary to make the reassignments in the sales file by creating the following as transactions that can be run through the update program written for Problem 7–6.

Number	Last name	Store	Department
0017	Payne	10	AP
0580	Dupree	10	AP
0859	Hutchens	10	AU
0956	Goltman	10	AU
1634	Vaughn	20	AP
2157	Young	20	AU
2269	Thompson	20	AP
2395	Matney	20	AP
2575	Cross	20	AP
2666	Barker	20	AU

Relative Files

Though not frequently used, relative file organization affords the opportunity to store data records in a file without the need for a separately maintained index as is the case with indexed files. It instead utilizes a relative record number, which represents a record's position in the file. Files whose organization is relative may be accessed either randomly, sequentially, or dynamically, just as is true with indexed files. Because a record in a relative file is accessed by the relative record number, there is no need for the system to create or access an index, thereby affording faster access to the data record when accessing on a random basis.

TERMS AND STATEMENTS

ACCESS clause	INVALID KEY	RELATIVE KEY
ASSIGN clause	clause	clause
CLOSE statement	OPEN statement	RELATIVE KEY
DELETE statement	ORGANIZATION IS	data-item
Digit extraction	RELATIVE	REWRITE statement
algorithm	RANDOM access	SELECT statement
Division/Remainder	Randomizing	SEQUENTIAL
algorithm	algorithm	access
DYNAMIC	READ statement	Squared value
EXCEPTION/	Record slot	algorithm
ERROR	Relative file	START statement
declarative	formatting	Synonyms
FILE STATUS	Relative record	WRITE statement
Folding algorithm	number	

Relative File Concepts

Relative files are chosen for applications that require rapid response time and that process a large number of transactions. An airline reservation system, for example, must support inquiries for thousands of reservations for a relatively few flights. A bank system, conversely, has relatively few inquiries from a large file of customer records. The airline system must support multiple, rapid-response inquiries from many sources and is best suited for relative file organization. The general rule of thumb is to choose relative file organization when a large number of inquiries occur on a comparatively small file; choose indexed organization when a small number of inquiries occur on a comparatively large file. Both organization methods support sequential access when necessary for those applications that dictate sequential processing.

When a record is stored in a relative file, it is first assigned a **relative record number.** The first record in the file is assigned relative record number 1; the second record is assigned relative record number 2, and so on. There is, however, no requirement that records be placed in contiguous record locations. That is, not all relative record numbers need to be filled with records.

The location used for a particular record can be thought of as a **record slot,** which may or may not be filled with a data record. Unlike indexed files, relative file organization requires that the programmer be knowledgeable of the method used to assign the relative record number, particularly when accessing the file randomly. When accessing the file sequentially, such as in a sequential report from the file, the system will appropriately access only used slots and will skip unused record slots.

Syntactical Requirements for Relative Files

The SELECT Statement

Figure 8–1 shows the format for the **SELECT statement** when using relative files.

Figure 8–1 *Format for the SELECT Statement for Relative Files*

```
SELECT file-name
     ASSIGN TO implementor-name
     [RESERVE integer [ AREA  ]]
                      [ AREAS ]
     ORGANIZATION IS RELATIVE
     [ACCESS MODE IS { SEQUENTIAL [RELATIVE KEY IS data-name-1] } ]
                     { { RANDOM  }                                }
                     { { DYNAMIC } RELATIVE KEY IS data-name-2     }
     [FILE STATUS IS data-name-3]
```

From the format shown in Figure 8–1, it can be seen that the **ASSIGN** and **ORGANIZATION IS RELATIVE** clauses are required. The **ACCESS** clause, if omitted, defaults to SEQUENTIAL access. The **FILE STATUS** clause, though optional, carries the same importance as with indexed files. When the ACCESS is specified as either **RANDOM access** or **DYNAMIC,** the RELATIVE KEY clause is required. With **SEQUENTIAL access** (whether the ACCESS clause is specified or omitted), the key is optional at the programmer's discretion.

The **RELATIVE KEY clause** identifies the relative record number for a specific logical record within the file. Only fixed-length records can be used with RELATIVE organization. Data-name-1 (or data-name-2) is the **RELATIVE KEY data-item,** which must be defined as an unsigned integer data item, and *cannot* be defined in a record associated with the relative file. Also note that there is no ability to define any alternate keys.

When ACCESS is SEQUENTIAL, data-name-1 need not be specified unless the START statement is to be used. When the START statement is used, the system uses the contents of the RELATIVE KEY data-item to determine the relative record number of the beginning record.

When RANDOM or DYNAMIC are specified as the access mode, data-name-2 must be specified for each random request because the content of the key is used to indicate the relative record number to the system. As with indexed files, when ACCESS is DYNAMIC is specified, the system interprets the access mode by the nature of the I/O request.

Input and Output Statements

Figure 8–2 illustrates the formats for all input and output statements for relative files.

Figure 8–2   *Input and Output Formats for Relative Files*

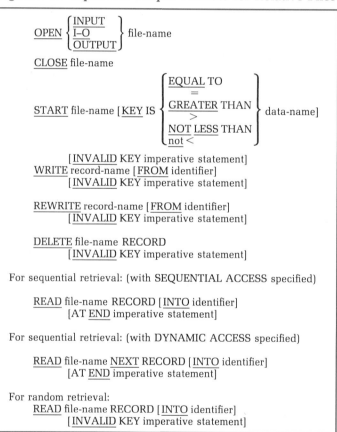

The formats shown in Figure 8–2 are essentially the same as for indexed files. As is always true, when in doubt, refer to the format of the particular statement desired.

Testing the Results of an I/O Operation   As with indexed files, the programmer has the option of three methods of error trapping with respect to input or output operations with relative files. These three include the use of an **EXCEPTION/ERROR declarative**, the testing of the FILE STA TUS, and the use of the INVALID KEY/AT END clauses or some combination of the three. The EXCEPTION/ERROR declaratives for relative files are used the same as with indexed files, and they must be specified when the INVALID KEY clause is omitted. In the programs in this text a dummy EXCEPTION/ERROR DECLARA-TIVE is used to satisfy this requirement, but the actual testing of the FILE STATUS occurs within the main logic of the program.

Testing the FILE STATUS allows the programmer to ascertain the results on any of the input or output operations, including the **OPEN, CLOSE, READ, WRITE, REWRITE, DELETE** and **START** statements. It also allows the programmer to omit the use of either the AT END clause or the **INVALID KEY clause.** The values associated with the FILE STATUS data item for relative files are shown in Figure 8–3.

Figure 8–3   *FILE STATUS Values for Relative Files*

FILE STATUS	Meaning
00	Successful completion.
10	End-of-file.
21	Sequence error.
22	Slot occupied.
23	No record found with current relative record number.
24	Boundary violation.
30	Permanent error.
9x	Other error—consult manual specific to vendor.

For any OPEN or CLOSE statement, if successful completion does not occur, the program should generally be terminated. If errors occur that cause file status values of 30 or 9x for any other I/O statement the program should also be terminated. FILE STATUS values in the 2x series can also be detected by the use of the INVALID KEY clause. For instance, a WRITE statement that included an INVALID KEY clause could cause the execution of an error paragraph if the INVALID KEY condition was found to be true. Throughout the programs in this chapter, the FILE STATUS values are tested rather than using the INVALID KEY clause, because the specific type of invalid key can be determined and documented with the program.

Sequential Creation of a Relative File

To illustrate the use of a relative file, consider an example of time series data shown in Figure 8–4. These data represent expected payroll expenses for the next 12 months in four departments.

Figure 8–4   *Budgetary Data for Twelve Months*

Month	Budget-dept 1	Budget-dept 2	Budget-dept 3	Budget-dept 4
January	24,000	22,000	23,000	21,000
February	25,000	26,000	25,000	23,000
March	25,000	28,000	27,000	26,000
April	30,000	32,000	31,000	28,000
May	35,000	35,000	36,000	29,000
June	42,000	44,000	40,000	38,000
July	45,000	48,000	44,000	42,000
August	53,000	57,000	52,000	50,000
September	47,000	52,000	49,000	35,000
October	40,000	53,000	42,000	32,000
November	18,000	25,000	21,000	15,000
December	18,000	10,000	15,000	8,000

The data are well-suited for use with a relative file because the month number can easily correspond to a relative record number. This budget data for four departments are to be created at the beginning of the year. Throughout the year both actual payroll amounts and budget amounts can be updated and reports can be produced on demand for all months and all departments or for some months and some departments.

Program 8–1 illustrates the creation of the relative file. Notice that the input data consists only of the budget data for each department for 12 months. Actual dollar amounts and changes to the budget amounts are processed with a later update program. When ACCESS IS SEQUENTIAL and the file is opened for OUTPUT, the system initially sets the relative record number to 1. The first WRITE statement, therefore, will cause the first record to be placed in the first slot. Accordingly, the data were previously sorted in ascending sequence using BI–PAY–PERIOD as the key. Notice the testing of the FILE STATUS after the OPEN and the WRITE statements. Also notice the omission of the specified RELATIVE KEY in the SELECT statement. When ACCESS IS SEQUENTIAL, the RELATIVE KEY is optional and, in this case, unnecessary since the system automatically increments the relative record number. No errors resulted from the execution of this program.

Program Example

Program 8–1

```
000010 IDENTIFICATION DIVISION.
000020 PROGRAM-ID.    RELCREAT.
000030*************************************************************
000040*        PROGRAM EXAMPLE 8-1 RELATIVE FILE CREATION         *
000050*************************************************************
000060 ENVIRONMENT DIVISION.
000070 CONFIGURATION SECTION.
000080    SOURCE-COMPUTER.  IBM-4341.
000090    OBJECT-COMPUTER.  IBM-4341.
000100 INPUT-OUTPUT SECTION.
000110 FILE-CONTROL.
000120    SELECT BUDGET-INPUT-FILE
000130        ASSIGN TO SYS016-UR-2501-S.
000140    SELECT BUDGET-DISK-FILE
000150        ASSIGN TO SYS025-DA-3375-BUDGET
000160        ORGANIZATION IS RELATIVE
000170        ACCESS IS SEQUENTIAL
000180        FILE STATUS IS EL-STATUS-ERROR.
000190    SELECT BUDGET-ERROR-REPORT
000200        ASSIGN TO SYS018-UR-3203-S.
000210*
000220 DATA DIVISION.
000230 FILE SECTION.
000240 FD  BUDGET-INPUT-FILE
000250     RECORD CONTAINS 26 CHARACTERS
000260     LABEL RECORDS STANDARD.
000270 01  BI-BUDGET-INPUT-RECORD.
000280     05  BI-PAY-PERIOD              PIC 9(2).
000290     05  BI-BUDGETED-DOLLARS        PIC 9(6)
000300             OCCURS 4 TIMES.
000310 FD  BUDGET-DISK-FILE
000320     RECORD CONTAINS 50 CHARACTERS
000330     LABEL RECORDS STANDARD.
000340 01  BD-BUDGET-DISK-RECORD.
000350     05  BD-PAY-PERIOD              PIC 9(2).
000360     05  BD-DEPARTMENT-BUDGET
000370             OCCURS 4 TIMES.
000380        10  BD-BUDGETED-DOLLARS     PIC 9(6).
000390        10  BD-ACTUAL-DOLLARS       PIC 9(6).
000400 FD  BUDGET-ERROR-REPORT
000410     RECORD CONTAINS 133 CHARACTERS
000420     LABEL RECORDS ARE OMITTED.
000430 01  BE-BUDGET-ERROR-LINE          PIC X(133).
000440*
000450 WORKING-STORAGE SECTION.
000460 01  WS-RECORD-INDICATORS.
000470     05  WS-EOF-INDICATOR          PIC X(3).
```

Program 8–1 *(concluded)*

```
000480          88 END-OF-BUDGET-FILE          VALUE 'END'.
000490      05  WS-NUMBER-OF-DEPARTMENTS        PIC 9(1).
000500 01  EL-ERROR-LINE.
000510      05  FILLER                         PIC X(1).
000520      05  EL-ERROR-OPERATION             PIC X(10).
000530      05  FILLER                         PIC X(5) VALUE SPACES.
000540      05  EL-STATUS-ERROR                PIC X(2).
000550          88 SUCCESSFUL-COMPLETION        VALUE '00'.
000560*
000570 PROCEDURE DIVISION.
000580 DECLARATIVES.
000590 DUMMY-ERROR-PROCEDURE SECTION.
000600     USE AFTER ERROR PROCEDURE ON BUDGET-DISK-FILE.
000610 END DECLARATIVES.
000620 A000-REL-CREATE.
000630     OPEN INPUT BUDGET-INPUT-FILE
000640          OUTPUT BUDGET-DISK-FILE
000650                 BUDGET-ERROR-REPORT.
000660     IF NOT SUCCESSFUL-COMPLETION
000670         PERFORM B100-OPEN-ABORT.
000680     MOVE 'NO' TO WS-EOF-INDICATOR.
000690     PERFORM Z100-READ-RECEIVE-RECORD.
000700     PERFORM B300-CREATE-FILE
000710         UNTIL END-OF-BUDGET-FILE.
000720     CLOSE BUDGET-INPUT-FILE
000730           BUDGET-DISK-FILE
000740           BUDGET-ERROR-REPORT.
000750     STOP RUN.
000760 B100-OPEN-ABORT.
000770     MOVE 'OPENING' TO EL-ERROR-OPERATION.
000780     WRITE BE-BUDGET-ERROR-LINE FROM EL-ERROR-LINE
000790         AFTER 1.
000800     CLOSE BUDGET-INPUT-FILE
000810           BUDGET-DISK-FILE
000820           BUDGET-ERROR-REPORT.
000830     STOP RUN.
000840 B300-CREATE-FILE.
000850     MOVE BI-PAY-PERIOD TO BD-PAY-PERIOD.
000860     PERFORM C100-CREATE-RECORD
000870         VARYING WS-NUMBER-OF-DEPARTMENTS
000880         FROM 1 BY 1
000890         UNTIL WS-NUMBER-OF-DEPARTMENTS > 4.
000900     WRITE BD-BUDGET-DISK-RECORD.
000910     IF NOT SUCCESSFUL-COMPLETION
000920         MOVE 'WRITING' TO EL-ERROR-OPERATION
000930         WRITE BE-BUDGET-ERROR-LINE FROM EL-ERROR-LINE
000940             AFTER 1.
000950     PERFORM Z100-READ-RECEIVE-RECORD.
000960 C100-CREATE-RECORD.
000970     MOVE BI-BUDGETED-DOLLARS(WS-NUMBER-OF-DEPARTMENTS)
000980         TO BD-BUDGETED-DOLLARS(WS-NUMBER-OF-DEPARTMENTS).
000990     MOVE ZEROS
001000         TO BD-ACTUAL-DOLLARS(WS-NUMBER-OF-DEPARTMENTS).
001010 Z100-READ-RECEIVE-RECORD.
001020     READ BUDGET-INPUT-FILE
001030         AT END MOVE 'END' TO WS-EOF-INDICATOR.
```

Reporting from a Relative File

Reports from a relative file may be done randomly or sequentially, depending on the nature of the desired report. Consider the data shown in Figure 8–5, which represent budget requests for specified periods and departments.

Figure 8–5 *Budget Report Request File*

Beginning month	Ending month	Beginning department	Ending department
1	12	1	4
1	1	1	1
2	4	1	4

For example, the first record would indicate that the requested budget report would cover months 1 through 12 and departments 1 through 4. In this case an entire sequential report would be indicated. The second request indicates that only department 1 is to be reported in month 1. This could be accomplished by a random access. The third request is for months 2 through 4 for all four departments. This request suggests a need to indicate a beginning relative record number (accomplished by the use of the START statement) and then to sequentially access the next two months. Program 8–2 illustrates the use of the START statement to select the beginning month.

Program Example

Program 8–2

```
000010 IDENTIFICATION DIVISION.
000020 PROGRAM-ID.    RELREPT.
000030*·····················································
000040*        PROGRAM EXAMPLE 8-2 RELATIVE FILE REPORT        *
000050*·····················································
000060 ENVIRONMENT DIVISION.
000070 CONFIGURATION SECTION.
000080    SOURCE-COMPUTER.   IBM-4341.
000090    OBJECT-COMPUTER.   IBM-4341.
000100 INPUT-OUTPUT SECTION.
000110 FILE-CONTROL.
000120    SELECT BUDGET-DISK-FILE
000130        ASSIGN TO SYS025-DA-3375-BUDGET
000140        ORGANIZATION IS RELATIVE
000150        ACCESS IS SEQUENTIAL
000160        RELATIVE KEY IS BR-BEGINNING-MONTH
000170        FILE STATUS IS EL-STATUS-ERROR.
000180    SELECT BUDGET-REPORT
000190        ASSIGN TO SYS018-UR-3203-S.
000200    SELECT BUDGET-REQUEST-FILE
000210        ASSIGN TO SYS016-UR-2501-S.
000220*
000230 DATA DIVISION.
000240 FILE SECTION.
000250 FD  BUDGET-DISK-FILE
000260     RECORD CONTAINS 50 CHARACTERS
000270     LABEL RECORDS STANDARD.
000280 01  BD-BUDGET-DISK-RECORD.
000290     05  BD-PAY-PERIOD            PIC 9(2).
000300     05  BD-DEPARTMENT-BUDGET
000310            OCCURS 4 TIMES.
000320        10  BD-BUDGETED-DOLLARS   PIC 9(6).
000330        10  BD-ACTUAL-DOLLARS     PIC 9(6).
000340 FD  BUDGET-REQUEST-FILE
000350     RECORD CONTAINS 6 CHARACTERS
000360     LABEL RECORDS ARE STANDARD.
000370 01  BR-BUDGET-REQUEST-RECORD.
000380     05  BR-BEGINNING-MONTH       PIC 9(2).
000390     05  BR-ENDING-MONTH          PIC 9(2).
```

Program 8–2 *(continued)*

```
000400      05  BR-BEGINNING-DEPARTMENT         PIC 9(1).
000410      05  BR-ENDING-DEPARTMENT            PIC 9(1).
000420 FD  BUDGET-REPORT
000430     RECORD CONTAINS 133 CHARACTERS
000440     LABEL RECORDS ARE OMITTED.
000450 01  BE-BUDGET-LINE                       PIC X(133).
000460*
000470 WORKING-STORAGE SECTION.
000480 01  WS-RECORD-INDICATORS.
000490      05  WS-EOF-INDICATOR               PIC X(3).
000500          88  END-OF-REQUEST-FILE        VALUE 'END'.
000510      05  WS-NUMBER-OF-DEPARTMENTS       PIC 9(1).
000520 01  HD-HEADING-LINE.
000530      05  FILLER                         PIC X(1).
000540      05  FILLER                         PIC X(13)
000550                                         VALUE 'BUDGET REPORT'.
000560 01  CH-COLUMN-HEADING.
000570      05  FILLER                         PIC X(1).
000580      05  FILLER                         PIC X(7) VALUE 'PERIOD'.
000590      05  FILLER                         PIC X(9)
000600                                         VALUE 'BUDGET 1'.
000610      05  FILLER                         PIC X(9)
000620                                         VALUE 'ACTUAL 1'.
000630      05  FILLER                         PIC X(9)
000640                                         VALUE 'VARIES 1'.
000650      05  FILLER                         PIC X(9)
000660                                         VALUE 'BUDGET 2'.
000670      05  FILLER                         PIC X(9)
000680                                         VALUE 'ACTUAL 2'.
000690      05  FILLER                         PIC X(9)
000700                                         VALUE 'VARIES 2'.
000710      05  FILLER                         PIC X(9)
000720                                         VALUE 'BUDGET 3'.
000730      05  FILLER                         PIC X(9)
000740                                         VALUE 'ACTUAL 3'.
000750      05  FILLER                         PIC X(9)
000760                                         VALUE 'VARIES 3'.
000770      05  FILLER                         PIC X(9)
000780                                         VALUE 'BUDGET 4'.
000790      05  FILLER                         PIC X(9)
000800                                         VALUE 'ACTUAL 4'.
000810      05  FILLER                         PIC X(9)
000820                                         VALUE 'VARIES 4'.
000830 01  DL-DETAIL-LINE.
000840      05  FILLER                         PIC X(1).
000850      05  DL-PAY-PERIOD                  PIC Z9.
000860      05  FILLER                         PIC X(5).
000870      05  DL-DEPARTMENT-BUDGETS
000880              OCCURS 4 TIMES.
000890          10  DL-BUDGETED-DOLLARS        PIC ZZZ,ZZ9.
000900          10  FILLER                     PIC X(2).
000910          10  DL-ACTUAL-DOLLARS          PIC ZZZ,ZZ9.
000920          10  FILLER                     PIC X(2).
000930          10  DL-VARIANCE                PIC ZZZ,ZZ9-.
000940          10  FILLER                     PIC X(1).
000950 01  EL-ERROR-LINE.
000960      05  FILLER                         PIC X(1).
000970      05  EL-ERROR-OPERATION             PIC X(10).
000980      05  FILLER                         PIC X(5) VALUE SPACES.
000990      05  EL-STATUS-ERROR                PIC XX.
001000          88  SUCCESSFUL-COMPLETION      VALUE '00'.
001010          88  END-OF-BUDGET-FILE         VALUE '10'.
001020*
001030 PROCEDURE DIVISION.
```

Program 8–2   *(continued)*

```
001040 DECLARATIVES.
001050 DUMMY-ERROR-PROCEDURE SECTION.
001060     USE AFTER ERROR PROCEDURE ON BUDGET-DISK-FILE.
001070 END DECLARATIVES.
001080 A000-BUDGET-REPORT.
001090     OPEN INPUT  BUDGET-REQUEST-FILE
001100                 BUDGET-DISK-FILE
001110          OUTPUT BUDGET-REPORT.
001120     IF NOT SUCCESSFUL-COMPLETION
001130          MOVE 'OPENING' TO EL-ERROR-OPERATION
001140          WRITE BE-BUDGET-LINE FROM EL-ERROR-LINE
001150               AFTER 1
001160          CLOSE BUDGET-REQUEST-FILE
001170                BUDGET-DISK-FILE
001180                BUDGET-REPORT
001190          STOP RUN.
001200     MOVE 'NO' TO WS-EOF-INDICATOR.
001210     PERFORM Z100-READ-BUDGET-RECORD.
001220     PERFORM B200-PRODUCE-REPORTS
001230          UNTIL END-OF-REQUEST-FILE.
001240     CLOSE BUDGET-REQUEST-FILE
001250           BUDGET-DISK-FILE
001260           BUDGET-REPORT.
001270     STOP RUN.
001280 B200-PRODUCE-REPORTS.
001290     START BUDGET-DISK-FILE.
001300     IF NOT SUCCESSFUL-COMPLETION
001310          MOVE 'STARTING' TO EL-ERROR-OPERATION
001320          WRITE BE-BUDGET-LINE FROM EL-ERROR-LINE
001330               AFTER 1
001340     ELSE
001350          PERFORM C200-PRINT-REPORT.
001360     PERFORM Z100-READ-BUDGET-RECORD.
001370 C200-PRINT-REPORT.
001380     PERFORM D100-PRINT-HEADINGS.
001390     READ BUDGET-DISK-FILE.
001400     PERFORM D300-CREATE-DETAIL-LINE
001410          UNTIL BD-PAY-PERIOD > BR-ENDING-MONTH
001420               OR END-OF-BUDGET-FILE.
001430 D100-PRINT-HEADINGS.
001440     WRITE BE-BUDGET-LINE FROM HD-HEADING-LINE
001450          AFTER PAGE.
001460     WRITE BE-BUDGET-LINE FROM CH-COLUMN-HEADING
001470          AFTER 2.
001480 D300-CREATE-DETAIL-LINE.
001490     MOVE SPACES TO DL-DETAIL-LINE.
001500     PERFORM E100-FORM-DETAIL-LINE
001510          VARYING WS-NUMBER-OF-DEPARTMENTS
001520          FROM BR-BEGINNING-DEPARTMENT BY 1
001530          UNTIL WS-NUMBER-OF-DEPARTMENTS >
001540               BR-ENDING-DEPARTMENT.
001550     WRITE BE-BUDGET-LINE FROM DL-DETAIL-LINE
001560          AFTER 2.
001570     READ BUDGET-DISK-FILE.
001580 E100-FORM-DETAIL-LINE.
001590     IF BD-ACTUAL-DOLLARS(WS-NUMBER-OF-DEPARTMENTS) NOT = ZEROS
001600          MOVE BD-ACTUAL-DOLLARS(WS-NUMBER-OF-DEPARTMENTS)
001610               TO DL-ACTUAL-DOLLARS(WS-NUMBER-OF-DEPARTMENTS)
001620          SUBTRACT BD-ACTUAL-DOLLARS(WS-NUMBER-OF-DEPARTMENTS)
001630               FROM BD-BUDGETED-DOLLARS(WS-NUMBER-OF-DEPARTMENTS)
001640               GIVING DL-VARIANCE(WS-NUMBER-OF-DEPARTMENTS).
001650     MOVE BD-PAY-PERIOD TO DL-PAY-PERIOD.
001660     MOVE BD-BUDGETED-DOLLARS(WS-NUMBER-OF-DEPARTMENTS)
001670          TO DL-BUDGETED-DOLLARS(WS-NUMBER-OF-DEPARTMENTS).
```

Program 8-2   *(concluded)*

```
001680 Z100-READ-BUDGET-RECORD.
001690     READ BUDGET-REQUEST-FILE
001700         AT END MOVE 'END' TO WS-EOF-INDICATOR.
```

Discussion

First, notice that the RELATIVE KEY has been specified as BR–BEGINNING–MONTH, which is defined in BR–BUDGET–REQUEST–RECORD. The contents of BR–BEGINNING–MONTH are then used by the START statement at line 1290 to find the requested record in the relative file. If the START operation is not successful it would indicate that no record exists with that particular relative record number. Notice it is possible to omit the use of the KEY clause of the START statement. When omitted the system assumes the KEY = condition is to be tested.

If the START is successful, C200–PRINT–REPORT is executed. In this module, the headings are printed and a priming READ of the relative file is accomplished. This READ obtains the record from the slot number determined by the START statement. Referring to the output in Figure 8–6, the first record obtained for the first budget request would be the record in slot 1; for the second budget request it would also be the record in slot 1; for the third budget request it would be the record in slot 2.

D300–CREATE–DETAIL–LINE is then performed until either the end of the file is detected (notice the use of END–OF–BUDGET–FILE defined at line 1010 as a tested condition related to EL–STATUS–ERROR, which is the FILE STATUS data-item) or BD–PAY–PERIOD is greater than BR–ENDING–MONTH. When the next record from the file obtained by the READ statement at line 1570, BD–PAY–PERIOD is compared to BR–ENDING–MONTH from the request file. As an example, for the second request, which has both BR–BEGINNING–MONTH and BR–ENDING–MONTH equal to 1, the subsequent READ at line 1570 causes BD–PAY–PERIOD to be 2, resulting in D300–CREATE–DETAIL–LINE being iterated only once. This situation could also have been handled by a random access to the single record by specifying DYNAMIC access. If access had been specified as DYNAMIC, the

Figure 8-6   *Output from Program 8-2 after Initial Creation*

```
BUDGET REPORT
PERIOD BUDGET 1 ACTUAL 1 VARIES 1 BUDGET 2 ACTUAL 2 VARIES 2 BUDGET 3 ACTUAL 3 VARIES 3 BUDGET 4 ACTUAL 4 VARIES 4
  1     24,000                      22,000                      23,000                      21,000
  2     25,000                      26,000                      25,000                      23,000
  3     25,000                      28,000                      27,000                      26,000
  4     30,000                      32,000                      31,000                      28,000
  5     35,000                      35,000                      36,000                      29,000
  6     42,000                      44,000                      40,000                      38,000
  7     45,000                      48,000                      44,000                      42,000
  8     53,000                      57,000                      52,000                      50,000
  9     47,000                      52,000                      49,000                      35,000
 10     40,000                      53,000                      42,000                      32,000
 11     18,000                      25,000                      21,000                      15,000
 12     18,000                      10,000                      15,000                       8,000

BUDGET REPORT
PERIOD BUDGET 1 ACTUAL 1 VARIES 1 BUDGET 2 ACTUAL 2 VARIES 2 BUDGET 3 ACTUAL 3 VARIES 3 BUDGET 4 ACTUAL 4 VARIES 4
  1     24,000

BUDGET REPORT
PERIOD BUDGET 1 ACTUAL 1 VARIES 1 BUDGET 2 ACTUAL 2 VARIES 2 BUDGET 3 ACTUAL 3 VARIES 3 BUDGET 4 ACTUAL 4 VARIES 4
  2     25,000                      26,000                      25,000                      23,000
  3     25,000                      28,000                      27,000                      26,000
  4     30,000                      32,000                      31,000                      28,000
```

READ statements at 1390 and 1570 would have to be modified to be READ BUDGET–DISK–FILE NEXT. NEXT is necessary when access is DYNAMIC and sequential access is desired.

Notice that the report format shown in the output from Program 8–2 in Figure 8–6 allows for the reporting of actual expenses and budget variances. This output was obtained by executing Program 8–2 immediately after the file was created. Therefore, neither actual expenses nor variance figures are included in the report.

Relative File Random Updating

The update to a relative file can take place either randomly or sequentially. However, in the case of the budget file created by Program 8–1, it would be more appropriate to accomplish a random update, because it is likely that only a few budget periods or departments would be updated at any one time. Program 8–3 illustrates the random updating of the budget file and allows for the updating of both the actual expenses and budgeted amounts. The input to the updating program includes not only the relative file but also the update transactions that are shown in Figure 8–7. Even though the records are in sequence, since a random update is being performed, any sequence is appropriate.

Figure 8–7 *Transactions to Update Budget File Randomly*

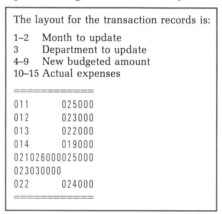

```
The layout for the transaction records is:

1–2    Month to update
3      Department to update
4–9    New budgeted amount
10–15  Actual expenses

=============
011       025000
012       023000
013       022000
014       019000
021026000025000
023030000
022       024000
=============
```

Note that when either the budgeted or actual dollars are included in the transaction record, that figure is used to update the appropriate record in the budget file. In this case, updating means that the amount from the transaction record will be moved to the appropriate location in the record.

Program Example

Program 8–3

```
000010 IDENTIFICATION DIVISION.
000020 PROGRAM-ID.    RELUPDT.
000030*··················································································
000040*          PROGRAM EXAMPLE 8-3 RELATIVE UPDATE PROGRAM           *
000050*··················································································
000060 ENVIRONMENT DIVISION.
000070 CONFIGURATION SECTION.
000080    SOURCE-COMPUTER.  IBM-4341.
000090    OBJECT-COMPUTER.  IBM-4341.
000100 INPUT-OUTPUT SECTION.
000110 FILE-CONTROL.
```

Program 8–3 *(continued)*

```
000120      SELECT BUDGET-DISK-FILE
000130          ASSIGN TO SYS025-DA-3375-BUDGET
000140          ORGANIZATION IS RELATIVE
000150          ACCESS IS RANDOM
000160          RELATIVE KEY IS BT-MONTH-TO-UPDATE
000170          FILE STATUS IS EL-STATUS-ERROR.
000180      SELECT BUDGET-REPORT
000190          ASSIGN TO SYS018-UR-3203-S.
000200      SELECT BUDGET-TRANS-FILE
000210          ASSIGN TO SYS016-UR-2501-S.
000220*
000230 DATA DIVISION.
000240 FILE SECTION.
000250 FD  BUDGET-DISK-FILE
000260      RECORD CONTAINS 50 CHARACTERS
000270      LABEL RECORDS STANDARD.
000280 01  BD-BUDGET-DISK-RECORD.
000290      05  BD-PAY-PERIOD              PIC 9(2).
000300      05  BD-DEPARTMENT-BUDGET
000310              OCCURS 4 TIMES.
000320          10  BD-BUDGETED-DOLLARS    PIC 9(6).
000330          10  BD-ACTUAL-DOLLARS      PIC 9(6).
000340 FD  BUDGET-TRANS-FILE
000350      RECORD CONTAINS 15 CHARACTERS
000360      LABEL RECORDS ARE STANDARD.
000370 01  BT-BUDGET-TRANS-RECORD.
000380      05  BT-MONTH-TO-UPDATE         PIC 9(2).
000390      05  BT-DEPARTMENT-TO-UPDATE    PIC 9(1).
000400      05  BT-BUDGETED-DOLLARS        PIC 9(6).
000410      05  BT-ACTUAL-DOLLARS          PIC 9(6).
000420 FD  BUDGET-REPORT
000430      RECORD CONTAINS 133 CHARACTERS
000440      LABEL RECORDS ARE OMITTED.
000450 01  BE-BUDGET-LINE                  PIC X(133).
000460*
000470 WORKING-STORAGE SECTION.
000480 01  WS-RECORD-INDICATORS.
000490      05  WS-EOF-INDICATOR           PIC X(3).
000500          88 END-OF-REQUEST-FILE     VALUE 'END'.
000510      05  WS-NUMBER-OF-DEPARTMENTS   PIC 9(1).
000520 01  HD-HEADING-LINE.
000530      05  FILLER                     PIC X(1).
000540      05  FILLER                     PIC X(25)
000550                                     VALUE 'UPDATE REPORT'.
000560 01  CH-COLUMN-HEADING.
000570      05  FILLER                     PIC X(1).
000580      05  FILLER                     PIC X(6) VALUE 'PERIOD'.
000590      05  FILLER                     PIC X(8)
000600                                     VALUE 'BUDGET 1'.
000610      05  FILLER                     PIC X(8)
000620                                     VALUE 'ACTUAL 1'.
000630      05  FILLER                     PIC X(8)
000640                                     VALUE 'VARIES 1'.
000650      05  FILLER                     PIC X(8)
000660                                     VALUE 'BUDGET 2'.
000670      05  FILLER                     PIC X(8)
000680                                     VALUE 'ACTUAL 2'.
000690      05  FILLER                     PIC X(8)
000700                                     VALUE 'VARIES 2'.
000710      05  FILLER                     PIC X(8)
000720                                     VALUE 'BUDGET 3'.
000730      05  FILLER                     PIC X(8)
000740                                     VALUE 'ACTUAL 3'.
000750      05  FILLER                     PIC X(8)
```

Program 8–3 *(continued)*

```
000760                                         VALUE 'VARIES 3'.
000770        05  FILLER                       PIC X(8)
000780                                         VALUE 'BUDGET 4'.
000790        05  FILLER                       PIC X(8)
000800                                         VALUE 'ACTUAL 4'.
000810        05  FILLER                       PIC X(8)
000820                                         VALUE 'VARIES 4'.
000830 01  DL-DETAIL-LINE.
000840        05  FILLER                       PIC X(1).
000850        05  DL-MONTH-TO-UPDATE           PIC X(2).
000860        05  FILLER                       PIC X(4).
000870        05  DL-DEPARTMENT-TO-UPDATE      PIC X(1).
000880        05  FILLER                       PIC X(4).
000890        05  DL-BUDGETED-DOLLARS          PIC ZZZ,ZZ9.
000900        05  FILLER                       PIC X(1).
000910        05  DL-ACTUAL-DOLLARS            PIC ZZZ,ZZ9.
000920        05  FILLER                       PIC X(1).
000930        05  DL-UPDATE-MESSAGE            PIC X(30).
000940 01  EL-ERROR-LINE.
000950        05  FILLER                       PIC X(1).
000960        05  EL-ERROR-OPERATION           PIC X(10).
000970        05  FILLER                       PIC X(5) VALUE SPACES.
000980        05  EL-STATUS-ERROR              PIC XX.
000990           88  SUCCESSFUL-COMPLETION     VALUE '00'.
001000           88  END-OF-BUDGET-FILE        VALUE '10'.
001010*
001020 PROCEDURE DIVISION.
001030 DECLARATIVES.
001040 DUMMY-ERROR-PROCEDURE SECTION.
001050     USE AFTER ERROR PROCEDURE ON BUDGET-DISK-FILE.
001060 END DECLARATIVES.
001070 A000-REL-UPDATE.
001080     OPEN INPUT  BUDGET-TRANS-FILE
001090          I-O    BUDGET-DISK-FILE
001100          OUTPUT BUDGET-REPORT.
001110     MOVE 'NO' TO WS-EOF-INDICATOR.
001120     PERFORM Z100-READ-UPDATE-RECORD.
001130     PERFORM B200-UPDATE-RECORDS
001140          UNTIL END-OF-REQUEST-FILE.
001150     CLOSE BUDGET-TRANS-FILE
001160           BUDGET-DISK-FILE
001170           BUDGET-REPORT.
001180     STOP RUN.
001190 B200-UPDATE-RECORDS.
001200     READ BUDGET-DISK-FILE.
001210     IF NOT SUCCESSFUL-COMPLETION
001220          MOVE 'READING' TO EL-ERROR-OPERATION
001230          WRITE BE-BUDGET-LINE FROM EL-ERROR-LINE
001240               AFTER 1
001250     ELSE
001260          PERFORM C300-DETERMINE-UPDATE.
001270     PERFORM Z100-READ-UPDATE-RECORD.
001280 C300-DETERMINE-UPDATE.
001290     MOVE SPACES TO DL-DETAIL-LINE.
001300     MOVE BT-MONTH-TO-UPDATE       TO DL-MONTH-TO-UPDATE.
001310     MOVE BT-DEPARTMENT-TO-UPDATE TO DL-DEPARTMENT-TO-UPDATE.
001320     IF BT-BUDGETED-DOLLARS NOT = SPACES
001330          MOVE BT-BUDGETED-DOLLARS
001340             TO BD-BUDGETED-DOLLARS(BT-DEPARTMENT-TO-UPDATE)
001350                DL-BUDGETED-DOLLARS
001360          MOVE 'BUDGET CHANGED' TO DL-UPDATE-MESSAGE
001370          IF BT-ACTUAL-DOLLARS NOT = SPACES
001380               MOVE BT-ACTUAL-DOLLARS
001390                  TO BD-ACTUAL-DOLLARS(BT-DEPARTMENT-TO-UPDATE)
```

Program 8–3 *(concluded)*

```
001400                      DL-ACTUAL-DOLLARS
001410            MOVE 'BOTH CHANGED' TO DL-UPDATE-MESSAGE
001420          ELSE
001430             NEXT SENTENCE
001440       ELSE
001450          IF BT-ACTUAL-DOLLARS NOT = SPACES
001460            MOVE BT-ACTUAL-DOLLARS
001470               TO BD-ACTUAL-DOLLARS(BT-DEPARTMENT-TO-UPDATE)
001480                     DL-ACTUAL-DOLLARS
001490            MOVE 'ACTUAL CHANGED' TO DL-UPDATE-MESSAGE.
001500       WRITE BE-BUDGET-LINE FROM DL-DETAIL-LINE
001510           AFTER 1.
001520       REWRITE BD-BUDGET-DISK-RECORD.
001530       IF NOT SUCCESSFUL-COMPLETION
001540          MOVE 'REWRITING' TO EL-ERROR-OPERATION
001550          WRITE BE-BUDGET-LINE FROM EL-ERROR-LINE
001560              AFTER 1.
001570  Z100-READ-UPDATE-RECORD.
001580       READ BUDGET-TRANS-FILE
001590           AT END MOVE 'END' TO WS-EOF-INDICATOR.
```

Discussion

BT–MONTH–TO–UPDATE is used as the RELATIVE KEY. Since the RELATIVE KEY is defined in a location that is not a part of the relative record, it does not have to be moved. With indexed files it is necessary to define the RECORD KEY as a part of the indexed record and ensure that an appropriate value is moved to the RECORD KEY before a random READ is attempted. With relative files, one MOVE statement is eliminated. Therefore, the READ statement at line 1200 will be successful so long as the BT–BUDGET–TRANS–RECORD contains a valid BT–MONTH–TO–UPDATE, the relative key.

If the READ is not successful, an error message is printed; otherwise C300–DETERMINE–UPDATE is performed. After appropriate updating occurs, the RE-WRITE statement at line 1520 accomplishes the in-place update. Figure 8–8 contains the output from the execution of Program 8–3. Figure 8–9 contains the output from executing Program 8–2 against the updated file. Compare the printed report before and after the update.

Figure 8–8 *Output from Program 8–3*

```
UPDATE REPORT

01    1                25,000 ACTUAL CHANGED
01    2                23,000 ACTUAL CHANGED
01    3                22,000 ACTUAL CHANGED
01    4                19,000 ACTUAL CHANGED
02    1       26,000   25,000 BOTH CHANGED
02    3       30,000          BUDGET CHANGED
02    2                24,000 ACTUAL CHANGED
```

Sequential Updating

As is true with indexed files, it is possible and sometimes desirable to sequentially update a relative file. In the budget example, a case in point would be at the end of the year. It may be desirable to use the existing budget file to prepare the file

Figure 8–9   *Output from Program 8–2 after Update*

```
BUDGET REPORT
PERIOD BUDGET 1 ACTUAL 1 VARIES 1 BUDGET 2 ACTUAL 2 VARIES 2 BUDGET 3 ACTUAL 3 VARIES 3 BUDGET 4 ACTUAL 4 VARIES 4
  1    24,000   25,000   1,000-  22,000   23,000   1,000-  23,000   22,000   1,000   21,000   19,000   2,000
  2    26,000   25,000   1,000   26,000   24,000   2,000   30,000                    23,000
  3    25,000                    28,000                    27,000                    26,000
  4    30,000                    32,000                    31,000                    28,000
  5    35,000                    35,000                    36,000                    29,000
  6    42,000                    44,000                    40,000                    38,000
  7    45,000                    48,000                    44,000                    42,000
  8    53,000                    57,000                    52,000                    50,000
  9    47,000                    52,000                    49,000                    35,000
 10    40,000                    53,000                    42,000                    32,000
 11    18,000                    25,000                    21,000                    15,000
 12    18,000                    10,000                    15,000                     8,000

BUDGET REPORT
PERIOD BUDGET 1 ACTUAL 1 VARIES 1 BUDGET 2 ACTUAL 2 VARIES 2 BUDGET 3 ACTUAL 3 VARIES 3 BUDGET 4 ACTUAL 4 VARIES 4
  1    24,000   25,000   1,000-

BUDGET REPORT
PERIOD BUDGET 1 ACTUAL 1 VARIES 1 BUDGET 2 ACTUAL 2 VARIES 2 BUDGET 3 ACTUAL 3 VARIES 3 BUDGET 4 ACTUAL 4 VARIES 4
  2    26,000   25,000   1,000   26,000   24,000   2,000   30,000                    23,000
  3    25,000                    28,000                    27,000                    26,000
  4    30,000                    32,000                    31,000                    28,000
```

for use in the following budget year, rather than creating an entirely new file. Program 8–4 illustrates this concept by moving the actual payroll expense to the budget amount, placing zeros in the actual amount fields and rewriting the record in-place sequentially. Note that access has been defined as SEQUENTIAL, and the file has been opened as I–O.

Program Example

Program 8–4

```
000010 IDENTIFICATION DIVISION.
000020 PROGRAM-ID.    RELUPDT.
000030*·····················································
000040*         PROGRAM EXAMPLE 8-4 RELATIVE SEQUENTIAL UPDATE PROGRAM *
000050*·····················································
000060 ENVIRONMENT DIVISION.
000070 CONFIGURATION SECTION.
000080    SOURCE-COMPUTER.   IBM-4341.
000090    OBJECT-COMPUTER.   IBM-4341.
000100 INPUT-OUTPUT SECTION.
000110 FILE-CONTROL.
000120    SELECT BUDGET-DISK-FILE
000130        ASSIGN TO SYS025-DA-3375-BUDGET
000140        ORGANIZATION IS RELATIVE
000150        ACCESS IS SEQUENTIAL
000160        FILE STATUS IS EL-STATUS-ERROR.
000170    SELECT BUDGET-REPORT
000180        ASSIGN TO SYS018-UR-3203-S.
000190*
000200 DATA DIVISION.
000210 FILE SECTION.
000220 FD  BUDGET-DISK-FILE
000230     RECORD CONTAINS 50 CHARACTERS
000240     LABEL RECORDS STANDARD.
000250 01  BD-BUDGET-DISK-RECORD.
000260     05  BD-PAY-PERIOD              PIC 9(2).
```

Program 8–4 *(continued)*

```
000270      05  BD-DEPARTMENT-BUDGET
000280              OCCURS 4 TIMES.
000290          10  BD-BUDGETED-DOLLARS      PIC 9(6).
000300          10  BD-ACTUAL-DOLLARS        PIC 9(6).
000310 FD  BUDGET-REPORT
000320     RECORD CONTAINS 133 CHARACTERS
000330     LABEL RECORDS ARE OMITTED.
000340 01  BR-BUDGET-REPORT-LINE             PIC X(133).
000350*
000360 WORKING-STORAGE SECTION.
000370 01  WS-NUMBER-OF-DEPARTMENTS          PIC 9.
000380 01  HD-HEADING-LINE.
000390      05  FILLER                       PIC X(1).
000400      05  FILLER                       PIC X(37)
000410              VALUE 'SEQUENTIAL UPDATE REPORT - NEW BUDGET'.
000420 01  DL-DETAIL-LINE.
000430      05  FILLER                       PIC X(1).
000440      05  DL-MONTH-TO-UPDATE           PIC X(2).
000450      05  FILLER OCCURS 4 TIMES.
000460          10  FILLER                   PIC X(4).
000470          10  DL-DEPARTMENT-TO-UPDATE  PIC X(1).
000480          10  FILLER                   PIC X(4).
000490          10  DL-BUDGETED-DOLLARS      PIC ZZZ,ZZ9.
000500          10  FILLER                   PIC X(4).
000510 01  EL-ERROR-LINE.
000520      05  FILLER                       PIC X(1).
000530      05  EL-ERROR-OPERATION           PIC X(10).
000540      05  FILLER                       PIC X(5) VALUE SPACES.
000550      05  EL-STATUS-ERROR              PIC XX.
000560          88  SUCCESSFUL-COMPLETION    VALUE '00'.
000570          88  END-OF-BUDGET-FILE       VALUE 'END'.
000580*
000590 PROCEDURE DIVISION.
000600 DECLARATIVES.
000610 DUMMY-ERROR-PROCEDURE SECTION.
000620     USE AFTER ERROR PROCEDURE ON BUDGET-DISK-FILE.
000630 END DECLARATIVES.
000640 A000-SEQ-RECEIVE.
000650     OPEN I-O    BUDGET-DISK-FILE
000660              OUTPUT BUDGET-REPORT.
000670     WRITE BR-BUDGET-REPORT-LINE FROM HD-HEADING-LINE
000680          AFTER PAGE.
000690     PERFORM Z100-READ-BUDGET-RECORD.
000700     PERFORM B400-UPDATE-RECORDS
000710          UNTIL END-OF-BUDGET-FILE.
000720     CLOSE BUDGET-DISK-FILE
000730           BUDGET-REPORT.
000740     STOP RUN.
000750 B400-UPDATE-RECORDS.
000760     MOVE SPACES TO DL-DETAIL-LINE.
000770     IF NOT SUCCESSFUL-COMPLETION
000780         MOVE 'READING' TO EL-ERROR-OPERATION
000790         WRITE BR-BUDGET-REPORT-LINE FROM EL-ERROR-LINE
000800              AFTER 1
000810     ELSE
000820         PERFORM C200-CREATE-NEW-RECORD.
000830     PERFORM Z100-READ-BUDGET-RECORD.
000840 C200-CREATE-NEW-RECORD.
000850     MOVE BD-PAY-PERIOD TO DL-MONTH-TO-UPDATE.
000860     PERFORM D100-DETERMINE-UPDATE
000870         VARYING WS-NUMBER-OF-DEPARTMENTS
000880         FROM 1 BY 1
000890         UNTIL WS-NUMBER-OF-DEPARTMENTS > 4.
000900     WRITE BR-BUDGET-REPORT-LINE FROM DL-DETAIL-LINE
```

Program 8–4 *(concluded)*

```
000910       AFTER 1.
000920       REWRITE BD-BUDGET-DISK-RECORD.
000930       IF NOT SUCCESSFUL-COMPLETION
000940           MOVE 'REWRITING' TO EL-ERROR-OPERATION
000950           WRITE BR-BUDGET-REPORT-LINE FROM EL-ERROR-LINE
000960               AFTER 1.
000970 D100-DETERMINE-UPDATE.
000980       MOVE WS-NUMBER-OF-DEPARTMENTS
000990           TO DL-DEPARTMENT-TO-UPDATE(WS-NUMBER-OF-DEPARTMENTS).
001000       MOVE BD-ACTUAL-DOLLARS(WS-NUMBER-OF-DEPARTMENTS)
001010           TO BD-BUDGETED-DOLLARS(WS-NUMBER-OF-DEPARTMENTS)
001020              DL-BUDGETED-DOLLARS(WS-NUMBER-OF-DEPARTMENTS).
001030       MOVE ZEROS TO BD-ACTUAL-DOLLARS(WS-NUMBER-OF-DEPARTMENTS).
001040 Z100-READ-BUDGET-RECORD.
001050       READ BUDGET-DISK-FILE.
```

Randomizing Algorithm

The previous examples illustrated the use of relative files when an item in a record can be used to directly determine the slot numbers. Not all files contain such a simple means of storing and retrieving a relative record. If it were desired to maintain a sales file as a relative file, what would be used as the RELATIVE KEY? The only candidate for the previously used sales file would be the salesperson number, which is a four-character field. Assuming that the highest salesperson number that could exist is 9999, that would necessitate allowance for the storage of that many records in as many slots. This would be true even if only 50 data records were to be stored. There would be thousands of unused slots, and the physical size of the file would be inordinately large.

Instead of using the salesperson number (or any number for a different file) as the slot number directly, a **randomizing algorithm** can be used to transform a number to an expected slot number. The advantage to this transformation process is that the required size of the file can be minimized.

Division/Remainder Algorithm

One of the commonly used randomizing algorithms is called the **division/remainder algorithm.** The first step in this technique is to estimate the number of slots that will be required. Next find the highest prime number that is lower than the number of slots estimated. Then the value that is to be transformed is divided by the prime number selected, and the remainder is determined. The expected slot number used is the remainder plus one. One is added because the slot number cannot be zero. The example in Figure 8–10 illustrates this concept.

From Figure 8–10 it is evident from the column for expected slot number that the transformation algorithm may result in **synonyms** for the expected slot number. When that occurs, a record is assigned the next available slot number as shown in the rightmost column. These actual slot numbers would be assigned if the data records were loaded into the file in the sequence they are listed. Any other input sequence would result in different assignments of actual slot numbers.

When a large number of synonyms occur during the transformation process, records are placed farther and farther away from the expected location. This necessitates searching for a record when it is not found in its expected location. An increase in file size (which also means a larger prime number) would decrease the number of synonyms but would also increase the number of unused slots in a file. Also an attempt to decrease the file size will not only increase the number of synonyms

Figure 8–10 *Division/Remainder Algorithm*

Assume: 30 records to be stored.
40 estimated slots required (allow for expansion).
37 highest prime number less than 40.

Salesperson number	Quotient division by 37	Remainder	Expected slot number	Actual slot number
125	3	14	15	15
529	14	11	12	12
746	20	6	7	7
859	23	8	9	9
1415	38	9	10	10
1634	44	6	7	8
1856	50	6	7	11
2157	58	11	12	13

but will also make it difficult (sometimes impossible) to assign a slot number that is larger than the expected slot number.

File Creation Using Division/Remainder

To illustrate the use of the transformation of a number to a slot number, Program 8–5 uses the same sales file as was previously used in Chapters 6 and 7. The same control considerations also apply. Thirty records are to be stored, so an estimate of 40 is used for the required number of slots. Assume that the file has been previously validated and sorted.

Program Example

Program 8–5

```
000010 IDENTIFICATION DIVISION.
000020 PROGRAM-ID.    RELCREAT.
000030*...........................................................
000040* PROGRAM EXAMPLE 8-5 RELATIVE CREATION - DIVISION/REMAINDER   *
000050*...........................................................
000060 ENVIRONMENT DIVISION.
000070 CONFIGURATION SECTION.
000080    SOURCE-COMPUTER.  IBM-4341.
000090    OBJECT-COMPUTER.  IBM-4341.
000100 INPUT-OUTPUT SECTION.
000110 FILE-CONTROL.
000120    SELECT RELATIVE-SALES-FILE
000130       ASSIGN TO SYS042-DA-3375-SALES
000140       ORGANIZATION IS RELATIVE
000150       ACCESS IS DYNAMIC
000160       RELATIVE KEY IS WS-SLOT-NUMBER
000170       FILE STATUS IS EL-STATUS-ERROR.
000180    SELECT SALES-BACKUP-FILE
000190       ASSIGN TO SYS026-UT-3375-SBACK.
000200    SELECT SALES-REPORT
000210       ASSIGN TO SYS018-UR-3203-S.
000220    SELECT SALES-INPUT-FILE
000230       ASSIGN TO SYS016-UR-2501-S.
000240    SELECT SALES-CONTROL-FILE
000250       ASSIGN TO SYS025-UT-3375-SALESCT.
000260*
000270 DATA DIVISION.
000280 FILE SECTION.
000290 FD  RELATIVE-SALES-FILE
000300    RECORD CONTAINS 55 CHARACTERS
000310    LABEL RECORDS STANDARD.
```

Program 8–5 *(continued)*

```
000320 01  RS-RELATIVE-SALES-RECORD.
000330     05  RS-SALESPERSON-NUMBER         PIC 9(4).
000340     05  RS-LAST-NAME                  PIC X(11).
000350     05  RS-FIRST-NAME                 PIC X(10).
000360     05  RS-YEAR-TO-DATE-SALES         PIC 9(5)V99.
000370     05  RS-YEAR-TO-DATE-SALES-RETURNS PIC 9(5)V99.
000380     05  RS-CURRENT-SALES              PIC 9(5)V99.
000390     05  RS-CURRENT-SALES-RETURNS      PIC 9(5)V99.
000400     05  RS-COMMISSION-RATE            PIC V99.
000410 FD  SALES-BACKUP-FILE
000420     RECORD CONTAINS 55 CHARACTERS
000430     LABEL RECORDS STANDARD.
000440 01  SB-SALES-BACKUP-RECORD            PIC X(55).
000450 FD  SALES-INPUT-FILE
000460     RECORD CONTAINS 44 CHARACTERS
000470     LABEL RECORDS ARE STANDARD.
000480 01  SI-SALES-INPUT-RECORD.
000490     05  SI-SALESPERSON-NUMBER         PIC 9(4).
000500     05  FILLER                        PIC X(1).
000510     05  SI-LAST-NAME                  PIC X(11).
000520     05  SI-FIRST-NAME                 PIC X(10).
000530     05  SI-YEAR-TO-DATE-SALES         PIC 9(5)V99.
000540     05  FILLER                        PIC X(1).
000550     05  SI-YEAR-TO-DATE-SALES-RETURNS PIC 9(5)V99.
000560     05  FILLER                        PIC X(1).
000570     05  SI-COMMISSION-RATE            PIC V99.
000580 FD  SALES-REPORT
000590     RECORD CONTAINS 133 CHARACTERS
000600     LABEL RECORDS ARE OMITTED.
000610 01  SR-SALES-REPORT-LINE              PIC X(133).
000620 FD  SALES-CONTROL-FILE
000630     RECORD CONTAINS 84 CHARACTERS
000640     LABEL RECORDS ARE STANDARD.
000650 01  SC-SALES-CONTROL-RECORD.
000660     05  SC-BEG-TOT-FIELDS.
000670         10  SC-BEG-TOT-RECORDS-STORED      PIC S9(4).
000680         10  SC-BEG-TOT-HASH-NUMBER         PIC S9(6).
000690         10  SC-BEG-TOT-YTD-SALES           PIC S9(6)V99.
000700         10  SC-BEG-TOT-YTD-SALES-RETURNS   PIC S9(6)V99.
000710         10  SC-BEG-TOT-CURRENT-SALES       PIC S9(6)V99.
000720         10  SC-BEG-TOT-CURRENT-RETURNS     PIC S9(6)V99.
000730     05  SC-CHG-TOT-FIELDS.
000740         10  SC-CHG-TOT-RECORDS-STORED      PIC S9(4).
000750         10  SC-CHG-TOT-HASH-NUMBER         PIC S9(6).
000760         10  SC-CHG-TOT-YTD-SALES           PIC S9(6)V99.
000770         10  SC-CHG-TOT-YTD-SALES-RETURNS   PIC S9(6)V99.
000780         10  SC-CHG-TOT-CURRENT-SALES       PIC S9(6)V99.
000790         10  SC-CHG-TOT-CURRENT-RETURNS     PIC S9(6)V99.
000800*
000810 WORKING-STORAGE SECTION.
000820 01  WS-ACCUMULATORS.
000830     05  WS-TOT-RECORDS-STORED         PIC S9(4).
000840     05  WS-TOT-HASH-NUMBER            PIC S9(6).
000850     05  WS-TOT-YTD-SALES              PIC S9(6)V99.
000860     05  WS-TOT-YTD-SALES-RETURNS      PIC S9(6)V99.
000870 01  WS-WORK-AREAS.
000880     05  WS-EOF-INDICATOR              PIC X(3).
000890         88  END-OF-INPUT-FILE         VALUE 'END'.
000900     05  WS-PRIME-NUMBER-DIVISOR       PIC 9(2) VALUE 37.
000910     05  WS-NUMBER-OF-SLOTS            PIC 9(2) VALUE 40.
000920     05  WS-SUBSCRIPT                  PIC 9(2).
000930     05  WS-QUOTIENT                   PIC 9(4).
000940     05  WS-REMAINDER                  PIC 9(2).
000950     05  WS-SLOT-NUMBER                PIC 9(2).
```

Program 8–5 *(continued)*

```
000960      05  WS-SEARCH-STEPS                    PIC 9(2) VALUE 20.
000970      05  WS-SEARCH-LIMIT                    PIC 9(2).
000980 01  HD-HEADING-LINE.
000990      05  FILLER                             PIC X(1).
001000      05  FILLER                             PIC X(28)
001010                                  VALUE 'RELATIVE SALES FILE TOTALS'.
001020 01  CH-COLUMN-HEADING-LINE.
001030      05  FILLER                             PIC X(20) VALUE SPACES.
001040      05  FILLER                             PIC X(8) VALUE 'RECORDS'.
001050      05  FILLER                             PIC X(11) VALUE SPACES.
001060      05  FILLER                             PIC X(5) VALUE 'SALES'.
001070      05  FILLER                             PIC X(8) VALUE SPACES.
001080      05  FILLER                             PIC X(8) VALUE 'RETURNS'.
001090      05  FILLER                             PIC X(1) VALUE SPACES.
001100      05  FILLER                             PIC X(11)
001110                                  VALUE 'HASH NUMBER'.
001120 01  TL-TOTAL-LINE.
001130      05  FILLER                             PIC X(1).
001140      05  TL-STUB-HEADING                    PIC X(20)
001150                                  VALUE 'BEGINNING TOTALS'.
001160      05  TL-TOT-RECORDS-STORED              PIC Z,ZZ9.
001170      05  FILLER                             PIC X(11) VALUE SPACES.
001180      05  TL-TOT-YTD-SALES                   PIC ZZZ,ZZZ.99-.
001190      05  FILLER                             PIC X(2) VALUE SPACES.
001200      05  TL-TOT-YTD-SALES-RETURNS           PIC ZZZ,ZZZ.99-.
001210      05  FILLER                             PIC X(2) VALUE SPACES.
001220      05  TL-TOT-HASH-NUMBER                 PIC ZZZ,ZZ9-.
001230 01  EL-ERROR-LINE.
001240      05  FILLER                             PIC X(1).
001250      05  EL-ERROR-OPERATION                 PIC X(30).
001260      05  FILLER                             PIC X(5) VALUE SPACES.
001270      05  EL-STATUS-ERROR                    PIC XX.
001280          88  SUCCESSFUL-COMPLETION          VALUE '00'.
001290          88  END-OF-SALES-FILE              VALUE '10'.
001300          88  SLOT-OCCUPIED                  VALUE '22'.
001310*
001320 PROCEDURE DIVISION.
001330 DECLARATIVES.
001340 DUMMY-ERROR-PROCEDURE SECTION.
001350     USE AFTER ERROR PROCEDURE ON RELATIVE-SALES-FILE.
001360 END DECLARATIVES.
001370 A000-CREATE.
001380     OPEN OUTPUT SALES-REPORT
001390                 SALES-CONTROL-FILE.
001400     PERFORM B100-INITIALIZE-VARIABLES.
001410     PERFORM B200-FORMAT-FILE.
001420     PERFORM B300-ADD-RECORDS.
001430     PERFORM B400-PROCESS-TOTALS.
001440     CLOSE SALES-REPORT
001450                 SALES-CONTROL-FILE.
001460     STOP RUN.
001470 B100-INITIALIZE-VARIABLES.
001480     MOVE 'NO'  TO WS-EOF-INDICATOR.
001490     MOVE ZEROS TO WS-ACCUMULATORS.
001500 B200-FORMAT-FILE.
001510     PERFORM C100-OPEN-TO-FORMAT.
001520     PERFORM C200-FORMAT-RECORDS
001530         VARYING WS-SUBSCRIPT
001540         FROM 1 BY 1
001550         UNTIL WS-SUBSCRIPT > WS-NUMBER-OF-SLOTS.
001560     CLOSE RELATIVE-SALES-FILE.
001570 B300-ADD-RECORDS.
001580     PERFORM C300-OPEN-TO-LOAD.
001590     PERFORM Z200-READ-NEW-RECORD.
```

Program 8–5   *(continued)*

```
001600        PERFORM C500-ADD-RECORDS
001610             UNTIL END-OF-INPUT-FILE.
001620        CLOSE SALES-INPUT-FILE
001630             RELATIVE-SALES-FILE
001640             SALES-BACKUP-FILE.
001650 B400-PROCESS-TOTALS.
001660        MOVE WS-TOT-RECORDS-STORED     TO SC-BEG-TOT-RECORDS-STORED
001670                                          TL-TOT-RECORDS-STORED.
001680        MOVE WS-TOT-HASH-NUMBER        TO SC-BEG-TOT-HASH-NUMBER
001690                                          TL-TOT-HASH-NUMBER.
001700        MOVE WS-TOT-YTD-SALES          TO SC-BEG-TOT-YTD-SALES
001710                                          TL-TOT-YTD-SALES.
001720        MOVE WS-TOT-YTD-SALES-RETURNS TO TL-TOT-YTD-SALES-RETURNS
001730                                          SC-BEG-TOT-YTD-SALES-RETURNS.
001740        MOVE ZEROS                     TO SC-BEG-TOT-CURRENT-SALES
001750                                          SC-BEG-TOT-CURRENT-RETURNS
001760                                          SC-CHG-TOT-FIELDS.
001770        WRITE SC-SALES-CONTROL-RECORD.
001780        WRITE SR-SALES-REPORT-LINE FROM HD-HEADING-LINE
001790             AFTER PAGE.
001800        WRITE SR-SALES-REPORT-LINE FROM CH-COLUMN-HEADING-LINE
001810             AFTER 2.
001820        WRITE SR-SALES-REPORT-LINE FROM TL-TOTAL-LINE
001830             AFTER 2.
001840 C100-OPEN-TO-FORMAT.
001850        OPEN OUTPUT RELATIVE-SALES-FILE.
001860        IF NOT SUCCESSFUL-COMPLETION
001870             MOVE 'FORMAT OPENING' TO EL-ERROR-OPERATION
001880             PERFORM Z100-ABORT-RUN
001890             STOP RUN.
001900 C200-FORMAT-RECORDS.
001910        MOVE WS-SUBSCRIPT TO WS-SLOT-NUMBER.
001920        MOVE HIGH-VALUES   TO RS-RELATIVE-SALES-RECORD.
001930        WRITE RS-RELATIVE-SALES-RECORD.
001940        IF NOT SUCCESSFUL-COMPLETION
001950             MOVE 'WRITE FORMATTING ERROR' TO EL-ERROR-OPERATION
001960             WRITE SR-SALES-REPORT-LINE     FROM EL-ERROR-LINE
001970                  AFTER 1.
001980 C300-OPEN-TO-LOAD.
001990        OPEN INPUT SALES-INPUT-FILE
002000             I-O   RELATIVE-SALES-FILE
002010             OUTPUT SALES-BACKUP-FILE.
002020        IF NOT SUCCESSFUL-COMPLETION
002030             MOVE 'LOAD OPENING' TO EL-ERROR-OPERATION
002040             PERFORM Z100-ABORT-RUN
002050             STOP RUN.
002060 C500-ADD-RECORDS.
002070        PERFORM D100-ACCUMULATE-TOTALS.
002080        DIVIDE SI-SALESPERSON-NUMBER BY WS-PRIME-NUMBER-DIVISOR
002090             GIVING WS-QUOTIENT
002100             REMAINDER WS-REMAINDER.
002110        COMPUTE WS-SLOT-NUMBER = WS-REMAINDER + 1.
002120        MOVE SI-SALESPERSON-NUMBER TO RS-SALESPERSON-NUMBER.
002130        MOVE SI-LAST-NAME          TO RS-LAST-NAME.
002140        MOVE SI-FIRST-NAME         TO RS-FIRST-NAME.
002150        MOVE SI-YEAR-TO-DATE-SALES TO RS-YEAR-TO-DATE-SALES.
002160        MOVE SI-YEAR-TO-DATE-SALES-RETURNS
002170             TO RS-YEAR-TO-DATE-SALES-RETURNS.
002180        MOVE ZEROS                 TO RS-CURRENT-SALES
002190                                      RS-CURRENT-SALES-RETURNS.
002200        MOVE SI-COMMISSION-RATE    TO RS-COMMISSION-RATE.
002210        WRITE RS-RELATIVE-SALES-RECORD.
002220        IF SLOT-OCCUPIED
002230             PERFORM D200-SEARCH-FOR-SLOT.
```

Program 8-5 *(concluded)*

```
002240     WRITE SB-SALES-BACKUP-RECORD
002250         FROM RS-RELATIVE-SALES-RECORD.
002260     PERFORM Z200-READ-NEW-RECORD.
002270 D100-ACCUMULATE-TOTALS.
002280     ADD 1                      TO WS-TOT-RECORDS-STORED.
002290     ADD SI-SALESPERSON-NUMBER TO WS-TOT-HASH-NUMBER.
002300     ADD SI-YEAR-TO-DATE-SALES TO WS-TOT-YTD-SALES.
002310     ADD SI-YEAR-TO-DATE-SALES-RETURNS
002320         TO WS-TOT-YTD-SALES-RETURNS.
002330 D200-SEARCH-FOR-SLOT.
002340     ADD WS-SLOT-NUMBER WS-SEARCH-STEPS
002350         GIVING WS-SEARCH-LIMIT.
002360     PERFORM E100-WRITE-SEARCH
002370         VARYING WS-SLOT-NUMBER
002380         FROM WS-SLOT-NUMBER BY 1
002390         UNTIL SUCCESSFUL-COMPLETION
002400             OR WS-SLOT-NUMBER > WS-SEARCH-LIMIT
002410             OR WS-SLOT-NUMBER > WS-NUMBER-OF-SLOTS.
002420     IF NOT SUCCESSFUL-COMPLETION
002430         MOVE 'INSUFFICIENT FILE SPACE' TO EL-ERROR-OPERATION
002440         PERFORM Z100-ABORT-RUN
002450         STOP RUN.
002460 E100-WRITE-SEARCH.
002470     WRITE RS-RELATIVE-SALES-RECORD.
002480 Z100-ABORT-RUN.
002490     WRITE SR-SALES-REPORT-LINE FROM EL-ERROR-LINE
002500         AFTER 1.
002510     CLOSE RELATIVE-SALES-FILE
002520           SALES-BACKUP-FILE
002530           SALES-REPORT.
002540 Z200-READ-NEW-RECORD.
002550     READ SALES-INPUT-FILE
002560         AT END MOVE 'END' TO WS-EOF-INDICATOR.
```

Discussion

In the DATA division, notice the items defined in WS–WORK–AREAS. Items WS–PRIME–NUMBER–DIVISOR through WS–SEARCH–LIMIT are used for the randomizing algorithm. WS–SUBSCRIPT is used in conjunction with WS–SEARCH–STEPS to find an available slot when a synonym occurs.

In the PROCEDURE division, the first major task is evidenced in B200–FORMAT–FILE. Some systems require that a relative file be initialized or formatted prior to data records being loaded. **Relative file formatting,** if required, places specified characters in the record and may be HIGH–VALUES, LOW–VALUES or SPACES, depending on the system. Check with the manual from the vendor to determine which characters are necessary and whether relative file formatting is necessary. Note the movement of HIGH–VALUES at line 1920 before the actual WRITE statement. Since the program contains both the need to format the file by opening the file as OUTPUT and the need to randomly load records into the formatted file, DYNAMIC access has been specified.

C500–ADD–RECORDS is iterated to actually load data records into the file. After the expected slot number is calculated in the DIVIDE statement at lines 2080 through the COMPUTE statement at line 2110, the input record is moved to the relative record, and a WRITE is attempted at line 2210. If SLOT–OCCUPIED is true, D200–SEARCH–FOR–SLOT is performed, which, in turn, performs E100–WRITE–SEARCH. E100–WRITE–SEARCH makes repeated attempts to find an available slot. If the attempts are unsuccessful, the program is terminated because of the inability to find an available slot. When that occurs, it would be necessary to increase the estimated number of slots required along with a concomitant increase in the prime number used in the transformation algorithm. This actually occurred with this data set when an initial estimate of 35 records was used. When the created file is later reported from, the slot numbers actually assigned will also be reported. The output from a sequential reporting program is shown in Figure 8–11.

File Reporting Using Division/Remainder

When reporting randomly from a relative file that uses the division/remainder transformation technique, an input value must be transformed to an expected slot number and a READ attempted. If the record is not the one desired, then a search similar to that performed in Program 8–5 would have to be performed. Since this method is used in Program 8–6, a random update program, a program using random reporting will not be shown.

Sequential reporting from a relative file poses no particular difficulties. The system automatically skips unused record slots and will provide the program with only records that actually exist. There is nothing to learn from showing the reader a sequential reporting program from a relative file, since it exactly parallels a sequential report from an indexed file. However, a sequential reporting program was written to be able to list the contents of the relative file, including the slot numbers that were assigned. The program was executed immediately after the file was initially

Figure 8–11 *Output from Report Program after Initial Creation*

```
SLOT REPORT
2294    HERMAN      JACK          484.65       87.47      .00       .00    .05    01
 927    BARCLAY     RICHARD     1,987.40      485.63      .00       .00    .11    03
1001    DILL        JEFF          586.40      284.56      .00       .00    .20    04
2186    SMITH       DOUGLAS       183.45      377.58      .00       .00    .20    05
 635    HUNT        ROBERT        453.20      475.34      .00       .00    .10    07
 746    JACKSON     JASON         784.50       84.78      .00       .00    .15    08
 859    HUTCHENS    JEFF          576.30       48.57      .00       .00    .14    09
1415    GOODMAN     EVE           645.42      238.47      .00       .00    .10    10
1634    VAUGHN      SYLVIA A.     478.99      456.78      .00       .00    .20    11
 529    PEACOCK     BARBARA       673.30      156.64      .00       .00    .08    12
1856    LOVELAND    GEORGE        462.75      276.56      .00       .00    .10    13
2157    YOUNG       KAREN L.    1,123.59       35.75      .00       .00    .30    14
 125    LISHER      JANET F.      500.00         .00      .00       .00    .15    15
1938    DWYER       JOHN D.       231.75       40.00      .00       .00    .10    16
2269    THOMPSON    LISA S.       500.00      100.00      .00       .00    .20    17
  17    PAYNE       MAX           987.00       56.73      .00       .00    .05    18
1867    STEWARD     KEVIN J.    1,150.00      175.00      .00       .00    .15    19
2341    ADAMS       ROBYN A.      231.75       40.00      .00       .00    .10    20
2485    PHILLIPS    TRACY L.      500.00      100.00      .00       .00    .30    21
 243    BROCKETT    JANE R.       750.00      900.00      .00       .00    .05    22
1132    UNLAND      KIM L.        475.64      395.85      .00       .00    .25    23
 356    GOLTMAN     LINDA S.    1,098.77       10.00      .00       .00    .10    24
2487    HUME        LETA          483.53      284.37      .00       .00    .20    25
 580    DUPREE      KELLY L.    3,578.88      275.82      .00       .00    .10    26
 396    VOLSKY      CHRIS         326.80       58.47      .00       .00    .08    27
2395    MATNEY      DELORES       795.74      857.46      .00       .00    .05    28
2575    CROSS       CHERYL        385.63      382.50      .00       .00    .10    29
1805    KIMBERLING  CARLA K.      500.00      100.00      .00       .00    .30    30
 401    OWENS       GEORGE        362.20       39.57      .00       .00    .09    32
 479    WETZEL      ROBERT D.   2,088.76       58.77      .00       .00    .15    36

                    RECORDS   HASH      SALES      RETURNS     SALES    RETURNS

BEGINNING - CONTROL    30    40,130   23,386.40   6,882.67      .00       .00

NET CHANGE - CONTROL    0         0         .00        .00      .00       .00

ENDING - CONTROL       30    40,130   23,386.40   6,882.67      .00       .00

ENDING - ACTUAL        30    40,130   23,386.40   6,882.67      .00       .00
```

loaded and resulted in the output in Figure 8–11. Notice that the data records are in slot number sequence (the slot numbers are in the rightmost column), not salesperson number sequence. Notice also that there are unused slot numbers as shown by the last column in the report.

Updating using Division/Remainder

To illustrate the ability to randomly update a relative file that has been created using a transformation technique (sequential updating poses no additional techniques), Program 8–6 uses the same transaction file as was used in the updates for both sequential and indexed files.

Program Example

Program 8–6

```
000010 IDENTIFICATION DIVISION.
000020 PROGRAM-ID.    RELUPDT.
000030**************************************************************
000040* PROGRAM EXAMPLE 8-6 RELATIVE RANDOM UPDATE                 *
000050**************************************************************
000060 ENVIRONMENT DIVISION.
000070 CONFIGURATION SECTION.
000080    SOURCE-COMPUTER.  IBM-4341.
000090    OBJECT-COMPUTER.  IBM-4341.
000100 INPUT-OUTPUT SECTION.
000110 FILE-CONTROL.
000120    SELECT RELATIVE-SALES-FILE
000130        ASSIGN TO SYS042-DA-3375-SALES
000140        ORGANIZATION IS RELATIVE
000150        ACCESS IS DYNAMIC
000160        RELATIVE KEY IS WS-SLOT-NUMBER
000170        FILE STATUS IS EL-STATUS-ERROR.
000180    SELECT SALES-REPORT-FILE
000190        ASSIGN TO SYS018-UR-3203-S.
000200    SELECT SALES-TRANSACTION-FILE
000210        ASSIGN TO SYS016-UR-2501-S.
000220    SELECT SALES-CONTROL-FILE
000230        ASSIGN TO SYS025-UT-3375-SALESCT.
000240*
000250 DATA DIVISION.
000260 FILE SECTION.
000270 FD  RELATIVE-SALES-FILE
000280     RECORD CONTAINS 55 CHARACTERS
000290     LABEL RECORDS STANDARD.
000300 01  RS-RELATIVE-SALES-RECORD.
000310     05  RS-SALESPERSON-NUMBER          PIC 9(4).
000320     05  RS-SALESPERSON-NUMBER-X
000330         REDEFINES RS-SALESPERSON-NUMBER  PIC X(4).
000340     05  RS-LAST-NAME                   PIC X(11).
000350     05  RS-FIRST-NAME                  PIC X(10).
000360     05  RS-YEAR-TO-DATE-SALES          PIC 9(5)V99.
000370     05  RS-YEAR-TO-DATE-SALES-RETURNS  PIC 9(5)V99.
000380     05  RS-CURRENT-SALES               PIC 9(5)V99.
000390     05  RS-CURRENT-SALES-RETURNS       PIC 9(5)V99.
000400     05  RS-COMMISSION-RATE             PIC V99.
000410 FD  SALES-TRANSACTION-FILE
000420     RECORD CONTAINS 46 CHARACTERS
000430     LABEL RECORDS ARE STANDARD.
000440 01  ST-SALES-TRANS-RECORD.
000450     05  ST-SALESPERSON-NUMBER          PIC 9(4).
000460     05  ST-SALESPERSON-NUMBER-X
000470         REDEFINES ST-SALESPERSON-NUMBER  PIC X(4).
```

Program 8–6 *(continued)*

```
000480     05  FILLER                      PIC X(1).
000490     05  ST-LAST-NAME                PIC X(11).
000500     05  ST-FIRST-NAME               PIC X(10).
000510     05  ST-CURRENT-SALES            PIC 9(5)V99.
000520     05  FILLER                      PIC X(1).
000530     05  ST-CURRENT-SALES-RETURNS    PIC 9(5)V99.
000540     05  FILLER                      PIC X(1).
000550     05  ST-COMMISSION-RATE          PIC V99.
000560     05  FILLER                      PIC X(1).
000570     05  ST-TRANSACTION-CODE         PIC X(1).
000580         88  ADDITION-OF-SALESPERSON     VALUE '1'.
000590         88  DELETION-OF-SALESPERSON     VALUE '2'.
000600         88  NAME-CHANGE                 VALUE '3'.
000610         88  UPDATE-CURRENT-SALES        VALUE '4'.
000620         88  UPDATE-CURRENT-SALES-RETURNS VALUE '5'.
000630         88  UPDATE-COMMISSION-RATE      VALUE '6'.
000640 FD  SALES-CONTROL-FILE
000650     RECORD CONTAINS 84 CHARACTERS
000660     LABEL RECORDS ARE STANDARD.
000670 01  SC-SALES-CONTROL-RECORD.
000680     05  SC-BEG-TOT-FIELDS.
000690         10  SC-BEG-TOT-RECORDS-STORED  PIC S9(4).
000700         10  SC-BEG-TOT-HASH-NUMBER     PIC S9(6).
000710         10  SC-BEG-TOT-YTD-SALES       PIC S9(6)V99.
000720         10  SC-BEG-TOT-YTD-SALES-RETURNS PIC S9(6)V99.
000730         10  SC-BEG-TOT-CURRENT-SALES   PIC S9(6)V99.
000740         10  SC-BEG-TOT-CURRENT-RETURNS PIC S9(6)V99.
000750     05  SC-CHG-TOT-FIELDS.
000760         10  SC-CHG-TOT-RECORDS-STORED  PIC S9(4).
000770         10  SC-CHG-TOT-HASH-NUMBER     PIC S9(6).
000780         10  SC-CHG-TOT-YTD-SALES       PIC S9(6)V99.
000790         10  SC-CHG-TOT-YTD-SALES-RETURNS PIC S9(6)V99.
000800         10  SC-CHG-TOT-CURRENT-SALES   PIC S9(6)V99.
000810         10  SC-CHG-TOT-CURRENT-RETURNS PIC S9(6)V99.
000820 FD  SALES-REPORT-FILE
000830     RECORD CONTAINS 133 CHARACTERS
000840     LABEL RECORDS ARE OMITTED.
000850 01  SR-SALES-REPORT-LINE            PIC X(133).
000860*
000870 WORKING-STORAGE SECTION.
000880 01  WS-ACCUMULATORS.
000890     05  WS-CHG-TOT-RECORDS-STORED   PIC S9(4).
000900     05  WS-CHG-TOT-HASH-NUMBER      PIC S9(6).
000910     05  WS-CHG-YTD-SALES            PIC S9(6)V99.
000920     05  WS-CHG-YTD-SALES-RETURNS    PIC S9(6)V99.
000930     05  WS-CHG-CURRENT-SALES        PIC S9(6)V99.
000940     05  WS-CHG-CURRENT-RETURNS      PIC S9(6)V99.
000950 01  WS-WORK-AREAS.
000960     05  WS-EOF-INDICATOR            PIC X(3).
000970         88  END-OF-TRANSACTION-FILE VALUE 'END'.
000980     05  WS-PRIME-NUMBER-DIVISOR     PIC 9(2) VALUE 37.
000990     05  WS-NUMBER-OF-SLOTS          PIC 9(2) VALUE 40.
001000     05  WS-SUBSCRIPT                PIC 9(2).
001010     05  WS-QUOTIENT                 PIC 9(4).
001020     05  WS-REMAINDER                PIC 9(2).
001030     05  WS-SLOT-NUMBER              PIC 9(2).
001040     05  WS-SEARCH-STEPS             PIC 9(2) VALUE 20.
001050     05  WS-SEARCH-LIMIT             PIC 9(2).
001060     05  WS-BEGINNING-SLOT           PIC 9(2).
001070 01  UC-UPDATE-CONTROL-AREAS.
001080     05  UC-MASTER-PENDING-SWITCH    PIC X(3).
001090         88  MASTER-IS-PENDING       VALUE 'YES'.
001100     05  UC-COUNT-SUB                PIC 9(4).
001110     05  UC-MASTER-HOLD-AREA         PIC X(41).
```

Program 8–6   *(continued)*

```
001120     05  UC-HEADING-CONTROL-VALUES.
001130         10  FILLER        PIC X(20) VALUE 'ADDITIONS'.
001140         10  FILLER        PIC X(20) VALUE 'DELETIONS'.
001150         10  FILLER        PIC X(20) VALUE 'NAME CHANGES'.
001160         10  FILLER        PIC X(20) VALUE 'YTD SALES CHANGES'.
001170         10  FILLER        PIC X(20) VALUE 'YTD RTNS CHANGES'.
001180         10  FILLER        PIC X(20) VALUE 'COM RATE CHANGES'.
001190         10  FILLER        PIC X(20) VALUE 'REJECTIONS'.
001200         10  FILLER        PIC X(20) VALUE 'TOTAL TRANSACTIONS'.
001210     05  FILLER REDEFINES UC-HEADING-CONTROL-VALUES.
001220         10  UC-HEADING-LINE       PIC X(20)
001230             OCCURS 8 TIMES.
001240     05  UC-RECORD-CONTROL-TOTALS.
001250         10  UC-NUM-OF-ADDS        PIC 9(4).
001260         10  UC-NUM-OF-DELETES     PIC 9(4).
001270         10  UC-NUM-OF-CHG-NAME    PIC 9(4).
001280         10  UC-NUM-OF-CHG-SALES   PIC 9(4).
001290         10  UC-NUM-OF-CHG-RTNS    PIC 9(4).
001300         10  UC-NUM-OF-CHG-COM-RATE PIC 9(4).
001310         10  UC-NUM-OF-REJECTIONS  PIC 9(4).
001320         10  UC-NUM-OF-TRANSACTIONS PIC 9(4).
001330     05  FILLER REDEFINES UC-RECORD-CONTROL-TOTALS.
001340         10  UC-RECORD-COUNT       PIC 9(4)
001350             OCCURS 8 TIMES.
001360 01  HD-HEADING-LINE.
001370     05  FILLER               PIC X(1).
001380     05  FILLER               PIC X(13)
001390                              VALUE 'UPDATE REPORT'.
001400 01  CH-COLUMN-HEADING-LINE.
001410     05  FILLER               PIC X(1).
001420     05  FILLER               PIC X(56)
001430                              VALUE 'RECORD IMAGE'.
001440     05  FILLER               PIC X(25)
001450                              VALUE 'UPDATE ACTION'.
001460     05  FILLER               PIC X(30)
001470                              VALUE 'ERROR MESSAGE'.
001480 01  CH-COLUMN-HEADING-LINE-2.
001490     05  FILLER               PIC X(1).
001500     05  FILLER               PIC X(20) VALUE SPACES.
001510     05  FILLER               PIC X(8) VALUE 'RECORDS'.
001520     05  FILLER               PIC X(2) VALUE SPACES.
001530     05  FILLER               PIC X(4) VALUE 'HASH'.
001540     05  FILLER               PIC X(5) VALUE SPACES.
001550     05  FILLER               PIC X(5) VALUE 'SALES'.
001560     05  FILLER               PIC X(8) VALUE SPACES.
001570     05  FILLER               PIC X(8) VALUE 'RETURNS'.
001580     05  FILLER               PIC X(5) VALUE SPACES.
001590     05  FILLER               PIC X(5) VALUE 'SALES'.
001600     05  FILLER               PIC X(8) VALUE SPACES.
001610     05  FILLER               PIC X(8) VALUE 'RETURNS'.
001620 01  DL-DETAIL-LINE.
001630     05  FILLER               PIC X(1).
001640     05  DL-RECORD-IMAGE      PIC X(50).
001650     05  FILLER               PIC X(2) VALUE SPACES.
001660     05  DL-SLOT-NUMBER       PIC 9(2).
001670     05  FILLER               PIC X(2) VALUE SPACES.
001680     05  DL-UPDATE-ACTION     PIC X(25).
001690     05  DL-ERROR-MESSAGE     PIC X(30).
001700 01  EL-ERROR-LINE.
001710     05  FILLER               PIC X(1).
001720     05  EL-ERROR-OPERATION   PIC X(30).
001730     05  FILLER               PIC X(5) VALUE SPACES.
001740     05  EL-STATUS-ERROR      PIC X(2).
001750         88  SUCCESSFUL-COMPLETION  VALUE '00'.
```

Program 8–6   *(continued)*

```
001760          88  SLOT-OCCUPIED              VALUE '22'.
001770          88  NO-RECORD-FOUND            VALUE '23'.
001780 01  TL-TOTAL-LINE-1.
001790     05  FILLER                          PIC X(1).
001800     05  TL-STUB-HEADING                 PIC X(20).
001810     05  TL-TOT-RECORDS-STORED           PIC Z,ZZ9-.
001820     05  FILLER                          PIC X(2) VALUE SPACES.
001830     05  TL-TOT-HASH-NUMBER              PIC ZZZ,ZZ9-.
001840     05  FILLER                          PIC X(2) VALUE SPACES.
001850     05  TL-TOT-YTD-SALES                PIC ZZZ,ZZZ.99-.
001860     05  FILLER                          PIC X(2) VALUE SPACES.
001870     05  TL-TOT-YTD-SALES-RETURNS        PIC ZZZ,ZZZ.99-.
001880     05  FILLER                          PIC X(2) VALUE SPACES.
001890     05  TL-TOT-CURRENT-SALES            PIC ZZZ,ZZZ.99-.
001900     05  FILLER                          PIC X(2) VALUE SPACES.
001910     05  TL-TOT-CURRENT-RETURNS          PIC ZZZ,ZZZ.99-.
001920 01  TL-TOTAL-LINE-2.
001930     05  FILLER                          PIC X(1).
001940     05  TL-HEADING                      PIC X(30).
001950     05  TL-COUNT                        PIC Z,ZZ9.
001960*
001970 PROCEDURE DIVISION.
001980 DECLARATIVES.
001990 DUMMY-ERROR-PROCEDURE SECTION.
002000     USE AFTER ERROR PROCEDURE ON RELATIVE-SALES-FILE.
002010 END DECLARATIVES.
002020 A000-UPDATE.
002030     PERFORM B100-OPEN-TO-UPDATE.
002040     PERFORM B200-INITIALIZE-VARIABLES.
002050     PERFORM B300-PRINT-HEADINGS.
002060     PERFORM Z100-READ-RECORD.
002070     PERFORM B500-UPDATE-RECORDS
002080          UNTIL END-OF-TRANSACTION-FILE.
002090     PERFORM B600-PROCESS-TOTALS.
002100     CLOSE RELATIVE-SALES-FILE
002110           SALES-TRANSACTION-FILE
002120           SALES-CONTROL-FILE
002130           SALES-REPORT-FILE.
002140     STOP RUN.
002150 B100-OPEN-TO-UPDATE.
002160     OPEN INPUT  SALES-TRANSACTION-FILE
002170          I-O    RELATIVE-SALES-FILE
002180                 SALES-CONTROL-FILE
002190          OUTPUT SALES-REPORT-FILE.
002200     IF NOT SUCCESSFUL-COMPLETION
002210        MOVE 'OPENING' TO EL-ERROR-OPERATION
002220        PERFORM Z300-ABORT-RUN
002230        STOP RUN.
002240 B200-INITIALIZE-VARIABLES.
002250     MOVE 'NO'  TO WS-EOF-INDICATOR.
002260     MOVE ZEROS TO WS-ACCUMULATORS
002270               UC-RECORD-CONTROL-TOTALS.
002280     MOVE 'NO'  TO UC-MASTER-PENDING-SWITCH.
002290 B300-PRINT-HEADINGS.
002300     WRITE SR-SALES-REPORT-LINE FROM HD-HEADING-LINE
002310          AFTER PAGE.
002320     WRITE SR-SALES-REPORT-LINE FROM CH-COLUMN-HEADING-LINE
002330          AFTER 1.
002340 B500-UPDATE-RECORDS.
002350     MOVE SPACES TO DL-DETAIL-LINE.
002360     MOVE ZEROS TO RS-SALESPERSON-NUMBER-X.
002370     PERFORM C100-DETERMINE-SLOT-NUMBER.
002380     PERFORM Z200-READ-RELATIVE-RECORD
002390          VARYING WS-SLOT-NUMBER
```

Program 8–6 *(continued)*

```
002400          FROM WS-BEGINNING-SLOT BY 1
002410          UNTIL ST-SALESPERSON-NUMBER-X = RS-SALESPERSON-NUMBER-X
002420          OR WS-SLOT-NUMBER > WS-SEARCH-LIMIT
002430          OR WS-SLOT-NUMBER > WS-NUMBER-OF-SLOTS.
002440      IF ADDITION-OF-SALESPERSON
002450          PERFORM C300-POSSIBLE-ADDITION
002460      ELSE
002470          PERFORM C400-POSSIBLE-UPDATE.
002480      PERFORM C500-WRITE-DETAIL-LINE.
002490      PERFORM Z100-READ-RECORD.
002500  B600-PROCESS-TOTALS.
002510      READ SALES-CONTROL-FILE.
002520      PERFORM C700-PRINT-BEG-TOTALS.
002530      PERFORM C800-PRINT-CHG-TOTALS.
002540      PERFORM C900-PRINT-END-TOTALS.
002550      PERFORM C1000-PRINT-COUNT-SUMMARY
002560          VARYING UC-COUNT-SUB
002570          FROM 1 BY 1
002580          UNTIL UC-COUNT-SUB > 8.
002590      REWRITE SC-SALES-CONTROL-RECORD.
002600  C100-DETERMINE-SLOT-NUMBER.
002610      DIVIDE ST-SALESPERSON-NUMBER BY WS-PRIME-NUMBER-DIVISOR
002620          GIVING WS-QUOTIENT
002630          REMAINDER WS-REMAINDER.
002640      ADD 1 WS-REMAINDER
002650          GIVING
002660          WS-SLOT-NUMBER
002670          WS-BEGINNING-SLOT.
002680      ADD WS-SLOT-NUMBER WS-SEARCH-STEPS
002690          GIVING WS-SEARCH-LIMIT.
002700  C300-POSSIBLE-ADDITION.
002710      IF ST-SALESPERSON-NUMBER-X = RS-SALESPERSON-NUMBER-X
002720          MOVE 'REJECTED'            TO DL-UPDATE-ACTION
002730          MOVE 'RECORD ALREADY EXISTS' TO DL-ERROR-MESSAGE
002740          ADD 1                      TO UC-NUM-OF-REJECTIONS
002750      ELSE
002760          PERFORM D200-ADD-RECORD.
002770  C400-POSSIBLE-UPDATE.
002780      IF WS-SLOT-NUMBER > WS-SEARCH-LIMIT
002790          OR WS-SLOT-NUMBER > WS-NUMBER-OF-SLOTS
002800          MOVE 'REJECTED' TO DL-UPDATE-ACTION
002810          MOVE 'RECORD NOT FOUND IN SEARCH' TO DL-ERROR-MESSAGE
002820          ADD 1 TO UC-NUM-OF-REJECTIONS
002830      ELSE
002840          PERFORM D400-UPDATE-RECORD.
002850  C500-WRITE-DETAIL-LINE.
002860      MOVE ST-SALES-TRANS-RECORD TO DL-RECORD-IMAGE.
002870      MOVE WS-SLOT-NUMBER         TO DL-SLOT-NUMBER.
002880      WRITE SR-SALES-REPORT-LINE FROM DL-DETAIL-LINE
002890          AFTER 1.
002900  C700-PRINT-BEG-TOTALS.
002910      WRITE SR-SALES-REPORT-LINE FROM CH-COLUMN-HEADING-LINE-2
002920          AFTER 2.
002930      MOVE 'BEGINNING  - CONTROL'   TO TL-STUB-HEADING.
002940      MOVE SC-BEG-TOT-RECORDS-STORED TO TL-TOT-RECORDS-STORED.
002950      MOVE SC-BEG-TOT-HASH-NUMBER     TO TL-TOT-HASH-NUMBER.
002960      MOVE SC-BEG-TOT-YTD-SALES       TO TL-TOT-YTD-SALES.
002970      MOVE SC-BEG-TOT-YTD-SALES-RETURNS
002980          TO TL-TOT-YTD-SALES-RETURNS.
002990      MOVE SC-BEG-TOT-CURRENT-SALES  TO TL-TOT-CURRENT-SALES.
003000      MOVE SC-BEG-TOT-CURRENT-RETURNS
003010          TO TL-TOT-CURRENT-RETURNS.
003020      WRITE SR-SALES-REPORT-LINE FROM TL-TOTAL-LINE-1
003030          AFTER 2.
```

Program 8–6 *(continued)*

```
003040 C800-PRINT-CHG-TOTALS.
003050     MOVE 'PREVIOUS CHANGES'        TO TL-STUB-HEADING.
003060     MOVE SC-CHG-TOT-RECORDS-STORED TO TL-TOT-RECORDS-STORED.
003070     MOVE SC-CHG-TOT-HASH-NUMBER    TO TL-TOT-HASH-NUMBER.
003080     MOVE SC-CHG-TOT-YTD-SALES      TO TL-TOT-YTD-SALES.
003090     MOVE SC-CHG-TOT-YTD-SALES-RETURNS
003100         TO TL-TOT-YTD-SALES-RETURNS.
003110     MOVE SC-CHG-TOT-CURRENT-SALES    TO TL-TOT-CURRENT-SALES.
003120     MOVE SC-CHG-TOT-CURRENT-RETURNS TO TL-TOT-CURRENT-RETURNS.
003130     WRITE SR-SALES-REPORT-LINE FROM TL-TOTAL-LINE-1
003140         AFTER 2.
003150     MOVE 'CURRENT CHANGES'         TO TL-STUB-HEADING.
003160     MOVE WS-CHG-TOT-RECORDS-STORED TO TL-TOT-RECORDS-STORED.
003170     MOVE WS-CHG-TOT-HASH-NUMBER    TO TL-TOT-HASH-NUMBER.
003180     MOVE WS-CHG-YTD-SALES          TO TL-TOT-YTD-SALES.
003190     MOVE WS-CHG-CURRENT-SALES      TO TL-TOT-CURRENT-SALES.
003200     MOVE WS-CHG-YTD-SALES-RETURNS
003210         TO TL-TOT-YTD-SALES-RETURNS.
003220     MOVE WS-CHG-YTD-SALES-RETURNS  TO TL-TOT-YTD-SALES-RETURNS.
003230     MOVE WS-CHG-CURRENT-RETURNS    TO TL-TOT-CURRENT-RETURNS.
003240     WRITE SR-SALES-REPORT-LINE FROM TL-TOTAL-LINE-1
003250         AFTER 2.
003260 C900-PRINT-END-TOTALS.
003270     MOVE 'ENDING - CONTROL'        TO TL-STUB-HEADING.
003280     ADD WS-CHG-TOT-RECORDS-STORED TO SC-CHG-TOT-RECORDS-STORED
003290     ADD WS-CHG-TOT-HASH-NUMBER    TO SC-CHG-TOT-HASH-NUMBER.
003300     ADD WS-CHG-YTD-SALES          TO SC-CHG-TOT-YTD-SALES.
003310     ADD WS-CHG-CURRENT-SALES      TO SC-CHG-TOT-CURRENT-SALES.
003320     ADD WS-CHG-YTD-SALES-RETURNS TO SC-CHG-TOT-YTD-SALES-RETURNS.
003330     ADD WS-CHG-CURRENT-RETURNS    TO SC-CHG-TOT-CURRENT-RETURNS.
003340     ADD SC-BEG-TOT-RECORDS-STORED SC-CHG-TOT-RECORDS-STORED
003350         GIVING TL-TOT-RECORDS-STORED.
003360     ADD SC-BEG-TOT-HASH-NUMBER SC-CHG-TOT-HASH-NUMBER
003370         GIVING TL-TOT-HASH-NUMBER.
003380     ADD SC-BEG-TOT-YTD-SALES SC-CHG-TOT-YTD-SALES
003390         GIVING TL-TOT-YTD-SALES.
003400     ADD SC-BEG-TOT-YTD-SALES-RETURNS SC-CHG-TOT-YTD-SALES-RETURNS
003410         GIVING TL-TOT-YTD-SALES-RETURNS.
003420     ADD SC-BEG-TOT-CURRENT-SALES SC-CHG-TOT-CURRENT-SALES
003430         GIVING TL-TOT-CURRENT-SALES.
003440     ADD SC-BEG-TOT-CURRENT-RETURNS SC-CHG-TOT-CURRENT-RETURNS
003450         GIVING TL-TOT-CURRENT-RETURNS.
003460     WRITE SR-SALES-REPORT-LINE FROM TL-TOTAL-LINE-1
003470         AFTER 2.
003480 C1000-PRINT-COUNT-SUMMARY.
003490     MOVE UC-HEADING-LINE(UC-COUNT-SUB) TO TL-HEADING.
003500     MOVE UC-RECORD-COUNT(UC-COUNT-SUB) TO TL-COUNT.
003510     WRITE SR-SALES-REPORT-LINE FROM TL-TOTAL-LINE-2
003520         AFTER 2.
003530 D200-ADD-RECORD.
003540     MOVE '00' TO EL-STATUS-ERROR.
003550     ADD 1                         TO WS-CHG-TOT-RECORDS-STORED
003560                                      UC-NUM-OF-ADDS.
003570     ADD ST-SALESPERSON-NUMBER TO WS-CHG-TOT-HASH-NUMBER.
003580     PERFORM Z200-READ-RELATIVE-RECORD
003590         VARYING WS-SLOT-NUMBER
003600         FROM WS-BEGINNING-SLOT BY 1
003610         UNTIL NO-RECORD-FOUND
003620         OR WS-SLOT-NUMBER > WS-SEARCH-LIMIT
003630         OR WS-SLOT-NUMBER > WS-NUMBER-OF-SLOTS.
003640     IF NO-RECORD-FOUND
003650         SUBTRACT 1                FROM WS-SLOT-NUMBER
003660         MOVE 'RECORD ADDED'       TO DL-UPDATE-ACTION
003670         MOVE ST-SALESPERSON-NUMBER TO RS-SALESPERSON-NUMBER
```

Program 8–6   *(continued)*

```
003680          MOVE ST-LAST-NAME          TO RS-LAST-NAME
003690          MOVE ST-FIRST-NAME         TO RS-FIRST-NAME
003700          MOVE ZEROS                 TO RS-YEAR-TO-DATE-SALES
003710                                     RS-YEAR-TO-DATE-SALES-RETURNS
003720                                     RS-CURRENT-SALES
003730                                     RS-CURRENT-SALES-RETURNS
003740          MOVE ST-COMMISSION-RATE    TO RS-COMMISSION-RATE
003750          WRITE RS-RELATIVE-SALES-RECORD
003760      ELSE
003770          MOVE 'REJECTED'      TO DL-UPDATE-ACTION
003780          MOVE 'SLOT NOT FOUND' TO DL-ERROR-MESSAGE
003790          ADD 1 TO UC-NUM-OF-REJECTIONS.
003800 D400-UPDATE-RECORD.
003810      MOVE '00' TO EL-STATUS-ERROR.
003820      SUBTRACT 1 FROM WS-SLOT-NUMBER.
003830      IF DELETION-OF-SALESPERSON
003840          MOVE 'RECORD DELETED'    TO DL-UPDATE-ACTION
003850          SUBTRACT 1               FROM WS-CHG-TOT-RECORDS-STORED
003860          SUBTRACT RS-SALESPERSON-NUMBER
003870              FROM WS-CHG-TOT-HASH-NUMBER
003880          SUBTRACT RS-YEAR-TO-DATE-SALES FROM WS-CHG-YTD-SALES
003890          SUBTRACT RS-YEAR-TO-DATE-SALES-RETURNS
003900              FROM WS-CHG-YTD-SALES-RETURNS
003910          SUBTRACT RS-CURRENT-SALES FROM WS-CHG-CURRENT-SALES
003920          SUBTRACT RS-CURRENT-SALES-RETURNS
003930              FROM WS-CHG-CURRENT-RETURNS
003940          ADD 1 TO UC-NUM-OF-DELETES.
003950      IF NAME-CHANGE
003960          MOVE 'NAME CHANGED'      TO DL-UPDATE-ACTION
003970          MOVE ST-LAST-NAME        TO RS-LAST-NAME
003980          MOVE ST-FIRST-NAME       TO RS-FIRST-NAME
003990          ADD 1 TO UC-NUM-OF-CHG-NAME.
004000      IF UPDATE-CURRENT-SALES
004010          MOVE 'YTD SALES UPDATED' TO DL-UPDATE-ACTION
004020          ADD ST-CURRENT-SALES     TO RS-YEAR-TO-DATE-SALES
004030                                   RS-CURRENT-SALES
004040                                   WS-CHG-YTD-SALES
004050                                   WS-CHG-CURRENT-SALES
004060          ADD 1                    TO UC-NUM-OF-CHG-SALES.
004070      IF UPDATE-CURRENT-SALES-RETURNS
004080          MOVE 'YTD SALES RETURNS UPDATED' TO DL-UPDATE-ACTION
004090          ADD ST-CURRENT-SALES-RETURNS
004100              TO RS-YEAR-TO-DATE-SALES-RETURNS
004110                 RS-CURRENT-SALES-RETURNS
004120                 WS-CHG-YTD-SALES-RETURNS
004130                 WS-CHG-CURRENT-RETURNS
004140          ADD 1 TO UC-NUM-OF-CHG-RTNS.
004150      IF UPDATE-COMMISSION-RATE
004160          MOVE 'COMMISSION RATE UPDATED' TO DL-UPDATE-ACTION
004170          MOVE ST-COMMISSION-RATE        TO RS-COMMISSION-RATE
004180          ADD 1 TO UC-NUM-OF-CHG-COM-RATE.
004190      IF DELETION-OF-SALESPERSON
004200          DELETE RELATIVE-SALES-FILE RECORD
004210      ELSE
004220          REWRITE RS-RELATIVE-SALES-RECORD.
004230      IF NOT SUCCESSFUL-COMPLETION
004240          MOVE 'UPDATING' TO EL-ERROR-OPERATION
004250          PERFORM Z300-ABORT-RUN
004260          STOP RUN.
004270 Z100-READ-RECORD.
004280      READ SALES-TRANSACTION-FILE
004290          AT END MOVE 'END' TO WS-EOF-INDICATOR.
004300      IF NOT END-OF-TRANSACTION-FILE
004310          ADD 1 TO UC-NUM-OF-TRANSACTIONS.
```

Program 8–6 *(concluded)*

```
004320 Z200-READ-RELATIVE-RECORD.
004330    READ RELATIVE-SALES-FILE.
004340 Z300-ABORT-RUN.
004350    WRITE SR-SALES-REPORT-LINE FROM EL-ERROR-LINE
004360       AFTER 1.
004370    CLOSE RELATIVE-SALES-FILE
004380        SALES-TRANSACTION-FILE
004390        SALES-REPORT-FILE.
```

Discussion

First, notice the definition of WS–WORK–AREAS, which uses the same data values for algorithm tasks as used in the creation program, with the addition of WS–BEGIN-NING–SLOT. It is used to initially define the search beginning point when attempting to find a record.

Next, study the logic of B500–UPDATE–RECORDS. First, the expected slot number is determined and the relative file is read until a record with a salesperson number equal to the transaction record number is encountered. Zero is moved to RS–SALESPERSON–NUMBER in line 2360 to ensure that the PERFORM at line 2380 is not terminated from a previous transaction. That search, however, is based on the expected location and is limited by the WS–SEARCH–LIMIT and the WS–NUM

Figure 8–12 *Output from Program 8–6*

```
UPDATE REPORT
RECORD IMAGE                              UPDATE ACTION        ERROR MESSAGE
0020 DOUGLAS     BRENT          05 1   31 RECORD ADDED
0125 LISHER      JANET F.          1   16 REJECTED             RECORD ALREADY EXISTS
0243                               2   22 RECORD DELETED
0356                               2   24 RECORD DELETED
2485                           25 6   21 COMMISSION RATE UPDATED
0396 VOLSKI      CHRIS             3   27 NAME CHANGED
0401                 0075000       4   32 YTD SALES UPDATED
0479                     0010000   5   36 YTD SALES RETURNS UPDATED
0590 DUPREE      KELLY L.          3   41 REJECTED             RECORD NOT FOUND IN SEARCH
0635 HUNT        ROBERT         10 1   08 REJECTED             RECORD ALREADY EXISTS
0017                 0020000       4   18 YTD SALES UPDATED
0020                 0072500       4   31 YTD SALES UPDATED
2485                     0005000   5   21 YTD SALES RETURNS UPDATED
1867                     0015000   5   19 YTD SALES RETURNS UPDATED
1805                               2   30 RECORD DELETED
```

	RECORDS	HASH	SALES	RETURNS	SALES	RETURNS
BEGINNING – CONTROL	30	40,130	23,386.40	6,882.67	.00	.00
PREVIOUS CHANGES	0	0	.00	.00	.00	.00
CURRENT CHANGES	2–	2,384–	673.77–	710.00–	1,675.00	300.00
ENDING – CONTROL	28	37,746	22,712.63	6,172.67	1,675.00	300.00
ADDITIONS	1					
DELETIONS	3					
NAME CHANGES	1					
YTD SALES CHANGES	3					
YTD RTNS CHANGES	3					
COM RATE CHANGES	1					
REJECTIONS	3					
TOTAL TRANSACTIONS	15					

BER–OF–SLOTS in the file. At this point in the program logic, a record with the correct salesperson number has either been found or not found. This was also the case with indexed files, though the determination for indexed files was obviously more direct. All that was necessary was a single READ that was preceded by moving a value to the RECORD KEY.

Follow the logic to C300–POSSIBLE–ADDITION. If a record was found that contains a salesperson number that is equal to the salesperson number from the transaction record, an addition cannot be made. Hence, the transaction is rejected. If this is not true, D200–ADD–RECORD is performed.

D200–ADD–RECORD begins by moving zeros to EL–STATUS–ERROR. This is done to ensure that NO–RECORD–FOUND cannot be true. If it were true, the PER FORM at line 3580 would never cause the iteration of Z200–READ–RELATIVE–RECORD because of the UNTIL clause at line 3610. The purpose of iterating Z200–READ–RELATIVE–RECORD is to find an available slot to store the record that is to be added. If the search results in NO–RECORD–FOUND, the record is written at statement 3750. First, however, WS–SLOT–NUMBER must be decremented at line 3650. This is done because the PERFORM/VARYING has incremented WS–SLOT–NUMBER and would currently be one value too high. If an available slot is not found, the transaction is rejected.

Next follow the logic of C400–POSSIBLE–UPDATE. Remember that at the point of entry to this module, a relative record has been read by the PERFORM/VARYING at line 2380. A valid update can occur only if ST–SALESPERSON–NUMBER is equal

Figure 8–13   *Output from Sequential Report Program after Updating*

```
SLOT REPORT
2294   HERMAN      JACK          484.65       87.47      .00        .00     .05   01
 927   BARCLAY     RICHARD     1,987.40      485.63      .00        .00     .11   03
1001   DILL        JEFF          586.40      284.56      .00        .00     .20   04
2186   SMITH       DOUGLAS       183.45      377.58      .00        .00     .20   05
 635   HUNT        ROBERT        453.20      475.34      .00        .00     .10   07
 746   JACKSON     JASON         784.50       84.78      .00        .00     .15   08
 859   HUTCHENS    JEFF          576.30       48.57      .00        .00     .14   09
1415   GOODMAN     EVE           645.42      238.47      .00        .00     .10   10
1634   VAUGHN      SYLVIA A.     478.99      456.78      .00        .00     .20   11
 529   PEACOCK     BARBARA       673.30      156.64      .00        .00     .08   12
1856   LOVELAND    GEORGE        462.75      276.56      .00        .00     .10   13
2157   YOUNG       KAREN L.    1,123.59       35.75      .00        .00     .30   14
 125   LISHER      JANET F.      500.00         .00      .00        .00     .15   15
1938   DWYER       JOHN D.       231.75       40.00      .00        .00     .10   16
2269   THOMPSON    LISA S.       500.00      100.00      .00        .00     .20   17
  17   PAYNE       MAX         1,187.00       56.73   200.00        .00     .05   18
1867   STEWARD     KEVIN J.    1,150.00      325.00      .00     150.00     .15   19
2341   ADAMS       ROBYN A.      231.75       40.00      .00        .00     .10   20
2485   PHILLIPS    TRACY L.      500.00      150.00      .00      50.00     .25   21
1132   UNLAND      KIM L.        475.64      395.85      .00        .00     .25   23
2487   HUME        LETA          483.53      284.37      .00        .00     .20   25
 580   DUPREE      KELLY L.    3,578.88      275.82      .00        .00     .10   26
 396   VOLSKI      CHRIS         326.80       58.47      .00        .00     .08   27
2395   MATNEY      DELORES       795.74      857.46      .00        .00     .05   28
2575   CROSS       CHERYL        385.63      382.50      .00        .00     .10   29
  20   DOUGLAS     BRENT         725.00         .00   725.00        .00     .05   31
 401   OWENS       GEORGE      1,112.20       39.57   750.00        .00     .09   32
 479   WETZEL      ROBERT D.   2,088.76      158.77      .00     100.00     .15   36
                   RECORDS    HASH       SALES      RETURNS    SALES    RETURNS

BEGINNING - CONTROL   30    40,130    23,386.40   6,882.67       .00       .00

NET CHANGE - CONTROL   2-    2,384-      673.77-    710.00-  1,675.00    300.00

ENDING - CONTROL      28    37,746    22,712.63   6,172.67  1,675.00    300.00

ENDING - ACTUAL       28    37,746    22,712.63   6,172.67  1,675.00    300.00
```

to RS–SALESPERSON–NUMBER. The IF statement at line 2780 rejects a transaction if the record was not found in the search. If it was found, D400–UPDATE–RECORD is performed.

In D400–UPDATE–RECORD, WS–SLOT–NUMBER is decremented because of the previous PERFORM/VARYING, and appropriate updates are performed, including the DELETE at line 4200 and the REWRITE at line 4220.

The major difference between a random update of a relative file and an indexed file, then, centers around the process by which a record in the relative file is located.

The output from Program 8–6, which the reader may compare with the corresponding output from the indexed file in Chapter 7, is found in Figure 8–12. The output from executing a sequential report program from the file after the update is shown in Figure 8–13. The reader should compare these two reports with the sequential report in Figure 8–11 before the update.

Other Randomizing Algorithms

There are several other randomizing algorithms that can be used to transform an identifying number to a relative record number. Some of the more common techniques include the **folding algorithm**, the **digit extraction algorithm**, and the **squared value algorithm**. Figure 8–14 illustrates how each of these algorithms can be used as the transformation technique. Each of these techniques would, of course, require logic modifications of the previous example programs. The choice of which method to use must utilize historical comparisons on a given data file, which must consider the percentage of synonyms and data access times.

Figure 8–14 *Commonly Used Randomizing Algorithms*

Assume: Up to 99 slots in file.		
Algorithm	*Explanation*	*Example calculation*
Folding	Split the key into two or more parts, add the parts, truncate if there are more digits than slots allocated.	Key: 0125 Split and add: 01 +25 = 26 Key: 2341 Split and add: 23 + 41 = 64
Digit extraction	Extract digit in digit position based on an analysis of digit distribution.	Assume: 2d and 4th are most evenly distributed digit positions. Key: 0125 Extract: 15 Key: 2341 Extract: 31
Squared value truncation	Square the key value and truncate to number of digits equal to file size.	Key: 0125 Square: 15625 Truncate: 25 Key: 2341 Square: 51938981 Truncate: 81

Programming Style

1. Make a choice as to the method of error detection with relative files and be consistent.

2. Use appropriate control and audit trail processes.

3. Precede any attempt at a random update with an attempt to READ a record with the relevant RELATIVE KEY. When using a transformation technique, a search must be conducted. Place a limit on the number of searches that will take place.

4. Make sure to include adequate validation of transaction records before attempting an update of a relative file.

Common Errors

1. Not decrementing the RELATIVE KEY after a search with a PERFORM/ VARYING when using a randomizing technique.
2. Not allowing a sufficiently large file size when using a randomizing technique.
3. Choosing an incorrect or invalid prime number divisor when using the division/remainder technique.
4. Failing to format a relative file when it is required by the system in use when using a randomizing technique.
5. Defining the RELATIVE KEY as a part of the record associated with a relative file. Remember, unlike a RECORD KEY, the RELATIVE KEY cannot be so defined.
6. Attempting to use RANDOM or DYNAMIC access without also defining the RELATIVE KEY. SEQUENTIAL access can omit the use of the RELATIVE KEY; the others cannot.
7. Failure to adequately use the testing of the FILE STATUS after each statement that accesses a relative file.
8. Using relative file organization when a number is not available to use for the slot number. This is true whether or not a transformation technique is used.

Exercises

1. What is the purpose and the concept of a transformation technique?
2. For the following estimated file sizes, determine the appropriate prime number divisor that would be used for the division/remainder algorithm.
   a. 50.
   b. 100.
   c. 1000.
   d. 5000.
3. For a file size of 100, determine expected slot number locations for the identifying numbers indicated using the division/remainder algorithm.
   a. 1479.
   b. 1987.
   c. 2597.
   d. 3025.
4. For a file size of 100, determine expected slot number locations for the identifying numbers indicated using the folding algorithm (split into two parts).
   a. 1479.
   b. 1987.
   c. 2597.
   d. 3025.
5. For a file size of 100, determine expected slot number locations for the identifying numbers indicated using the squared value truncation algorithm.
   a. 1479.
   b. 1987.
   c. 2597.
   d. 3025.

Problems

1. Modify the creation program, update program, and report program for the sales file written in Chapter 7 on indexed files to use RELATIVE ORGANIZATION. This would mean modifying Problems 7-1, 7-5, and 7-6.

2. Modify the creation program, update program and report programs for the inventory file written in Chapter 7 on indexed files to use RELATIVE ORGANIZATION. This would mean modifying Problems 7–3, 7–5 and 7–7.

3. The following data are to be placed in a relative file and represent income and expenses for the first quarter of the year. Write a program that will create the relative file.

Week	Income	Expenses
1	23,000	15,000
2	35,000	17,800
3	47,000	31,000
4	42,000	45,000
5	28,000	47,000
6	37,000	45,000
7	47,000	38,000
8	86,000	37,000
9	93,000	47,000
10	47,000	30,000
11	98,000	51,000
12	102,000	84,000

4. Write a program that will produce each of the following reports from the file created in Problem 1.
    a. A complete listing of all the data to include net income (or loss) for each week and the average gross income, average expenses and average net income for all 12 weeks.
    b. The same data as reported in *a* above but only for weeks 4 through 8.
    c. The same data as reported in *a* above but only for every other week beginning with week 2.
    d. The same data as reported in *a* above but only for every other week beginning with week 1.

9

Subprograms

It is not unusual for a COBOL program to consist of several thousand lines of code. The programming effort for long programs can lead to problems such as difficulty with programming logic, the length of the time period to write the program, debugging the program, and program maintenance. In addition, many times a procedure in the program being developed is the same as one already written, debugged, and tested for one or more other programs. An approach used to aid in the programming effort for such programs is the use of subprograms or subroutines.

Concepts

Subroutines were introduced to the programmer earlier in COBOL by the use of the PERFORM statement. Much of the structured programming technique involves **subroutines** (modules) that divide the main procedure into a series of subroutines that are called by PERFORM statements. Since these subroutines are enclosed entirely within the program to be executed, they are referred to as **open subroutines.** Other programs cannot access these modules, but they are open (that is they can be accessed) to any statement within the program.

In order to make a subroutine in a program available to other programs, COBOL has a method where the subroutine is made into an entirely separate entity from any one program. This involves the use of subprograms. A **subprogram** is actually a program by itself which has the ability to be accessed by other programs as it is needed. These subprograms are referred to as **closed subroutines** because they are external to a program and cannot be referenced by PERFORM statements. Special COBOL statements are necessary to use a subprogram as part of a regular program.

Subprograms also allow the division of a program into parts to be solved. A programmer can be assigned the task of developing and testing a subprogram independently of the other parts of the program. When all of the parts are completed they can be brought together by a main program. This technique can shorten the time period in which to complete a large complex program and also make the program easier to maintain at a later date.

Transfer of Control

If a program uses one or more subprograms, that program is referred to as the **calling program.** The subprogram that is referenced is the **called program.** During the execution of the called program, control can be returned to the calling program, and reference can be made to another subprogram. The job can be terminated within the called subprogram; however this would be an extemely poor technique.

A called program itself can become a calling program. That is, it can call another subprogram. When a subprogram calls another program it is termed **nesting subprograms.** A called program cannot directly or indirectly call its caller. If that happens the system's knowledge of which subprogram is the calling or called program is lost, and the results are unpredictable. Figure 9–1 is an illustration of transferring control between programs and subprograms.

The program MAIN in Figure 9–1 is a calling program on two different occasions. As a calling program it calls the program SUBONE first. After the execution of the program SUBONE, control is returned to the program MAIN. The program MAIN becomes a calling program a second time when the program SUBTWO is called.

Figure 9–1 *Transfer of Control*

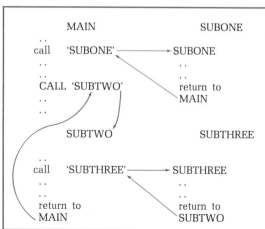

During the execution of SUBTWO, it becomes a calling program for the called program SUBTHREE. The program SUBTHREE returns control to the program SUBTWO, which in turn returns control to the program MAIN. These programs and subprograms interact with each other as if they were one program and are referred to as a **run unit.**

Common Data

There are times when a called program must be supplied with data from the calling program. If this is necessary, COBOL allows the system to provide a **common data** area to store the data. The data area is described only once for all subprograms in the **main program.** A called program can access the data stored in the main program as if the data were part of the subprogram. The calling program must supply the called program with the addresses of the data locations. If a called program becomes a calling program, it in turn must supply its called program with the addresses of any common data that are needed.

Subprogram Linkage

There are two ways to link subprograms with a main program. The standard COBOL available to all systems is the **static linkage** method. The other method is with **dynamic linkage** and is not available on all systems.

Static Linkage

When the static linkage method is used, the calling and called programs are compiled separately. The object programs are then link-edited to form a single load module, also called a phase. When the calling program references the called program for the first time, the values and conditions of the called program are as originally initialized. Each subsequent time the called program is entered, the program is in the same state as when exited from the previous call. If it is necessary, the programmer must reinitialize the subprogram. This is not necessary very often, but the programmer should be aware of any data-items that should be reset to zero and the condition of switches and PERFORM statements. Figure 9–2 shows the format for invoking a subprogram.

Figure 9–2   *CALL Statement*

<u>CALL</u> literal [<u>USING</u> data-name-1 [data-name-2] . . .].

In Figure 9–2 each literal must be nonnumeric. Standard COBOL always enters the called program at the first nondeclarative statement in the PROCEDURE division. This requires that the literal in the **CALL statement** be the PROGRAM–ID name of the called program. If the called program is to use data common to the calling program, the data-name(s) in the calling program tell the called program the addresses of the common data. A called program *cannot* contain a CALL statement that directly or indirectly refers to the calling program.

Dynamic Linkage

Using this method causes the called program to be compiled and link-edited as a separate program and stored as a separate load module. The major advantage of this method is that it can reduce CPU storage requirements during the execution of the run unit. The CALL format is the same as for that used for static linkage. This simply allows any COBOL program to access the separately stored COBOL program.

PROCEDURE Division Entries

The CALL Statement

The transfer of control from a calling program to a called program is made with the CALL statement described in Figure 9–2. Examples of its use are shown in Figure 9–3.

Figure 9–3   *Examples of the CALL Statement*

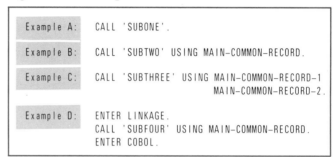

```
Example A:   CALL 'SUBONE'.

Example B:   CALL 'SUBTWO' USING MAIN-COMMON-RECORD.

Example C:   CALL 'SUBTHREE' USING MAIN-COMMON-RECORD-1
                                    MAIN-COMMON-RECORD-2.

Example D:   ENTER LINKAGE.
             CALL 'SUBFOUR' USING MAIN-COMMON-RECORD.
             ENTER COBOL.
```

In all of the examples of Figure 9–3 the literal contains the PROGRAM–ID name of the called program. The CALL statement resides in the calling program. If there are no common data to be used between the calling and called programs, a CALL statement of the format in Example A is needed. The statement transfers control to the first nondeclarative statement in the subprogram SUBONE.

A COBOL program can transfer control to other COBOL programs or non-COBOL programs. Example D shows the calling of an Assembler program.

If common data are to be used for a main program and subprograms, these data are stored in the main program in either the FILE or WORKING–STORAGE section. (A subprogram can also pass data from its LINKAGE section to another subprogram.) The **USING option** of the CALL statement allows for the addresses (referred to as **arguments**) to be sent to the subprograms. MAIN–COMMON–RE CORD in Example B is a data-name in the main program. Its address is being passed to the subprogram. Example C illustrates that the address of more than one data-name can be given to a subprogram.

There are several rules that govern the use of the USING option:

- READ and WRITE statements can only appear in the program that defines their FD.
- The specified data names must be defined at the 01 level in the FILE or WORKING–STORAGE sections of the main program and the LINKAGE section of the subprogram. They can be either group or elementary items.
- If the USING option is used in a calling program the called program must have a USING option with the PROCEDURE division header.
- The called subprogram must have a LINKAGE section to receive the addresses of the data-names.
- No actual storage space is allocated to the LINKAGE section by the COBOL compiler; therefore, no VALUE clauses can be used in the LINKAGE section except for 88-level condition names.
- The data-names in the USING option do not have to be spelled the same in the calling and called programs (in fact they seldom are). However, there must be the same number of arguments for the USING option in both the calling and called programs. Also, if more than one argument is specified, as in Example C, they must appear in the same order in each USING option.
- Index-names must be initialized in the called program and cannot be SET in the calling program; therefore, they cannot appear in the USING option.

■ Subscript values that have been defined in the calling program can be used in the called program.

The USING Option in the Called Program

The format of the USING option in the PROCEDURE division header is given in Figure 9–4.

Figure 9–4 *Format of PROCEDURE DIVISION USING Option*

PROCEDURE DIVISION [USING data-name-1 [data-name-2] . . .].

Notice that the USING option in Figure 9–4 is in the same sentence as the procedure heading. If the calling program does not have a USING option, this option is also omitted from the called program. Figure 9–5 illustrates the use of the called program's procedure heading.

Figure 9–5 *The USING Option in the PROCEDURE DIVISION*

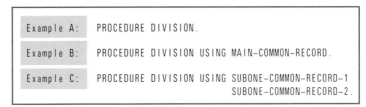

Example A: PROCEDURE DIVISION.

Example B: PROCEDURE DIVISION USING MAIN-COMMON-RECORD.

Example C: PROCEDURE DIVISION USING SUBONE-COMMON-RECORD-1
                                       SUBONE-COMMON-RECORD-2.

Example A of Figure 9–3 does not have a USING option. No common data exist between the calling and called programs. The PROCEDURE division header in the called program would be the same as Example A of Figure 9–5.

Example B of Figures 9–3 and 9–5 illustrate the USING option with one argument. Notice that the argument has the same name in both the calling and called programs. Since subprograms are independent of other programs, the names used have no relationship to names outside of the subprogram. Although it is less confusing if identical names are used between programs, it is seldom a practical occurrence.

Example C of these same figures show two arguments in the USING option. The argument names in the called program are different from those in the calling program. Different names are valid. However, the number of positions of the arguments must be the same. That is, when there are two or more arguments in the called program, the first argument must be able to handle the number of characters in the first argument of the calling program, and so forth for the remaining arguments. In addition, the order of the arguments in the called program must be the same as those in the calling program.

The EXIT PROGRAM Statement

To return control from a called program back to its calling program the **EXIT PROGRAM statement** must be used. The format for this statement is given in Figure 9–6.

Figure 9–6
Format of EXIT PROGRAM Statement

procedure-name.
   EXIT PROGRAM.

The exit statement must be the only statement within a procedure. When the EXIT PROGRAM is executed in a subprogram, control is returned to the CALL statement in the calling program. If the EXIT PROGRAM statement is used in a program other than a called subprogram, it is treated as a no-operation statement (just like the EXIT statement).

DATA Division Entries

WORKING–STORAGE Section

The **WORKING–STORAGE section** of the main program usually contains the common data used in a run unit. (On occasion it is the FILE section.) The addresses of the data locations are given to subprograms through the arguments of the USING option.

Communication between the calling and called programs is done through the CALL statement. If common data are to be shared between programs, these data must be defined at the 01 level. Appropriate PIC and VALUE clauses are used to describe the format of the data.

LINKAGE Section

The **LINKAGE section** is only found in subprograms. Its purpose is to accept the addresses of common data stored in the main program or the calling program from the arguments in the USING option of the CALL statement. This section does not take up any storage space. It uses the space allocated to the WORKING–STORAGE section of the main program or the calling program.

Calling and Called Programs

Figures 9–7 and 9–8 are examples of intercommunications between programs.

In Figure 9–7 the program MAIN is a calling program on three different occasions. It first communicates with SUBONE and uses the common data COMMON–RECORD–1 and COMMON–RECORD–2. The called program must have a **LINKAGE section** that can contain 40 characters for COMMON–RECORD–1 and 20 characters for COMMON–RECORD–2, in that order. SUBONE must also have a USING option for the procedure heading. The entry point into SUBONE is the first nondeclarative statement in the PROCEDURE division.

The statement PROCEDURE DIVISION USING COMMON–RECORD–1 COMMON–RECORD–2 accepts the addresses of the arguments from the calling program MAIN. Notice that the names of the arguments happen to be the same in this example for both the calling and called programs. The LINKAGE section of SUBONE allows the use of the common data area defined in the calling program MAIN. After execution of SUBONE, the statement EXIT PROGRAM returns control to the statement following the CALL 'SUBONE' statement in the calling program. The data fields MAIN–AMOUNT and MAIN–MAJOR in the common data area contain the value 5 and INFORMATION SYSTEMS, respectively.

The second time the program MAIN in Figure 9–7 becomes a calling program is when CALL 'SUBTWO' is executed. Since no arguments are present in this statement, there are no common data between the calling and called programs. SUBTWO does not have a LINKAGE section. SUBTWO does, however, have a declaratives area. The entry point into SUBTWO is at 0000–NONDECLARATIVES SECTION, the first nondeclaratives statements in the called program. EXIT PROGRAM returns control to the calling program MAIN. If SUBTWO is called again, the programmer must remember that the condition of SWITCH–ON may have been changed during the previous execution of the program. If so, that condition remains changed, and the programmer must allow for the logic to correctly execute SUBTWO.

Figure 9–7 *Example of Calling Program*

```
(main program)
  IDENTIFICATION DIVISION.
  PROGRAM-ID.  MAIN
  .
  FILE SECTION.
  FD  . . . .
  01  IN-INVENTORY-RECORD       PIC X(80).
  .
  .
  WORKING-STORAGE SECTION.
  .
  .
*****COMMON DATA STORED IN MAIN PROGRAM*****
  01  COMMON-RECORD-1.
      05  MAIN-NAME             PIC X(20).
      05  FILLER                PIC X(5) VALUE SPACES.
      05  MAIN-ID               PIC 9(6).
      05  FILLER                PIC X(5) VALUE SPACES.
      05  MAIN-AMOUNT           PIC 9(4) VALUE ZEROS.
  01  COMMON-RECORD-2.
      05  MAIN-MAJOR            PIC X(11).
      05  MAIN-NUMBER           PIC 9(9).
  .
  .
      CALL 'SUBONE' USING COMMON-RECORD-1
                          COMMON-RECORD-2.
  .
  .
      CALL 'SUBTWO'.
  .
  .
      CALL 'SUBTHREE' USING IN-INVENTORY-RECORD.
  .
  .
```

CALL 'SUBTHREE' USING IN–INVENTORY–RECORD of Figure 9–7 is the third communication with a called program by the calling program MAIN. Notice that IN–INVENTORY–RECORD is in the FILE SECTION because it consists of data that have been input to the calling program. It is now treated as common data for the called program SUBTHREE.

The called program receives the arguments in the data-name SUB–RECORD of the USING option. In this example the names used for the common data are different. This is valid because all names used in a subprogram are independent of those used in other programs. IN–INVENTORY–RECORD is an elementary item in the calling program, and SUB–RECORD is a group item in the called program. This is valid because each data-name contains the same number of characters, in this case 80. SUB–F1, SUB–F2, and SUB–F3 can be used as necessary in the called program.

SUBTHREE becomes a calling program when CALL 'SUBFOUR' USING SUB–RECORD WS–TOTAL is executed. Control is transferred to the called program SUBFOUR.

SUB–SUB–RECORD of SUBFOUR's USING option receives the address of the common data SUB–RECORD from SUBTHREE. This allows SUBFOUR to use the common data IN–INVENTORY–RECORD of the program MAIN. Note that when a subprogram passes arguments of common data from a main program to another subprogram, it must use its LINKAGE section. If the data are common between only the two subprograms such as WS–TOTAL, the WORKING–STORAGE section, in the calling program is used.

Figure 9–8   *Examples of Called Programs*

```
Example A:

      .
      .

   PROGRAM-ID.  SUBONE.
      .
      .

   LINKAGE SECTION.
   01  COMMON-RECORD-1.
       05  MAIN-NAME          PIC X(20).
       05  FILLER             PIC X(5).
       05  MAIN-ID            PIC 9(6).
       05  FILLER             PIC X(5).
       05  MAIN-AMOUNT        PIC 9(4).
   01  COMMON-RECORD-2.
       05  MAIN-MAJOR         PIC X(11).
       05  MAIN-NUMBER        PIC 9(9).
      .
      .

   PROCEDURE DIVISION USING COMMON-RECORD-1
                            COMMON-RECORD-2.
      .
      .

         MOVE 5 TO MAIN-AMOUNT.
         MOVE 'INFORMATION' TO MAIN-MAJOR.
      .
      .

   D400-EXIT.
       EXIT PROGRAM.

Example B:

      .
      .

   PROGRAM-ID.  SUBTWO.
      .
      .

   WORKING-STORAGE SECTION.
   01  WS-SWITCH-1            PIC X(3).
       88  SWITCH-ON          VALUE 'ON'.
      .
      .

   PROCEDURE DIVISION.
   DECLARATIVES.
      .
      .

   END DECLARATIVES.
   0000-NONDECLARATIVES SECTION.
   A000-SUBTWO-LOGIC.
      .
      .

       IF SWITCH-ON MOVE 'OFF' TO WS-SWITCH-1.
      .
      .

   D400-EXIT.  EXIT PROGRAM.

Example C:

      .
      .

   PROGRAM-ID.  SUBTHREE.
      .
      .

   FILE SECTION.
      .
      .
```

Figure 9–8 *(concluded)*

```
WORKING-STORAGE SECTION.
*****COMMON DATA STORED IN CALLING PROGRAM*****
01  WS-TOTAL                    PIC 9(3) VALUE ZEROS.


    .
LINKAGE SECTION.
01  SUB-RECORD.
    05  SUB-F1                  PIC X(20).
    05  SUB-F2                  PIC 9(7).
    05  SUB-F3                  PIC 9(3).
    05  FILLER                  PIC X(50).
PROCEDURE DIVISION USING SUB-RECORD.



    .


    .
D400-EXIT.
    EXIT PROGRAM.

Example D:


    .
PROGRAM-ID.   SUBFOUR.


LINKAGE SECTION.
01  WS-TOTAL                    PIC 9(3)
01  SUB-SUB-RECORD.
    05  SUB-SUB-F1              PIC X(20).
    05  SUB-SUB-F2              PIC 9(7).
    05  SUB-SUB-F3              PIC 9(3).
    05  FILLER                  PIC X(50).
PROCEDURE DIVISION USING SUB-SUB-RECORD
                         WS-TOTAL.


    .
    IF SUB-SUB-F2 = ZERO
        STOP RUN.

    .
D400-EXIT.
    EXIT PROGRAM.
```

Execution of the run unit can be terminated within a subprogram. If the statement IF SUB–SUB–F2 = ZERO is true, the run unit will terminate, otherwise, EXIT PROGRAM returns control to SUBTHREE. The next statement after the CALL statement in SUBTHREE, EXIT PROGRAM, is executed. Control is then returned to the program MAIN.

Program Example

Statement of the Problem

This problem is the same as for Program 2–1, except for the use of subprograms. The subprograms are used for the creation of the tables used to determine each employee's pay-rate and to print out department and region names. These subprograms could then be used in other programs as needed. Also, the calculations for gross pay, overtime pay, and regular pay will be placed in a subprogram, thus enabling standardized payroll calculations when needed.

Whenever changes or additions are to be made to these tables or calculations, only subprograms need to be changed, and the main program will remain the same.

More specifically, there are three subprograms used in the problem solution. The first subprogram (called TABLDEF) defines the department name table, the region name table, and the shift worked table using VALUE clauses. The second subprogram (called TABLLD) input-loads the pay-rate table. During execution of the run unit, the first subprogram calls the second subprogram. The third subprogram (called CALCPAY) calculates gross pay, overtime pay, and regular pay.

The main program and subprograms together are to input employee data records stored in random order to:

1. Check for valid department number, valid region number, and valid shift number.

2. Calculate gross pay, overtime pay, and regular pay for each employee based on the pay-rate according to the region worked in, the shift worked, and their job level.

3. Calculate summary gross pay for all employees by region worked in, the shift worked, and the job level. This is to be printed beginning on a new page at the end of the report in table form.

Overtime is calculated for any person who has worked more than 80 hours this two-week pay period at the rate of 1.5 times the normal pay-rate for those hours over 80. No one works more than 100 hours.

The main program will utilize tables that are defined and loaded in subprograms to determine each employee's pay-rate, to print out department and region names, and to store the final totals. The pay-rate table shown in Figure 9–9 is a three level table with the page being the region; the row, the job level; and the column, the shift worked. This table is to be input-loaded because of the volatility of pay-rate tables. It is input-loaded by the second subprogram.

Figure 9–9 · Pay-Rate Table

Eastern region				Central region			
Job level	Shift			Job level	Shift		
	1	2	3		1	2	3
1	7.70	7.90	8.20	1	7.35	7.60	7.85
2	8.00	8.40	8.80	2	7.65	7.95	8.25
3	8.50	8.90	9.30	3	8.15	8.55	8.95
4	9.00	9.50	10.00	4	8.65	9.15	9.65
5	9.75	10.25	11.00	5	9.40	9.90	10.50

Western region			
Job level	Shift		
	1	2	3
1	7.60	7.75	8.05
2	7.90	8.35	8.70
3	8.40	8.85	9.00
4	8.90	9.45	9.75
5	9.65	10.15	10.80

The table shown in Figure 9–10 is a one level table for department names. Because of the static nature of the data it will be hard-coded. This is done in the first subprogram.

Figure 9–10 *Department Name Table*

Department	
Name	*Number*
Shipping	10
Assembly	15
Receiving	20
Accounting	25
Maintenance	30
Production	35

Figure 9–11 shows the table for the region names and is used in a similar fashion as the department name table.

Figure 9–11 *Region Name Table*

Region	
Name	*Number*
Eastern	1
Central	2
Western	3

Another table is to be created by the program. This table will be initialized and manipulated only in the main program. It is a three level table to store the totals of all employees by region, job level, and shift. Its format is similar to Figure 9–9, except that an employee's gross pay will be accumulated into the proper page, row and column, replacing the pay-rate. The printer spacing chart in Figure 9–13 illustrates its format when printed in the report.

Input

The data records shown in Figure 9–12 are to be used for input. The first 15 records are to be input-loaded into the pay- rate table and the remaining records contain the employee data that are to be used as input to calculate employee gross pay and totals for region, job level, and shift.

Figure 9–12 *Input Data File for Program 9–1*

The record definition for the pay rate table is:

1–4	Shift 1 pay rate (two assumed decimal positions)
5–8	Shift 2 pay rate (two assumed decimal positions)
9–12	Shift 3 pay rate (two assumed decimal positions)

```
============
077007900820
080008400880
085008900930
090009501000
097510251100
073507600785
076507950825
081508550895
086509150965
094009901050
076007750805
079008350870
```

Figure 9–12 *(concluded)*

```
084008850900
089009450975
096510151080
============
```

The record definition for the payroll data is:

1– 2	Department number
3	Region number
4– 6	Employee number
8	Job level
10	Shift worked
12–14	Hours worked (no decimals)

```
==============
101022 2 2 075
102042 1 1 067
102059 3 3 071
153111 4 1 080
151122 5 2 013
152123 1 2 080
202126 3 1 049
202159 5 3 093
201175 4 2 080
203176 2 3 080
253222 5 1 080
252226 4 2 100
302242 3 3 084
304999 4 4 080
303277 3 2 007
352299 2 1 100
353311 3 1 082
354322 3 2 057
351411 4 1 012
351420 4 2 094
202421 1 1 085
203422 2 2 043
253459 3 1 012
303477 3 2 092
302499 5 1 070
301517 2 2 080
353522 4 2 100
104542 1 3 010
202611 3 2 058
303621 4 3 099
151677 1 3 072
252777 3 2 097
252799 5 3 084
151811 1 2 022
253821 1 3 011
353822 3 3 082
302826 3 5 095
201859 3 1 093
152842 3 1 081
153899 4 2 008
253921 4 1 076
352922 5 1 010
101926 4 1 014
401982 3 2 080
101995 3 3 080
==============
```

Output

The output will be a printed report in the format shown in Figure 9–13.

Figure 9–13 *Printer Spacing Chart for Program 9–1*

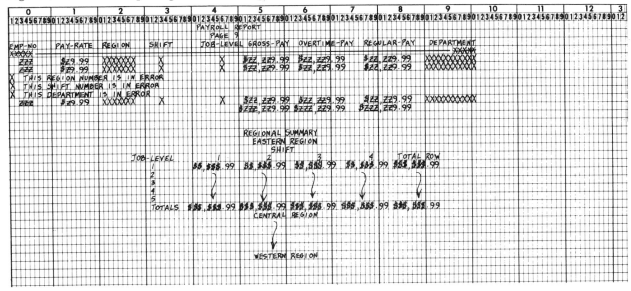

Main Program

Program 9–1

```
000010 IDENTIFICATION DIVISION.
000020 PROGRAM-ID.  PAYROLL.
000030***************************************************************
000040* PROGRAM EXAMPLE 9-1.  THIS PROGRAM USES THREE SUBPROGRAMS   *
000050***************************************************************
000060 ENVIRONMENT DIVISION.
000070 CONFIGURATION SECTION.
000080    SOURCE-COMPUTER.  IBM-4341.
000090    OBJECT-COMPUTER.  IBM-4341.
000100 INPUT-OUTPUT SECTION.
000110    FILE-CONTROL.
000120       SELECT PAYROLL-FILE  ASSIGN TO UT-S-PAY.
000130       SELECT REPORT-FILE   ASSIGN TO UT-S-PRINTER.
000140*
000150 DATA DIVISION.
000160 FILE SECTION.
000170 FD  PAYROLL-FILE
000180     RECORD CONTAINS 14 CHARACTERS
000190     LABEL RECORDS STANDARD.
000200 01  PR-PAYROLL-RECORD.
000210     05  PR-DEPARTMENT-NUMBER    PIC 9(2).
000220     05  PR-REGION-NUMBER        PIC 9(1).
000230     05  PR-EMPLOYEE-NUMBER      PIC 9(3).
000240     05  FILLER                  PIC X(1).
```

Program 9–1 *(continued)*

```
000250       05  PR-JOB-LEVEL              PIC 9(1).
000260       05  FILLER                    PIC X(1).
000270       05  PR-SHIFT                  PIC 9(1).
000280       05  FILLER                    PIC X(1).
000290       05  PR-HOURS-WORKED           PIC 9(3).
000300 FD  REPORT-FILE
000310       RECORD CONTAINS 132 CHARACTERS
000320       LABEL RECORDS STANDARD.
000330 01  RR-REPORT-RECORD               PIC X(132).
000340 WORKING-STORAGE SECTION.
000350 01  WS-REPORT-INDICATORS.
000360       05  WS-END-OF-FILE-INDICATOR PIC X(3).
000370           88  END-OF-FILE          VALUE 'END'.
000380       05  DEPT-FOUND-INDICATOR     PIC X(3).
000390           88  DEPARTMENT-FOUND     VALUE 'YES'.
000400       05  REGION-FOUND-INDICATOR   PIC X(3).
000410           88  REGION-FOUND         VALUE 'YES'.
000420       05  SHIFT-FOUND-INDICATOR    PIC X(3).
000430           88  SHIFT-FOUND          VALUE 'YES'.
000440       05  WS-LINES-PER-PAGE        PIC 9(2) VALUE 40.
000450       05  MISC-REGION              PIC 9(5).
000460 01  WS-WORK-AREAS.
000470       05  WS-GROSS-PAY             PIC 9(4)V99.
000480       05  WS-OVERTIME-PAY          PIC 9(4)V99.
000490       05  WS-REGULAR-PAY           PIC 9(4)V99.
000500 01  WS-ACCUMULATORS.
000510       05  T-TOTAL-ACCUMULATORS.
000520           10  TOT-GROSS-PAY        PIC 9(6)V99.
000530           10  TOT-OVERTIME-PAY     PIC 9(6)V99.
000540           10  TOT-REGULAR-PAY      PIC 9(6)V99.
000550       05  WS-PAGE-NUMBER           PIC 9(2).
000560       05  WS-LINES-USED            PIC 9(2).
000570       05  WS-JOB-LEVEL-NUMBER      PIC 9(1).
000580 01  PAY-RATE-TABLE.
000590       05  REGION                       OCCURS 3 TIMES
000600                                        INDEXED BY R-INDEX.
000610           10  JOB-LEVEL                OCCURS 5 TIMES
000620                                        INDEXED BY J-INDEX.
000630               15  SHIFT-RATE  PIC 99V99 OCCURS 3 TIMES
000640                                        INDEXED BY S-INDEX.
000650 01  TOTALS-TABLE.
000660       05  REGION-TOTAL                 OCCURS 3 TIMES
000670                                        INDEXED BY REGION-INDEX.
000680           10  JOB-LEVEL-TOTAL          OCCURS 6 TIMES
000690                                        INDEXED BY LEVEL-INDEX.
000700               15  SHIFT-TOTAL PIC 9(6)V99 OCCURS 4 TIMES
000710                                        INDEXED BY SHIFT-INDEX.
000720 01  DEPARTMENT-NAME-TABLE.
000730       05  DEPARTMENT-TABLE         OCCURS 6 TIMES
000740                                    ASCENDING KEY DEPARTMENT-NUMBER
000750                                    INDEXED BY DEPARTMENT-INDEX.
000760           10  DEPARTMENT-NAME      PIC X(11).
000770           10  DEPARTMENT-NUMBER    PIC X(2).
000780 01  REGION-NAME-TABLE.
000790       05  REGION-TABLE             OCCURS 3 TIMES
000800                                    ASCENDING KEY REGION-NUMBER
000810                                    INDEXED BY R-TABLE-INDEX.
000820           10  REGION-NAME          PIC X(7).
000830           10  REGION-NUMBER        PIC 9(1).
000840 01  SHIFT-NUMBER-TABLE.
000850       05  SHIFT-TABLE              OCCURS 3 TIMES
000860                                    ASCENDING KEY SHIFT-NUMBER
000870                                    INDEXED BY S-WORKED-INDEX.
000880           10  SHIFT-NUMBER         PIC 9(1).
```

Program 9-1   *(continued)*

```
000890 01  DL-DETAIL-LINE.
000900     05  FILLER                    PIC X(2) VALUE SPACES.
000910     05  DL-EMPLOYEE-NUMBER        PIC X(3).
000920     05  FILLER                    PIC X(6) VALUE SPACES.
000930     05  DL-PAY-RATE               PIC $Z9.99.
000940     05  FILLER                    PIC X(3) VALUE SPACES.
000950     05  DL-REGION-NAME            PIC X(7).
000960     05  FILLER                    PIC X(5) VALUE SPACES.
000970     05  DL-SHIFT                  PIC X(1).
000980     05  FILLER                    PIC X(11) VALUE SPACES.
000990     05  DL-JOB-LEVEL              PIC X(1).
001000     05  FILLER                    PIC X(5) VALUE SPACES.
001010     05  DL-GROSS-PAY              PIC $ZZ,ZZ9.99.
001020     05  FILLER                    PIC X(2) VALUE SPACES.
001030     05  DL-OVERTIME-PAY           PIC $ZZ,ZZ9.99.
001040     05  FILLER                    PIC X(4) VALUE SPACES.
001050     05  DL-REGULAR-PAY            PIC $ZZ,ZZ9.99.
001060     05  FILLER                    PIC X(3) VALUE SPACES.
001070     05  DL-DEPARTMENT-NAME        PIC X(11).
001080 01  ER-ERROR-LINE.
001090     05  ER-NUMBER                 PIC ZZ9.
001100     05  FILLER                    PIC X(2) VALUE SPACES.
001110     05  ER-MESSAGE                PIC X(50).
001120 01  HD-HEADING-LINE-1.
001130     05  FILLER          PIC X(40) VALUE SPACES.
001140     05  FILLER          PIC X(14) VALUE 'PAYROLL REPORT'.
001150 01  HD-HEADING-LINE-2.
001160     05  FILLER          PIC X(43) VALUE SPACES.
001170     05  FILLER          PIC X(5)  VALUE 'PAGE'.
001180     05  HD-PAGE-NUMBER  PIC Z9.
001190 01  HD-HEADING-LINE-3.
001200     05  FILLER          PIC X(10) VALUE 'EMP-NO'.
001210     05  FILLER          PIC X(10) VALUE 'PAY-RATE'.
001220     05  FILLER          PIC X(10) VALUE 'REGION'.
001230     05  FILLER          PIC X(10) VALUE 'SHIFT'.
001240     05  FILLER          PIC X(11) VALUE 'JOB-LEVEL'.
001250     05  FILLER          PIC X(11) VALUE 'GROSS-PAY'.
001260     05  FILLER          PIC X(14) VALUE 'OVERTIME-PAY'.
001270     05  FILLER          PIC X(14) VALUE 'REGULAR-PAY'.
001280     05  FILLER          PIC X(10) VALUE 'DEPARTMENT'.
001290 01  ASTERISK-LINE.
001300     05  FILLER          PIC X(100) VALUE ALL '*'.
001310 01  TL-TOTAL-LINE.
001320     05  FILLER          PIC X(49) VALUE 'TOTALS'.
001330     05  TL-GROSS-PAY    PIC $ZZZ,ZZ9.99.
001340     05  FILLER          PIC X(1)  VALUE SPACES.
001350     05  TL-OVERTIME-PAY PIC $ZZZ,ZZ9.99.
001360     05  FILLER          PIC X(3)  VALUE SPACES.
001370     05  TL-REGULAR-PAY  PIC $ZZZ,ZZ9.99.
001380 01  SL-SUMMARY-LINE-1.
001390     05  FILLER          PIC X(50) VALUE SPACES.
001400     05  FILLER          PIC X(20) VALUE 'REGIONAL SUMMARY'.
001410 01  SL-SUMMARY-LINE-2.
001420     05  FILLER          PIC X(52) VALUE SPACES.
001430     05  SL-REGION-NAME  PIC X(8).
001440     05  FILLER          PIC X(6)  VALUE 'REGION'.
001450 01  SL-SUMMARY-LINE-3.
001460     05  FILLER          PIC X(56) VALUE SPACES.
001470     05  FILLER          PIC X(5)  VALUE 'SHIFT'.
001480 01  SL-SUMMARY-LINE-4.
001490     05  FILLER          PIC X(26) VALUE SPACES.
001500     05  FILLER          PIC X(15) VALUE 'JOB-LEVEL'.
001510     05  FILLER          PIC X(49)
001520         VALUE '    1         2         3      TOTAL ROW'.
```

Program 9–1   *(continued)*

```
001530 01  SL-SUMMARY-LINE-5.
001540     05  FILLER                PIC X(30) VALUE SPACES.
001550     05  SL-JOB-LEVEL          PIC X(7).
001560     05  SL-SHIFT              OCCURS 4 TIMES.
001570         10  SL-SHIFT-VALUE    PIC $$$$,$$$.99.
001580*
001590 PROCEDURE DIVISION.
001600 A000-PAYROLL-REPORT.
001610     OPEN INPUT  PAYROLL-FILE
001620          OUTPUT REPORT-FILE.
001630     CALL 'TABLDEF' USING PAY-RATE-TABLE
001640                          DEPARTMENT-NAME-TABLE
001650                          REGION-NAME-TABLE
001660                          SHIFT-NUMBER-TABLE.
001670     PERFORM B200-INITIALIZE-VARIABLES.
001680     PERFORM Z100-PRINT-REPORT-HEADINGS.
001690     PERFORM Z200-READ-PAYROLL.
001700     PERFORM B500-PROCESS-RECORDS
001710         UNTIL END-OF-FILE.
001720     PERFORM B600-FINAL-TOTALS.
001730     PERFORM B700-SUMMARIES.
001740     CLOSE PAYROLL-FILE
001750           REPORT-FILE.
001760     STOP RUN.
001770 B200-INITIALIZE-VARIABLES.
001780     MOVE 'NO'   TO WS-END-OF-FILE-INDICATOR.
001790     MOVE ZEROES TO WS-ACCUMULATORS
001800                    TOTALS-TABLE.
001810 B500-PROCESS-RECORDS.
001820     CALL 'CALCPAY' USING PR-PAYROLL-RECORD
001830                          WS-WORK-AREAS
001840                          PAY-RATE-TABLE.
001850     PERFORM C200-DETAIL-LINE.
001860     PERFORM Z200-READ-PAYROLL.
001870 B600-FINAL-TOTALS.
001880     MOVE TOT-GROSS-PAY     TO TL-GROSS-PAY.
001890     MOVE TOT-OVERTIME-PAY  TO TL-OVERTIME-PAY.
001900     MOVE TOT-REGULAR-PAY   TO TL-REGULAR-PAY.
001910     WRITE RR-REPORT-RECORD FROM TL-TOTAL-LINE
001920         AFTER 2.
001930 B700-SUMMARIES.
001940     WRITE RR-REPORT-RECORD FROM SL-SUMMARY-LINE-1
001950         AFTER PAGE.
001960     PERFORM C400-PRINT-REGION-NAME
001970         VARYING REGION-INDEX
001980         FROM 1 BY 1
001990         UNTIL REGION-INDEX > 3.
002000 C200-DETAIL-LINE.
002010     PERFORM D100-PAGE-OVERFLOW-CHECK.
002020     PERFORM D200-FIND-DEPT-NAME.
002030     PERFORM D300-FIND-REGION-NAME.
002040     PERFORM D400-FIND-SHIFT.
002050     IF DEPARTMENT-FOUND
002060        AND REGION-FOUND
002070        AND SHIFT-FOUND
002080           PERFORM D500-CREATE-DETAIL-LINE
002090           PERFORM D600-PRINT-DETAIL-LINE
002100           PERFORM D700-ADD-TO-ACCUMULATORS.
002110 C400-PRINT-REGION-NAME.
002120     SET MISC-REGION              TO REGION-INDEX.
002130     MOVE REGION-NAME(MISC-REGION) TO SL-REGION-NAME.
002140     WRITE RR-REPORT-RECORD FROM SL-SUMMARY-LINE-2
002150         AFTER 3.
002160     WRITE RR-REPORT-RECORD FROM SL-SUMMARY-LINE-3
```

Program 9–1   *(continued)*

```
002170          AFTER 1.
002180      WRITE RR-REPORT-RECORD FROM SL-SUMMARY-LINE-4
002190          AFTER 1.
002200      MOVE ZERO TO WS-JOB-LEVEL-NUMBER.
002210      PERFORM D800-PRINT-REGION-SUMMARY
002220          VARYING LEVEL-INDEX
002230          FROM 1 BY 1
002240          UNTIL LEVEL-INDEX > 6.
002250 D100-PAGE-OVERFLOW-CHECK.
002260      IF WS-LINES-USED > WS-LINES-PER-PAGE
002270          PERFORM Z100-PRINT-REPORT-HEADINGS.
002280 D200-FIND-DEPT-NAME.
002290      SEARCH ALL DEPARTMENT-TABLE
002300          AT END MOVE PR-DEPARTMENT-NUMBER TO ER-NUMBER
002310              MOVE 'THIS DEPARTMENT NUMBER IS IN ERROR'
002320                  TO ER-MESSAGE
002330              WRITE RR-REPORT-RECORD FROM ER-ERROR-LINE
002340                  AFTER 1
002350              MOVE 'NO' TO DEPT-FOUND-INDICATOR
002360          WHEN DEPARTMENT-NUMBER(DEPARTMENT-INDEX)
002370              = PR-DEPARTMENT-NUMBER
002380              MOVE 'YES' TO DEPT-FOUND-INDICATOR.
002390 D300-FIND-REGION-NAME.
002400      SEARCH ALL REGION-TABLE
002410          AT END MOVE PR-REGION-NUMBER TO ER-NUMBER
002420              MOVE 'THIS REGION NUMBER IS IN ERROR' TO ER-MESSAGE
002430              WRITE RR-REPORT-RECORD FROM ER-ERROR-LINE
002440                  AFTER 1
002450              MOVE 'NO' TO REGION-FOUND-INDICATOR
002460          WHEN REGION-NUMBER(R-TABLE-INDEX) = PR-REGION-NUMBER
002470              MOVE 'YES' TO REGION-FOUND-INDICATOR.
002480 D400-FIND-SHIFT.
002490      SEARCH ALL SHIFT-TABLE
002500          AT END MOVE PR-SHIFT TO ER-NUMBER
002510              MOVE 'THIS SHIFT NUMBER IS IN ERROR' TO ER-MESSAGE
002520              WRITE RR-REPORT-RECORD FROM ER-ERROR-LINE
002530                  AFTER 1
002540              MOVE 'NO' TO SHIFT-FOUND-INDICATOR
002550          WHEN SHIFT-NUMBER(S-WORKED-INDEX) = PR-SHIFT
002560              MOVE 'YES' TO SHIFT-FOUND-INDICATOR.
002570 D500-CREATE-DETAIL-LINE.
002580      MOVE PR-EMPLOYEE-NUMBER              TO DL-EMPLOYEE-NUMBER.
002590      MOVE SHIFT-RATE(PR-REGION-NUMBER PR-JOB-LEVEL PR-SHIFT)
002600          TO DL-PAY-RATE.
002610      MOVE REGION-NAME(PR-REGION-NUMBER) TO DL-REGION-NAME.
002620      MOVE PR-SHIFT                       TO DL-SHIFT.
002630      MOVE PR-JOB-LEVEL                   TO DL-JOB-LEVEL.
002640      MOVE WS-GROSS-PAY                   TO DL-GROSS-PAY.
002650      MOVE WS-OVERTIME-PAY                TO DL-OVERTIME-PAY.
002660      MOVE WS-REGULAR-PAY                 TO DL-REGULAR-PAY.
002670      MOVE DEPARTMENT-NAME(DEPARTMENT-INDEX)
002680          TO DL-DEPARTMENT-NAME.
002690      MOVE DL-DETAIL-LINE                 TO RR-REPORT-RECORD.
002700 D600-PRINT-DETAIL-LINE.
002710      WRITE RR-REPORT-RECORD
002720          AFTER 1.
002730 *    ADD 1 TO WS-LINES-USED.
002740 D700-ADD-TO-ACCUMULATORS.
002750      ADD WS-GROSS-PAY    TO TOT-GROSS-PAY
002760      ADD WS-GROSS-PAY    TO
002770          SHIFT-TOTAL(PR-REGION-NUMBER PR-JOB-LEVEL PR-SHIFT)
002780      ADD WS-GROSS-PAY    TO
002790          SHIFT-TOTAL(PR-REGION-NUMBER PR-JOB-LEVEL 4)
002800      ADD WS-GROSS-PAY    TO
```

Program 9–1   *(concluded)*

```
002810          SHIFT-TOTAL(PR-REGION-NUMBER 6 PR-SHIFT).
002820      ADD WS-GROSS-PAY      TO
002830          SHIFT-TOTAL(PR-REGION-NUMBER 6 4).
002840      ADD WS-OVERTIME-PAY TO TOT-OVERTIME-PAY.
002850      ADD WS-REGULAR-PAY   TO  TOT-REGULAR-PAY.
002860 D800-PRINT-REGION-SUMMARY.
002870      ADD 1 TO WS-JOB-LEVEL-NUMBER.
002880      IF WS-JOB-LEVEL-NUMBER = 6
002890          MOVE 'TOTALS' TO SL-JOB-LEVEL
002900      ELSE
002910          MOVE WS-JOB-LEVEL-NUMBER TO SL-JOB-LEVEL.
002920      PERFORM E200-FILL-SUMMARY-ROW
002930          VARYING SHIFT-INDEX
002940          FROM 1 BY 1
002950          UNTIL SHIFT-INDEX > 4.
002960      WRITE RR-REPORT-RECORD FROM SL-SUMMARY-LINE-5
002970          AFTER 1.
002980 E200-FILL-SUMMARY-ROW.
002990      MOVE SHIFT-TOTAL (REGION-INDEX LEVEL-INDEX SHIFT-INDEX)
003000          TO SL-SHIFT-VALUE(SHIFT-INDEX).
003010 Z100-PRINT-REPORT-HEADINGS.
003020      ADD 1          TO WS-PAGE-NUMBER.
003030      MOVE WS-PAGE-NUMBER TO HD-PAGE-NUMBER.
003040      MOVE 5          TO WS-LINES-USED.
003050      WRITE RR-REPORT-RECORD FROM HD-HEADING-LINE-1
003060          AFTER PAGE.
003070      WRITE RR-REPORT-RECORD FROM HD-HEADING-LINE-2
003080          AFTER 1.
003090      WRITE RR-REPORT-RECORD FROM HD-HEADING-LINE-3
003100          AFTER 2.
003110      WRITE RR-REPORT-RECORD FROM ASTERISK-LINE
003120          AFTER 1.
003130 Z200-READ-PAYROLL.
003140      READ PAYROLL-FILE
003150          AT END MOVE 'END' TO WS-END-OF-FILE-INDICATOR.
```

Table Definition Subprogram

```
000010 IDENTIFICATION DIVISION.
000020 PROGRAM-ID.  TABLDEF.
000030**********************************************************
000040* PROGRAM EXAMPLE 9-1.  THIS SUBPROGRAM DEFINES AND LOADS   *
000050*                       SEVERAL TABLES FOR USE BY THE MAIN  *
000060**********************************************************
000070 ENVIRONMENT DIVISION.
000080 CONFIGURATION SECTION.
000090   SOURCE-COMPUTER.  IBM-4341.
000100   OBJECT-COMPUTER.  IBM-4341.
000110 INPUT-OUTPUT SECTION.
000120   FILE-CONTROL.
000130*
000140 DATA DIVISION.
000150 WORKING-STORAGE SECTION.
000160 01  DEPARTMENT-NAME-VALUES.
000170     05  FILLER          PIC X(13) VALUE 'SHIPPING   10'.
000180     05  FILLER          PIC X(13) VALUE 'ASSEMBLY   15'.
000190     05  FILLER          PIC X(13) VALUE 'RECEIVING  20'.
000200     05  FILLER          PIC X(13) VALUE 'ACCOUNTING 25'.
000210     05  FILLER          PIC X(13) VALUE 'MAINTENANCE30'.
```

Table Definition Subprogram   *(concluded)*

```
000220      05  FILLER              PIC X(13) VALUE 'PRODUCTION 35'.
000230 01  DEPARTMENT-NAME-TABLE REDEFINES DEPARTMENT-NAME-VALUES.
000240      05  DEPARTMENT-TABLE       OCCURS 6 TIMES.
000250          10  DEPARTMENT-NAME   PIC X(11).
000260          10  DEPARTMENT-NUMBER PIC X(2).
000270 01  REGION-NAME-VALUES.
000280      05  FILLER              PIC X(8) VALUE 'EASTERN1'.
000290      05  FILLER              PIC X(8) VALUE 'CENTRAL2'.
000300      05  FILLER              PIC X(8) VALUE 'WESTERN3'.
000310 01  REGION-NAME-TABLE REDEFINES REGION-NAME-VALUES.
000320      05  REGION-TABLE          OCCURS 3 TIMES.
000330          10  REGION-NAME      PIC X(7).
000340          10  REGION-NUMBER    PIC 9(1).
000350 01  SHIFT-NUMBER-VALUES.
000360      05  FILLER              PIC 9(3) VALUE 123.
000370 01  SHIFT-NUMBER-TABLE REDEFINES SHIFT-NUMBER-VALUES.
000380      05  SHIFT-TABLE           OCCURS 3 TIMES.
000390          10  SHIFT-NUMBER     PIC 9(1).
000400 LINKAGE SECTION.
000410 01  PAY-RATE-TABLE.
000420      05  REGION                      OCCURS 3 TIMES
000430                                      INDEXED BY R-INDEX.
000440          10  JOB-LEVEL               OCCURS 5 TIMES
000450                                      INDEXED BY J-INDEX.
000460              15  SHIFT-RATE  PIC 99V99 OCCURS 3 TIMES
000470                                      INDEXED BY S-INDEX.
000480 01  DEPARTMENT-NAME-TABLE-MAIN.
000490      05  DEPARTMENT-TABLE       OCCURS 6 TIMES.
000500          10  DEPARTMENT-NAME   PIC X(11).
000510          10  DEPARTMENT-NUMBER PIC X(2).
000520 01  REGION-NAME-TABLE-MAIN.
000530      05  REGION-TABLE          OCCURS 3 TIMES.
000540          10  REGION-NAME      PIC X(7).
000550          10  REGION-NUMBER    PIC 9(1).
000560 01  SHIFT-NUMBER-TABLE-MAIN.
000570      05  SHIFT-TABLE           OCCURS 3 TIMES.
000580          10  SHIFT-NUMBER     PIC 9(1).
000590*
000600 PROCEDURE DIVISION USING PAY-RATE-TABLE
000610                           DEPARTMENT-NAME-TABLE-MAIN
000620                           REGION-NAME-TABLE-MAIN
000630                           SHIFT-NUMBER-TABLE-MAIN.
000640 A000-TABLE-DEFINE.
000650      MOVE DEPARTMENT-NAME-TABLE TO DEPARTMENT-NAME-TABLE-MAIN.
000660      MOVE REGION-NAME-TABLE     TO REGION-NAME-TABLE-MAIN.
000670      MOVE SHIFT-NUMBER-TABLE    TO SHIFT-NUMBER-TABLE-MAIN.
000680      CALL 'TABLLD' USING PAY-RATE-TABLE.
000690 A000-PROGRAM-EXIT.
000700      EXIT PROGRAM.
```

Table Load Subprogram

```
000010 IDENTIFICATION DIVISION.
000020 PROGRAM-ID.  TABLLD.
000030**************************************************
000040* PROGRAM EXAMPLE 9-1.  THIS SUBPROGRAM LOADS THE PAY TABLE   *
000050**************************************************
000060 ENVIRONMENT DIVISION.
000070 CONFIGURATION SECTION.
```

Table Load Subprogram   *(concluded)*

```
000080    SOURCE-COMPUTER.  IBM-4341.
000090    OBJECT-COMPUTER.  IBM-4341.
000100 INPUT-OUTPUT SECTION.
000110    FILE-CONTROL.
000120       SELECT PAY-RATE-FILE ASSIGN TO UT-S-RATE.
000130*
000140 DATA DIVISION.
000150 FILE SECTION.
000160 FD  PAY-RATE-FILE
000170     RECORD CONTAINS 12 CHARACTERS
000180     LABEL RECORDS STANDARD.
000190 01  PAY-RATE-RECORD.
000200     05  PAY-RATE-ROW.
000210         10  PAY-RATE-VALUES        PIC 99V99 OCCURS 3 TIMES.
000220 LINKAGE SECTION.
000230 01  PAY-RATE-TABLE.
000240     05  REGION                     OCCURS 3 TIMES
000250                                     INDEXED BY R-INDEX.
000260         10  JOB-LEVEL               OCCURS 5 TIMES
000270                                     INDEXED BY J-INDEX.
000280             15  SHIFT-RATE PIC 99V99 OCCURS 3 TIMES
000290                                     INDEXED BY S-INDEX.
000300*
000310 PROCEDURE DIVISION USING PAY-RATE-TABLE.
000320 A000-TABLE-LOAD.
000330     OPEN INPUT PAY-RATE-FILE.
000340     PERFORM B100-LOAD-PAY-RATE-TABLE
000350       VARYING R-INDEX
000360         FROM 1 BY 1
000370           UNTIL R-INDEX > 3
000380       AFTER J-INDEX
000390         FROM 1 BY 1
000400           UNTIL J-INDEX > 5.
000410     CLOSE PAY-RATE-FILE.
000420 A000-PROGRAM-EXIT.
000430     EXIT PROGRAM.
000440 B100-LOAD-PAY-RATE-TABLE.
000450     READ PAY-RATE-FILE.
000460     MOVE PAY-RATE-ROW TO JOB-LEVEL(R-INDEX, J-INDEX).
```

Pay Calculation Subprogram

```
000010 IDENTIFICATION DIVISION.
000020 PROGRAM-ID.  CALCPAY.
000030***************************************************
000040* PROGRAM EXAMPLE 9-1.  THIS SUBPROGRAM CALCULATES OVERTIME,  *
000050*                       REGULAR AND GROSS PAY                  *
000060***************************************************
000070 ENVIRONMENT DIVISION.
000080 CONFIGURATION SECTION.
000090    SOURCE-COMPUTER.  IBM-4341.
000100    OBJECT-COMPUTER.  IBM-4341.
000110*
000120 DATA DIVISION.
000130 LINKAGE SECTION.
000140 01  PR-PAYROLL-RECORD.
000150     05  PR-DEPARTMENT-NUMBER      PIC 9(2).
000160     05  PR-REGION-NUMBER          PIC 9(1).
000170     05  PR-EMPLOYEE-NUMBER        PIC 9(3).
```

Pay Calculation Subprogram *(concluded)*

```
000180        05  FILLER                    PIC X(1).
000190        05  PR-JOB-LEVEL              PIC 9(1).
000200        05  FILLER                    PIC X(1).
000210        05  PR-SHIFT                  PIC 9(1).
000220        05  FILLER                    PIC X(1).
000230        05  PR-HOURS-WORKED           PIC 9(3).
000240 01  WS-WORK-AREAS.
000250        05  WS-GROSS-PAY              PIC 9(4)V99.
000260        05  WS-OVERTIME-PAY           PIC 9(4)V99.
000270        05  WS-REGULAR-PAY            PIC 9(4)V99.
000280 01  PAY-RATE-TABLE.
000290        05  REGION                         OCCURS 3 TIMES
000300                                            INDEXED BY R-INDEX.
000310            10  JOB-LEVEL                   OCCURS 5 TIMES
000320                                            INDEXED BY J-INDEX.
000330                15  SHIFT-RATE PIC 99V99 OCCURS 3 TIMES
000340                                            INDEXED BY S-INDEX.
000350*
000360 PROCEDURE DIVISION USING PR-PAYROLL-RECORD
000370                          WS-WORK-AREAS
000380                          PAY-RATE-TABLE.
000390 A000-PAYROLL-CALCULATION.
000400     IF PR-HOURS-WORKED > 80
000410         PERFORM B100-CALCULATE-OVERTIME
000420     ELSE
000430         MOVE ZEROS TO WS-OVERTIME-PAY.
000440     PERFORM B300-CALCULATE-REGULAR.
000450     PERFORM B400-CALCULATE-GROSS-PAY.
000460 A000-PROGRAM-EXIT.
000470     EXIT PROGRAM.
000480 B100-CALCULATE-OVERTIME.
000490     COMPUTE WS-OVERTIME-PAY ROUNDED = (PR-HOURS-WORKED - 80) *
000500         SHIFT-RATE(PR-REGION-NUMBER, PR-JOB-LEVEL, PR-SHIFT)
000510         * 1.5.
000520 B300-CALCULATE-REGULAR.
000530     IF PR-HOURS-WORKED > 80
000540         COMPUTE WS-REGULAR-PAY ROUNDED = 80 *
000550             SHIFT-RATE(PR-REGION-NUMBER, PR-JOB-LEVEL, PR-SHIFT)
000560     ELSE
000570         COMPUTE WS-REGULAR-PAY ROUNDED = PR-HOURS-WORKED *
000580             SHIFT-RATE(PR-REGION-NUMBER, PR-JOB-LEVEL, PR-SHIFT).
000590 B400-CALCULATE-GROSS-PAY.
000600     COMPUTE WS-GROSS-PAY = WS-OVERTIME-PAY + WS-REGULAR-PAY.
```

Structure Chart

The structure chart for Program 2–1 is shown in Figure 9–14.

Discussion

The main program has defined an area in lines 580 through 880 to hold the data for each of the tables. B100–LOAD–DEFINE–TABLES calls the subprogram TABLDEF to place data values into four of these tables. When TABLDEF is run, it initializes three of the tables and in turn calls the subprogram TABLLD to input-load the pay-rate table. TABLLD's only function is to input-load the pay-rate table in the addresses provided by its LINKAGE section. This allows the LINKAGE section of TABLDEF access to the records input by TABLLD.

326   *Chapter 9*

Figure 9–14   *Structure Chart for Program 9–1*

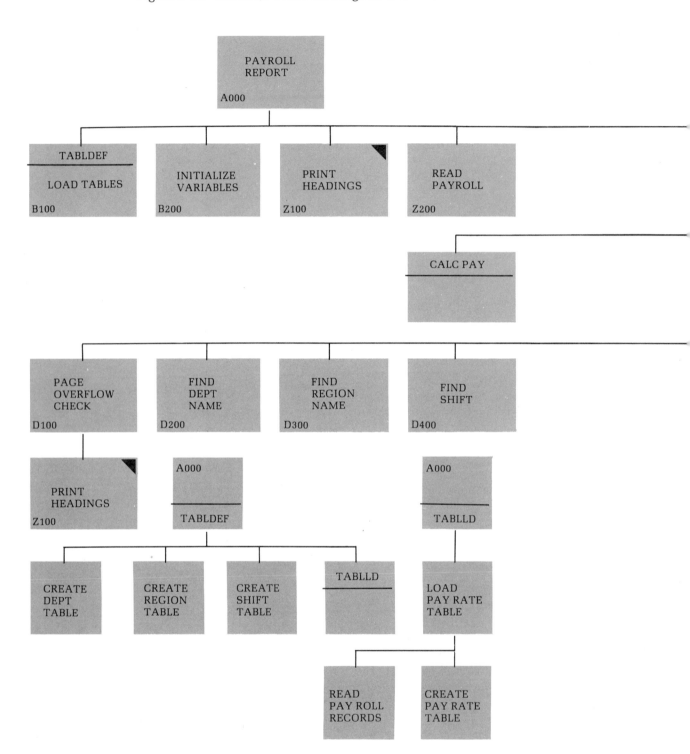

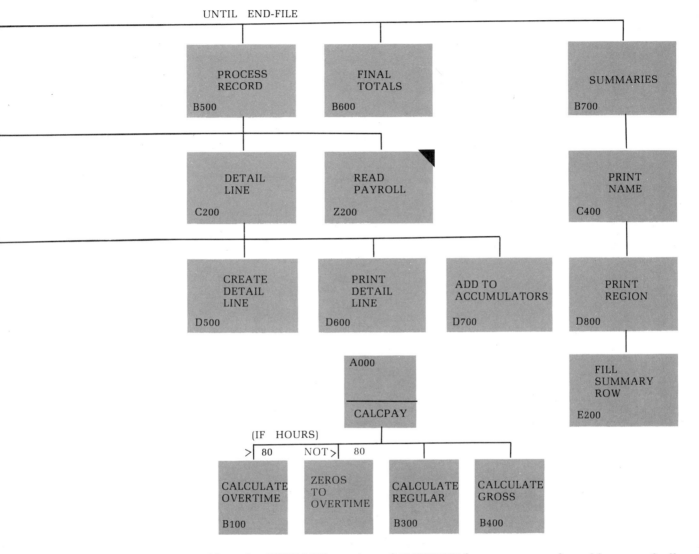

Now the LINKAGE section of TABLDEF has access to the addresses of all table data and control returns to the main program, which also now has access to all values in the defined and loaded tables.

The CALL statement at line 1820 in the main program calls on the subprogram CALCPAY to access the input record PR–PAYROLL–RECORD, WS–WORK–AREAS and the data in the PAY–RATE–TABLE through the USING clause. When CALCPAY operates on each input record, it will calculate overtime pay, regular, and overtime pay. These results are made available to the main program by lines 140 through 340 of the subprogram CALCPAY.

The remainder of the processing takes place in the main program and is the same as for Program 2–1. The results of executing the main program and the three subprograms are shown in Figure 9–15. This output is identical to that produced by the Program 2–1.

Figure 9–15 *Output from Program 9–1*

```
                                    PAYROLL REPORT
                                       PAGE  1
  EMP-NO    PAY-RATE   REGION    SHIFT    JOB-LEVEL  GROSS-PAY    OVERTIME-PAY   REGULAR-PAY    DEPARTMENT
  ............................................................................................................

    022     $  8.40   EASTERN      2         2     $    630.00  $     0.00     $    630.00    SHIPPING
    042     $  7.35   CENTRAL      1         1     $    492.45  $     0.00     $    492.45    SHIPPING
    059     $  8.95   CENTRAL      3         3     $    635.45  $     0.00     $    635.45    SHIPPING
    111     $  8.90   WESTERN      1         4     $    712.00  $     0.00     $    712.00    ASSEMBLY
    122     $ 10.25   EASTERN      2         5     $    133.25  $     0.00     $    133.25    ASSEMBLY
    123     $  7.60   CENTRAL      2         1     $    608.00  $     0.00     $    608.00    ASSEMBLY
    126     $  8.15   CEMTRAL      1         3     $    399.35  $     0.00     $    399.35    RECEIVING
    159     $ 10.50   CENTRAL      3         5     $  1,044.75  $   204.75     $    840.00    RECEIVING
    175     $  9.50   EASTERN      2         4     $    760.00  $     0.00     $    760.00    RECEIVING
    176     $  8.70   WESTERN      3         2     $    696.00  $     0.00     $    696.00    RECEIVING
    222     $  9.65   WESTERN      1         5     $    772.00  $     0.00     $    772.00    ACCOUNTING
    226     $  9.15   CENTRAL      2         4     $  1,006.50  $   274.50     $    732.00    ACCOUNTING
    242     $  8.95   CENTRAL      3         3     $    769.70  $    53.70     $    716.00    MAINTENANCE
     4   THIS REGION NUMBER IS IN ERROR
     4   THIS SHIFT NUMBER IS IN ERROR
    277     $  8.85   WESTERN      2         3     $     61.95  $     0.00     $     61.95    MAINTENANCE
    299     $  7.65   CENTRAL      1         2     $    841.50  $   229.50     $    612.00    PRODUCTION
    311     $  8.40   WESTERN      1         3     $    697.20  $    25.20     $    672.00    PRODUCTION
     4   THIS REGION NUMBER IS IN ERROR
    411     $  9.00   EASTERN      1         4     $    108.00  $     0.00     $    108.00    PRODUCTION
    420     $  9.50   EASTERN      2         4     $    959.50  $   199.50     $    760.00    PRODUCTION
    421     $  7.35   CENTRAL      1         1     $    643.13  $    55.13     $    588.00    RECEIVING
    422     $  8.35   WESTERN      2         2     $    359.05  $     0.00     $    359.05    RECEIVING
    459     $  8.40   WESTERN      1         3     $    100.80  $     0.00     $    100.80    ACCOUNTING
    477     $  8.85   WESTERN      2         3     $    867.30  $   159.30     $    708.00    MAINTENANCE
    499     $  9.40   CENTRAL      1         5     $    658.00  $     0.00     $    658.00    MAINTENANCE
    517     $  8.40   EASTERN      2         2     $    672.00  $     0.00     $    672.00    MAINTENANCE
    522     $  9.45   WESTERN      2         4     $  1,039.50  $   283.50     $    756.00    PRODUCTION
     4   THIS REGION NUMBER IS IN ERROR
    611     $  8.55   CENTRAL      2         3     $    495.90  $     0.00     $    495.90    RECEIVING
    621     $  9.75   WESTERN      3         4     $  1,057.88  $   277.88     $    780.00    MAINTENANCE
    677     $  8.20   EASTERN      3         1     $    590.40  $     0.00     $    590.40    ASSEMBLY
    777     $  8.55   CENTRAL      2         3     $    902.03  $   218.03     $    684.00    ACCOUNTING
    799     $ 10.50   CENTRAL      3         5     $    903.00  $    63.00     $    840.00    ACCOUNTING
    811     $  7.90   EASTERN      2         1     $    173.80  $     0.00     $    173.80    ASSEMBLY
    821     $  8.05   WESTERN      3         1     $     88.55  $     0.00     $     88.55    ACCOUNTING
    822     $  9.00   WESTERN      3         3     $    747.00  $    27.00     $    720.00    PRODUCTION
     5   THIS SHIFT NUMBER IS IN ERROR
    859     $  8.50   EASTERN      1         3     $    845.75  $   165.75     $    680.00    RECEIVING
    842     $  8.15   CENTRAL      1         3     $    664.23  $    12.23     $    652.00    ASSEMBLY
    899     $  9.45   WESTERN      2         4     $     75.60  $     0.00     $     75.60    ASSEMBLY
                                    PAYROLL REPORT
                                       PAGE  2
  EMP-NO    PAY-RATE   REGION    SHIFT    JOB-LEVEL  GROSS-PAY    OVERTIME-PAY   REGULAR-PAY    DEPARTMENT
  ............................................................................................................

    921     $  8.90   WESTERN      1         4     $    676.40  $     0.00     $    676.40    ACCOUNTING
    922     $  9.40   CENTRAL      1         5     $     94.00  $     0.00     $     94.00    PRODUCTION
    926     $  9.00   EASTERN      1         4     $    126.00  $     0.00     $    126.00    SHIPPING
    40   THIS DEPARTMENT NUMBER IS IN ERROR
    995     $  9.30   EASTERN      3         3     $    744.00  $     0.00     $    744.00    SHIPPING
  TOTALS                                           $ 23,851.92  $ 2,248.97     $ 21,602.95
                                    REGIONAL SUMMARY
                                     EASTERN REGION
                                         SHIFT
                JOB-LEVEL            1            2            3        TOTAL ROW
                    1             $.00       $173.80      $590.40       $764.20
                    2             $.00     $1,302.00         $.00     $1,302.00
                    3          $845.75          $.00      $744.00     $1,589.75
                    4          $234.00     $1,719.50         $.00     $1,953.50
                    5             $.00       $133.25         $.00       $133.25
                 TOTALS       $1,079.75    $3,328.55    $1,334.40     $5,742.70
```

Figure 9–15 *(concluded)*

```
                              CENTRAL REGION
                                 SHIFT
           JOB–LEVEL      1          2          3      TOTAL ROW
               1      $1,135.58    $608.00      $.00   $1,743.58
               2        $841.50       $.00      $.00     $841.50
               3      $1,063.58  $1,397.93  $1,405.15   $3,866.66
               4           $.00  $1,006.50      $.00   $1,006.50
               5        $752.00       $.00  $1,947.75   $2,699.75
           TOTALS     $3,792.66  $3,012.43  $3,352.90  $10,157.99
                              WESTERN REGION
                                 SHIFT
           JOB–LEVEL      1          2          3      TOTAL ROW
               1           $.00       $.00    $88.55      $88.55
               2           $.00    $359.05   $696.00   $1,055.05
               3        $798.00    $929.25   $747.00   $2,474.25
               4      $1,388.40  $1,115.10  $1,057.88   $3,561.38
               5        $772.00       $.00      $.00     $772.00
           TOTALS     $2,958.40  $2,403.40  $2,589.43   $7,951.23
```

Programming Style

1. Use subprograms when a procedure is to be used in several different programs.
2. Use subprograms when a large program is to be divided into two or more parts and programmed by different programmers.
3. Although data-names in subprograms are independent of other programs, construct data-names so they help the programmer to understand their use.
4. Code common data as one group whenever possible.
5. When using several subprograms using static linkage, stack the subprograms after the main program. If one of the subprograms uses the SORT statement, place it at the end of the stack (required on some systems).
6. If used, place the LINKAGE section last in the DATA division.
7. Avoid the use of STOP RUN in a subprogram whenever possible. The fewer points of exit in a program the better the program structure.

Common Errors

1. Omitting the USING option in the called subprogram when arguments are to be passed.
2. Receiving the arguments in the USING option of the called subprogram in the wrong order.
3. Receiving area in the LINKAGE section has fewer positions than the sending area of the WORKING–STORAGE section.
4. Using as an argument a data-name that was not defined at the 01 level.
5. Using an index as an argument.
6. Calling a called program a second time and not allowing for any data or condition changes having occurred on the first entry.
7. Not placing the EXIT PROGRAM statement in a procedure by itself.
8. Using VALUE clauses in the LINKAGE section for non-88-level entries.
9. Not using a literal as the entry point location when using the static CALL statement.
10. Having a calling program directly or indirectly call itself.

Exercises

1. What are the advantages of using subprograms?

2. What is the purpose of the following:
   a. The CALL literal clause of the static CALL statement.
   b. The USING option of the CALL statement.
   c. The EXIT PROGRAM statement.
   d. The LINKAGE section.

3. Define the following:
   a. Subprogram.
   b. Calling program.
   c. Called program.
   d. Nested subprogram.
   e. Run unit.
   f. Main program.
   g. Arguments.

4. Given the following:

```
WORKING-STORAGE SECTION.
01  COMMON-RECORD-A          PIC X(80).
01  COMMON-RECORD-B.
    05  COMMON-NAME          PIC X(20).
    05  COMMON-ADDRESS       PIC X(20).
01  COMMON-RECORD-C.
    05  COMMON-ID            PIC 9(9).
    05  COMMON-HOURLY-RATE   PIC 99V99.
    05  COMMON-HOURS-WORKED  PIC 9(3).
```

   Write COBOL statements to do the following:
   a. Create a LINKAGE section for subprogram SUBONE to process the data for COMMON–RECORD–A and COMMON–NAME.
   b. Create a LINKAGE section subprogram SUBONE to process the data for COMMON–ID, COMMON–HOURLY–RATE and COMMON–HOURS–WORKED.
   c. Create LINKAGE sections for subprogram SUBONE to process the data for COMMON–RECORD–B and subprogram SUBTWO to process COMMON–RECORD–A and COMMON–RECORD–B when SUBONE is its calling program.

5. Using the WORKING–STORAGE section in exercise 4, write COBOL statements to do the following: (show the necessary statements in both the calling and called programs including the LINKAGE section)
   a. Transfer control to subprogram SUBTWO.
   b. Transfer control to subprogram SUBTHREE and the arguments for COMMON–RECORD–A.
   c. Transfer control to subprogram SUBFOUR and the arguments for COMMON–HOURLY–RATE, COMMON–HOURS–WORKED, COMMON–NAME, and COMMON–ADDRESS, in that order.

6. Given the following entries correct only those that are in error. Assume all programmer-defined names have been properly defined.

   a. `CALL PROGRAM3 USING RECORD-1   RECORD-2.`
   b. `IF WS-AMOUNT = ZERO CALL 'SUBPROG' ELSE CALL PROGRAM 3.`
   c. `EXIT SUBPROGRAM.`
   d.
   ```
   LINKAGE SECTION.
   01 COMMON-DATA.
       05  FD-1    PIC X(20).
       05  FD-2    PIC 9(5).
   ```

```
PROCEDURE DIVISION.

    CALL 'SUBTWO' USING FD-1 FD-2.

    EXIT PROGRAM.
```
e.
```
IF WS-AMOUNT = ZERO NEXT SENTENCE
ELSE PERFORM CALL 'SUBFIVE' UNTIL END-OF-FILE.
```
f.
```
WORKING-STORAGE SECTION.
01  SUM-ACCUMULATOR     PIC 99.
LINKAGE SECTION.
01  COMMON-COUNTER      PIC 99.



    CALL 'SUBSIX' USING SUM-ACCUMULATOR   COMMON-COUNTER.
```

7. In Figure 9–8 change the PROCEDURE division in Example C to :
```
PROCEDURE DIVISION USING SUB-RECORD.
    MOVE 10 TO SUB-F3.
    PERFORM D300 3 TIMES.
D300.
    CALL 'SUBFOUR' USING SUB-RECORD.
D400.  EXIT PROGRAM.
```
and change the PROCEDURE division in Example D to:
```
PROCEDURE DIVISION USING SUB-SUB-RECORD.
    COMPUTE SUB-SUB-F2 = SUB-SUB-F3 / 3.
    IF SUB-SUB-F2 < ZERO STOP RUN.
D400.   EXIT PROGRAM.
```
What are the values of SUB–SUB–F2, SUB–SUB–F3, SUB–F2, and SUB–F3 when control is returned to SUBTHREE?

Problems

1. Write a program to read in customer's account number, age, and current credit balance. Store the data in table form. The table data is to be transferred to a subprogram, which will calculate average age and average credit balance and send the results back to the main program. The main program will print out the results. Use as data the following:

Account number	Age	Credit balance
		(2 decimals)
61246	35	020034
58541	40	100515
13355	56	073922
41231	39	006050
32198	63	007583
40037	45	276870
35610	49	116000
56585	51	134598
29109	50	017080
24164	37	031145

2. Recode a chapter sample program of your choice from any chapter in this text. Divide the job into a main program and two or more subprograms. Have one subprogram call another subprogram. Check to see if the results of this program match the results of the program sample selected. Use the data given for the sample program.

3. Use three subprograms in this problem. Using the data described below as input, create a report that includes for each record a new field that contains the average

for all grades in the record. Create another report that contains the records of all students with an average five or more points higher than the average for all students combined. Create a final report that assigns a letter grade of A for an average of 90–100, B for an average of 80 and under 90, C for an average of 70 and under 80, D for an average of 60 and under 70, and F for under 60.

Student Data

Student ID	Test 1	Test 2	Test 3
527128888	090	093	097
524364785	070	085	060
333431996	040	056	034
691325574	080	081	082
615114891	085	100	095
512113466	069	075	076
781236630	082	080	073
520803322	089	094	095
448431518	069	072	075
651324693	080	065	080

Report Writer

Writing reports is a major task in most organizations. This task typically requires such activities as the proper formatting of data, controlling for page overflow, controlling breaks for various levels of totals, performing arithmetic, and writing headings, detail lines, footings, and so forth. If a programmer has written many programs in COBOL, it is evident that such programs become quite large and complex and require a lot of time to develop and debug. A special feature is provided by the standard COBOL language called the **Report Writer** to ease the burden of writing reports.

TERMS AND STATEMENTS

Absolute value	LAST DETAIL	Report group
COLUMN clause	clause	REPORT HEADING
CONTROL clause	LINE–COUNTER	clause
CONTROL	LINE NUMBER	REPORT SECTION
FOOTING clause	clause	Report Writer
CONTROL	NEXT GROUP	RESET option
HEADING clause	NEXT PAGE	SOURCE clause
DETAIL clause	PAGE clause	SUM clause
FINAL	PAGE–COUNTER	SUPPRESS
FIRST DETAIL	PAGE FOOTING	statement
clause	clause	TERMINATE
FOOTING clause	PAGE HEADING	statement
GENERATE	clause	UPON option
statement	PRINT–SWITCH	USE BEFORE
GROUP INDICATE	RD entry	REPORTING
clause	Relative value	statement
HEADING clause	REPORT clause	USAGE clause
INITIATE statement	REPORT FOOTING	VALUE clause
	clause	

Report Writer Concepts

The **Report Writer** feature of COBOL is designed to simplify the programming for report output. Procedures for constructing output lines, totaling, moving data, and writing are automatically provided. Many of COBOL's reserved words are used with the Report Writer. It is like a language within the COBOL language.

The programmer can describe the report both physically and logically in the **REPORT SECTION** of the DATA division. Within the PROCEDURE division only a few simple statements are necessary to execute the Report Writer's special subroutines.

The concepts behind the use of the Report Writer are simple, but at first sight seem somewhat confusing. This has historically led programmers to avoid the use of this extremely powerful and worthwhile feature of COBOL. After using the Report Writer, however, many programmers have found it to be a very important tool in the writing of many types of programs.

In recent times, many computer centers have started to use the Report Writer feature on a regular basis. It is an important part of the COBOL language, and a programmer should know how to use it.

DATA Division

FILE Section

Formats, names, file descriptions, and record descriptions used in a program are defined in the FILE SECTION. In addition, a REPORT SECTION is added at the end of the DATA division to define the format of one or more reports to be generated by the Report Writer.

REPORT Clause

The first new entry using the Report Writer is found in the FD. The DATA RECORD clause is replaced with a **REPORT clause.** This clause is used to list the name of the report(s) to be created. Figure 10–1 shows its general format.

Figure 10–1　*Format of the REPORT Clause*

Figure 10–2　*Examples of using REPORT Clause*

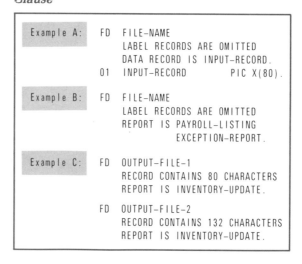

Figure 10–2 illustrates how the REPORT clause is used. Example A is a regular FD entry followed by an 01 to describe the data. Example B is an FD entry using the REPORT clause. The differences between the two examples are that the 01 level number and the DATA RECORD clause must be omitted when using the RE PORT clause. Example B also shows that more than one report may be defined for one file. The REPORT names can be in any order. Example C is where the same report can be defined and used in two different files. However, OUTPUT–FILE–1 will only contain the first 80 positions of the report's record, and OUTPUT–FILE–2 will contain the entire 132 positions.

REPORT SECTION

If a REPORT clause is used in a program, there must be a REPORT SECTION. Within this section each report must be described by an **RD entry.** The RD is analogous to an FD and begins in area A followed by the report name in area B. The report's physical structure and organization are then described. This is followed by an 01 level number in area A and the report group name in area B. The **report group** name describes the format of the report's elements and its sources of information. The report group may be an elementary or group item, and there may be several report groups for an RD entry.

RD Entry

The general format for the RD entry is given in Figure 10–3.

Figure 10–3   *Format of the RD Entry*

```
RD report-name
   [[{CONTROL  IS  } {identifier-1 [identifier-2] ...        }]]
   [[{CONTROLS ARE}  {FINAL identifier-1 [identifier-2] ...}]]
   [      [{LIMIT  IS }]            {LINE }]
   [PAGE  [{           }] integer-1 {     }]
   [      [{LIMITS ARE}]            {LINES}]
   [HEADING        integer-2]
   [FIRST DETAIL   integer-3]
   [LAST DETAIL    integer-4]
   [FOOTING        integer-5]
```

RD Clauses

CONTROL Clause. The **CONTROL clause** defines the hierarchy of control breaks in a report. This clause is required when any control report groups are used. When only a FINAL total is used the clause may be omitted. Referring to Figure 10–3, **FINAL** represents the highest level of control; and identifier-1, the major control. Identifier-2 represents the intermediate control, and the last identifier represents the minor control. A control break occurs when a control item has changed in value since the last time it was tested.

PAGE Clause. The purpose of the **PAGE clause** is to define the page size and any vertical subdivisions of the page. It is only required if the page format is controlled by the Report Writer; otherwise, it can be omitted. If omitted, vertical subdivisions of the page are controlled by the reserved words LINE or NEXT GROUP, and relative spacing is not allowed. Integer-1 defines the maximum length of each report page and must not exceed 999.

Other Clauses. Integer-2 of the **HEADING clause** defines the first line of which anything may be printed and is usually for the first line of a heading. **FIRST DETAIL clause** defines the first line where a detail line can be printed. Integer-4 of the **LAST DETAIL clause** defines the last line on which a detail line can be printed. Integer-5 of the **FOOTING clause** is the first line where a footing can be printed.

Examples of RD Entry Clauses

Figure 10–4 illustrates several examples of the RD entry clauses.

Figure 10–4   *Examples of Using RD Entry Clauses*

```
Example A:   RD  INVENTORY-LISTING
                 PAGE LIMIT   40 LINES.

Example B:   RD  INVENTORY-LISTING
                 CONTROL IS ITEM-TOTAL
                 PAGE LIMIT   40
                 HEADING      2
                 FIRST DETAIL 4
                 FOOTING      40.

Example C:   RD  INVENTORY-LISTING
                 CONTROL IS FINAL
                             ITEM-NUMBER
                 PAGE-LIMIT   40
                 HEADING      2
                 FIRST DETAIL 5
                 LAST DETAIL  30
                 FOOTING      35.
```

Example A of Figure 10–4 is a complete RD entry. In this case the entry is defining each page in the report to have a maximum of 40 lines before a page overflow is to take place.

Example B is more detailed in defining the physical structure and organization of the report. The CONTROL clause has one control item identified, ITEM–NUMBER. Whenever its value changes, a total is printed. There are 40 lines per page. The page heading will print starting at line 2 and the page footing will print at line 40. All other lines to be printed will be between lines 2 and 40.

A more structured report is defined in Example C. Here the CONTROL clause has two control items. The minor control break is taken whenever the value of ITEM–NUMBER changes, and this value is accumulated in a final total area defined by the reserved word FINAL. After the last record has been input, the end-of-file condition triggers a control break, which prints the last total for ITEM–NUMBER, followed by the printing of the accumulated FINAL total.

Again there are 40 lines per page with the page heading printed starting at line 2. Since the first line of the report after the page heading starts at line 6, the page heading can be four lines long if desired (lines 2 through 5). The clause LAST DETAIL 30 will leave four blank lines prior to the page footing (lines 31 through 34). FOOTING 35 means that six lines can be printed for the page footing before the page limit of 40 is reached.

Omitted PAGE Clause Options

If the PAGE clause is specified and optional clauses are omitted from the RD entry, certain default values are assumed. These are listed in Figure 10–5.

Figure 10–5   *Default Values for PAGE Clause*

Omitted entry	Default value assumed
HEADING integer-2	integer-2 = 1
FIRST DETAIL integer-3	integer-3 = integer-2
LAST DETAIL integer-4	integer-4 = integer-5
FOOTING integer-5	integer-5 = integer-4
Both LAST DETAIL	integer-4 = 1
And FOOTING omitted	integer-5 = 1

Counters for the PAGE Clause

The **PAGE clause** automatically generates two numeric counters for a program when used in the RD entry. They are identified by the reserved words PAGE–COUNTER and LINE–COUNTER.

PAGE–COUNTER. The initial value of **PAGE–COUNTER** is 1 and is incremented by 1 whenever a page overflow occurs. It is an unsigned integer and can have a value as large as 999999. Its actual size is specified by the PIC clause associated with the SOURCE PAGE–COUNTER statement. The value of PAGE–COUNTER can be changed by statements in the PROCEDURE division. This value can also be displayed. However, if more than one PAGE–COUNTER exists in a program, it must be qualified by the report-name.

LINE–COUNTER. The reserved word **LINE–COUNTER** is used to determine page breaks and to control vertical subdivisions of a page. Its initial value is zero, and it is automatically set to zero on a page break. It is incremented as necessary by the Report Writer. Its size and the rules governing its use are the same as those for PAGE–COUNTER.

Report Group

Various types of lines may be printed by the Report Writer. A **report group** is one or more of these lines in a report. Following each RD entry there must be at least one 01-level entry which is used to define these report groups.

TYPE Clauses

The general format of the various TYPE clauses are shown in Figure 10–6.

Figure 10–6 *Formats of the TYPE Clauses*

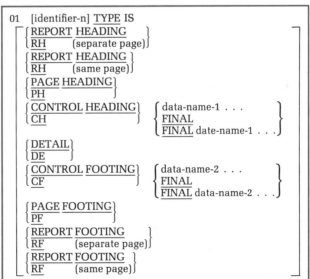

The rules for the use of TYPE clauses are:

- The **REPORT HEADING clause** can occur only once, at the beginning of a report or at the top of the first page in a report. It differs in form and content from the rest of the report, and its use is optional. To use this clause at the top of the first page in a report the FIRST DETAIL clause and the PAGE LIMIT clause are required.
- The **PAGE HEADING clause** can cause a page heading to be printed on every page of the report. Page numbers can be printed with a page heading

using the PAGE–COUNTER. The first page number is 2 if REPORT HEADINGS is on a page by itself; otherwise, the first page number is 1.

■ A collection of lines may have heading information printed prior to another collection of lines, if desired. This is done with the **CONTROL HEADING clause** and a data-name. A special CONTROL HEADING can be defined by the reserved word FINAL and a data-name. This line or set of lines can be written only once. The PAGE LIMIT clause is required.

■ If a PAGE FOOTING precedes a REPORT FOOTING on the same page or if a PAGE HEADING follows a REPORT HEADING on the same page, both must be printable in that area of the page.

■ The **CONTROL FOOTING clause** is used to summarize a group of data at the end of a control group. Whenever the controlled data-item changes its value, a control break occurs. When more than one control break is to be used, any lower-level control footing as well as the current control footing is printed. When FINAL is used, this total is only printed once, after the last control footing. The PAGE LIMIT clause is required.

■ The **PAGE FOOTING clause** allows for each page, except for a REPORT HEADING or REPORT FOOTING on a separate page, to contain summary lines at the bottom of a page. The PAGE LIMIT, LAST DETAIL, and FOOTING clauses are required.

■ The **REPORT FOOTING clause** will print summary lines once, at the end of the report. If the summary is printed on the same page as other footings, the clauses PAGE LIMIT, LAST DETAIL, and FOOTING must be used. If the summary lines are to print on a separate page, only the PAGE LIMIT clause is required.

■ The **DETAIL clause** is always under the direct control of the programmer and must be preceded by an identifier. There may be several different types of detail lines in a report. When this is the case, the desired detail line must be generated. The PAGE LIMIT clause is required.

Report Description Entries

The general format of the various report description entries are shown in Figure 10–7.

Format 1 is the beginning of a report group description entry. Format 2 is used for level numbers 02–48 to specify the line number of subordinate entries and to group these entries together. Format 3 is used for an elementary entry with level numbers 02–49 to describe an elementary DETAIL entry for items to be summed and to define a counter for a CONTROL FOOTING entry. Format 4 is to describe one elementary item.

LINE NUMBER Clause. The **LINE NUMBER clause** is used for within-group spacing at the 01 level or as part of a description of an elementary item. LINE NUMBER IS 1 **(absolute value)** means to position the printer at the first line of the report. LINE PLUS 2 **(relative value)** means to position the printer two lines from the last line printed. **NEXT PAGE** means to skip to the next page first, then execute the clause.

NEXT GROUP Clause. **NEXT GROUP** indicates the spacing between the current report group being defined and the next group to be printed. NEXT GROUP NEXT PAGE means to start the next group on a new page after any headings. NEXT GROUP IS PLUS 3 is to triple space between report groups. NEXT GROUP IS 30 would indicate an absolute line number on which to begin the next group. This clause can be used only at the 01 level.

COLUMN Clause. The **COLUMN clause** specifies the horizontal positioning of the leftmost character of a field. The clause can be used only at the elementary level, and integer-5 must be positive. If the integer value is omitted, the item is not printed at execution time.

Figure 10–7 *Formats of Description Entries*

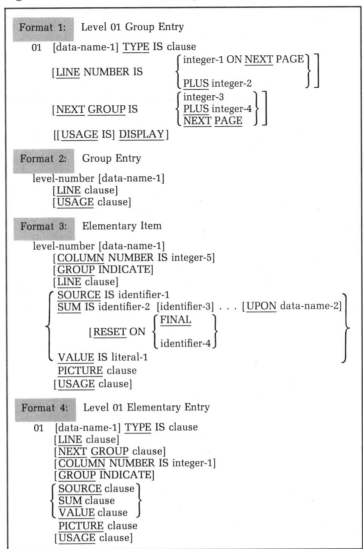

GROUP INDICATE Clause. The **GROUP INDICATE clause** allows the printing of an elementary item only the first time it occurs or after a control or page break. At all other times the contents of the item are suppressed. It can be used only for elementary items in a DETAIL report group.

SOURCE Clause. This clause moves data from a source defined by a data-name outside of the REPORT SECTION to the PIC clause associated with a **SOURCE clause.** In addition, it can specify a data-name to be summed in a CONTROL FOOTING report group.

SUM Clause. The **SUM clause** sets up an elementary item as a receiving field for addition using SOURCE data items and other SUM accumulators. It can be used only at the elementary level within a CONTROL report group. In Format 3 of Figure 10–7, identifiers 2 and 3 are SUM operands. These operands must be defined in the DATA division as numeric data-items or as another SUM counter in a CONTROL REPORT GROUP. The size of the SUM counter is determined by the PIC clause that accompanies the SUM clause description. SUM counters may be added to other SUM counters to obtain minor, intermediate, and major totals.
The **UPON option** allows selective summing of certain data-items named as

source items in DETAIL report groups. The **RESET option** will allow the SUM counter being used to be reset to zero only after the named (identifier-4) higher level control break occurs or after the FINAL control break. If the RESET option is not specified the SUM counter is automatically set to zero after the control break for that report group.

VALUE Clause. The **VALUE clause** allows an elementary item to assume a literal value whenever that report group is executed. It must be accompanied by a proper PIC clause. Remember, if a GROUP INDICATE clause is present, existing conditions may suppress printing of the value.

USAGE Clause. The **USAGE clause** must only refer to DISPLAY data or not be used in the statement.

Examples of Report Description Entries   Figures 10–8 through 10–10 show examples of report description entries.

Figure 10–8   *Examples of Line Spaces*

```
Example A:

   01   TYPE IS REPORT HEADING
        LINE NUMBER IS 25.
        05   COLUMN NUMBER IS 56 PIC X(19)
             VALUE 'NAME OF THIS REPORT'.

Example B:

   01   TYPE IS REPORT HEADING.
        05   LINE NUMBER IS 1
             COLUMN NUMBER IS 59 PIC X(4)
             VALUE 'THIS IS LINE 1'.
        05   LINE NUMBER PLUS 2
             COLUMN NUMBER IS 59 PIC X(14)
             VALUE 'THIS IS LINE 3'.

Example C:

   01   TYPE IS PAGE HEADING.
        05   LINE NUMBER IS 1
             COLUMN NUMBER IS 16 PIC X(17)
             VALUE IS 'INVENTORY LISTING'.
        05   LINE NUMBER PLUS 2
             10   COLUMN NUMBER IS 14 PIC X(8) VALUE 'SOFTWARE'.
             10   COLUMN NUMBER IS 28 PIC X(8) VALUE 'HARDWARE'.
```

Example A of Figure 10–8 is a one-line report heading printed on line 25 of the page. The heading NAME OF THIS REPORT starts in column 56 and is 19 positions in length. The LINE NUMBER clause could have been placed at the 05 level.

Example B is a two-line report heading. Line 1 will have the heading THIS IS LINE 1 starting in position 59. The second line in the heading is positioned two lines after the first line, which is line 3 on the page. THIS IS LINE 3 will be printed starting in column 59. Here the LINE NUMBER clause must be placed at the 05 level. In both Examples A and B the 05 level described a line to be printed.

The arrangement of the heading in Example C allows for a two-line page heading. On line 1, INVENTORY LISTING will be printed starting in position 16. The second line will print on line 3; it has two fields. The first field starts in position 14 and prints the word SOFTWARE, and the second field prints the word HARDWARE starting in position 28. Notice that the level number 10 was needed to indicate the presence of more than one field on that line.

Figure 10–9   *Examples of the SOURCE and SUM Clauses*

```
  Example A:

    01   DETAIL-NAME TYPE DETAIL LINE.
         05  LINE NUMBER IS PLUS 1.
             10   COLUMN  5 PIC X(20) GROUP INDICATE
                                      SOURCE IN-SALESPERSON.
             10   COLUMN 30 PIC 9(5)  SOURCE IN-ITEM-NUM.
             10   COLUMN 55 PIC ZZ9   SOURCE IN-ITEM-QTY.

  Example B:

    01   TYPE CONTROL FOOTING DEPT-NUMBER
         LINE PLUS 2 NEXT GROUP NEXT PAGE.
         05  COLUMN 10 PIC X(12) VALUE 'DEPT-NAME IS'.
         05  COLUMN 25 PIC X(10) SOURCE DEPT-NAME(INDEX-NUMBER).
         05  COLUMN 40 PIC $ZZ,ZZ9.99 SUM IN-ITEM-QTY.
```

Example A of Figure 10–9 has a GROUP INDICATE clause for IN–SALESPER SON. If there were 10 input records in sequential order for this person, the name would be printed only when the first of these records was processed, and again, only if a page break occurred. SOURCE will find the values in the named data fields and move the values to their respective PIC clauses. There are three data fields per record. Whenever this detail record is printed, LINE NUMBER PLUS 1 will cause the printer to single space.

Example B will double space from the last detail line before printing a total when a control break is taken on DEPT–NUMBER. NEXT GROUP NEXT PAGE will skip to the next page after the control total is printed for the report group. The total to be printed is the SUM of all the IN–ITEM–QTY fields. This SUM will be set to zero after it is printed and is ready to start accumulating for the next report group. The individual values for IN–ITEM–QTY were printed in Example A when the DETAIL record was processed. Notice that three fields are to be printed for each control break on DEPT–NUMBER. DEPT–NAME(INDEX–NUMBER) is a value stored in a table.

Figure 10–10   *Examples of Rolling Forward Totals*

```
    01   DETAIL-NAME TYPE DETAIL LINE
         LINE NUMBER IS PLUS 1.
         05  COLUMN 40 PIC Z,ZZ9 SOURCE EMPLOYEE-HOURS.
    01   TYPE CONTROL FOOTING EMPLOYEE-NUMBER
         LINE NUMBER IS PLUS 2.
         05  DEPT-TOTAL
             COLUMN 42 PIC Z,ZZ9 SOURCE SUM EMPLOYEE-HOURS.
    01   TYPE CONTROL FOOTING FINAL
         LINE NUMBER IS PLUS 2.
         05  COLUMN 44 PIC Z,ZZ9 SOURCE SUM DEPT-TOTAL.
```

Figure 10–10 illustrates one of several methods of accumulating more than one total. This method is referred to as rolling forward.

The value of EMPLOYEE–HOURS is printed after single spacing each time the detail record is processed. This value is accumulated (rolled forward) by the SUM EMPLOYEE–HOURS clause. When a control break is taken on EMPLOYEE–NUM BER, the current report group's last detail record is processed. Then after double spacing, SUM EMPLOYEE–HOURS total is printed and its value accumulated (rolled forward) to DEPT–TOTAL. The total of SUM EMPLOYEE–HOURS is set to zero, and processing begins on the next report group.

This process continues until a control break is taken on FINAL. When this break occurs, the last report group's detail record is processed. After double spacing, the SUM EMPLOYEE–HOURS total is printed and accumulated in DEPT–TOTAL. The total of EMPLOYEE–HOURS is set to zero. After double spacing, SUM DEPT–TOTAL is printed. Since the FINAL control break has been encountered, it is not necessary to accumulate SUM DEPT–TOTAL. Its value is set to zero and the totaling process is complete. Notice, that to accumulate a total and save it, a data-name must be defined after the level-number in the same statement where the SUM is located.

PROCEDURE Division

Three basic statements control the Report Writer in the PROCEDURE division. Figure 10–11 gives their general format.

Figure 10–11 *Formats of PROCEDURE Division Statements*

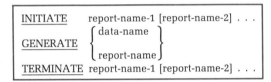

INITIATE Statement

The purpose of the **INITIATE statement** is to begin processing a report. The report name(s) have been defined in the FD that contains the REPORT clauses. It also appears in an RD in the REPORT SECTION. Execution of this statement sets the value of all SUM entries, sets the LINE–COUNTER to zero, and sets the value of PAGE–COUNTER to 1. A second INITIATE cannot be executed until the first has been terminated.

GENERATE Statement

The **GENERATE statement** controls the printing of the report. When the data-name option is used, detail reporting is done. If the report-name option is used summary reporting is done.

The first GENERATE statement executed produces the following report groups: report heading, page heading, control headings, and the detail, if specified. Subsequent execution of the GENERATE statement will produce appropriate detail groups, increment any counters as needed, increment SUM operands, and reset them as specified.

TERMINATE Statement

A **TERMINATE statement** must be executed to complete the processing of a report. Execution of this statement will automatically add all SUM operands; save current values of all control items; produce remaining control footings, FINAL control footings, page footings, and report footings. A second TERMINATE statement for a particular file may not be executed unless a second INITIATE statement has been executed.

Program Execution

Perhaps the best way to analyze the use of the Report Writer feature is to examine actual programs where it has been used. The following data records shown in Figure 10–12 have been used as input to all of the programs in this chapter.

Figure 10–12   *Input to Report Writer Programs*

```
1- 3  IN-SALESPERSON
6-30  IN-DESCRIPTION
33-40 IN-STOCK-NUMBER
43-50 IN-TYPE
53-59 IN-PRICE
62-64 IN-NUMBER-SOLD


===================================================================
050   300 BAUD MODEM            M4575    HARDWARE  0008900  001
050   1200/300 EXEC MODEM       M4571    HARDWARE  0059900  001
050   VOLTAGE REGULATOR         V1317E   HARDWARE  0038500  002
050   SURGE PROTECTOR           S6112    HARDWARE  0007900  004
050   SURGE PROTECTOR           S6112A   HARDWARE  0006300  001
050   SURGE PROTECTOR           S6112A   HARDWARE  0006300  001
050   POWERLINE MONITOR         P4029    HARDWARE  0096000  001
050   RIBBON-DIABLO             R8135    SUPPLIES  0000750  006
050   RIBBON-DIABLO             R8135    SUPPLIES  0000750  012
050   RIBBON-DIABLO             R8135    SUPPLIES  0000750  006
100   WORD-STAR                 P1654P   SOFTWARE  0042500  001
100   WORD-STAR                 P1654P   SOFTWARE  0042500  001
100   WORD-STAR PROFESSIONAL    P1664P   SOFTWARE  0075000  001
100   LOTUS 1-2-3               P1764Q   SOFTWARE  0056000  001
100   12 DS/DD 5 1/4            D4444    SUPPLIES  0004800  001
100   12 DS/DD 5 1/4            D4444    SUPPLIES  0004800  001
100   12 SS/SD 5 1/4            D4000    SUPPLIES  0003300  001
100   RIBBON OKIDATA            R9991    SUPPLIES  0000350  006
100   RIBBON OKIDATA            D9991    SUPPLIES  0000350  012
100   SURGE PROTECTOR           S6112    HARDWARE  0007900  002
===================================================================
```

Use of Headings and Final Totals

Program 10–1 uses a report heading, a page heading, a listing of detail records and a final total.

Program 10–1

```
000010 IDENTIFICATION DIVISION.
000020   PROGRAM-ID.  CHAP10.
000030*........................................................
000040* PROGRAM EXAMPLE 10-1                                    *
000050*........................................................
000060 ENVIRONMENT DIVISION.
000070 CONFIGURATION SECTION.
000080   SOURCE-COMPUTER.  VAX.
000090   OBJECT-COMPUTER.  VAX.
000100 INPUT-OUTPUT SECTION.
000110   FILE-CONTROL.
000120     SELECT INVENTORY-FILE ASSIGN TO INVEN.
000130     SELECT REPORT-FILE    ASSIGN TO PRINTER.
000140*
000150 DATA DIVISION.
000160 FILE SECTION.
000170 FD  INVENTORY-FILE
000180     RECORD CONTAINS 64 CHARACTERS
000190     LABEL RECORDS STANDARD.
000200 01  IN-INVENTORY-RECORD.
000210     05  IN-SALESPERSON      PIC X(3).
000220     05  FILLER              PIC X(2).
000230     05  IN-DESCRIPTION      PIC X(25).
000240     05  FILLER              PIC X(2).
000250     05  IN-STOCK-NUMBER     PIC X(8).
```

Program 10–1 *(continued)*

```
000260      05  FILLER                PIC X(2).
000270      05  IN-TYPE               PIC X(8).
000280      05  FILLER                PIC X(2).
000290      05  IN-PRICE              PIC 9(5)V9(2).
000300      05  FILLER                PIC X(2).
000310      05  IN-NUMBER-SOLD        PIC 9(3).
000320 FD  REPORT-FILE
000330      LABEL RECORDS ARE OMITTED
000340      REPORT IS INVENTORY-REPORT.
000350 WORKING-STORAGE SECTION.
000360 01  WS-REPORT-INDICATORS.
000370      05  WS-END-OF-FILE-INDICATOR PIC X(3).
000380          88  END-OF-FILE           VALUE 'END'.
000390 01  WS-ACCUMULATORS.
000400      05  WS-SALES-AMOUNT        PIC 9(3)V9(2).
000410*
000420 REPORT SECTION.
000430 RD  INVENTORY-REPORT
000440      PAGE LIMIT 50 LINES
000450      HEADING         1
000460      FIRST DETAIL    6
000470      LAST DETAIL    48.
000480 01  TYPE IS REPORT HEADING
000490      NEXT GROUP NEXT PAGE.
000500      05  LINE NUMBER 25.
000510          10  COLUMN 32    PIC X(22)
000520              VALUE 'APRIL INVENTORY REPORT'.
000530      05  LINE NUMBER PLUS 2.
000540          10  COLUMN 30    PIC X(25)
000550              VALUE 'QUALITY COMPUTER SUPPLIES'.
000560 01  TYPE IS PAGE HEADING.
000570      05  LINE NUMBER 1.
000580          10  COLUMN 32    PIC X(16)
000590              VALUE 'INVENTORY REPORT'.
000600          10  COLUMN 74    PIC X(4)  VALUE 'PAGE'.
000610          10  COLUMN 79    PIC Z9    SOURCE PAGE-COUNTER.
000620      05  LINE NUMBER PLUS 2.
000630          10  COLUMN 38    PIC X(5)  VALUE 'STOCK'.
000640          10  COLUMN 65    PIC X(6)  VALUE 'NUMBER'.
000650          10  COLUMN 73    PIC X(5)  VALUE 'SALES'.
000660      05  LINE NUMBER PLUS 1.
000670          10  COLUMN  1    PIC X(11) VALUE 'SALESPERSON'.
000680          10  COLUMN 14    PIC X(11) VALUE 'DESCRIPTION'.
000690          10  COLUMN 38    PIC X(6)  VALUE 'NUMBER'.
000700          10  COLUMN 45    PIC X(4)  VALUE 'TYPE'.
000710          10  COLUMN 57    PIC X(5)  VALUE 'PRICE'.
000720          10  COLUMN 67    PIC X(4)  VALUE 'SOLD'.
000730          10  COLUMN 73    PIC X(6)  VALUE 'AMOUNT'.
000740 01  DETAIL-LINE TYPE IS DETAIL.
000750      05  LINE NUMBER PLUS 1.
000760          10  COLUMN  5    PIC ZZ9         SOURCE IN-SALESPERSON.
000770          10  COLUMN 14    PIC X(25)       SOURCE IN-DESCRIPTION.
000780          10  COLUMN 38    PIC X(8)        SOURCE IN-STOCK-NUMBER.
000790          10  COLUMN 45    PIC X(8)        SOURCE IN-TYPE.
000800          10  COLUMN 54    PIC $$$,$$9.99 SOURCE IN-PRICE.
000810          10  COLUMN 66    PIC ZZ9         SOURCE IN-NUMBER-SOLD.
000820          10  COLUMN 71    PIC $$,$$9.99  SOURCE WS-SALES-AMOUNT.
000830 01  TYPE IS CONTROL FOOTING FINAL.
000840      05  LINE NUMBER PLUS 2.
000850          10  COLUMN 33    PIC X(16)       VALUE 'INVENTORY REPORT'.
000860          10  COLUMN 70    PIC $ZZ,ZZ9.99 SUM WS-SALES-AMOUNT.
000870*
000880 PROCEDURE DIVISION.
000890 A000-INVENTORY-LISTING.
```

Program 10–1 *(concluded)*

```
000900      OPEN INPUT  INVENTORY-FILE
000910          OUTPUT REPORT-FILE.
000920      INITIATE INVENTORY-REPORT.
000930      PERFORM Z100-READ-INVENTORY-RECORD.
000940      PERFORM B200-PROCESS-RECORDS
000950          UNTIL END-OF-FILE.
000960      TERMINATE INVENTORY-REPORT.
000970      CLOSE INVENTORY-FILE
000980          REPORT-FILE.
000990      STOP RUN.
001000  B200-PROCESS-RECORDS.
001010      COMPUTE WS-SALES-AMOUNT = IN-PRICE * IN-NUMBER-SOLD.
001020      GENERATE DETAIL-LINE.
001030      PERFORM Z100-READ-INVENTORY-RECORD.
001040  Z100-READ-INVENTORY-RECORD.
001050      READ INVENTORY-FILE
001060          AT END MOVE 'END' TO WS-END-OF-FILE-INDICATOR.
```

Figure 10–13 *Output from Program 10–1*

```
                         APRIL INVENTORY REPORT
                         QUALITY COMPUTER SUPPLIES


                         INVENTORY REPORT                      PAGE  2

                              STOCK                   NUMBER SALES
   SALESPERSON  DESCRIPTION      NUMBER TYPE     PRICE    SOLD AMOUNT

        50    300 BAUD MODEM        M4575  HARDWARE   $89.00    1     $89.00
        50    1200/300 EXEC MODEM   M4571  HARDWARE  $599.00    1    $599.00
        50    VOLTAGE REGULATOR     V1317E HARDWARE  $385.00    2    $770.00
        50    SURGE PROTECTOR       S6112  HARDWARE   $79.00    4    $316.00
        50    SURGE PROTECTOR       S6112A HARDWARE   $63.00    1     $63.00
        50    SURGE PROTECTOR       S6112A HARDWARE   $63.00    1     $63.00
        50    POWERLINE MONITOR     P4029  HARDWARE  $960.00    1    $960.00
        50    RIBBON-DIABLO         R8135  SUPPLIES    $7.50    6     $45.00
        50    RIBBON-DIABLO         R8135  SUPPLIES    $7.50   12     $90.00
        50    RIBBON-DIABLO         R8135  SUPPLIES    $7.50    6     $45.00
       100    WORD-STAR             P1654P SOFTWARE  $425.00    1    $425.00
       100    WORD-STAR             P1654P SOFTWARE  $425.00    1    $425.00
       100    WORD-STAR PROFESSIONAL P1664P SOFTWARE $750.00    1    $750.00
       100    LOTUS 1-2-3           P1764Q SOFTWARE  $560.00    1    $560.00
       100    12 DS/DD 5 1/4        D4444  SUPPLIES   $48.00    1     $48.00
       100    12 DS/DD 5 1/4        D4444  SUPPLIES   $48.00    1     $48.00
       100    12 SS/SD 5 1/4        D4000  SUPPLIES   $33.00    1     $33.00
       100    RIBBON OKIDATA        R9991  SUPPLIES    $3.50    6     $21.00
       100    RIBBON OKIDATA        R9991  SUPPLIES    $3.50   12     $42.00
       100    SURGE PROTECTOR       S6112  HARDWARE   $79.00    2    $158.00
                         INVENTORY REPORT              $ 5,550.00
```

The name of the report is INVENTORY–REPORT and is defined in the FD clause for the REPORT–FILE. The REPORT SECTION defines the format of all records to be printed.

Each page in the report has a maximum length of 50 lines. The first detail line on each page cannot be printed before line 6, and the last detail line cannot be printed after line 48.

The REPORT HEADING statement causes a report page to be the first page printed. The title will be on two lines. The first line of the title, APRIL INVENTORY REPORT, will print on line 25. The second line, QUALITY COMPUTER SUPPLIES, will print on line 27. The NEXT GROUP NEXT PAGE clause must be placed at the 01 level and will cause any additional printing to be on another page.

Starting on line 1 of the second page will be the page heading. The third and fourth lines of the page have the column headings. The first detail line will print at the first opportunity available at line 6 or after. Since the page heading was completed at line 4, the first detail can be printed at line 6. All detail lines are to be single spaced.

The DETAIL statement describes the format of each detail line. COLUMN indicates where the first position of each field will print according to the PIC clause. SOURCE precedes the name of the field to be printed which is defined either in the input or the working-storage areas.

The control statement FINAL will allow a total to be accumulated and printed. The value of WS–SALES–AMOUNT is accumulated by the reserved word SUM and stored in an internal area of the system until needed.

When INITIATE INVENTORY–REPORT is executed, the values of the LINE–COUNTER and the SUM entry will be set to zero; the value of the PAGE–COUNTER will be set to 1. The first time GENERATE DETAIL–LINE is executed, the report heading, the page heading, and the first detail line are printed. Each additional time GENERATE DETAIL–LINE is executed, LINE–NUMBER, PAGE–COUNTER, and SUM entries are incremented, and the detail line printed. Upon reaching the end of the data file TERMINATE INVENTORY–REPORT is executed. This will cause the printing of the final total.

In this program the report is two pages long. There are 20 input records read and 20 detail lines printed. The final total of WS–SALES–AMOUNT has been accumulated in a SUM area and printed double spaced after the last detail line. Most of the program was defined and controlled by the TYPE statements. The PROCEDURE division contains only a few statements.

Use of Multiple Totals

Program 10–2 will print report headings and page headings on the same page. Printing is suppressed for certain data on detail lines. Control headings, control footings, and page footings are printed. Three control breaks are taken.

Program 10–2

```
000010 IDENTIFICATION DIVISION.
000020 PROGRAM-ID.  CHAP10.
000030************************************************************
000040* PROGRAM EXAMPLE 10-2                                      *
000050************************************************************
000060 ENVIRONMENT DIVISION.
000070 CONFIGURATION SECTION.
000080    SOURCE-COMPUTER.  VAX.
000090    OBJECT-COMPUTER.  VAX.
000100 INPUT-OUTPUT SECTION.
000110    FILE-CONTROL.
000120       SELECT INVENTORY-FILE ASSIGN TO INVEN.
000130       SELECT REPORT-FILE    ASSIGN TO PRINTER.
000140*
000150 DATA DIVISION.
000160 FILE SECTION.
000170 FD  INVENTORY-FILE
000180     RECORD CONTAINS 64 CHARACTERS
000190     LABEL RECORDS STANDARD.
000200 01  IN-INVENTORY-RECORD.
000210     05  IN-SALESPERSON     PIC X(3).
000220     05  FILLER             PIC X(2).
000230     05  IN-DESCRIPTION     PIC X(25).
```

Program 10–2 *(continued)*

```
000240       05  FILLER              PIC X(2).
000250       05  IN-STOCK-NUMBER     PIC X(8).
000260       05  FILLER              PIC X(2).
000270       05  IN-TYPE             PIC X(8).
000280       05  FILLER              PIC X(2).
000290       05  IN-PRICE            PIC 9(5)V9(2).
000300       05  FILLER              PIC X(2).
000310       05  IN-NUMBER-SOLD      PIC 9(3).
000320 FD  REPORT-FILE
000330      LABEL RECORDS ARE OMITTED
000340      REPORT IS INVENTORY-REPORT.
000350 WORKING-STORAGE SECTION.
000360 01  WS-REPORT-INDICATORS.
000370      05  WS-END-OF-FILE-INDICATOR  PIC X(3).
000380          88  END-OF-FILE    VALUE 'END'.
000390 01  WS-ACCUMULATORS.
000400      05  WS-SALES-AMOUNT     PIC 9(4)V9(2).
000410*
000420 REPORT SECTION.
000430 RD  INVENTORY-REPORT
000440      CONTROLS ARE FINAL
000450                  IN-SALESPERSON
000460                  IN-TYPE
000470      PAGE LIMIT 40 LINES
000480      HEADING         1
000490      FIRST DETAIL    9
000500      LAST DETAIL    35
000510      FOOTING        37.
000520 01  TYPE IS REPORT HEADING.
000530      05  LINE NUMBER 1.
000540          10  COLUMN 28  PIC X(25)
000550              VALUE 'QUALITY COMPUTER SUPPLIES'.
000560      05  LINE NUMBER 2.
000570          10  COLUMN 1  PIC X(80) VALUE ALL '*'.
000580 01  TYPE PAGE HEADING.
000590      05  LINE NUMBER 3.
000600          10  COLUMN 32  PIC X(16) VALUE 'INVENTORY REPORT'.
000610          10  COLUMN 74  PIC X(4)  VALUE 'PAGE'.
000620          10  COLUMN 79  PIC Z9    SOURCE PAGE-COUNTER.
000630      05  LINE NUMBER PLUS 2.
000640          10  COLUMN 38  PIC X(5)  VALUE 'STOCK'.
000650          10  COLUMN 65  PIC X(6)  VALUE 'NUMBER'.
000660          10  COLUMN 73  PIC X(5)  VALUE 'SALES'.
000670      05  LINE NUMBER PLUS 1.
000680          10  COLUMN 1   PIC X(11) VALUE 'SALESPERSON'.
000690          10  COLUMN 14  PIC X(11) VALUE 'DESCRIPTION'.
000700          10  COLUMN 38  PIC X(6)  VALUE 'NUMBER'.
000710          10  COLUMN 45  PIC X(4)  VALUE 'TYPE'.
000720          10  COLUMN 57  PIC X(5)  VALUE 'PRICE'.
000730          10  COLUMN 65  PIC X(4)  VALUE 'SOLD'.
000740          10  COLUMN 73  PIC X(6)  VALUE 'AMOUNT'.
000750      05  LINE NUMBER PLUS 1.
000760          10  COLUMN 1   PIC X(80) VALUE ALL '*'.
000770 01  TYPE IS CONTROL HEADING IN-SALESPERSON.
000780      05  LINE NUMBER PLUS 2.
000790          10  COLUMN 1   PIC X(21) VALUE 'SALESPERSON NUMBER IS'.
000800          10  COLUMN 24  PIC ZZ9   SOURCE IS IN-SALESPERSON.
000810      05  LINE NUMBER PLUS 1.
000820 01  DETAIL-LINE TYPE IS DETAIL.
000830      05  LINE NUMBER PLUS 1.
000840          10  COLUMN 5  PIC ZZ9  GROUP INDICATE
000850                               SOURCE IN-SALESPERSON.
000860          10  COLUMN 14  PIC X(25) SOURCE IN-DESCRIPTION.
000870          10  COLUMN 38  PIC X(8)  SOURCE IN-STOCK-NUMBER.
```

348   *Chapter 10*

Program 10-2 *(concluded)*

```
000880          10  COLUMN 45  PIC X(8)  GROUP INDICATE
000890                                   SOURCE IN-TYPE.
000900          10  COLUMN 54  PIC $$$,$$9.99 SOURCE IN-PRICE.
000910          10  COLUMN 66  PIC ZZ9   SOURCE IN-NUMBER-SOLD.
000920          10  COLUMN 71  PIC $$,$$9.99 SOURCE WS-SALES-AMOUNT.
000930 01  TYPE IS CONTROL FOOTING IN-TYPE.
000940      05  LINE NUMBER PLUS 2.
000950          10  COLUMN 44  PIC X(12) VALUE '*TYPE TOTAL*'.
000960          10  SALESPERSON-TOTAL
000970              COLUMN 70  PIC $$$,$$9.99 SUM WS-SALES-AMOUNT.
000980      05  LINE NUMBER PLUS 1.
000990 01  TYPE IS CONTROL FOOTING IN-SALESPERSON.
001000      05  LINE NUMBER PLUS 2.
001010          10  COLUMN 43  PIC X(21) VALUE '**SALESPERSON TOTAL**'.
001020          10  STORE-TOTAL
001030              COLUMN 70  PIC $$$,$$9.99 SUM SALESPERSON-TOTAL.
001040      05  LINE NUMBER PLUS 1.
001050 01  TYPE IS CONTROL FOOTING FINAL.
001060      05  LINE NUMBER PLUS 2.
001070          10  COLUMN 42  PIC X(17) VALUE '***FINAL TOTAL***'.
001080          10  COLUMN 70  PIC $$$,$$9.99 SUM STORE-TOTAL.
001090 01  TYPE IS PAGE FOOTING.
001100      05  LINE NUMBER 40.
001110          10  COLUMN  1  PIC X(22) VALUE 'APRIL INVENTORY REPORT'
001120*
001130 PROCEDURE DIVISION.
001140 A000-INVENTORY-LISTING.
001150      OPEN INPUT  INVENTORY-FILE
001160           OUTPUT REPORT-FILE.
001170      INITIATE INVENTORY-REPORT.
001180      PERFORM Z100-READ-INVENTORY-RECORD.
001190      PERFORM B200-PROCESS-RECORDS
001200          UNTIL END-OF-FILE.
001210      TERMINATE INVENTORY-REPORT.
001220      CLOSE INVENTORY-FILE
001230            REPORT-FILE.
001240      STOP RUN.
001250 B200-PROCESS-RECORDS.
001260      COMPUTE WS-SALES-AMOUNT = IN-PRICE * IN-NUMBER-SOLD.
001270      GENERATE DETAIL-LINE.
001280      PERFORM Z100-READ-INVENTORY-RECORD.
001290 Z100-READ-INVENTORY-RECORD.
001300      READ INVENTORY-FILE
001310          AT END MOVE 'END' TO WS-END-OF-FILE-INDICATOR.
```

The REPORT SECTION defines three control breaks: FINAL, IN-SALESPERSON, and IN-TYPE. Each page in the report can be 40 lines in length. The first detail line can start on line 9 or after; the last detail line can be line 35. The footing can be on lines 37-40.

Both report and page headings are on the first page of the report. QUALITY COMPUTER COMPANY will print on line 1 and a row of asterisks on line 2. Line 3 will contain the heading INVENTORY REPORT, and lines 5 and 6 will contain the column headings. SALESPERSON NUMBER IS will print on line 9 and then skip to line 10. On the first page of the report the first available line for a detail line to be printed is line 10.

Detail lines are single spaced and the fields IN-SALESPERSON and IN-TYPE have the GROUP INDICATE clause. This will suppress the printing of these fields after their first occurrence until a different value appears in the field or either a

Figure 10–14 *Output from Program 10–2*

```
                         QUALITY COMPUTER SUPPLIES
...................................................................................
                         INVENTORY REPORT                         PAGE   1
                                STOCK                      NUMBER SALES
SALESPERSON  DESCRIPTION        NUMBER TYPE       PRICE    SOLD   AMOUNT
...................................................................................

SALESPERSON NUMBER IS   50

    50     300 BAUD MODEM       M4575   HARDWARE   $89.00    1     $89.00
           1200/300 EXEC MODEM  M4571             $599.00    1    $599.00
           VOLTAGE REGULATOR    V1317E            $385.00    2    $770.00
           SURGE PROTECTOR      S6112              $79.00    4    $316.00
           SURGE PROTECTOR      S6112A             $63.00    1     $63.00
           SURGE PROTECTOR      S6112A             $63.00    1     $63.00
           POWERLINE MONITOR    P4029             $960.00    1    $960.00

                                *TYPE TOTAL*               $2,860.00

    50     RIBBON-DIABLO        R8135   SUPPLIES    $7.50    6     $45.00
           RIBBON-DIABLO        R8135              $7.50    12     $90.00
           RIBBON-DIABLO        R8135              $7.50     6     $45.00

                                *TYPE TOTAL*                 $180.00


                            **SALESPERSON TOTAL**         $3,040.00



SALESPERSON NUMBER IS  100

   100     WORD-STAR            P1654P SOFTWARE   $425.00    1    $425.00
           WORD-STAR            P1654P            $425.00    1    $425.00
           WORD-STAR PROFESSIONAL P1664P          $750.00    1    $750.00



APRIL INVENTORY REPORT

                         INVENTORY REPORT                         PAGE   2
                                STOCK                      NUMBER SALES
SALESPERSON  DESCRIPTION        NUMBER TYPE       PRICE    SOLD   AMOUNT
...................................................................................

   100     LOTUS 1-2-3          P1764Q SOFTWARE   $560.00    1    $560.00
                                *TYPE TOTAL*               $2,160.00

   100     12 DS/DD 5 1/4       D4444   SUPPLIES   $48.00    1     $48.00
           12 DS/DD 5 1/4       D4444              $48.00    1     $48.00
           12 SS/SD 5 1/4       D4000              $33.00    1     $33.00
           RIBBON OKIDATA       R9991              $3.50     6     $21.00
           RIBBON OKIDATA       R9991              $3.50    12     $42.00

                                *TYPE TOTAL*                 $192.00
   100     SURGE PROTECTOR      S6112   HARDWARE   $79.00    2    $158.00
                                *TYPE TOTAL*                 $158.00


                            **SALESPERSON TOTAL**         $2,510.00


                            ***FINAL TOTAL***            $5,550.00


APRIL INVENTORY REPORT
```

control or page break occurs. Notice that a control break is taken on HARDWARE. That brings in a new type, SUPPLIES, and causes the salesperson number 50 to be printed again. The page break for page 2 will cause the printing of IN–SALESPER SON and IN–TYPE for the first detail line in the continued report group.

The minor control is IN–TYPE. This will accumulate the SUM of WS–SALES–AMOUNT into SALESPERSON–TOTAL, print the message *TYPE TOTAL*, and print the sum of WS–SALES–AMOUNT after double spacing. After the control total is printed another line is skipped. The next record group is then printed. Notice that the salesperson number and the type are suppressed for all detail lines except the first in this report group. When the intermediate control IN–SALESPERSON is encountered, it prints the minor total for SUM WS–SALES–AMOUNT, accumulates it into STORE–TOTAL, sets SUM WS–SALES–AMOUNT and SUM SALESPERSON–TOTAL to zero, double spaces and prints the value of **SALESPERSON TOTAL**. It then adds 1 to the LINE–COUNTER and skips a line.

The next CONTROL HEADING is printed after double spacing and then adds 2 to the LINE–COUNTER. The processing of the detail line is continued. At line 35 the last detail line for that page is printed. The page footing APRIL INVENTORY REPORT is printed on line 40.

On page 2 only the page heading is printed starting on line 3. Since no control heading is to be printed at this time the first detail line for the page is printed on line 9. When the major total FINAL is reached, the values for the minor and intermediate totals are printed, spaced accordingly and accumulated. ***FINAL TOTAL*** and SUM STORE–TOTAL are then printed. The last line of the report is the page footing which is printed on line 40.

Again the logic of the PROCEDURE division is quite simple and short. The INITIATE, GENERATE, and TERMINATE statements cause the TYPE statements to control the processing of the report.

Using the PROCEDURE Division

Program 10–3 manipulates the use of tables along with using the Report Writer. The result is a program that prints two records per line, splitting the report into two parts.

Program 10–3

```
000010 IDENTIFICATION DIVISION.
000020 PROGRAM-ID.  CHAP10.
000030**************************************************************
000040* PROGRAM EXAMPLE 10-3                                       *
000050**************************************************************
000060 ENVIRONMENT DIVISION.
000070 CONFIGURATION SECTION.
000080    SOURCE-COMPUTER.  VAX.
000090    OBJECT-COMPUTER.  VAX.
000100 INPUT-OUTPUT SECTION.
000110    FILE-CONTROL.
000120       SELECT INVENTORY-FILE ASSIGN TO INVEN.
000130       SELECT REPORT-FILE    ASSIGN TO PRINTER.
000140*
000150 DATA DIVISION.
000160 FILE SECTION.
000170 FD  INVENTORY-FILE
000180     RECORD CONTAINS 64 CHARACTERS
000190     LABEL RECORDS STANDARD.
000200 01  IN-INVENTORY-RECORD.
000210     05  IN-SALESPERSON    PIC X(3).
000220     05  FILLER            PIC X(2).
000230     05  IN-DESCRIPTION    PIC X(25).
000240     05  FILLER            PIC X(2).
```

Program 10–3 *(continued)*

```
000250      05   IN-STOCK-NUMBER     PIC X(8).
000260      05   FILLER              PIC X(2).
000270      05   IN-TYPE             PIC X(8).
000280      05   FILLER              PIC X(2).
000290      05   IN-PRICE            PIC 9(5)V9(2).
000300      05   FILLER              PIC X(2).
000310      05   IN-NUMBER-SOLD      PIC 9(3).
000320 FD  REPORT-FILE
000330     LABEL RECORDS ARE OMITTED
000340     REPORT IS INVENTORY-REPORT.
000350 WORKING-STORAGE SECTION.
000360 01  WS-REPORT-INDICATORS.
000370      05   WS-END-OF-FILE-INDICATOR PIC X(3).
000380          88   END-OF-FILE     VALUE 'END'.
000390 01  WS-ACCUMULATORS.
000400      05   WS-SALES-AMOUNT     PIC 9(4)V9(2).
000410 01  WS-SUBSCRIPTS.
000420      05   SUB1                PIC 99.
000430      05   SUB2                PIC 99.
000440 01  INVENTORY-TABLE.
000450      05   TABLE-RECORD        OCCURS 20 TIMES.
000460          10   SALESPERSON     PIC X(3).
000470          10   STOCK-NUMBER    PIC X(8).
000480          10   ITEM-TYPE       PIC X(8).
000490          10   PRICE           PIC 9(5)V99.
000500          10   NUMBER-SOLD     PIC 9(3).
000510*
000520 REPORT SECTION.
000530 RD  INVENTORY-REPORT
000540     PAGE LIMIT 40 LINES
000550     FIRST DETAIL   7
000560     LAST DETAIL   40.
000570 01  TYPE IS PAGE HEADING.
000580      05   LINE NUMBER 1.
000590          10   COLUMN 46       PIC X(16) VALUE 'INVENTORY REPORT'.
000600      05   LINE NUMBER PLUS 2.
000610          10   COLUMN   1      PIC X(5)  VALUE 'SALES'.
000620          10   COLUMN  10      PIC X(5)  VALUE 'STOCK'.
000630          10   COLUMN  41      PIC X(6)  VALUE 'NUMBER'.
000640          10   COLUMN  61      PIC X(5)  VALUE 'SALES'.
000650          10   COLUMN  70      PIC X(5)  VALUE 'STOCK'.
000660          10   COLUMN 111      PIC X(6)  VALUE 'NUMBER'.
000670      05   LINE NUMBER PLUS 1.
000680          10   COLUMN   1      PIC X(6)  VALUE 'PERSON'.
000690          10   COLUMN  10      PIC X(16) VALUE 'NUMBER'.
000700          10   COLUMN  18      PIC X(4)  VALUE 'TYPE'.
000710          10   COLUMN  31      PIC X(5)  VALUE 'PRICE'.
000720          10   COLUMN  41      PIC X(4)  VALUE 'SOLD'.
000730          10   COLUMN  61      PIC X(6)  VALUE 'PERSON'.
000740          10   COLUMN  70      PIC X(6)  VALUE 'NUMBER'.
000750          10   COLUMN  88      PIC X(4)  VALUE 'TYPE'.
000760          10   COLUMN 102      PIC X(5)  VALUE 'PRICE'.
000770          10   COLUMN 111      PIC X(4)  VALUE 'SOLD'.
000780      05   LINE NUMBER PLUS 2.
000790 01  DETAIL-LINE TYPE IS DETAIL.
000800      05   LINE NUMBER PLUS 1.
000810          10   COLUMN   1      PIC ZZ9 SOURCE SALESPERSON(SUB1).
000820          10   COLUMN  10      PIC X(8) SOURCE STOCK-NUMBER(SUB1).
000830          10   COLUMN  18      PIC X(8) SOURCE ITEM-TYPE(SUB1).
000840          10   COLUMN  29      PIC $$$,$$9.99 SOURCE PRICE(SUB1).
000850          10   COLUMN  41      PIC ZZ9 SOURCE NUMBER-SOLD(SUB1).
000860          10   COLUMN  61      PIC ZZ9 SOURCE SALESPERSON(SUB2).
000870          10   COLUMN  70      PIC X(8) SOURCE STOCK-NUMBER(SUB2).
000880          10   COLUMN  88      PIC X(8) SOURCE ITEM-TYPE(SUB2).
```

Program 10-3   *(concluded)*

```
000890        10    COLUMN  99     PIC $$$,$$9.99 SOURCE PRICE(SUB2).
000900        10    COLUMN 111     PIC ZZ9  SOURCE NUMBER-SOLD(SUB2).
000910*
000920 PROCEDURE DIVISION.
000930 A000-INVENTORY-LISTING.
000940     OPEN INPUT  INVENTORY-FILE
000950          OUTPUT REPORT-FILE.
000960     PERFORM B100-CREATE-TABLE
000970        VARYING SUB1
000980        FROM 1 BY 1
000990        UNTIL SUB1 > 20.
001000     INITIATE INVENTORY-REPORT.
001010     PERFORM B200-PROCESS-DATA
001020        VARYING SUB1
001030        FROM 1 BY 1
001040        UNTIL SUB1 > 10.
001050     TERMINATE INVENTORY-REPORT.
001060     CLOSE INVENTORY-FILE
001070           REPORT-FILE.
001080     STOP RUN.
001090 B100-CREATE-TABLE.
001100     PERFORM Z100-READ-INVENTORY-RECORD.
001110     MOVE IN-SALESPERSON  TO SALESPERSON(SUB1).
001120     MOVE IN-STOCK-NUMBER TO STOCK-NUMBER(SUB1).
001130     MOVE IN-TYPE         TO ITEM-TYPE(SUB1).
001140     MOVE IN-PRICE        TO PRICE(SUB1).
001150     MOVE IN-NUMBER-SOLD  TO NUMBER-SOLD(SUB1).
001160 B200-PROCESS-DATA.
001170     COMPUTE SUB2 = SUB1 + 10.
001180     GENERATE DETAIL-LINE.
001190 Z100-READ-INVENTORY-RECORD.
001200     READ INVENTORY-FILE
001210        AT END MOVE 'END' TO WS-END-OF-FILE-INDICATOR.
```

Figure 10-15   *Output from Program 10-3*

```
                                     INVENTORY REPORT
SALES    STOCK                     NUMBER        SALES    STOCK                          NUMBER
PERSON   NUMBER  TYPE      PRICE     SOLD        PERSON   NUMBER   TYPE       PRICE        SOLD

  50     M4575   HARDWARE  $89.00     1           100     P1654P   SOFTWARE   $425.00       1
  50     M4571   HARDWARE  $599.00    1           100     P1654P   SOFTWARE   $425.00       1
  50     V1317E  HARDWARE  $385.00    2           100     P1664P   SOFTWARE   $750.00       1
  50     S6112   HARDWARE  $79.00     4           100     P1764Q   SOFTWARE   $560.00       1
  50     S6112A  HARDWARE  $63.00     1           100     D4444    SUPPLIES   $48.00        1
  50     S6112A  HARDWARE  $63.00     1           100     D4444    SUPPLIES   $48.00        1
  50     P4029   HARDWARE  $960.00    1           100     D4000    SUPPLIES   $33.00        1
  50     R8135   SUPPLIES  $7.50      6           100     R9991    SUPPLIES   $3.50         6
  50     R8135   SUPPLIES  $7.50     12           100     R9991    SUPPLIES   $3.50        12
  50     R8135   SUPPLIES  $7.50      6           100     S6112    HARDWARE   $79.00        2
```

The PAGE HEADING has two sets of column headings spaced accordingly. The DETAIL line has used subscripted data-names. SUB1 is used for the first record to be printed in each line and SUB2 for the second record. The detail lines will be single spaced when printed. Double spacing occurs after the heading INVENTORY REPORT and the second line of column headings. This is caused by the two LINE PLUS 2 clauses in the TYPE IS PAGE HEADING statement.

In the PROCEDURE division a table is created at B100-CREATE-TABLE. Twenty input records are read and their data fields moved into the table. The report is initiated next. The first time GENERATE DETAIL–LINE is encountered in B200–PROCESS–DATA, the page heading and the first detail line are printed with appropriate spacing. Each additional execution of GENERATE DETAIL–LINE will print a detail line. This program does not have control footing, so no control breaks are taken. The output is just a simple listing.

DECLARATIVES

Although the Report Writer has many features it cannot always print a report in the format needed by the programmer. The DECLARATIVES procedure can be used to direct the Report Writer to take certain actions when special conditions exist during the execution of the program.

When used in a program, all entries for the DECLARATIVES procedure must be placed together at the beginning of the PROCEDURE division. The reserved word DECLARATIVES followed by a period on a line by itself indicates that these procedures are to follow. The reserved words END DECLARATIVES followed by a period on a line by itself indicates the end of the procedure. The remaining portion of the PROCEDURE division must begin with a section name.

USE BEFORE REPORTING Sentence

The **USE BEFORE REPORTING statement** must be used within a section of the declaratives portion of a program. Its purpose is to identify declarative procedures to be executed just before a specified heading or footing is produced by the Report Writer. The general format for this sentence is shown in Figure 10–16.

Figure 10–16 *USE BEFORE REPORTING Statement*

```
USE BEFORE REPORTING group-name
```

Rules for the use of this sentence are

- Group-name identifies a control heading or control footing report group.
- A programmer-supplied section name must precede the USE sentence.
- There may be any number of sections in a program each with its own USE sentence.
- Each USE sentence is followed by one or more programmer-supplied paragraph names.
- Paragraphs in one section can be referenced in another section by the use of a PERFORM.
- Procedures in the declarative portion of the program cannot contain statements that refer to any procedures within the nondeclaratives portion.

Special Switches

COBOL compilers use either the **PRINT–SWITCH** or the **SUPPRESS statement** in the DECLARATIVES procedure to suppress printing of a report group. Most compilers allow the use of only one of these alternatives. The general formats of these statements are found in Figure 10–17.

Figure 10–17 *Suppress Printing Statements*

```
[MOVE 1 TO PRINT–SWITCH.]
[SUPPRESS PRINTING.]
```

Whenever one of these special switches is encountered in a program the printing of the report group is suppressed, the LINE–COUNTER is not changed, and the special switch used is set back to zero. Check your system to determine which of these special switches is available for use by your program.

Using the DECLARATIVES Procedure

Figure 10–18 illustrates examples of the DECLARATIVES procedure.

Figure 10–18   *Examples Using the DECLARATIVES Procedure*

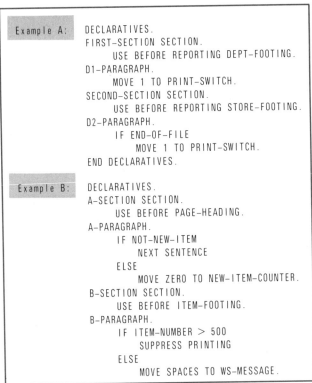

```
Example A:    DECLARATIVES.
              FIRST-SECTION SECTION.
                    USE BEFORE REPORTING DEPT-FOOTING.
              D1-PARAGRAPH.
                    MOVE 1 TO PRINT-SWITCH.
              SECOND-SECTION SECTION.
                    USE BEFORE REPORTING STORE-FOOTING.
              D2-PARAGRAPH.
                    IF END-OF-FILE
                        MOVE 1 TO PRINT-SWITCH.
              END DECLARATIVES.

Example B:    DECLARATIVES.
              A-SECTION SECTION.
                    USE BEFORE PAGE-HEADING.
              A-PARAGRAPH.
                    IF NOT-NEW-ITEM
                        NEXT SENTENCE
                    ELSE
                        MOVE ZERO TO NEW-ITEM-COUNTER.
              B-SECTION SECTION.
                    USE BEFORE ITEM-FOOTING.
              B-PARAGRAPH.
                    IF ITEM-NUMBER > 500
                        SUPPRESS PRINTING
                    ELSE
                        MOVE SPACES TO WS-MESSAGE.
```

Example A of Figure 10–18 has two sections. Each section has its own USE sentence. The data-names DEPT–FOOTING AND STORE–FOOTING are the names of TYPE statements and can be used in only one USE statement in the program. During the processing of the program when the TYPE statement DEPT–FOOTING is encountered, its printing will be suppressed by the MOVE 1 TO PRINT–SWITCH statement. When the TYPE statement STORE–FOOTING is encountered, the printing of the TYPE statement is suppressed only when END–OF–FILE is true.

Example B will zero out NEW–ITEM–COUNTER when the conditions tested are false after encountering the PAGE–HEADING TYPE statement. The ITEM–FOOTING TYPE statement will be suppressed if ITEM–NUMBER > 500; otherwise, WS–MESSAGE will contain spaces.

The use of DECLARATIVES with the Report Writer allows the programmer much more flexibility in printing reports.

Program Example

Statement of the Problem

Write a program to read a data file and produce two different reports in the same program. One report is to take control breaks and print out headings, detail lines, and totals. This is basically the same as Program 10–2. The second report is to print only the summary totals for type of product by salesperson and a final total. The same data file will need to be used a second time for this report.

Output

The output for the two reports is to be listed on a 132-column line printer. See Figure 10–19 for the output format.

Structure Chart

The structure chart for Program 10–4 is shown in Figure 10–20.

Program

Program 10–4

```
000010 IDENTIFICATION DIVISION.
000020 PROGRAM-ID.  CHAP10.
000030*************************************************************
000040* PROGRAM EXAMPLE 10-4.                                      *
000050*************************************************************
000060 ENVIRONMENT DIVISION.
000070 CONFIGURATION SECTION.
000080    SOURCE-COMPUTER.  VAX.
000090    OBJECT-COMPUTER.  VAX.
000100 INPUT-OUTPUT SECTION.
000110    FILE-CONTROL.
000120       SELECT INVENTORY-FILE ASSIGN TO INVEN.
000130       SELECT REPORT-FILE    ASSIGN TO PRINTER.
000140*
000150 DATA DIVISION.
000160 FILE SECTION.
000170 FD  INVENTORY-FILE
000180     RECORD CONTAINS 64 CHARACTERS
000190     LABEL RECORDS STANDARD.
000200 01  IN-INVENTORY-RECORD.
000210     05  IN-SALESPERSON     PIC X(3).
000220     05  FILLER             PIC X(2).
000230     05  IN-DESCRIPTION     PIC X(25).
000240     05  FILLER             PIC X(2).
000250     05  IN-STOCK-NUMBER    PIC X(8).
000260     05  FILLER             PIC X(2).
000270     05  IN-TYPE            PIC X(8).
000280     05  FILLER             PIC X(2).
000290     05  IN-PRICE           PIC 9(5)V9(2).
000300     05  FILLER             PIC X(2).
000310     05  IN-NUMBER-SOLD     PIC 9(3).
000320 01  SM-SUMMARY-RECORD.
000330     05  SM-SALESPERSON     PIC X(3).
000340     05  FILLER             PIC X(2).
000350     05  SM-DESCRIPTION     PIC X(25).
000360     05  FILLER             PIC X(2).
000370     05  SM-STOCK-NUMBER    PIC X(8).
000380     05  FILLER             PIC X(2).
000390     05  SM-TYPE            PIC X(8).
000400     05  FILLER             PIC X(2).
000410     05  SM-PRICE           PIC 9(5)V9(2).
000420     05  FILLER             PIC X(2).
000430     05  SM-NUMBER-SOLD     PIC 9(3).
000440 FD  REPORT-FILE
000450     LABEL RECORDS ARE OMITTED
```

Program 10–4 *(continued)*

```
000460        REPORTS ARE INVENTORY-REPORT
000470                  SUMMARY-REPORT.
000480 WORKING-STORAGE SECTION.
000490 01  WS-REPORT-INDICATORS.
000500     05  WS-END-OF-FILE-INDICATOR  PIC X(3).
000510         88  END-OF-FILE    VALUE 'END'.
000520 01  WS-ACCUMULATORS.
000530     05  WS-SALES-AMOUNT      PIC 9(4)V9(2).
000540 01  WS-TYPE-COMPARE         PIC X(8).
000550*
000560 REPORT SECTION.
000570 RD  INVENTORY-REPORT
000580     CONTROLS ARE FINAL
000590                IN-SALESPERSON
000600                IN-TYPE
000610     PAGE LIMIT 40 LINES
000620     HEADING      1
000630     FIRST DETAIL   9
000640     LAST DETAIL   35
000650     FOOTING       37.
000660 01  TYPE IS REPORT HEADING.
000670     05  LINE NUMBER 1.
000680         10  COLUMN 28   PIC X(25)
000690             VALUE 'QUALITY COMPUTER SUPPLIES'.
000700     05  LINE NUMBER 2.
000710         10  COLUMN  1   PIC X(80) VALUE ALL '*'.
000720 01  TYPE IS PAGE HEADING.
000730     05  LINE NUMBER 3.
000740         10  COLUMN 32   PIC X(16)    VALUE 'INVENTORY REPORT'.
000750         10  COLUMN 74   PIC X(4)     VALUE 'PAGE'.
000760         10  COLUMN 79   PIC Z9       SOURCE PAGE-COUNTER
000770                                          OF INVENTORY-REPORT.
000780     05  LINE NUMBER PLUS 2.
000790         10  COLUMN 38   PIC X(5)     VALUE 'STOCK'.
000800         10  COLUMN 65   PIC X(6)     VALUE 'NUMBER'.
000810         10  COLUMN 73   PIC X(5)     VALUE 'SALES'.
000820     05  LINE NUMBER PLUS 1.
000830         10  COLUMN  1   PIC X(11)    VALUE 'SALESPERSON'.
000840         10  COLUMN 14   PIC X(11)    VALUE 'DESCRIPTION'.
000850         10  COLUMN 38   PIC X(6)     VALUE 'NUMBER'.
000860         10  COLUMN 45   PIC X(4)     VALUE 'TYPE'.
000870         10  COLUMN 57   PIC X(5)     VALUE 'PRICE'.
000880         10  COLUMN 65   PIC X(4)     VALUE 'SOLD'.
000890         10  COLUMN 73   PIC X(6)     VALUE 'AMOUNT'.
000900     05  LINE NUMBER PLUS 1.
000910         10  COLUMN  1   PIC X(80)    VALUE ALL '*'.
000920 01  TYPE CONTROL HEADING IN-SALESPERSON.
000930     05  LINE NUMBER PLUS 2.
000940         10  COLUMN  1   PIC X(21)  VALUE 'SALESPERSON NUMBER'.
000950         10  COLUMN 24   PIC ZZ9       SOURCE IS IN-SALESPERSON.
000960     05  LINE NUMBER PLUS 1.
000970 01  DETAIL-LINE TYPE IS DETAIL.
000980     05  LINE NUMBER PLUS 1.
000990         10  COLUMN  5   PIC ZZ9       GROUP INDICATE
001000                                       SOURCE IN-SALESPERSON.
001010         10  COLUMN 14   PIC X(22)     SOURCE IN-DESCRIPTION.
001020         10  COLUMN 38   PIC X(6)      SOURCE IN-STOCK-NUMBER.
001030         10  COLUMN 45   PIC X(8)      GROUP INDICATE
001040                                       SOURCE IN-TYPE.
001050         10  COLUMN 54   PIC $$$,$$9.99 SOURCE IN-PRICE.
001060         10  COLUMN 66   PIC ZZ9       SOURCE IN-NUMBER-SOLD.
001070         10  COLUMN 71   PIC $$,$$9.99 SOURCE WS-SALES-AMOUNT.
001080 01  BOTTOM-CONTINUATION TYPE IS DETAIL.
001090     05  LINE NUMBER PLUS 2.
```

Program 10–4 *(continued)*

```
001100          10  COLUMN 29      PIC X(24) VALUE
001110                                '(CONTINUED ON NEXT PAGE)'.
001120 01  IN-TYPE-CLASS TYPE IS CONTROL FOOTING IN-TYPE.
001130     05  LINE NUMBER PLUS 2.
001140          10  COLUMN 44      PIC X(12)   VALUE '*TYPE TOTAL*'.
001150          10  SALESPERSON-TOTAL
001160              COLUMN 70      PIC $$$,$$9.99 SUM WS-SALES-AMOUNT.
001170     05  LINE NUMBER PLUS 1.
001180 01  TYPE IS CONTROL FOOTING IN-SALESPERSON.
001190     05  LINE NUMBER PLUS 2.
001200          10  COLUMN 43      PIC X(21) VALUE '**SALESPERSON TOTAL*'.
001210          10  STORE-TOTAL
001220              COLUMN 70      PIC $$$,$$9.99 SUM SALESPERSON-TOTAL.
001230     05  LINE NUMBER PLUS 1.
001240 01  TYPE IS CONTROL FOOTING FINAL.
001250     05  LINE NUMBER PLUS 2.
001260          10  COLUMN 42      PIC X(17)   VALUE '***FINAL TOTAL***'.
001270          10  COLUMN 70      PIC $$$,$$9.99 SUM STORE-TOTAL.
001280 01  TYPE IS PAGE FOOTING.
001290     05  LINE NUMBER 40.
001300          10  COLUMN  1   PIC X(22) VALUE 'APRIL INVENTORY REPORT'.
001310 RD  SUMMARY-REPORT
001320     CONTROLS ARE FINAL
001330                  SM-SALESPERSON
001340                  SM-TYPE
001350     PAGE LIMIT 50 LINES
001360     HEADING        1.
001370 01  SUMMARY-DETAIL-LINE TYPE IS DETAIL.
001380     05  LINE NUMBER PLUS 1.
001390          10  COLUMN  5      PIC ZZ9      GROUP INDICATE
001400                                          SOURCE SM-SALESPERSON.
001410          10  COLUMN 14      PIC X(25)    SOURCE SM-DESCRIPTION.
001420          10  COLUMN 38      PIC X(8)     SOURCE SM-STOCK-NUMBER.
001430          10  COLUMN 45      PIC X(8)     GROUP INDICATE
001440                                          SOURCE SM-TYPE.
001450          10  COLUMN 54      PIC $$$,$$9.99 SOURCE SM-PRICE.
001460          10  COLUMN 66      PIC ZZ9      SOURCE SM-NUMBER-SOLD.
001470          10  COLUMN 70      PIC $$,$$9.99 SOURCE WS-SALES-AMOUNT.
001480 01  TYPE IS CONTROL FOOTING SM-TYPE.
001490     05  LINE NUMBER PLUS 2.
001500          10  COLUMN  1      PIC ZZ9      SOURCE SM-SALESPERSON.
001510          10  COLUMN 10      PIC X(8)     SOURCE SM-TYPE.
001520          10  COLUMN 44      PIC X(12)    VALUE '*TYPE TOTÁL*'.
001530          10  SALESPERSON-TOTAL
001540              COLUMN 70      PIC $$$,$$9.99 SUM WS-SALES-AMOUNT.
001550     05  LINE NUMBER PLUS 1.
001560 01  TYPE IS CONTROL FOOTING SM-SALESPERSON.
001570     05  LINE NUMBER PLUS 2.
001580          10  COLUMN  1      PIC ZZ9      SOURCE SM-SALESPERSON.
001590          10  COLUMN 43      PIC X(21) VALUE '**SALESPERSON TOTAL*'.
001600          10  STORE-TOTAL
001610              COLUMN 70      PIC $$$,$$9.99 SUM SALESPERSON-TOTAL.
001620     05  LINE NUMBER PLUS 1.
001630 01  TYPE IS CONTROL FOOTING FINAL.
001640     05  LINE NUMBER PLUS 2.
001650          10  COLUMN 42      PIC X(17)   VALUE '***FINAL TOTAL***'.
001660          10  COLUMN 70      PIC $$$,$$9.99 SUM STORE-TOTAL.
001670*
001680 PROCEDURE DIVISION.
001690 DECLARATIVES.
001700 SUPPRESS-IN-TYPE-CLASS SECTION.
001710     USE BEFORE REPORTING IN-TYPE-CLASS.
001720 IN-TYPE-CLASS-PARAGRAPH.
001730     MOVE 1 TO PRINT-SWITCH.
```

Program 10–4   *(concluded)*

```
001740 END DECLARATIVES.
001750 A000-INVENTORY-LISTING SECTION.
001760     PERFORM B100-DETAIL-REPORT.
001770     PERFORM B200-SUMMARY-REPORT.
001780     STOP RUN.
001790 B100-DETAIL-REPORT.
001800     PERFORM C100-INITIALIZE-DETAIL-RPT.
001810     PERFORM C200-PROCESS-DETAIL
001820         UNTIL END-OF-FILE.
001830     PERFORM C300-TERMINATE-DETAIL.
001840 B200-SUMMARY-REPORT.
001850     PERFORM C400-INITIALIZE-SUMMARY-RPT.
001860     PERFORM C500-PROCESS-SUMMARY
001870         UNTIL END-OF-FILE.
001880     PERFORM C600-TERMINATE-SUMMARY.
001890 C100-INITIALIZE-DETAIL-RPT.
001900     OPEN INPUT  INVENTORY-FILE
001910          OUTPUT REPORT-FILE.
001920     INITIATE INVENTORY-REPORT.
001930     PERFORM Z100-READ-INVENTORY-RECORD.
001940 C200-PROCESS-DETAIL.
001950     IF LINE-COUNTER OF INVENTORY-REPORT  = 33
001960         IF IN-TYPE = WS-TYPE-COMPARE
001970             GENERATE BOTTOM-CONTINUATION.
001980     COMPUTE WS-SALES-AMOUNT = IN-PRICE * IN-NUMBER-SOLD.
001990     GENERATE DETAIL-LINE.
002000     MOVE IN-TYPE TO WS-TYPE-COMPARE.
002010     PERFORM Z100-READ-INVENTORY-RECORD.
002020 C300-TERMINATE-DETAIL.
002030     TERMINATE INVENTORY-REPORT.
002040     CLOSE INVENTORY-FILE.
002050 C400-INITIALIZE-SUMMARY-RPT.
002060     OPEN INPUT INVENTORY-FILE.
002070     MOVE SPACES TO WS-END-OF-FILE-INDICATOR.
002080     INITIATE SUMMARY-REPORT.
002090     PERFORM Z100-READ-INVENTORY-RECORD.
002100 C500-PROCESS-SUMMARY.
002110     COMPUTE WS-SALES-AMOUNT = SM-PRICE * SM-NUMBER-SOLD.
002120     GENERATE SUMMARY-REPORT.
002130     PERFORM Z100-READ-INVENTORY-RECORD.
002140 C600-TERMINATE-SUMMARY.
002150     TERMINATE SUMMARY-REPORT.
002160     CLOSE INVENTORY-FILE
002170          REPORT-FILE.
002180 Z100-READ-INVENTORY-RECORD.
002190     READ INVENTORY-FILE
002200         AT END MOVE 'END' TO WS-END-OF-FILE-INDICATOR.
```

Discussion

There are two input files and one output file in the program. Two different reports are output on the REPORT–FILE. The two reports are named INVENTORY–REPORT and SUMMARY–REPORT in lines 460 and 470. The RDs for these reports start on lines 570 and 1310.

The INVENTORY–REPORT is initiated at line 1920. Then C200–PROCESS–DETAIL processes the two detail lines. If the LINE–COUNTER OF INVENTORY–REPORT has a detail line of a report group that is to be continued on the next page, the two IF statements cause BOTTOM–CONTINUATION to be printed. Then the next DETAIL–LINE is generated as the first detail line of the next page.

Although the program has three control footings, only two of them are printed.

Figure 10–19 *Printer Spacing Chart for Program 10–4*

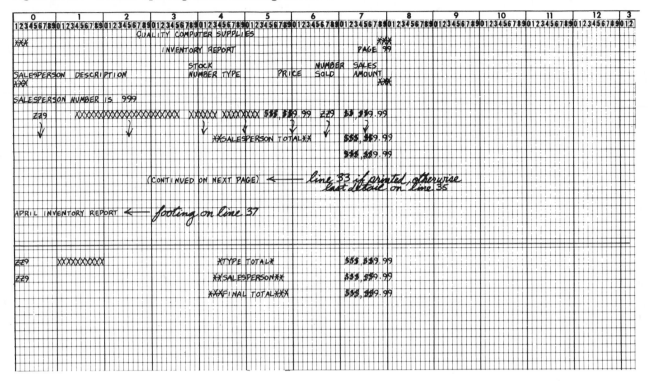

When the control footing IN–TYPE–CLASS at line 1120 is encountered, control of the program is given to the DECLARATIVES procedure by the USE BEFORE REPORTING sentence. The PRINT–SWITCH is set to 1, which causes the printing of that footing to be suppressed. The system then sets PRINT–SWITCH back to zero, and normal processing continues.

The LINE–COUNTER at line 1950 has to be qualified because there is more than one report to be produced by the program. At the end-of-file condition, C300–

Figure 10–20 *Structure Chart for Program 10–4*

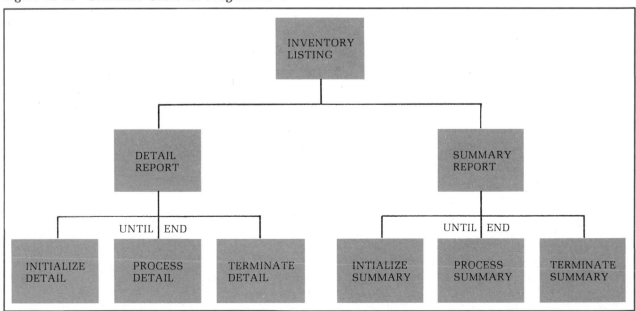

TERMINATE–DETAIL is executed, and the printing of the INVENTORY–REPORT is complete.

C400–INITIALIZE–SUMMARY–RPT opens the second input file, resets the WS–END–OF–FILE–INDICATOR, and initializes the SUMMARY–REPORT. C500–PRO CESS–SUMMARY produces the report. Notice the GENERATE SUMMARY–REPORT statement at line 2120. This statement causes all of the TYPE statements in the report to be processed except the printing of the SUMMARY–DETAIL–LINE. This is called summary reporting.

Figure 10–21 shows the results of printing the INVENTORY–REPORT. Compare this output to Figure 10–15. It is the same except for the suppression of the *TYPE TOTAL* line. Figure 10–22 shows the results of printing the SUMMARY–REPORT. Only the three levels of totals are printed. These totals have the same values as both Figure 10–15 and Figure 10–21.

Figure 10–21 *Output from Program 10–4*

```
                          QUALITY COMPUTER SUPPLIES
 ..........................................................................

                          INVENTORY  REPORT                         PAGE   1
                                STOCK                    NUMBER  SALES
      SALESPERSON  DESCRIPTION   NUMBER TYPE      PRICE   SOLD    AMOUNT
 ..........................................................................

      SALESPERSON NUMBER      50

         50    300 BAUD MODEM         M4575   HARDWARE   $89.00    1     $89.00
               1200/300 EXEC MODEM    M4571             $599.00    1    $599.00
               VOLTAGE REGULATOR      V1317E            $385.00    2    $770.00
               SURGE PROTECTOR        S6112              $79.00    4    $316.00
               SURGE PROTECTOR        S6112A             $63.00    1     $63.00
               SURGE PROTECTOR        S6112A             $63.00    1     $63.00
               POWERLINE MONITOR      P4029             $960.00    1    $960.00
         50    RIBBON-DIABLO          R8135   SUPPLIES    $7.50    6     $45.00
               RIBBON-DIABLO          R8135               $7.50   12     $90.00
               RIBBON-DIABLO          R8135               $7.50    6     $45.00

                                    **SALESPERSON TOTAL*        $3,040.00


      SALESPERSON NUMBER     100

        100    WORD-STAR              P1654P  SOFTWARE  $425.00    1    $425.00
               WORD-STAR              P1654P            $425.00    1    $425.00
               WORD-STAR PROFESSIONAL P1664P            $750.00    1    $750.00
               LOTUS 1-2-3            P1764Q            $560.00    1    $560.00
        100    12 DS/DD 5 1/4         D4444   SUPPLIES   $48.00    1     $48.00
               12 DS/DD 5 1/4         D4444              $48.00    1     $48.00
               12 SS/SD 5 1/4         D4000              $33.00    1     $33.00

                              (CONTINUED ON NEXT PAGE)


      APRIL INVENTORY REPORT

                          INVENTORY  REPORT                         PAGE   2
                                STOCK                    NUMBER  SALES
      SALESPERSON  DESCRIPTION   NUMBER TYPE      PRICE   SOLD    AMOUNT
 ..........................................................................
        100    RIBBON OKIDATA         R9991   SUPPLIES    $3.50    6     $21.00
               RIBBON OKIDATA         R9991               $3.50   12     $42.00
        100    SURGE PROTECTOR        S6112   HARDWARE   $79.00    2    $158.00

                                    **SALESPERSON TOTAL*        $2,510.00

                                    ***FINAL TOTAL***          $5,550.00


      APRIL INVENTORY REPORT
```

Figure 10–22 *Summary Report from Program 10–4*

50	HARDWARE	*TYPE TOTAL*	$2,860.00
50	SUPPLIES	*TYPE TOTAL*	$180.00
50		**SALESPERSON TOTAL*	$3,040.00
100	SOFTWARE	*TYPE TOTAL*	$2,160.00
100	SUPPLIES	*TYPE TOTAL*	$192.00
100	HARDWARE	*TYPE TOTAL*	$158.00
100		**SALESPERSON TOTAL*	$2,510.00
		FINAL TOTAL	$5,550.00

Programming Style

1. Spell out the type of TYPE statement instead of using the abbreviations. This provides better documentation.
2. Place the TYPE statements in the order which they will be executed by the program (required by some systems).
3. Place the LINE NUMBER clause at the 05 level by itself whenever the logic or syntax allows. Although there are times when it is necessary to place it at the 01 level, keep these occurrences to a minimum.
4. Place the COLUMN clause at the 10 level.
5. The NEXT GROUP clause is used for vertical spacing after printing a report group. The clause is ignored in a program when a control break is taken or at an end-of-file condition. This is a very useful feature. However, there are times when using LINE PLUS n will improve the logic of the program and might be preferred to the NEXT GROUP clause.
6. Using the GROUP INDICATE usually makes the report easier to read.

Common Errors

1. Not placing the REPORT SECTION as the last section in the DATA division.
2. Omitting the CONTROL clause when totals are to be taken.
3. Omitting the PAGE clause when vertical line spacing is to be controlled by the Report Writer.
4. Naming the levels of control breaks in the wrong order.
5. Omitting the word FINAL when it is to be used as a control break.
6. Using the NEXT GROUP clause at a number level other than 01.
7. Using the NEXT GROUP clause in a PAGE HEADING or REPORT FOOTING statement.
8. Not giving a SUM field a name to accumulate values when the accumulated values are to be used elsewhere in the program.
9. Using a GENERATE with a wrong TYPE statement.
10. Using a second INITIATE before the first INITIATE has been terminated.
11. Not remembering the default values when certain entries are omitted when using the PAGE clause. (Review Figure 10–5 carefully.)
12. Not using the PAGE LIMIT, LAST DETAIL, and FOOTING clauses with the PAGE FOOTING statement.
13. Not using the PAGE LIMIT clause with CONTROL FOOTING, CONTROL HEADING, and DETAIL statements.
14. Not using the PAGE LIMIT, LAST DETAIL, and FOOTING clauses with the PAGE FOOTING statement.

15. Using a PERFORM statement in the DECLARATIVES area to reference a procedure in the nondeclaratives area and vice versa.

16. Omitting a section name in the DECLARATIVES area.

Exercises

1. Define the purpose of Report Writer.

2. Explain what the following RD entries attempt to do.
   a. ```
      RD SALES-REPORT PAGE LIMIT 40
              FIRST DETAIL 5 LAST DETAIL 40.
      ```
   b. ```
      RD  SALES-REPORT PAGE LIMIT 50.
      ```
   c. ```
      RD SALES-REPORT CONTROL IS FINAL STORE-NUM   DEPT-NUM
             PAGE LIMIT 40 HEADING 1
             FIRST DETAIL 6 LAST DETAIL 38 FOOTING 40.
      ```

3. Explain the purpose of the following TYPE statements:
   a. REPORT HEADING.
   b. PAGE HEADING.
   c. CONTROL FOOTING.
   d. PAGE FOOTING.
   e. DETAIL.

4. What is the difference between relative and absolute line spacing?

5. When would the NEXT GROUP clause be used?

6. Explain the differences between the following:
   a. NEXT GROUP PLUS 2.
   b. NEXT GROUP IS 20.
   c. NEXT GROUP NEXT PAGE.

7. Write the COBOL statements for each of the following:
   a. Write a report heading on a page by itself. The name of the report is SALES REPORT and is to be printed on the fifth line of the page starting in position 11. The second line of the heading is MIDWEST REGION and is to be printed on the eighth line of the page starting in position 10.
   b. Write a page heading that will start on line 3 of a page in position 20. The name of the title is APRIL SUMMARY. Skip a line and print the column headings NAME, NUMBER, ITEM, TOTAL, starting in positions 5, 15, 25, and 35, respectively. Place a row of 80 asterisks after the column headings.
   c. Write a control footing that will triple space from the last detail line before printing a total when a control break is taken on IN–NUMBER. Then skip to the next page for the next report group. The total to be printed is the sum of all the IN–NUMBER–AMT fields that have been printed in detail lines. In addition, save this sum in MINOR–TOTAL for later use in another control footing.

8. Given the following entries, correct only those that are in error. Assume programmer-supplied names have been properly defined.
   a. ```
      RD  INVENTORY-REPORT HEADING 1 FIRST DETAIL 5.
      ```
   b. ```
      01 IDENTIFIER-1 TYPE CONTROL FOOTING TOTAL-1 FINAL.
      ```
   c. ```
      05  NEXT GROUP NEXT PAGE.
             10 COLUMN 50 PIC X(10) SOURCE IN-NAME.
      ```
   d. ```
      10 DEPT-TOTAL COLUMN 10 PIC ZZ9 SUM IN-DEPT-AMOUNT.
      ```
   e. ```
      01  TYPE CONTROL FOOTING DEPT-NUMBER.
             LINE PLUS 2 NEXT GROUP PLUS 2.
      ```
   f. ```
      INITIATE INVENTORY-REPORT. PERFORM B200-PROCESS.   TERMINATE.
      ```
      ```

9. Correct any logic and/or syntax errors in the following:

a.
```
DELCARATIVES.
    FIRST SECTION.
        USE BEFORE REPORTING PAGE-LINE.
    SECOND SECTION.
        IF END-OF-JOB MOVE 1 TO PRINT-SWITCH.
```

b.
```
DECLARATIVES.
    FIRST-GROUP.
        USE BEFORE REPORTING HEAD-LINE.
    SECOND-GROUP.
        MOVE ZERO TO IN-DEPT-NUMBER.
END DECLARATIVES.
```

c.
```
DECLARATIVES.
SUPPRESS-PRODUCT SECTION.
    USE BEFORE REPORTING PRODUCT-FOOTINGS.
SUPPRESS-PRODUCT-PARA.
    MOVE 1 TO PRINT-SWITCH.
SUPPRESS-CLASS SECTION.
    USE BEFORE REPORTING CLASS-FOOTINGS.
SUPPRESS-CLASS-PARA.
    MOVE 1 TO PRINT-SWITCH.
```

Problems

1. Modify Program 10–2 as follows:
   a. Combine the report heading and page heading into a report heading with the same spacing.
   b. Do not GROUP INDICATE.
   c. Use four controls: FINAL, IN–SALESPERSON, IN–TYPE, and IN–DESCRIPTION.
   d. Omit the control heading.
   e. Print a report footing on a separate page instead of a page footing on each page.

2. Modify Program 10–2 to sort the records on IN–TYPE. Take a control break on IN–TYPE only, and print each new report group on a separate page. Omit the GROUP INDICATE and the control heading.

3. Write a program to determine the premium to be paid for a 10-year term policy. Depending on an individual's sex, age, and policy amount, the monthly premium can be found in the tables given below for persons between the ages of 20 and 55 for either a $25,000 or $50,000 policy.

	Female			*Male*	
Age	*$25,000*	*$50,000*	*Age*	*$25,000*	*$50,000*
20 to 25	$10.00	$18.00	20 to 25	$ 7.90	$14.90
25 to 30	12.50	20.50	25 to 30	9.45	16.85
30 to 35	16.20	25.25	30 to 35	13.05	21.00
35 to 40	20.15	29.30	35 to 40	17.05	24.95
40 to 45	25.00	34.10	40 to 45	22.60	33.90
45 to 50	30.20	39.00	45 to 50	26.90	35.05
50 to 55	36.90	48.15	50 to 55	32.10	43.50

Hard-code the above table and use as input the following:

Name	*Sex*	*Age*	*Amount*
Alice Hartman	F	35	25000
Joe Biship	M	49	25000
Dan Tinsley	M	23	50000
Mable Washington	F	30	50000
Brenda Cruise	F	55	50000
Matt Zen	M	40	25000
Judy Chin	F	20	25000

The output from the program is to be a one-page report of the following format for each person:

```
FEDERAL BANK OF USA
1776 FREEDOM STREET
NEW YORK, NY  10000


DEAR (NAME)

THE MONTHLY PREMIUM ON A 10 YEAR $$$,$$$ TERM
POLICY FOR A PERSON OF AGE NN AND WHO IS (SEX)

IS $$$.$$.

THANK YOU FOR YOUR INQUIRY.

SINCERELY,

A. J. LOPEZ
V. P. INSURANCE DEPARTMENT
```

11

Character Manipulation

Like many other languages, COBOL has the ability to manipulate individual characters in a program. Sets of characters, often referred to as **strings,** at times need to be separated or joined with other strings (**concatenation**). In text editing, application fields or record strings can be split apart for the rearrangement of characters. Examples of this are the printing of mailing labels or the listing of records in a report.

When data are to be stored on tape or disk, character manipulation can be used to accomplish the job of condensing data so that the files require less storage space. Also, when data have been stored in a condensed format it is usually necessary to convert it to an expanded format.

This chapter addresses the need to search for a substring within a larger string, to determine the number of characters in a string, to concatenate two or more strings, and to replace characters in a string.

TERMS AND STATEMENTS

Concatenation	INSPECT statement	TALLYING option
COUNT IN option	ON OVERFLOW	UNSTRING
DELIMITED BY	option	statement
clause	REPLACING option	WITH POINTER
DELIMITED BY ALL	STRING statement	option
option	Strings	
DELIMITER IN	TALLYING IN	
option	option	

The STRING Statement

The purpose of the **STRING statement** is to concatenate two or more fields of data into a single field or record. The general format of this statement is given in Figure 11–1.

Figure 11–1   *General Format of the STRING Statement*

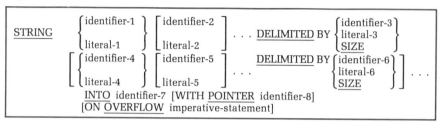

The identifiers and the literals 1, 2, 4, and 5 are the sending fields in Figure 11–1. Identifier-7 is the receiving field. The identifiers and literals 3 and 6 and the reserved word SIZE are delimiter values. They terminate the concatenation of data from the sending fields to the receiving field. Identifier-8 is the value of POINTER. This is used to establish the position of where the data will be sent in the receiving field.

Characters are transferred, starting with the first sending field, one at a time from left to right into the receiving field. The POINTER keeps track of the position in the receiving field to receive the first character. Characters will continue to be transferred until all characters to be sent from the sending field have been transferred or the receiving field is filled. Any unfilled positions in the received field retain their original characters; they are not filled with blank spaces as with a MOVE statement.

DELIMITED BY Clause

The use of at least one **DELIMITED BY clause** is required when using the STRING statement. If the identifiers or literals 3 and/or 6 are specified the leftmost character of a sending field is transferred to the receiving field. This continues from left to right until the rightmost character of the sending field has been transferred or a delimiter for that sending field has been reached. If another sending field is present this process is repeated. The delimiter itself is never transferred to the receiving field.

When SIZE is specified in this clause the entire sending field is transferred to the receiving field. The operation is terminated when all of the sending fields have been transferred.

If the receiving field becomes full before a sending field completes its transfer of characters, the operation is terminated and an error may have occurred.

WITH POINTER Option

If the **WITH POINTER option** is used in the STRING statement, it provides an explicit pointer field for the programmer's use to control where a character is to be placed in the receiving field. Identifier-8 is a programmer supplied integer data-name and must be initialized with an integer value between 1 and the length of the receiving field. When this option is not used, the system implicitly initializes the value of the pointer to 1, and the programmer does not have access to its value.

The initial value of the pointer is the position of where the first character is to be transferred in the receiving field. Transfer of characters continues from that position, from left to right, one character at a time. After each character has been transferred to the receiving field, the system increments the current value of the pointer by 1. The value of the pointer tells the system where the next value from a sending field is to be positioned. Hence, the value of the pointer is always one position greater than the position of the last character transferred to the receiving field.

If the value of the pointer exceeds the length of the receiving field and another character attempts to be transferred an overflow condition occurs.

ON OVERFLOW Option

The major purpose of the **ON OVERFLOW option** is to detect if the receiving field is shorter in length then the combined length of the fields to be concatenated. If the receiving field cannot accept characters yet to be transferred, the value of the pointer will be greater than the length of the receiving field. This will set an overflow condition.

When the ON OVERFLOW option is specified and an overflow occurs the imperative statement is executed. If an overflow occurs and the ON OVERFLOW option is not specified, the transferring is terminated and the next statement in the program is executed.

Rules for the STRING Statement

- All literals used must be nonnumeric.
- When a figurative constant is used, it is treated as a one-character nonnumeric literal.
- There can be any number of sending fields.
- If the sending field is an elementary numeric field, it must be an integer field, and the PIC clause cannot contain the edit symbol P.
- Receiving fields must be elementary alphanumeric items without edit symbols and without the JUSTIFIED RIGHT clause.
- The pointer field must be an elementary numeric item which can contain a value one position larger than the length of the receiving field. The PIC clause cannot contain the edit symbol P.
- When identifier-8 is used the programmer must define the field and give it an initial value between 1 and the length of the field.
- Unused portions of the receiving field contain their initial values, they are not changed to spaces.
- Data in the sending fields remain unchanged after the statement is executed.

Examples of the STRING Statement

Use of DELIMITED BY Clause

Figure 11–2 illustrates several ways the DELIMITED BY clause can be used. In Example A since SIZE is the delimiter for both F1 and F2, all of the characters in both fields are transferred. F1 starts in position 1 of FA, and F2 starts in position 6. Since the concatenation of F1 and F2 is only a string of eight characters, the ninth character in FA remains unchanged with a ? after the statement is executed. Remember, the STRING statement does not fill unused positions with spaces like the MOVE statement.

Example B is similar to Example A. In this case the remaining characters in FB were spaces, and F2 started in position 1 because it was the first sending field in the statement. Since F2 is numeric, the field must contain only integer values.

Each sending field in Example C has a delimiter. F2 is to have the entire field transferred and F5 is to transfer characters only until the delimiter /* is reached.

Figure 11–2   *Using the DELIMITED BY Clause*

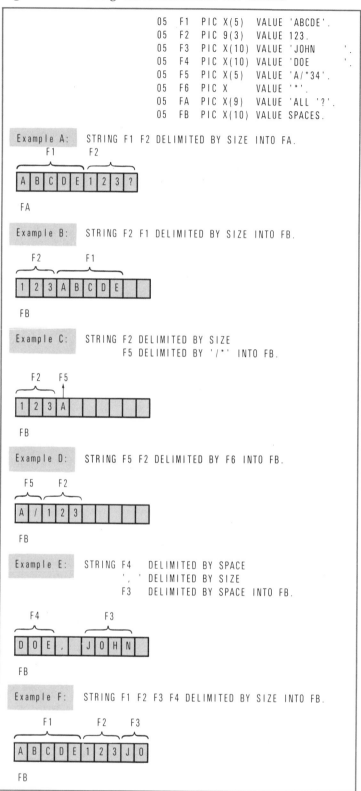

FB receives the characters 123 from F2 but only the character A from F5. That is because when the /* was encountered, it caused the transfer of characters from F5 to be terminated. Note the delimiter /* was not transferred, and the sending field's contents of 123 for F2 and A/*34 for F5 remain unchanged.

The delimiter for Example D is the data-name F6 which contains the value *. This is a one-character delimiter where in Example C there was a two-character delimiter. The delimiter * terminated the transfer of any more characters after A/ in F5. Since the delimiter * was not found in F2 the contents of the entire field were transferred.

Example E uses the DELIMITED BY clause three times. The delimiter SPACE is a figurative constant and is treated as a single character. In this case a comma and a space are inserted between F4 and F3. The STRING rearranges the data and inserts editing characters. Both F3 and F4 are 10-position fields. They are condensed into one 10-position field with a position to spare.

An overflow condition occurs in Example F. Since all of the sending fields are delimited by SIZE, some of these fields will not fit into FB. F3 can transfer only the characters JO before FB is filled and the attempt of transferring the next character H, causes the overflow condition. The remaining characters in F3 and all of the characters in F4 are ignored. Since the OVERFLOW option is not being used, the STRING is terminated and control is given to the next statement in the program.

Use of the WITH POINTER Option

One common use of the POINTER option is to count the number of characters in a field. Another is to move data to a receiving field beginning at a point other than the first position.

Suppose that single-word department names of varying lengths will be input into a program. At certain points in a program the department name is to be printed left-justified and at other times right-justified. Figure 11–3 is an example of how the data can be defined for printing the department name either left- or right-justified.

Figure 11–3 *Using the POINTER Option*

```
FD  SALES-FILE
    .
    .
01  SALES-RECORD.
    05   SALES-DEPARTMENT-NAME           PIC X(10).
         .
         .

01  WS-RIGHT-DEPARTMENT-NAME     PIC X(10).
01  WS-CHARACTER-COUNT           PIC 99.
    .

    PERFORM Z100-READ-SALES.
    .

    MOVE 1 TO WS-CHARACTER-COUNT.
    PERFORM C100-RIGHT-PRINT.
    COMPUTE WS-CHARACTER-COUNT = 12 - WS-CHARACTER-COUNT.
    MOVE SPACES TO WS-RIGHT-DEPARTMENT-NAME.
    PERFORM C100-RIGHT-PRINT.
    .

C100-RIGHT-PRINT.
    STRING SALES-DEPARTMENT-NAME DELIMITED BY SPACE
        INTO WS-RIGHT-DEPARTMENT-NAME
        WITH POINTER WS-CHARACTER-COUNT.
```

SALES–DEPARTMENT–NAME is input into a partial program illustrated by Figure 11–3. The PIC X(10) clause will left-justify the name starting in position 1 of the field. This is a 10-position field for all department names. To right-justify these names one can use the STRING statement with the POINTER option.

First set the pointer value to 1 with the statement MOVE 1 TO WS–CHARAC TER–COUNT. This assures that the transfer of the first character of SALES–DEPART

MENT–NAME will be transferred to the first position of WS–RIGHT–DEPART
MENT–NAME. As the characters are transferred one at a time the value of WS–
CHARACTER–COUNT is incremented by 1. If a space is encountered in the field,
the value of WS–CHARACTER–COUNT will be the length of the field plus 1. If
no spaces are found its value will be 11.

To determine the position to start the transfer of characters in the receiving
field so that department names are always right-justified, a new value for WS–
CHARACTER–COUNT must be computed. Just take the current value of the pointer
(which is 1 greater than the length of the field) and subtract it from 12. This gives
the value where the first position of the department name is to be transferred when
C100–RIGHT–PRINT is performed a second time. MOVE SPACES TO WS–RIGHT–
DEPARTMENT–NAME initializes the field to all spaces. Figure 11–4 shows the contents of the fields before and after execution of the STRING statement.

Figure 11–4   *Value of Fields from Figure 11–3*

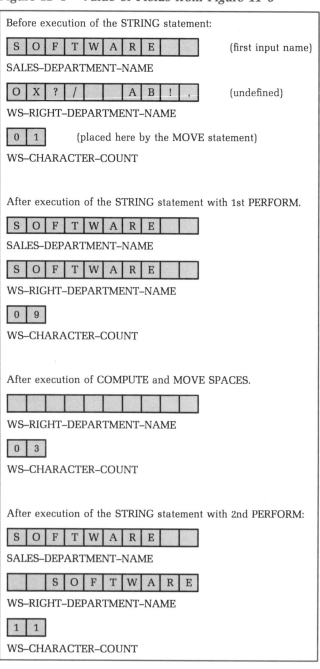

**Use of the
OVERFLOW
Option**

Several clauses and options of the STRING statement are used in Figure 11–5. After the sending fields have transferred all of the characters to OUTPUT–AREA the value of the pointer is 43. The pointer must have a value of 51 and another character must be attempting to transfer to OUTPUT–AREA before an overflow condition occurs. If this were to happen PERFORM E200–ERROR–IN–LENGTH would be executed.

Figure 11–5   *Using the OVERFLOW Option*

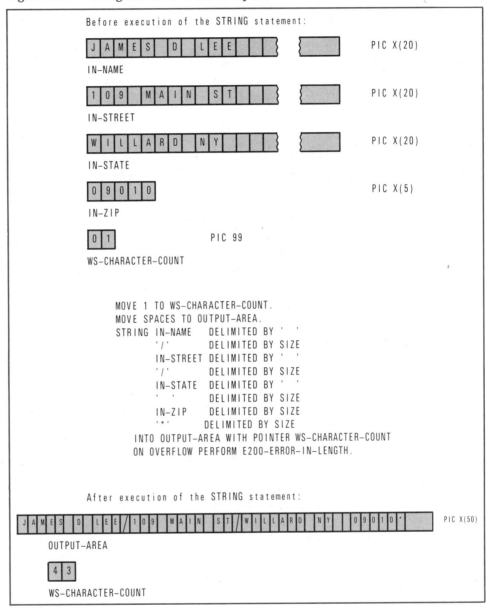

The UNSTRING Statement

The purpose of the **UNSTRING statement** is to separate the contents of a sending field into one or more receiving fields. The general format of this statement is given in Figure 11–6.

Identifier-1 of Figure 11–6 is the sending field. Identifiers-2, 3 and literals-1, 2 are delimiters for the sending field. Receiving fields for data characters represented

Figure 11–6 *General Format of the UNSTRING Statement*

```
UNSTRING identifier-1

    [DELIMITED BY [ALL] {identifier-2}  [OR [ALL] {identifier-3}  ] . . .]
                        {literal-1   }               {literal-2   }

    INTO identifier-4 [DELIMITER IN identifier-5][COUNT IN identifier-6]
         [identifier-7 [DELIMITER IN identifier-8 [COUNT IN identifier-9]] . . .
         [WITH POINTER identifier-10] [TALLYING IN identifier-11]
         [ON OVERFLOW imperative-statement]
```

by identifiers-4 and 7. If the DELIMITED BY clause is specified identifiers-5 and 8 are delimiting character receiving fields. Identifiers-6 and 9 are receiving fields to store the count of the number of characters that are transferred to identifiers-4 and 7. The pointer value is placed in identifier-10. The number of fields that receive characters from the sending field are tallied and stored in identifier-11.

Characters are transferred one at a time from left to right to the receiving fields for data characters. The POINTER keeps track of the position in the receiving field to receive the first character. Characters will continue to be transferred until all characters to be sent from the sending field have been transferred or the receiving field is filled. This process continues for all of the receiving fields.

DELIMITED BY Clause

The DELIMITED BY clause is optional in the STRING statement. If it is not specified and the receiving field is nonnumeric the number of characters transferred can be equal to the length of the receiving field. If the receiving field is numeric, the number of characters transferred can be equal only to the number of integer positions in the receiving field.

The **DELIMITED BY ALL option** causes consecutive occurrences of the delimiter to be treated as only one occurrence of the delimiter. The DELIMITED BY causes each consecutive occurrence of the delimiter to be treated as a separate delimiter character. If it is necessary to use two or more different delimiters, the OR condition is used with the DELIMITED clause. The delimiter itself is never transferred to the receiving fields for data characters. Delimiters must be alphanumeric and up to 15 may be specified for an UNSTRING statement. When two or more delimiters are in adjacent locations of the sending field, no characters from the sending field are transferred.

When the number of characters transferred to any receiving field for data characters is less than the length of the field, the rightmost positions are filled with spaces. A special situation occurs when two or more separate delimiters appear in consecutive positions. When the receiving field is alphanumeric the entire field is filled with spaces. If the receiving field is numeric the entire field is filled with zeros.

DELIMITER IN Option

The **DELIMITER IN option** can only be used if the DELIMITED BY clause has been specified. Its purpose is to save the value of the delimiter from the receiving field in the delimiter's receiving field. These receiving fields must be alphanumeric.

The delimiter is left-justified in its receiving field. Use of the ALL option causes only one occurrence of the delimiter to be moved. If the receiving field is larger than the delimiter, the rightmost positions are filled with spaces. The receiving field is filled with all spaces if the delimiting condition is the end of the sending field.

COUNT IN Option

The **COUNT IN option** will keep a count of the number of characters transferred to a data receiving field. The count field can be specified for each data receiving field and it must be defined as numeric. This option cannot be used unless the DELIMITED BY clause is specified.

WITH POINTER Option

If the WITH POINTER option is used in an UNSTRING statement, it provides an explicit pointer field for the programmer's use to control where a character is to be placed in the data receiving field. Identifier-10 is a programmer-supplied numeric integer data-name (PIC clause cannot contain the edit symbol P) and must be initialized with an integer value between 1 and the length of the receiving field. If this option is not used the system implicitly initializes the value of the pointer to 1, and the programmer is denied access to its value.

The position of where the first character is to be transferred in the receiving field is the initial value of the pointer. Transfer of characters continues from that position, from left to right one character at a time. After each character has been transferred to the receiving field the system increments the current value of the pointer by 1. The value of the pointer tells the system where the next value from the sending field is coming from. The value of the pointer is always one position greater than the position of the last position transferred from the receiving field.

TALLYING IN Option

The purpose of the **TALLYING IN option** is to count the number of data receiving fields operated on. If a data receiving field is skipped because of two adjacent delimiters, it is still counted as a field that was operated on. The TALLYING field is a programmer-supplied, elementary numeric integer item. Its PIC clause cannot contain the edit symbol P.

ON OVERFLOW Option

An overflow condition exists when: (1) the value of the pointer was initialized to a value greater than the length of the sending field and (2) all of the data receiving fields have been used, but there are still characters to transfer in the sending field.

When the ON OVERFLOW option is specified and an overflow occurs, the imperative statement is executed. If an overflow occurs and the ON OVERFLOW option is not specified, the statement is terminated and the next statement in the program is executed.

Rules for the UNSTRING Statement

- All literals used must be nonnumeric.
- The sending field must be an elementary alphanumeric item.
- Receiving fields may be nonnumeric (edit symbol B cannot be used in PIC clause) or numeric (edit symbol P cannot be used in PIC clause).
- DELIMITER IN and COUNT options cannot be used without the DELIMITED BY clause.
- COUNT, POINT, and TALLY receiving fields must be elementary numeric integer data-items. The PIC clauses cannot contain the edit symbol P.
- The programmer may initialize the count, pointer, and tallying receiving fields.
- If a delimiter contains more than one character, the characters must be in consecutive positions in the sending field.

- If two different delimiters are in consecutive locations in the sending field the data receiving field becomes a "null" field.
- Characters are transferred to data receiving fields until the receiving fields are full or the sending field has no characters to send.
- The final contents of TALLY are its initial value plus the number of data receiving fields acted on.
- The final contents of COUNT are its initial value plus the number of characters transferred to its related data receiving field.
- The final contents of DELIMITER IN are the delimiting character(s).
- After the transfer of characters to a data receiving field, unused positions of the field are filled with spaces (even numeric fields).

Examples of the UNSTRING Statement

Use of DELIMITED BY Clause   Figure 11–7 illustrates different ways to use the DELIMITED BY clause. In Example A the clause is omitted. The transfer of characters will continue until either the data receiving fields are filled or the sending field is out of data. F1 receives the first 10 characters and F2 receives the last 7 characters from FA.

Figure 11–7   *Using the DELIMITED BY Clause*

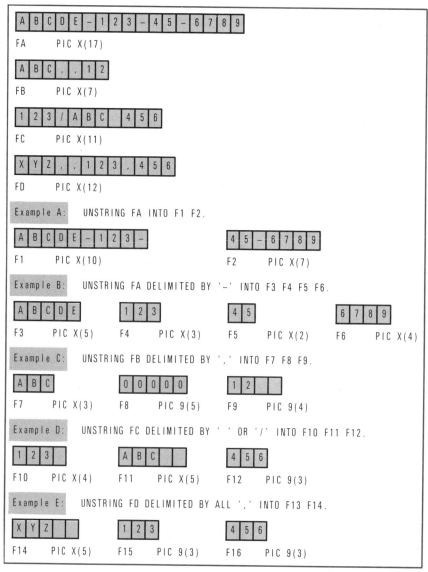

Example B has one delimiter and four data receiving fields. Whenever the delimiter '-' is examined it terminates further transfer of characters into that field. Transferring of characters stops when the last character in FA has been transferred to F6. Notice that the delimiter itself was not transferred.

There are two different consecutive delimiters in FB of Example C. This will cause F8 to become a "null" field. Since it is a numeric field it is filled with zeros. Transfer continues until the 2 is located in F9 and the sending field is out of data. Even though F9 is a numeric field, all unused positions in a data receiving field after a transfer are filled with spaces. The space in the last two positions of the field made this an invalid numeric field.

Two different delimiters are used for the sending field FC in Example D. When either a space or a / are examined in FC, the transferring of characters into a data receiving field is terminated. F10 contains the characters 123 and a filled space. F11 contains ABC and two filled spaces. F12 is filled with the normal transfer of 456. Notice that F12 is a numeric field. In this case it still is because all of the values placed in the field are numeric.

The ALL option is used in Example E. All of the consecutive locations of a comma are treated as a single delimiter. F14 will contain XYZ, and two spaces after the two commas are treated as one delimiter. F15 contains 123, and F16 contains 456. The single comma was treated as a delimiter just like the two commas. This is because ALL treats the multiple consecutive occurrences of a delimiter's value as a single-valued delimiter.

Use of the DELIMITER IN Option

In Figure 11–8 the example uses three delimiter value fields for the DELIMITER IN option. This option moves the delimiter that causes termination of a transfer into a delimiter value field. After the execution of the statement D1 contains a / and D2 contains a hyphen. D4 contains a blank because no named delimiter was found. Since there was no DELIMITER IN option for F19 its delimiter was not saved.

Figure 11–8 *Using the DELIMITER IN Option*

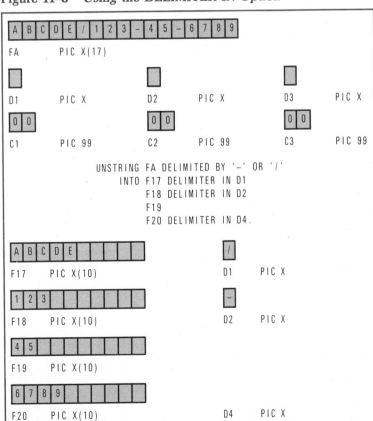

Use of the COUNT IN Option

Using the same data fields as Figure 11–8 the example in Figure 11–9 adds the COUNT IN option to the UNSTRING statement. After its execution C1, C2, and C3 contain the values 5, 3, and 4. These values represent the number of characters transferred to each of the fields from the sending field.

Figure 11–9   *Using the COUNT IN Option*

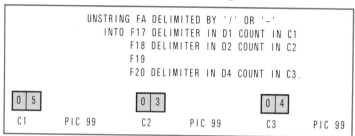

Use of the TALLYING IN and POINTER Options

The pointer value was initialized to 3 and the tallying value to 0 in Figure 11–10. After the execution of the statement, T1 has a value of 2, the number of data receiving fields operated on. P1's initial value of 3 started the examining of characters with the A. It was incremented by one each time another character was examined. The five characters A//B* were examined and this value was added to 3. The final value for P1 is 8.

Figure 11–10   *Using the TALLYING and POINTER Options*

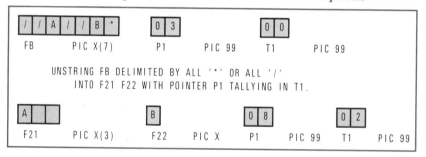

Use of the OVERFLOW Option

The sending field in Figure 11–11 does not have the delimiter SPACE. After F23 is filled the transfer of characters is still being attempted because the delimiter has not been found. The execution of the statement is terminated, F24 remains unchanged, and an overflow condition is set. The statement PERFORM D400–OVERFLOW–ERROR is executed. If the OVERFLOW option has been omitted, control would be given to the next statement in the program.

Figure 11–11   *Using the OVERFLOW Option*

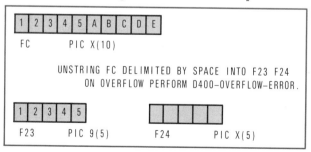

Use of the Complete UNSTRING Statement

The results from executing the statement in Figure 11–12 are as follows: D1, D2, and D3 have the values of the delimiters /. C1, C2, and C3 have the number of characters transferred to the fields LABEL–NAME, LABEL–STREET, and LABEL–STATE. Since three fields were operated on the value of T1 is 3. Although there was room in the last receiving field LABEL–STATE for more characters, at position 42 the sending field had completed its transfer of characters so the statement had a normal termination. No overflow condition exists, and the next statement in the program is executed.

Figure 11–12   *Using the UNSTRING Statement*

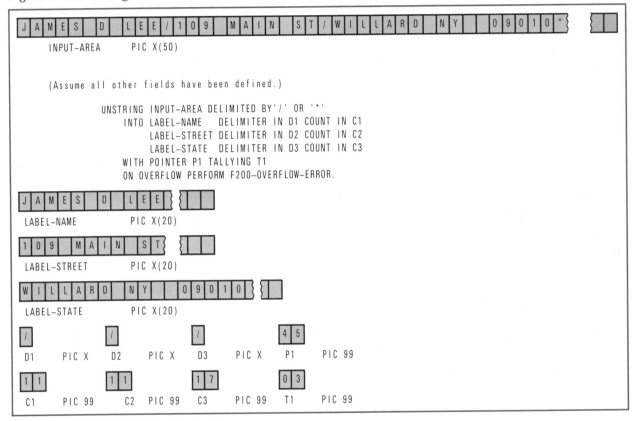

The INSPECT Statement

The purpose of the **INSPECT statement** is to examine characters in a data-item, specified by the programmer, that are to be counted, replaced, or both counted and replaced. Figure 11–13 shows its general format.

Identifier-1 is a group or elementary item with USAGE DISPLAY to be inspected. When used, identifier-2 is the tallying field and must be an elementary integer item defined without the symbol P in its PIC clause. It must be initialized by the programmer before the INSPECT statement is executed. All other identifiers must be elementary items and are treated as alphanumeric items. Literals must be nonnumeric. Either the TALLYING or the REPLACING option must be specified in the statement. If both are specified, all tallying is executed before any replacing is done.

TALLYING Option

The **TALLYING option** is used for character counting applications. Identifier-3 or literal-1 is the tallied field. When ALL is specified the tallying field is increased

Figure 11–13 *Format of the INSPECT Statement*

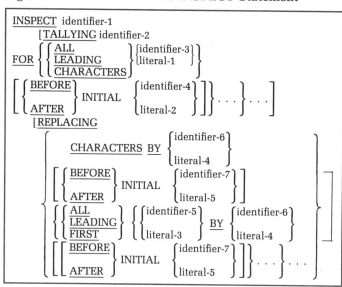

by 1 for each nonoverlapping occurrence in the inspected item, starting in the leftmost position of the item and continuing to the rightmost position. When LEADING is used, the tallying field is increased by 1 for each contiguous nonoverlapping occurrence in the inspected item. If CHARACTERS is specified, the tallying field is increased by 1 for each character in the inspected item.

If either BEFORE or AFTER is used with this option, identifier-4 and literal-2 are delimiters. If literal-2 is a figurative constant it is considered to be one character in length. The BEFORE causes counting to occur at the leftmost character of the inspected item and continues until the first occurrence of the delimiter or until the end of the item. The AFTER begins counting with the first character to the right of the delimiter. If the delimiter is not present, no counting is done. Figure 11–14 illustrates examples of using the TALLYING option.

TALLYING/ALL is used Examples A through C. Example A compares each character in A1 and counts the number of times X appeared. In this case WS–COUNT–1 will contain a value of 1. In example B, UV is compared to VW, then VW is compared to VW, and so on. One match is found. No matches are found in Example C, so WS–COUNT–1 has a value of zeros.

TALLYING/LEADING is used in Example D and E. Example D has three leading zeros so WS–COUNT–2 has a value of 3, and Example E does not have any leading values of '4' so WS–COUNT–2 is zero.

The CHARACTERS/BEFORE–AFTER option is used in Examples F through H. WS–COUNT–3 in Example F has a value of 3 because the characters UVW precede X. In Example G, WS–COUNT–3 is 1 because only the character Y is after the X. Since there are no characters after Z in Example H, WS–COUNT–3 is zero.

In Example I and J, two tallying fields are used. For example I there is one leading U before the first W and one leading X after the first W. In Example J, three leading zeros appear before the initial '5' and there are a total of three zeros after the initial zero.

REPLACING Option

The **REPLACING option** is used for character manipulation applications. Identifier-5 or literal-3 is the subject field, and identifier-6 or literal-4 is the substitution field. These fields must be the same length. If the subject field is a figurative constant it is treated as a one-character nonnumeric literal. When the substitution field is

Figure 11–14 *Examples of the TALLYING Option*

```
                01  A1           PIC X(5) VALUE 'UVWXY'.
                01  A2           PIC X(5) VALUE '00050'.
                01  WS-COUNT-1 PIC 9(2) VALUE ZEROS.
                01  WS-COUNT-2 PIC 9(2) VALUE ZEROS.
                01  WS-COUNT-3 PIC 9(2) VALUE ZEROS.
                01  WS-COUNT-4 PIC 9(2) VALUE ZEROS.
                01  WS-COUNT-5 PIC 9(2) VALUE ZEROS.

Example A:

                INSPECT A1
                     TALLYING WS-COUNT-1
                     FOR ALL 'X'.

Example B:

                INSPECT A1
                     TALLYING WS-COUNT-1
                     FOR ALL 'VW'.

Example C:

                INSPECT A1
                     TALLYING WS-COUNT-1
                     FOR ALL 'Z'.

Example D:

                INSPECT A2
                     TALLYING WS-COUNT-2
                     FOR LEADING '0'.

Example E:

                INSPECT A2
                     TALLYING WS-COUNT-2
                     FOR LEADING '4'.

Example F:

                INSPECT A1
                     TALLYING WS-COUNT-3
                     FOR CHARACTERS BEFORE INITIAL 'X'.

Example G:

                INSPECT A1
                     TALLYING WS-COUNT-3
                     FOR CHARACTERS AFTER INITIAL 'X'.

Example H:

                INSPECT A1
                     TALLYING WS-COUNT-3
                     FOR CHARACTERS AFTER INITIAL 'Z'.

Example I:

                INSPECT A1
                     TALLYING WS-COUNT-4
                     FOR LEADING 'U' BEFORE INITIAL 'W'.
                     WS-COUNT-5
                     FOR LEADING 'X' AFTER INITIAL 'W'.

Example J:

                INSPECT A2
                     TALLYING WS-COUNT-4
                     FOR LEADING ZERO BEFORE INITIAL '5'
                     WS-COUNT-5
                     FOR ALL ZEROS AFTER INITIAL ZERO.
```

a figurative constant, the field is considered to be the same length as the subject field.

When CHARACTERS is specified, the substitution field must be one character in length. Substitution is made beginning at the leftmost character of the inspected item and continuing to the end of the item. When ALL is specified each nonoverlapping occurrence of the subject field is replaced by the substitution field. LEADING causes each nonoverlapping occurrence of the subject field to be replaced by the substitution field. FIRST allows only the leftmost occurrence of the subject field to be replaced by the substitution field.

If either BEFORE or AFTER is used with this option, identifier-7 and literal-5 are delimiters. The delimiters must be one character in length. The BEFORE causes replacement to occur at the leftmost character of the inspected item and continues until the first occurrence of the delimiter or the end of the item. The AFTER begins replacement with the first character to the right of the delimiter. If the delimiter is not present, replacement does not occur. Figure 11–15 shows examples of the REPLACING option.

The REPLACING ALL option is used in Examples A through D. After execution of the INSPECT statements, B1 has the value 123–45–6789, B2 the value ABCABCWXYZ, B3 the value AAAAAAAAAA, and B4 the value AAAAYZXXYW.

In Example E the four leading values of X are replaced, and the value of B4 becomes 1111YZXXYW. FIRST is used in Example F, and the new value of B4 is XXXXWZXXYW.

Examples G and H use multiple replacements. The final value of B4 in Example G is WWWWYWWWYW. Example H is somewhat tricky. There are four replacements that take place. After FIRST 'Y' BY 'W' is executed, B4 is XXXXWZXXYW. After FIRST 'X' BY 'W' is changed to WXXXWZXXYW. LEADING 'X' BY 'Z' AFTER INITIAL 'Z' gives the value WXXXWZZZYW to B4, and finally after LEADING 'W' BY 'Y' is executed B4 has the value YXXXWZZZYW.

Both the TALLYING and REPLACING options are used in Example I. When this occurs the INSPECT statement is executed as if an INSPECT TALLYING statement were specified as one statement followed by an INSPECT REPLACING statement. In this example WS–COUNT–1 has a value of 6, and B4 has a value of XXXXYZZZZYW.

Program Example

Statement of the Problem

Each week a group of records for magazine subscriptions are received. A program is to be written that will:

a. Create a coded label entry for each new subscription.
b. Create a condensed record for each subscriber.
c. Create an audit report that will list the coded label, a three-line mailing label, and a copy of the condensed record.
d. Create a transaction file to be stored on disk of the condensed records.

The transaction file is to be used at a later time to update the master subscriber's file. The transaction file is to have fixed-length records, but the master file may contain variable length records. Mailings for subscribers are printed from the master file.

Construct the coded label in the following order:

a. First 2 characters from magazine name.
b. Zip code.
c. First 4 characters from last name.
d. First 4 characters of street/apartment.

Figure 11–15 *Examples of the REPLACING Option*

```
                    01  B1 PIC X(11) VALUE '123 45 6789'.
                    01  B2 PIC X(10) VALUE 'ABC123WXYZ'.
                    01  B3 PIC X(10) VALUE 'ABABABABAB'.
                    01  B4 PIC X(10) VALUE 'XXXXYZXXYW'.

  Example A:

                    INSPECT B1
                        REPLACING ALL SPACES BY '-'.

  Example B:

                    INSPECT B2
                        REPLACING ALL '123' BY 'ABC'.

  Example C:

                    INSPECT B3
                        REPLACING ALL 'B' BY 'A'.

  Example D:

                    INSPECT B4
                        REPLACING ALL 'X' BY 'A' BEFORE 'Z'.

  Example E:

                    INSPECT B4
                        REPLACING LEADING 'X' BY '1'.

  Example F:

                    INSPECT B4
                        REPLACING FIRST 'Y' BY 'W'.

  Example G:

                    INSPECT B4
                        REPLACING ALL 'X' BY 'W'
                                      'Z' BY 'W' AFTER INITIAL 'Y'.

  Example H:

                    INSPECT B4
                        REPLACING FIRST 'Y' BY 'W'
                                        'X' BY 'W'
                                  LEADING 'X' BY 'Z' AFTER INITIAL 'Z'
                                        'W' BY 'Y'.

  Example I:

                    INSPECT B4
                        TALLYING WS-COUNT-1 FOR ALL 'X'
                        BEFORE
                        REPLACING LEADING 'X' BY 'Z'
                            AFTER INITIAL 'Z'.
```

 e. First 3 characters of month subscription expires.

 f. Characters for the year subscription expires.

Print the three-line mailing label as follows (each line is to be 35 positions in length):

 a. First name, one space, and last name.

 b. Street or apartment number, one space, and name of street or building.

 c. City name, one space, state, two spaces, and the zip code. Construct the condensed record in the following order:

a. A two-position field for the length of the condensed record (to be used when updating the variable length record master file).

b. The 20-position coded label followed by a slash.

c. The first line of the mailing label followed by a slash.

d. The second line of the mailing label followed by a slash.

e. The third line of the mailing label followed by an asterisk.

Input

The records are each 80 columns long and are stored on a disk file. The format of these records is shown in Figure 11–16.

Figure 11–16   *Input to Program 11–1*

```
          1-10    Last name
         11-20    First name
         21-32    Street/apartment number
         33-44    Street/building name
         45-56    City/state name
         57-61    Zip code
         62-70    Expiration month
         71-72    Expiration year
         73-80    Magazine name

==============================================================================
MATSUDA    TATSUO     3144       AVENUE CT   HUGO WA     98221MARCH     89NEWSWEEK
WILLIAMS   KEITH      2332       19TH ST     MORNING OH  44890NOVEMBER  90NEWSWEEK
FURROW     RICK       33126      CTY RD 64   SUNDIAL MI  48122JANUARY   89TIME
GILFRY     MAJOR      800        SOUTH 1ST   AIMES NE    68105MAY       91NATLGEOG
CIMMIYOTTID            3500       JFK PKWY    BIGGS TX    69146APRIL     90TIME
GREEN      ROBERT     206 APT5B  PLAZA BLDG  SWAN IA     50293OCTOBER   88NEWSWEEK
COMPANY    KLOSMISCKICITY BANK   SUITE 301   ALFRED MO   65882JULY      89NEWSWEEK
ADDERSON   JAMES      1141       MED CENTER  WUPLIFT LA  71511SEPTEMBER91TIME
COMPANY    HAL-IRWIN  2044       FAIRWAY LN  ROCK FORD CO80710DECEMBER  89TIME
LIPVAK     KAREEN     161615     ELLIOTT CT  FERRIS NY   09871MARCH     90NATLGEOG
==============================================================================
```

Program

Program 11–1

```
000010 IDENTIFICATION DIVISION.
000020 PROGRAM-ID.    LABELS.
000030************************************************************
000040* PROGRAM EXAMPLE 11-1 USES THE STRING AND UNSTRING STATEMENTS   *
000050************************************************************
000060 ENVIRONMENT DIVISION.
000070 CONFIGURATION SECTION.
000080    SOURCE-COMPUTER.    IBM-4341.
000090    OBJECT-COMPUTER.    IBM-4341.
000100 INPUT-OUTPUT SECTION.
000110 FILE-CONTROL.
000120    SELECT NEW-LABEL-FILE
000130       ASSIGN TO UT-S-NEWLAB.
000140    SELECT AUDIT-FILE
000150       ASSIGN TO UT-S-PRINTER.
000160    SELECT TRANS-LABEL-FILE
000170       ASSIGN TO UT-S-TRANS.
000180*
000190 DATA DIVISION.
000200 FILE SECTION.
```

Program 11–1   *(continued)*

```
000210 FD  NEW-LABEL-FILE
000220     RECORD CONTAINS 80 CHARACTERS
000230     LABEL RECORDS ARE STANDARD.
000240 01  NL-NEW-LABEL-RECORD.
000250     05  NL-NAME.
000260         10  NL-LAST-NAME           PIC X(10).
000270         10  NL-FIRST-NAME          PIC X(10).
000280     05  NL-ADDRESS.
000290         10  NL-STREET-APT          PIC X(12).
000300         10  NL-STREET-NAME         PIC X(12).
000310         10  NL-CITY-STATE          PIC X(12).
000320         10  NL-ZIP                 PIC X(5).
000330     05  NL-EXPIRATION-DATE.
000340         10  NL-MONTH-EXPIRES       PIC X(9).
000350         10  NL-YEAR-EXPIRES        PIC X(2).
000360     05  NL-MAGAZINE-NAME           PIC X(8).
000370 FD  AUDIT-FILE
000380     RECORD CONTAINS 132 CHARACTERS
000390     LABEL RECORD OMITTED.
000400 01  AR-AUDIT-RECORD                PIC X(132).
000410 FD  TRANS-LABEL-FILE
000420     RECORD CONTAINS 92 CHARACTERS
000430     LABEL RECORDS STANDARD.
000440 01  TL-TRANS-LABEL-RECORD          PIC X(92).
000450*
000460 WORKING-STORAGE SECTION.
000470 01  WS-WORK-AREAS.
000480     05  WS-EOF-INDICATOR           PIC X(3).
000490         88 END-OF-INPUT-FILE       VALUE 'END'.
000500 01  WS-LABEL-CODE.
000510     05  WS-MAGAZINE-NAME           PIC X(2).
000520     05  WS-ZIP                     PIC X(5).
000530     05  WS-LAST-NAME               PIC X(4).
000540     05  WS-STREET-APT              PIC X(4).
000550     05  WS-MONTH-EXPIRES           PIC X(3).
000560     05  WS-YEAR-EXPIRES            PIC X(2).
000570 01  WS-LABEL-PRINT-LINE-1.
000580     05  WS-SUBSCRIBER-NAME         PIC X(35).
000590 01  WS-LABEL-PRINT-LINE-2.
000600     05  WS-STREET-ADDRESS          PIC X(35).
000610 01  WS-LABEL-PRINT-LINE-3.
000620     05  WS-LOCATION-ADDRESS        PIC X(35).
000630 01  WS-CONDENSED-RECORD.
000640     05  WS-LENGTH-OF-RECORD        PIC 9(2).
000650     05  FILLER                     PIC X(1) VALUE '/'.
000660     05  WS-CONDENSED-LABEL-CODE    PIC X(20).
000670     05  FILLER                     PIC X(1) VALUE '/'.
000680     05  WS-LABEL-RECORD            PIC X(68).
000690 01  HD-HEADING-LINE.
000700     05  FILLER                     PIC X(40)
000710             VALUE 'AUDIT REPORT FOR NEW SUBSCRIBER RECORDS'.
000720*
000730 PROCEDURE DIVISION.
000740 A000-LABELS.
000750     OPEN INPUT  NEW-LABEL-FILE
000760          OUTPUT AUDIT-FILE
000770                 TRANS-LABEL-FILE.
000780     PERFORM B100-PRINT-HEADINGS.
000790     PERFORM Z100-READ-NEW-RECORD.
000800     PERFORM B300-PROCESS-RECORDS
000810         UNTIL END-OF-INPUT-FILE.
000820     CLOSE NEW-LABEL-FILE
000830           AUDIT-FILE
000840           TRANS-LABEL-FILE.
```

Program 11–1   *(concluded)*

```
000850      STOP RUN.
000860 B100-PRINT-HEADINGS.
000870      WRITE AR-AUDIT-RECORD FROM HD-HEADING-LINE
000880           AFTER PAGE.
000890 B300-PROCESS-RECORDS.
000900      PERFORM C100-INITIALIZE-VARIABLES.
000910      PERFORM C200-CHARACTER-PROCESSING.
000920      PERFORM C300-OUTPUT-PROCESSING.
000930      PERFORM Z100-READ-NEW-RECORD.
000940 C100-INITIALIZE-VARIABLES.
000950      MOVE SPACES TO WS-LABEL-RECORD.
000960      MOVE 1       TO WS-LENGTH-OF-RECORD.
000970 C200-CHARACTER-PROCESSING.
000980      MOVE NL-MAGAZINE-NAME TO WS-MAGAZINE-NAME.
000990      MOVE NL-ZIP           TO WS-ZIP.
001000      MOVE NL-LAST-NAME     TO WS-LAST-NAME.
001010      MOVE NL-STREET-APT    TO WS-STREET-APT.
001020      MOVE NL-MONTH-EXPIRES TO WS-MONTH-EXPIRES.
001030      MOVE NL-YEAR-EXPIRES  TO WS-YEAR-EXPIRES.
001040      MOVE WS-LABEL-CODE    TO WS-CONDENSED-LABEL-CODE.
001050      STRING NL-FIRST-NAME    DELIMITED BY ' '
001060             ' '              DELIMITED BY SIZE
001070             NL-LAST-NAME     DELIMITED BY ' '
001080             '/'              DELIMITED BY SIZE
001090             NL-STREET-APT    DELIMITED BY ' '
001100             ' '              DELIMITED BY SIZE
001110             NL-STREET-NAME   DELIMITED BY ' '
001120             '/'              DELIMITED BY SIZE
001130             NL-CITY-STATE    DELIMITED BY ' '
001140             ' '              DELIMITED BY SIZE
001150             NL-ZIP           DELIMITED BY ' '
001160             '*'              DELIMITED BY SIZE
001170         INTO WS-LABEL-RECORD
001180         WITH POINTER WS-LENGTH-OF-RECORD.
001190      ADD 23 TO WS-LENGTH-OF-RECORD.
001200      UNSTRING WS-LABEL-RECORD DELIMITED BY '/' OR '*'
001210         INTO WS-SUBSCRIBER-NAME
001220              WS-STREET-ADDRESS
001230              WS-LOCATION-ADDRESS.
001240 C300-OUTPUT-PROCESSING.
001250      MOVE SPACES TO AR-AUDIT-RECORD.
001260      WRITE AR-AUDIT-RECORD
001270           AFTER 1.
001280      WRITE AR-AUDIT-RECORD          FROM WS-CONDENSED-LABEL-CODE
001290           AFTER 1.
001300      WRITE AR-AUDIT-RECORD          FROM WS-SUBSCRIBER-NAME
001310           AFTER 1.
001320      WRITE AR-AUDIT-RECORD          FROM WS-STREET-ADDRESS
001330           AFTER 1.
001340      WRITE AR-AUDIT-RECORD          FROM WS-LOCATION-ADDRESS
001350           AFTER 1.
001360      WRITE AR-AUDIT-RECORD          FROM WS-CONDENSED-RECORD
001370           AFTER 1.
001380      WRITE TL-TRANS-LABEL-RECORD FROM WS-CONDENSED-RECORD.
001390 Z100-READ-NEW-RECORD.
001400      READ NEW-LABEL-FILE
001410           AT END MOVE 'END' TO WS-EOF-INDICATOR.
```

Discussion

The initialize procedure is not found in its normal place in the main paragraph. It is the first statement in B300–PROCESS–RECORDS. If this were not done, unused positions in WS–LABEL–RECORD would contain unwanted data because the

STRING statement does not replace unused positions with spaces. Also, since the program is to use the WITH POINTER option, its counter must be initialized to 1.

All of the character processing is done in C200–CHARACTER–PROCESSING. First the fields to be used to make up WS–LABEL–CODE are moved to the appropriate fields and the unused portions truncated. Next the STRING statement will condense the input record into WS–LABEL–RECORD. Notice that the name fields must contain single names and if blanks are present they are placed to the right of the name. The reason for this is that a space or the last character in the field is used as a delimiter in the STRING statement. The address fields may contain a single space between entries. The delimiters for these fields are two consecutive spaces or the last character in the field. The character / is placed in the receiving field after each entry from the sending field except for the last entry. An asterisk is used here (instead of the 1) to indicate that this is the end of the data for this record.

The ADD 23 TO WS–LENGTH–OF–RECORD is used to determine the number of characters in WS–CONDENSED–RECORD. This is done by adding the field length of WS–LENGTH–RECORD (which is 2), the length of WS–CONDENSED–LABEL–RECORD (which is 20), the length of each of the FILLER's (1 each) and the number of characters that were strung into WS–LABEL–RECORD. The number of characters in WS–LABEL–RECORD will vary depending on the data in the input record and is determined by the POINTER option. Therefore, when adding 2 + 20 + 1 + 1, for a value of 24, a value of 1 must be subtracted to adjust the value of the POINTER counter so it will contain the correct number of positions. (It is always 1 greater than the number of characters in the receiving field.) Hence 23 is added and not 24. The value of WS–LENGTH–OF–RECORD would be used to change the fixed length of WS–CONDENSED–RECORD when it is used as a variable length record in the master subscriber file, while it is used to update in another program.

UNSTRING WS–LABEL–RECORD will place these appropriate data from the string field into three receiving fields that will be printed as label lines in the audit report.

C300–OUTPUT–PROCESSING creates the audit report and creates the transaction record to be placed into the TRANS–LABEL–FILE. The results of the audit report are shown in Figure 11–17, and the contents of the created file are shown in Figure 11–18.

Notice the lines in Figure 11–17 that contain the coded label. These characters are used in identifying a subscriber. The three lines following the coded label are what should print out when these records become part of the master file. The next line is a copy of what has been placed in the transaction file.

Check the first line in the transaction file in Figure 11–18. The value of 69 is the number of characters in this record. The slashes are delimiters to be used in another program to unstring this record. NE98221MATS3144MAR89 is the coded label. TATSUO MATSUDA is the first line of the label, 3144 AVENUE CT and HUGO WA 98221 will be the second and third lines of the label.

Programming Style

1. Place STRING and UNSTRING statements in a separate procedure to be performed whenever practical.

2. Always initialize receiving fields for the STRING statement with spaces before it is executed.

3. Use the STRING statement to condense data for storage on tape or disk.

4. Use the UNSTRING statement to accept terminal data and convert it to an appropriate format for use in a program in an interactive environment.

Figure 11–17   *Audit Output from Program 11–1*

```
AUDIT REPORT FOR NEW SUBSCRIBER RECORDS

NE98221MATS3144MAR89
TATSUO MATSUDA
3144 AVENUE CT
HUGO WA  98221
69/NE98221MATS3144MAR89/TATSUO MATSUDA/3144 AVENUE CT/HUGO WA   98221*

NE44890WILL2332NOV90
KEITH WILLIAMS
2332 19TH ST
MORNING OH  44890
70/NE44890WILL2332NOV90/KEITH WILLIAMS/2332 19TH ST/MORNING OH   44890*

TI48122FURR3312JAN89
RICK FURROW
33126 CTY RD 64
SUNDIAL MI  48122
70/TI48122FURR3312JAN89/RICK FURROW/33126 CTY RD 64/SUNDIAL MI   48122*

NA68105GILF800 MAY91
MAJOR GILFRY
800 SOUTH 1ST
AIMES NE  68105
67/NA68105GILF800 MAY91/MAJOR GILFRY/800 SOUTH 1ST/AIMES NE   68105*

TI69146CIMM3500APR90
D CIMMIYOTTI
3500 JFK PKWY
BIGGS TX  69146
67/TI69146CIMM3500APR90/D CIMMIYOTTI/3500 JFK PKWY/BIGGS TX   69146*

NE50293GREE206 OCT88
ROBERT GREEN
206 APT5B PLAZA BLDG
SWAN IA  50293
73/NE50293GREE206 OCT88/ROBERT GREEN/206 APT5B PLAZA BLDG/SWAN IA   50293*

NE65882COMPCITYJUL89
KLOSMISCKI COMPANY
CITY BANK SUITE 301
ALFRED MO  65882
80/NE65882COMPCITYJUL89/KLOSMISCKI COMPANY/CITY BANK SUITE 301/ALFRED MO 65882*

TI71511ADDE1141SEP91
JAMES ADDERSON
1141 MED CENTER W
UPLIFT LA  71511
74/TI71511ADDE1141SEP91/JAMES ADDERSON/1141 MED CENTER W/UPLIFT LA   71511*

TI80710COMP2044DEC89
HAL-IRWIN COMPANY
2044 FAIRWAY LN
ROCK FORD CO  80710
78/TI80710COMP2044DEC89/HAL-IRWIN COMPANY/2044 FAIRWAY LN/ROCK FORD CO   80710*

NA09871LIPV1616MAR90
KAREEN LIPVAK
161615 ELLIOTT CT
FERRIS NY  09871
73/NA09871LIPV1616MAR90/KAREEN LIPVAK/161615 ELLIOTT CT/FERRIS NY   09871*
```

5. Use the STRING statement to count the number of characters actually moved to a field.
6. When variable length names are placed in fixed-length fields, use the STRING statement to either left- or right-justify the data.

Figure 11–18 *Contents of TRANS–LABLE–FILE*

```
69/NE98221MATS3144MAR89/TATSUO MATSUDA/3144 AVENUE CT/HUGO WA  98221*
70/NE44890WILL2332NOV90/KEITH WILLIAMS/2332 19TH ST/MORNING OH  44890*
70/TI48122FURR3312JAN89/RICK FURROW/33126 CTY RD 64/SUNDIAL MI 48122*
67/NA68105GILF800 MAY91/MAJOR GILFRY/800 SOUTH 1ST/AIMES NE  68105*
67/TI69146CIMM3500APR90/D CIMMIYOTTI/3500 JFK PKWY/BIGGS TX  69146*
73/NE50293GREE206 OCT88/ROBERT GREEN/206 APT5B PLAZA BLDG/SWAN IA  50293*
80/NE65882COMPCITYJUL89/KLOSMISCKI COMPANY/CITY BANK SUITE 301/ALFRED MO  65882*
74/TI71511ADDE1141SEP91/JAMES ADDERSON/1141 MED CENTER W/UPLIFT LA  71511*
78/TI80710COMP2044DEC89/HAL-IRWIN COMPANY/2044 FAIRWAY LN/ROCK FORD CO  80710*
73/NA09871LIPV1616MAR90/KAREEN LIPVAK/161615 ELLIOTT CT/FERRIS NY  09871*
```

Common Errors

1. Misusing different consecutive delimiters in the sending field of an UN STRING.
2. Misusing the ALL option using delimiters in the sending field of an UN STRING.
3. Not initializing receiving fields in a STRING.
4. Using numeric literals in either the STRING or UNSTRING.
5. Not defining the field and giving it an initial value when using the value of the pointer in a program.
6. Not defining numeric fields as integers.
7. Not using alphanumeric fields as sending fields.
8. Not accounting for spaces in a numeric data receiving field in an UN-STRING.
9. Not checking for overflow conditions when necessary.
10. Misusing the DELIMITER IN option.

Exercises

1. Give an example (other than that discussed in this chapter) of the need to accomplish character manipulation in COBOL.

2. What is the purpose of the following:
    a. STRING statement.
    b. DELIMITED BY of the STRING statement.
    c. INTO of the STRING statement.
    d. WITH POINTER of the UNSTRING statement.
    e. OVERFLOW of the UNSTRING statement.
    f. DELIMITER IN of the UNSTRING statement.
    g. COUNT IN of the UNSTRING statement.

3. Define the following:
    a. Strings.
    b. Concatenation.
    c. Null.

4. Given:
```
05  F1  PIC XXX VALUE '123'.
05  F2  PIC X.
05  F3  PIC X.
```
What are the values of these fields after the execution of:
```
UNSTRING F1 INTO F2 F3.
```

5. Given:
```
05  F1  PIC XXX VALUE 'XYZ'.
05  F2  PIC XX.
05  F3  PIC XXXXX.
```
What are the values of F1, F2, and F3 after the execution of:
```
UNSTRING F1 DELIMITED BY ' ' INTO F2 F3.
```

6. Given:
```
01  ADDRESS-RECORD.
    05  ADD-NAME    PIC X(15).
    05  FILLER      PIC X.
    05  ADD-STREET  PIC X(15).
    05  FILLER      PIC X.
    05  ADD-STATE   PIC X(15).
```

    a. Write a STRING statement that will condense ADDRESS-RECORD into the field called CONDENSED-RECORD. Assume each sending field has as a delimiter two or more spaces at the end of the data to be transferred. Each field in CONDENSED-RECORD should be separated by *** or **.

    b. Write an UNSTRING statement to restore CONDENSED-RECORD into its original form.

7. Given:
```
01  NAME-RECORD.
    05  FIRST   PIC X(10) VALUE 'JOHN'.
    05  MIDDLE  PIC X     VALUE 'E'.
    05  LAST    PIC X(10) VALUE 'REVERE'.
```

Write a STRING statement to condense NAME-RECORD into the field CONDENSED-RECORD. The format of the condensed record is to be LAST, MIDDLE, and FIRST name order; a comma and a space after LAST; and a period and a space after MIDDLE. Allow for an overflow condition, and count the number of positions used in CONDENSED-RECORD.

8. Given: `F1 is ???165/1965/ABCDE*-M/X`

Write the UNSTRING statement for F1 that will hold the transferred data. Use five data receiving fields. Both the / and * are used as single character delimiters. Do not transfer the ??? into a receiving field. Keep track of the value of the pointer, the delimiter, the counter, and the tally for each field.

9. Given the following entries, correct only those that are in error. Assume all programmer-defined names have been properly defined.
    a. `UNSTRING F1 INTO F2 WITH POINTER.`
    b. `UNSTRING F1 F2 INTO F3 ON OVERFLOW PERFORM E100.`
    c. `UNSTRING F1 DELIMITED BY F2 OR F3 INTO F4 F5 F6.`
    d. `UNSTRING F1 DELIMITED BY ALL '*' INTO F2 DELIMITER IN D1`
          `F3 DELIMITER IN COUNT IN CL WITH POINTER P1.`
    e. `UNSTRING F1 DELIMITED BY SPACE OR '/' OR '*' INTO F2`
          `TALLING IN T1 WHEN OVERFLOW MOVE 1 TO ERROR-TOTAL.`
    f. `STRING F10 INTO F9 WITH POINTER P1.`
    g. `STRING F10 DELIMITED BY SPACE F11 DELIMITED BY SIZE`
          `',' INTO F9 WITH POINTER P2.`
    h. `STRING F10 DELIMITED BY ALL '*' INTO F9 AND F8.`
    i. `STRING F10 F11 F12 DELIMITED BY SIZE.`
    j. `STRING F15 DELIMITED BY SIZE INTO F20 F20.`

10. Given: `01  F5 PIC X(10) VALUE 'AABBCDEFAB'.`

What is the value of F5 after the execution of the following mutually exclusive INSPECT statements.
    a. `INSPECT F5 REPLACING ALL 'AB' BY 'XX'.`
    b. `INSPECT F5 REPLACING ALL 'B' BY 'C' BEFORE 'D'.`
    c. `INSPECT F5 REPLACING LEADING 'A' BY '?'.`

    d. INSPECT F5 REPLACING CHARACTERS BY ' ' BEFORE INITIAL 'F'.
    e. INSPECT F5 REPLACING LEADING 'A' BY 'B' ALL 'B' BY 'F' 'CDE' BY
        'FFF' FIRST 'A' BY 'F' BEFORE INITIAL 'F'.

11. Given: 01 F6 PIC X(10) VALUE 'ABCABC1233'.

What is the value of F6 after the execution of the following mutually exclusive
INSPECT statements. Assume initial values of WS–TALLY and WS–COUNT
are both zero.

    a. INSPECT F6 TALLYING WS–TALLY FOR CHARACTERS AFTER INITIAL 'C'.
    b. INSPECT F6 TALLYING WS–COUNT FOR ALL 'X'.
    c. INSPECT F6 TALLYING WS–TALLY FOR LEADING 'A' AFTER INITIAL 'C' WS–COUNT
        FOR ALL 'B' BEFORE INITIAL '2'.
    d. INSPECT F6 TALLYING WS–TALLY FOR ALL 'ABC'.
    e. INSPECT F6 TALLYING WS–COUNT FOR ALL 'C' AFTER INITIAL 'B' BEFORE REPLACING
        LEADING '3' BY 'C' AFTER INITIAL '1'.

Problems

1. Write a program that will print a one-page letter with the following format:

```
(NAME)
(STREET ADDRESS)
(CITY,STATE,ZIP)

DEAR (FIRST NAME):
     CONGRATULATIONS, YOUR COMMUNITY OF (CITY NAME) HAS BEEN
SELECTED AS A TEST MARKET FOR OUR NEW "WHIZ" PROMOTION.  ALL
MEMBERS OF YOUR FAMILY THAT RESIDE AT (STREET ADDRESS)
IN (CITY NAME) WILL RECEIVE A TEN DOLLAR GIFT CERTIFICATE.
     TO RECEIVE YOUR GIFT PLEASE FILL OUT THE ENCLOSED FORM
AND MAIL IT BACK TO US NO LATER THAN APRIL 1.  WE ARE SURE THAT
THE (LAST NAME) FAMILY WILL ENJOY OUR PRODUCTS.
     SINCERELY,
     THE CARE COMPANY
```

The following rules are to be followed:

    a. The name is to be printed in the order first and last with one space
        between words.
    b. The street address is to be printed as it appears on the data record.
    c. The state name is to be followed by two spaces and the zip code.
    d. The first name is to be followed by a colon on the salutations.
    e. The city name, street address, and last name in the body of the letter
        have a single space before and after the entry.
    f. Use the following data as input to the program:

Name	Street Address	City-state-zip
Matsuda, Tatsuo	3144 Avenue Ct	Hugo, Washington 98221
Williams, Keith	2332 19th Street	Morning, Ohio 44890
Gilfry, Major	800 South First	Aimes, Nebraska 68105
Cimmiyotti, D	3500 JFK Parkway	Biggs, Texas 69143
Green, Robert	206 Apt 5B Plaza Bldg	Swan, Iowa 50293

12

Interactive Systems

The development of interactive systems presents the most challenging and rewarding opportunities for the COBOL programmer. It is challenging because of the complexities of developing systems of programs that are interrelated to bring the interactive capabilities to the user. It is challenging because each vendor provides its own unique methods of developing systems, thus precluding a presentation of a standard COBOL implementation. It is challenging because of the need to make the system acceptable to the user. It is rewarding to complete a fully developed interactive system that users are comfortable with and enjoy. It is rewarding to be able to be creative in presenting to the user a system that not only satisfies their perceived needs, but also provides procedures that cannot be accomplished with batch systems.

TERMS AND STATEMENTS

ACCEPT statement	Hybrid systems	SPECIAL–NAMES
Batch systems	Interactive systems	paragraph
Cathode ray tube	Light pen	Screen development
CONSOLE IS entry	Line scrolling	guidelines
Conversational	Menu-driven	Selection screen
programming	systems	format
Customer	Multiprogramming	Teleprinter terminal
Information	Multitasking	Transaction
Control System	Multithreading	identifier
(CICS/VS)	Page scrolling	Vendor extensions
DISPLAY statement	Program function	Video Display
File browsing	keys	Terminal
Fill-in screen format	Pseudoconversational	
Hierarchical	programming	
development	Reentrant code	

Interactive Systems Concepts

Batch systems require the use of programs submitted to an operating system to process collected batches of transactions. The execution of a single batch job may include the execution of many programs, each of which may need access to several different files. Additionally, the job executes with little or no operator intervention once initiated. Each execution step must be precisely predetermined and communicated to the operating system. This is done in most systems by preparing job control statements that are submitted to the system along with COBOL programs and other system utility programs.

Conversely, **interactive systems** enable a user (usually not data processing personnel) to initiate, monitor, and change processing steps by directly interacting with the operating system through COBOL and other programs. If the user decides that a different procedure now is appropriate, a single command or selection among several commands is all that is normally necessary. Instead of the job instructions directing the system to function, the user directs the system to function.

In reality, few systems are purely interactive or purely batch. Most systems are **hybrid systems,** which indicates that both interactive and batch processes occur in the system. As an example, a user may use the interactive portion of the system throughout the day and then initiate a series of batch procedures at the end of the day. In most systems both interactive and batch procedures execute concurrently throughout the life of the system. One interactive user may be updating customer credit information, another user may be creating purchases interactively, and another user may be recording a customer sale at a point-of-sale terminal. Concurrently, a batch job may be producing commission checks for salespersons, another batch job may be updating an inventory file for orders received, and another batch job may be preparing revenue and expense projections.

The concurrent execution of both interactive and batch systems is made possible by **multiprogramming** software, which enables multiple programs to reside in the CPU at the same time. When several users are using terminals for the same purpose, the system is said to be in a **multitasking** environment. Each task request calls for the execution of a program or series of programs, and these programs may already be in use by another user. Multitasking allows multiple task requests to access the same program. Needless to say, the multiprogramming and multitasking software is extremely complex, but is of concern to the COBOL programmer only if the system affects the way COBOL programs are written.

Audit trails and file control are no less important with interactive systems and may in fact present a larger problem to consider since the system is screen oriented. When the user enters transactions into the system, a transaction register or transaction log should be maintained. This register may be the only hard-copy evidence supporting the transaction. An interactive system could totally destroy data files and their contents and accordingly warrants additional attention to control and audit trail concerns.

Interactive Terminals

Terminals used to enable the user to interact with the system are generally of two types. One type is the **teleprinter terminal,** which has a keyboard for the user to enter commands or data and a character printer, which the computer system uses to print messages on continuous-form paper. This type of terminal was widely used before the introduction of the **Video Display Terminal** (VDT). Many video display terminals utilize **cathode ray tube** technology and are called CRTs. Visual display terminals utilize a keyboard or a **light pen** for the user to enter data and a screen for the computer system to display messages to the user. An automated teller machine (ATM) is an example of a visual display terminal.

Visual display terminals enable the use of either **line scrolling** or **page scrolling** to display information. Line scrolling means that messages are displayed one line at a time, which is the same as would occur on a teleprinter. First, the computer system displays messages to the user and then the user enters appropriate responses to the system. Page scrolling means that an entire screen of information is presented to the user at one time. After the screen is presented, the user responds appropriately to the system, which may include the user entering data in several locations on the screen. Page scrolling represents the most flexible means for interactive systems.

Screen Development

Before screen development can begin, the programmer needs to know the particular characteristics of the terminal in use. For instance, most full-screen terminals allow for 24 lines of data and 80 columns to be displayed. Additionally, some systems allow highlighting, blinking, reverse video, underscoring, and color. Judicious use of a terminal's characteristics helps to make the screen more attractive and more usable for interactive users. Some terminals allow data to be entered only by a keyed entry. Others additionally allow the use of a light pen. Still others allow the use of **program function keys.** The use of a light pen or program function keys is simply a means of allowing a program to sense input other than through a keyed entry.

Screens developed for interactive systems generally take the form of either a **selection screen format** or a **fill-in screen format.** Figure 12–1 illustrates a selection format, in which the user is prompted to choose among several alternatives that are available. Once selected, the procedure is initiated, which may call for another screen to be displayed.

Figure 12–2 illustrates a fill-in format. In this format the user may enter data into appropriate locations on the screen for each field, just like filling in a form manually.

Screen Guidelines

The developer of online systems must pay particular attention to screen layout. There are several **screen development** guidelines that are covered in the following

Figure 12–1   *Selection Screen Format Example*

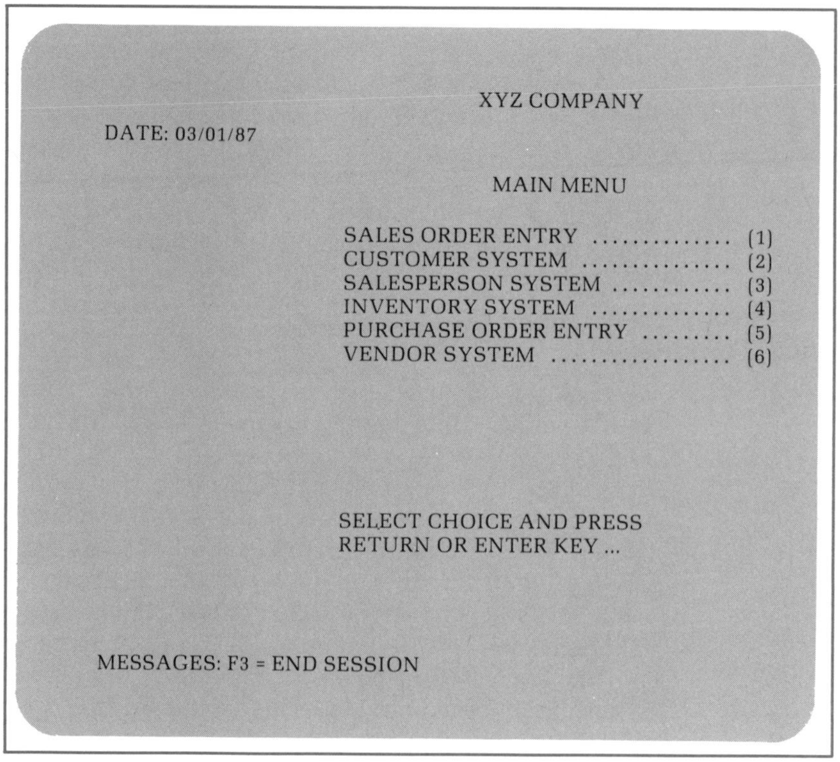

```
                              XYZ COMPANY
           DATE: 03/01/87

                              MAIN MENU

                    SALES ORDER ENTRY .............. (1)
                    CUSTOMER SYSTEM ............... (2)
                    SALESPERSON SYSTEM ........... (3)
                    INVENTORY SYSTEM  .............. (4)
                    PURCHASE ORDER ENTRY ......... (5)
                    VENDOR SYSTEM .................. (6)




                    SELECT CHOICE AND PRESS
                    RETURN OR ENTER KEY ...



           MESSAGES: F3 = END SESSION
```

Figure 12–2 *Fill-in Screen Format Example*

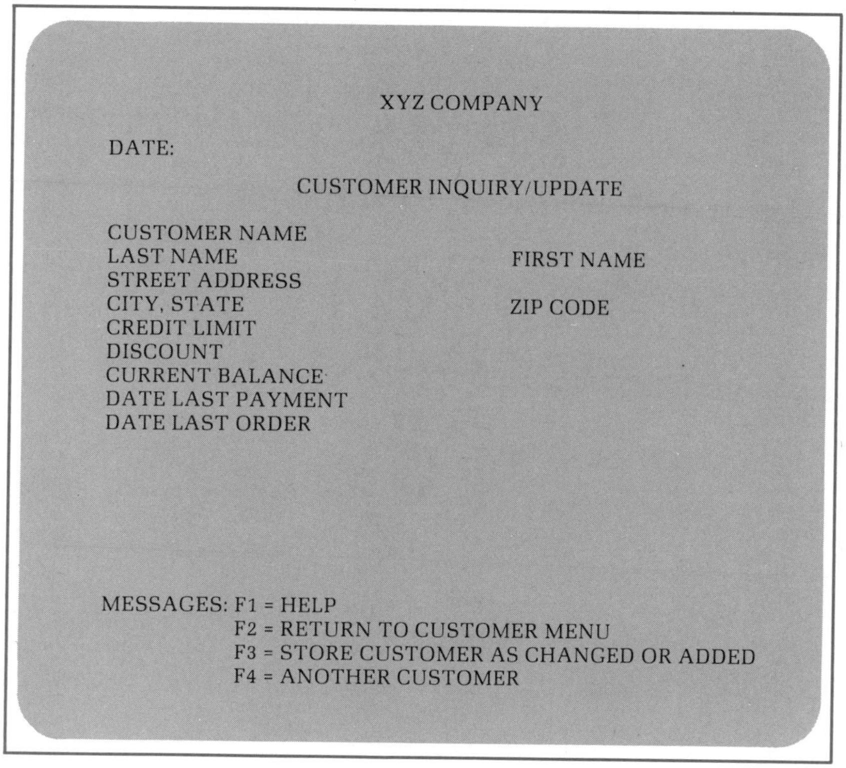

```
                        XYZ COMPANY

        DATE:

                    CUSTOMER INQUIRY/UPDATE

        CUSTOMER NAME
        LAST NAME                        FIRST NAME
        STREET ADDRESS
        CITY, STATE                      ZIP CODE
        CREDIT LIMIT
        DISCOUNT
        CURRENT BALANCE
        DATE LAST PAYMENT
        DATE LAST ORDER




        MESSAGES: F1 = HELP
                  F2 = RETURN TO CUSTOMER MENU
                  F3 = STORE CUSTOMER AS CHANGED OR ADDED
                  F4 = ANOTHER CUSTOMER
```

discussion which can be of benefit to take advantage of a full-screen visual display terminal.

1. *Involve the user.* Many organizations let the user define the screen layout. The user is the ultimate consumer of the screen and should be intimately involved in how they will interact with the system.

2. *Be consistent.* Most systems involve a series of screens. Inconsistent use of screen layouts can be very confusing. Be consistent by placing items that appear on several screens in the same location. If available, the program function keys should be used consistently from screen to screen. The screens presented in this chapter exhibit consistency as to the location of the screen name and date, the use of program function keys, and the location of messages.

3. *Use titles and dates.* Each screen should be conspicuously titled and dated so that the user does not have to guess what the screen's purpose is. If the screen is one of two or more screens for the same purpose, number the screens. For instance, data related to a particular customer may not fit on one screen. Inform the user that there are multiple screens.

4. *Do not clutter the screen.* It would be better to use multiple screens than to attempt to put everything on one screen, which may tend to make the screen confusing and frustrating.

5. *Use informative messages.* Place messages in a consistent location and ensure that the form of the message is brief and to the point. Avoid unnecessary humor and scolding. When the user makes an error, messages should be helpful, not punitive.

6. *Consider help screens.* If deemed necessary, the system could include an expanded help function for each screen, which the user could invoke when they do not understand the use of a particular screen. The amount of detail provided as messages may also vary depending on the user. A casual user

may need considerably more detailed explanations. A frequent user may not need much detail and may resent such detail, if presented.

7. *Make effective use of terminal characteristics.* Each terminal's characteristics must be taken into account when designing screens. Most terminals allow highlighting, reverse video, and color combinations. Titles and captions

Figure 12–3   *Hierarchical Menu-Driven System*

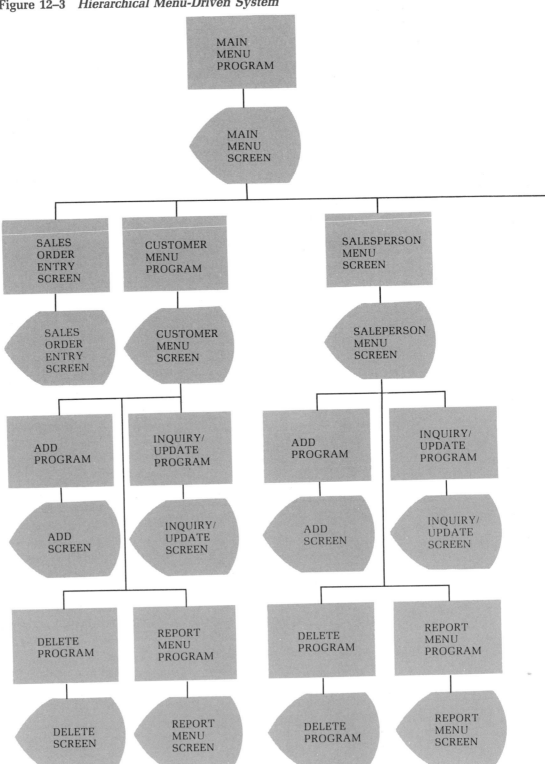

should not be highlighted, but data that are supplied by the user or the program should be highlighted. If color is available, titles and captions could be one color, user-supplied data another color, and messages still another color. Reverse video allows an item to stand out, another form of highlighting. For instance, if white on black is the normal screen mode, reverse video could make the item black on white.

8. *Use field protection.* Certain fields that contain data supplied by a program should be precluded from change by the user. For example, the date obtained from the system by the COBOL program should not be changed by the user. Other examples would be the protection of a field that a particular user is not authorized to change. A sales clerk, for instance, would not be allowed to change a customer's credit limit or current balance. The credit manager, however, may have such authorization. The screen used by these people may be the same; the protection level on given fields may be different.

9. *Use numeric lock.* Most systems allow the keyboard to be locked in numeric mode. For fields that must be filled only with numeric data, this feature precludes the user from entering nonnumeric characters and relieves the

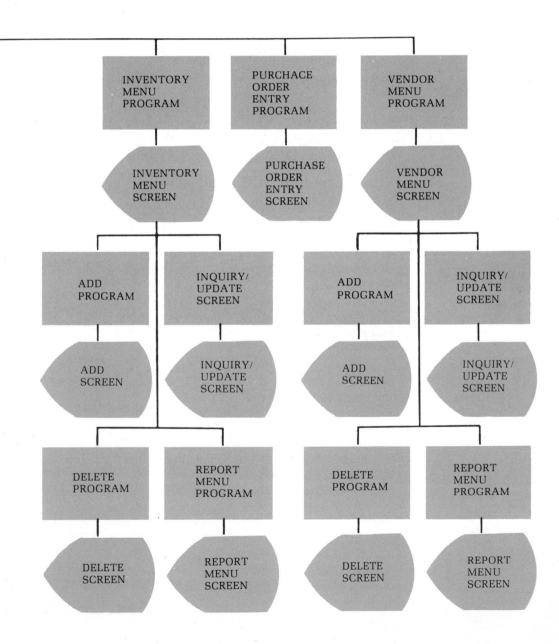

COBOL program of the need to validate for numeric characters in such fields.

Menu-Driven Systems

Many interactive systems are developed as **menu-driven systems.** That is, a user selects among various alternatives that are available in order to accomplish a desired result. Figure 12–3 presents an example structure of a menu-driven system developed in a **hierarchical development** process. Each block on this diagram represents a program, and each program may call for one or more screens to accomplish the desired result.

In this system the user would first invoke the execution of the main menu program and make a selection from among the six alternatives using the main menu screen previously shown in Figure 12–1. The selection made invokes the execution of one of the programs at the second level. Programs invoked at this level may invoke screens that allow the user to enter data into a fill-in format as would be the case for both sales order and purchase order entries or may be a sub-menu program, which allows the user to make additional selections. Menu or sub-menu programs (those that use the selection format) generally do not access online files. Fill-in formats generally do access online files.

To illustrate further development of this system, assume that the sub-menu screen invoked by the salesperson menu program was developed as shown in Figure 12–4.

In this sub-menu the user is allowed to choose among four alternatives. Once the screen is displayed and the user makes a selection, the COBOL program will need to test to determine which selection was made by the user. This selection, in turn, will invoke another COBOL program, which may also invoke another screen. At any given time during the development of an interactive system, it is possible that all parts of the system may not be available. The statements in Figure 12–5 illustrate the logic necessary to test the selection and illustrate what to do when any portion of the system is not yet developed.

Note in Figure 12–5 that a linear nested IF statement is used to ensure that only an acceptable user response has been made and to trap any invalid response. This logic assumes that the customer inquiry/update portion of the system is the only selection currently available. When that selection is made another COBOL program (and another screen) is invoked by the CALL statement. If that selection is made, an appropriate message is sent to the screen (the location of which would be at the bottom of the screen), or if program function key 3 is pressed, the system returns to the main menu.

At a later time when additional systems are brought online, the moving of a message to the comment would be replaced by an appropriate CALL statement to invoke the added system.

Figure 12–6 presents a screen that could be used for the salesperson inquiry/update function. Notice in this example, data has been provided by the COBOL program for the user to see. This is the first point in this system that a program has actually accessed a data file. Unlike batch systems that immediately process data files, menu-driven, interactive systems many times require considerable development and front-end programs before a data file is accessed.

The salesperson inquiry/update screen has several possible purposes. When first invoked, the user could enter a salesperson's number or name and have the program complete a random search for the person, either by primary or alternate key. If an update is to be made to a record, the user could enter the correct information by typing over the existing entry and then pressing program function key 5. Note that many of these fields would be protected, which would preclude their being changed by a given user of this screen. YTD SALES, for example, would

Figure 12–4   *Salesperson Sub-Menu Screen*

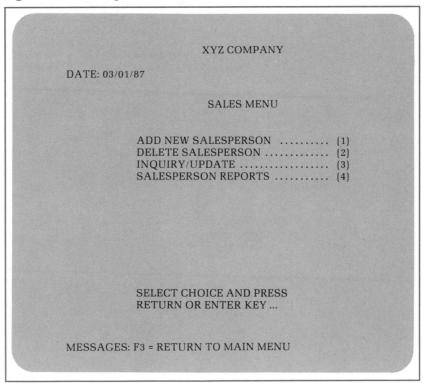

```
                          XYZ COMPANY

        DATE: 03/01/87


                           SALES MENU


            ADD NEW SALESPERSON  .........  (1)
            DELETE SALESPERSON ............  (2)
            INQUIRY/UPDATE .................  (3)
            SALESPERSON REPORTS ...........  (4)






               SELECT CHOICE AND PRESS
               RETURN OR ENTER KEY ...


        MESSAGES: F3 = RETURN TO MAIN MENU
```

Figure 12–5   *COBOL Logic to Test Selection*

```
IF ADD-NEW-SALESPERSON-REQUEST
    MOVE 'ADDING SALESPERSON NOT YET AVAILABLE' TO COMMENT
ELSE
    IF DELETE-SALESPERSON-REQUEST
        MOVE 'DELETING SALESPERSON NOT YET AVAILABLE'
            TO COMMENT
    ELSE
        IF INQUIRE-UPDATE-REQUEST
            CALL 'SALESINQ'
        ELSE
            IF SALESPERSON-REPORTS
                MOVE 'SALESPERSON REPORTS NOT YET AVAILABLE'
                    TO COMMENT
            ELSE
                IF PF3
                    MOVE 'YES' TO END-OF-SESSION-SWITCH
                ELSE
                    MOVE 'INVALID RESPONSE' TO COMMENT.
```

probably be updated when a sale is recorded in the sales order entry system and not allowed to be changed during an online inquiry. One feature inherent in online systems that is not available in batch systems is the ability to browse a file. **File browsing** means that the user can sequentially scroll through the contents of the file until the desired record is found. This is particularly beneficial when a user does not know the relevant primary key and is unsure of an alternate key. Additionally, it allows a user to simply look through the file contents on a purely informational basis. At a later time, it may be appropriate to enter into the reporting subsystem to produce more formalized, hard-copy reports. It is important to realize that there are several possible points in this system when batch processing may be invoked.

Figure 12–6 *Salesperson inquiry/Update Screen*

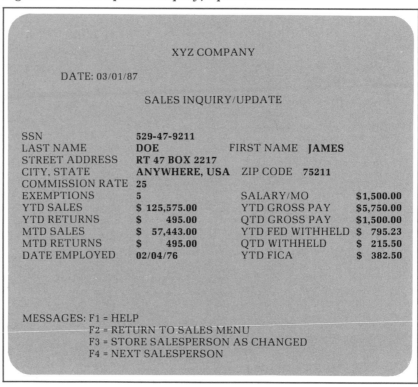

XYZ COMPANY

DATE: 03/01/87

SALES INQUIRY/UPDATE

SSN	529-47-9211		
LAST NAME	DOE	FIRST NAME	JAMES
STREET ADDRESS	RT 47 BOX 2217		
CITY, STATE	ANYWHERE, USA	ZIP CODE	75211
COMMISSION RATE	25		
EXEMPTIONS	5	SALARY/MO	$1,500.00
YTD SALES	$ 125,575.00	YTD GROSS PAY	$5,750.00
YTD RETURNS	$ 495.00	QTD GROSS PAY	$1,500.00
MTD SALES	$ 57,443.00	YTD FED WITHHELD	$ 795.23
MTD RETURNS	$ 495.00	QTD WITHHELD	$ 215.50
DATE EMPLOYED	02/04/76	YTD FICA	$ 382.50

MESSAGES: F1 = HELP
F2 = RETURN TO SALES MENU
F3 = STORE SALESPERSON AS CHANGED
F4 = NEXT SALESPERSON

Creating Screens

The actual production of interactive messages to the user and responses from the user in COBOL varies widely. Most any COBOL compiler can display and accept data from a terminal in a line-scrolling environment, and the method is fairly straightforward and standard. Creating full screens with page scrolling is a different matter, in that some vendors provide COBOL extensions to the ACCEPT and the DISPLAY statements in order to create screens, and other vendors supply systems that are external to COBOL in order to develop screens. Full-screen development in either the case of vendor-supplied COBOL extensions or vendor-supplied external systems is not standardized. There are almost as many different methods as there are vendors.

Line-Scrolling Techniques

To use COBOL in a line-scrolling environment, the **ACCEPT statement** is used to receive responses from the user, and the **DISPLAY statement** is used to provide prompting messages to the user. In order to inform the system that a terminal is to be used for input and output some systems require the use of an entry in the **SPECIAL–NAMES paragraph** of the ENVIRONMENT division. Figure 12–7 illustrates the use of the SPECIAL–NAMES entry and the standard formats of the ACCEPT and DISPLAY statements.

Note that the entry in the SPECIAL-NAMES paragraph is vendor-dependent and must be determined by referring to appropriate reference materials. The DISPLAY and ACCEPT statements are used in conjunction with each other to provide the user with appropriate messages and to allow the user to enter responses. Realize that in the line-scrolling environment the contents of the screen will change each time another ACCEPT or DISPLAY statement is executed. If a teleprinter terminal is in use the continuous-form paper will be scrolled through the carriage system, one line at a time.

Figure 12-7   *Line-Scrolling Requirements*

```
CONFIGURATION SECTION.
          .
SPECIAL-NAMES.
          .
    CONSOLE IS mnemonic-name.
          .
PROCEDURE DIVISION.
                  ⎰literal   ⎱
    DISPLAY ⎨          ⎬ UPON  mnemonic-name
                  ⎱identifier⎰
    ACCEPT identifier FROM mnemonic-name
```

Vendor Extensions for Page Scrolling

To display a full screen in a page-scrolling environment, some vendors provide COBOL extensions to the ACCEPT and DISPLAY statements. These **vendor extensions** allow text and data to be displayed in particular locations on the screen, allow data to be entered by the user at appropriate locations on the screen by controlling cursor location, and allow for other terminal characteristics such as field protection, numeric lock, reverse video, and color.

Since COBOL compilers are not standard in their COBOL extensions (some do not use COBOL extensions) it is impossible to present a standard format for either the ACCEPT or the DISPLAY statement. However, the formats shown in Figure 12-8 can be considered representative of the types of features that the reader is likely to encounter. The formats shown are a compilation of several vendors and are not representative of any single vendor.

Vendor Utilities for Page Scrolling

Several vendors supply utilities for screen development and interface systems that are necessary for a COBOL program to invoke the screen, to enable the COBOL program to load data into the screen, and to enable the COBOL program to unload data from the screen. The most widely used such system is supplied by IBM and is called **Customer Information Control System (CICS/VS).**

CICS/VS   CICS/VS is both a terminal control monitoring system and a file control system. It provides the user an interface between application programs (including COBOL and other languages) and the operating system. Several features inherent in CICS/

Figure 12-8   *Example of COBOL Extensions*

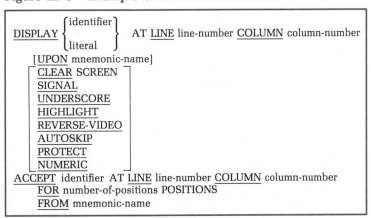

VS are important to consider because they affect the way the COBOL program using CICS/VS is written.

Multiple users executing similar tasks use only one copy of the PROCEDURE division, but a unique copy of the DATA division. This feature, called **multithreading** saves main storage but suggests that the COBOL program maintain literals as a part of the PROCEDURE division instead of the DATA division.

Since multithreading requires all users to use the same copy of the PROCEDURE division, the code must be serially reusable. This concept, called **reentrant code,** means that any values changed during the execution of the program by any given user must be restored to its original value before the task is suspended. If this is not accomplished, the next task that requests the program will not function correctly. Reentrant code also necessitates a drastic change in the structure of the COBOL program. First, the program should be limited in size. (This is true of all interactive programs.) Second, it should be written exclusively in straight-line logic. PERFORM statements and GO TO statements should be minimized and, if used at all, a branching statement should reference a procedure as close as possible to the branching statement itself.

The screen development and interface routines are developed by writing IBM Assembler programs using macros. Figure 12–9 is an example program which creates the main menu screen previously discussed.

In addition to the creation of the screen layout, executing the previously shown Assembler program creates COBOL code that the user copies into the WORKING–STORAGE section so that each relevant field can be accessed by the COBOL program. The COBOL code produced by CICS from the Assembler program is shown in Figure 12–10. Note the corresponding entries for DATECU, SYSSEL, and MESSAGE in the Assembler program to the same named fields in the COBOL code. DATECU is expressed in the COBOL code by several subfields, DATECUL, DATECUF,

Figure 12–9   *Assembler to Create Main Screen in CICS/VS*

```
MAINS1  DFHMSD  TYPE=MAP,MODE=INOUT,CTRL=FREEKB,LANG=COBOL,      X
                STORAGE=AUTO,TIOAPFX=YES
MAINA1  DFHMDI  SIZE=(24,80)
        DFHMDF  POS=(1,30),LENGTH=21,ATTRB=(ASKIP,BRT),          X
                INITIAL='X Y Z   C O M P A N Y'
        DFHMDF  POS=(3,1),LENGTH=6,INITIAL='DATE: '
DATECU  DFHMDF  POS=(3,8),LENGTH=8,ATTRB=(ASKIP,BRT)
        DFHMDF  POS=(3,34),LENGTH=9,INITIAL='MAIN MENU'
        DFHMDF  POS=(8,26),LENGTH=27,                            X
                INITIAL='SALES ORDER ENTRY...... (1)'
        DFHMDF  POS=(9,26),LENGTH=27,                            X
                INITIAL='CUSTOMER SYSTEM........ (2)'
        DFHMDF  POS=(10,26),LENGTH=27,                           X
                INITIAL='SALESPERSON SYSTEM..... (3)'
        DFHMDF  POS=(11,26),LENGTH=27,                           X
                INITIAL='INVENTORY SYSTEM....... (4)'
        DFHMDF  POS=(12,26),LENGTH=27,                           X
                INITIAL='PURCHASE ORDER ENTRY... (5)'
        DFHMDF  POS=(13,26),LENGTH=27,                           X
                INITIAL='VENDOR SYSTEM.......... (6)'
        DFHMDF  POS=(19,26),LENGTH=27,                           X
                INITIAL='SELECT CHOICE AND PRESS   '
        DFHMDF  POS=(20,26),LENGTH=23,                           X
                INITIAL='RETURN OR ENTER KEY....'
SYSSEL  DFHMDF  POS=(20,50),LENGTH=1,ATTRB=(NUM,BRT,IC)
        DFHMDF  POS=(23,1),LENGTH=26,                            X
                INITIAL='MESSAGES: F3 = END SESSION'
MESSAGE DFHMDF  POS=(24,1),LENGTH=79,ATTRB=(ASKIP,BRT)
        DFHMSD  TYPE=FINAL
        END
```

DATECUA, and DATECUI in MAINA1I and DATECUO in MAINA1O. MAINA1I is the definition of the input screen that can be read by the COBOL program, and MAINA1O is the definition of the screen that will be displayed. DATECUI is the actual definition of the field that can be read from the screen. DATECUO can be used to display the date. The other subfields are used for the length of the field entered (DATECUL), an indicator of whether the field was changed (DATECUF) and the attribute of the field (DATECUA). Notice that the PIC clause of the input field (DATECUI) is X(8), the length that was specified in the Assembler program.

Figure 12–10 *COBOL Code Generated by CICS*

```
00012    000120 WORKING-STORAGE SECTION.
00013    000130   COPY MAINA1.
00014 C       01  MAINA1I.
00015 C           02  FILLER PIC X(12).
00016 C           02  DATECUL   COMP  PIC  S9(4).
00017 C           02  DATECUF   PICTURE X.
00018 C           02  FILLER REDEFINES DATECUF.
00019 C              03 DATECUA   PICTURE X.
00020 C           02  DATECUI PIC X(8).
00021 C           02  SYSSELL   COMP  PIC  S9(4).
00022 C           02  SYSSELF   PICTURE X.
00023 C           02  FILLER REDEFINES SYSSELF.
00024 C              03 SYSSELA   PICTURE X.
00025 C           02  SYSSELI PIC X(1).
00026 C           02  MESSAGEL   COMP  PIC  S9(4).
00027 C           02  MESSAGEF   PICTURE X.
00028 C           02  FILLER REDEFINES MESSAGEF.
00029 C              03 MESSAGEA   PICTURE X.
00030 C           02  MESSAGEI PIC X(79).
00031 C       01  MAINA1O REDEFINES MAINA1I.
00032 C           02  FILLER PIC X(12).
00033 C           02  FILLER PICTURE X(3).
00034 C           02  DATECUO PIC X(8).
00035 C           02  FILLER PICTURE X(3).
00036 C           02  SYSSELO PIC X(1).
00037 C           02  FILLER PICTURE X(3).
00038 C           02  MESSAGEO PIC X(79).
```

Program 12–1 is an example of a COBOL program using command-level CICS that invokes the display of the main menu screen developed by the previous Assembler program. It also invokes another COBOL program that is to be used to read the screen to determine what action should take place next.

Programs written in CICS may be conversational or pseudoconversational. **Conversational programming** means that the COBOL program will display the screen and wait for the user's response. **Pseudoconversational programming** means that the COBOL program will invoke the screen display and then suspend operation. The reading of the user's response (by another COBOL program) will not take place until the user actually responds. The advantage of this approach is that the programs are executing only when necessary and not residing in main storage in a wait status. This concept is enabled by means of a **transaction identifier.** In batch programs, the execution of a program is invoked by submitting a job stream with appropriate JCL. To invoke a CICS program the user (or another COBOL program) enters a transaction identifier that invokes a program.

There are several COBOL statements that cannot be used when writing CICS programs. These include the use of the OPEN, CLOSE, READ, WRITE, ACCEPT, DISPLAY, EXHIBIT, INSPECT, SORT, TRACE, and UNSTRING statements. Additionally, several other features such as the use of Report Writer and CURRENT-DATE cannot be used. However, IBM has replaced many of these functions with

Program 12–1

```
000010 IDENTIFICATION DIVISION.
000020 PROGRAM-ID.    MAINA1A.
000030·······································································
000040* MAIN MENU SYSTEM - CICS/VS                                        ·
000050·······································································
000060 ENVIRONMENT DIVISION.
000070 CONFIGURATION SECTION.
000080    SOURCE-COMPUTER.  IBM-4341.
000090    OBJECT-COMPUTER.  IBM-4341.
000100·
000110 DATA DIVISION.
000120 WORKING-STORAGE SECTION.
000130      COPY MAINA1.
000140 PROCEDURE DIVISION.
000150 A000-MAIN-MENU.
000160 B100-DISPLAY-MAIN-MENU.
000170      EXEC CICS SEND MAP ('MAINA1')
000180               FREEKB
000190               ERASE
000200               MAPONLY
000210      END-EXEC.
000220 B200-LINK-TO-READ-PROGRAM.
000230      EXEC CICS LINK PROGRAM('MAINA1B') END-EXEC.
000240 B300-RETURN-TO-CICS.
000250      EXEC CICS RETURN END-EXEC.
000260      GOBACK.
```

CICS commands, such as CICS READ, CICS WRITE, CICS READNEXT (for file browsing), and CICS REWRITE. Other functions, such as opening a file are handled dynamically when access to a file is requested.

When Program 12–1 was actually compiled and stored in the library, the listing shown in Figure 12–11 was produced. The additional items from line 00039 through 00106 are automatically added by CICS and can be used by the program. For instance, EIBDATE can be used to obtain the Julian date and EIDTRNID can be used to obtain the transaction identifier.

The reader should consider this only a brief introduction to the use of CICS/VS and is referred to appropriate reference material if the system in use requires the use of CICS/VS.

Figure 12–11   *Results of Compiling Program 12–1*

```
00001    000010 IDENTIFICATION DIVISION.
00002    000020 PROGRAM-ID.    MAINA1A.
00003    000030 ·······································································
00004    000040* MAIN MENU SYSTEM - CICS/VS                                        ·
00005    000050 ·······································································
00006    000060 ENVIRONMENT DIVISION.
00007    000070 CONFIGURATION SECTION.
00008    000080    SOURCE-COMPUTER.  IBM-4341.
00009    000090    OBJECT-COMPUTER.  IBM-4341.
00010    000100·
00011    000110 DATA DIVISION.
 )12     000120 WORKING-STORAGE SECTION.
   13    000130      COPY MAINA1.
   14 C         01  MAINA1I.
```

Figure 12–11 *(continued)*

```
00015 C              02  FILLER PIC X(12).
00016 C              02  DATECUL   COMP PIC S9(4).
00017 C              02  DATECUF   PICTURE X.
00018 C              02  FILLER REDEFINES DATECUF.
00019 C                  03 DATECUA   PICTURE X.
00020 C              02  DATECUI PIC X(8).
00021 C              02  SYSSELL   COMP PIC S9(4).
00022 C              02  SYSSELF   PICTURE X.
00023 C              02  FILLER REDEFINES SYSSELF.
00024 C                  03 SYSSELA   PICTURE X.
00025 C              02  SYSSELI PIC X(1).
00026 C              02  MESSAGEL   COMP PIC S9(4).
00027 C              02  MESSAGEF   PICTURE X.
00028 C              02  FILLER REDEFINES MESSAGEF.
00029 C                  03 MESSAGEA   PICTURE X.
00030 C              02  MESSAGEI PIC X(79).
00031 C         01  MAINA1O REDEFINES MAINA1I.
00032 C              02  FILLER PIC X(12).
00033 C              02  FILLER PICTURE X(3).
00034 C              02  DATECUO  PIC X(8).
00035 C              02  FILLER PICTURE X(3).
00036 C              02  SYSSELO  PIC X(1).
00037 C              02  FILLER PICTURE X(3).
00038 C              02  MESSAGED  PIC X(79).
00039          01  DFHLDVER PIC X(22) VALUE 'LD TABLE DFHEITAB 1-6.'.
00040          01  DFHEIDO PICTURE S9(7) COMPUTATIONAL-3 VALUE ZERO.
00041          01  DFHEIBO PICTURE S9(4) COMPUTATIONAL VALUE ZERO.
00042          01  DFHEICB  PICTURE X(8) VALUE IS '        '.
00043
00044          01  DFHEIV16  COMP PIC S9(8).
00045          01  DFHEIV11  COMP PIC S9(4).
00046          01  DFHEIV12  COMP PIC S9(4).
00047          01  DFHEIV13  COMP PIC S9(4).
00048          01  DFHEIV14  COMP PIC S9(4).
00049          01  DFHEIV15  COMP PIC S9(4).
00050          01  DFHB0025  COMP PIC S9(4).
00051          01  DFHEIV5   PIC X(4).
00052          01  DFHEIV6   PIC X(4).
00053          01  DFHEIV17  PIC X(4).
00054          01  DFHEIV18  PIC X(4).
00055          01  DFHEIV19  PIC X(4).
00056          01  DFHEIV1   PIC X(8).
00057          01  DFHEIV2   PIC X(8).
00058          01  DFHEIV3   PIC X(8).
00059          01  DFHEIV20  PIC X(8).
00060          01  DFHC0084  PIC X(8).
00061          01  DFHC0085  PIC X(8).
00062          01  DFHC0320  PIC X(32).
00063          01  DFHEIV7   PIC X(2).
00064          01  DFHEIV8   PIC X(2).
00065          01  DFHC0022  PIC X(2).
00066          01  DFHC0023  PIC X(2).
00067          01  DFHEIV9   PIC X(1).
00068          01  DFHEIV10  PIC S9(7) COMP-3.
00069          01  DFHEIV4   PIC X(6).
00070          01  DFHC0070  PIC X(7).
00071          01  DFHC0071  PIC X(7).
00072          01  DFHDUMMY COMP PIC S9(4).
00073          01  DFHEIVO  PICTURE X(29).
00074          LINKAGE SECTION.
00075          01  DFHEIBLK.
00076          02  EIBTIME PIC S9(7) COMP-3.
00077          02  EIBDATE PIC S9(7) COMP-3.
00078          02  EIBTRNID PIC X(4).
```

Figure 12–11 *(concluded)*

```
00079              02      EIBTASKN PIC S9(7) COMP-3.
00080              02      EIBTRMID PIC X(4).
00081              02      DFHEIGDI COMP PIC S9(4).
00082              02      EIBCPOSN COMP PIC S9(4).
00083              02      EIBCALEN COMP PIC S9(4).
00084              02      EIBAID   PIC X(1).
00085              02      EIBFN    PIC X(2).
00086              02      EIBRCODE PIC X(6).
00087              02      EIBDS    PIC X(8).
00088              02      EIBREQID PIC X(8).
00089              02      EIBRSRCE PIC X(8).
00090              02      EIBSYNC  PIC X(1).
00091              02      EIBFREE  PIC X(1).
00092              02      EIBRECV  PIC X(1).
00093              02      EIBFIL02 PIC X(1).
00094              02      EIBATT   PIC X(1).
00095              02      EIBEOC   PIC X(1).
00096              02      EIBFMH   PIC X(1).
00097              02      EIBCOMPL PIC X(1).
00098              02      EIBSIG   PIC X(1).
00099              02      EIBCONF  PIC X(1).
00100              02      EIBERR   PIC X(1).
00101              02      EIBERRCD PIC X(4).
00102              02      EIBSYNRB PIC X(1).
00103              02      EIBNODAT PIC X(1).
00104            01    DFHCOMMAREA PICTURE X(1).
00105            01    DFHBLLSLOT1 PICTURE X(1).
00106            01    DFHBLLSLOT2 PICTURE X(1).
00107   000140 PROCEDURE DIVISION USING DFHEIBLK DFHCOMMAREA.
00108   000150 A000-IMAIN.
00109   000160 B100-DISPLAY-MAIN-MENU.
00110          *EXEC CICS SEND MAP ('MAINA1')
00111          *          FREEKB
00112          *          ERASE
00113          *          MAPONLY
00114          *END-EXEC.
00115   000170    MOVE '{     B000170  ' TO DFHEIV0
00116             MOVE 'MAINA1' TO DFHC0070
00117             CALL 'DFHEI1' USING DFHEIV0  DFHC0070 DFHEICB.
00118
00119
00120   000220 B200-LINK-TO-READ-PROGRAM.
00121          *EXEC CICS LINK PROGRAM('MAINA1B') END-EXEC.
00122   00230     MOVE '     000230  ' TO DFHEIV0
00123             MOVE 'MAINA1B' TO DFHEIV1
00124             CALL 'DFHEI1' USING DFHEIV0  DFHEIV1.
00125   000240 B300-RETURN-TO-CICS.
00126          *EXEC CICS RETURN END-EXEC.
00127   000250    MOVE '     000250  ' TO DFHEIV0
00128             CALL 'DFHEI1' USING DFHEIV0.
00129   000260    GOBACK.
```

Exercises

1. Determine if the **CONSOLE IS** entry is usable in your system and determine how the system implements line-scrolling interactive techniques.

2. Determine how your particular system accomplishes full-screen development.

Problems

1. Using line-scrolling techniques, develop and test a series of COBOL programs to create and display the screens in the chapter for the main menu, customer menu, sales menu, and inventory menu. It would be expedient to have one main program with three subprograms for the sub-menus.

2. Using full-screen techniques, develop and test a series of programs that would accomplish the same results as 1 above.

3. Using either line- or page-scrolling techniques, develop and test an interactive program that allows the inquiry/update function for the sales file in Data Set F in Appendix C.

4. Using either line- or page-scrolling techniques, develop and test an interactive program that allows the inquiry/update function for the inventory file in Data Set E in Appendix C.

5. Using either line- or page-scrolling techniques, develop and test an interactive program that allows the inquiry/update function for the customer file in Data Set P in Appendix C.

COBOL Language Formats

General Format for Identification Division

IDENTIFICATION DIVISION.

PROGRAM-ID.   program-name.

$$\begin{bmatrix} \text{AUTHOR.} & [\text{comment-entry}] \ldots \end{bmatrix}$$

$$\begin{bmatrix} \text{INSTALLATION.} & [\text{comment-entry}] \ldots \end{bmatrix}$$

$$\begin{bmatrix} \text{DATE-WRITTEN.} & [\text{comment-entry}] \ldots \end{bmatrix}$$

$$\begin{bmatrix} \text{DATE-COMPILED.} & [\text{comment-entry}] \ldots \end{bmatrix}$$

$$\begin{bmatrix} \text{SECURITY.} & [\text{comment-entry}] \ldots \end{bmatrix}$$

General Format for Environment Division

ENVIRONMENT DIVISION.

CONFIGURATION SECTION.

SOURCE-COMPUTER.   computer-name [WITH DEBUGGING MODE].

OBJECT-COMPUTER.   computer-name

$$\begin{bmatrix} \text{MEMORY SIZE integer} & \begin{Bmatrix} \text{WORDS} \\ \text{CHARACTERS} \\ \text{MODULES} \end{Bmatrix} \end{bmatrix}$$

[PROGRAM COLLATING SEQUENCE IS alphabet-name]

[SEGMENT-LIMIT IS segment-number].

[SPECIAL-NAMES. [implementor-name

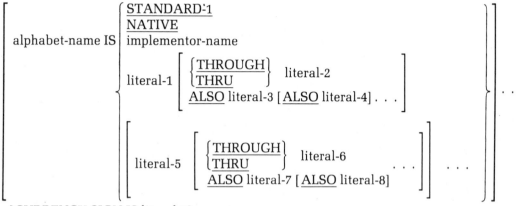

$$
\begin{Bmatrix}
\begin{bmatrix}
\text{IS mnemonic-name} \left[\underline{\text{ON}}\ \text{STATUS}\ \underline{\text{IS}}\ \text{condition-name-1}\ [\underline{\text{OFF}}\ \text{STATUS}\ \underline{\text{IS}}\ \text{condition-name-2}] \right] \\
\text{IS mnemonic-name} \left[\underline{\text{OFF}}\ \text{STATUS}\ \underline{\text{IS}}\ \text{condition-name-2}\ [\underline{\text{ON}}\ \text{STATUS}\ \underline{\text{IS}}\ \text{condition-name-1}] \right] \\
\underline{\text{ON}}\ \text{STATUS}\ \underline{\text{IS}}\ \text{condition-name-1}\ [\underline{\text{OFF}}\ \text{STATUS}\ \underline{\text{IS}}\ \text{condition-name-2}] \\
\underline{\text{OFF}}\ \text{STATUS}\ \underline{\text{IS}}\ \text{condition-name-2}\ [\underline{\text{ON}}\ \text{STATUS}\ \underline{\text{IS}}\ \text{condition-name-1}]
\end{bmatrix}
\end{Bmatrix}
$$

$$
\left[\text{alphabet-name IS} \begin{Bmatrix} \underline{\text{STANDARD-1}} \\ \underline{\text{NATIVE}} \\ \text{implementor-name} \\ \text{literal-1} \begin{bmatrix} \begin{Bmatrix} \underline{\text{THROUGH}} \\ \underline{\text{THRU}} \end{Bmatrix} \text{literal-2} \\ \underline{\text{ALSO}}\ \text{literal-3}\ [\underline{\text{ALSO}}\ \text{literal-4}]\ldots \end{bmatrix} \\ \begin{bmatrix} \text{literal-5} \begin{bmatrix} \begin{Bmatrix} \underline{\text{THROUGH}} \\ \underline{\text{THRU}} \end{Bmatrix} \text{literal-6} \\ \underline{\text{ALSO}}\ \text{literal-7}\ [\underline{\text{ALSO}}\ \text{literal-8}] \end{bmatrix} \ldots \end{bmatrix} \ldots \end{Bmatrix} \right]\ldots
$$

[CURRENCY SIGN IS literal-9]

[DECIMAL-POINT IS COMMA].]

[INPUT-OUTPUT SECTION.

FILE-CONTROL.

{file-control-entry} . . .

[I-O-CONTROL.

$$
\left[\underline{\text{RERUN}} \left[\underline{\text{ON}} \begin{Bmatrix} \text{file-name-1} \\ \text{implementor-name} \end{Bmatrix} \right] \right.
$$

$$
\left. \underline{\text{EVERY}} \begin{Bmatrix} \begin{Bmatrix} [\underline{\text{END}}\ \text{OF}] \begin{Bmatrix} \underline{\text{REEL}} \\ \underline{\text{UNIT}} \end{Bmatrix} \\ \text{integer-1}\ \underline{\text{RECORDS}} \end{Bmatrix} \text{OF file-name-2} \\ \text{integer-2}\ \underline{\text{CLOCK-UNITS}} \\ \text{condition-name} \end{Bmatrix} \right] \ldots
$$

$$
\left[\underline{\text{SAME}} \begin{bmatrix} \underline{\text{RECORD}} \\ \underline{\text{SORT}} \\ \underline{\text{SORT-MERGE}} \end{bmatrix} \text{AREA FOR file-name-3 {file-name-4}} \ldots \right] \ldots
$$

$$
\left[\underline{\text{MULTIPLE}}\ \underline{\text{FILE}}\ \text{TAPE CONTAINS file-name-5}\ [\underline{\text{POSITION}}\ \text{integer-3}] \right.
$$

$$
\left. \left[\text{file-name-6}\ [\underline{\text{POSITION}}\ \text{integer-4}] \right] \ldots \right] \ldots \Big]
$$

General Format for File Control Entry

Format 1

SELECT [OPTIONAL] file-name

    ASSIGN TO implementor-name-1 [implementor-name-2] . . .

$$\left[\text{RESERVE integer-1} \begin{bmatrix} \text{AREA} \\ \text{AREAS} \end{bmatrix} \right]$$

    [ORGANIZATION IS SEQUENTIAL]

    [ACCESS MODE IS SEQUENTIAL]

    [FILE STATUS IS data-name-1].

Format 2

SELECT file-name

    ASSIGN TO implementor-name-1 [implementor-name-2] . . .

$$\left[\text{RESERVE integer-1} \begin{bmatrix} \text{AREA} \\ \text{AREAS} \end{bmatrix} \right]$$

    ORGANIZATION IS RELATIVE

$$\left[\text{ACCESS MODE IS} \left\{ \begin{array}{l} \text{SEQUENTIAL [RELATIVE KEY IS data-name-1]} \\ \left\{ \begin{array}{l} \text{RANDOM} \\ \text{DYNAMIC} \end{array} \right\} \text{RELATIVE KEY IS data-name-1} \end{array} \right\} \right]$$

    [FILE STATUS IS data-name-2].

Format 3

SELECT file-name

    ASSIGN TO implementor-name-1 [implementor-name-2] . . .

$$\left[\text{RESERVE integer-1} \begin{bmatrix} \text{AREA} \\ \text{AREAS} \end{bmatrix} \right]$$

    ORGANIZATION IS INDEXED

$$\left[\text{ACCESS MODE IS} \left\{ \begin{array}{l} \text{SEQUENTIAL} \\ \text{RANDOM} \\ \text{DYNAMIC} \end{array} \right\} \right]$$

    RECORD KEY IS data-name-1

$$\left[\text{ALTERNATE RECORD KEY IS data-name-2 [WITH DUPLICATES]} \right] . . .$$

    [FILE STATUS IS data-name-3].

Format 4

SELECT file-name ASSIGN TO implementor-name-1 [implementor-name-2] . . .

General Format for Data Division

DATA DIVISION.

[FILE SECTION.

[FD file-name

$$\left[\underline{BLOCK} \text{ CONTAINS } [\text{integer-1 } \underline{TO}] \text{ integer-2} \begin{Bmatrix} \underline{RECORDS} \\ \underline{CHARACTERS} \end{Bmatrix} \right]$$

[RECORD CONTAINS [integer-3 TO] integer-4 CHARACTERS]

$$\underline{LABEL} \begin{Bmatrix} \underline{RECORD} \text{ IS} \\ \underline{RECORDS} \text{ ARE} \end{Bmatrix} \begin{Bmatrix} \underline{STANDARD} \\ \underline{OMITTED} \end{Bmatrix}$$

$$\left[\underline{VALUE} \ \underline{OF} \text{ implementor-name-1 IS} \begin{Bmatrix} \text{data-name-1} \\ \text{literal-1} \end{Bmatrix} \right.$$

$$\left[\text{implementor-name-2 IS} \begin{Bmatrix} \text{data-name-2} \\ \text{literal-2} \end{Bmatrix} \right] \dots \bigg]$$

$$\left[\underline{DATA} \begin{Bmatrix} \underline{RECORD} \text{ IS} \\ \underline{RECORDS} \text{ ARE} \end{Bmatrix} \text{data-name-3 [data-name-4]} \dots \right]$$

$$\left[\underline{LINAGE} \text{ IS} \begin{Bmatrix} \text{data-name-5} \\ \text{integer-5} \end{Bmatrix} \text{LINES} \left[\text{WITH } \underline{FOOTING} \text{ AT} \begin{Bmatrix} \text{data-name-6} \\ \text{integer-6} \end{Bmatrix} \right] \right.$$

$$\left. \left[\text{LINES AT } \underline{TOP} \begin{Bmatrix} \text{data-name-7} \\ \text{integer-7} \end{Bmatrix} \right] \left[\text{LINES AT } \underline{BOTTOM} \begin{Bmatrix} \text{data-name-8} \\ \text{integer-8} \end{Bmatrix} \right] \right]$$

[CODE-SET IS alphabet-name]

$$\left[\begin{Bmatrix} \underline{REPORT} \text{ IS} \\ \underline{REPORTS} \text{ ARE} \end{Bmatrix} \text{report-name-1 [report-name-2]} \dots \right].$$

[record-description-entry] . . .] . . .

[SD file-name

[RECORD CONTAINS [integer-1 TO] integer-2 CHARACTERS]

$$\left[\underline{DATA} \begin{Bmatrix} \underline{RECORD} \text{ IS} \\ \underline{RECORDS} \text{ ARE} \end{Bmatrix} \text{data-name-1 [data-name-2]} \dots \right].$$

{record-description-entry} . . .] . . .]

[WORKING-STORAGE SECTION.

$$\begin{bmatrix} \text{77-level-description-entry} \\ \text{record-description-entry} \end{bmatrix} \dots \bigg]$$

[LINKAGE SECTION.

$$\begin{bmatrix} \text{77-level-description-entry} \\ \text{record-description-entry} \end{bmatrix} \ldots]$$

[COMMUNICATION SECTION.

[communication-description-entry

[record-description-entry] . . .] . . .]

[REPORT SECTION.

[RD report-name

    [CODE literal-1]

$$\begin{bmatrix} \left\{ \begin{matrix} \text{CONTROL IS} \\ \text{CONTROLS ARE} \end{matrix} \right\} \left\{ \begin{matrix} \text{data-name-1 [data-name-2]} \ldots \\ \text{FINAL [data-name-1 [data-name-2]} \ldots] \end{matrix} \right\} \end{bmatrix}$$

$$\begin{bmatrix} \text{PAGE} \begin{bmatrix} \text{LIMIT IS} \\ \text{LIMITS ARE} \end{bmatrix} \text{integer-1} \begin{bmatrix} \text{LINE} \\ \text{LINES} \end{bmatrix} [\text{HEADING integer-2}] \end{bmatrix}$$

        [FIRST DETAIL integer-3] [LAST DETAIL integer-4]

$$\begin{matrix} [\text{FOOTING integer-5}] \end{matrix} \Big].$$

  {report-group-description-entry} . . .] . . .]

General Format for Data Description Entry

Format 1

$$\text{level-number} \left\{ \begin{matrix} \text{data-name-1} \\ \text{FILLER} \end{matrix} \right\}$$

    [REDEFINES data-name-2]

$$\begin{bmatrix} \left\{ \begin{matrix} \text{PICTURE} \\ \text{PIC} \end{matrix} \right\} \text{IS character-string} \end{bmatrix}$$

$$\begin{bmatrix} [\text{USAGE IS}] \left\{ \begin{matrix} \text{COMPUTATIONAL} \\ \text{COMP} \\ \text{DISPLAY} \\ \text{INDEX} \end{matrix} \right\} \end{bmatrix}$$

$$\begin{bmatrix} [\text{SIGN IS}] \left\{ \begin{matrix} \text{LEADING} \\ \text{TRAILING} \end{matrix} \right\} [\text{SEPARATE CHARACTER}] \end{bmatrix}$$

$$\begin{bmatrix} \text{OCCURS} \left\{ \begin{matrix} \text{integer-1 TO integer-2 TIMES DEPENDING ON data-name-3} \\ \text{integer-2 TIMES} \end{matrix} \right. \end{bmatrix}$$

$$\left[\begin{Bmatrix} \underline{\text{ASCENDING}} \\ \underline{\text{DESCENDING}} \end{Bmatrix} \text{KEY IS data-name-4 [data-name-5]} \ldots \right] \ldots$$

$$[\underline{\text{INDEXED}} \text{ BY index-name-1 [index-name-2]} \ldots]$$

$$\left[\begin{Bmatrix} \underline{\text{SYNCHRONIZED}} \\ \underline{\text{SYNC}} \end{Bmatrix} \begin{bmatrix} \underline{\text{LEFT}} \\ \underline{\text{RIGHT}} \end{bmatrix} \right]$$

$$\left[\begin{Bmatrix} \underline{\text{JUSTIFIED}} \\ \underline{\text{JUST}} \end{Bmatrix} \text{RIGHT} \right]$$

$$[\underline{\text{BLANK}} \text{ WHEN } \underline{\text{ZERO}}]$$

$$[\underline{\text{VALUE}} \text{ IS literal}].$$

Format 2

$$\text{66 data-name-1 } \underline{\text{RENAMES}} \text{ data-name-2} \left[\begin{Bmatrix} \underline{\text{THROUGH}} \\ \underline{\text{THRU}} \end{Bmatrix} \text{data-name-3} \right].$$

Format 3

$$\text{88 condition-name} \begin{Bmatrix} \underline{\text{VALUE}} \text{ IS} \\ \underline{\text{VALUES}} \text{ ARE} \end{Bmatrix} \text{literal-1} \left[\begin{Bmatrix} \underline{\text{THROUGH}} \\ \underline{\text{THRU}} \end{Bmatrix} \text{literal-2} \right]$$

$$\left[\text{literal-3} \left[\begin{Bmatrix} \underline{\text{THROUGH}} \\ \underline{\text{THRU}} \end{Bmatrix} \text{literal-4} \right] \right] \ldots .$$

General Format for Communication Description Entry

Format 1

$$\underline{\text{CD}} \text{ cd-name}$$

$$\text{FOR [}\underline{\text{INITIAL}}\text{] } \underline{\text{INPUT}} \left[\begin{array}{l} [\text{SYMBOLIC } \underline{\text{QUEUE}} \text{ IS data-name-1}] \\ [\text{SYMBOLIC } \underline{\text{SUB-QUEUE-1}} \text{ IS data-name-2}] \\ [\text{SYMBOLIC } \underline{\text{SUB-QUEUE-2}} \text{ IS data-name-3}] \\ [\text{SYMBOLIC } \underline{\text{SUB-QUEUE-3}} \text{ IS data-name-4}] \\ [\underline{\text{MESSAGE}} \ \underline{\text{DATE}} \text{ IS data-name-5}] \\ [\underline{\text{MESSAGE}} \ \underline{\text{TIME}} \text{ IS data-name-6}] \\ [\text{SYMBOLIC } \underline{\text{SOURCE}} \text{ IS data-name-7}] \\ [\underline{\text{TEXT}} \ \underline{\text{LENGTH}} \text{ IS data-name-8}] \\ [\underline{\text{END}} \ \underline{\text{KEY}} \text{ IS data-name-9}] \\ [\underline{\text{STATUS}} \ \underline{\text{KEY}} \text{ IS data-name-10}] \\ [\underline{\text{MESSAGE}} \ \underline{\text{COUNT}} \text{ IS data-name-11}] \\ [\text{data-name-1 \ data-name-2} \ldots \text{data-name-11}] \end{array} \right]$$

Format 2

CD cd-name; FOR OUTPUT

    [DESTINATION COUNT IS data-name-1]

    [TEXT LENGTH IS data-name-2]

    [STATUS KEY IS data-name-3]

    [DESTINATION TABLE OCCURS integer-2 TIMES

        $\left[\text{INDEXED BY index-name-1 [index-name-2]} \ldots \right]$]

    [ERROR KEY IS data-name-4]

    [SYMBOLIC DESTINATION IS data-name-5].

General Format for Report Group Description Entry

Format 1

01 [data-name-1]

$$\left[\text{LINE NUMBER IS} \begin{Bmatrix} \text{integer-1 [ON NEXT PAGE]} \\ \text{PLUS integer-2} \end{Bmatrix} \right]$$

$$\left[\text{NEXT GROUP IS} \begin{Bmatrix} \text{integer-3} \\ \text{PLUS integer-4} \\ \text{NEXT PAGE} \end{Bmatrix} \right]$$

$$\underline{\text{TYPE}} \text{ IS} \begin{Bmatrix} \begin{Bmatrix} \text{REPORT HEADING} \\ \text{RH} \end{Bmatrix} \\ \begin{Bmatrix} \text{PAGE HEADING} \\ \text{PH} \end{Bmatrix} \\ \begin{Bmatrix} \text{CONTROL HEADING} \\ \text{CH} \end{Bmatrix} \begin{Bmatrix} \text{data-name-2} \\ \text{FINAL} \end{Bmatrix} \\ \begin{Bmatrix} \text{DETAIL} \\ \text{DE} \end{Bmatrix} \\ \begin{Bmatrix} \text{CONTROL FOOTING} \\ \text{CF} \end{Bmatrix} \begin{Bmatrix} \text{data-name-3} \\ \text{FINAL} \end{Bmatrix} \\ \begin{Bmatrix} \text{PAGE FOOTING} \\ \text{PF} \end{Bmatrix} \\ \begin{Bmatrix} \text{REPORT FOOTING} \\ \text{RF} \end{Bmatrix} \end{Bmatrix}$$

$$\left[\text{[USAGE IS] DISPLAY} \right].$$

Format 2

level-number [data-name-1]

$$\left[\text{LINE NUMBER IS} \begin{Bmatrix} \text{integer-1 [ON NEXT PAGE]} \\ \text{PLUS integer-2} \end{Bmatrix} \right]$$

$$\left[\text{[USAGE IS] DISPLAY} \right].$$

Format 3

level-number [data-name-1]

[BLANK WHEN ZERO]

[GROUP INDICATE]

$$\left[\left\{ \begin{array}{l} \underline{\text{JUSTIFIED}} \\ \underline{\text{JUST}} \end{array} \right\} \text{RIGHT} \right]$$

$$\left[\underline{\text{LINE}} \text{ NUMBER IS} \left\{ \begin{array}{l} \text{integer-1 [ON } \underline{\text{NEXT}}\ \underline{\text{PAGE}}] \\ \underline{\text{PLUS}} \text{ integer-2} \end{array} \right\} \right]$$

[COLUMN NUMBER IS integer-3]

$$\left\{ \begin{array}{l} \underline{\text{PICTURE}} \\ \underline{\text{PIC}} \end{array} \right\} \text{IS character-string}$$

$$\left\{ \begin{array}{l} \underline{\text{SOURCE}} \text{ IS identifier-1} \\ \\ \underline{\text{VALUE}} \text{ IS literal} \\ \\ \{\underline{\text{SUM}} \text{ identifier-2 [identifier-3]} \ldots \\ \qquad \left[\underline{\text{UPON}} \text{ data-name-2 [data-name-3]} \ldots \right] \} \ldots \\ \qquad \left[\underline{\text{RESET}} \text{ ON} \left\{ \begin{array}{l} \text{data-name-4} \\ \underline{\text{FINAL}} \end{array} \right\} \right] \end{array} \right\}$$

$$\left[\text{[}\underline{\text{USAGE}} \text{ IS]} \ \underline{\text{DISPLAY}} \right].$$

General Format for Procedure Division

Format 1

PROCEDURE DIVISION [USING data-name-1 [data-name-2] . . .] .

[DECLARATIVES.

{section-name SECTION [segment-number] . declarative-sentence

[paragraph-name. [sentence] . . .] . . . } . . .

END DECLARATIVES.]

$$\left\{ \begin{array}{l} \text{section-name } \underline{\text{SECTION}} \text{ [segment-number].} \\ \left[\text{paragraph-name. [sentence]} \ldots \right] \ldots \end{array} \right\} \ldots$$

Format 2

$$\text{PROCEDURE DIVISION} \left[\underline{\text{USING}} \text{ data-name-1 [data-name-2]} \ldots \right].$$

{paragraph-name. [sentence] . . . } . . .

General Format for Verbs

ACCEPT identifier [FROM mnemonic-name]

ACCEPT identifier FROM $\begin{Bmatrix} \text{DATE} \\ \text{DAY} \\ \text{TIME} \end{Bmatrix}$

ACCEPT cd-name MESSAGE COUNT

ADD $\begin{Bmatrix} \text{identifier-1} \\ \text{literal-1} \end{Bmatrix}$ $\begin{bmatrix} \text{identifier-2} \\ \text{literal-2} \end{bmatrix}$ . . . TO identifier-m [ROUNDED]

$\begin{bmatrix} \text{identifier-n [ROUNDED]} \end{bmatrix}$ . . . [ON SIZE ERROR imperative-statement]

ADD $\begin{Bmatrix} \text{identifier-1} \\ \text{literal-1} \end{Bmatrix}$ $\begin{Bmatrix} \text{identifier-2} \\ \text{literal-2} \end{Bmatrix}$ $\begin{bmatrix} \text{identifier-3} \\ \text{literal-3} \end{bmatrix}$ . . .

GIVING identifier-m [ROUNDED] $\begin{bmatrix} \text{identifier-n [ROUNDED]} \end{bmatrix}$ . . .

[ON SIZE ERROR imperative-statement]

ADD $\begin{Bmatrix} \text{CORRESPONDING} \\ \text{CORR} \end{Bmatrix}$ identifier-1 TO identifier-2 [ROUNDED]

[ON SIZE ERROR imperative-statement]

ALTER procedure-name-1 TO [PROCEED TO] procedure-name-2

$\begin{bmatrix} \text{procedure-name-3 TO [PROCEED TO] procedure-name-4} \end{bmatrix}$ . . .

CALL $\begin{Bmatrix} \text{identifier-1} \\ \text{literal-1} \end{Bmatrix}$ $\begin{bmatrix} \text{USING data-name-1 [data-name-2] . . .} \end{bmatrix}$

[ON OVERFLOW imperative-statement]

CANCEL $\begin{Bmatrix} \text{identifier-1} \\ \text{literal-1} \end{Bmatrix}$ $\begin{bmatrix} \text{identifier-2} \\ \text{literal-2} \end{bmatrix}$ . . .

CLOSE file-name-1 $\begin{bmatrix} \begin{Bmatrix} \text{REEL} \\ \text{UNIT} \end{Bmatrix} \begin{bmatrix} \text{WITH NO REWIND} \\ \text{FOR REMOVAL} \end{bmatrix} \\ \text{With } \begin{Bmatrix} \text{NO REWIND} \\ \text{LOCK} \end{Bmatrix} \end{bmatrix}$

$\begin{bmatrix} \text{file-name-2} \begin{bmatrix} \begin{Bmatrix} \text{REEL} \\ \text{UNIT} \end{Bmatrix} \begin{bmatrix} \text{WITH NO REWIND} \\ \text{FOR REMOVAL} \end{bmatrix} \\ \text{WITH } \begin{Bmatrix} \text{NO REWIND} \\ \text{LOCK} \end{Bmatrix} \end{bmatrix} \end{bmatrix}$ . . .

CLOSE file-name-1 [WITH LOCK] $\begin{bmatrix} \text{file-name-2 [WITH LOCK]} \end{bmatrix}$ . . .

COMPUTE identifier-1 [ROUNDED] $\begin{bmatrix} \text{identifier-2 [ROUNDED]} \end{bmatrix}$ . . .

= arithmetic-expression [ON SIZE ERROR imperative-statement]

DELETE file-name RECORD [INVALID KEY imperative-statement]

DISABLE $\begin{Bmatrix} \text{INPUT [TERMINAL]} \\ \text{OUTPUT} \end{Bmatrix}$ cd-name WITH KEY $\begin{Bmatrix} \text{identifier-1} \\ \text{literal-1} \end{Bmatrix}$

DISPLAY $\begin{Bmatrix} \text{identifier-1} \\ \text{literal-1} \end{Bmatrix}$ $\begin{bmatrix} \text{identifier-2} \\ \text{literal-2} \end{bmatrix}$ . . . [UPON mnemonic-name]

DIVIDE $\begin{Bmatrix} \text{identifier-1} \\ \text{literal-1} \end{Bmatrix}$ INTO identifier-2 [ROUNDED]

$\begin{bmatrix} \text{identifier-3 [ROUNDED]} \end{bmatrix}$ . . . [ON SIZE ERROR imperative-statement]

DIVIDE $\begin{Bmatrix} \text{identifier-1} \\ \text{literal-1} \end{Bmatrix}$ INTO $\begin{Bmatrix} \text{identifier-2} \\ \text{literal-2} \end{Bmatrix}$ GIVING identifier-3 [ROUNDED]

$\begin{bmatrix} \text{identifier-4 [ROUNDED]} \end{bmatrix}$ . . . [ON SIZE ERROR imperative-statement]

DIVIDE $\begin{Bmatrix} \text{identifier-1} \\ \text{literal-1} \end{Bmatrix}$ BY $\begin{Bmatrix} \text{identifier-2} \\ \text{literal-2} \end{Bmatrix}$ GIVING identifier-3 [ROUNDED]

$\begin{bmatrix} \text{identifier-4 [ROUNDED]} \end{bmatrix}$ . . . [ON SIZE ERROR imperative-statement]

DIVIDE $\begin{Bmatrix} \text{identifier-1} \\ \text{literal-1} \end{Bmatrix}$ INTO $\begin{Bmatrix} \text{identifier-2} \\ \text{literal-2} \end{Bmatrix}$ GIVING identifier-3 [ROUNDED]

REMAINDER identifier-4 [ON SIZE ERROR imperative-statement]

DIVIDE $\begin{Bmatrix} \text{identifier-1} \\ \text{literal-1} \end{Bmatrix}$ BY $\begin{Bmatrix} \text{identifier-2} \\ \text{literal-2} \end{Bmatrix}$ GIVING identifier-3 [ROUNDED]

REMAINDER identifier-4 [ON SIZE ERROR imperative-statement]

ENABLE $\begin{Bmatrix} \text{INPUT [TERMINAL]} \\ \text{OUTPUT} \end{Bmatrix}$ cd-name WITH KEY $\begin{Bmatrix} \text{identifier-1} \\ \text{literal-1} \end{Bmatrix}$

ENTER language-name [routine-name].

EXIT [PROGRAM].

GENERATE $\begin{Bmatrix} \text{data-name} \\ \text{report-name} \end{Bmatrix}$

GO TO [procedure-name-1]

GO TO procedure-name-1 [procedure-name-2] . . . procedure-name-n

DEPENDING ON identifier

IF condition; $\begin{Bmatrix} \text{statement-1} \\ \text{NEXT SENTENCE} \end{Bmatrix}$ $\begin{Bmatrix} \text{ELSE statement-2} \\ \text{ELSE NEXT SENTENCE} \end{Bmatrix}$

INITIATE report-name-1 [report-name-2] . . .

INSPECT identifier-1 TALLYING

$$\left\{ \text{identifier-2 } \underline{\text{FOR}} \left\{ \left\{ \begin{array}{l} \underline{\text{ALL}} \\ \underline{\text{LEADING}} \\ \underline{\text{CHARACTERS}} \end{array} \right\} \left\{ \begin{array}{l} \text{identifier-3} \\ \text{literal-1} \end{array} \right\} \right\} \left[\left\{ \begin{array}{l} \underline{\text{BEFORE}} \\ \underline{\text{AFTER}} \end{array} \right\} \text{INITIAL} \left\{ \begin{array}{l} \text{identifier-4} \\ \text{literal-2} \end{array} \right\} \right] \right\} \cdots \right\} \cdots$$

$\underline{\text{INSPECT}}$ identifier-1 $\underline{\text{REPLACING}}$

$$\left\{ \begin{array}{l} \underline{\text{CHARACTERS}} \underline{\text{BY}} \left\{ \begin{array}{l} \text{identifier-6} \\ \text{literal-4} \end{array} \right\} \left[\left\{ \begin{array}{l} \underline{\text{BEFORE}} \\ \underline{\text{AFTER}} \end{array} \right\} \text{INITIAL} \left\{ \begin{array}{l} \text{identifier-7} \\ \text{literal-5} \end{array} \right\} \right] \\ \left\{ \left\{ \begin{array}{l} \underline{\text{ALL}} \\ \underline{\text{LEADING}} \\ \underline{\text{FIRST}} \end{array} \right\} \left\{ \begin{array}{l} \text{identifier-5} \\ \text{literal-3} \end{array} \right\} \underline{\text{BY}} \left\{ \begin{array}{l} \text{identifier-6} \\ \text{literal-4} \end{array} \right\} \left[\left\{ \begin{array}{l} \underline{\text{BEFORE}} \\ \underline{\text{AFTER}} \end{array} \right\} \text{INITIAL} \left\{ \begin{array}{l} \text{identifier-7} \\ \text{literal-5} \end{array} \right\} \right] \right\} \cdots \right\} \cdots \end{array} \right\}$$

$\underline{\text{INSPECT}}$ identifier-1 $\underline{\text{TALLYING}}$

$$\left\{ \text{identifier-2 } \underline{\text{FOR}} \left\{ \left\{ \begin{array}{l} \underline{\text{ALL}} \\ \underline{\text{LEADING}} \\ \underline{\text{CHARACTERS}} \end{array} \right\} \left\{ \begin{array}{l} \text{identifier-3} \\ \text{literal-1} \end{array} \right\} \right\} \left[\left\{ \begin{array}{l} \underline{\text{BEFORE}} \\ \underline{\text{AFTER}} \end{array} \right\} \text{INITIAL} \left\{ \begin{array}{l} \text{identifier-4} \\ \text{literal-2} \end{array} \right\} \right] \right\} \cdots \right\} \cdots$$

$\underline{\text{REPLACING}}$

$$\left\{ \begin{array}{l} \underline{\text{CHARACTERS}} \underline{\text{BY}} \left\{ \begin{array}{l} \text{identifier-6} \\ \text{literal-4} \end{array} \right\} \left[\left\{ \begin{array}{l} \underline{\text{BEFORE}} \\ \underline{\text{AFTER}} \end{array} \right\} \text{INITIAL} \left\{ \begin{array}{l} \text{identifier-7} \\ \text{literal-5} \end{array} \right\} \right] \\ \left\{ \left\{ \begin{array}{l} \underline{\text{ALL}} \\ \underline{\text{LEADING}} \\ \underline{\text{FIRST}} \end{array} \right\} \left\{ \begin{array}{l} \text{identifier-5} \\ \text{literal-3} \end{array} \right\} \underline{\text{BY}} \left\{ \begin{array}{l} \text{identifier-6} \\ \text{literal-4} \end{array} \right\} \left[\left\{ \begin{array}{l} \underline{\text{BEFORE}} \\ \underline{\text{AFTER}} \end{array} \right\} \text{INITIAL} \left\{ \begin{array}{l} \text{identifier-7} \\ \text{literal-5} \end{array} \right\} \right] \right\} \cdots \right\} \cdots \end{array} \right\}$$

$\underline{\text{MERGE}}$ file-name-1 ON $\left\{ \begin{array}{l} \underline{\text{ASCENDING}} \\ \underline{\text{DESCENDING}} \end{array} \right\}$ KEY data-name-1 [data-name-2] . . .

$$\left[\text{ON} \left\{ \begin{array}{l} \underline{\text{ASCENDING}} \\ \underline{\text{DESCENDING}} \end{array} \right\} \text{KEY data-name-3 [data-name-4]} \cdots \right] \cdots$$

[COLLATING $\underline{\text{SEQUENCE}}$ IS alphabet-name]

$\underline{\text{USING}}$ file-name-2 file-name-3 [file-name-4] . . .

$$\left\{ \begin{array}{l} \underline{\text{OUTPUT}} \underline{\text{PROCEDURE}} \text{ IS section-name-1} \left[\left\{ \begin{array}{l} \underline{\text{THROUGH}} \\ \underline{\text{THRU}} \end{array} \right\} \text{section-name-2} \right] \\ \underline{\text{GIVING}} \text{ file-name-5} \end{array} \right\}$$

$\underline{\text{MOVE}}$ $\left\{ \begin{array}{l} \text{identifier-1} \\ \text{literal-1} \end{array} \right\}$ $\underline{\text{TO}}$ identifier-2 [identifier-3] . . .

$\underline{\text{MOVE}}$ $\left\{ \begin{array}{l} \underline{\text{CORRESPONDING}} \\ \underline{\text{CORR}} \end{array} \right\}$ identifier-1 $\underline{\text{TO}}$ identifier-2

$\underline{\text{MULTIPLY}}$ $\left\{ \begin{array}{l} \text{identifier-1} \\ \text{literal-1} \end{array} \right\}$ $\underline{\text{BY}}$ identifier-2 [$\underline{\text{ROUNDED}}$]

$\left[\text{identifier-3 [}\underline{\text{ROUNDED}}\text{]} \right]$ . . . [ON $\underline{\text{SIZE}}$ $\underline{\text{ERROR}}$ imperative-statement]

$\underline{\text{MULTIPLY}}$ $\left\{ \begin{array}{l} \text{identifier-1} \\ \text{literal-1} \end{array} \right\}$ $\underline{\text{BY}}$ $\left\{ \begin{array}{l} \text{identifier-2} \\ \text{literal-2} \end{array} \right\}$ $\underline{\text{GIVING}}$ identifier-3 [$\underline{\text{ROUNDED}}$]

$\left[\text{identifier-4 [}\underline{\text{ROUNDED}}\text{]} \right]$ . . . [ON $\underline{\text{SIZE}}$ $\underline{\text{ERROR}}$ imperative-statement]

$$\underline{\text{OPEN}} \begin{Bmatrix} \underline{\text{INPUT}} \text{ file-name-1} \begin{bmatrix} \underline{\text{REVERSED}} \\ \text{WITH } \underline{\text{NO}} \text{ REWIND} \end{bmatrix} \begin{bmatrix} \text{file-name-2} \begin{bmatrix} \underline{\text{REVERSED}} \\ \text{WITH } \underline{\text{NO}} \text{ REWIND} \end{bmatrix} \end{bmatrix} \dots \\ \underline{\text{OUTPUT}} \text{ file-name-3 [WITH } \underline{\text{NO}} \text{ REWIND]} \begin{bmatrix} \text{file-name-4 [WITH } \underline{\text{NO}} \text{ REWIND]} \end{bmatrix} \dots \\ \underline{\text{I-O}} \text{ file-name-5 [file-name-6]} \dots \\ \underline{\text{EXTEND}} \text{ file-name-7 [file-name-8]} \dots \end{Bmatrix} \dots$$

$$\underline{\text{OPEN}} \begin{Bmatrix} \underline{\text{INPUT}} \text{ file-name-1 [file-name-2]} \dots \\ \underline{\text{OUTPUT}} \text{ file-name-3 [file-name-4]} \dots \\ \underline{\text{I-O}} \text{ file-name-5 [file-name-6]} \dots \end{Bmatrix} \dots$$

$$\underline{\text{PERFORM}} \text{ procedure-name-1} \begin{bmatrix} \begin{Bmatrix} \underline{\text{THROUGH}} \\ \underline{\text{THRU}} \end{Bmatrix} \text{procedure-name-2} \end{bmatrix}$$

$$\underline{\text{PERFORM}} \text{ procedure-name-1} \begin{bmatrix} \begin{Bmatrix} \underline{\text{THROUGH}} \\ \underline{\text{THRU}} \end{Bmatrix} \text{procedure-name-2} \end{bmatrix} \begin{Bmatrix} \text{identifier-1} \\ \text{integer-1} \end{Bmatrix} \underline{\text{TIMES}}$$

$$\underline{\text{PERFORM}} \text{ procedure-name-1} \begin{bmatrix} \begin{Bmatrix} \underline{\text{THROUGH}} \\ \underline{\text{THRU}} \end{Bmatrix} \text{procedure-name-2} \end{bmatrix} \underline{\text{UNTIL}} \text{ condition-1}$$

$$\underline{\text{PERFORM}} \text{ procedure-name-1} \begin{bmatrix} \begin{Bmatrix} \underline{\text{THROUGH}} \\ \underline{\text{THRU}} \end{Bmatrix} \text{procedure-name-2} \end{bmatrix}$$

$$\underline{\text{VARYING}} \begin{Bmatrix} \text{identifier-2} \\ \text{index-name-1} \end{Bmatrix} \underline{\text{FROM}} \begin{Bmatrix} \text{identifier-3} \\ \text{index-name-2} \\ \text{literal-1} \end{Bmatrix}$$

$$\underline{\text{BY}} \begin{Bmatrix} \text{identifier-4} \\ \text{literal-3} \end{Bmatrix} \underline{\text{UNTIL}} \text{ condition-1}$$

$$\begin{bmatrix} \underline{\text{AFTER}} \begin{Bmatrix} \text{identifier-5} \\ \text{index-name-3} \end{Bmatrix} \underline{\text{FROM}} \begin{Bmatrix} \text{identifier-6} \\ \text{index-name-4} \\ \text{literal-3} \end{Bmatrix} \end{bmatrix}$$

$$\underline{\text{BY}} \begin{Bmatrix} \text{identifier-7} \\ \text{literal-4} \end{Bmatrix} \underline{\text{UNTIL}} \text{ condition-2}$$

$$\begin{bmatrix} \underline{\text{AFTER}} \begin{Bmatrix} \text{identifier-8} \\ \text{index-name-5} \end{Bmatrix} \underline{\text{FROM}} \begin{Bmatrix} \text{identifier-9} \\ \text{index-name-6} \\ \text{literal-5} \end{Bmatrix} \end{bmatrix}$$

$$\underline{\text{BY}} \begin{Bmatrix} \text{identifier-10} \\ \text{literal-6} \end{Bmatrix} \underline{\text{UNTIL}} \text{ condition-3}$$

$\underline{\text{READ}}$ file-name RECORD [$\underline{\text{INTO}}$ identifier] [AT $\underline{\text{END}}$ imperative-statement]

$\underline{\text{Read}}$ file-name [$\underline{\text{NEXT}}$] RECORD [$\underline{\text{INTO}}$ identifier]

[AT $\underline{\text{END}}$ imperative-statement]

$\underline{\text{READ}}$ file-name RECORD [$\underline{\text{INTO}}$ identifier] [$\underline{\text{INVALID}}$ KEY imperative-statement]

$\underline{\text{READ}}$ file-name RECORD [$\underline{\text{INTO}}$ identifier]

[$\underline{\text{KEY}}$ IS data-name]

[$\underline{\text{INVALID}}$ KEY imperative-statement]

$\underline{\text{RECEIVE}}$ cd-name $\begin{Bmatrix} \underline{\text{MESSAGE}} \\ \underline{\text{SEGMENT}} \end{Bmatrix}$ $\underline{\text{INTO}}$ identifier-1 [$\underline{\text{NO}}$ $\underline{\text{DATA}}$ imperative-statement]

RELEASE record-name [FROM identifier]

RETURN file-name RECORD [INTO identifier] AT END imperative-statement

REWRITE record-name [FROM identifier]

REWRITE record-name [FROM identifier] [INVALID KEY imperative-statement]

SEARCH identifier-1 $\left[\text{VARYING} \begin{Bmatrix} \text{identifier-2} \\ \text{index-name-1} \end{Bmatrix}\right]$ [AT END imperative-statement-1]

$\quad$ WHEN condition-1 $\begin{Bmatrix} \text{imperative-statement-2} \\ \text{NEXT SENTENCE} \end{Bmatrix}$

$\quad \left[\text{WHEN condition-2} \begin{Bmatrix} \text{imperative-statement-3} \\ \text{NEXT SENTENCE} \end{Bmatrix}\right] \ldots$

SEARCH ALL identifier-1 [AT END imperative-statement-1]

$\quad$ WHEN $\begin{Bmatrix} \text{data-name-1} \begin{Bmatrix} \text{IS EQUAL TO} \\ \text{IS} = \end{Bmatrix} \begin{Bmatrix} \text{identifier-3} \\ \text{literal-1} \\ \text{arithmetic-expression-1} \end{Bmatrix} \\ \text{condition-name-1} \end{Bmatrix}$

$\quad \left[\underline{\text{AND}} \begin{Bmatrix} \text{data-name-2} \begin{Bmatrix} \text{IS EQUAL TO} \\ \text{IS} = \end{Bmatrix} \begin{Bmatrix} \text{identifier-4} \\ \text{literal-2} \\ \text{arithmetic-expression-2} \end{Bmatrix} \\ \text{condition-name-2} \end{Bmatrix}\right] \ldots$

$\quad \begin{Bmatrix} \text{imperative-statement-2} \\ \text{NEXT SENTENCE} \end{Bmatrix}$

SEND cd-name FROM identifier-1

SEND cd-name [FROM identifier-1] $\begin{Bmatrix} \text{WITH identifier-2} \\ \text{WITH ESI} \\ \text{WITH EMI} \\ \text{WITH EGI} \end{Bmatrix}$

$\quad \left[\begin{Bmatrix} \text{BEFORE} \\ \text{AFTER} \end{Bmatrix} \text{ADVANCING} \begin{Bmatrix} \left\{\begin{Bmatrix} \text{identifier-3} \\ \text{integer} \end{Bmatrix} \begin{bmatrix} \text{LINE} \\ \text{LINES} \end{bmatrix}\right\} \\ \text{mnemonic-name} \\ \text{PAGE} \end{Bmatrix}\right]$

SET $\begin{Bmatrix} \text{identifier-1} \quad [\text{identifier-2}] \quad \ldots \\ \text{index-name-1} [\text{index-name-2}] \ldots \end{Bmatrix}$ TO $\begin{Bmatrix} \text{identifier-3} \\ \text{index-name-3} \\ \text{integer-1} \end{Bmatrix}$

SET index-name-4 [index-name-5] . . . $\begin{Bmatrix} \text{UP BY} \\ \text{DOWN BY} \end{Bmatrix} \begin{Bmatrix} \text{identifier-4} \\ \text{integer-2} \end{Bmatrix}$

SORT file-name-1 ON $\begin{Bmatrix} \text{ASCENDING} \\ \text{DESCENDING} \end{Bmatrix}$ KEY data-name-1 [data-name-2] . . .

$\quad \left[\text{ON} \begin{Bmatrix} \text{ASCENDING} \\ \text{DESCENDING} \end{Bmatrix} \text{KEY data-name-3 [data-name-4] . . .}\right] \ldots$

[COLLATING SEQUENCE IS alphabet-name]

$$\left\{ \begin{array}{l} \underline{\text{INPUT}}\ \underline{\text{PROCEDURE}}\ \text{IS section-name-1} \left[\left\{ \begin{array}{l} \underline{\text{THROUGH}} \\ \underline{\text{THRU}} \end{array} \right\} \text{section-name-2} \right] \\ \underline{\text{USING}}\ \text{file-name-2 [file-name-3]} \ldots \end{array} \right\}$$

$$\left\{ \begin{array}{l} \underline{\text{OUTPUT}}\ \underline{\text{PROCEDURE}}\ \text{IS section-name-3} \left[\left\{ \begin{array}{l} \underline{\text{THROUGH}} \\ \underline{\text{THRU}} \end{array} \right\} \text{section-name-4} \right] \\ \underline{\text{GIVING}}\ \text{file-name-4} \end{array} \right\}$$

$$\underline{\text{START}}\ \text{file-name} \left[\underline{\text{KEY}} \left\{ \begin{array}{l} \text{IS } \underline{\text{EQUAL}}\ \text{TO} \\ \text{IS} = \\ \text{IS } \underline{\text{GREATER}}\ \text{THAN} \\ \text{IS} > \\ \text{IS } \underline{\text{NOT}}\ \underline{\text{LESS}}\ \text{THAN} \\ \text{IS } \underline{\text{NOT}} < \end{array} \right\} \text{data-name} \right]$$

[INVALID KEY imperative-statement]

$$\underline{\text{STOP}} \left\{ \begin{array}{l} \underline{\text{RUN}} \\ \text{literal} \end{array} \right\}$$

$$\underline{\text{STRING}} \left\{ \begin{array}{l} \text{identifier-1} \\ \text{literal-1} \end{array} \right\} \left[\begin{array}{l} \text{identifier-2} \\ \text{literal-2} \end{array} \right] \ldots \underline{\text{DELIMITED}}\ \text{BY} \left\{ \begin{array}{l} \text{identifier-3} \\ \text{literal-3} \\ \underline{\text{SIZE}} \end{array} \right\}$$

$$\left[\left\{ \begin{array}{l} \text{identifier-4} \\ \text{literal-4} \end{array} \right\} \left[\begin{array}{l} \text{identifier-5} \\ \text{literal-5} \end{array} \right] \ldots \underline{\text{DELIMITED}}\ \text{BY} \left\{ \begin{array}{l} \text{identifier-6} \\ \text{literal-6} \\ \underline{\text{SIZE}} \end{array} \right\} \right] \ldots$$

INTO identifier-7 [WITH POINTER identifier-8]

[ON OVERFLOW imperative-statement]

$$\underline{\text{SUBTRACT}} \left\{ \begin{array}{l} \text{identifier-1} \\ \text{literal-1} \end{array} \right\} \left[\begin{array}{l} \text{identifier-2} \\ \text{literal-2} \end{array} \right] \ldots \underline{\text{FROM}}\ \text{identifier-m [}\underline{\text{ROUNDED}}\text{]}$$

$$\left[\text{identifier-n [}\underline{\text{ROUNDED}}\text{]} \right] \ldots \text{[ON } \underline{\text{SIZE}}\ \underline{\text{ERROR}}\ \text{imperative-statement]}$$

$$\underline{\text{SUBTRACT}} \left\{ \begin{array}{l} \text{identifier-1} \\ \text{literal-1} \end{array} \right\} \left[\begin{array}{l} \text{identifier-2} \\ \text{literal-2} \end{array} \right] \ldots \underline{\text{FROM}} \left\{ \begin{array}{l} \text{identifier-m} \\ \text{literal-m} \end{array} \right\}$$

$$\underline{\text{GIVING}}\ \text{identifier-n [}\underline{\text{ROUNDED}}\text{]} \left[\text{identifier-o [}\underline{\text{ROUNDED}}\text{]} \right] \ldots$$

[ON SIZE ERROR imperative-statement]

$$\underline{\text{SUBTRACT}} \left\{ \begin{array}{l} \underline{\text{CORRESPONDING}} \\ \underline{\text{CORR}} \end{array} \right\} \text{identifier-1} \underline{\text{FROM}}\ \text{identifier-2 [}\underline{\text{ROUNDED}}\text{]}$$

[ON SIZE ERROR imperative-statement]

$$\underline{\text{SUPPRESS}}\ \text{PRINTING}$$

TERMINATE report-name-1 [report-name-2] . . .

UNSTRING identifier-1

$$\left[\underline{\text{DELIMITED}}\text{ BY }[\underline{\text{ALL}}]\begin{Bmatrix}\text{identifier-2}\\\text{literal-1}\end{Bmatrix}\left[\underline{\text{OR}}\text{ }[\underline{\text{ALL}}]\begin{Bmatrix}\text{identifier-3}\\\text{literal-2}\end{Bmatrix}\right]\text{ . . .}\right]$$

INTO identifier-4 [DELIMITER IN identifier-5] [COUNT IN identifier-6]

$$\left[\text{identifier-7 }[\underline{\text{DELIMITER}}\text{ IN identifier-8}]\text{ }[\underline{\text{COUNT}}\text{ IN identifier-9}]\right]\text{ . . .}$$

[WITH POINTER identifier-10] [TALLYING IN identifier-11]

[ON OVERFLOW imperative-statement]

$$\underline{\text{USE}}\text{ }\underline{\text{AFTER}}\text{ STANDARD }\begin{Bmatrix}\underline{\text{EXCEPTION}}\\\underline{\text{ERROR}}\end{Bmatrix}\text{ PROCEDURE ON }\begin{Bmatrix}\text{file-name-1 [file-name-2] . . .}\\\underline{\text{INPUT}}\\\underline{\text{OUTPUT}}\\\underline{\text{I-O}}\\\underline{\text{EXTEND}}\end{Bmatrix}.$$

$$\underline{\text{USE}}\text{ }\underline{\text{AFTER}}\text{ STANDARD }\begin{Bmatrix}\underline{\text{EXCEPTION}}\\\underline{\text{ERROR}}\end{Bmatrix}\text{ PROCEDURE ON }\begin{Bmatrix}\text{file-name-1 [file-name-2] . . .}\\\underline{\text{INPUT}}\\\underline{\text{OUTPUT}}\\\underline{\text{I-O}}\end{Bmatrix}.$$

USE BEFORE REPORTING identifier.

$$\underline{\text{USE}}\text{ FOR }\underline{\text{DEBUGGING}}\text{ ON}\begin{Bmatrix}\text{cd-name-1}\\[\underline{\text{ALL}}\text{ REFERENCES OF] identifier-1}\\\text{file-name-1}\\\text{procedure-name-1}\\\underline{\text{ALL}}\text{ }\underline{\text{PROCEDURES}}\end{Bmatrix}$$

$$\left[\begin{Bmatrix}\text{cd-name-2}\\[\underline{\text{ALL}}\text{ REFERENCES OF] identifier-2}\\\text{file-name-2}\\\text{procedure-name-2}\\\underline{\text{ALL}}\text{ }\underline{\text{PROCEDURES}}\end{Bmatrix}\text{ . . .}\right].$$

WRITE record-name [FROM identifier-1]

$$\left[\begin{Bmatrix}\underline{\text{BEFORE}}\\\underline{\text{AFTER}}\end{Bmatrix}\text{ ADVANCING}\begin{Bmatrix}\begin{Bmatrix}\text{identifier-2}\\\text{integer}\end{Bmatrix}\begin{bmatrix}\text{LINE}\\\text{LINES}\end{bmatrix}\\\\\begin{Bmatrix}\text{mnemonic-name}\\\underline{\text{PAGE}}\end{Bmatrix}\end{Bmatrix}\right]$$

$$\left[\text{AT}\begin{Bmatrix}\underline{\text{END-OF-PAGE}}\\\underline{\text{EOP}}\end{Bmatrix}\text{imperative-statement}\right]$$

WRITE record-name [FROM identifier] [INVALID KEY imperative-statement]

General Format for Conditions

Relation Condition

$$\left\{ \begin{array}{l} \text{identifier-1} \\ \text{literal-1} \\ \text{arithmetic-expression-1} \\ \text{index-name-1} \end{array} \right\} \left\{ \begin{array}{l} \text{IS [\underline{NOT}] \underline{GREATER} THAN} \\ \text{IS [\underline{NOT}] \underline{LESS} THAN} \\ \text{IS [\underline{NOT}] \underline{EQUAL} TO} \\ \text{IS [\underline{NOT}] >} \\ \text{IS [\underline{NOT}] <} \\ \text{IS [\underline{NOT}] =} \end{array} \right\} \left\{ \begin{array}{l} \text{identifier-2} \\ \text{literal-2} \\ \text{arithmetic-expression-2} \\ \text{index-name-2} \end{array} \right\}$$

Class Condition

$$\text{identifier IS [\underline{NOT}]} \left\{ \begin{array}{l} \underline{\text{NUMERIC}} \\ \underline{\text{ALPHABETIC}} \end{array} \right\}$$

Sign Condition

$$\text{arithmetic-expression IS [\underline{NOT}]} \left\{ \begin{array}{l} \underline{\text{POSITIVE}} \\ \underline{\text{NEGATIVE}} \\ \underline{\text{ZERO}} \end{array} \right\}$$

Condition-Name Condition

condition-name

Switch-Status Condition

condition-name

Negated Simple Condition

<u>NOT</u> simple-condition

Combined Condition

$$\text{condition} \left\{ \left\{ \begin{array}{l} \underline{\text{AND}} \\ \underline{\text{OR}} \end{array} \right\} \text{condition} \right\} \ldots$$

Abbreviated Combined Relation Condition

$$\text{relation-condition} \left\{ \left\{ \begin{array}{l} \underline{\text{AND}} \\ \underline{\text{OR}} \end{array} \right\} \text{[\underline{NOT}] [relational-operator] object} \right\} \ldots$$

Miscellaneous Formats

Qualification

$$\left\{ \begin{array}{l} \text{data-name-1} \\ \text{condition-name} \end{array} \right\} \left[\left\{ \begin{array}{l} \underline{\text{OF}} \\ \underline{\text{IN}} \end{array} \right\} \text{data-name-2} \right] \ldots$$

$$\text{paragraph-name} \left[\left\{ \begin{array}{l} \underline{\text{OF}} \\ \underline{\text{IN}} \end{array} \right\} \text{section-name} \right]$$

$$\text{text-name}\left[\left\{\frac{\underline{OF}}{\underline{IN}}\right\}\text{library-name}\right]$$

Subscripting

$$\left\{\begin{matrix}\text{data-name}\\\text{condition-name}\end{matrix}\right\}(\text{subscript-1 [subscript-2 [subscript-3]}])$$

Indexing

$$\left\{\begin{matrix}\text{data-name}\\\text{condition-name}\end{matrix}\right\}\left(\left\{\begin{matrix}\text{index-name-1 [\{±\} literal-2]}\\\text{literal-1}\end{matrix}\right\}\right.$$

$$\left.\left[\left\{\begin{matrix}\text{index-name-2 [\{±\} literal-4]}\\\text{literal-3}\end{matrix}\right\}\right]\left[\left\{\begin{matrix}\text{index-name-3 [\{±\} literal-6]}\\\text{literal-5}\end{matrix}\right\}\right]\right]\right)$$

Identifier: Format 1

$$\text{data-name-1}\left[\left\{\frac{\underline{OF}}{\underline{IN}}\right\}\text{data-name-2}\right]\ldots[[\text{(subscript-1 [subscript-2}$$

$$\left.\text{[subscript-3]])}\right]$$

Identifier: Format 2

$$\text{data-name-1}\left[\left\{\frac{\underline{OF}}{\underline{IN}}\right\}\text{data-name-2}\right]\ldots\left[\left(\left\{\begin{matrix}\text{index-name-1 [\{±\} literal-2]}\\\text{literal-1}\end{matrix}\right\}\right.\right.$$

$$\left.\left.\left[\left\{\begin{matrix}\text{index-name-2 [\{±\} literal-4]}\\\text{literal-3}\end{matrix}\right\}\right]\left[\left\{\begin{matrix}\text{index-name-3 [\{±\} literal-6]}\\\text{literal-5}\end{matrix}\right\}\right]\right)\right]$$

General Format for Copy Statement

$$\underline{COPY}\text{ text-name}\left[\left\{\frac{\underline{OF}}{\underline{IN}}\right\}\text{library-name}\right]$$

$$\left[\underline{REPLACING}\left\{\begin{matrix}\text{==pseudo-text-1==}\\\text{identifier-1}\\\text{literal-1}\\\text{word-1}\end{matrix}\right\}\underline{BY}\left\{\begin{matrix}\text{==pseudo-text-2==}\\\text{identifier-2}\\\text{literal-2}\\\text{word-2}\end{matrix}\right\}\right]\ldots$$

COBOL Reserved Words

 Check your COBOL manual for the reserved words used on your system. It may have some minor changes from this list.

ACCEPT	COMPUTATIONAL-2	ELSE
ACCESS	COMPUTATIONAL-3	EMI
ADD	COMPUTATIONAL-4	ENABLE
ADVANCING	COMPUTE	END
AFTER	CONFIGURATION	END-OF-PAGE
ALL	CONTAINS	ENTER
ALPHABETIC	CONTROL	ENVIRONMENT
ALSO	CONTROLS	EOP
ALTER	COPY	EQUAL
ALTERNATE	CORR	ERROR
AND	CORRESPONDING	ESI
ARE	COUNT	EVERY
AREA	CURRENCY	EXCEPTION
AREAS	DATA	EXHIBIT
ASCENDING	DATE	EXIT
ASSIGN	DATE-COMPILED	EXTEND
AT	DATE-WRITTEN	FD
AUTHOR	DAY	FILE
BEFORE	DE	FILE-CONTROL
BLANK	DEBUG-CONTENTS	FILLER
BEGINNING	DEBUG-ITEM	FINAL
BLOCK	DEBUG-LINE	FIRST
BOTTOM	DEBUG-NAME	FOOTING
BY	DEBUG-SUB-1	FOR
CALL	DEBUG-SUB-2	FROM
CANCEL	DEBUG-SUB-3	GENERATE
CD	DEBUGGING	GIVING
CF	DECIMAL-POINT	GO
CH	DECLARATIVES	GREATER
CHARACTER	DELETE	GROUP
CHARACTERS	DELIMITED	HEADING
CLOCK-UNITS	DELIMITER	HIGH-VALUE
CLOSE	DESCENDING	HIGH-VALUES
COBOL	DESTINATION	HOLD
CODE	DETAIL	I-O
CODE-SET	DISABLE	I-O-CONTROL
COLLATING	DISPLAY	IDENTIFICATION
COLUMN	DIVIDE	IF
COMMA	DIVISION	IN
COMMUNICATION	DOWN	INDEX
COMP	DUPLICATES	INDEXED
COMPUTATIONAL	DYNAMIC	INDICATE
COMPUTATIONAL-1	EGI	INITIAL

COBOL Reserved Words
(continued)

INITIATE	PF	SEQUENCE
INPUT	PH	SEQUENTIAL
INPUT-OUTPUT	PIC	SET
INSPECT	PICTURE	SIGN
INSTALLATION	PLUS	SIZE
INTO	POINTER	SORT
INVALID	POSITION	SORT-MERGE
IS	POSITIVE	SOURCE
JUST	PRINTING	SOURCE-COMPUTER
JUSTIFIED	PROCEDURE	SPACE
KEY	PROCEDURES	SPACES
LABEL	PROCEED	SPECIAL-NAMES
LAST	PROCESS	STANDARD
LEADING	PROCESSING	STANDARD-1
LEFT	PROGRAM	START
LENGTH	PROGRAM-ID	STATUS
LESS	QUEUE	STOP
LIBRARY	QUOTE	STRING
LIMIT	QUOTES	SUB-QUEUE-1
LIMITS	RANDOM	SUB-QUEUE-2
LINAGE	RD	SUB-QUEUE-3
LINAGE-COUNTER	READ	SUBTRACT
LINE	RECEIVE	SUM
LINE-COUNTER	RECORD	SUPPRESS
LINES	RECORDS	SYMBOLIC
LINKAGE	REDEFINES	SYNC
LOCK	REEL	SYNCHRONIZED
LOW-VALUE	REFERENCES	TABLE
LOW-VALUES	RELATIVE	TALLYING
MASTER-INDEX	RELEASE	TAPE
MEMORY	REMAINDER	TERMINAL
MERGE	REMOVAL	TERMINATE
MESSAGE	RENAMES	TEXT
MODE	REPLACING	THAN
MODULES	REPORT	THROUGH
MOVE	REPORTING	THRU
MULTIPLE	REPORTS	TIME
MULTIPLY	RERUN	TIMES
NATIVE	RESERVE	TO
NEGATIVE	RESET	TOP
NEXT	RETURN	TRAILING
NO	REVERSED	TYPE
NOT	REWIND	UNIT
NUMBER	REWRITE	UNSTRING
NUMERIC	RF	UNTIL
NUMERIC-EDITED	RH	UP
OBJECT-COMPUTER	RIGHT	UPON
OCCURS	ROUNDED	USAGE
OF	RUN	USE
OFF	SA	USING
OMITTED	SAME	VALUE
ON	SD	VALUES
OPEN	SEARCH	VARYING
OPTIONAL	SECTION	WHEN
OR	SECURITY	WITH
ORGANIZATION	SEGMENT	WORDS
OUTPUT	SEGMENT-LIMIT	WORKING-STORAGE
OVERFLOW	SELECT	WRITE
PAGE	SEND	ZERO
PAGE-COUNTER	SENTENCE	ZEROS
PERFORM	SEPARATE	

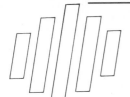

Data Sets for Use with Textbook Problems

Data Set A

These records contain payroll data and are 80 characters long.
The field definitions are:

Column	Field name	Type of data
1–20	Employee name	Alphanumeric or Alphabetic
21–29	Social security number	Numeric or Alphanumeric
30–33	Hourly pay rate	Numeric, 2 decimal places
34–37	Hours worked	Numeric, 1 decimal place
38–39	Exemptions	Numeric
40–41	Department number	Numeric
42–43	Plant number	Numeric
44	Region number	Numeric
45–52	YTD gross pay	Numeric, 2 decimal places
53–60	YTD federal income tax	Numeric, 2 decimal places
61–68	YTD FICA	Numeric, 2 decimal places
69–76	YTD state income tax	Numeric, 2 decimal places
77–79	FILLER	Blanks
80	Marital status	Numeric

```
                 1111111111222222222233333333334444444444555555555566666666667777777777 8
       1234567890123456789012345678901234567890123456789012345678901234567890123456 7890

ESPINOZA RAMON J      444996111050004800405011010405030016641700083244000249 82    2
HARRIS FLOYD K        437187777060004000306011009612160017282300076840000259 91    1
LAMOTHE EDITH L       399176051090004000406011014411930023946200115261000345 21    3
PATTON RONALD B       523171700085004000608011013600560021765200108840000326 24    5
PATTON DONALD A       123231111117504070108011019293450034720500154389000521 13    1
QUIROZ PEDRO S        311115657080003400301021010888510019584100087062000293 77    3
CAPOZZI ANTHONY D     519889916092503800301021014060870025306600112431000379 93    2
AYARS HARRY P         312614312090004000301021014408230025922000115205000388 80    2
CAREY MICHAEL A       781913468056003600602021009360110014976000074880000224 64    3
SMITH JOE Z           851111444095004801002021019760190023812400158169000355 48    1
EDIT KEVIN S          512891967065004000304021010425610018724600083232000280 85    2
EDWARDS SUE E         513161185075003850304021011550760020791700092415000311 88    3
SCHMANSKI ANN H       500179898090004000105021014416560025922100115221000388 21    2
FRY BELVA G           314812224090004000405021014423150023043000115262000345 63    4
WEITZEL DAVID B       212003033067504210407021011651430018646700093231000279 71    1
```

```
UBOSKIE ANGELINA H     99911310008250400040702101319961002112900010566900031637    3
QUINTANA MANUEL B      20067333109250410020702101535553002763160012289000041488     1
GOODFELLOW HARRY O     28064185012000400020702101920000003456000015300000051840     3
FABRIZIO THOMAS L      55511660005000385030802100771692001386290006169300020791     2
PARRO JOHN D           24023311608500420020802101462162002631320011692400039445     1
KITCHELL FAY R         63451234507500420020902101290000002322000010320000034830     2
WYMAN OTHO Y           63513579006210410031002101037592001867180008308100028015     2
HERNANDEZ MARTINA T    42812651106500400021002101040000001872000008320000028080     2
LEUENBERGER FRITZ A    78901178906500480051002101352000002163200010016000032448     1
VANCE BURTON E         61112314510000400000103101603510003200100012801100048016     1
WAAG ROBERT D          62101234510000440000103101846162003680350014721200055217     1
UZCATEGI RICARDO R     33433660308000400010503101280011002304260010246000034535     1
ANDERSON GILBERT E     60013312109000400030903101441366002592510011526000038806     3
UPTON THOMAS G         40688612609500400010501201520621002761830012169800041076     2
NEERGAARD JOYCE E      17899340109000400000601201441125002880190011521700043275     1
SAKURARI SAKA I        80803145007500480000103201573184003120920012485500046891     1
PROCHOWNIK PETER F     11515111510000400030103201612265002880180012801700043212     2
GARCIA SANTOS R        31416555511000400040203201760000000281600014080000042240     1
ROY ROBERT J           67676767608500400070203201361577001904410010881100028561     1
MWANKWO CHIN C         20861888809500400030303201520000002736000012160000041040     3
VANDERLOO MARNE G      21113336306750400030403201080832001944870008644100029163     2
PUENTE ARTURO M        21100301509000375040403201356143002160220010802300032416     1
TANNENBAUM ORLEAN M    77700563008000360050503201152128001843560009217000027640     1
JURGENS JAMES J        50666310106500400020503201061230001900810008180300026615     1
BENNETT JOYCE N        58713198705000400080603200806293001120100006407100016831     3
SMITH JOE A            80904312306500400010603201040532001872870008325700028174     2
GALLEGOS ISABELL A     30416128011500400010603201848162003312140014728100049681     2
REEVES CLARA P         33355444408000400010703201280598002304630010241000034578     5
DANHOFF GREG M         78130016306500500030703201434073002574330011444000038613     1
YAMAGUCHI HAJIME L     31833123409000375030803201350000002430000010800000036450     1
ZACZKOWSKI IVAN P      63145611105000400000803200808075001600160006401500024000     1
DAVIS KIM S            33310103606500400050903201040304001664560008321700024930     3
XAVIER SAM L           62314681608000381020903201219211002194560009753600032918     2
MACKENZIE EMMETT Z     80161777709500400060903201520000002432000012160000036480     1
LOPEZ ALFONSO M        80156565610000500041003200200000000320000016000000004800     1
KIM TIPAWAN I          67890123407500400041003201200000001920000009600000028800     1
OBRIEN DONALD R        39987121208500410071003201411000001975400011288000029631     1
BALES BETTY D          51241246809000400051003201440057002304730011521100034560     1
ARCHER JOHN S          28024176310000400011003201605610002880100012801200043200     1
SEARS ANITA N          49917631308000400000701301288671002561630010243200038462     1
PAPAS HENRY M          24020177709000360020701301296014002332410010365200034943     2
YBABEN FLORENCIO H     70899224405500400001001300880061001760330007041600026490     2
OCONNELL DANIEL J      60101331208250420040202301419176002270920011355300034031     2
ZABKA MARY M           10535151507750360000702301116932002232200008922300033463     1
CHIN LEE S             71728112208500400051003301655123002176560010886500032611     2
============================================================================
```

Data Set B

These records contain sales data and are 51 characters long.
The field definitions are:

Column	Field name	Type of data
1–4	Salesperson number	Alphanumeric
6–25	Salesperson name	Alphanumeric
26–27	Store number	Alphanumeric
29–30	Department mnemonic	Alphanumeric
32	Employee code	Alphanumeric
	1 = Full time	
	2 = Part time	
	3 = Full-time trainee	
	4 = Part-time trainee	
	5 = Store manager	
34–40	Year-to-date sales	Numeric, 2 decimal places
42–48	Year-to-date sales returns	Numeric, 2 decimal places
50–51	Commission rate	Numeric, 2 decimal places

```
                    1111111111222222222233333333334444444444455
           1234567890123456789012345678901234567890123456789012345678901
```

```
9730 CROSSLAND, BRENDA R.10 FO 2    23175     4000 08
2487 HUME, LETA            10 FO 2    48353    28437 20
3902 JENKINS, KIM A.       10 FO 2   112359     3575 08
5906 EAKINS, CHERYL R.     10 FO 2   115000    17500 08
1938 DWYER, JOHN D.        10 JE 3    23175     4000 10
7807 NEWALL, NANCY R.      10 JE 3    23175          10
4123 JACKSON, EARL         10 LG 1    68473    49959 27
2963 BRADY, CURTIS         20 AP 3   W00039    68473 10
4233 MURPHY, ALICE         20 EL 3    21763     2847 15
5958 KINCADE, MICHAEL D.   20 FO 2    50000    10000 08
2963 BRADY, CURTIS         20 AP 3   W00039    68473 10
4233 MURPHY, ALICE         20 EL 3    21763     2847 15
5958 KINCADE, MICHAEL D.   20 FO 2    50000    10000 08
3810 EAGAN, DEBBIE R.      20 FO 2   115000    17500 08
7924                       20 FO 6   115000    17500 08
1805 KIMBERLING, CARLA K.  20 GA 2    50000    10000 30
2157 YOUNG, KAREN L.       20 GA 2   112359     3575 30
0479 WETZEL, ROBERT D.     20 GA 2   208876     5877
2186 SMITH, DOUGLAS        20 HD 3    18345    37758 20
4189 HEYDT, MARY J.        20 H8 1    50000    10000 15
5749 GIBSON, MICHELLE R.   20 IC 2    23175     4000 15
3967 MOORE, EDWARD W.      20 JE 2    23175     4000 10
8239 ASTON, ARNOLD A.      20 JE 3              3575 10
     PAYNE, MAX            30 FH 2    98700     5673 05
0356 GOLTMAN, LINDA S.     30 FO 1   109877     1000 10
4362 QUIGLEY, BRETT E.     30 FO 2    23175     4000 08
5638 SHELBY, JODI D.       03 FO 2    50000    10000 08
7731 HUTTON, JOANN H.      30 FO 2   112359     E575 08
0580 DUPREE, KELLY L.      30 FO 3   357888    27582 10
3735 LOYD, JAMES R.        30 HO 1    50000    10000 15
2269 THOMPSON, LISA S.     30 HO 1    50000    10000 20
4231 RICE, BRAD S.         30 HO 1   115000    17500 15
2871 WELCH, JAMES          30 HO 5    64530    37857 25
8110 ZIMMERMAN, BETTY B.   30 IC B    50000    10000 15
1867 STEWARD, KEVIN J.     30 IC 1   115000    17500 1T
0396 VOLSKY, CHRIS         3P IS 3    32680     5847 08
7660 BUEHLER, JENNIFER M.  30 JE 3    50000    10000 10
6197 JONES, JILL A.        30 JE 3   115000    17500 10
1856 LOVELAND, GEORGE      30 SP 1    46275    27656 10
4853 BENNETT, BRENDA       30 2S 2    95720    48684 10
1634 VAUGHN, SYLVIA A.     40 FO 1    47899    45678 20
3669 TAYLOR, STEVE M.      40 FO 2    23175     4000 08
6278 MCQUEEN, ANGIE L.     40 FO 2    23175     4000 08
0635 HUNT, ROBERT             FO 2    45320    47534 10
0243 BROCKETT, JANE R.     40 FO 4    75000    90000 05
4454 MAPLES, LAURIE A.     40 GA 2   115000    17500 30
0529 PEACOCK, BARBARA      40    3    67330    15664 08
2341 ADAMS, ROBYN A.       40 JE 3    23175     4000 10
0401 OWENS, GEORGE         40 MS      36220     3957 09
0746 JACKSON, JASON        40 MU 3    78450     8478 15
1415 GOODMAN, EVE          40 RA 2    64542    23847 10
2666 BARKER, MARY          50 AU 4    45746     2743 20
2758 WELLS, LARRY          50 BC 3    36440    22204 10
4997 JESSON, WAYNE         50 BS 1    28546     5885 20
3219 BOYER, CATHY          50 CH 2    47656    36680 10
1132 UNLAND, KIM L.        50 EL 5    47564    39585 25
3033 ASHLEY, SHELLEY       50 FH 2    85443    43765 20
1001 DILL, JEFF            50 FO 1    58640    28456 20
4587 WOLFE, KATHY L.       50 FO 2   112359     3575 08
6405 ARNOLD, JULIE D.      50 FO 2   115000    17500 08
6341 YORK, BOB Q.          50 GA 2    23175     4000 30
2485 PHILLIPS, TRACY L.    50 GA 2    50000    10000 30
2294 HERMAN, JACK          50 GA 4    48465     8747 05
```

```
3874 DAILEY, GREG        50 HO 3   48945          20
2575 CROSS, CHERYL       50 IC 3   38563    38250 10
0125 LISHER, JANET F.    50 JE 2   50000          15
2577 IRWIN, ANGELA M.    50 JE 3  115000    17500 10
0927 BARCLAY, RICHARD    50 JE 3  198740    48563 11
2395 MATNEY, DELORES     50 LG 4   79574    85746 05
4043 MYERS, JACKIE       50 MU 4   87755    48672 10
0859 HUTCHENS, JEFF      50 MW 2   57630     4857 14
3957 JONES, NEIL         50 SP 4   87867    39777 08
=============================================
```

Data Set C

These records contain inventory data and are 69 characters long. The field definitions are:

Column	Field name	Type of data
1–2	Store number	Alphanumeric
4–5	Department mnemonic	Alphanumeric
7–9	Item number	Alphanumeric
11–35	Item description	Alphanumeric
36–41	Quantity on hand	Numeric
43–48	Sales price per unit	Numeric, 2 decimal places
50–55	Cost per unit	Numeric, 2 decimal places
57–62	Year-to-date quantity sold	Numeric
64–69	Year-to-date quantity purchased	Numeric

```
============================================================
          1111111111222222222233333333334444444444555555555566666666666
123456789012345678901234567890123456789012345678901234567890123456789
============================================================
10 AP 190 12.1 CU. FT. FREEZER     11   85575  45345    44    55
10 AP 191 30-IN. GAS RANGE         19   34995  20997    76    95
10 AP 192 AMANA RADAR RANGE        57   47599          228   285
10 AP 990 ELECTRIC WOK             42   10172   6103   168   210
10 AP 200 3-CLCLE MAYTAG WASHER   190   52988  31792   760   950
10 AP 201 TOUCH MICROWAVE          80   48575  29145   320   400
10 AP     11-CYCLE DISHWASHER     440   40995  24597   176   220
10 AP 211 9-CYCLE DISHWASHER      100   38995  23397   400   500
10 AP 220 SLIDE-IN ELECTRIC RANGE       42995  2 797   400   500
10 AP 616 EUREKA POWER PLUS VACUUM 19   14488   8692    76    95
10 AP 617 SEWING TABLE             31   24995  14997   124   155
10 AP 619 GE MICROWAVE OVEN        23   48995  29397    92   115
   AP 620 GE MICROWAVE W/PROBE     33          35397   132   165
10 AU 208 BOOSTER CABLES           54    1599   1199   162   108
10 AU 209                         301    1249    936   903   602
10     211 POWER DOOR LOCK         50     649    486   120    Y0
10 AU 213 ZT-10 CRUISE CONTROL     31    6999   5249    93    62
10 AU 876 440 BATTERY              47    4499   3374   141    94
10 AU 877 AUTO COVER                5    3030   2272    15    10
10 AU 881 STEADY RIDER SHOCKS      47    2998   2248          94
10 AU 883 INFLATE AIR COMPRESSOR   40    2475   1856   120    80
20 BD 191 30-IN. GAS RANGE         25   34995  20997    96    85
20 AP 220 SLIDE-IN ELECTRIC RANGE 200   42995  25797   300   400
20 AP 616 EUREKA POWER PLUS VACUUM 29   14488   8692    76    85
20 AP 617 SEWING TABLE             54   24995  14997   275   165
20 AP 619 GE MICROWAVE OVEN        35   48995  29397   192
30 AU 211 12V SPORT BATTERY        25    8199   5399    75    50
20 AU 212 40WATT BOOSTER AMP       12    6000   4500    36    24
20 AU 876 440 BATTERY              57    4499   3374   1T1   104
20 AU 877 AUTO COVER               25    3030   2272   215   110
20 AU 881 STEADY RIDER SHOCKS    B057    2998   2248   241   115
20 AU 898 MUZZLER MUFFLER          96    2499   1874   288   192
============================================================
```

Data Set D

These records contain sales data and are 51 characters long.
The field definitions are:

Column	Field name	Type of data
1–4	Salesperson number	Alphanumeric
6–25	Salesperson name	Alphanumeric
26–27	Store number	Alphanumeric
29–30	Department mnemonic	Alphanumeric
32	Employee code	Alphanumeric
	1 = Full time	
	2 = Part time	
	3 = Full-time trainee	
	4 = Part-time trainee	
	5 = Store manager	
34–40	Year-to-date sales	Numeric, 2 decimal places
42–48	Year-to-date sales returns	Numeric, 2 decimal places
50–51	Commission rate	Numeric, 2 decimal places

```
          1111111111222222222233333333334444444444455
123456789012345678901234567890123456789012345678901

9730 CROSSLAND, BRENDA R.10 FO 2 0023175 0004000 08
2487 HUME, LETA         10 FO 2 0048353 0028437 20
3902 JENKINS, KIM A.     10 FO 2 0112359 0003575 08
5906 EAKINS, CHERYL R.   10 FO 2 0115000 0017500 08
1938 DWYER, JOHN D.      10 JE 3 0023175 0004000 10
7807 NEWALL, NANCY R.    10 JE 3 0023175 0004000 10
4123 JACKSON, EARL       10 LG 1 0068473 0049959 27
2963 BRADY, CURTIS       20 AP 3 0100039 0068473 10
4233 MURPHY, ALICE       20 EL 3 0021763 0002847 15
5958 KINCADE, MICHAEL D. 20 FO 2 0050000 0010000 08
3810 EAGAN, DEBBIE R.    20 FO 2 0115000 0017500 08
7924 TUCKER, GENA E.     20 FO 2 0115000 0017500 08
1805 KIMBERLING, CARLA K.20 GA 2 0050000 0010000 30
2157 YOUNG, KAREN L.     20 GA 2 0112359 0003575 30
0479 WETZEL, ROBERT D.   20 GA 2 0208876 0005877 15
2186 SMITH, DOUGLAS      20 HD 3 0018345 0037758 20
4189 HEYDT, MARY J.      20 HO 1 0050000 0010000 15
5749 GIBSON, MICHELLE R. 20 IC 2 0023175 0004000 15
3967 MOORE, EDWARD W.    20 JE 2 0023175 0004000 10
8239 ASTON, ARNOLD A.    20 JE 3 0112359 0003575 10
0017 PAYNE, MAX          30 FH 2 0098700 0005673 05
0356 GOLTMAN, LINDA S.   30 FO 1 0109877 0001000 10
4362 QUIGLEY, BRETT E.   30 FO 2 0023175 0004000 08
5638 SHELBY, JODI D.     30 FO 2 0050000 0010000 08
7731 HUTTON, JOANN H.    30 FO 2 0112359 0003575 08
0580 DUPREE, KELLY L.    30 FO 3 0357888 0027582 10
3735 LOYD, JAMES R.      30 HO 1 0050000 0010000 15
2269 THOMPSON, LISA S.   30 HO 1 0050000 0010000 20
4231 RICE, BRAD S.       30 HO 1 0115000 0017500 15
2871 WELCH, JAMES        30 HO 5 0064530 0037857 25
8110 ZIMMERMAN, BETTY B. 30 IC 1 0050000 0010000 15
1867 STEWARD, KEVIN J.   30 IC 1 0115000 0017500 15
0396 VOLSKY, CHRIS       30 IS 3 0032680 0005847 08
7660 BUEHLER, JENNIFER M.30 JE 3 0050000 0010000 10
6197 JONES, JILL A.      30 JE 3 0115000 0017500 10
1856 LOVELAND, GEORGE    30 SP 1 0046275 0027656 10
4853 BENNETT, BRENDA     30 WS 2 0095720 0048684 10
1634 VAUGHN, SYLVIA A.   40 FO 1 0047899 0045678 20
3669 TAYLOR, STEVE M.    40 FO 2 0023175 0004000 08
```

```
6278 MCQUEEN, ANGIE L.    40 FO 2 0023175 0004000 08
0635 HUNT, ROBERT         40 FO 2 0045320 0047534 10
0243 BROCKETT, JANE R.    40 FO 4 0075000 0090000 05
4454 MAPLES, LAURIE A.    40 GA 2 0115000 0017500 30
0529 PEACOCK, BARBARA     40 GS 3 0067330 0015664 08
2341 ADAMS, ROBYN A.      40 JE 3 0023175 0004000 10
0401 OWENS, GEORGE        40 MS 4 0036220 0003957 09
0746 JACKSON, JASON       40 MU 3 0078450 0008478 15
1415 GOODMAN, EVE         40 RA 2 0064542 0023847 10
2666 BARKER, MARY         50 AU 4 0045746 0002743 20
2758 WELLS, LARRY         50 BC 3 0036440 0022204 10
4997 JESSON, WAYNE        50 BS 1 0028546 0005885 20
3219 BOYER, CATHY         50 CH 2 0047656 0036680 10
1132 UNLAND, KIM L.       50 EL 5 0047564 0039585 25
3033 ASHLEY, SHELLEY      50 FH 2 0085443 0043765 20
1001 DILL, JEFF           50 FO 1 0058640 0028456 20
4587 WOLFE, KATHY L.      50 FO 2 0112359 0003575 08
6405 ARNOLD, JULIE D.     50 FO 2 0115000 0017500 08
6341 YORK, BOB Q.         50 GA 2 0023175 0004000 30
2485 PHILLIPS, TRACY L.   50 GA 2 0050000 0010000 30
2294 HERMAN, JACK         50 GA 4 0048465 0008747 05
3874 DAILEY, GREG         50 HO 3 0048945 0000000 20
2575 CROSS, CHERYL        50 IC 3 0038563 0038250 10
0125 LISHER, JANET F.     50 JE 2 0050000 0000000 15
2577 IRWIN, ANGELA M.     50 JE 3 0115000 0017500 10
0927 BARCLAY, RICHARD     50 JE 3 0198740 0048563 11
2395 MATNEY, DELORES      50 LG 4 0079574 0085746 05
4043 MYERS, JACKIE        50 MU 4 0087755 0048672 10
0859 HUTCHENS, JEFF       50 MW 2 0057630 0004857 14
3957 JONES, NEIL          50 SP 4 0087867 0039777 08
===============================================
```

Data Set E

These records contain inventory data and are 69 characters long. The field definitions are:

Column	Field name	Type of data
1–2	Store number	Alphanumeric
4–5	Department mnemonic	Alphanumeric
7–9	Item number	Alphanumeric
11–35	Item description	Alphanumeric
36–41	Quantity on hand	Numeric
43–48	Sales price per unit	Numeric, 2 decimal places
50–55	Cost per unit	Numeric, 2 decimal places
57–62	Year-to-date quantity sold	Numeric
64–69	Year-to-date quantity purchased	Numeric

```
          1111111111222222222233333333334444444444555555555566666666
 1234567890123456789012345678901234567890123456789012345678901234567890
=========================================================================

10 AP 190 12.1 CU. FT. FREEZER     000011 075575 045345 000044 000055
10 AP 191 30-IN. GAS RANGE         000019 034995 020997 000076 000095
10 AP 192 AMANA RADAR RANGE        000057 047599 028559 000228 000285
10 AP 193 ELECTRIC WOK             000042 010172 006103 000168 000210
10 AP 200 3-CLCLE MAYTAG WASHER    000190 052988 031792 000760 000950
10 AP 201 TOUCH MICROWAVE          000080 048575 029145 000320 000400
10 AP 210 11-CYCLE DISHWASHER      000440 040995 024597 000176 000220
```

```
10 AP 211 9-CYCLE DISHWASHER         000100 038995 023397 000400 000500
10 AP 220 SLIDE-IN ELECTRIC RANGE    000100 042995 025797 000400 000500
10 AP 616 EUREKA POWER PLUS VACUUM   000019 014488 008692 000076 000095
10 AP 617 SEWING TABLE               000031 024995 014997 000124 000155
10 AP 619 GE MICROWAVE OVEN          000023 048995 029397 000092 000115
10 AP 620 GE MICROWAVE W/PROBE       000033 058995 035397 000132 000165
10 AU 208 BOOSTER CABLES             000054 001599 001199 000162 000108
10 AU 209 BULLET-STYLE CAR MIRROR    000301 001249 000936 000903 000602
10 AU 212 POWER DOOR LOCK            000040 000649 000486 000120 000080
10 AU 213 ZT-10 CRUISE CONTROL       000031 006999 005249 000093 000062
10 AU 876 440 BATTERY                000047 004499 003374 000141 000094
10 AU 877 AUTO COVER                 000005 003030 002272 000015 000010
10 AU 881 STEADY RIDER SHOCKS        000047 002998 002248 000141 000094
10 AU 883 INFLATE AIR COMPRESSOR     000040 002475 001856 000120 000080
20 AP 191 30-IN. GAS RANGE           000025 034995 020997 000096 000085
20 AP 220 SLIDE-IN ELECTRIC RANGE    000200 042995 025797 000300 000400
20 AP 616 EUREKA POWER PLUS VACUUM   000029 014488 008692 000076 000085
20 AP 617 SEWING TABLE               000054 024995 014997 000275 000165
20 AP 619 GE MICROWAVE OVEN          000033 048995 029397 000192 000125
20 AU 211 12V SPORT BATTERY          000025 007199 005399 000075 000050
20 AU 212 40WATT BOOSTER AMP         000012 006000 004500 000036 000024
20 AU 876 440 BATTERY                000057 004499 003374 000161 000104
20 AU 877 AUTO COVER                 000025 003030 002272 000215 000110
20 AU 881 STEADY RIDER SHOCKS        000057 002998 002248 000241 000115
20 AU 898 MUZZLER MUFFLER            000096 002499 001874 000288 000192
=================================================================
```

Data Set F

These records contain sales data and are 51 characters long.
The field definitions are:

Column	Field name	Type of data
1–4	Salesperson number	Alphanumeric
6–25	Salesperson name	Alphanumeric
26–27	Store number	Alphanumeric
29–30	Department mnemonic	Alphanumeric
32	Employee code	Alphanumeric
	1 = Full time	
	2 = Part time	
	3 = Full-time trainee	
	4 = Part-time trainee	
	5 = Store manager	
34–40	Year-to-date sales	Numeric, 2 decimal places
42–48	Year-to-date sales returns	Numeric, 2 decimal places
50–51	Commission rate	Numeric, 2 decimal places

```
=================================================
          1111111111222222222233333333334444444444 55
1234567890123456789012345678901234567890123456789 01
=================================================
0017 PAYNE, MAX         30 FH 2 0098700 0005673 05
0125 LISHER, JANET F.   50 JE 2 0050000 0000000 15
0243 BROCKETT, JANE R.  40 FO 4 0075000 0090000 05
0356 GOLTMAN, LINDA S.  30 FO 1 0109877 0001000 10
0396 VOLSKY, CHRIS      30 IS 3 0032680 0005847 08
0401 OWENS, GEORGE      40 MS 4 0036220 0003957 09
0479 WETZEL, ROBERT D.  20 GA 2 0208876 0005877 15
0529 PEACOCK, BARBARA   40 GS 3 0067330 0015664 08
0580 DUPREE, KELLY L.   30 FO 3 0357888 0027582 10
0635 HUNT, ROBERT       40 FO 2 0045320 0047534 10
```

```
0746 JACKSON, JASON       40 MU 3 0078450 0008478 15
0859 HUTCHENS, JEFF       50 MW 2 0057630 0004857 14
0927 BARCLAY, RICHARD     50 JE 3 0198740 0048563 11
1001 DILL, JEFF           50 FO 1 0058640 0028456 20
1132 UNLAND, KIM L.       50 EL 5 0047564 0039585 25
1415 GOODMAN, EVE         40 RA 2 0064542 0023847 10
1634 VAUGHN, SYLVIA A.    40 FO 1 0047899 0045678 20
1805 KIMBERLING, CARLA K. 20 GA 2 0050000 0010000 30
1856 LOVELAND, GEORGE     30 SP 1 0046275 0027656 10
1867 STEWARD, KEVIN J.    30 IC 1 0115000 0017500 15
1938 DWYER, JOHN D.       10 JE 3 0023175 0004000 10
2157 YOUNG, KAREN L.      20 GA 2 0112359 0003575 30
2186 SMITH, DOUGLAS       20 HD 3 0018345 0037758 20
2269 THOMPSON, LISA S.    30 HO 1 0050000 0010000 20
2294 HERMAN, JACK         50 GA 4 0048465 0008747 05
2341 ADAMS, ROBYN A.      40 JE 3 0023175 0004000 10
2395 MATNEY, DELORES      50 LG 4 0079574 0085746 05
2485 PHILLIPS, TRACY L.   50 GA 2 0050000 0010000 30
2487 HUME, LETA           10 FO 2 0048353 0028437 20
2575 CROSS, CHERYL        50 IC 3 0038563 0038250 10
2577 IRWIN, ANGELA M.     50 JE 3 0115000 0017500 10
2666 BARKER, MARY         50 AU 4 0045746 0002743 20
2758 WELLS, LARRY         50 BC 3 0036440 0022204 10
2871 WELCH, JAMES         30 HO 5 0064530 0037857 25
2963 BRADY, CURTIS        20 AP 3 0100039 0068473 10
3033 ASHLEY, SHELLEY      50 FH 2 0085443 0043765 20
3219 BOYER, CATHY         50 CH 2 0047656 0036680 10
3669 TAYLOR, STEVE M.     40 FO 2 0023175 0004000 08
3735 LOYD, JAMES R.       30 HO 1 0050000 0010000 15
3810 EAGAN, DEBBIE R.     20 FO 2 0115000 0017500 08
3874 DAILEY, GREG         50 HO 3 0048945 0000000 20
3902 JENKINS, KIM A.      10 FO 2 0112359 0003575 08
3957 JONES, NEIL          50 SP 4 0087867 0039777 08
3967 MOORE, EDWARD W.     20 JE 2 0023175 0004000 10
4043 MYERS, JACKIE        50 MU 4 0087755 0048672 10
4123 JACKSON, EARL        10 LG 1 0068473 0049959 27
4189 HEYDT, MARY J.       20 HO 1 0050000 0010000 15
4231 RICE, BRAD S.        30 HO 1 0115000 0017500 15
4233 MURPHY, ALICE        20 EL 3 0021763 0002847 15
4362 QUIGLEY, BRETT E.    30 FO 2 0023175 0004000 08
4454 MAPLES, LAURIE A.    40 GA 2 0115000 0017500 30
4587 WOLFE, KATHY L.      50 FO 2 0112359 0003575 08
4853 BENNETT, BRENDA      30 WS 2 0095720 0048684 10
4997 JESSON, WAYNE        50 BS 1 0028546 0005885 20
5638 SHELBY, JODI D.      30 FO 2 0050000 0010000 08
5749 GIBSON, MICHELLE R.  20 IC 2 0023175 0004000 15
5906 EAKINS, CHERYL R.    10 FO 2 0115000 0017500 08
5958 KINCADE, MICHAEL D.  20 FO 2 0050000 0010000 08
6197 JONES, JILL A.       30 JE 3 0115000 0017500 10
6278 MCQUEEN, ANGIE L.    40 FO 2 0023175 0004000 08
6341 YORK, BOB Q.         50 GA 2 0023175 0004000 30
6405 ARNOLD, JULIE D.     50 FO 2 0115000 0017500 08
7660 BUEHLER, JENNIFER M. 30 JE 3 0050000 0010000 10
7731 HUTTON, JOANN H.     30 FO 2 0112359 0003575 08
7807 NEWALL, NANCY R.     10 JE 3 0023175 0004000 10
7924 TUCKER, GENA E.      20 FO 2 0115000 0017500 08
8110 ZIMMERMAN, BETTY B.  30 IC 1 0050000 0010000 15
8239 ASTON, ARNOLD A.     20 JE 3 0112359 0003575 10
9730 CROSSLAND, BRENDA R. 10 FO 2 0023175 0004000 08
===================================================
```

Data Set G

These records contain inventory data and are 69 characters long.
The field definitions are:

Column	Field name	Type of data
1–2	Store number	Alphanumeric
4–5	Department mnemonic	Alphanumeric
7–9	Item number	Alphanumeric
11–35	Item description	Alphanumeric
36–41	Quantity on hand	Numeric
43–48	Sales price per unit	Numeric, 2 decimal places
50–55	Cost per unit	Numeric, 2 decimal places
57–62	Year-to-date quantity sold	Numeric
64–69	Year-to-date quantity purchased	Numeric

```
                    1111111111222222222233333333334444444444555555555566666666666
          1234567890123456789012345678901234567890123456789012345678901234567890123456789

10 AP 210 11-CYCLE DISHWASHER         000440 040995 024597 000176 000220
10 AP 190 12.1 CU. FT. FREEZER        000011 075575 045345 000044 000055
20 AU 211 12V SPORT BATTERY           000025 007199 005399 000075 000050
10 AP 200 3-CLCLE MAYTAG WASHER       000190 052988 031792 000760 000950
10 AP 191 30-IN. GAS RANGE            000019 034995 020997 000076 000095
20 AP 191 30-IN. GAS RANGE            000025 034995 020997 000096 000085
20 AU 212 40WATT BOOSTER AMP          000012 006000 004500 000036 000024
10 AU 876 440 BATTERY                 000047 004499 003374 000141 000094
20 AU 876 440 BATTERY                 000057 004499 003374 000161 000104
10 AP 211 9-CYCLE DISHWASHER          000100 038995 023397 000400 000500
10 AP 192 AMANA RADAR RANGE           000057 047599 028559 000228 000285
10 AU 876 AUTO COVER                  000005 003030 002272 000015 000010
20 AU 876 AUTO COVER                  000025 003030 002272 000215 000110
10 AU 208 BOOSTER CABLES              000054 001599 001199 000162 000108
10 AU 209 BULLET-STYLE CAR MIRROR     000301 001249 000936 000903 000602
10 AP 193 ELECTRIC WOK                000042 010172 006103 000168 000210
10 AP 616 EUREKA POWER PLUS VACUUM    000019 014488 008692 000076 000095
20 AP 616 EUREKA POWER PLUS VACUUM    000029 014488 008692 000076 000085
10 AP 619 GE MICROWAVE OVEN           000023 048995 029397 000092 000115
20 AP 619 GE MICROWAVE OVEN           000033 048995 029397 000192 000125
10 AP 620 GE MICROWAVE W/PROBE        000033 058995 035397 000132 000165
10 AU 883 INFLATE AIR COMPRESSOR      000040 002475 001856 000120 000080
20 AU 898 MUZZLER MUFFLER             000096 002499 001874 000288 000192
10 AU 212 POWER DOOR LOCK             000040 000649 000486 000120 000080
10 AP 617 SEWING TABLE                000031 024995 014997 000124 000155
20 AP 617 SEWING TABLE                000054 024995 014997 000275 000165
10 AP 220 SLIDE-IN ELECTRIC RANGE     000100 042995 025797 000400 000500
20 AP 220 SLIDE-IN ELECTRIC RANGE     000200 042995 025797 000300 000400
10 AU 881 STEADY RIDER SHOCKS         000047 002998 002248 000141 000094
20 AU 881 STEADY RIDER SHOCKS         000057 002998 002248 000241 000115
10 AP 201 TOUCH MICROWAVE             000080 048575 029145 000320 000400
10 AU 213 ZT-10 CRUISE CONTROL        000031 006999 005249 000093 000062
```

Data Set H

These records contain sales data and are 51 characters long.
The field definitions are:

Column	Field name	Type of data
1–4	Salesperson number	Alphanumeric
6–25	Salesperson name	Alphanumeric
26–27	Store number	Alphanumeric
29–30	Department mnemonic	Alphanumeric
32	Employee code	Alphanumeric
	1 = Full time	
	2 = Part time	
	3 = Full-time trainee	
	4 = Part-time trainee	
	5 = Store manager	
34–40	Year-to-date sales	Numeric, 2 decimal places
42–48	Year-to-date sales returns	Numeric, 2 decimal places
50–51	Commission rate	Numeric, 2 decimal places

```
=========================================
         11111111112222222222333333333344444444445 5
1234567890123456789012345678901234567890123456789 01
=========================================
      PAYNE, MAX            30 FH 2   98700    5673 05
0125 LISHER, JANET F.       50 JE 2   50000         15
0243 BROCKETT, JANE R.      40 FO 4   75000   90000 05
0356 GOLTMAN, LINDA S.      30 FO 1  109877    1000 10
0396 VOLSKY, CHRIS          3P IS 3   32680    5847 08
0401 OWENS, GEORGE          40 MS     36220    3957 09
0479 WETZEL, ROBERT D.      20 GA 2  208876    5877
0529 PEACOCK, BARBARA       40    3   67330   15664 08
0580 DUPREE, KELLY L.       30 FO 3  357888   27582 10
0635 HUNT, ROBERT              FO 2   45320   47534 10
0746 JACKSON, JASON         40 MU 3   78450    8478 15
0859 HUTCHENS, JEFF         50 MW 2   57630    4857 14
0927 BARCLAY, RICHARD       50 JE 3  198740   48563 11
1001 DILL, JEFF             50 FO 1   58640   28456 20
1132 UNLAND, KIM L.         50 EL 5   47564   39585 25
1415 GOODMAN, EVE           40 RA 2   64542   23847 10
1634 VAUGHN, SYLVIA A.      40 FO 1   47899   45678 20
1805 KIMBERLING, CARLA K.   20 GA 2   50000   10000 30
1856 LOVELAND, GEORGE       30 SP 1   46275   27656 10
1867 STEWARD, KEVIN J.      30 IC 1  115000   17500 1T
1938 DWYER, JOHN D.         10 JE 3   23175    4000 10
2157 YOUNG, KAREN L.        20 GA 2  112359    3575 30
2186 SMITH, DOUGLAS         20 HD 3   18345   37758 20
2269 THOMPSON, LISA S.      30 HO 1   50000   10000 20
2294 HERMAN, JACK           50 GA 4   48465    8747 05
2341 ADAMS, ROBYN A.        40 JE 3   23175    4000 10
2395 MATNEY, DELORES        50 LG 4   79574   85746 05
2485 PHILLIPS, TRACY L.     50 GA 2   50000   10000 30
2487 HUME, LETA             10 FO 2   48353   28437 20
2575 CROSS, CHERYL          50 IC 3   38563   38250 10
2577 IRWIN, ANGELA M.       50 JE 3  115000   17500 10
2666 BARKER, MARY           50 AU 4   45746    2743 20
2758 WELLS, LARRY           50 BC 3   36440   22204 10
2871  WELCH, JAMES          30 HO 5   64530   37857 25
2963 BRADY, CURTIS          20 AP 3  W00039   68473 10
3033 ASHLEY, SHELLEY        50 FH 2   85443   43765 20
3219 BOYER, CATHY           50 CH 2   47656   36680 10
3669 TAYLOR, STEVE M.       40 FO 2   23175    4000 08
3735 LOYD, JAMES R.         30 HO 1   50000   10000 15
3810 EAGAN, DEBBIE R.       20 FO 2  115000   17500 08
3874 DAILEY, GREG           50 HO 3   48945         20
3902 JENKINS, KIM A.        10 FO 2  112359    3575 08
3957 JONES, NEIL            50 SP 4   87867   39777 08
3967 MOORE, EDWARD W.       20 JE 2   23175    4000 10
```

```
4043 MYERS, JACKIE        50 MU 4    87755   48672 10
4123 JACKSON, EARL        10 LG 1    68473   49959 27
4189 HEYDT, MARY J.       20 H8 1    50000   10000 15
4231 RICE, BRAD S.        30 HO 1   115000   17500 15
4233 MURPHY, ALICE        20 EL 3    21763    2847 15
4362 QUIGLEY, BRETT E.    30 FO 2    23175    4000 08
4454 MAPLES, LAURIE A.    40 GA 2   115000   17500 30
4587 WOLFE, KATHY L.      50 FO 2   112359    3575 08
4853 BENNETT, BRENDA      30 2S 2    95720   48684 10
4997 JESSON, WAYNE        50 BS 1    28546    5885 20
5638 SHELBY, JODI D.      03 FO 2    50000   10000 08
5749 GIBSON, MICHELLE R.  20 IC 2    23175    4000 15
5906 EAKINS, CHERYL R.    10 FO 2   115000   17500 08
5958 KINCADE, MICHAEL D.  20 FO 2    50000   10000 08
6197 JONES, JILL A.       30 JE 3   115000   17500 10
6278 MCQUEEN, ANGIE L.    40 FO 2    23175    4000 08
6341 YORK, BOB Q.         50 GA 2    23175    4000 30
6405 ARNOLD, JULIE D.     50 FO 2   115000   17500 08
7660 BUEHLER, JENNIFER M. 30 JE 3    50000   10000 10
7731 HUTTON, JOANN H.     30 FO 2   112359    E575 08
7807 NEWALL, NANCY R.     10 JE 3    23175          10
7924                      20 FO 6   115000   17500 08
8110 ZIMMERMAN, BETTY B.  30 IC B    50000   10000 15
8239 ASTON, ARNOLD A.     20 JE 3             3575 10
9730 CROSSLAND, BRENDA R. 10 FO 2    23175    4000 08
====================================================
```

Data Set I

These records contain inventory data and are 69 characters long. The field definitions are:

Column	Field name	Type of data
1–2	Store number	Alphanumeric
4–5	Department mnemonic	Alphanumeric
7–9	Item number	Alphanumeric
11–35	Item description	Alphanumeric
36–41	Quantity on hand	Numeric
43–48	Sales price per unit	Numeric, 2 decimal places
50–55	Cost per unit	Numeric, 2 decimal places
57–62	Year-to-date quantity sold	Numeric
64–69	Year-to-date quantity purchased	Numeric

```
=============================================================
          1111111111222222222233333333334444444444555555555566666666666
1234567890123456789012345678901234567890123456789012345678901234567890123456789
=============================================================
10 AU 208                        301    1249    936   903    602
10    212  POWER DOOR LOCK        50     649    486   120     Y0
10 AP     11-CYCLE DISHWASHER    440   40995  24597   176    220
10 AP 190 12.1 CU. FT. FREEZER    11   85575  45345    44     55
30 AU 211 12V SPORT BATTERY       25    8199   5399    75     50
10 AP 200 3-CLCLE MAYTAG WASHER  190   52988  31792   760    950
10 AP 191 30-IN. GAS RANGE        19   34995  20997    76     95
20 BD 191 30-IN. GAS RANGE        25   34995  20997    96     85
20 AU 212 40WATT BOOSTER AMP      12    6000   4500    36     24
10 AU 876 440 BATTERY             47    4499   3374   141     94
20 AU 876 440 BATTERY             57    4499   3374   1T1    104
```

```
10 AP 211 9-CYCLE DISHWASHER            100   38995  23397   400   500
10 AP 192 AMANA RADAR RANGE              57   47599          228   285
10 AU 877 AUTO COVER                      5    3030   2272    15    10
20 AU 877 AUTO COVER                     25    3030   2272   215   110
10 AU 208 BOOSTER CABLES                 54    1599   1199   162   108
10 AP 990 ELECTRIC WOK                   42   10172   6103   168   210
10 AP 616 EUREKA POWER PLUS VACUUM       19   14488   8692    76    95
20 AP 616 EUREKA POWER PLUS VACUUM       29   14488   8692    76    85
10 AP 619 GE MICROWAVE OVEN              23   48995  29397    92   115
20 AP 619 GE MICROWAVE OVEN              35   48995  29397   192
   AP 620 GE MICROWAVE W/PROBE           33          35397   132   165
10 AU 883 INFLATE AIR COMPRESSOR         40    2475   1856   120    80
20 AU 898 MUZZLER MUFFLER                96    2499   1874   288   192
10 AP 617 SEWING TABLE                   31   24995  14997   124   155
20 AP 617 SEWING TABLE                   54   24995  14997   275   165
10 AP 220 SLIDE-IN ELECTRIC RANGE             42995   2 797   400   500
20 AP 220 SLIDE-IN ELECTRIC RANGE       200   42995  25797   300   400
10 AU 881 STEADY RIDER SHOCKS            47    2998   2248          94
20 AU 881 STEADY RIDER SHOCKS          B057    2998   2248   241   115
10 AP 201 TOUCH MICROWAVE                80   48575  29145   320   400
10 AU 213 ZT-10 CRUISE CONTROL           31    6999   5249    93    62
=================================================================
```

Data Set J

These records contain payroll data.
The following records are to be used for the pay scales.

```
=======
123456789
=======
300350400
325375425
335400450
400425475
500550675
625675725
750800950
800900975
950975985
=======
```

The following records are the records to be used to calculate payroll.
The field definitions are:

Column	Field name
1–2	Department number
4–6	Employee number
8	Pay code
10–12	Hours worked
14	Employee type

```
==========
         11111
12345678901234
==========
10 022 1 075 1
10 042 6 067 2
10 059 5 071 2
15 111 2 080 1
15 122 8 013 2
```

```
15  123  1  080  3
20  126  9  049  1
20  159  5  093  1
20  175  3  080  2
20  176  6  080  3
25  222  8  080  2
25  226  9  100  2
30  242  6  084  2
30  247  4  080  2
30  277  3  007  3
35  299  2  100  1
35  311  7  082  2
35  322  8  057  2
35  411  7  012  1
35  420  8  094  1
20  421  4  085  3
20  422  8  043  2
25  459  5  012  2
30  477  3  092  1
30  499  2  070  2
30  517  9  080  1
35  522  1  100  1
10  542  6  010  2
20  611  7  058  2
30  621  4  099  2
15  677  3  072  2
25  777  3  097  3
25  799  2  084  1
15  811  7  022  1
25  821  4  011  2
35  822  1  082  1
30  826  9  095  2
20  859  5  093  2
15  842  6  081  2
15  899  2  008  3
25  921  4  076  1
35  922  1  010  2
10  926  9  014  1
40  982  5  080  1
10  995  7  080  3
===========
```

Data Set K

These records contain shipment data.

The following records are to be used for the base-rate table.

The field definitions are:

Column	Field name
1–8	Origin Name
9–23	Base rates

```
===================
          11111111112222
12345678901234567890123
===================
Portland110230340442456
Chicago 315230325390399
Atlanta 575410105225325
Miami   515410225225475
Boston  375402325485225
===================
```

The following records are to be used for the shipment data.
The field definitions are:

Column	Field name
1–4	Commodity number
6–11	Shipment weight
13	Origin number
15	Destination number

```
============
            111111
123456789012345
============
8850 021000 1 2
8863 021000 3 1
8920 021000 3 2
8920 020000 4 1
8890 010500 1 3
8990 029000 2 3
8990 030000 2 4
8890 012000 5 1
9900 036000 5 4
8963 020000 4 2
8990 036000 4 3
8890 013000 3 4
8850 025000 3 5
8920 170500 1 4
8985 011500 2 1
8963 002000 1 5
8850 024000 4 5
7850 024000 5 2
8962 020000 5 3
8985 130500 2 5
============
```

Data Set L

These records contain sales data and contain both header and transaction records that are to be combined into one file. The header records are 55 characters long. The transaction records are 33 characters long.

The field definitions for the header records are:

Column	Field name	Type of data
1–2	Record type, SH=header	Alphanumeric
4–7	Salesperson number	Alphanumeric
9–28	Salesperson name	Alphanumeric
29–30	Store number	Alphanumeric
32–33	Department mnemonic	Alphanumeric
35	Employee code	Alphanumeric
	1 = Full time	
	2 = Part time	
	3 = Full-time trainee	
	4 = Part-time trainee	
	5 = Store manager	
37–43	Year-to-date sales	Numeric, 2 decimal places
45–51	Year-to-date sales returns	Numeric, 2 decimal places
53–54	Commission rate	Numeric, 2 decimal places

The field definitions for the transaction records are:

Column	Field name	Type of data
1–2	Record type, ST=header	Alphanumeric
4–7	Salesperson number	Alphanumeric
9	Transaction Code	Alphanumeric
	1 = New salesperson	
	2 = Delete salesperson	
	3 = Change store number	
	4 = Change department mnemonic	
	5 = Change name	
	6 = Update current sales	
	7 = Update current returns	
	8 = Change commission rate	
11–17	Amount involved	Numeric, 2 decimal places
19–26	Transaction date	Alphanumeric
29–30	Store number	Alphanumeric
32–33	Department mnemonic	Alphanumeric

```
=================================================
         1111111111222222222233333333334444444444455555
1234567890123456789012345678901234567890123456789012345
=================================================

SH 0017 PAYNE, MAX          30 FH 2 0098700 0005673 05
SH 0125 LISHER, JANET F.    50 JE 2 0050000 0000000 15
SH 0243 BROCKETT, JANE R.   40 FO 4 0075000 0090000 05
SH 0356 GOLTMAN, LINDA S.   30 FO 1 0109877 0001000 10
SH 0396 VOLSKY, CHRIS       30 IS 3 0032680 0005847 08
SH 0401 OWENS, GEORGE       40 MS 4 0036220 0003957 09
SH 0479 WETZEL, ROBERT D.   20 GA 2 0208876 0005877 15
SH 0529 PEACOCK, BARBARA    40 GS 3 0067330 0015664 08
SH 0580 DUPREE, KELLY L.    30 FO 3 0357888 0027582 10
SH 0635 HUNT, ROBERT        40 FO 2 0045320 0047534 10
SH 0746 JACKSON, JASON      40 MU 3 0078450 0008478 15
SH 0859 HUTCHENS, JEFF      50 MW 2 0057630 0004857 14
SH 0927 BARCLAY, RICHARD    50 JE 3 0198740 0048563 11
SH 1001 DILL, JEFF          50 FO 1 0058640 0028456 20
SH 1132 UNLAND, KIM L.      50 EL 5 0047564 0039585 25
SH 1415 GOODMAN, EVE        40 RA 2 0064542 0023847 10
SH 1634 VAUGHN, SYLVIA A.   40 FO 1 0047899 0045678 20
SH 1805 KIMBERLING, CARLA K.20 GA 2 0050000 0010000 30
SH 1856 LOVELAND, GEORGE    30 SP 1 0046275 0027656 10
SH 1867 STEWARD, KEVIN J.   30 IC 1 0115000 0017500 15
SH 1938 DWYER, JOHN D.      10 JE 3 0023175 0004000 10
SH 2157 YOUNG, KAREN L.     20 GA 2 0112359 0003575 30
SH 2186 SMITH, DOUGLAS      20 HD 3 0018345 0037758 20
SH 2269 THOMPSON, LISA S.   30 HO 1 0050000 0010000 20
SH 2294 HERMAN, JACK        50 GA 4 0048465 0008747 05
SH 2341 ADAMS, ROBYN A.     40 JE 3 0023175 0004000 10
SH 2395 MATNEY, DELORES     50 LG 4 0079574 0085746 05
SH 2485 PHILLIPS, TRACY L.  50 GA 2 0050000 0010000 30
SH 2487 HUME, LETA          10 FO 2 0048353 0028437 20
SH 2575 CROSS, CHERYL       50 IC 3 0038563 0038250 10
SH 2577 IRWIN, ANGELA M.    50 JE 3 0115000 0017500 10
SH 2666 BARKER, MARY        50 AU 4 0045746 0002743 20
SH 2758 WELLS, LARRY        50 BC 3 0036440 0022204 10
SH 2871 WELCH, JAMES        30 HO 5 0064530 0037857 25
SH 2963 BRADY, CURTIS       20 AP 3 0100039 0068473 10
SH 3033 ASHLEY, SHELLEY     50 FH 2 0085443 0043765 20
SH 3219 BOYER, CATHY        50 CH 2 0047656 0036680 10
SH 3669 TAYLOR, STEVE M.    40 FO 2 0023175 0004000 08
SH 3735 LOYD, JAMES R.      30 HO 1 0050000 0010000 15
SH 3810 EAGAN, DEBBIE R.    20 FO 2 0115000 0017500 08
SH 3874 DAILEY, GREG        50 HO 3 0048945 0000000 20
SH 3902 JENKINS, KIM A.     10 FO 2 0112359 0003575 08
```

```
SH 3957 JONES, NEIL         50 SP 4 0087867 0039777 08
SH 3967 MOORE, EDWARD W.     20 JE 2 0023175 0004000 10
SH 4043 MYERS, JACKIE        50 MU 4 0087755 0048672 10
SH 4123 JACKSON, EARL        10 LG 1 0068473 0049959 27
SH 4189 HEYDT, MARY J.       20 HO 1 0050000 0010000 15
SH 4231 RICE, BRAD S.        30 HO 1 0115000 0017500 15
SH 4233 MURPHY, ALICE        20 EL 3 0021763 0002847 15
SH 4362 QUIGLEY, BRETT E.    30 FO 2 0023175 0004000 08
SH 4454 MAPLES, LAURIE A.    40 GA 2 0115000 0017500 30
SH 4587 WOLFE, KATHY L.      50 FO 2 0112359 0003575 08
SH 4853 BENNETT, BRENDA      30 WS 2 0095720 0048684 10
SH 4997 JESSON, WAYNE        50 BS 1 0028546 0005885 20
SH 5638 SHELBY, JODI D.      30 FO 2 0050000 0010000 08
SH 5749 GIBSON, MICHELLE R.  20 IC 2 0023175 0004000 15
SH 5906 EAKINS, CHERYL .R.   10 FO 2 0115000 0017500 08
SH 5958 KINCADE, MICHAEL D.  20 FO 2 0050000 0010000 08
SH 6197 JONES, JILL A.       30 JE 3 0115000 0017500 10
SH 6278 MCQUEEN, ANGIE L.    40 FO 2 0023175 0004000 08
SH 6341 YORK, BOB Q.         50 GA 2 0023175 0004000 30
SH 6405 ARNOLD, JULIE D.     50 FO 2 0115000 0017500 08
SH 7660 BUEHLER, JENNIFER M.30 JE 3 0050000 0010000 10
SH 7731 HUTTON, JOANN H.     30 FO 2 0112359 0003575 08
SH 7807 NEWALL, NANCY R.     10 JE 3 0023175 0004000 10
SH 7924 TUCKER, GENA E.      20 FO 2 0115000 0017500 08
SH 8110 ZIMMERMAN, BETTY B.  30 IC 1 0050000 0010000 15
SH 8239 ASTON, ARNOLD A.     20 JE 3 0112359 0003575 10
SH 9730 CROSSLAND, BRENDA R.10 FO 2 0023175 0004000 08
ST 7731 7 0027500 10/01/86   30 FO
ST 7731 6 0027500 10/01/86   30 FO
ST 0927 6 0037500 10/05/86   50 JE
ST 0927 7 0015000 10/05/86   50 JE
ST 0017 6 0037500 10/11/86   30 FH
ST 3033 6 0017500 10/05/86   50 FH
ST 3033 7 0022500 10/25/86   50 FH
ST 0927 6 0045000 10/05/86   50 JE
ST 0017 6 0012300 10/02/86   30 FH
ST 0017 6 0025000 10/10/86   30 FH
ST 7731 6 0052500 10/01/86   30 FO
ST 7731 6 0047500 10/01/86   30 FO
ST 0927 6 0025000 10/05/86   50 JE
ST 0017 7 0005000 10/13/86   30 FH
ST 0017 6 0025500 10/01/86   30 FH
ST 3033 6 0025000 10/22/86   50 FH
ST 3033 6 0005200 10/21/86   50 FH
```

===

Data Set M

These records contain inventory data and contain both header records and transaction records that are to be combined into one file with different length records. The header records are 72 characters long. The transaction records are 56 characters long.

The field definitions for the header records are:

Column	Field name	Type of data
1–2	Record type, IH=header	Alphanumeric
4–5	Store number	Alphanumeric
7–8	Department mnemonic	Alphanumeric
10–12	Item number	Alphanumeric
14–38	Item description	Alphanumeric
39–44	Quantity on hand	Numeric
46–51	Sales price per unit	Numeric, 2 decimal places
53–58	Cost per unit	Numeric, 2 decimal places
60–65	Year-to-date quantity sold	Numeric
67–72	Year-to-date quantity purchased	Numeric

The field definitions for the transaction records are:

Column	Field name	Type of data
1–2	Record type, TH=header	Alphanumeric
4–5	Store number	Alphanumeric
7–8	Department mnemonic	Alphanumeric
10–12	Item number	Alphanumeric
14–38	Item description	Alphanumeric
40	Transaction code	Alphanumeric
	1 = New inventory item	
	2 = Delete inventory item	
	(no longer to be sold)	
	3 = New item description	
	4 = New sales price	
	5 = New cost per unit	
	6 = Update quantity sold	
	7 = Update quantity purchased	
42–47	Quantity sold or purchased	
49–56	Date of transaction	

```
                        1111111111222222222233333333334444444444555555555566666666667777
               1234567890123456789012345678901234567890123456789012345678901234567890
IH 10 AP 190 12.1 CU. FT. FREEZER       000011 075575 045345 000044 000055
IH 10 AP 191 30-IN. GAS RANGE           000019 034995 020997 000076 000095
IH 20 AP 220 SLIDE-IN ELECTRIC RANGE    000200 042995 025797 000300 000400
IH 20 AP 616 EUREKA POWER PLUS VACUUM   000029 014488 008692 000076 000085
IH 20 AU 212 40WATT BOOSTER AMP         000012 006000 004500 000036 000024
IH 10 AP 200 3-CLCLE MAYTAG WASHER      000190 052988 031792 000760 000950
IH 10 AP 201 TOUCH MICROWAVE            000080 048575 029145 000320 000400
IH 10 AP 210 11-CYCLE DISHWASHER        000440 040995 024597 000176 000220
IH 20 AU 876 440 BATTERY                000057 004499 003374 000161 000104
IH 20 AU 881 STEADY RIDER SHOCKS        000057 002998 002248 000241 000115
IH 20 AU 898 MUZZLER MUFFLER            000096 002499 001874 000288 000192
IH 10 AP 211 9-CYCLE DISHWASHER         000100 038995 023397 000400 000500
IH 10 AP 220 SLIDE-IN ELECTRIC RANGE    000100 042995 025797 000400 000500
IH 10 AP 616 EUREKA POWER PLUS VACUUM   000019 014488 008692 000076 000095
IH 10 AP 617 SEWING TABLE               000031 024995 014997 000124 000155
IH 10 AP 619 GE MICROWAVE OVEN          000023 048995 029397 000092 000115
IH 10 AP 620 GE MICROWAVE W/PROBE       000033 058995 035397 000132 000165
IH 10 AU 208 BOOSTER CABLES             000054 001599 001199 000162 000108
IH 10 AU 212 POWER DOOR LOCK            000040 000649 000486 000120 000080
IH 10 AU 213 ZT-10 CRUISE CONTROL       000031 006999 005249 000093 000062
IH 10 AU 876 440 BATTERY                000047 004499 003374 000141 000094
IH 10 AU 877 AUTO COVER                 000005 003030 002272 000015 000010
IH 10 AP 191 AMANA RADAR RANGE          000057 047599 028559 000228 000285
IH 10 AP 193 ELECTRIC WOK               000042 010172 006103 000168 000210
IH 10 AU 209 BULLET-STYLE CAR MIRROR    000301 001249 000936 000903 000602
IH 10 AU 881 STEADY RIDER SHOCKS        000047 002998 002248 000141 000094
IH 20 AU 877 AUTO COVER                 000025 003030 002272 000215 000110
IH 10 AU 883 INFLATE AIR COMPRESSOR     000040 002475 001856 000120 000080
IH 20 AP 191 30-IN. GAS RANGE           000025 034995 020997 000096 000085
IH 20 AP 617 SEWING TABLE               000054 024995 014997 000275 000165
IH 20 AP 619 GE MICROWAVE OVEN          000033 048995 029397 000192 000125
IH 20 AU 211 12V SPORT BATTERY          000025 007199 005399 000075 000050
TH 10 AU 881 STEADY RIDER SHOCKS        6 000003 10/03/86
TH 10 AU 881 STEADY RIDER SHOCKS        6 000005 10/04/86
TH 10 AU 881 STEADY RIDER SHOCKS        6 000012 10/02/86
TH 10 AP 616 EUREKA POWER PLUS VACUUM   6 000011 10/10/86
TH 10 AP 616 EUREKA POWER PLUS VACUUM   6 000002 10/10/86
TH 10 AP 616 EUREKA POWER PLUS VACUUM   6 000001 10/06/86
```

```
TH 10 AP 616 EUREKA POWER PLUS VACUUM   7 000010 10/01/86
TH 10 AP 616 EUREKA POWER PLUS VACUUM   6 000015 10/05/86
TH 10 AP 190 12.1 CU. FT. FREEZER       6 000002 10/01/86
TH 10 AP 190 12.1 CU. FT. FREEZER       7 000020 10/07/86
TH 10 AP 190 12.1 CU. FT. FREEZER       6 000003 10/05/86
TH 10 AP 190 12.1 CU. FT. FREEZER       6 000010 10/10/86
TH 20 AU 212 40WATT BOOSTER AMP         7 000030 10/02/86
TH 20 AU 212 40WATT BOOSTER AMP         6 000002 10/01/86
TH 20 AU 212 40WATT BOOSTER AMP         6 000010 10/08/86
```

Data Set N

These records contain sales transaction records and are 51 characters long. The field definitions for the transaction records are:

Column	Field name	Type of data
1–4	Salesperson number	Alphanumeric
6–25	Salesperson name	Alphanumeric
26–27	Store number	Alphanumeric
29–30	Department mnemonic	Alphanumeric
32	Employee code	Alphanumeric
34	Transaction Code	Alphanumeric
	1 = New salesperson	
	2 = Delete salesperson	
	3 = Change store number	
	4 = Change department mnemonic	
	5 = Change name	
	6 = Update current sales	
	7 = Update current returns	
	8 = Change commission rate	
	9 = Change employee code	
36–42	Amount involved	Numeric, 2 decimal places
	(Used for current sales,	9(5)V99 for sales and returns,
	returns and commission rate)	V99 for commission rate
44–51	Transaction date	Alphanumeric

```
                1111111111222222222233333333334444444444455
      123456789012345678901234567890123456789012345678901
      ===================================================
9730                          1 9            10/01/86
  17                            6     25500   10/01/86
 356                            2            10/01/86
7731                            7     27500   10/01/86
7731                            6     27500   10/01/86
                                6            10/01/86
7731                            6     47500   10/01/86
  17                            6     12300   10/02/86
  20  DOUGLAS, BRENT      50 JE 1 1 15        10/02/86
 396  VOLSKI, CHRIS              5            10/02/86
  2 0                           6     20000   10/02/86
1001                    40      3            10/02/86
6197                            8 15         10/02/86
1001                    MU      4            10/02/86
 243                            2            10/03/86
 125  LISHER, JANET F.    50 JE 2 1 15        10/05/86
3033                            6     17500   10/05/86
 927                            6    3 500   10/05/86
 927                            6     25B00   10/05/86
 927                                 15000   10/05/86
 927                            6     45000   10/05/86
 125                            6     17500   10/06/86
```

```
    125                              U    5225 10/10/86
     17                              6   25000 10/10/86
     17                              6   37500 10/11/86
     17                          4 9       10/12/86
     17                              7    5000 10/13/86
   3033                             6    5200 10/21/86
   3559                  75 JE 2 1 15      10/21/86
   3033                             6   25000 10/22/86
   3033                             7   22500 10/25/87
   ================================================
```

Data Set O

These records contain inventory transaction records. The transaction records are 59 characters long.

The field definitions for the transaction records are:

Column	Field name	Type of data
1–2	Store number	Alphanumeric
4–5	Department mnemonic	Alphanumeric
7–9	Item number	Alphanumeric
11–35	Item description	Alphanumeric
36–41	Price or cost per unit	Numeric
43	Transaction code	Alphanumeric
	1 = New inventory item	
	2 = Delete inventory item (no longer to be sold)	
	3 = New item description	
	4 = New sales price	
	5 = New cost per unit	
	6 = Update quantity sold	
	7 = Update quantity purchased	
45–50	Quantity sold or purchased	
52–59	Date of transaction	

```
=========================================================
          1111111111222222222233333333334444444444555555555
1234567890123456789012345678901234567890123456789012345678 9
=========================================================
10 AP 190                              6     2 10/01/86
20 AU 21W                              6     2 10/01/86
10 AO 616                              7    10 10/01/86
19 AP 190                       69995 4       10/02/86
10 AP 618  SINGER SEWING MACHINE       1       10/02/86
10 AP 618                              7    20 10/02/86
10 AP 618                       18750 4       10/02/86
10 AP 618                       9 75 5        10/02/86
10 AU 881                              6    12 10/02/86
20 AU 212                              7    30 10/02/86
20 AP 191                              2       10/03/86
10 AP 190                              6     3 10/05/86
10 AP 616                              6    15 10/05/86
20 AP 192  32-IN. GAS RANGE            1       10/05/86
20 AP 192                       27595 4       10/05/86
20 AP 192                       12350 5       10/05/86
20 AP 192                              7    11 10/05/86
10 AU 213                              2       10/05/86
10 AO 616                              6    P1 10/06/86
10 AP 190                              8    20 10/07/86
10 AU 881  STEADY RIDER PLUS                   10/07/86
20 AU 212                              A    10 10/08/86
20 AP 192                              7     1 10/08/86
```

```
20 AU 876                               1      10/10/86
20 AU 876                               7    5 10/10/86
30 AU 886                          4499 4      10/10/86
20 AU 876                          2850 5      10/10/86
10 AP 616                               6   11 10/10/86
10 AP 616                          9590 5      10/10/86
20 AU 877                               6   10 10/10/86
20 AU 881                               6    2 10/10/86
10 AP 616                               6    2 10/10/86
10 AP 190                               6   10 10/32/86
10 AU 881                               6    3 10/03/87
10 AU 881                               6    5 11/04/86
============================================================
```

Data Set P

These records contains customer accounts receivable data and are 78 characters long.

The record layout is:

1–4	Customer number
6–24	Customer name
25–39	Street address
40–54	City
55–56	State abbreviation
58–62	Zip code
64–70	Beginning balance (i.e., $650.75)
72–78	Credit Limit (i.e., $800)

```
============================================================
         1111111111222222222233333333334444444444555555555566666666667777777777
123456789012345678901234567890123456789012345678901234567890123456789012345678
============================================================
1057 ABC CO.            1715 RIDGE RD. NEW BEDFORD      NH 00123 0065075 0080000
1092 XYZ CO.            1922 ROSE LANE TULSA            OK 69999 0010019 0890000
1159 HILLDEBRAND        2909 FAIRMONT   SALEM           OR 92257 0021975 0020000
1347 MASTER MECHANICS   3298 14TH STR   WAUKEGON        MN 56509 0042400 0075000
1596 PLUMBERS UNION     6557 NE         WASHINGTON      DC 34506 0097800 0100000
1678 SEVEN ELEVEN       732 MONTCLAIR   FLINTRIDGE      MI 68130 0027600 0100000
1990 TENTH STR. TEXACO  3245 10TH ST    GREENFIELD      AL 40998 0005000 0010000
2003 BATTLEFIELD MALL   5578 BARBER ST PEORIA           IL 55801 0090000 0200000
2417 MUMFORD            2118 18TH ST    EUREKA          CA 97908 0102709 0110000
2923 SMSU               19201 BENTON DRCLINTON          IA 65804 0042250 0100000
3075 NHPG               RT 13 BX 179    AUGSBURG        NJ 20639 0150000 0190000
4139 SPRINGFIELD DINER  7497 BLAKE      SPRINGFIELD     IL 55802 0010500 0080000
4765 EDWARDS CHEVROLET  6116 E 6TH      PORTALES        NM 72201 0232011 0250000
4983 BUNTING TRASH      4456 N 4TH      BENTON HARBOR   MI 70631 0458700 0500000
5217 WARDS TRUCKS       RT 50 BX 971    BRANSON         MO 65550 1000000 2000000
6082 BARCLAY PAINT      RT 975 BX 2245 BARCLAY          NV 85803 0010219 0090000
6153 ALLEN PLUMBING     5128 WAVERLY    WINSTON         MS 45802 0022975 0050000
6157 ACME MANUFACTURING 5209 MAIN       ACME            GE 35907 0055075 0100000
6547 JUNIOR'S DINER     9 E MAIN        SENECA          NY 11579 0152400 0200000
6576 TEAMSTERS UNION    3211 CENTRAL    LUBBOCK         TX 73705 0000810 0030000
6679 EZ SHOP            RR 24 BX 12235 NEW ORLEANS      LA 45507 0135400 0150000
6890 KEARNEY CHEVRON    32987 KEARNEY   GRANTS PASS     OR 95803 0015500 0020000
7083 BATTLEFIELD TEXACO 114 N 5TH AVE   ANCHORAGE       AK 99901 0082200 0085000
7117 WANG LABS          21198 RAMBLE DRBERKELEY         SC 12104 0113409 0375000
============================================================
```

Data Set Q

These records contain transactions and are used to concurrently update the customer accounts, salesperson file, and inventory file. The records are 41 characters long.
The record format is:

1–4	Customer number
6–7	Store number
9–10	Department mnemonic
12–15	Salesperson number
17–19	Item number
21	Transaction code
	1 = Credit sale
	2 = Customer Payment
	3 = Credit return
	4 = Cash sale
	5 = Cash return
23–25	Quantity of transaction (i.e., 50)
27–32	Dollar amount (i.e., $550.75)
33–41	Transaction date

```
=====================================
         11111111112222222222333333333344
1234567890123456789012345678901234567890 1
=====================================
1057 10 AP 0017 191 1 001        02/02/87
6157 20 JE 3967     2     055075 02/12/87
6153 10 LG 4123     2     010000 02/22/87
6082 20 AP 1634 619 1 002        02/03/87
     20 JE 7924     2     075500 02/05/87
2417 20 GA 0479     2     004500 02/04/87
2003 20 AP 2575 193 1 010        02/01/87
7083 20 AU 2157     2     082200 02/12/87
4983 10 AP 0017 619 1 001        02/22/87
6890 10 AP 0017 200 1 001        02/15/87
8565 10 AU 0580 876 1 002        02/14/87
7375 20 AP 2575 619 1 001        02/12/87
6679 10 FO 2487     2     200000 02/13/87
1159 20 AP 1634 617 1 002        02/11/87
8993 20 AU 2157 898 1 003        02/10/87
6157 20 AP 2963 220 1 004        02/09/87
1159 20 IS 5749     2     021975 02/08/87
6547 20 AP 1634     2     152400 02/01/87
4765 20 AP 1634 619 1 001        02/01/87
2923 20 AP 2395     2     050000 02/04/87
4139 20 AU 2666 881 1 003        02/01/87
6890 20 AP 2963     2     015500 02/22/87
1596 20 AP 2269 191 3 001        02/15/87
7479 20 AU 2157 876 1 001        02/14/87
8317 10 AP 0411 193 1 001        02/30/87
1678 20 AP 2395 616 1 002        02/01/87
2923 20 AP 2395 617 1 002        02/03/87
4139 20 AU 2666 211 3 001        02/04/87
     20 AP 2395 220 4 001        02/03/87
     10 AU 0580 212 4 002        02/02/87
7479 10 AP 1634     2     150000 02/01/87
6576 10 AP 0017 210 1 002        02/08/87
     10 AU 0580 213 4 001        02/08/87
7083 10 AU 0580 213 1 001        02/07/87
     20 AP 1634 616 4 001        02/07/87
     20 AU 2666 877 5 001        02/06/87
7375 20 AU 2157 881 3 002        02/04/87
```

```
1347 10 AU 0859 883 1 001          02/05/87
     10 AU 0859 883 4 001          02/04/87
     10 AP 0017 616 5 002          02/03/87
1092 10 AU 0580 208 1 010          02/01/87
1990 10 AP 0580 620 1 001          02/02/87
8993 10 FO 3902      2      087500 02/02/87
     20 AU 2157 877 5 005          02/02/87
3075 20 AU 2157      2      200000 02/03/87
7117 20 AP 1634 191 1 002          02/03/87
1092 20 AP 2269 617 1 035          02/02/87
5217 20 AU 2666 898 1 006          02/04/87
=========================================
```

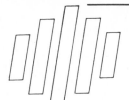

Answers to Selected Exercises

Chapter 2

1. Both are compiler-generated indexes. The index-name is associated with a particular table and must be specified with the INDEXED BY clause. An index-data item is specified with a USAGE IS INDEX clause and can be used with any table.

3. A subscript is any numeric literal or elementary data-name that represents a positive integer and is used to locate an element in a table. An index is either an index-name specified as part of the OCCURS clause or an index data-item defined in WORKING–STORAGE and is also used to locate an element in a table.

5. 05 PAY–RATE PIC 99V99 OCCURS 10 TIMES.

7.

    a.

Storage positions	Storage locations
120	10
75	10
144	24
1500	300
350	100

    b.

MONTH–NAME	1
DEPT–VALUES	1
D–ITEM	1
DEPT–NAMES	1
AIRLINE–TO	1
AIRLINE–RATE	2
SHIPMENT–ORIGIN	1
FREIGHT–OUT	2
F1	2

9.
```
01  TABLE-1.
    05  FILLER PIC X(12) VALUE '10AUTOMOTIVE'.
    05  FILLER PIC X(12) VALUE '15APPLIANCE '.
    05  FILLER PIC X(12) VALUE '23TV        '.
    05  FILLER PIC X(12) VALUE '45CLOTHING  '.
    05  FILLER PIC X(12) VALUE '36HARDWARE  '.
```

```
01  FILLER REDEFINES TABLE-1.
    05  TABLE-VALUES
            OCCURS 5 TIMES
            INDEXED BY TABLE-INDEX.
        10  DEPT-NUMBER PIC 9(2).
        10  DEPT-NAME   PIC X(10).
```

11.

a. Missing PIC clause.

b. Valid.

c. Missing OCCURS clause.

d. Valid.

e. > invalid, only condition can be =.

f. 1 must be index-name.

g. Valid.

h. Either IN-TOTAL or IN-TOTAL(R1, R2) will cause an error.

i. PIC clause with wrong OCCURS.

13.

a.
```
PERFORM COPY-ROUTINE
        VARYING SUB-1 FROM 1 BY 1
        UNTIL SUB-1 > 10.
COPY-ROUTINE.
    MOVE A-TABLE-DATA(SUB-1) TO   B-TABLE-DATA(SUB-1).
```

b.
```
MOVE 10 TO SUB-2.
PERFORM COPY-ROUTINE
    VARYING SUB-1 FROM 1 BY 1 UNTIL SUB-1 > 10.
COPY-ROUTINE.
    MOVE A-TABLE-DATA(SUB-1) TO   B-TABLE-DATA(SUB-2).
    SUBTRACT 1 FROM SUB-2.
```

c.
```
MOVE A-FIELD(1) TO B-SMALL.
PERFORM FIND-SMALLEST-VALUE
    VARYING SUB-1 FROM 2 BY 1 UNTIL SUB-1 > 20.
FIND-SMALLEST-VALUE.
    IF A-FIELD(SUB-1) < B-SMALL
        MOVE A-FIELD(SUB-1) TO B-SMALL.
```

d.
```
PERFORM TABLE-SEARCH
    VARYING SUB-1 FROM 1 BY 1 UNTIL WS-END-FILE =   'END'
    AFTER SUB-2 FROM 1 BY 1 UNTIL WS-END-FILE =   'END'
                                    OR SUB-2 > 6.
TABLE-SEARCH.
    IF TABLE-VALUE(SUB-1, SUB-2) = B-VALUE
        PERFORM VALUE-FOUND
        MOVE 'END' TO WS-END-FILE
    ELSE
        IF SUB-1 = 5 AND SUB-2 = 6
            PERFORM VALUE-NOT-FOUND
            MOVE 'END' TO WS-END-FILE.
```

15.

```
B200-PROCESS
    PERFORM C100-ROW-SEARCH
        IF ROW-FOUND
            PERFORM C200-COL-SEARCH
            IF COL-FOUND
                PERFORM VALUE-FOUND
            ELSE
                PERFORM VALUE-NOT-FOUND
```

```
                    ELSE
                         PERFORM VALUE-NOT-FOUND.
        C100-ROW-SEARCH.
            SET ROW-INDEX TO 1.
            SEARCH ROW-VALUE
                 AT END MOVE 'END' TO WS-END-ROW
              WHEN ROW-VALUE(ROW-INDEX) = SOME-VALUE
                 MOVE 'YES' TO WS-END-ROW.
        C200-COL-SEARCH.
            SET COL-INDEX TO 1.
            SEARCH COL-VALUE
                 AT END MOVE 'END' TO WS-END-COL
              WHEN COL-VALUE(ROW-INDEX, COL-INDEX) = B-VALUE
                 MOVE 'YES' TO WS-END-COL.
```

Chapter 3

1.

    a. Sort key—the field to be sorted on.

    b. Major sort field—the first key in the SORT statement. All data are arranged within the order of this field.

    c. SD—sort description.

    d. ASCENDING KEY clause—sorts from low to high value order.

3. Add a SELECT and SD for SORT-WORK-FILE, including record description. Add a GO TO B100-REFORMAT-EXIT at the end of the paragraph labeled B100-REFORMAT-DATA-PARA. Change the statement MOVE UI-YTD-SALES TO SW-UNIT-PRICE to MOVE UI-YTD-SALES TO SW-YTD-SALES. Change the statement RETURN SW-SORT-WORK-RECORD to RE LEASE SW-SORT-WORK-RECORD in the B100-REFORMAT-DATA section.

```
        INPUT-OUTPUT SECTION.
        FILE-CONTROL.
            SELECT UNSORTED-SALES ASSIGN TO UNSORT.
            SELECT REPORT-FILE     ASSIGN TO SYSPRINT.
            SELECT SORT-WORK-FILE ASSIGN TO SORTWK1.
        DATA DIVISION.
        FILE SECTION.
        FD  UNSORTED-SALES
            RECORD CONTAINS 14 CHARACTERS
            LABEL RECORDS ARE OMITTED.
        01  UI-UNSORTED-SALES-RECORD.
            05  UI-SALES-NUMBER             PIC X(2).
            05  UI-YTD-SALES                PIC 99V99.
        FD  REPORT-FILE
            RECORD CONTAINS 133 CHARACTERS
            LABEL RECORDS ARE OMITTED.
        01  REPORT-RECORD                   PIC X(133).
        SD  SORT-WORK-FILE
            LABEL RECORDS STANDARD.
        01  SW-SORT-WORK-RECORD.
            05  SW-SALES-NUMBER             PIC X(2).
            05  SW-YTD-SALES                PIC 99V99.
        WORKING-STORAGE SECTION.
        PROCEDURE DIVISION.
        A000-MAINLINE SECTION.
```

```
A000-NUMBER-ORDER.
    SORT SORT-WORK-FILE
        ASCENDING KEY SW-SALES-NUMBER
        INPUT PROCEDURE B100-REFORMAT-DATA
        OUTPUT PROCEDURE B200-PRINT-REPORT.
    STOP RUN.
B100-REFORMAT-DATA SECTION.
B100-REFORMAT-DATA-PARA.
    OPEN INPUT UNSORTED-SALES
        OUTPUT REPORT-FILE.
    READ UNSORTED-SALES
        AT END MOVE 'END' TO WS-END-OF-FILE-INDICATOR.
PERFORM B100-READ-UNSORTED
        UNTIL END-OF-FILE.
    CLOSE UNSORTED-SALES.
    GO TO B100-REFORMAT-EXIT.
B100-READ-UNSORTED.
    MOVE 'NO' TO WS-INVALID-RECORD-INDICATOR.
    PERFORM B100-VALIDATE-ROUTINE.
    IF RECORD-NOT-VALID
        PERFORM B100-PRINT-ERROR-MESSAGE
    ELSE MOVE UI-SALES-NUMBER       TO SW-SALES-NUMBER
        MOVE UI-YTD-SALES           TO SW-YTD-SALES
        RELEASE SW-SORT-WORK-RECORD.
    READ UNSORTED-SALES
        AT END MOVE 'END' TO WS-END-OF-FILE-INDICATOR.
B100-VALIDATE-ROUTINE.

B100-REFORMAT-EXIT.
    EXIT.
B200-PRINT-REPORT SECTION.
B200-PRINT-REPORT-PARA.
    RETURN SORT-WORK-FILE
        AT END MOVE 'END' TO WS-END-OF-FILE-INDICATOR.
    PERFORM B200-INITIALIZE-VARIABLES.
    PERFORM B200-PRINT-DETAIL
        UNTIL END-OF-FILE.
    PERFORM B200-GRAND-TOTAL-ROUTINE.
    CLOSE REPORT-FILE.
    GO TO B200-PRINT-EXIT.
B200-INITIALIZE-VARIABLES.

B200-PRINT-DETAIL.

    RETURN SORT-WORK-FILE
        AT END MOVE 'END' TO WS-END-OF-FILE-INDICATOR.
B200-PRINT-EXIT.
    EXIT.
```

Chapter 4

1. The process of eliminating syntax, logic and data errors from a data set.
3.
   a. Prints out the name of the data-item and its value when the statement is executed.

  b. Will print the data-item's name and value only if the value of the data-item has changed since a previous execution of the statement.

  c. Just like *b* except the name of the data-item is never printed.

5.

  a. The compile-time switch is left off.

  b. All lines with a D in column 7 are treated as comments as are any debugging sections.

  c. No debugging takes place.

7.

  a. USE statement starts in the B area. No hyphen in END DECLARA-TIVES.

  b. Need END DECLARATIVES.

  c. Need hyphens in paragraph names. D500–TOTALS invalid, must be a name in the declaratives portion to be performed.

Chapter 5

1. Existence, justification, numeric, alphabetic, sign, check digit, date, inter-file.

3.

  a. Salesperson number—existence, fill with leading zeros, numeric, valid salesperson number.

  b. Salesperson name—existence, left-justification.

  c. Store number—existence, fill with leading zeros, numeric, valid store number.

  d. Department code—existence, fill with leading zeros, numeric (or alphabetic, depending on code), valid department code.

  e. Employee code—existence, fill with leading zeros, numeric (or alphabetic, depending on code), valid employee code.

  f. Year-to-date sales—existence, fill with leading zeros, numeric.

  g. Year to date sales returns—existence, fill with leading zeros, numeric.

  h. Commission rate—existence, fill with leading zeros, numeric.

5.

  a. No message.

  b. FIELD NOT NUMERIC.

  c. FIELD > 8000.

  d. FIELD DOES NOT EXIST.

  e. No message.

  f. FIELD DOES NOT EXIST.

  g. FIELD NOT JUSTIFIED.

Chapter 6

1. File creation is taking a data set, validating and sorting the data and storing the results in a file for future use. File updating is taking a file that has been created and adding, deleting, or changing records in that file as needed in a given time period. File reporting is accessing an updated file and processing a report using data from the file.

3. File control helps ensure the integrity of the data in a file as well as the integrity of the programs that access a file. File control helps to ensure that records are not lost, misplaced, or erroneously recorded. It also helps to ensure that the interrelationships among files in the system are kept intact.

5.
    a. 1,2,3,4,5.
    b. No.
    c. 1,3,4,6,8.
    d. ID 6 has a transaction code of add and that ID already exists on the master file. Also what do you do with ID 9 when it has code of D?
    e. The transaction file continues to be processed. However, only transactions with a code of A are valid.

7. It is a figurative constant that contains the highest value in your system's collating sequence. It is used as a switch to determine when the processing of a particular file is complete. HIGH–VALUES is used because no value in the system can possibly be larger.

Chapter 7

1. A logical record is the data for one complete data record. A physical record may contain one or more logical records (often referred to as a block) and is treated as one record.

3. Add: Refers to a new record being added to the file.
Delete: Refers to a record being deleted from the file.
Changes: Refers to the contents of one or more fields in the master file being changed to reflect the new data.

5. File creation, file maintenance of updating, file reporting.

7.
    a. Valid.
    b. SEQUENTIAL should be replaced with a programmer-supplied name that refers to an error condition.
    c. Omit either INPUT OR I–O.
    d. Valid.
    e. Must include RECORD before KEY.
    f. AT ALTERNATE KEY is in error; should be a condition followed by a data name.
    g. Valid.
    h. Valid.
    i. Valid.

Chapter 8

1. A transformation technique is used to change a numeric value to a relative record number, which is used as the key of the record.

3. Expected slot
    a. 25.
    b. 48.
    c. 76.
    d. 16.

5. Expected slot
    a. 41.
    b. 69.
    c. 9.
    d. 25.

Chapter 10

1. The Report Writer is designed to minimize the logic necessary to prepare hard-copy reports.

3.
    a. Can occur only once at the beginning of a report or at the top of the first page. Used to identify a report.

    b. Can cause a page heading to be printed on every page of the report. Used to identify pages in a report.

    c. Used to summarize a group of data at the end of a control group.

    d. Allows each page except a REPORT HEADING or a REPORT FOOTING to contain summary lines at the bottom of a page.

    e. Allows the programmer to control the printing of a detail line. Prints the detail of input and other records.

5. To indicate the spacing between the current report group and the next report group to be printed.

7.
    a.
```
01 TYPE IS REPORT HEADING.
   05 LINE NUMBER IS 5.
      10 COLUMN 11 PIC X(12) VALUE 'SALES REPORT'.
   05 LINE NUMBER IS 8.
      10 COLUMN 10 PIC X(14) VALUE 'MIDWEST REGION'.
```
    b.
```
01 TYPE IS PAGE HEADING.
   05 LINE NUMBER IS 3.
      10 COLUMN 20 PIC X(13) VALUE 'APRIL SUMMARY'.
   05 LINE NUMBER IS 5.  (or PLUS 2)
      10 COLUMN  5 PIC X(4) VALUE 'NAME'.
      10 COLUMN 15 PIC X(6) VALUE 'NUMBER'.
      10 COLUMN 25 PIC X(4) VALUE 'ITEM'.
      10 COLUMN 35 PIC X(5) VALUE 'TOTAL'.
   05 LINE NUMBER IS 6.  (or PLUS 1)
      10 COLUMN  1 PIC X(80) VALUE ALL '*'.
```
    c.
```
01 TYPE CONTROL FOOTING IN-NUMBER
   LINE PLUS 3 NEXT GROUP NEXT PAGE.
   10 MINOR-TOTAL COLUMN 50
      PIC ZZ,ZZZ SOURCE  SUM IN-NUMBER-AMT.
```

9.
    a. SECOND SECTION must be paragraph name.

    b. FIRST GROUP must be section name.

    c. OTHER–PRINT–SWITCH is invalid.

Chapter 11

1. Validation of input data (INSPECT). Editing data—somewhat like a text editor (STRING and INSPECT). Changing variable length records to fixed-length records (STRING).

3.
    a. Sets of characters.

    b. Joining a set of characters (string) with another set of characters.

    c. A null field is a field that does not receive any data from a sending field.

5. F1 = XYZ
F2 = XYZ
F3 = Spaces (because an overflow occurred when the delimiter was not found for F2.

7.
```
MOVE 1 TO WS-CHARACTER-COUNT
MOVE SPACES TO OUTPUT-AREA.
STRING LAST       DELIMITED BY ' '
      ', '        DELIMITED BY SIZE
      MIDDLE       DELIMITED BY SIZE
      '. '         DELIMITED BY SIZE
      FIRST        DELIMITED BY ' '
   INTO CONDENSED-RECORD
      WITH POINTER WS-CHARACTER-COUNT
      ON OVERFLOW PERFORM E100-ERROR-ROUTINE.
```

9.

   a. Need data-name to store value of POINTER.

   b. Cannot unstring both F1 and F2. Only one sending field valid.

   c. No errors.

   d. Need data-name such as D2 after F3 DELIMITER.

   e. Delete WHEN.

   f. No errors.

   g. Need DELIMITED BY SPACE after ','.

   h. Missing INTO data-name.

   i. ALL and AND invalid in STRING statement.

11.

   a. 7.

   b. 0.

   c. WS–TALLY = 1.
      WS–COUNT=2.

   d. 2.

   e. 2.

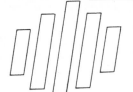

Text Editors

CMS XEDIT

CMS (Conversational Monitor System) is an IBM operating system which includes XEDIT as its prime means of creating source programs. XEDIT may be used as a line editor, but it is used mostly as a full screen editor. The following demonstration introduces the reader to a subset of XEDIT commands.

Editing a New File

1. Enter XEDIT fn ft fm, where fn is an 8-character or less file name, ft is an 8-character file type, and fm is a 1-character file mode indicating the logged disk. This is normally 'A' and can be omitted when working on the A disk.

   For example, if you wanted to create a COBOL program named test, the following command would be entered:
   ```
   XEDIT TEST COBOL
   ```

2. The system responds by creating a full screen that looks like Figure E–1.

   Figure E–1 *New File Screen*

   ```
   TEST     COBOL    A1  F 80  TRUNC=72 SIZE=0 LINE=0 COL=1 ALT=0
   ====>
          ]...+....1....+....2....+....3....+....4....+....5....+....6....+....7.>.
   00000 * * * TOP OF FILE * * *
   00001 * * * END OF FILE * * *
   ```

3. At the top of the screen you will find file information. The second line with the ====> represents the command line, on which you may enter XEDIT commands, such as INPUT, TOP, BOTTOM, CHANGE, etc. The third line contains the scale line, indicating positions within a given line. The remainder of the screen is the file area, in which you enter and/or change the file. Note the line numbers to the left of the TOP and END OF FILE lines. Each entered line is given a number and is placed in what is called the prefix area. The prefix area is used to enter some of the XEDIT commands.

4. To enter lines, type INPUT on the command line and press the enter key. The screen now appears as shown in Figure E–2.

   Figure E–2 *Input Mode*

   ```
    INPUT MODE:
    ====>
    ]...+....1....+....2....+....3....+....4....+....5....+....6....+....7..
    * * * TOP OF FILE * * *
   ```

You may now enter lines, pressing the new line key for each new line. Pressing the enter key once causes the last line typed to move to the top of the screen and leaves the rest of the screen blank. You may continue to enter lines. Pressing the enter key twice causes the cursor to return to the command line. You are now in the edit mode and can enter additional XEDIT commands, such as the FILE command. Issuing the FILE command saves the file under fn ft fm shown at the top left of the screen and ends the editing session.

Editing an Existing File

1. The same format of the XEDIT command is used to edit an existing file. To determine what files exist on your disk, you may issue the FILELIST command.
2. When editing an existing file, the screen that is displayed contains a full screen of the existing file.

Inputting Lines in the File

1. With the cursor on the command line, enter INPUT and press the enter key. The INPUT command allows the entering of lines in the file after the current line. The current line (CURLINE) is the line immediately following the scale line (for a new file CURLINE is initially the TOP OF FILE line). Note: you may change the location of CURLINE with the SET CURLINE command, but it is initially set below the scale line. CURLINE is always highlighted for ease of identification.
2. The cursor is placed after CURLINE—you may now enter lines to be entered in the file. Use the newline key to enter subsequent lines.
3. To leave the input mode, press the enter key twice.
4. While entering lines, you may use the insert key, the delete key, backspace key, and arrow keys on the terminal as necessary.

Scrolling through a File

1. Some of the scrolling commands must be entered on the command line while some may be effected with PF keys. The following table is useful:

Figure E–3 *Miscellaneous Commands*

Synonym	Command	PF key (if applicable)	Effect
TOP	TOP		CURLINE set at TOP
BOT	BOTTOM		CURLINE set at BOTTOM
F	FORWARD	PF8	Forward one screen
B	BACKWARD	PF7	Backward one screen
D	DOWN N		CURLINE down n lines
U	UP N		CURLINE up n lines
	/0000	Entering a slash in the prefix area of a line causes that line to be made CURLINE	

F 3 would scroll forward 3 screens
B 4 would scroll backward 4 screens

Locating a String

1. Use the LOCATE /target/ command to locate a given string, where target is the desired string.
2. You may wish to use the TOP command before issuing the LOCATE command since the LOCATE begins its search on the line following CURLINE.

You may combine commands by using #, as the following sequence indicates:
TOP # LOCATE /PROCEDURE DIVISION/

The above command would first position CURLINE at the top of the file and then search downward until the target is found. If the search is successful, CURLINE is set to the line that contains the target. If unsuccessful, a message is displayed.

3. Searching may also take place beginning with the line above CURLINE and proceeding backward, such as:
LOCATE -/PIC X(4)/

4. The LOCATE command is implied if you enter a string only. The following command would direct a search for the string 'PERFORM B1'.
/PERFORM B1/

Adding and Deleting Lines

1. Though you could add lines by entering the input mode, if only a few lines are needed and you know how many, you may issue the ADD n command with the cursor on the command line. This causes the addition of n lines after CURLINE. The same thing is true of the DELETE n command. DELETE 5 would delete CURLINE and the following four lines.

2. The more efficient method of adding and deleting lines uses the prefix area. The following examples illustrate. The example in Figure E–4 adds one line after line 4. Note the A is placed in the prefix area and the enter key is pressed to execute the command.

Figure E–4 *Adding Lines*

```
Before:

00000 * * * TOP OF FILE * * *
00001        IDENTIFICATION DIVISION.
00002        PROGRAM-ID.  SALESREP.
00003        ENVIRONMENT DIVISION.
A0004        CONFIGURATION SECTION.
00005           SOURCE-COMPUTER.  IBM.
00006 * * * END OF FILE * * *

After:

00000 * * * TOP OF FILE * * *
00001        IDENTIFICATION DIVISION.
00002        PROGRAM-ID.  SALESREP.
00003        ENVIRONMENT DIVISION.
00004        CONFIGURATION SECTION.
00005
00006           SOURCE-COMPUTER.  IBM.
00007 * * * END OF FILE * * *
```

Similarly, placing A5 in the prefix area of a line adds five lines after CURLINE. Placing a D in the prefix area of a line, and pressing the enter key, causes the deletion of CURLINE. If D10 OR 10D were placed in the prefix area and the enter key was pressed, CURLINE and the following nine lines would be deleted. If you do not wish to count the number of lines to be deleted (common if you want to delete a series of lines that are not on the same screen), place DD in both the beginning and ending lines that you want deleted. (You may scroll between placing DD in the beginning line and placing DD in the ending line.) Note: The use of any prefix commands that indicate a block may span any number of screens backward or forward.

For example, if the following was entered, lines 3 through 5 would be deleted simply by pressing the enter key.

Figure E–5 *Deleting Lines*

```
Before:

00000 * * * TOP OF FILE * * *
00001          IDENTIFICATION DIVISION.
00002          PROGRAM-ID.  SALESREP.
DD003          ENVIRONMENT DIVISION.
00004          CONFIGURATION SECTION.
DD005              SOURCE-COMPUTER.  IBM.
00006 * * * END OF FILE * * *

After:

00000 * * * TOP OF FILE * * *
00001          IDENTIFICATION DIVISION.
00002          PROGRAM-ID.  SALESREP.
00003 * * * END OF FILE * * *
```

3. If it is necessary to remove any pending prefix commands (before pressing the enter key), issue the RESET command from the command line.
4. You may also recover deleted lines by using the RECOVER n command or the RECOVER * command to recover all lines that had been previously deleted with a D prefix command.

Changing Lines

1. Entries can be changed by positioning the cursor at the desired location of the change. The change can then be made by typing over the wrong entries, using the delete key or the insert key, and then typing in the correct entries.
2. Changes can also be effected by the CHANGE command. The CHANGE command has the format:
   CHANGE /oldstring/newstring/[* *]
   This command changes whatever is indicated as oldstring to newstring in CURLINE, if the oldstring is found. Global changes can be made from CURLINE to the bottom of the file by adding * *. You may wish to precede a CHANGE command by a TOP, such as the following command, which sets CURLINE to TOP and changes all occurrences of EMPLOYEE-RECORD to SALES-RECORD in the entire file.
   TOP # CHANGE /EMPLOYEE-RECORD/SALES-RECORD/ * *

Copying and Moving Lines

1. Copying and moving lines can be done with commands from the command line. However, the easier method uses the prefix area. The following example, shown in Figure E–6, causes line 4 to be copied after line 6. The C indicates the line to copy and the F indicates that the copied line is to be placed following line 6. A P in the prefix area of line 6 would cause the copied line to be placed previous to line 6. The result is shown in the next screen.

Figure E–6 *Copying Lines*

```
Before:

C0004          CONFIGURATION SECTION.
00005             SOURCE-COMPUTER.  IBM.
F0006             OBJECT-COMPUTER.  IBM.
00007          INPUT-OUTPUT SECTION.

After:

00004          CONFIGURATION SECTION.
00005             SOURCE-COMPUTER.  IBM.
00006             OBJECT-COMPUTER.  IBM.
00007          CONFIGURATION SECTION.
00008          INPUT-OUTPUT SECTION.
```

2. If blocks of lines are to be copied, then CC is placed in the prefix area of the first line to be copied and in the prefix area of the last line to be copied. The use of F and P remain the same.
3. Similarly, the M or MM commands in the prefix area are used to move lines. The use of F and P remains the same.
4. You may also duplicate a line by placing " or "n in the prefix area. For example, Figure E–7 shows how to duplicate line 9 three times, and place the three lines immediately following line 9. If you wish to duplicate a block of lines, use " " in the prefix area in two lines.

Figure E–7 *Duplicating Lines*

```
Before:

"3009          05 FILLER   PIC X(5) VALUE SPACES.

After:

00009          05 FILLER   PIC X(5) VALUE SPACES.
00010          05 FILLER   PIC X(5) VALUE SPACES.
00011          05 FILLER   PIC X(5) VALUE SPACES.
00012          05 FILLER   PIC X(5) VALUE SPACES.
```

5. Remember to press the enter key for all commands that use the prefix area.

Merging Files

1. To bring an existing file into the file currently being edited, use the GET command, which merges the file named in the GET command after CURLINE. The format of the GET command is:
GET fn ft fm

Saving Files

1. To save the file that is currently being edited, and remain in the editor, issue the following command.
SAVE fn ft fm
Fn ft fm can be used to change the name of the file from what it is currently named. If omitted, the current fn ft fm is used.
2. To save the file that is currently being edited and to leave the editor, issue

the FILE fn ft fm command. Its use in allowing the changing of the name is the same as that for the SAVE command.

3. If you wish to leave the editor, issue the QUIT command. If changes have been made to the current file since a previous SAVE command, the system requires the use of QUIT to leave the editor.

EDT

The editor program referenced here is one that is used on Digital Equipment Corporation systems and is call EDT. To use this editor one must do the following:

1. Log on the system.
2. When the system is READY
   a. Enter EDT file-name. File-name is a six position name of alphabetic and/or characters. It can be the name of a new file to be created or the name of an old file that is to be brought back into the system.
   b. Create or modify the file.
   c. Leave EDT by entering QUIT or EXIT. When the system responses with READY, the user is free to continue with whatever needs to be done.
   d. Log off the system.

This line editor can operate in two modes; the EDT mode, which is used to enter various commands, and the INSERT mode which is used to create text in a file or add lines to an existing file. When in the EDT mode, an asterisk is always displayed on the input device. When in the INSERT mode, the asterisk does not appear, and the cursor is positioned at column one of that line.

Invoking the Editor

Enter EDT NAME1, where NAME1 is the name of an old edited file that is being brought back into the system or the name of a new file that is going to be edited. Once you are in the EDT mode, entering INSERT puts you into the INSERT mode.

Creating Lines in the File

To place a new line in a file you must be in the INSERT mode. The editor is positioned at character one of the line to be created. You may space to a certain position in the line, or enter characters (up to 80 per line). When you have completed a line, depress the RETURN key. The line just entered is saved, and again the system has positioned you at column 1 of a new line.

If an error is discovered before you depress the RETURN key, it can be corrected by one of the following:

1. Depress the RUBOUT or DELETE key for each character to be corrected, and then enter the correct character. To see if the correction was properly made, depress the CTRL and R keys at the same time. This displays the entire line the exact way it is residing in the system.
2. Depress the CTRL and U keys at the same time. This deletes the entire line just entered and positions the system at column 1 of the line. Enter the data again.

To get out of the INSERT mode and back into the EDT mode, depress the keys CTRL and Z at the same time. When an asterisk appears on the input device, the EDT mode is awaiting a command.

Displaying Lines of the File

When in the EDT mode, one may look at all or selected lines in the file. Each line of text in the file will have been given a line number to identify it; the lines are usually in increments of 10.

1. To display the entire file, enter T%WH or just %WH. This lists the file with line numbers being shown on the left side of the line. While the file is being listed, do not attempt to stop it. This causes either the file to be erased or unpredictable results to occur.
2. To display only one line of a file, determine the line number in the file you want (usually a complete listing of the file is obtained ahead of time so that the user can look for the lines in question and find the line number); enter T50. T means to type a line, and 50 refers to a particular line and could be any line number in the file.
3. To display a group of lines, enter T50:100. This displays all of the lines between 50 and 100. These line numbers can be any numbers listed within the file and must be in ascending order.
4. To display a selection of lines, enter T 100, 200, 300. The three lines 100, 200, and 300 will be displayed. Any number of lines can be selected.

Deleting Lines in the File

To delete a line or group of lines while in the EDT mode, do one of the following:

1. To delete a single line, enter D100 (where 100 can be any line number).
2. To delete a group of lines, enter D100:300. All the lines from 100 through 300 are deleted from the file. 100 and 300 can be any line numbers in ascending order.
3. To delete selected lines enter D110, 230, 450. The three lines 110, 230, 450 are deleted. Any number of lines can be selected.

Selective Corrections in the EDT Mode

Selective corrections can be made to lines without changing the whole line. Either the SUBSTITUTE, or S, command is used with the delimiter / or ' to separate characters to be changed.

1. Below is an example of substitutions to a single line:

Figure E–8 *Substitutions*

```
T100              (to find the line to change)
S'ABD'ABC         (changes ABD to ABC)
S/ABC/  ABC       (inserts 2 spaces before ABC)
S'ABC'A B C       (inserts spaces between letters)
S/ABC/            (deletes ABC)
```

2. To make a substitution throughout the entire file (a global search), enter S/DATA RECORD/DATA-RECORD/%WH. The %WH starts the search for DATA RECORD at the beginning of the file, and each time it is encountered it is replaced by DATA-RECORD.
3. To make a selective substitution throughout the entire file, enter S/DATE/ DATA/%WH/Q. The %WH causes a global search, and the Q stops the search each time it locates a DATE; this allows the user to answer yes or no about making the substitution for that occurrence of DATE. This procedure continues until the end of the file is reached.

Entering Lines in an Existing File

If it is necessary to insert lines in an existing file, enter the INSERT mode as given below.

1. To enter statements before a given line number, enter INSERT 300. You are now at column one, and in the INSERT mode at line 291. You can enter

as many new lines as necessary. They are given line numbers in increments of one until line 299. Since the next line is 300, it does not duplicate the line number; therefore the remaining lines entered at this point are not given line numbers at this time. Remember, to get out of the INSERT mode, you must depress the keys CTRL and Z at the same time.

2. To place lines after the last line in the file, enter INSERT %E. Line numbers are again in increments of 10, starting after the number of the last line in the file.

As has been seen, the lines entered in a file may be given line numbers in increments of 10, 1, or none at all. After lines have been entered, deleted, or changed, enter RES to resequence the line numbers, if desired, with new line numbers in increments of 10.

Merging Files

While in the EDT mode, one can merge two or more files.

1. To merge a file before a certain line in the file, enter INC 500/FI: FILE1. This merges a file called FILE1 ahead of line 500 in the file with which you are working.
2. To merge a file after the last line in the file, enter INC %E/FI: FILE3. The %E causes the file FILE3 to be placed at the end of the file being edited.

Moving Lines

Lines can be moved from one area of a file to another.

1. To move one line, enter M 300 % TO 35. This places the contents of line 300 at line 35, where 35 must be an unused line number, and erases line 300 from the file.
2. To move a group of lines, enter M 300:310 % TO 325:327. Lines 325 through 327 must have been unused. After the move, lines 300 through 310 are erased.

Copying Lines

Lines can be copied from one area of a file to another.

1. To copy one line, enter CO 610 % TO 805. The statement at line 610 is duplicated at line 805. Line 805 must be unused.
2. To copy a group of lines, enter CO 610:650 % TO 310:350. Lines 310 through 350 must be unused before the copy.

Leaving the Editing Program

One can leave the edit session in two ways.

1. Enter EXIT. This terminates the session. If this was an old file, and changes were made to it during the edit session, a copy of the old file before any changes is saved as a backup file; and the copy of the file with changes is also saved.
2. Enter QUIT. This also terminates the session. If this was an old file, it is saved as it was before any changes had been made to it. If it is a new file, it is not saved.

Renaming a File

To change the name of a saved edited file and at the same time to make a duplicate copy of the file enter EDT NAME5=NAME4. The contents of the file NAME4 are left unchanged but a copy of this file is placed in the file NAME5. There are now two files with the same contents but different names. If it is necessary to purge the file NAME4 from the system enter UNSAVE NAME5 after you have left the EDT mode.

Virtual Storage Access Method (VSAM)

Virtual Storage Access Method (VSAM) is an IBM product that enables the interface between COBOL (and other languages) and the physical storage on magnetic disk for both indexed and relative files. VSAM is a physical approach to the storage of these files and is also a series of utilities called **Access Method Services**. The following IBM materials should be available in any installation using VSAM:

- VSE/VSAM General Information, GC24–5143
- Using VSE/VSAM Commands and Macros, SC24–5144
- VSE/VSAM Messages and Codes, SC24–5146
- VSE/VSAM Programmer's Reference, SC24–5145
- Using the VSE/VSAM Space Management for SAM Feature, SC24–5192
- Using the VSE/VSAM Backup/Restore Feature, SC24–5216
- VSE/VSAM Documentation Subset, SC24–5191

VSAM as a Physical Concept

To understand VSAM as a physical concept or approach to data storage, the reader is referred to Figure F–1.

In this example, an indexed file has been loaded into a VSAM cluster, which contains among other things an index set, a sequence set, control areas, and control intervals. The data are loaded into **control intervals**, into which the records and associated keys are placed in contiguous locations. The record locations are indicated in this example by the key numbers 123, 385, and so forth. The cross-hatched portions of each control interval contain necessary control information used by the system.

Notice the purpose of the contents of the sequence sets and the index set. The **sequence set** contains the highest key of related control intervals and the **index set** contains the highest key of related control areas. These allow a relatively fast means of determining the likely location of a record in the cluster during additions, deletions, and changes.

When a READ is issued, VSAM locates the appropriate control interval by using the index set and the sequence sets. For example, if a READ was issued to do an update on the record that has a key of 920, the index set is first accessed, and it is determined that the record, if it exists, would be located in the second control area. The second sequence set is then accessed, and it indicates that the second control interval in the second control area is the correct control interval. Then the entire control interval is read into the computer for further processing. If another READ was issued by the COBOL program for a record with a key of 903, the system already has the appropriate control interval in memory, thereby eliminating the need for another physical read to be issued.

Figure F-1 *Indexed File Storage in VSAM*

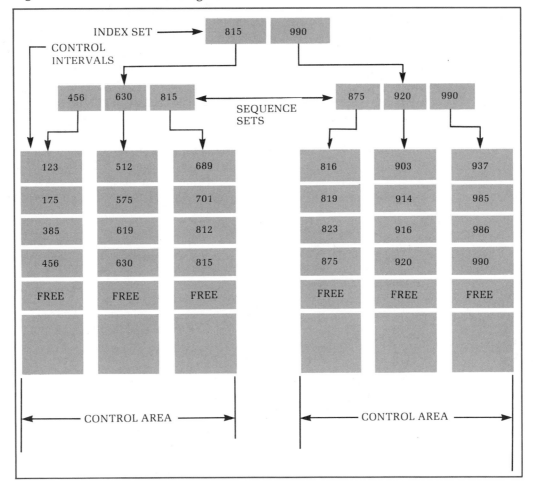

In each control interval it is possible to allocate a portion of the control interval as free space. The purpose of the free space is to allow the addition of records into a control interval, while still maintaining physical sequence. As an example, if a record with a key of 259 was to be added to the VSAM cluster, record 456 could be moved to the free space, record 385 would be moved to the position previously occupied by record 456, and the new record would be added into the space previously occupied by record 385. Unlike many indexed file systems, VSAM is in a continual process of reorganizing the data in the cluster.

If insufficient free space exists in a control interval when another record is added, records can be shifted to the right in another control interval within the same control area. A **control area** is comprised of two or more control intervals. This shifting of data records within a control area is called a **control interval split**. Should insufficient free space exist in a control area, data records can be shifted to a control interval in another control area, causing a **control area split**. Both the number of control interval and control area splits should be minimized and should occur primarily during file expansion. When record deletion occurs, VSAM can reclaim unused space due to the deletion by causing records to be shifted to the left. On balance, deletions and additions tend to keep the cluster relatively stable.

VSAM as a Series of Programs

IBM supplies a series of powerful utility programs to work with VSAM clusters. They enable such tasks as cluster definition, building of alternate indexes, cluster deletion, cluster backup, cluster statistics, cluster printing, and migrating indexed files that were formerly non-VSAM. An introduction to the more important commands for the COBOL programmer are presented in the following discussion. Additionally, JCL used for both OS/VSE and DOS/VSE are included to enable VSAM users to run the programs in this text with minor modification.

Figure F–2 lists the formats of the major VSAM commands that are necessary to work with indexed and relative files.

First, it is important to note the format of access methods services commands. Many commands require parentheses (and, of course, must balance). If an entry cannot be completed on one line, the continuation character (-) must be used.

Second, there are specific rules regarding the construction of names. Cluster-names, alternate-index-names, data-names, and index-names, must all be unique in the system. These names can be a maximum of 44 characters, can contain a maximum of 5 segments separated by a period, and each name segment (which

Figure F–2 *Major VSAM Commands for the COBOL Programmer*

```
To delete an existing cluster:
    DELETE (cluster-name) CLUSTER PURGE

    DELETE (alternate-index-name) ALTERNATEINDEX PURGE

To define a key-sequenced-cluster:
    DEFINE CLUSTER -
        (NAME(cluster-name) -
        INDEXED -
        RECORDS(primary-records secondary-records) -
        FOR(number-of-days-to-retain) -
        FREESPACE(%-free-CI %-free-CA) -
        KEYS(length-of-key offset-of-key) -
        SHAREOPTIONS(2) -
        SPEED -
        VOLUME(volume-id)) -
    DATA -
        (NAME(data-name) -
        RECORDSIZE(average-lrecl maximum-lrecl) -
        CISZ(control-interval-size)) -
    INDEX -
        (NAME(index-name)) -
    CATALOG(CATALOG.catalog-name catalog-name)

To define an alternate index:
    DEFINE ALTERNATEINDEX -
        (NAME(alternate-index-name) -
        RELATE(cluster-name) -
        KEYS(length-of-key offset-of-key) -
        SHAREOPTIONS(3) -
        VOLUME(volume-id) -
        RECORDS(number-of-primary-records number-of-secondary-records) -
        NONUNIQUEKEY -
        UPGRADE) -
     DATA -
        (NAME(alternate-index-data-name) -
        RECORDSIZE(average-lrecl maximum-lrecl) -
        CISZ(control-interval-size)) -
     INDEX -
        (NAME(alternate-index-index-name))
    DEFINE PATH -
        (NAME(path-name) -
        PATHENTRY(alternate-index-name) -
        UPDATE)
    BLDINDEX -
        INDATASET(cluster-name) -
        OUTDATASET(alternate-index-name) -
        WORKVOLUMES(volume-id) -
        CATALOG(CATALOG.catalog-name)
```

Figure F–2 *(concluded)*

To define a relative cluster:

```
DEFINE CLUSTER –
     (NAME(relative-cluster-name) –
     NUMBERED –
     FOR(number-of-days-to-retain) –
     SHAREOPTIONS(2) –
     RECORDSIZE(average-lrecl maximum-lrecl) –
     TRACKS(primary-no-of-tracks secondary-no-of-tracks) –
     SPEED –
     VOLUME(volume-id)) –
CATALOG(CATALOG.catalog-name)
```

To update catalog entries and to close an opened file:

```
VERIFY DATASET (cluster-name)
```

To print data records from an existing cluster:

```
PRINT INFILE (system-name) COUNT(number-to-print) DUMP
```

To print statistics relative to an existing cluster:

```
LISTCAT ENTRIES (cluster-or-other-name) ALL
```

Figure F–3 *DOS Job Stream Used to Run Programs 7–1, 7–2, and 7–3*

```
// EXEC IDCAMS,SIZE=AUTO
   DELETE (INDEXED.SALES.KD) –
           CLUSTER –
           PURGE
   DEFINE CLUSTER –
       (NAME(INDEXED.SALES.KD) –
        INDEXED –
        RECORDS(20 20) –
        FOR(50) –
        FREESPACE(10 0) –
        KEYS(4 0) –
        SHAREOPTIONS(2) –
        SPEED –
        VOLUME(ACAWK2)) –
     DATA –
        (NAME(INDEXED.SALES.DATA) –
         RECORDSIZE(55 55) –
         CISZ(4096)) –
     INDEX –
        (NAME(INDEXED.SALES.INDEX)) –
     CATALOG(CATALOG.ACAD01 ACAD01)
/*
// OPTION LINK,NOSYM,NOLIST,NODUMP
// EXEC FCOBOL
===Program 7–1===
/*
// EXEC LNKEDT
// DLBL SALES,'INDEXED.SALES.KD',,VSAM
// DLBL SALESCT,'%%INDEXED.CONTROL.KD',0,VSAM
// EXTENT ,ACAWK2,,,1,2
// DLBL SBACK,'%%INDEXED.BACKUP.KD',0,VSAM
// EXTENT ,ACAWK2,,,1,2
// EXEC
===input data===
/*
// EXEC IDCAMS,SIZE=AUTO
   VERIFY DATASET (INDEXED.SALES.KD)
   DELETE (COM.RATE.AIX) –
          ALTERNATEINDEX –
          PURGE
```

Figure F–3 *(concluded)*

```
   DEFINE -
     ALTERNATEINDEX -
       (NAME(COM.RATE.AIX) -
        RELATE(INDEXED.SALES.KD) -
        KEYS(2 53) -
        SHAREOPTIONS(3) -
        VOLUME(ACAWK2) -
        RECORDS(20 20) -
        NONUNIQUEKEY -
        UPGRADE) -
     DATA -
       (NAME(COM.RATE.AIX.DATA) -
        RECORDSIZE(12 47) -
        CISZ(2048)) -
     INDEX -
       (NAME(COM.RATE.AIX.INDEX))
   DEFINE PATH -
       (NAME(COM.RATE.PATH) -
        PATHENTRY(COM.RATE.AIX) -
        UPDATE)
   BLDINDEX -
        INDATASET(INDEXED.SALES.KD) -
        OUTDATASET(COM.RATE.AIX) -
        WORKVOLUMES(ACAWK2) -
        CATALOG(CATALOG.ACAD01)
===other entries for other alternate indexes
/*
// OPTION LINK,NOSYM,NOLIST,NODUMP
// EXEC FCOBOL
===Program 7-2===
/*
// EXEC LNKEDT
// DLBL SALES,'INDEXED.SALES.KD',,VSAM
// DLBL SALES1,'LAST.NAME.PATH',,VSAM
// DLBL SALES2,'YTD.SALES.PATH',,VSAM
// DLBL SALES3,'COM.RATE.PATH',,VSAM
// DLBL SALESCT,'%%INDEXED.CONTROL.KD',,VSAM
// EXEC
1
2
3
4
/*
// OPTION LINK,NOSYM,NOLIST,NODUMP
// EXEC FCOBOL
===Program 7-3===
/*
// EXEC LNKEDT
// DLBL SALESCT,'%%INDEXED.CONTROL.KD',0,VSAM
// DLBL SALES,'INDEXED.SALES.KD',,VSAM
// DLBL SALES1,'LAST.NAME.PATH',,VSAM
// DLBL SALES2,'YTD.SALES.PATH',,VSAM
// DLBL SALES3,'COM.RATE.PATH',,VSAM
// EXEC
===sales transaction data===
/*
```

must start with an alphabetic character) can be a maximum of 8 characters. Examples of valid names can be seen in Figures F–3 and F–4.

The **DEFINE CLUSTER** establishes parameters for a cluster by first providing the **NAME** of the cluster, then indicating the type of cluster (**INDEXED** for an indexed cluster, **NUMBERED** for a relative cluster). The number of **RECORDS**, both for a

Figure F–4 *OS Job Stream Used to Run Programs 7–1, 7–2, and 7–3*

```
//FILESTP EXEC PGM=IDCAMS
//SYSPRINT DD SYSOUT=A
//SYSIN    DD *
   DELETE (INDEXED.SALES.KD) -
          CLUSTER -
          PURGE
   DEFINE CLUSTER -
       (NAME(INDEXED.SALES.KD) -
        INDEXED -
        RECORDS(20 20) -
        FOR(50) -
        FREESPACE(10 0) -
        KEYS(4 0) -
        SHAREOPTIONS(2) -
        SPEED -
        VOLUME(ACAWK2)) -
   DATA -
       (NAME(INDEXED.SALES.DATA) -
        RECORDSIZE(55 55) -
        CISZ(4096)) -
   INDEX -
       (NAME(INDEXED.SALES.INDEX)) -
   CATALOG(CATALOG.ACAD01 ACAD01)
/*
//COBOL1 EXEC COBUCLG
//SYSIN    DD *
===Program 7-1===
/*
//GO.SALES   DD DSN=INDEXED.SALES.KD,DISP=OLD
//GO.SALESCT DD DSN=%%INDEXED.CONTROL.KD,DISP=NEW,KEEP,
//   SPACE=(TRK,(2),,CONTIG)
//GO.SBACK   DD DSN=%%INDEXED.BACKUP.KD,DISP=NEW,KEEP,
//   SPACE=(TRK,(2),,CONTIG)
//GO.READER  DD *
===input data===
/*
//ALTSTEP EXEC PGM=IDCAMS
   VERIFY DATASET (INDEXED.SALES.KD)
   DELETE (COM.RATE.AIX) -
       ALTERNATEINDEX -
       PURGE
   DEFINE -
     ALTERNATEINDEX -
       (NAME(COM.RATE.AIX) -
        RELATE(INDEXED.SALES.KD) -
        KEYS(2 53) -
        SHAREOPTIONS(3) -
        VOLUME(ACAWK2) -
        RECORDS(20 20) -
        NONUNIQUEKEY -
        UPGRADE) -
     DATA -
       (NAME(COM.RATE.AIX.DATA) -
        RECORDSIZE(12 47) -
        CISZ(2048)) -
     INDEX -
       (NAME(COM.RATE.AIX.INDEX))
   DEFINE PATH -
       (NAME(COM.RATE.PATH) -
        PATHENTRY(COM.RATE.AIX) -
        UPDATE)
   BLDINDEX -
       INDATASET(INDEXED.SALES.KD) -
```

Figure F–4 *(concluded)*

```
         OUTDATASET(COM.RATE.AIX) -
         WORKVOLUMES(ACAWK2) -
         CATALOG(CATALOG.ACAD01)
===other entries for other alternate indexes===
/*
//COBOL2 EXEC COBUCLG
//SYSIN DD *
===Program 7-2===
/*
//GO.SALES    DD DSN=INDEXED.SALES.KD,DISP=OLD
//GO.SALES1   DD DSN=LAST.NAME.PATH,DISP=OLD
//GO.SALES2   DD DSN=YTD.SALES.PATH,DISP=OLD
//GO.SALES3   DD DSN=COM.RATE.PATH,DISP=OLD
//GO.SALESCT DD DSN=%%INDEXED.CONTROL.KD,DISP=OLD
//GO.READER   DD *
===input data===
/*
//COBOL3 EXEC COBUCLG
//SYSIN DD*
===Program 7-3===
/*
//GO.SALES    DD DSN=INDEXED.SALES.KD,DISP=OLD
//GO.SALES1   DD DSN=LAST.NAME.PATH,DISP=OLD
//GO.SALES2   DD DSN=YTD.SALES.PATH,DISP=OLD
//GO.SALES3   DD DSN=COM.RATE.PATH,DISP=OLD
//GO.SALESCT DD DSN=%%INDEXED.CONTROL.KD,DISP=OLD
//GO.READER   DD *
===input data for transactions===
/*
```

primary number of records and for a secondary allocation is requested. It is also possible to indicate that the cluster is to be retained **FOR** a certain number of days. The **FREESPACE** is indicated by a percentage for both the amount of freespace that is to be maintained after a control interval and/or a control area split. The length and offset of the **KEY** is also specified. A key that was 10 characters long and located in position 35 of the record would be indicated by KEY(10 34). **SHAREOPTION**, **SPEED**, and **VOLUME** are additional requirements. The actual record size is indicated by the **RECORDSIZE** entry. The size of the control interval is specified by the **CISZ** entry and ranges from 512 to 32768. When the size is between 512 and 8192 a multiple of 512 must be used. When greater than 8192, the control interval size must be a multiple of 2048.

Figure F–3 illustrates the DOS job stream used to run Programs 7–1, 7–2 and 7–3 in the chapter on indexed files. It is presumed that from this presentation and the preceding DEFINE commands to define a relative cluster, that the programmer would be able to create the job stream necessary to run the programs contained in Chapter 8 for relative files. Figure F–4 illustrates the OS job stream used to run Programs 7–1, 7–2, and 7–3 in the chapter on indexed files.

Two items of particular importance in the preceding and following job streams should be highlighted. They are the RECORDSIZE entry when defining the alternate indexes and the DLBL statements when accessing a cluster that contains alternate indexes. In the example, an alternate index is to be defined and built using commission rate as the alternate key. Commission rate is located in positions 54 and 55 of the indexed record. The formula to determine the maximum logical length is 5 + alternate key size + (prime key size × number of prime keys with alternate index). In this example, this would be 5 + 2 + (4 × 10) = 47. The 10 is an estimate of the number of records that would have a particular alternate key. If the estimate is too low, the system will inform you.

The DLBL statements in the previous job stream using DOS and the GO steps in the following job stream using OS are of particular importance. First, the system-name used, SALES1, SALES2, and SALES3 come from the system-name in the AS-SIGN clause of the SELECT statement (in this case, it was SALES), and the system-name used in the JCL statements must concatenate a 1, 2, 3, and so on because an alternate index does not have a separate ASSIGN clause. Also the path names must be used in the order that these alternate indexes are specified in the SELECT statement.

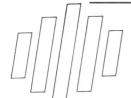

Valid Combinations of I/O Statements

File Organization	Access Mode	Open Mode	Valid I/O Entries	Relevant FILE STATUS Values
Sequential	Sequential	INPUT	READ f-name [INTO] [AT END] USE EXCEPTION/ERROR	10 - end-of-file

		I-0	READ f-name
			[INTO]
			[AT END]
			REWRITE r-name
			[FROM]
			WRITE r-name
			[FROM]
			USE
			  EXCEPTION/ERROR
				10 - end-of-file
				
				21 - key not equal to
				     last record read
				34 - boundary violation

		OUTPUT	WRITE r-name [FROM] USE EXCEPTION/ERROR	34 - boundary violation
		EXTEND	WRITE r-name [FROM] USE EXCEPTION/ERROR	34 - boundary violation

File Organization	Access Mode	Open Mode	Valid I/O Entries	Relevant FILE STATUS Values
Indexed	Sequential	INPUT	READ f-name [NEXT] [INTO] [AT END] START f-name [KEY] [INVALID KEY] USE EXCEPTION/ERROR	10 - end-of-file 23 - record key not found
		I-0	READ f-name [NEXT] [INTO] [AT END]	10 - end-of-file

		START f—name [KEY] [INVALID KEY]	23 — record key not found
		REWRITE r—name [FROM] [INVALID KEY]	02 — duplicate alternate key (WITH DUPLICATES specified)
			21 — key not equal to last key read
			22 — duplicate alternate key (without duplicates)
		DELETE f—name [RECORD] [INVALID KEY] USE EXCEPTION/ERROR	21 — key not equal to last key read
	OUTPUT	WRITE r—name [FROM] [INVALID KEY]	02 — duplicate alternate key (WITH DUPLICATES specified)
			21 — sequence error (prime) key not greater than last record written)
			22 — duplicate prime or alternate key (without duplicates)
			24 — boundary violation
		USE EXCEPTION/ERROR	
Random	INPUT	READ f—name [INTO]	10 — end-of-file
		[INVALID KEY] USE EXCEPTION/ERROR	23 — key not found
	I-0	READ f—name [INTO] [INVALID KEY]	23 — key not found
		REWRITE r—name [FROM] [INVALID KEY]	02 — duplicate alternate key (WITH DUPLICATES specified)
			22 — duplicate alternate key (without duplicates)
			23 — record key not found
		WRITE r—name [FROM] [INVALID KEY]	02 — duplicate alternate key (WITH DUPLICATES specified)
			22 — duplicate prime or alternate key (without duplicates)
			24 — boundary violation
		DELETE f—name [RECORD] [INVALID KEY] USE EXCEPTION/ERROR	23 — record key not found
	OUTPUT	WRITE r—name [FROM] [INVALID KEY]	02 — duplicate alternate key (WITH DUPLICATES specified
			21 — sequence error

			22 – duplicate prime or alternate key (without duplicates)
			24 – boundary violation
		USE EXCEPTION/ERROR	
Dynamic	INPUT	USE EXCEPTION/ERROR (Sequential request)	
		READ f-name NEXT [INTO] [AT END]	10 – end-of-file
		START f-name [KEY] [INVALID KEY] (Random request)	23 – record key not found
		READ f-name [INTO] [INVALID KEY]	23 – record key not found
	I-O	USE EXCEPTION/ERROR (Sequential request)	
		READ f-name NEXT [INTO] [AT END]	10 – end-of-file
		START f-name [KEY] [INVALID KEY] (Random request)	23 – record key not found
		READ f-name [INTO] [INVALID KEY]	23 – record key not found
		REWRITE r-name [FROM] [INVALID KEY]	02 – duplicate alternate key (WITH DUPLICATES specified)
			22 – duplicate alternate key (without duplicates)
			23 – record key not found
		WRITE r-name [FROM] [INVALID KEY]	02 – duplicate alternate key (WITH DUPLICATES specified)
			22 – duplicate prime or alternate key (without duplicates)
			24 – boundary violation
		DELETE f-name [RECORD] [INVALID KEY]	23 – record key not found
	OUTPUT	WRITE r-name [FROM] [INVALID KEY]	02 – duplicate alternate key (WITH DUPLICATES specified)
			22 – duplicate prime or alternate key (without duplicates
			24 – boundary violation
		USE EXCEPTION/ERROR	

Relative	Sequential	INPUT	READ f-name [NEXT] [INTO] [AT END] START f-name [KEY] [INVALID KEY] USE EXCEPTION/ERROR	10 - end-of-file 23 - relative key not found
		I-0	READ f-name [NEXT] [INTO] [AT END] START f-name [KEY] [INVALID KEY] REWRITE r-name [FROM] [INVALID KEY] DELETE f-name [RECORD] [INVALID KEY] USE EXCEPTION/ERROR	10 - end-of-file 23 - relative key not found 23 - relative key not found 21 - relative key not equal to last record read 21 - relative key not equal to last record read
		OUTPUT	WRITE r-name [FROM] [INVALID KEY] USE EXCEPTION/ERROR	24 - boundary violation
	Random	INPUT	READ f-name [INTO] [INVALID KEY] USE EXCEPTION/ERROR	23 - relative key not found
		I-0	READ f-name [INTO] [INVALID KEY] REWRITE r-name [FROM] [INVALID KEY] WRITE r-name [FROM] [INVALID KEY] DELETE f-name [RECORD] [INVALID KEY] USE EXCEPTION/ERROR	23 - relative key not found 23 - relative key not found 22 - duplicate relative key 24 - boundary violation 23 - relative key not found
		OUTPUT	WRITE r-name [FROM] [INVALID KEY] USE EXCEPTION/ERROR	22 - duplicate relative key 24 - boundary violation
	Dynamic	INPUT	USE EXCEPTION/ERROR (Sequential request) READ f-name NEXT	 10 - end-of-file

		[INTO] [AT END]	

		START f-name
		  [KEY]
		  INVALID KEY]
		(Random request)
			23 — relative key not
			        found

		READ f-name
		  [INTO]
		  [INVALID KEY]
			23 — relative key not
			        found

	I-O	USE EXCEPTION/ERROR (Sequential request)	

		READ f-name
		  NEXT
		  [INTO]
		  [AT END]
			10 — end-of-file

		START f-name
		  [KEY]
		  [INVALID KEY]
		(Random request)
			23 — relative key not
			        found

		READ f-name
		  [INTO]
		  [INVALID KEY]
			23 — relative key not
			        found

		REWRITE r-name
		  [FROM]
		  [INVALID KEY]
			23 — relative key not
			        found

		WRITE r-name
		  [FROM]
		  [INVALID KEY]
			22 — duplicate relative
			        key
			24 — boundary violation

		DELETE f-name
		  [RECORD]
		  [INVALID KEY]
			21 — relative key not
			        equal to last record
			        read

	OUTPUT	WRITE r-name
		  [FROM]
		  [INVALID KEY]
		USE
		  EXCEPTION/ERROR
			22 — duplicate relative
			        key
			24 — boundary violation

Additionally, **FILE STATUS** values of '00', successful completion, '30', permanent I/O error, and values in the 9x series may be encountered.

INDEX

This book has been set VideoComp in 10 and 9 point Melior, leaded 2 points. Computer programs and computer type extracts are set 8 point Universal Monospace, leaded 2 points. Chapter numbers are 62 point and chapter titles are 36 point Melior Bold Italic. The size of the type area is 40½ by 60½ picas.